PLANTS

David F. Avery  Dwight G. Smith  Marcia Schultz, Editor

Southern Connecticut State University

D1404341

PEARSON

Custom Publishing

PEARSON CUSTOM PUBLISHING
75 Arlington Street, Suite 300, Boston, MA 02116
A Pearson Education Company

Contents

◀ · · · · · · ◀ · · · ◀ · · · · · · · · · · · · ·

Preface

The writing of a textbook is an exciting event filled with problems and compromises. This text is no exception. Botanists for generations have been confronted with the problem of how to approach Botany in an organized way that is also meaningful. The main problem with plants is that they do not adapt themselves to this kind of treatment. Most all plants are angiosperms, which are the summit of evolution, and their structure and function is the most complex. Yet if we discuss them in a phylogenetic way, we must leave them until last. An approach has been developed over the past century of dealing with angiosperms in a botany class by treating normal angiosperm morphology and function as normal plant morphology and function. This means that most of the discussions in this book are based on angiosperms. We have followed tradition by leaving the discussion of other plant groups and their uniqueness until later chapters when we present a plant survey. This is good in that it gives angiosperms proper weight in an economically based general botany class, but it also provided some problems. All life forms have evolved in a sequence of simple to complex, hence, the logical sequence for such a class would be to begin with the simplest and build upon that. Unfortunately that approach does not adapt itself well to Botany and we have avoided it here.

This book is prepared as a general requirement for students who need to learn to appreciate the subject matter for its impact on their future lives and avocations. For this reason this book is not highly technical, although we have tried to include the basics needed by a non-major who might decide to switch to the field of biology. For this reason, we also stress the economic impact and importance of plants in everyday life. We hope that students will obtain from this work and the experience of the class, an appreciation of life in general, and of plants for their uniqueness. We also hope that issues of conservation, ecology and evolution that have been raised here, will impact them to the point where they will be better and informed citizens in their future lives.

Few people write textbooks alone. We have had a lot of help with this effort and wish to thank especially Dave Canny, Trevor Becker, Stephanie Tobin, Liz Samander, Julie Hall, Tara Casonova, Carrie Bradley, Mary Anne Flood, and Dwight G. Smith, Jr. We are especially indebted to our colleagues Noble Proctor, Al Turko, Ken Petit, and Gerald Schultz for their unfailing encouragement in this and many other projects.

Gerald Schultz, Scott Schultz, and Erika Avery, in particular, read and corrected most of the chapters in this book several times. Carolyn Alling provided valuable technical adivce regarding illustrations, diagrams, and figures for the current textbook. As always, our botany students have been most helpful in pointing out typos and other errors in early versions of this manuscript.

Dwight Glenn Smith
David F. Avery
Marcia H. Schultz
New Haven, Connecticut
September 2000

Chapter 1

A Science Called Botany

What Are Plants?
Botany as a Science
    History of Botany
    Diversity of Botany
    Future of Botanical Science
Characteristics of Life

Plants and the science of plants has always figured importantly in human history. Plants represent our source of food, clothing, and medicine. Since earliest times, much of our historical culture has centered on plants. In fact, the most seminal event in this millennium was really all about plants: in 1492 Columbus sailed across the Atlantic Ocean to touch land on a small island at the eastern edge of the Caribbean Sea. Columbus had set sail on his epic voyage of discovery because of plants. He was actually searching for a new route to the "Spice Islands" of the East Indies. Columbus had been granted permission to sail west to the Spice Islands by the Spanish king and queen (Ferdinand and Isabella) who wanted to break the Portuguese trade monopoly on spices and other plant products with Asia—a trade which centered on spices from the East Indies. Spices were then very much in demand in Europe to flavor the otherwise drab tasting food of that era. The Portuguese were able to exploit the European market for spices because earlier, their mariners had discovered a trade route south around the Cape of Good Hope of Africa and on eastward across the Indian Ocean to Asia and the Spice Islands. Since the Portuguese held the southern route, Columbus convinced the Spanish monarchs to finance an exploration to search for a new trade route to the Spice Islands westward, directly across the Atlantic Ocean (Columbus, of course, was unaware that the New World was between Spain and Asia). Later, this same driving force in search of plants and plant products would send Henrik Hudson to New York and John Cabot to Newfoundland; both explorers were searching for a Northwest Passage to the fabulous and fabled Spice Islands. Seen in this context, plants, plant products, and botany have played a major role in politics and trade in the Middle Ages, as they have in almost every age of human endeavor.

What Are Plants?

A dictionary defines plants as living organisms that grow by synthesizing organic substances (e.g., sugars) from inorganic materials (e.g., water and carbon dioxide), that have cell walls made of cellulose, and that are limited or lacking in their ability to move about (locomotion). The critical feature in this definition of plants is that they can manufacture their own food, in contrast to animals, which must obtain food from other sources. Traditionally, the study of plants at the introductory level also includes the study of related organisms such as the viruses, bacteria and fungi as well as green plants. The kinds and variety of plants discussed in this textbook are given in Table 1-1 below.

Plants are organisms that manufacture their own food by photosynthesis while animals must obtain their food by eating plants or other animals or a combination of plants and animals.

Table 1–1 A brief survey of the major kinds of plants studied in botany.

Major Plant Groups	Descriptive Features of the Plant Group
Bacteria	one celled, or colonial, prokaryotes, blue-green bacteria, parasites, saprophytes
Fungi	usually multicellular and eukaryotic, molds, mushrooms, rusts, smuts
Lichens	symbiotic combination of fungi and algae, e.g., British Soldier Lichen
Protistans: The Algae	one-celled or colonial, eukaryotes, desmids, diatoms, green, brown, red algae
Liverworts and Mosses	multicellular, small, creeping or erect green plants; mosses with spore capsules
Ferns	multi celled, vascular green plants that bear spores, e.g., ferns, club mosses, horsetails
Conifers	mostly evergreen, needle-leaved trees or shrubs, seeds confined in cones ,e.g., pines, spruces, firs, cedars
Flowering Plants	green flowering plants with seeds contained within fruits, e.g., herbs, grasses, trees and shrubs.

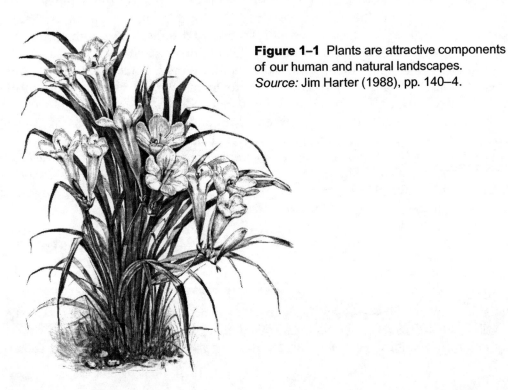

Figure 1–1 Plants are attractive components of our human and natural landscapes. *Source:* Jim Harter (1988), pp. 140–4.

Plants have always been pivotal in the activities of humans as components of the human landscape and of the global biosphere. The importance of plants is far reaching for many reasons.

ECOLOGICAL VALUE OF PLANTS

Ecologically, plants are the biosphere's producers and form the base of the food chain upon which all animals depend. They are the only living organisms with the ability to trap energy from the sun. Through the process of photosynthesis, plants use some of the sun's solar energy (sunlight) to chemically combine water and carbon dioxide to produce organic molecules such as the simple sugars. In essence, plants have the ability to convert some of the kinetic energy in a beam of sunlight into the potential energy that "glues" the molecules of water and carbon dioxide together to make the sugar molecule. The synthesized sugars are also the food for the plant. They are used as an energy source to power the plant's activities as well as provide the initial substrates from which plants can synthesize other organic molecules—the lipids, proteins, vitamins and nucleic acids, for example, which comprise the plant's biomass. Because plants can produce their own food they are called **autotrophs**, which means self-nourishing—that is, the plant (the auto part of autotroph) manufactures its own food supply (troph = to obtain food). All other organisms, including all of the animals must obtain their food by eating plants or other animals and are called **heterotrophs** (heter = other, trophs = nourishing).

Since plants are the only organisms that have the ability to manufacture their own food, all other life forms ultimately depend on plants for sugars and for the many other organic chemicals that plants manufacture. For example, animals, in the traditional sense, must obtain their food by eating plants or other animals which have fed on plants. Animals thus consume plant tissue as a food source for energy to power animal activities and also as a source of many other chemicals which they can convert or incorporate into animal tissue (animal flesh).

All life depends on the organic molecules (food) that are first manufactured by plants.

Plants are also ecologically important because they generate oxygen as a by-product of photosynthesis. The ability of plants to photosynthetically produce oxygen has played a pivotal role in the history of life on earth. For millions of years during the early history of the earth, almost all oxygen was chemically bound in the form of mineral oxides such as iron oxide or aluminum oxide that were common in the rocks and soils. Consequently, the earth's early atmosphere was comprised mostly of nitrogen and carbon dioxide and other gases, but little, if any, free oxygen. The evolutionary appearance of plants marked the beginning of an enormous outpouring of free oxygen into the atmosphere, in essence, transforming the gaseous composition of the atmosphere to one higher in oxygen, which now comprises 21 % of atmosphere, almost all due to the metabolic release of oxygen into the atmosphere by plants. All aerobic animals have greatly benefitted from the increased availability of free oxygen (provided by plant processes), which they require for respiration. The dependence of animals on plants is not one-sided however, as animals produce carbon dioxide which plants require for photosynthesis. As a result, an interdependence has developed between both plants and animals.

Plants are also functionally important as decomposers. All organisms eventually die and decompose, during which their body is chemically broken down and the minerals that comprise their tissues are released back to the environment. This process of ecological recycling is performed by certain kinds of plants, mainly bacteria and fungi. For example, when you create a compost pile in your backyard bacteria and fungi consume and chemically process the grass clippings and weeds, breaking them down to obtain food and energy for themselves and in the process, releasing the minerals and other materials. The same process occurs when an animal dies and decomposes. In another example of how decomposition works, consider the bones of vertebrates, which contain important minerals such as calcium and phosphorous. When a small bird or squirrel dies, the bacteria and fungi chemically decompose the bones, freeing the calcium and phosphate minerals into the soil.

PLANTS AS FOOD FOR HUMANS

Plants are the basic source of food for most of the human population. Humans eat vegetables, seeds, nuts, berries and other fruits of plants. They provide us with our daily nutritional needs for carbohydrates, proteins, fats and also furnish necessary vitamins and minerals.

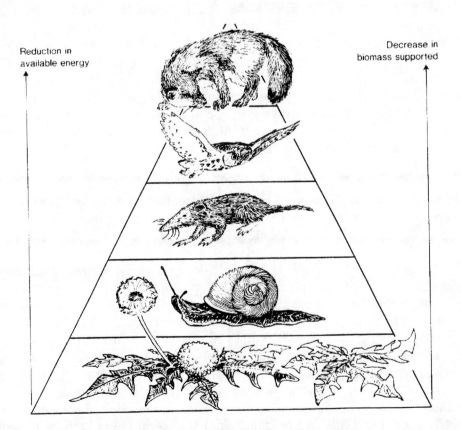

Reduction in available energy

Decrease in biomass supported

Figure 1–2 The pyramid of living organisms. Plants are the producers at the base of this pyramid. By converting the energy of sunlight into the biomass of plant tissue, plants provide the food energy for all other organisms in an ecosystem. *Source:* Tom M. Graham (1997), p. 170.

More than half of the world's human population relies almost entirely on plants to provide their daily nutritional requirements.

Grains (the cereals) are especially important kinds of plants. Three species of grains, rice, wheat and corn supply most of the carbohydrates consumed by humans. In fact, rice is the staple diet of just about half of the world's populations; the peoples of many pantropic countries of the world such as India, China, Indonesia and the Philippines depend on this single plant to supply almost all of their food. Other grains such as oats, barley and rye are forage for cattle, sheep and other livestock, and so contribute indirectly to our food supply.

Both cultivated and wild plants also are an important and enjoyable food for humans. For third world country peoples, berries, nuts, roots and mushrooms constitute essential food resources but people everywhere enjoy berries, truffles, morels and other delicacies collected in the wild.

COMMERCIAL VALUE OF PLANTS

We also obtain many materials other than food from the plants we cultivate or harvest in the wild. We flavor our foods with spices, color our cloth with dyes, glue things together with adhesives, manufacture cloth, ropes and strings with plant fibers, and

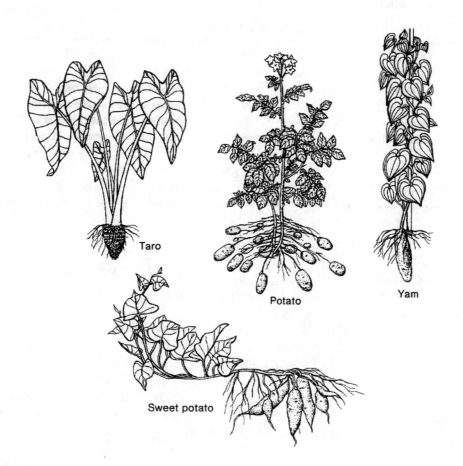

Taro

Potato

Yam

Sweet potato

Figure 1–3 Varieties of starchy root crops humans use as food. *Source:* James F. Hancock (1992), p. 243.

change the nature of foods with food stabilizers and emulsifiers—all obtained from plants. We also build houses and other structures out of wood. We change wood into paper for many purposes, we burn fossil wood in the form of coal for heating homes, and, in some countries, for making power in local power plants. In addition to wood and wood products, some of the many other commercially valuable plant products include rubber, resins, gums, tannin, turpentine, waxes and pectins.

The beer, wine and whiskey industries use plant products to promote fermentation of sugars. In fermentation, plant sugars from grain, fruits, berries, and flowers are chemically broken down to produce the alcohols in alcoholic beverages. Alcohols derived from plants are also used in a variety of commercial and pharmaceutical industries. Within the past three decades the fuel crisis has stimulated the production of gasohol, a gasoline-alcohol mix derived from plant biomass which is mixed with gasoline, typically in a 9:1 ratio. The use of gasohol as an alternative fuel for vehicles promises to help stretch gasoline supplies.

More than half of all the medicines and natural remedies used in the treatment of ailments in the United States contain products manufactured by plants.

Table 1–2 Some of the many natural plant products used in treatment of human diseases.

Plant	Medicine	Use
Bacterium	Tetracycline	antibiotic
Fungus	Penicillin	antibiotic
Poppy	Morphine	analgesic
Chincona	Quinine	antimalarial drug
American Yew	Taxol	anticancer drug
Periwinkle Plant	Vinblastine	anticancer drug
Foxglove	Digitalis	heart stimulant
Yam	Diosgenin	birth-control drug
Yam	Cortisone	anti-inflammation

MEDICINAL VALUE OF PLANTS

Plants have also been used for centuries as sources of **medicines** and **drugs.** The earliest forms of treatment for many human ailments were herbal medicines. Today, plants and plant products are used as drugs or as a primary substance for the manufacture of drugs. These plant derived drugs are extensively used for the treatment of many kinds of diseases and other ailments that occur in humans: they provide antibiotics, analgesics, anticancer drugs, antiparasitic drugs, drugs to regulate blood pressure, pharmaceuticals, laxatives and hormones and enzymes to supplement or direct many specific physiological processes. Even many of our most common drugs come from plants—aspirin, for example, is obtained from tree bark. The search continues for new and ever more potent plant products useful in treating disease.

CONSERVATION VALUE AND BEAUTY OF PLANTS

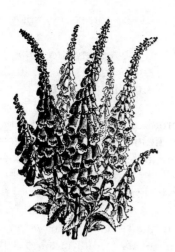

Figure 1–4 The foxglove plant from which digitalis is obtained to be used as a heart stimulant. *Source:* Jim Harter (1988), p. 231.

Plants clothe our landscapes in shades of green, gold and brown. Their fantastic variety of forms, color, shapes and markings are endlessly interesting and beautiful. Leaves, stems, fruits and, especially flowers color the human landscape and add beauty and diversity to our otherwise drab residential and commercial settings.

Plants are also important agents of soil and water conservation. Communities of plants cover the fragile earth, preventing water and wind erosion and scouring of soils. Vegetated landscapes also retain water, preventing floods and severe erosion during and following rainstorms. Plants are also cultivated as wind breaks. For example, the plantations of pines and other conifers planted around water courses and reservoirs shade the water and help prevent evaporation of water from our reservoirs. Lines of trees also act as excellent wind breaks and green belts, alleviating visual and noise pollution.

Plants are also the main organisms that restore stressed or ruined habitats. For example, if a woodlot is burned, logged or plowed over and then left undisturbed plants invade, colonize and eventually transform the barren land into the original habitat of plants and animals. This process of natural restoration is called ecological succession.

PLANTS AS AGENTS OF DISEASE

Some diseases may be caused by plants or plant products. Bacterial and fungal infections are the cause of many maladies of humankind. Some of the worst kinds of human diseases such as dysentery, cholera, typhoid and paratyphoid fevers are caused by bacteria. Other bacteria cause syphilis, gonorrhea and anthrax. Some of the many kinds of viral diseases of humans include AIDS, measles, rabies and smallpox.

Bacteria and fungi also cause many plant diseases. Fungi such as rusts, smuts, mildews and molds cause billions of dollars worth of damage to crops each year. Some bacteria and fungi also attack and destroy plants and animals of our natural habitats. For example, the American Chestnut tree, once an important and valuable lumber tree of the eastern forests of North America, was devastated by a fungi called the chestnut blight. Similarly, the American Elm has been almost eliminated from the countryside and cityscapes by another fungi that causes the Dutch Elm disease. Other rusts, smuts and fungi attack and destroy economically and ecologically valuable trees such as White Pine, Eastern Hemlock and Red Pine.

PLANTS USED IN EXPERIMENTAL SCIENCE

Plants are also important in scientific experimentation. Within the last few decades, there has developed an appreciation of the suffering that experimental animals endure; consequently, scientists have turned to plants as a source of experimental material, especially at the cellular level of investigation. Plants are very useful in this way as they are simpler in structure than animals and less responsive to invasive experimental techniques. Furthermore, scientific experiments on and with plants don't seem to cause the same moral and ethical concerns that are so commonly raised when experiments are conducted on animals.

Genetic engineering is one of the many areas of current research to benefit from the use of plants. In genetic engineering, genes from other organisms are artificially implanted within plant cells to alter their physiology or structure. Using this technique, genetic engineers can produce new strains of bacteria, some of which can mass produce critical substances needed by humans such as medicines now in short supply. In the future, the production of substances such as insulin and other hormones—originally animal products—may be entirely produced by bacteria and other plants for human use. Because plants are so important as a source of medicine and drugs, their conservation is a major environmental and political concern today. For example, tropical rain forests comprise just seven percent of the world's terrestrial habitats, but hold some 90 percent of the different kinds of plant and animal species in the world, many of which may produce important drugs and other chemicals for humankind. Unfortunately, tropical areas of the world are being destroyed at a very rapid rate—they are removed for logging, to provide space for pastures and to provide homes for native towns and villages. The loss of tropical rain forests means the loss of potentially important (and as yet unknown) plant sources of drugs and other useful products. In another context, the loss of these forests is important because the trees are some of the major oxygen producers of the world. In tropical rain forests and elsewhere around the world, the seemingly mad rush to convert natural habitats into human types of habitats means that many species of plants (and animals too) are being driven to extinction before we acquire any knowledge of their genuine ecological value or potential economic value. With the extinction of these plants, the possible cures for diseases will be lost to humankind forever.

To summarize, the usefulness of plants far exceeds the economic value that we humans tend to put on them. As human populations continue to grow and spread across the earth's natural habitats, our success in conserving plant life on Earth will increasingly become of vital importance, both on economic grounds and also from an ethical sense of the worth of all organisms.

The History of Botany

Botany is formally recognized as the scientific study of plants. This was not always the case. The history of botany begins thousands of years ago, as humans learned to sort out which plants provided food and medicines and which plants should be avoided.

PLANTS AND PREHISTORIC HUMANS

Plants and knowledge of plant use had a major impact on the life of early humans. Evidence from the fossil record indicates that distant ancestors of humans were hunter-gatherers. Small bands of these early humans spent their days wandering in search of food, probably very much like the primate troops of baboons or chimpanzees are observed to do today. These early humans were opportunists as they would take advantage of any food source that they encountered. They ate carrion obtained from predatory animal kills, or killed animals themselves whenever possible. They also gathered fruits, nuts, berries, roots and other plant parts to supplement their diet. It has sometimes been stated that the difference between these early humans and other scavenging animals is the fact that they scavenged and brought material back to the campsite to share.

The first humans were also the first botanists who knew and used plants for many purposes, most especially for food and medicines.

During the period in which modern forms of humans were evolving much of the northern half of the earths' surface was in the grip of a massive Ice Age. This created a situation where the prey species that human hunters sought were concentrated in small areas. As a result humans often decimated the herds of animals that they depended upon for food. Hunting was good and easy and soon many species were driven into extinction by over hunting. This Pleistocene "overkill," as it has since been termed, resulted in the destruction of many of the large mammals in North America, Africa and Eurasia that exceeded one hundred pounds in weight. At the end of the Pleistocene the "good life" of easy hunting for readily available prey was over. Faced with starvation, humans were increasingly forced to supplement their diet with plants (as their distant ancestors had done). At some point in our prehistory, the peoples in a number of areas of the world deliberately began to cultivate plants rather than simply gather them from the wild. The introduction of **plant cultivation,** or **agriculture,** can be traced back to perhaps between 35,000 and 15,000 years ago.

The cultivation and harvesting of crops may be considered to mark the transformation of humans from nomadic wanderers to city and suburb dwellers and at some later time, marked the beginnings of civilization. Evidence from the near East and the Indus Valley of India indicates that the cultivation of crops was well established and became the focal point of early civilizations just 8,000 years ago or so. Water works, irrigation canals, the first plows and other implements of agriculture developed as a consequence of this dependence upon plants rather than animals as the food source of these early civilizations. Increasingly, the scientists of those civilizations concentrated on crop production and ways to improve it. For example, the large monolithic structures such as Stonehenge in England and other astronomical clocks in North and Central America apparently represent calendars that enabled these peoples to keep track of the yearly cycle of seasons and provide a timetable of sorts for planting and harvesting their crops.

Cultivation of plants provided humans with a dependable food source that enabled the establishment and growth of the first civilizations along the Nile River in Egypt, the Indus River in India and between the Tigris and Euphrates Rivers of Mesopotamia.

Cultivation had a major impact on the history of humankind as it led to a fundamental change in human lifestyle. Agricultural protocol requires that crops be planted, tended and harvested at specific times. This in turn necessitated the establishment of permanent settlements nearby. In time, the settlements became towns which grew into cities and into city states, the earliest forms of governments. Cultivation was particularly important in the warmer areas of the world where climate allowed a long growing season. Ancient Assyrians, Babylonians and Egyptians, for example, cultivated legumes, grains, fruits, figs, olives, pomegranates, and dates as well as many other grains and vegetables. Grapes, in particular were important as they could be fermented to produce wines. Among their other crops, Egyptians discovered and cultivated wheat to make bread and barley to make beer.

Associated with the cultivation of plants for food, was the collection of information about plants that might be useful in the treatment of disease. Assyrians, Egyptians and other early civilizations collected and transmitted such information from generation to generation as part of their cultural heritage. The credit for the greatest investigations of the medicinal use of plants must go to the Chinese. By 2737 BC they had invented the plow and had seed-sowing ceremonies to support their agriculture. The Chinese also produced a 40 volume work called a **pharmacopoeia,** a kind of listing of herbs and other plant and animal information relating to medicinal uses.

BOTANY BECOMES A SCIENCE

The transformation of knowledge of plants and plant biology acquired by the ancients into the science of plant biology or botany took place over many centuries of time. In order to understand this major step we must understand the nature of science as a discipline. A science is not just a body of knowledge, as in the case of a pharmacopoeia, but it is an organized attempt to study and understand related phenomena of the natural world. Far more than a collection of information, science is a way of obtaining information by using a specific protocol called the scientific method. In fact, science is a body of knowledge that is based on observation, recording, organization and classification of facts.

The Scientific Method

In science we develop our understanding of natural events and processes by collecting and interpreting information in a prescribed way to arrive at the correct conclusions without bias. This prescribed way is called the **scientific method** which involves four steps. First, the scientific method begins with an **observation.** A scientist observes a process or phenomena or event that requires an explanation. For example, a scientist might observe that light availability seems to be related to plant growth. Second, the scientist makes an educated guess or **hypothesis** as to what might have caused the process or event to occur. To continue our example, the scientist might hypothesize that light is necessary for plants to grow because plants wither and die if they are deprived of light for any length of time. Therefore, light is something plants need. In the third step, the hypothesis must be tested to be proven correct or incorrect. A scientist tests a hypothesis through an **experiment** or in a series of experiments. Experiments are tests that are designed to collect the type of information that can confirm or deny the hypothesis. The scientist next designs a series of experiments to test the idea that light is important to plants. Some plants could be grown in light and some grown without light to test the importance of light. Some might be grown in different kinds of light to determine if wavelength of light is an important factor. The experiments revealed that when plants are deprived of light they wither and die. His experiments might also show that the intensity of light and the type of light might stimulate or retard different kinds of plant growth. The information collected by this series of experiments is called **data**. Once the data are analyzed the scientist can draw conclusions. Conclusions are ideas based on fact. These conclusions can be presented in the form of a **theory**. A theory is an explanation for a phenomenon that is based on facts or data. A reasonable theory to fit our example could be that light is necessary for the growth of plants because light provides energy for the manufacture of food. Theories are subject to change as more facts are collected and data is reinterpreted in view of new facts. The end result of these changing theories is an attempt to find truth by examining facts.

The scientific method consists of four steps; making an observation, formulating a working hypothesis, testing the hypothesis by means of an experiment, and constructing a scientific theory based on results of the experiment.

When a theory is proven beyond all doubt, it is called a **scientific law**. There are very few laws in botany as there are usually a few exceptions to almost all phenomena. In botany, as in all sciences, even laws are subject to revision as new information provides a more complete picture of the scientific processes that define and describe life.

Early Botany as a Science

Botany slowly developed into the scientific study of plants. Today, it is one of the principal subdivisions of **biology,** which is the study of life. Other major subdivisions of biology include **zoology,** the study of animals and **microbiology,** in which viruses and bacteria are investigated. Traditionally, most introductory textbooks of botany also include one or more chapters on viruses and bacteria. The evolutionary history of plants, animals, and bacteria is usually presented in a more specialized course in paleontology, commonly taught as a branch of geology.

The word botany is actually derived from the French word botanique which in turn is related to the Greek words botanikos, and botanica. Related Greek and Latin words include botane, meaning plant or herb, and boskein meaning to eat. As can be seen by these Greek and Latin words the initial interest in botany came from using plants as food, in planting crops to use for materials and for feeding the population. It was not until historical times that botany developed into a systematic collection of information and a formalized study making it into a science. Scientific botany appeared in its earliest form in ancient Greece. The Greeks had a practical interest in plants as sources of food and drugs. Early Greek physicians and pharmacists recognized many kinds of plants useful for treating disease.

In fact, the formal study of botany began with a Greek philosopher named Aristotle. Aristotle, who died in 322 BC, was a student of the great philosopher Plato. He was among the earliest investigators to systematically observe, analyze and record a remarkable amount of biological phenomena—in short, he was one of the first modern scientists. Aristotle experimentally investigated the relationships of plants and animals and developed a classification scheme to place each kind of organism in their proper place in relation to others. Aristotle was so important that his ideas about nature were accepted as gospel by the early Christian church in Europe and the value of his writings was accepted almost as much as the *Bible* itself. His interest in botany is illustrated by the fact that he created a botanical garden in Athens and wrote extensively about plants he had collected there.

When Aristotle died, his botanical gardens were taken over by **Theophrastus,** one of his former students. Theophrastus furthered Aristotle's studies of plants into an important avocation. The extent of Theophrastus' importance to the science of plant biology can be found in that he had over 2,000 students, and wrote over 200 scholarly papers on botanical subjects. He was one of the first scientists to concentrate on botany and collect botanical information in an organized way.

Theophrastus, a student of Aristotle, is the father of the science of botany.

Because of his extensive scholarship and writings, Theophrastus is considered to be the father of modern botany. Among his many scholarly writings are two exceptionally important books; *History of Plants*, and *Causes of Plants*. These books represented the encyclopedic collections of all that was known about the biology of plants at that time and became models for many of the future botany textbooks that were actually written down through the centuries.

The Rise of Herbalism

The knowledge that plants were useful in the treatment of many diseases of humans and other animals (such as livestock) was apparent since prehistoric times. At first, the rise of scientific botany centered on the collection and storing, in written form, of this information. One of the first works to chronicle the importance of plants in the treatment of diseases was penned in the second century by the Roman scientist, soldier, and traveler, named Pliny. Pliny traveled extensively, gathered all sorts of information about plants and animals that he encountered, and eventually wrote a multi volume work called *Historia Naturalis*. In it, Pliny tried to list and describe all of the accepted knowledge of plants and animals known at that time. His works were encyclopedic in scope and were important reference works for future botanists.

Another very important book of this Roman era, entitled *Material Medica,* was written by the Greek, Disoscorides, who was also the first to illustrate plants. His book was used to identify useful plants for medicinal purposes. This work is also considered to be the first **Herbal.** Herbals were books of tremendous importance through the Middle Ages as they were the main source of information on how to treat many diseases using plants, plant juices or plant seeds. The state of medical science was in its infancy and the physicians of that time as such were rather crude and uneducated. Most sick folk were self-treated or helped by friends and relatives who used various folk remedies as cures for their various ailments. Herbals were really the only source of medical information available for common people at that time, and as such, were of tremendous importance. In fact, if one went into a house in Europe during the Middle Ages, and if the family was affluent enough to have books, they would have at least two; the *Bible* and an Herbal. Early books were handwritten and it was not until the invention of the printing press in the 1500's that Herbals became cheap enough to be mass produced for everyone. The period of time from 1500 to 1700 is considered to be the golden age of Herbals. During this period many varieties of Herbals were produced, especially in Germany, where the greatest interest in Herbals was maintained. Germany hosted a large number of Herbalists who wrote many popular Herbals, along with a few Italian and English authors as well. The most famous of the German herbalists was Otto Brunfels, who wrote a massive, three volume Herbal in 1530.

Households of the Middle Ages almost invariably had a library of two books, the *Bible* and an Herbal, the latter a kind of home remedy book that specified what herbs should be used to treat each ailment.

Brunfels and the other medieval herbalists were really only interested in the medicinal values of plants. They cultivated and studied the various herbs in large and well maintained gardens and proposed cures based on a philosophy called the Doctrine of Signatures. This idea was rooted in the philosophy that if a plant structure was shaped like an organ or other part of the human body that plant would be useful for the treatment of diseases of that organ. For example, since the kidney bean looks like a kidney it can be used in treating diseases of the kidney and urinary tract. We know today that this is not true but in some parts of the world the Doctrine of Signatures is still used in folk medicine. For example, in Asia, ginseng, a plant with a root that resembles the shape of a human, is often used to treat diseases although its actual effectiveness has never been scientifically proven. Despite the fact that the Doctrine of Signatures is false, the interest in plants as natural cures continues even today. For example naturopathic physicians prescribe naturopathic medicines as herbal cures for a number of human diseases and ailments. Furthermore, the abundance of health food stores is testimony to our continued interest in the relationships between plants and our health.

New Tools for the Investigation of Plants

Microscopes

Of necessity, the earliest scientific studies of plants conducted by Aristotle, Theophrastus and others were limited to observation. The first scientific instruments to provide further insights into the scientific study of plants were the early microscopes. In 1590 the first **simple microscope** was invented by the Dutch scientist named **Zacharias Janssen.** Although Janssen was not a biologist, his crude arrangements of magnifying lenses enabled other people to see objects magnified many times. Prior to the invention of microscopes people could only see macroscopic objects, that is, things visible to the naked eye. The microscopic world of plant structures, bacteria and other animals was too small to be seen and was totally unknown. The microscope very quickly became popular as an important instrument of science. One of the earliest microscopists to study plants was another Dutch worker, **Anton von Leeuwenhoek** (1632–1723). Leeuwenhoek constructed his own microscopes based on those of Zacharias Janssen and improved them to produce greater powers of magnification. Leeuwenhoek's microscope which is something like our magnifying glasses of today, enabled him to discover and study bacteria, sperm, and thousands of tiny, single celled animals such as the green algae and protozoa. At their best, Leeuwenhoek's microscopes could magnify objects up to 200 times.

The simple microscopes used by the early microscopists consisted of a single magnifying lens. Today's microscopes may use several lenses in combination and are called compound microscopes. Electron microscopes allow us to see into the molecular world.

Since those early times microscopes have been much improved and are a common and useful instrument of science laboratories. Today modern **compound microscopes** use several magnifying lenses in combination and can magnify objects many thousands of times. Another common instrument that seems to be an important feature of modern botany research laboratories is the **Electron microscope.** Unlike light microscopes, which depend on light as a medium of magnification, the electron microscope uses a beam of electrons to magnify objects millions of times. With the best electron microscopes, scientists can actually see individual atoms that comprise the chemical makeup of an object. Regardless of its form, since its discovery, the different kinds of microscopes have proven exceptionally important in gathering the basic structure and functional details that have led to a major understanding of the biology of plants.

Figure 1–5 An early light microscope used by Robert Hooke and other early microscopists. *Source:* Teresa Audesirk and Gerald Audesirk (1996), p. 76.

Herbaria

Herbaria are museums that store large or small collections of plant specimens. The largest herbaria may hold millions of specimens, each carefully labeled with the name of the species, where and when it was collected along with other important information such as the name of the collector. Herbaria represent a storehouse of knowledge about the plants much like a library represents a store house, of sorts, of books. Using herbaria, plant biologists can study the relationships of plants to one another (their taxonomy) their distribution (plant geography) and which plants occur in which habitats (plant ecology).

Botany as a Science

Botany is a biological science that involves the study of plants. Two other basic biological sciences are zoology, the study of animals, and microbiology, the study of bacteria and viruses. Traditionally, most botany courses also include the study of four special groups of organisms, the bacteria, viruses, the protistans, and the fungi. Viruses and bacteria are comparatively simple organisms that lack a nucleus. Many viruses, in fact, don't even have their own DNA. Protistans are more advanced than bacteria in having DNA protected by a nucleus. Although existing in unicellular forms, the protistans also exhibit a greater complexity of structure and life history than bacteria and viruses. The

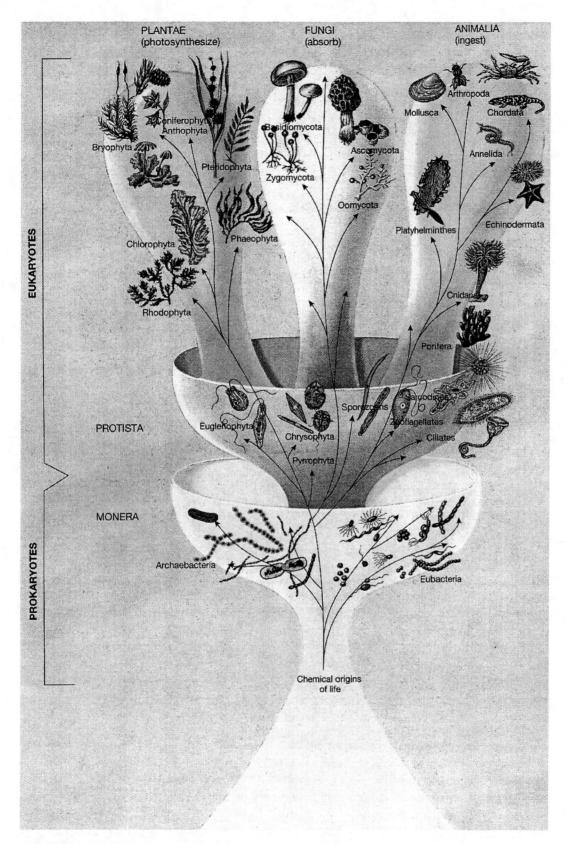

Figure 1–6 The kinds of plants and their positions within the tree of life. *Source*: Teresa Audesirk and Gerald Audesirk (1996), p. 392.

fungi are a highly specialized group of organisms that have evolved the ability to obtain their food by directly absorbing organic materials from their environment. Their body plan is unique in consisting of a series of tubules called hyphae. Green plants are the primary focus of most botany courses. They are the only organisms in nature that have the ability to photosynthetically produce their own food using the energy of sunlight. Like animals, green plants are typically larger, more complex organisms with often intricate life histories. However, green plants differ from animals in producing their own food, and in having a rigid cell wall that surrounds, protects and provides a structure for their cells.

THE DIVERSITY OF BOTANY AS A SCIENCE

Modern botany is a complex science with many disciplines. In fact, the science of plant biology has become so large and so information oriented, that, of necessity, botanists generally specialize in the study of one or two related disciplines. We usually divide the scientific study of botany into a number of interrelated subfields, or disciplines.

Plant Anatomy is the study of the internal structure of plants. Plant anatomy is basic to understanding how plants are built, and how they function. The study of plant anatomy was made possible by the development of the microscope and early investigations by the Italian philosopher and investigator, Malpighi (1628–1694). He discovered and studied the tissues found in plant stems and roots. Another early student of plant anatomy was Nehemiah Grew (1628–1711) who discovered the structure of wood.

Plant Physiology is the study of how plants function at the chemical, or molecular, level. A plant physiologist might investigate how plants absorb water, or how sunlight influences the rate of photosynthesis or perhaps how plants distribute sugars and other nutrients. Plant physiologists may also study how plants react to and interact with their environment. J.B. von Helmont (1577–1644) was one of the first plant physiologists; he experimentally demonstrated that plants have different nutritional needs than animals.

Plant Taxonomy, or **Systematic Botany,** is the botanical science that deals with identifying, naming and classifying plants. The naming of plants is basic to all other studies in botany (as well as in studies of animals and other organisms). Scientists can't compare results of their investigations with other scientists unless they know, in fact, which particular species were studied. The science of classification of plants and animals was pioneered by Linnaeus (1707–1778) a Swede who developed the basis for the current system of classification and naming of all living organisms. Today, we still use Linneaus' method to classify plants in plant biology courses and studies.

Plant Geography is the study of where, why, and how plants are distributed on the earth. Very few plants occur across the globe. Geographically, most plants are restricted to particular locales or, in a few cases, to particular continents. Some of the original studies in plant geography were developed by Carl Willdenow (1765–1812) and Alexander von Humboldt (1769–1859) who published books on the relationships of seed dispersal to plant distribution. Joseph D. Hooker (1817–1911) published surveys of the floras of Northern and Southern Hemispheres. Interest in plant geography is important in studies of how plants adapt to specific environments, how they disperse from one area to another, and how plants can successfully colonize new habitats. Plant Geography studies can also shed light on the evolution of plants and the development of plant species.

Plant Ecology is a study of the interaction of plants with one another and with their environment. The ability of plants to survive in a particular environment and their relationships to each other and animals in that environment is of tremendous importance to us. Because plants are the only organisms capable of manufacturing energy by photosynthesis, they are essentially the ultimate limiting factors in the biological world. Ecologically, plants provide food and cover for animals and can also alter both local and global environmental conditions. The ability of animals to survive in particular habitats is often tied closely to the plant species which provide food, shelter or refuge for the animals.

Plant Morphology developed as a separate science in the 19th century. Although morphology is another term for form and form can be considered to be anatomy, the field of plant morphology is different from that of plant anatomy. Plant Morphology is the study of the shape and form of plants and plant structures (i.e., shapes of leaves, fruits, stems, roots), and how these forms contribute to the functioning of plant structures. Such information is used in comparing plants for classification and evolution studies.

Plant Genetics is the study of inheritance in plants. Plant geneticists specifically study how genes are transmitted from parents to offspring and compare how they are expressed in offspring. Genetics was established as a science with the work of Gregor Mendel (1822–1884) who discovered many of the elementary processes and laws that govern inheritance. Today, genetics is used in studies on plant breeding to select the most desirable traits of plants or produce better plant products. Another aspect of plant genetics involves **genetic engineering,** a process whereby we are able to make plants into life forms that are useful to us in performing specific functions. The use of bacteria to produce insulin is one outstanding example of how useful genetic engineering can be. This was made possible because scientists learned to implant an animal gene which controlled the production of insulin into the chromosomal strand of a bacterium. Equipped with this gene as part of its normal genetic makeup, the modified bacterium then manufactured the insulin. Such bacteria can be grown in large colonies and the insulin they produce can be harvested to treat diabetic conditions in humans.

Molecular Plant Biology is the study of the organic chemistry of plants. The molecular plant biologist uses such tools as the scanning electron microscope to determine the intricacies of plant molecules from carbohydrates to nucleic acids. Information about plant molecules has important applications in developing techniques that can help in the artificial synthesis of vitamins and many other extremely important chemicals that only plants can naturally manufacture.

Plant Cytology. Lastly, the discipline of **Cytology** has developed as a separate science. Cytology is the study of cells, the basic units of organisms. In this sense it is a highly specialized version of plant physiology. Plant scientists that study cytology are called cytologists. They study the structure and chemistry of biochemical systems and actions at the cellular level in an attempt to understand the chemical basis and processes of life.

THE FUTURE OF BOTANY

Today, as always during the history of the human population, plants and plant products contribute enormous benefits—food, medicines, clothing and shelter—to a growing human population that is placing ever increasing demands for such resources on the environment. Plant scientists are constantly exploring new avenues of research and searching for new species of plants that may be used to meet these demands. It is interesting to note that botanists estimate that about one third of all plants have yet to be discovered and named. In particular the algae and fungi are poorly investigated groups. At the same time wild plants are becoming extinct rapidly. The rain forests in tropical areas of the world are being destroyed at exceptionally rapid rates and being lost with them are plants that can provide us with as yet unknown drugs and other chemicals that could be of great value to us. Plant scientists are racing to discover useful products of tropical plants before they disappear from the face of the earth. For all of these reasons, botany promises to remain a central and progressive science for humans.

The Characteristics of Life

Plants, like animals and bacteria are living organisms. All living organisms have in common a unique set of properties which distinguishes them from lifeless materials that comprise the nonliving aspects of habitats. The major characteristics of living organisms are described as follows:

Organization. All living organisms exhibit a kind of structured organization. By organization it is meant that there is complexity, composition and nonrandom structure. That is, its makeup is nonuniform—it has parts.

Life Chemistry. Living organisms are chemically comprised of organic compounds, substances which they have manufactured from inorganic chemicals originally obtained from their environment. The major organic compounds that make up organisms include carbohydrates, lipids, proteins and nucleic acids.

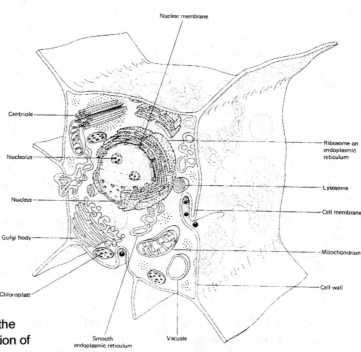

Figure 1–7 Cells represent the fundamental unit of organization of all life. *Source:* Tom M. Graham (1997) p. 31.

Life History. All living organisms go through a sequence of events during their life history. They germinate, or in the case of animals may be born or hatched, for example. They exhibit a period of growth, a time of maturity during which they usually reproduce and then a decline, or "old age" era which terminates when they die.

Metabolism. Organisms are the only physical entities that have the ability to extract nutrients from the environment, chemically transform them to fit their own needs, either as a source of energy or to synthesize tissues for growth. The series of physiological transformations—respiration, anabolism, catabolism and excretion is usually given the collective term, metabolism.

Growth. Growth implies a change in size and often in form as well. However, growth is sometimes relative as some organisms grow by changing form rather than by increasing in size. Growth is also related to metabolism, which provides the energy and molecule building blocks to support growth.

Reproduction. Reproduction is the process of duplication or replication of structures. Nucleic acids can replicate themselves, to produce copies. At the species level, all living organisms have the capability to reproduce. The new individuals are the products of one or more parents.

Movement. Living things move themselves or their structures. Things that are nonlife can be moved, but they don't initiate that movement. Most organisms are capable of movement of some or all parts of the organisms' body. In general, animals exhibit greater mobility than plants, but plant reproductive cells migrate during the fertilization process and plant structures may move. For example, the leaves of the Sensitive Plant close quickly in response to touch and Jewelweed pods twist rapidly to spray their seeds when brushed. Generally, plant movements are much slower and more subtle, especially when compared to animals. Thus, plant leaves, flowers, and even stems move in response to changing conditions of light, water and temperature. The twining of plant tendrils around objects for support, and the movement of leaves as they track the sun are all examples of the mobility of plants.

Response. Life has adapted to and exists in environments where various conditions of light, water and temperature, for example are often changing. The ability of organisms to respond to changing conditions exemplifies a stimulus-response feature unique to organisms. Long term adaptation to changing environmental conditions at the genetic level of the organism is called evolution.

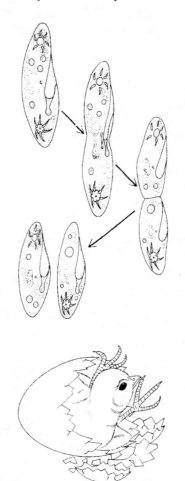

Figure 1–8 Reproduction is a fundamental characteristic of life.
Source: Tom M. Graham (1997), p. 34.

The Basic Characteristics of Life

Unique Life Chemistry	Genetic Content (DNA or RNA or both)
Life History	Reproduction
Response to Environment	Evolutionary Adaptation
Metabolic Events	Movement
Growth	Physiology Processes

Processes. Finally, it must be noted that all of these features define life. That is, life can't be reduced to a definition based on chemicals (everything is made of chemicals), movement (air and water can be in motion), organization (crystals and most other non-living entities are recognized by their organization) or even necessarily evolution or other adaptive characteristics (the sun and earth exhibit an evolution of sorts). Rather, life is all of these processes—respiration, digestion, metabolism, gas exchange and the others. Therefore, we recognize life by its effects. We cannot tell exactly what it is, only what it does and how it reacts. This fact that life transforms matter into new forms through a variety of metabolic processes that occur only in living organisms is the fundamental secret of life.

Key Words and Phrases

autotroph	heterotroph	biology
botany	zoology	observation
scientific method	hypothesis	experiment
theory	scientific law	Aristotle
simple microscope	compound microscope	Herbals
electron microscope	Zacharias Janssen	Pliny
Theophrastus	Anton von Leeuwenhoek	J. B. von Helmont
herbalists	genetic engineering	genetics
plant morphology	cytology	plant ecology
plant geography	plant anatomy	plant taxonomy
plant physiology	systematic botany	Linneaus
characteristics of life	life chemistry	life cycle
metabolism	evolution	movement
processes	life history	growth
reproduction	organization	

Selected References and Resources

Anderson, F. J. 1985. *An Illustrated History of the Herbals*. Columbia University Press. New York.

Anon. 1989. *Botany. Encyclopedia Britannica*. Macropedia.

Ewan, J. Ed. 1969. *A Short History of Botany in the United States*. Lubrecht & Cramer Publishers. Forestburgh, New York

Forbes, J. R. 1992. *Plants in Agriculture*. Cambridge University Press. New York.

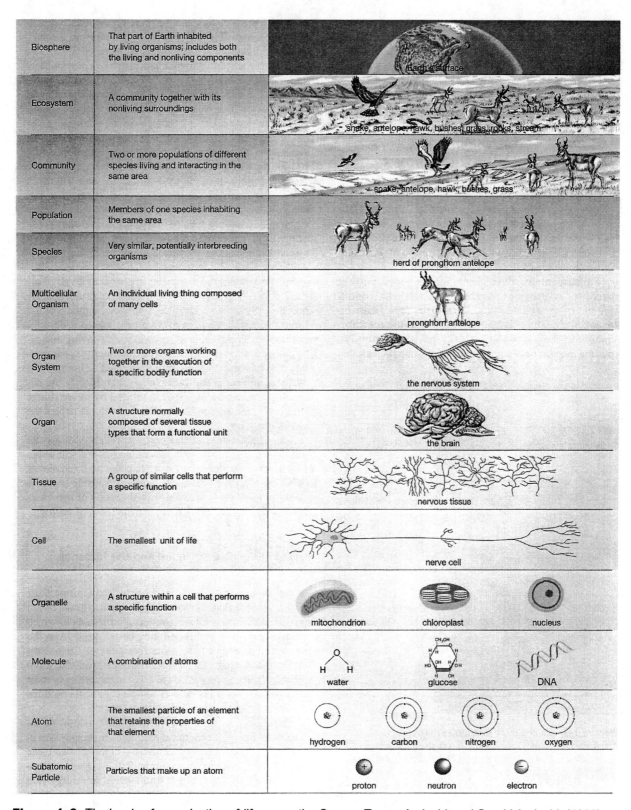

Biosphere	That part of Earth inhabited by living organisms; includes both the living and nonliving components	
Ecosystem	A community together with its nonliving surroundings	snake, antelope, hawk, bushes, grass, rocks, stream
Community	Two or more populations of different species living and interacting in the same area	snake, antelope, hawk, bushes, grass
Population	Members of one species inhabiting the same area	
Species	Very similar, potentially interbreeding organisms	herd of pronghorn antelope
Multicellular Organism	An individual living thing composed of many cells	pronghorn antelope
Organ System	Two or more organs working together in the execution of a specific bodily function	the nervous system
Organ	A structure normally composed of several tissue types that form a functional unit	the brain
Tissue	A group of similar cells that perform a specific function	nervous tissue
Cell	The smallest unit of life	nerve cell
Organelle	A structure within a cell that performs a specific function	mitochondrion chloroplast nucleus
Molecule	A combination of atoms	water glucose DNA
Atom	The smallest particle of an element that retains the properties of that element	hydrogen carbon nitrogen oxygen
Subatomic Particle	Particles that make up an atom	proton neutron electron

Figure 1–9 The levels of organization of life on earth. *Source:* Teresa Audesirk and Gerald Audesirk (1999), p. 3.

Harlan, J. R. 1995. *The Living Fields. Our Agricultural Heritage.* Cambridge University Press. New York.

Harvey-Gibson, R. J. 1981. *Outlines of the History of Botany.* Ayer Company. Salem, New Hampshire.

Judson, H. F. 1979. *The Eighth Day of Creation.* Simon and Schuster. Boston, Massachusetts.

King, J. 1997. *Reaching for the Sun. How Plants Work.* Cambridge University Press. New York.

Mabberley, D. J. 1997. *The Plant Book. A Portable Dictionary of the Vascular Plants.* Cambridge University Press. New York.

Margulis, L. 1982. *Early Life.* Science Books International, Inc. Boston, Massachusetts.

Mayr. E. 1982. *The Growth of Biological Thought: Diversity, Evolution, and Inheritance.* Belknap Press of the Harvard University Press. Cambridge, Massachusetts.

Medawar, P. B. 1989. *Introduction and Intuition in Scientific Thought.* Methuen & Company. London.

Moore, J. A. 1993. *Science as a Way of Knowing the Foundations of Modern Biology.* Harvard University Press. Cambridge, Massachusetts.

Review and Discussion Questions

1. How would you use the scientific method to design an experiment that could test whether plants use water and energy at night?

2. Compare and contrast the development of early agricultural practices in Mesopotamia with those of the Mayan civilization of Mesoamerica. What plants were domesticated and used as principle crops to sustain each of these early civilizations?

3. Trade in plants and plant products has been closely linked with explorations of discovery such as that of Columbus for centuries. What New World plants were adopted for agricultural use in the Old World?

4. The tropical rain forests of the world are being lost because of deforestation at the rate of just about 1 percent each year. What are the potential consequences of this rapid loss for humans?

5. What is the field of ethnobotany? Trace the rise in interest and importance attached to this rapidly developing aspect of the science of botany.

Chapter 2

Chemistry of Life

Some Basic Chemistry
Organic Chemistry of Life
Chemistry of Protoplasm
From Chemicals to Living Organisms

Life is made up of chemical matter and chemical energy. In fact, everything in the universe is made up of chemical matter and energy. **Matter** is anything that occupies space and has mass while energy is the capacity to do work, that is, to promote transformations. Examples of matter are everywhere—the food we eat, the rocks we step on and the stars we see are all commonplace examples of matter. Light, heat, motion, and gravitation are examples of energy. Matter and energy are actually interrelated phenomena as they can be converted one into the other and back, a fact shown by Einstein's equation $E = mc2$, where E = energy, m = mass and c = the speed of light. This equation tells us that matter can be changed into energy and energy into matter.

Matter is structured energy. Energy is randomized matter in motion.

Matter exists in a number of different kinds that are called elements. All life and other substances are made up of elements and combinations of elements. Chemically, elements are the simplest substances that have uniquely different properties and cannot be further subdivided by normal chemical and physical means. Elements such as gold, copper, silver and sulfur were known for centuries, however, most of the elements have been discovered only within the last 100 years. Today, we recognize 92 kinds of naturally occurring elements and another 18 have been artificially manufactured in cyclotrons and nuclear reactors.

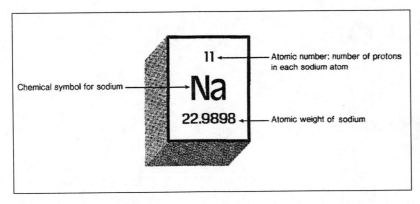

Figure 2–1 The chemical element sodium as displayed in the periodic table. The chemical symbol, atomic number, and the atomic weight of the element are all displayed. *Source:* Tom M. Graham (1997), p. 49.

About 40 of the naturally occurring elements are found in living organisms. Four of these, carbon, hydrogen, oxygen, and nitrogen comprise about 95 percent of the element makeup of all organisms while the remaining are present in considerably smaller amounts. Whether found in nature or in life, each element is known by its chemical name and by a one or two letter symbol. For example, carbon is C, nitrogen is N, iron is Fe and Chlorine is Cl.

The fundamental unit of elements are atoms. Elements differ from one another in the size and chemical activity of their atoms. Atoms of elements may chemically bind together to form a seemingly endless variety of substances. These substances can be represented by a common name and a chemical formula that includes the list of elements which comprise the substance along with the number of atoms of each element. For example, the simple sugar glucose (blood sugar in humans) is chemically $C_6H_{12}O_6$ which tells us that glucose is comprised of 6 atoms of the element carbon, 12 atoms of the element hydrogen, and 6 atoms of the element oxygen. To understand how atoms of elements differ from one another and also chemically bind together we must consider the atomic structure and activity of atoms.

Atomic Structure

Atoms are like building blocks which, when put together, can produce an infinite variety of substances. Atoms have the ability to make variations of substances because not all atoms are identical. It has been found that atoms have an atomic structure reminiscent of a solar system with a central sun and revolving planets. The central mass of the atom is a positively charged structure called the **nucleus**. The nucleus is the most massive part of the atom and consists of a cluster of **protons** and **neutrons**. Protons are atomic particles that have a positive electrical charge. Neutrons are similar in mass to protons, but are particles that are neutral, that is, they do not carry an electrical charge.

Atoms are the basic building blocks of nature. Each atom consists of protons, neutrons and electrons.

Revolving (or orbiting) around the central nucleus are negatively charged atomic particles called **electrons,** each with a mass about 1/1836 of that of a proton or neutron. The electrons are important for several reasons. The negative charge of the electrons balances the positive charge of the protons in the nucleus. The number of electrons always equals the number of protons (except in the case of certain kinds of atoms called ions), so an atom is normally electrically neutral.

Figure 2–2 The atomic structure of several biologically important atoms. *Source:* Teresa Audesirk and Gerald Audesirk (1996), p. 24.

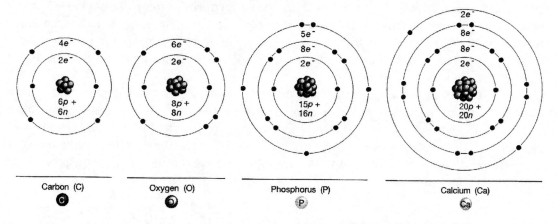

The electrons of an atom occupy a series of **orbits** or **energy shells** around the nucleus and are constantly in motion, forming a kind of electron cloud around the nucleus. Electrons not only rotate within their energy shell (orbit) but can change from one energy shell to another if the atom gains or loses energy. These energy shells with their electrons form a specific configuration around the nucleus of the atom. Each energy shell around a nucleus can hold a maximum number of electrons. The energy shell nearest the nucleus can hold a maximum of 2 electrons occupying it at any point in time. The next electron energy shell (orbit) can hold a maximum of 8 electrons at any one time. While some of the larger atoms have an energy shell that can hold more than eight electrons, the outer energy shell of all atoms (of all elements) can hold a maximum of 8 electrons at any one time. Since the inner shells are filled first, the last or outermost energy shell may be filled or may be incompletely filled. For example, atoms of hydrogen, the simplest element, are comprised of a single proton in the nucleus and a single electron occupying the first energy shell. Since the first energy shell can hold two electrons, the energy shell of a hydrogen atom is incomplete. Atoms of helium (which are the next smallest atoms found in nature) are comprised of two protons and two neutrons in the nucleus and two electrons in the first energy shell. Since this energy shell can only hold two electrons, it is completely filled.

To compare atoms of hydrogen and helium with atoms of larger elements, consider oxygen, which has 8 protons, 8 neutrons, and 8 electrons. An oxygen atom has 2 electrons in its first energy shell and the remaining 6 electrons in the second energy shell. Since the second energy shell can hold a maximum of 8 electrons, it is incomplete.

The atoms of different elements can also be distinguished by their **atomic number** and **atomic mass**. The atomic number of an element refers to the number of protons making up each atom of an element. Comparatively, the atomic mass of an element is the sum of its protons, neutrons, and electrons.

Isotopes. While all of the atoms of a particular element have the same number of protons and electrons, some elements have atoms that differ in their number of neutrons. These different kinds of atoms of the same element are called **isotopes**. For example, most atoms of hydrogen consist of 1 proton and 1 electron. Two rarer forms of hydrogen are known; deuterium, which consists of 1 proton, 1 neutron, and 1 electron, and tritium, which has atoms comprised of one proton, 2 neutrons, and 1 electron. Both deuterium and tritium are, therefore, isotopes of the element hydrogen. Uranium is another well known example of an element that has several isotopes.

Uranium exists in a variety of forms (U^{233}, U^{235}, U^{238}). The most abundant form, U^{238} has a nucleus containing 92 protons and 146 neutrons and a series of electron energy shells that contain a total of 92 electrons. The other forms of uranium also have 92 protons and electrons, but differ in the number of neutrons in their nucleus. Because neutrons have much less affect on the chemical activity of atoms compared to protons and electrons, most isotopes are indistinguishable from "normal" atoms of an element but their atomic mass differs.

Some isotopes, however, are unstable and emit particles of gamma rays, beta rays (electrons), or alpha rays (helium nuclei). In the process, these isotopes decay into smaller and eventually more stable atoms. Atoms of uranium, for example, spontaneously decay into stable atoms of lead over billions of years. Researchers make use of radioisotopes to trace chemical pathways of metabolism and other physiological events in plants and animals.

Molecules and Compounds

In nature, atoms of helium, neon, and argon have filled outer electron shells and are chemically stable. Conversely, all other atoms have unfilled outer electron shells and are chemically unstable. Given proper conditions, these unstable atoms can gain, lose, or share electrons by combining with other atoms to become stable. Carbon dioxide (CO_2), for example, is a combination of one atom of the element carbon and two atoms of the element oxygen. Even the oxygen that we breathe is actually comprised of two atoms of oxygen bonded together (O_2). Combinations of atoms are called **molecules** or **compounds**.

A **molecule** is comprised of two or more atoms of the same or different elements. Thus, the water molecule, H_2O, is comprised of two atoms of hydrogen and one atom of oxygen while the sugar glucose ($C_6H_{12}O_6$) is made up of 6 atoms of carbon, 6 atoms of oxygen and 12 atoms of hydrogen. Glucose is therefore also a chemical molecule.

A **compound** is comprised of two or more molecules, usually bound together in very specific ratios. Two common examples of compounds include sucrose, which is made up of a molecule of glucose bonded with a molecule of fructose, and cellulose, which is comprised of several thousand glucose molecules bonded together forming long chains.

To a chemist, both molecules and compounds are combinations of atoms but only compounds represent aggregates of atoms of different elements. Thus, of our examples, water, carbon dioxide and glucose are molecules and also compounds (they are comprised of different elements) but only respiratory oxygen (O_2) is a molecule in the strict chemical definition.

Chemical Bonding

The number of electrons in the outer energy shell of an atom determines the stability and chemical activity of the atom. Atoms that have a single energy shell holding 2 electrons are stable and chemically inactive. Larger atoms that have an outer energy shell containing eight electrons are also filled and are chemically stable. If the total number of electrons in the outer energy shell of an atom is less than four the atom may lose electrons to a more active atom. In this interaction, the atom with fewer than four electrons in its outer shell is called an **electron donor** because it donates electrons to another atom. An electron donor is also called a **metal**. If the number of electrons in the outer shell is five or more but less than eight, the atom is an electron acceptor and is called a **non-metal**.

The number of electrons in the atom's outer energy shell also determines the electrical charge or **oxidation number (valence)** of the atom. An atom that has one electron in its outer energy shell can donate its electron to an active non-metal and is said to have an oxidation number of $+1$. If an atom has seven electrons in its outer energy shell it can accept one electron from a donor atom and has an oxidation number of -1. All atoms with electrical charges are called **ions**.

The number of electrons in the outer energy shell of an atom determines its chemical stability and activity.

When atoms are placed together they may interact in the form of a chemical reaction. Usually the end products of these reactions are different both chemically and physically from the free atoms. When atoms combine into molecules (or molecules split into atoms), energy may be consumed or released in the process of the chemical reaction.

The electromagnetic forces that hold atoms bonded together in molecules are called **chemical bonds**. There are several types of chemical bonds and they differ in their strength of attraction and their importance in biological systems.

Ionic Bonds. The strongest kind of chemical bond is the **ionic bond**. This type of chemical bond occurs when a metal and non-metal combine to produce a substance called a **salt**. The ionic bond is formed by the transfer of an electron from the outer energy shell of one atom (the donor) to the outer energy shell of another atom (the acceptor). The two atoms are bound together by this process and at the same time the outer energy shells of both atoms are filled.

To illustrate ionic bonding, consider how atoms of sodium (Na) and chlorine (Cl) bond to form salt (NaCl). Atoms of sodium are comprised of 11 protons, 11 neutrons, and 11 electrons. In terms of its atomic structure, 2 electrons occupy the first energy shell, 8 the second energy shell and 1 occupies the third energy shell. The single electron in the outer shell gives sodium a valence of $+1$. Atoms of chlorine have 17 electrons, 2 in the inner shell, 8 in the next shell, and 7 in the outer shell. Since the outer shell of a sodium atom can hold another electron, chlorine can be an acceptor and has a valence of -1. When an atom of sodium ionically bonds with an atom of chlorine one electron from sodium is transferred to chlorine. With that electron gone, the sodium atom has one less energy shell but now its outermost energy shell has eight electrons in it and is completely full and chemically stable. The chlorine atom accepts the electron from sodium and thereby completes its outer energy shell from seven to eight electrons. Since it gave up an electron to chlorine, the sodium atom has 11 protons and 10 electrons and is positively charged. Conversely, the chlorine atom now has 17 protons and 18 electrons and therefore is negatively charged. Since unlike atoms attract one another, the positive sodium atom is attracted to and bonds with the negative chlorine atom to form NaCl, which is chemically stable. Chemical processes in which an atom loses one or more electrons are called **oxidation reactions** while those in which an atom gains electrons are called **reduction reactions**. Since both kinds of reactions occur at the same time they are usually called **oxidation-reduction reactions** or **redox reactions**.

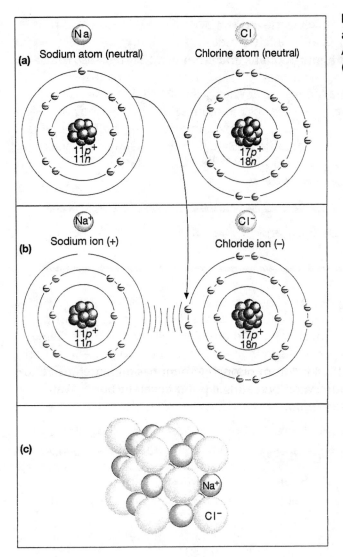

Figure 2–3 The formation of ions and ionic bonds. *Source:* Teresa Audesirk and Gerald Audesir (1999), p. 25.

(a)
Na
Sodium atom (neutral)
Cl
Chlorine atom (neutral)
$11p^+$
$11n$
$17p^+$
$18n$

(b)
Na$^+$
Sodium ion (+)
Cl$^-$
Chloride ion (–)
$11p^+$
$11n$
$17p^+$
$18n$

(c)
Na$^+$
Cl$^-$

Ionic bonding is the most common form of chemical activity in inorganic compounds, (that is, compounds outside of living systems). Ionic bonds may also occur in living systems as well. Ionic bonds are strong and require a lot of energy to disrupt them and split the molecule.

Covalent Bonds. One of the most common types of chemical bonds found in living organisms is the covalent bond. Covalent bonds involve a kind of "sharing" of electrons between the bonded atoms. That is, the electron or electrons spend time in the outer energy shells of each of the atoms bonded together so in a sense they are shared by the two bonded atoms.

Most of the organic molecules found in living organisms are examples of covalent bonding of atoms of carbon with other carbon atoms and with hydrogen and oxygen atoms. Carbon is a very unique element; each carbon atom has four electrons in its outer energy shell. Since carbon's outer energy shell can normally hold 8 electrons, carbon's shell is half empty (or half full). This means that carbon can donate electrons to, or accept electrons from, other atoms. Carbon atoms are also distinctive because they can bond with one another, sharing the electrons in their outer shells. This unique ability of carbon atoms to bond with one another can produce long chains of carbon-to-carbon molecules which serve as a kind of skeletal framework on which atoms of other elements (e.g., hydrogen and oxygen) can be bonded.

One of the most common elements in plants and other living systems is hydrogen, which is usually covalently bonded to carbon. Compared to carbon, hydrogen can act as an electron donor or electron acceptor. When an atom of hydrogen bonds with an atom of carbon they each "share" the hydrogen's electron. For example, if four hydrogen atoms covalently bond with carbon, they form a chemical compound known as methane (CH_4). The carbon atom in methane now has eight electrons (four from the carbon atom and one each from the four hydrogen atoms) in its outer shell and is filled. Similarly, because of the "sharing" of electrons between carbon and hydrogen, each of the hydrogen atoms sometimes has two electrons in its outer shell and is also filled.

Since electrons are equally shared between atoms in covalent bonds, this type of chemical bonding is considered to be stronger than the ionic bonding that occurs in salts. Furthermore, the sharing of electrons in covalent bonds produces molecules of considerable flexibility—that is, molecules can be more easily formed and more easily broken compared to most other types of chemical bonds. Since the metabolic activities of plants require that organic molecules (with covalent bonds) often have to be converted into other organic molecules (proteins to sugars, or the reverse, for example), the covalent bonds require lower energies and shorter times for conversions.

In most examples of covalent bonding the electrons are equally shared by the two atoms. In some molecules, however, the atom of one element has a greater attraction for the shared electron than the other atom, creating a **polar covalent bond**. Water is a familiar example of a polar covalent bond. A molecule of water consists of two atoms of hydrogen covalently bonded to an atom of oxygen. However, the oxygen atom more

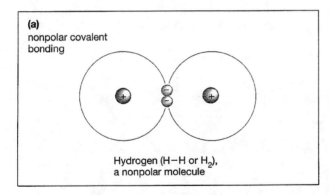

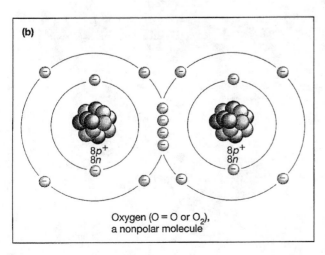

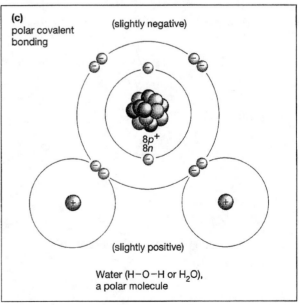

Figure 2–4 The formation of covalent bonds.
Source: Teresa Audesirk and Gerald Audesir (1999), p. 26.

strongly attracts the "shared" electrons, which consequently spend more time in oxygen's outer electron shell. The mostly "electron less" hydrogens become slightly positive (the proton is not always balanced by a negative electron) while the oxygen atom becomes slightly negative as it sometimes has two extra negative electrons. Since the electron sharing is unequal, polar covalent bonds are somewhat weaker than covalent bonds.

Hydrogen Bonds. A third basic type of chemical bond found in organic compounds involves chemical attractions between hydrogen atoms. As a result of its single proton and single electron the hydrogen atom exhibits a polarity. That means the atom has a positive side and a negative side. The positive side of a hydrogen atom can be attracted to a negative charge of another hydrogen atom (or other atoms of another element) while the negative side can be attracted to a positive charge of another molecule, including hydrogen. One of the effects of hydrogen bonding is seen in water, in which hydrogen atoms are attracted to one another, creating a surface tension at the air-water interface that slows water evaporation and acts as a barrier to the entry and exit of small animals into and out of the water. The attraction of hydrogen atoms to one another can act as chemical connecting bridges between adjacent organic molecules. For example, hydrogen bonds are the main attractive forces that hold the molecules of proteins, DNA, and other nucleic acids together.

Although comparatively weak, hydrogen bonds are of great importance in maintaining the shape and orientation of nucleic acids and many other organic compounds. Very often the three-dimensional shape of an organic chemical is more important than its structural composition in determining its properties and reactivity. For example, the very specific chemical configuration of many enzymes is due to the hydrogen bonds which maintain their shape.

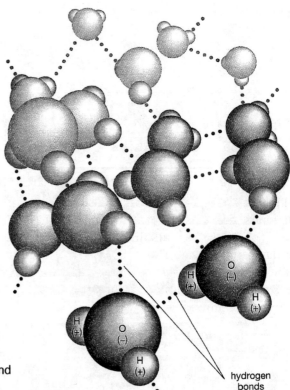

Figure 2–5 Hydrogen bonds of water molecules. *Source:* Teresa Audesirk and Gerald Audesir (1999), p. 28.

hydrogen bonds

Disulfide Bonds. A fourth type of bonding between atoms involves sulfur (S) and is called a disulfide bond. The bonds form between hydrocarbons and sulfur in the same way they form with hydrogen. The shape of the sulfur atom exhibits a polarity that allows it to create magnetic attractions between different molecules or different parts of the same molecule. Disulfide bonds are particularly important in maintaining the complex shapes of proteins.

Acids, Bases, Salts, and pH

Chemical and physiological processes that occur within animals operate most efficiently only within a fairly narrow acid-base (pH) range. In fact, at higher or lower pH enzymes may be disrupted or destroyed and physiological events stopped.

An **acid** is any chemical substance that releases hydrogen (H^+) ions when it is dissolved in water. For example, when placed in an aqueous solution, hydrochloric acid (HCl) dissolves, releasing H^+ and Cl^- ions. An acid is a strong acid if it dissolves completely or almost completely in an aqueous solution. Conversely, a weak acid dissolves only partially in an aqueous solution and releases only a comparatively few H^+ ions. Hydrochloric acid and nitric acid (HNO_3) are two examples of strong acids which dissolve almost completely. Carbonic acid (H_2CO_3) only partially dissolves in water and is therefore considered a weak acid. The introduction of H^+ ions in a solution is important because they lower the pH, i.e., making the solution more acidic.

A **base** is any substance that releases hydroxyl ions (OH^-) when dissolved, and strong bases dissolve completely or almost completely. A strong base like sodium hydroxide (NaOH), for example, will fragment into Na^+ and OH^- ions in water.

A **salt** is a molecular combination of an acid and a base. To illustrate, if hydrochloric acid (HCl) and sodium hydroxide (NaOH) are introduced in an aqueous solution they will dissolve into H^+ and Cl^- and Na^+ and OH^- ions respectively. The Na^+ and Cl^- ions bond to form a salt NaCl (table salt) while the H^+ and OH^- ions combine to form H_2O.

Fluids of plants and animals and solutions of all kinds are classified as **acidic, basic** (more commonly called **alkaline**), or **neutral,** depending on the proportion of H^+ and OH^- ions they contain. In acidic solutions there are more H^+ ions, in alkaline solutions the OH^- ions are more abundant and, of course, in neutral solutions the two ions are present in equal concentrations. The degree of acidity or alkalinity of a solution is expressed as the **pH** of that solution. Most plant fluids are slightly

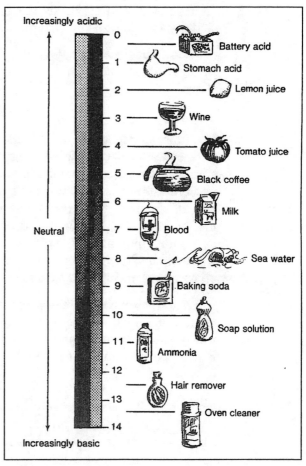

Figure 2–6 The pH scale. *Source:* Tom M. Graham 1997, p. 75.

alkaline (about 7.2–7.4 pH) although fluids secreted by root tips may be acidic at pH 2.5 or so.

The pH of fluids is closely maintained by substances called **buffers**. Buffers are chemicals that can combine with strong acids or strong bases and convert them into weaker acids and bases, thereby preventing changes in the overall pH. An example of a common buffer is sodium bicarbonate ($NaHCO_3$), a salt which strongly dissociates into Na^+ and the bicarbonate ion HCO_3^-. Thus, when a strong acid such as HCl is added to the solution and dissociates into H^+ and Cl^- ions the HCO_3 combines with the H^+ ions liberated from HCl to produce H_2CO_3 (carbonic acid). Since carbonic is a weak acid and dissociates only slowly and slightly the pH of the solution remains almost unchanged. Conversely, if a strong base such as NaOH is added to a solution containing $NaHCO_3$ the OH^- ions from the base react with the H^+ ions released from sodium bicarbonate to form H_2O and again, the pH of the solution is unchanged.

Types of Chemical Reactions

Chemical reactions drive the activity of cells and ultimately of living organisms. In fact, chemical reactions comprise most of a cell's biochemical activities. Chemical reactions involve atoms and molecules called **reactants** that are chemically altered to form **products**. Some typical kinds of chemical reactions include exchange reactions, decomposition reactions, and synthesis reactions. In living systems, most of these chemical reactions are catalyzed by enzymes.

Decomposition Reactions. In decomposition reactions larger molecules are broken down into smaller molecules or atoms. A generic decomposition reaction is as follows:

$$AB \longrightarrow A + B.$$

Almost all decomposition reactions in living systems involve the addition of water and are often called **hydrolysis** or **hydrolytic** reactions. Decomposition reactions in animals include the enzymatic breakdown of food during digestion. For example, animals typically consume foodstuffs in the form of fats, proteins, and carbohydrates. Since all of these organic molecules are too large and too complex to be absorbed they must be chemically decomposed. Proteins (the reactants) are enzymatically decomposed into amino acids (the products), fats into fatty acids and glycerol molecules and carbohydrates into monosaccharides, all of which can then be absorbed. Decomposition reactions in cells are also called **catabolism**.

Synthesis Reactions. Also known as **anabolism** when occurring in cells, synthesis reactions are the opposite of decomposition reactions in that molecules are assembled from reactants, that is, larger molecules are assembled from smaller molecules. The form a typical synthesis reaction takes is as follows:

$$A + B \longrightarrow AB.$$

Most synthesis reactions involve the removal of water or dehydration during the reactions. The growth of cells and of organisms involves synthesis reactions in which new cellular components are manufactured which ultimately contribute to an overall increase in size of the organism.

Exchange Reactions. Exchange reactions involve two reactants which transfer some of their atoms or molecules to form two products as follows:

$$AB + BC = AC + BD.$$

Many of the exchange reactions that occur in plants involve the activity of buffers. To illustrate how an exchange reaction involving a buffer works, consider, for example, how hydrochloric acid (HCl) from the human stomach is effectively buffered by sodium bicarbonate ($NaHCO_3$) secreted by the small intestine, liver, and pancreas as follows:

$$HCl + NaHCO_3 \longrightarrow NaCl + H_2CO_3$$

Reversible Reactions. Most chemical reactions that occur in cells and plant fluids are reversible as illustrated as follows:

$$AB \leftrightarrow A + B$$

In reversible reactions, chemical reactions continue until the concentrations of reactants and products on either side of the equation come to an equilibrium. Note that in reversible reactions either side of the equation may represent products or reactants. That is, if the reaction is going from left to right AB is the reactant and A and B are the products and the reaction is a decomposition reaction. Conversely, if the reaction is going from right to left then (of course) A and B are the reactants and AB is the product in a synthesis reaction.

The Chemistry of Life

Living organisms are a complex chemical mixture of water, minerals, gases, carbohydrates, fats, and proteins, most of which can be variously labeled as either **nutrients** or **metabolites**. Nutrients include water, **inorganic** minerals, and other substances obtained in the diet while metabolites are substances living organisms manufacture through synthesis or decomposition reactions. Nutrients and metabolites can be classed into either **inorganic** or **organic** chemicals.

INORGANIC CHEMISTRY OF LIFE

The most important inorganic chemicals in living organisms include water, oxygen, carbon dioxide, and a variety of inorganic salts, acids, and bases. Of these, water is the single most abundant inorganic substance and also the most important. Depending on the specific type of cell, water comprises some 60–90 percent of it, by content. In comparison, other inorganic chemicals generally make up less than one percent of plant cells and tissues. Water has several unique properties that make it important to life.

Chemical reactions take place in solution. Almost all of the thousands of different chemical reactions that occur in cells take place in water (aqueous) solutions. Water is often a participant in these reactions, as the addition of water (hydrolysis) accompanies the chemical decomposition of substances into products. Conversely, many synthesis biochemical reactions also involve the removal of water (dehydrolysis).

Water and Cell Shape and Form. Water dictates the shape and form of most plant cells. If water is removed from a cell the cell shrinks and changes form and usually cell

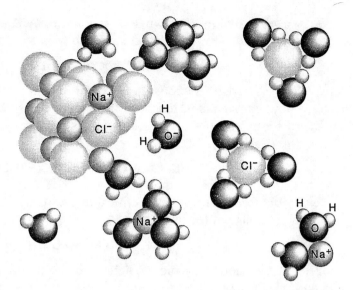

Figure 2–7 The use of water as a solvent. *Source:* Teresa Audesirk and Gerald Audesirk (1999), p. 28.

function is impaired as well. If water is added to a cell the cell swells to maintain turgor pressure.

Water and Temperature. Water has a very high specific heat, which allows it to absorb or give off heat with very little change in overall temperature. This means that cells can absorb or lose much heat without experiencing a serious increase or decline in temperature which might damage the cell or impair its physiological activities.

Water as a lubricant. Water is an excellent lubricant for reducing friction between adjacent surfaces. Even thin films of water greatly reduce friction. In humans, for example, a thin film of water lubricates joints, bones, muscles, and organs that otherwise would rub against one another.

Water as a Solvent. Water is almost a universal solvent as many substances will dissolve in it, forming a solution in which water is the **solvent** and the ions, minerals, and other dissolved substances are the **solute**. Generally there are three types of mixtures involving water as a solvent or a medium: solutions, suspensions, and colloid suspensions.

Solutions. One type of mixture is called a **solution**. Solutions consist of a solvent in which extremely small solute particles are dissolved. These small particles cannot be filtered out and will not settle out if left undisturbed. When we make tea or coffee we are making a solution.

Suspensions. A second type of a aqueous mixture is a **suspension**. In suspensions, larger solute particles are dissolved in the solvent. If the mixture is left undisturbed these larger particles will tend to precipitate, or settle out. For example, to make lemonade we mix a solution of bits of lemon, sugar and water. If left standing the particles of lemon settle to the bottom of the glass.

Colloidal Suspensions. The third type of aqueous mixture is a **colloidal suspension**. In colloidal suspensions, particles of solute may be large or small but most are intermediate in size. Particles suspended in colloids do not separate out because the molecules are electrically charged. Similar electrical charges repel each other: thus in colloids the molecules are kept in a continual state of movement because of constantly being repelled by other molecules. This form of interaction results in a mixture in which molecules are held in place and do not settle out despite the particle size.

Colloids have several distinct properties compared to other types of mixtures. For example, due to particle size colloids do not easily pass through membranes. Thus they can be retained in the living system easily. The large size of some organic compounds in colloids creates a tremendous surface area for chemical action. Lastly, there is the phenomenon of phase reversal or **sol-gel transformation**. Colloids can change to a spongy solid (gel) which holds liquids and other particles or it can become a fluid (sol). Colloids can take different forms, depending on temperature, electrical charge, or pH. This phase reversal phenomena is characteristic of protoplasm and is responsible for the contraction of cells, movement of organs, and thousands of other activities of life.

ORGANIC CHEMISTRY OF LIFE

In common usage organic molecules refer to all chemical substances that are manufactured by plants and animals and that have a basic carbon-to-carbon bonding structure. Organic chemicals are the chemical compounds that form most of the physical structure of plants and other living organisms. They are also the most important chemicals in the physiology of living systems.

The organic chemicals of living organisms are often called **hydrocarbons** because they consist of combinations of atoms of carbon and hydrogen to which atoms of other elements, chiefly oxygen but also nitrogen, calcium, phosphorous, iron, and many others, for example, may be bonded. These hydrocarbons of life are held together by covalent bonds. The versatility of the carbon atom and the simplicity of the hydrogen atom can produce an infinite number of compounds of varying complexity. Over a million organic molecules have been identified and the potential variety is almost endless. The most important types of organic chemicals in living organisms are carbohydrates, lipids, proteins, and nucleic acids.

Carbohydrates

Carbohydrates are the most abundant organic compounds in nature. The major carbohydrates include the sugars, starches, and cellulose. All carbohydrates consist of atoms of carbon, hydrogen and oxygen. Typically carbohydrates are comprised of equal numbers of carbon and oxygen atoms and twice as many hydrogen atoms, occurring in a H-C-OH groupings. For example, glucose, a common sugar found in candy, has the chemical formula $C_6H_{12}O_6$.

Carbohydrates serve three basic functions in living organisms. Simple sugars are the principal energy molecules that provide the energy to power the vast range of physiological activities in cells. For example, all plants (and animals too) rely on the glucose for most of their energy needs. Glucose is a simple sugar that plants photosynthetically produce by combining a molecule of water and a molecule of carbon dioxide using the energy of sunlight.

Carbohydrates are also important structural components of plasma membranes and other cellular structures. Some carbohydrates bound with proteins to form **glycoproteins** which help strengthen the plasma membranes. More complex carbohydrates such as cellulose provide a rigid and protective outer wall that forms, shapes, and protects plants. Animals also store carbohydrate energy in their tissues in the form of larger carbohydrates such as glycogen (animal starch). Three basic kinds of carbohydrates are common in living systems, monosaccharides, disaccharides, and polysaccharides.

Figure 2–8 The chemical structure of several monosaccharides. *Source:* Teresa Audesirk and Gerald Audesirk (1996), p. 40.

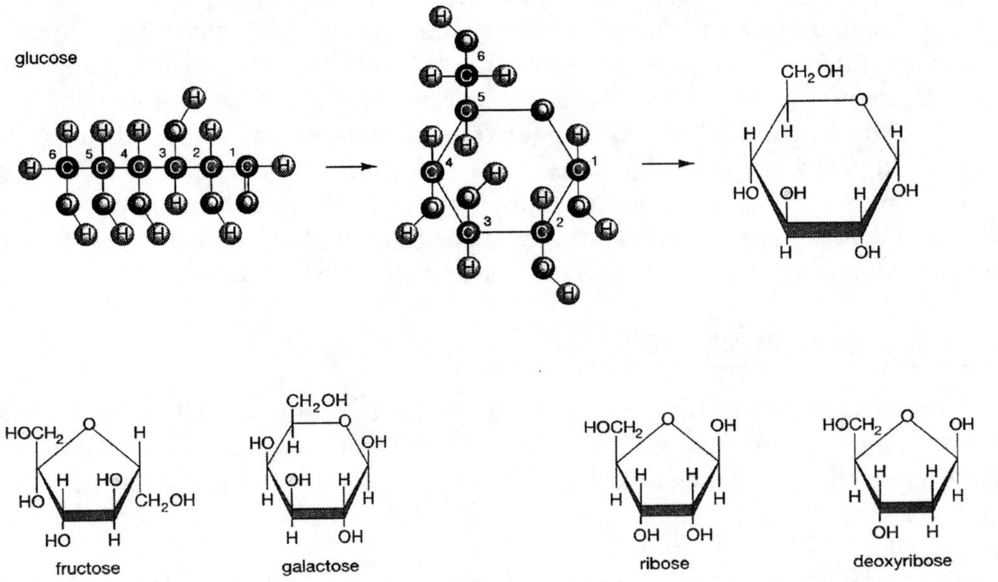

Monosaccharides. The simplest kinds of carbohydrates are monosaccharides (mono = one, saccharides = sugar), which, as their name implies, consist of a single sugar molecule. Simple sugars consisting of four carbons are called **tetroses**, with five carbons are **pentoses**, with six carbons they are called **hexoses**, and with seven carbons they are **heptoses**. While all simple sugars are illustrated as a straight chain of carbons to which are bonded hydrogen and oxygen atoms, in water their active ends tend to bond, thereby forming ring structures.

Examples of simple sugars include glucose, galactose, ribose and fructose; the last is a common sugar found in fruits. Glucose is the energy molecule used by almost all living organisms. When a plant cell requires energy to do work a molecule of glucose is enzymatically broken down and the energy contained in its chemical bonds is extracted to do the cell's work. Other monosaccharides such as ribose are used as structural components of nucleic acids and other organic compounds. Monosaccharides can also be chemically combined to form disaccharides and polysaccharides.

Disaccharides. Carbohydrates made up of two sugar molecules are called disaccharides. Disaccharides are generally manufactured by a condensation reaction in which two monosaccharides are covalently bonded and water is removed (dehydration). A common example of a disaccharide is sucrose (cane sugar or table sugar), which is comprised of a molecule of glucose and a molecule of fructose bonded together. Sucrose is used to transport sugars from one part of the plant to another. Other examples of disaccharides include maltose, composed of two glucose molecules, and lactose (milk sugar) which is made up of a molecule of glucose and galactose.

Polysaccharides. Carbohydrates comprised of many molecules of simple sugars bonded together to form long chains are called polysaccharides. Polysaccharides and other large, complex organic molecules which are comprised of long chains of similar units are called **polymers**.

Figure 2–9 The molecular structure of cellulose as a polysaccharide. *Source:* Teresa Audesirk and Gerald Audesirk (1996), p. 39.

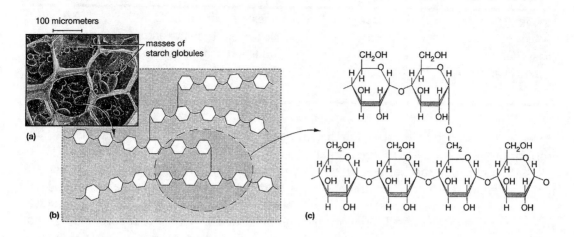

Figure 2–10 The molecular structure of cellulose as a polysaccharide. *Source:* Teresa Audesirk and Gerald Audesirk (1996), p. 40.

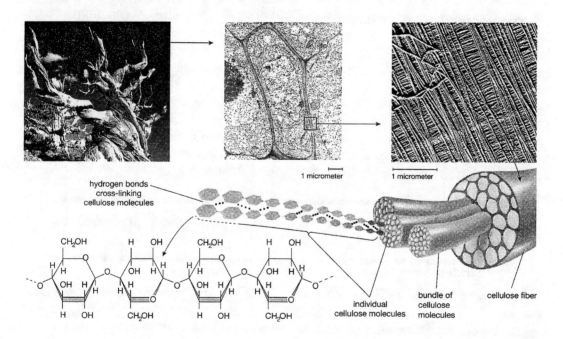

Polysaccharides are among the most common substances in nature. Two of them, cellulose and starch are especially important to plants and animals as well. Cellulose has been called the most common organic molecule in nature. Almost all of a plant's structural tissues are comprised of cellulose. Chemically, cellulose is a large polysaccharide comprised of about 2,000 glucose molecules bonded together to form a long chain. Cellulose is a basic component of plant cell walls and provides a strong structure that helps support the weight of the plant. Although cellulose is abundant in nature animals have difficulty digesting cellulose and instead rely mostly on starch for food. Com-

Table 2-1 Examples of plant carbohydrates.

Type or Class	Examples	Function in Plants
Monosaccharides	glucose	Energy source for cells
	ribose	Nucleic acid component
Disaccharides	sucrose	Transport and storage sugar
Polysaccharides	starch	Storage molecule for carbohydrate energy
	cellulose	Structural component of plant cell walls

prised of 68 glucose molecules, starch is the plant's way of storing sugars and is also an important food source for many animals.

Two other polysaccharides that are important components of plant structure include pectin and lignin. Pectins are sticky carbohydrates that act as a kind of plant "glue" to hold the cells, tissues, and other plant structures in place. Lignins permeate many cells and tissues to solidify and strengthen tissues. In some cases layers of lignins form an impenetrable barrier that helps prevent bacteria and fungi from invading plant tissues.

Lipids

Lipids are a class of hydrocarbons that include the fats and substances that have fat-like properties. Lipids are comprised of carbon, hydrogen, and oxygen atoms. Structurally, they resemble carbohydrates but have much less oxygen per molecule than carbon and hydrogen. Lipid molecules form fatty or oily substances which are insoluble in water but are soluble in substances such as ether and acetone.

Lipids have many important functions in plants. Since most lipids contain many high energy bonds they can be oxidized to provide large quantities of energy when needed. Many plants also store energy in the form of lipids such as plant oils. As energy storage molecules, lipids are actually more efficient than carbohydrates because they are mostly hydrocarbons. Some kinds of lipids are also integral features of cellular structures such as ribosomes, mitochondria and cell membranes.

Four basic kinds of lipids are common in nature: triglycerides, phospholipids, waxes and steroids.

Triglycerides. Also known as neutral fats, triglycerides are especially abundant as fats and are an important source of fuels. Triglycerides are compounds made up of four molecules: three fatty acid molecules and a glycerol molecule all covalently bonded together. Glycerol is a three-carbon molecule to which is bonded hydrogen and oxygen. Fatty acids are typically long chains of carbons, generally varying from 14 to 24 carbons in length. Two other kinds of neutral fats are **diglycerides**, which consist of a glycerol molecule and two fatty acids, and **monoglycerides**, which have a single fatty acid chain bonded to the glycerol molecule.

Fatty acids come in two varieties, saturated and unsaturated fatty acids. In **saturated fatty acids** every carbon atom of the carbon-to-carbon chain is bonded to two hydrogen atoms. Because their bonding points are all filled, saturated fatty acids are less active chemically; most are solid at room temperature. They function primarily as energy storage and transport compounds. Examples of saturated fatty acids include dairy butter, lard, and bacon fat. In comparison, some of the carbon atoms of **unsatu-**

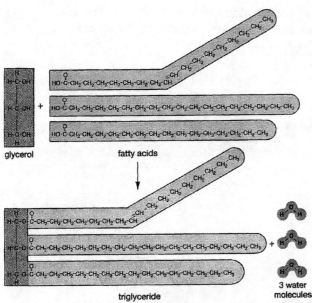

Figure 2–11 The chemical structure of triglycerides. *Source:* Teresa Audesirk and Gerald Audesirk (1996), p. 44.

rated fatty acids are bonded to a single hydrogen molecule, consequently, the bonding points are vacant (meaning that they are not bonded with hydrogen or oxygen atoms); instead, the carbons are said to be double-bonded with each other. Due to the energy storage in these vacant bonds, unsaturated fatty acid molecules are generally much more chemically active. Fatty acids that have several double-bonded carbons along the carbon-to-carbon chain are termed polyunsaturated fatty acids. Most unsaturated fatty acids are liquid at room temperature. They are especially common in plants and include peanut oil, corn oil, and olive oil. The plant oils used to manufacture margarine are also an example of unsaturated fatty acids.

Phospholipids resemble triglycerides except that one of the fatty acids has a phospholipid molecule attached along with a nitrogen-containing base. Phospholipids are unique among lipids in that they have a soluble and insoluble component. Although the glycerol and fatty acids are insoluble in water the phosphate molecule is charged and polar, thereby permitting phospholipids to bind proteins and other water-soluble molecules to molecules that are insoluble.

The phosphate tails of phospholipids also bind with one another, forming the unique, double-membrane that bounds and protects plant and animal cells. Phospholipids are also important in the makeup of membranes that bound and protect the organelles of the cytoplasm and the nuclear membrane.

Waxes. Waxes are a kind of lipid-like substances constructed by combining fatty acids and an alcohol. Like all lipids, waxes are insoluble in water. A chief function of plant waxes is to form a waterproof coating on the surfaces of stems and leaves of the plant. This layer is important as it prevents excess water loss or desiccation. The first land plants may have developed a layer of waxes as protection from the harsh, dry terrestrial environment.

Steroids. Composed mostly of complex alcohols, steroids are larger molecules that have many lipid-like properties. Structurally, most steroids occur as complexes of ring-like structures. Examples of steroids include cholesterol, which is an important structural component of cell membranes, and, in animals, several sex hormones, corticoid steroid hormones, and Vitamin D.

Figure 2–12 The chemical structure of phospholipids. Note that a phospholipid consists of two fatty acids and a phospholipid tail. *Source:* Teresa Audesirk and Gerald Audesirk (1996), p. 45.

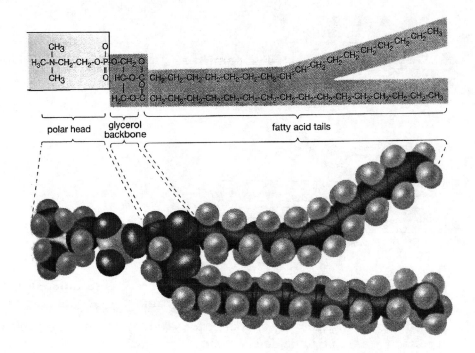

polar head   glycerol backbone   fatty acid tails

Steroids seem to play a more important role in animals, and are often known for their adverse effects. Excess cholesterol, for example, can cause hardening of the arteries and other circulatory problems. In a similar vein, some athletics deliberately inject steroids into their bodies to stimulate production of sex hormones. In turn, sex hormones enhance the development of secondary sexual characteristics; in males this results in a larger body mass and musculature, all very desirable from the standpoint of a football player, professional wrestler, or other professional athlete.

The role of steroids in plants is uncertain. Certain plants such as the tropical vines called yams produce and store large amounts of steroids in root tubers, which are then commercially harvested and used to produce drugs such as cortisone and sex hormones that in turn, are used in the production of some oral contraceptives.

Proteins

Proteins are abundant and valuable organic substances in plants, generally comprising from 3–8 percent of the plant's organic makeup. Chemically, proteins are large, complex macromolecules formed from carbon, hydrogen, oxygen, and nitrogen. Many proteins may also include sulfur and phosphorous, or small amounts of other elements. Proteins perform many important functions in plants. They form part of the structural makeup of many plants, especially at the cellular level. They also make up the basic structure of most enzymes and hormones used by plants for metabolism and directional activities. Some proteins also act as buffers in maintaining the pH of cells and tissue fluids. Lastly, some proteins are regulatory in function as they control the action of nucleic acids such as DNA and RNA. We will discuss this at length later.

Proteins are important structural elements of cells, function as buffers of plant fluids, direct responses as hormones and act as enzymes to cause specific metabolic activities.

Structurally, proteins are long chains of **amino acid** molecules bonded together. All amino acids are hydrocarbon molecules that have the same basic structure. They consist of a central carbon to which four groups are bonded; an amine group (NH^+) bearing a positive charge, a carboxyl group ($COOH^-$) carrying a negative charge, a hydrogen (H), and a variable group which by tradition is labeled R. Thus amino acids are similar to one another but differ in the complexity of atoms included in the R (variable) group, which promotes different sizes, shapes, water solubility, and other chemical and physical properties between amino acids. Another interesting aspect of amino acids is that they have the positively charged amine group and the negatively charged carboxyl group. This enables amino acids to react with acids or bases, thereby functioning as buffers of the plants' cellular and interstitial fluids. This property is called **amphoteric**.

About 28 different kinds of amino acids are known, but only 20 of these have been found in the proteins of animals. Plant cells can synthesize all 20 amino acids while animal cells, especially liver cells in higher animals, can assemble all but seven of the needed animo acids from precursor molecules. For animals, the remaining seven amino acids are called **essential amino acids** because they must be supplied in the diet by eating plants.

Chemically, a protein is constructed from a specific mix of amino acids which are linked together by covalent **peptide bonds** that join the amine group of one amino acid to the carboxyl group of a second amino acid. Since all proteins are made up of the 20 amino acids there can theoretically be an almost unlimited number of different proteins. Proteins differ from one another in their length, that is, in the number of amino acids

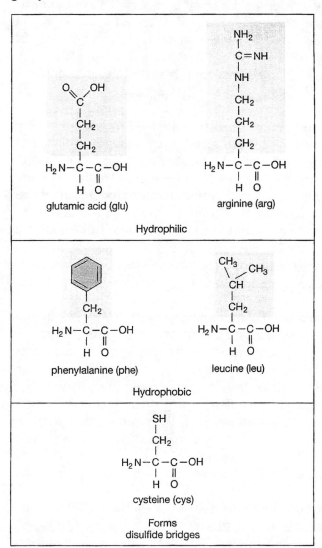

Figure 2–13 The diversity of amino acids. *Source:* Teresa Audesirk and Gerald Audesirk (1999), p. 45.

Figure 2–14 How proteins are synthesized from amino acids. *Source:* Teresa Audesirk and Gerald Audesirk (1999), p. 47.

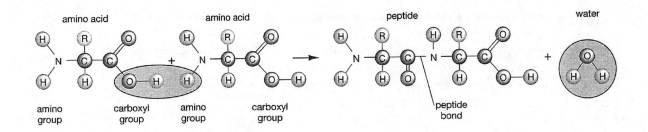

in the protein, in the sequence of amino acids that make up each particular protein, and in their spatial configuration.

The sequence of amino acids that comprises a particular protein is called the **primary structure** of the protein. The long chain of amino acids is folded in the form of a helix, a fact first observed by the Nobel Laureate Linus Pauling. This helical twisting of the chain constitutes the **secondary structure** of the protein and is maintained by hydrogen and disulfide bonds. These molecular twists may also fold again to obtain a three dimensional spatial configuration which is called the **tertiary structure** of the protein.

The intricate foldings inherent in the tertiary structure are held in place by either disulfide, hydrogen, or ionic bonds that form a bridge between adjacent amino acid groups. This intricate bonding also helps stabilize the specific size and shape of proteins. Some proteins are actually comprised of several polypeptide chains, all complexed together in a **quaternary** structure. The oxygen-binding **hemoglobin** of red blood cells is a familiar and abundant example of an animal protein with a quaternary structure. Hemoglobin consists of four polypeptide chains, all bonded together and held in place by ionic and covalent bonds between amino acid groups of adjacent polypeptides, the whole forming a structurally complex three-dimensional protein. Its close relative, the chlorophyll molecule of plants has a similar structure but with a central atom of magnesium.

This emphasis on the spatial configuration of proteins is a critical feature, for in proteins the ultimate shape of the molecule is at least as important as the string of amino acids that forms it. It is the shape of the protein molecule that confers chemical activity upon it. Working as enzymes, protein molecules of various shapes fit into spaces within other molecules to produce chemical reactions. To relate this to our human culture, we search for natural products to use in drugs and medicines. Very often the natural source of that compound is limited and we can't harvest much of it. We can synthesize these compounds in the laboratory and produce copies of the original. Even though the laboratory version is different chemically from the natural product, it causes the same activity, as the shape of the synthetic compound mimics the molecular shape as the original.

Proteins exhibit one of two basic configurations, **fibrous** or **globular**. Fibrous proteins are, as their name implies, long thread-like strands which are most commonly used as structural components of cells and tissues. Globular or globus proteins are more nearly circular in configuration. Most enzymes and hormones are globular.

Because of their complexity, many proteins can often operate only within the specific environments of living systems, where conditions such as pH and temperature are very carefully controlled. If proteins are subjected to changes in pH or excessive temperatures, the weak hydrogen and disulfide bonds can be broken and the secondary and tertiary structures of the protein are destroyed. This process is called **denaturization**. For example, when you fry an egg, the heat from the stove causes the hydrogen and disulfide bonds in the egg white proteins to rupture and the egg white is denatured. It changes the structure from a liquid to a solid.

Protein Enzymes. One of the most important groups of proteins are **enzymes**. Enzymes are proteins that react with other chemical substances to produce a product. All metabolic activities that occur in cells are mediated by protein enzymes. Enzymes participate in the process but are not altered, hence a single enzyme can catalyze many reactions. Enzymes are named for the compound they react with. For example the disaccharide sucrose is broken apart by an enzyme sucrase. The ending on the enzyme name is standardized and *-ase* at the end of a chemical name denotes an enzyme. Enzymes operate because of their specific shape. The activity of an enzyme can be summarized as follows:

$$\text{substrate} \longrightarrow \text{substrate + enzyme} \longrightarrow \text{product + enzyme}$$

Note that the enzyme acts by combining with the substrate, which is chemically altered to produce a product. The enzyme emerges from the reaction unchanged and may combine with additional substrates.

The shape of the enzyme is a mirror image of the shape of the **substrate**, or molecule to be acted upon. Since each enzyme has a unique shape, enzymes combine only with a specific molecule operating in a "lock and key" manner. Some enzymes rupture chemical bonds to fragment compounds while others enable the formation of bonds between molecules or attach atoms to molecules. Enzymes cause and promote chemical reactions and may also increase the speed of reactions but are themselves not changed during the process. Enzymes are therefore called **catalysts**.

Some enzymes are specific for particular substrates, while others are general, acting on groups of compounds. Sucrase, for example, is a specific enzyme acting only on sucrose, breaking it down into the sugar molecules glucose and fructose. Lipase on the other hand is a general enzyme that acts on many different kinds of lipids.

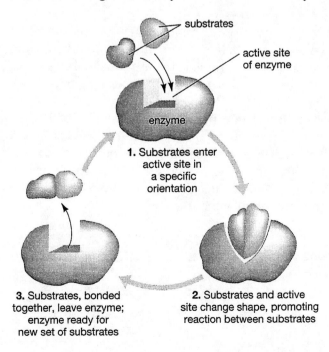

Figure 2–15 An example of how an enzyme works. *Source:* Teresa Audesirk and Gerald Audesirk (1999), p. 62.

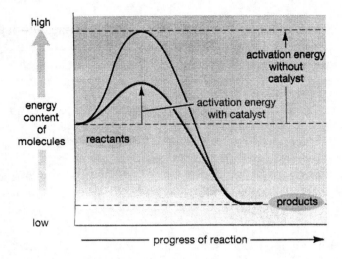

Figure 2–16 How an enzyme works by lowering the activation energy. *Source:* Teresa Audesirk and Gerald Audesirk (1999), p. 61.

Some enzymes are comprised entirely of protein but many enzymes are complexed with other components such as vitamins and minerals. In enzymes that consist of a protein and vitamin complex, the vitamin is termed a **coenzyme**. In enzymes of protein and minerals the mineral component is termed a **cofactor**. Enzymes that require vitamins or minerals will not function if they are not available. Plants can synthesize vitamins and absorb the minerals directly from their environment but animals must obtain them from their diet. Dietary deficiencies thus create problems because they interfere with enzyme reactions.

The environment of an enzyme is also important. The pH and temperature are especially crucial. If the temperature of the reaction medium (the cytoplasmic interior, for example) is too hot the enzyme can be denatured the same as any other protein. If the pH is too acidic or too basic the enzyme can be destroyed or become inactive. There are also enzyme inhibitors that keep the substrate from being treated too fast. In this way the system can be kept from being overloaded by products produced by the enzymatic activity.

NUCLEIC ACIDS

In general, nucleic acids are even larger and more complex organic molecules than proteins. Like proteins, nucleic acids are chemically comprised of carbon, hydrogen, oxygen, nitrogen and phosphorous atoms. Unlike proteins, these atoms make up three distinct subunits of nucleic acids; nitrogenous bases, phosphate molecules, and ribose sugars.

Nucleic acids are chemical repositories of information at the cellular level. They also regulate the activities of cells and are the structural components of the genes and chromosomes—the units of heredity. Thus, nucleic acids determine our inheritance of eye color, hair color, height, and many other inheritable features. Nucleic acids also regulate almost all cell activities including metabolic rates and growth by controlling the rate and types of protein enzymes that are manufactured.

Forms of Nucleic Acids

Two basic kinds of nucleic acids are known. One form is represented by the molecule **deoxyribose nucleic acid,** better known by its abbreviated form, **DNA**. DNA molecules have a ladder-like configuration which is twisted into the form of a double helix. The second molecular form of nucleic acids is called **ribose nucleic acid** or **RNA**. RNA somewhat resembles one-half of a DNA molecule—it is actually the copy of one side of the ladder-like structure of DNA.

DNA as Chromosomes

As chromosomes, DNA molecules also play a central role in heredity, for it is the chromosomes that contain the genes. Each chromosome contains hundreds and sometimes thousands of genes located along its length, each gene providing the instructions that direct and control a specific event of life. To see how this works, we must first examine the structure of the DNA molecule.

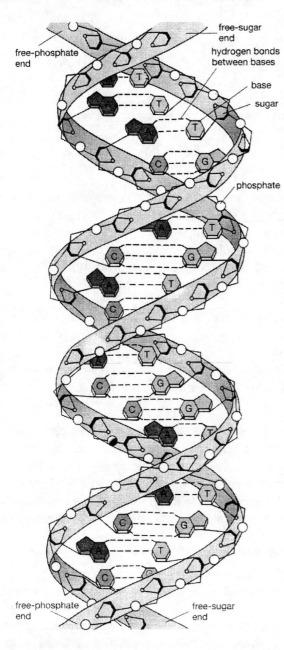

Figure 2–17 The base pairing sequence of DNA. Also illustrated is the helical nature of the DNA molecule. *Source:* Teresa Audesirk and Gerald Audesirk (1999), p. 147.

Structure of Nucleic Acids

The complex structure of nucleic acids is built up of repeating units of three molecules which are chemically bonded together in synthesis (dehydration) reactions to form subunits called nucleotides. Each nucleotide consists of a **phosphate group, a sugar molecule,** and **a nitrogenous base.**

The sugar molecule is a five carbon pentose sugar called ribose which is found in RNA or deoxyribose which occurs in DNA molecules. Each ribose or deoxyribose molecule is bonded to a phosphate molecule at one end and a nitrogenous base at the other end. Nitrogenous bases are so-called because they are ring structures that contain nitrogen groups. Five nitrogenous bases are found in plants—adenine (A), cytosine (C), guanine (G), thymine (T), and uracil (U). DNA molecules contain adenine, cytosine, guanine, and thymine while RNA molecules are comprised of adenine, cytosine, guanine, and uracil.

DNA Form and Function. At the molecular level, a typical DNA molecule resembles a spiral staircase. The sides of the staircase are comprised of the phosphate and sugar molecules which are chemically bonded to one another to form a long, spiraling chain. Each of the interior steps of the DNA molecule consists of two nucleotides that are held together by hydrogen bonds in the middle, thereby forming the rungs of the helical ladder. The nucleotides of DNA are

Figure 2–18 The structure and diversity of nucleotides. *Source:* Teresa Audesirk and Gerald Audesirk (1999), p. 50.

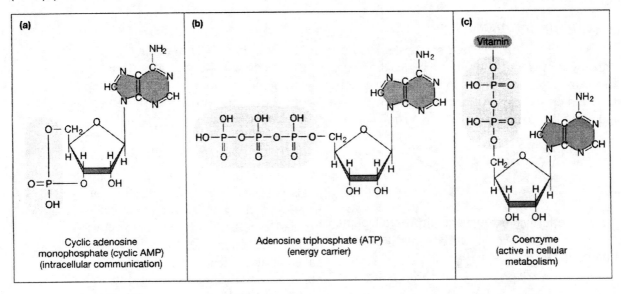

(a) Cyclic adenosine monophosphate (cyclic AMP) (intracellular communication)

(b) Adenosine triphosphate (ATP) (energy carrier)

(c) Coenzyme (active in cellular metabolism)

organized in a very specific fashion. For example, adenine (A) always pairs with thymine (T) to form an A-T rung while cytosine (C) and guanine (G) always pair to form a C-G rung. Rungs of the ladder are formed from complementary base pairs and are arranged throughout the length of the DNA molecule. The sequence of nucleotides along a DNA molecule actually spells out a chemical code, or blueprint, utilized by the cell as a kind of chemical blueprint to construct a particular protein or perform a specific function.

DNA molecules play a central role in heredity as chromosomes. The chromosomes, in turn, are divided into segments which correspond to the genes that control all of the characteristics and activities of organisms. That is, each chromosome (DNA molecule) actually consists of dozens and sometimes hundreds of genes located along its length, each gene providing the instructions that direct and control one or more specific events of life.

RNA Form and Function. Molecules of RNA resemble a single strand, or one-half of a DNA molecule. RNA thus consists of a long backbone of phosphate and sugar molecules to which are attached the nitrogenous bases adenine, cytosine, guanine, and uracil. Three kinds of RNA molecules occur in cells, messenger RNA (mRNA), transfer RNA (tRNA), and ribosomal RNA (rRNA). Together, these three kinds of RNA molecules function to manufacture proteins using the chemical codes specified by DNA molecules.

Differences between DNA and RNA Molecules

DNA and RNA molecules differ from one another in their structural makeup and in their functions. The most obvious molecular difference is that DNA consists of two strands of nucleotides bound together by hydrogen bonds while RNA consists of a single strand. RNA nucleotides also differ from DNA nucleotides in two important ways. First, RNA nucleotides consist of ribose sugar while DNA consist of deoxyribose sugar. Second, DNA nucleotides include adenine, cytosine, guanine and thymine nitrogenous bases while RNA nucleotides substitute uracil nitrogenous bases for thymine.

Table 2–4 Major differences between DNA and RNA nucleic acids.

Characteristic	DNA	RNA
Structure	double helix	single helical strand
sugar	deoxyribose	ribose
nitrogenous bases	adenine, cytosine, guanine, thymine	adenine, cytosine, guanine, uracil
functions	storage of genetic information, that controls protein synthesis, RNA synthesis, and mitosis	mRNA carries blueprints to and directs protein synthesis at ribosomes with help of RNA which translates message and tRNA which delivers amino acids to ribosomes.

High Energy Nucleic Acids

The energy currency of almost all plant cells is a nucleic acid molecule called adenosine tri-phosphate (ATP). ATP is an adenine nucleotide bonded to three phosphates. In cells, ATP is created by the addition of a phosphate group to adenosine-diphosphate (ADP) molecule in a process called phosphorylation. Furthermore, since it takes a considerable amount of energy to add the third phosphate group the last bond is called a high-energy bond. The ATP represents an important high energy storage that can be readily broken by enzymes to liberate the energy contained in the high energy bond as follows:

$$\text{ATP} + \text{H2O} \longrightarrow \text{ADP} + \text{phosphate group} + \text{energy.}$$

The reaction is easily reversible, given the appropriate enzymes and the need for energy liberation or energy storage. Thus, when energy is needed ATP is broken down so that the high energy of the third phosphate bond can be used to do cellular work. Conversely, if excess energy is available, cells convert the ADP and phosphate back into ATP for energy storage.

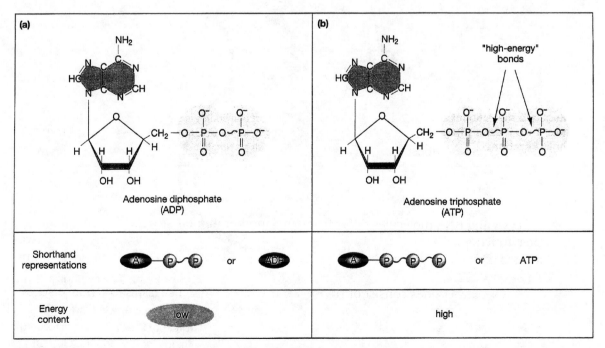

Figure 2–19 High energy molecules of ATP and ADP. *Source:* Teresa Audesirk and Gerald Audesirk (1999), p. 65.

How DNA → RNA Directs Cell Activities

In plant cells most of the DNA is found in the nucleus where it is encased in the chromosomes. (The chromosomes are actually DNA molecules complexed with proteins for support). Strands of DNA also occur in mitochondria and chloroplasts, where they participate in manufacturing enzymes that control and direct the metabolic and structural operations of these organelles and also direct their reproduction. The simplest organisms, bacteria, lack a central nucleus but have a single strand of DNA called a nucleoid.

The primary function of the DNA-RNA complex of molecules is to direct the activity of cells. This is done by synthesizing enzymes or a series of enzymes that cause a particular activity to occur within the cell or at the cell surface.

The sequence of events in cell direction begins at the DNA molecule, which is the cell's library of blueprints (in chemical form) for manufacturing specific enzymes. Under the influence of an internal or external stimulus, the segment of the DNA molecule containing the chemical instructions for manufacturing the needed enzyme (which is technically, a gene) separates or "unzips" along the hydrogen bonds that connect the nitrogenous bases forming the interior of the ladder-shaped DNA molecule, exposing the active chemical ends of the nitrogenous bases. Next, an enzyme called RNA polymerase constructs an RNA molecule along the exposed DNA half from building blocks of sugar, phosphoric acid and nitrogenous bases available in the nucleoplasm. The sequence of exposed DNA nitrogenous bases serves as a template which dictates the sequence of bases along the newly forming RNA molecule, with C-G and A-U base pairing arrangements. For example, a DNA nitrogenous base sequence of A-T-A-C-G will produce a corresponding sequence of U-A-U-G-C nitrogenous bases in the RNA molecule being made.

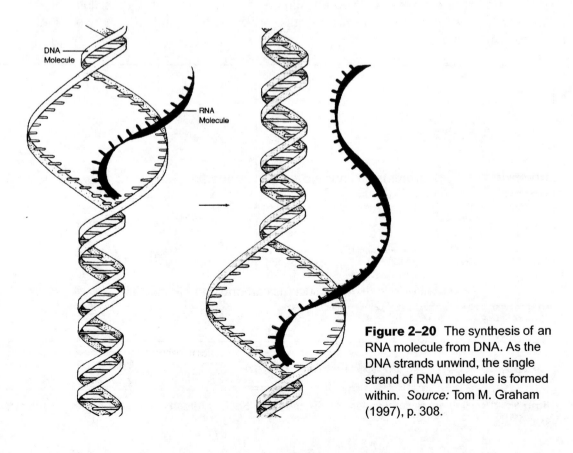

DNA Molecule

RNA Molecule

Figure 2–20 The synthesis of an RNA molecule from DNA. As the DNA strands unwind, the single strand of RNA molecule is formed within. *Source:* Tom M. Graham (1997), p. 308.

Once formed, the resulting RNA molecule is called messenger RNA (mRNA) and is stripped from the DNA molecule. Next, the mRNA molecule migrates from the nucleus to the cytoplasm, where it complexes with a cell organelle called a ribosome. Using the template provided by the sequence of nitrogenous bases along the mRNA molecule, the ribosome constructs the needed enzyme. (That is, the ribosome translates the message and produces the enzyme).

The sequence of cell directional activities is:
DNA $\longrightarrow$ messenger RNA $\longrightarrow$ ribosome $\longrightarrow$ transfer RNA
+ amino acids $\longrightarrow$ enzyme $\longrightarrow$ activity.

At the ribosome a second kind of RNA, called **transfer RNA (tRNA)** delivers amino acids to the mRNA-ribosome complex. There are 20 different kinds of tRNA molecules in the cell, each of which can bind with one of the 20 different amino acids found in proteins. Structurally, tRNA molecules have a binding site for an amino acid and another active site of nitrogenous bases, which will temporarily pair with the nitrogenous bases along the mRNA chain. Every three nitrogenous bases along the mRNA constitute a codon which is matched by a triplex of three nitrogenous bases on the tRNA molecule, called an anticodon. For example, a small stretch of mRNA molecule with the following bases A-U-C G-C-U will bind with two tRNA molecules, the first with the anticodon U-A-G and the second C-G-A. Since the two tRNA molecules carry different amino acids the resulting chain of amino acids along the mRNA molecule will be built with a very specific sequence. Once the amino acids are carried to their respective sites peptide bonds form, and the chain becomes the primary structure of a particular protein.

The newly formed protein is somehow stripped away from the mRNA-ribosome complex, then is folded by other enzymes to produce the three dimensional structure of the completed protein. Such finished proteins can now be used to build structure in the plant or function as enzymes to cause a particular activity.

Secondary Plant Compounds

Carbohydrates, lipids, proteins and nucleic acids are sometimes called the primary compounds manufactured by all plants. Many plants also manufacture a variety of other hydrocarbon compounds which are collectively called secondary compounds, some of which are commercially or medically important substances. Most of these other hydrocarbons manufactured by plants are chemically "built up" from metabolites.

Alkaloids. Consisting mostly of nitrogenous bases such as purine, many alkaloids affect animals; in small doses alkaloids such as caffeine and nicotine are stimulants, in larger doses they can be hallucinogenic (e.g., cocaine, derived from the cocoa leaf) and in still larger doses they are poisonous (e.g., conine, from Poison Hemlock, strychnine).

Terpenes. Consisting of five-carbon isoprene rings, plant terpenes include volatile oils such as peppermint, lemon, lavender and rose oils, resins, carotenoids that give fungi and plants their reds, yellows and oranges and also serve as accessory photosynthetic pigments. The largest terpenes are comprised of several thousand isoprenes and include the commercially valuable plant product rubber, manufactured by the tropical tree, *Hevea*.

Tannins. Chemically complex but containing at least one benzene ring, tannins are deposited in leaves, twigs, bark, roots and fruits of many species, especially of oaks, hemlocks and sumacs. Tannins make plants less palatable to herbivores. They are used in the fur industry to tan skins and in small amounts provide the astringent taste of tea and other beverages.

The Chemistry of Protoplasm

PHYSICAL PROPERTIES OF PROTOPLASM

The mixture of chemical compounds in living systems is called **protoplasm**. All life is made of protoplasm (proto = first, plasma = form). Protoplasm is the general term for the living material of plants and animals. If protoplasm is encased in a cell it is called cytoplasm, but regardless it is the same material. Protoplasm resembles the white of an egg in that it is nearly transparent, and may be fluid, jelly-like or solid. Protoplasm has many organic substances dissolved in it, but it is mostly water. Besides organic compounds, protoplasm usually includes inorganic salts and traces of many elements.

Protoplasm exhibits the physical and chemical properties of a mixture. Chemically, a mixture is a combination of free atoms, molecules or compounds in varying proportions which are dissolved in a **solvent**. In the case of protoplasm the solvent is water, which can comprise from 60–95 percent of a cell. Materials called the **solutes** are dissolved within the solvent. The interactions of solvents and solutes can occur in three basic ways.

Solutions. One type of mixture is called a **solution**. Solutions consist of a solvent in which extremely small solute particles are dissolved. These small particles cannot be filtered out and will not settle out if left undisturbed. When we make tea or coffee we are making a solution.

Suspensions. A second type of a mixture is a **suspension**. In suspensions, larger solute particles are dissolved in the solvent. If the mixture is left undisturbed these larger particles will tend to precipitate, or settle out. For example, to make lemonade we mix a solution of bits of lemon, sugar and water. If left standing the particles of lemon settle to the bottom of the glass.

Colloidal Suspensions. The third type of mixture is a **colloidal suspension**. In colloidal suspensions, particles of solute may be large or small but most are intermediate in size. Particles suspended in colloids do not separate out because the molecules are electrically charged. Similar electrical charges repel each other, thus in colloids the molecules are kept in a continual state of movement because of constantly being repelled by other molecules. This form of interaction results in a mixture in which molecules are held in place and do not settle out despite the particle size.

Protoplasm is a colloidal suspension in which water is the solvent and the lipids, carbohydrates, proteins and other chemicals are the solutes.

Colloids have several distinct properties compared to other types of mixtures. For example, due to particle size colloids do not easily pass through membranes. Thus they can be retained in the living system easily. The large size of some organic compounds in colloids creates a tremendous surface area for chemical action. Lastly, there is the phenomenon of phase reversal or **sol-gel transformation**. Colloids can change to a spongy solid (gel) which holds liquids and other particles or it can become a fluid (sol). Colloids can take different forms, depending on temperature, electrical charge, or pH. This phase reversal phenomena is characteristic of protoplasm and is responsible for the contraction of cells, movement of organs, and thousands of other activities of life.

BIOLOGICAL PROPERTIES OF PROTOPLASM

In living systems, protoplasm is always bound by membranes which partially control the properties and activities of the confined and complex chemical mix. There are several kinds of membranes but three are of special importance to plants.

Permeable membranes are those that have large openings in them that allow molecules to pass through unimpeded. Cheesecloth serves as an example of a permeable membrane.

Impermeable membranes allow nothing to pass because the structure of the membrane either lacks pores or has a structural barrier which hinders passage of molecules through the membrane. The cuticle of plants and the outer layer of our skin are examples of impermeable membranes. Materials that pass through these barriers does so only by using special organs or glands.

Semipermeable membranes. Many membranes found in living organisms allow the passage of some rather than all materials, so they are termed semipermeable membranes. Properties specific to the membrane control the types and rates of substances that pass through it. A semipermeable membrane can also be termed selectively permeable or differentially permeable.

Substances can pass through membranes by either passive movement or active transport. **Passive transport** of materials is done without the expenditure of energy and relies on laws of physics to accomplish the task. A common example of passive transport is **diffusion**, which refers to the movement of materials other than water across a membrane following a concentration gradient from an area of higher concentration to an area of lower concentration. For example if perfume is released in a room, the kinetic energy of perfume molecules colliding with each other causes a gradual dispersal until the gas molecules are evenly distributed throughout the room. Diffusion is the major means of passage for many liquids, gases and solids in non-biological systems but also operates for many ions and smaller molecules in cells.

The movement of water across a semipermeable membrane is called **osmosis**. In osmosis, water is following a diffusion gradient created by the presence or absence of salts and their concentration. Salts have a tendency to draw water to them rather than water drawing salts to it. As a result water is actually moving along a **concentration gradient**, from an area of low salt concentration (and therefore higher water concentration) to an area of high salt concentration (and lower water concentration). This is important to plants that live in the water because the gain or loss of water can be determined by respective salt concentrations of the plant to its environment. Plants living in **hypertonic** environments have salt concentrations outside the plant higher than inside. Thus water tends to be lost to the surrounding environment. The plant must compensate for this in some way. Some marine algae have thick cuticles to prevent such water loss. If the concentration of salts is larger inside the plant than outside the environment is said to be **hypotonic**. In this condition, a plant would tend to gain water and bloat. Again cuticles and other plant structures help to prevent excessive water loss. In situations where salt concentration inside the plant is equal to salt concentrations outside we say the plant is **isotonic** to its environment. Under these conditions water will pass by osmosis equally in either direction.

In living systems many ions and organic molecules are small and can easily pass through semipermeable membranes, but larger molecules are blocked from passage. The cell obtains or excretes these large molecules by a mechanism of **active transport**. In active transport materials may be moved against a concentration gradient and also may be moved despite the large size of the molecules. In the process, energy is consumed by the cell in moving the molecules, hence the name active transport. In this process the substance to be moved forms a chemical complex with the semipermeable membrane. Enzymes called **permiases** and **translocases** move the molecule through the membrane chemically. In essence they dissolve the membrane, move the molecule and then reform the membrane behind it. Once the molecule is moved through the membrane the chemical complex it formed with the membrane is disrupted and the molecule is freed from the membrane.

From Chemicals to Protoplasm to Living Organisms

Protoplasm is the stuff of life but how did living organisms first originate? Scientists have argued extensively about the origins of life. Life is very old and may exceed 3.5 billion years in age. The life forms on earth show a consistent relationship to each other and thus are thought to have evolved here and be related to each other. These early life forms evolved in conditions that are different from those on earth today. The very first forms of life may have been small strands of nucleic acids such as DNA and RNA which developed the ability to replicate themselves. These nucleic acid molecules existed in pools of free chemical compounds that provided the necessary building blocks for replication of the molecules. In essence, these nucleic acids functioned as genes to control their own reproduction.

Such early nucleic acid genes in the environment could be swamped or disrupted by other free chemical compounds in the environment. Thus there was a strong evolutionary drive for the development of a membrane to protect the primitive enzyme and nucleic acid system. Eventually, some nucleic acids produced a protective membrane that encapsulated the naked nucleic acids. This membrane bound mix of nucleic acids and organic chemicals marked the beginnings of the first cell-like structures. These early cells lived in a dilute solution of organic molecules and probably obtained energy to power their enzymatic activities through a process called **fermentation**. The earth on which they lived had a different atmosphere than we have today. Free oxygen was lacking and so they functioned as anaerobes, obtaining energy by the process of fermentation. A simple fermentation reaction is illustrated as follows:

$$C_6H_{12}O_6 \longrightarrow 2CO_2 + 2C_2H_5OH + 2H_2 + energy$$

A fermenting organism chemically fragments a sugar molecule to produce carbon dioxide, an alcohol, and energy. Fermenting organisms face two basic problems. First, the organism may eventually consume all of its food supply and starve to death. Secondly, a by-product of the above reaction is C_2H_5OH, an alcohol, that is toxic and can kill organisms at even low concentrations. To provide an example, yeast is commonly used in beer and wine industries to make alcohol, which actually represents a by-product of the yeast metabolically harvesting energy from sugar by the process of fermentation. An examination of the labels on wine bottles reveals that no wine contains over 12 percent alcohol by content. This is because the alcohol kills the yeast culture when it reaches 12 percent concentration.

Another important by-product of fermentation is the production of carbon dioxide, which is released into the atmosphere. The accumulation of carbon dioxide made possible the evolutionary development of organisms that could trap energy from the sun. The process is called **photosynthesis** and the organisms are called plants. A general formula for photosynthesis is given below:

$$\text{Sunlight} + 6H2O + 6CO2 + \text{chlorophyll} \longrightarrow C_6H_{12}O_6 + 6O_2 + 6H_2O$$

Early plants developed a way of trapping energy from the sun using a pigment called chlorophyll. They saved that trapped energy in the form of sugars and released oxygen and water in the process. The release of oxygen as a product of photosynthesis is tremendously important because it became the main source of oxygen in the atmosphere. The availability of oxygen made possible the evolution of a new and more efficient means of producing energy by **oxidative respiration**. Organisms that function as oxidative respirators can systematically fragment sugars and other organic molecules in a process called respiration. A general formula for respiration is as follows:

$$C_6H_{12}O_6 + 6O_2 \longrightarrow 6 CO_2 + 6H_2O + \text{energy}$$

Most plants and animals function as oxidative respirators. This form of energy produces far more usable energy for the organism than any other energy production method and has made possible the increasing complexity and abundance of life that we find today.

Key Words and Phrases

matter	energy	element
atom	proton	neutron
electron	ions	isotope
molecule	compound	ionic bond
covalent bond	hydrogen bond	disulfide bond
carbohydrate	monosaccharide	disaccharide
polysaccharide	lipid	triglyceride
phospholipid	wax	steroid
protein	amino acid	denaturization
enzyme	catalyst	cofactor
coenzyme	mRNA	tRNA
deoxyribonucleic acid (DNA)		ribosome
ribonucleic acid (RNA)	codon	anticodon
protoplasm	solution	colloid
semipermeable membrane	passive transport	active transport
diffusion	osmosis	hypertonic
hypotonic	isotonic	characteristics of life
photosynthesis	respiration	fermentation
pectin	lignin	steroid

Selected References and Resources

Alberts, B., D. Bray, A. Johnson, J. Lewis, M. Raff, K. Roberts, and P. Walter. 1997. *Essential Cell Biology*. McGraw-Hill Publishers. New York.

Creighton, T. E., Editor. 1992. *Protein folding*. W. H. Freeman and Company. New York.

Dickerson, R., and I. Geis. 1976. *Chemistry, Matter, and the Living Universe*. Benjamin/ Cummings. Menlo Park, California.

Fruton, J. S. 1972. *Molecules and Life*. Wiley Interscience. New York.

Lehninger, A. L. 1993. *Principles of Biochemistry*. 2nd Edition. Worth Publishers Inc., New York.

Lodish, H., D. Baltimore, A. Bert, S. L. Zipursky, P. Matsuidira, and J. Darnell. 1995. *Molecular Cell Biology*. 2nd Edition. Scientific American Books. New York, New York.

Robinson, T. 1983. *The Organic Constituents of Higher Plants*. 3rd. Ed. Cordus Press. North Amherst, Mass.

Sheeler, P., and D. E. Bianchi. 1987. *Cell biology: structure, biochemistry, and function*. 2nd Edition. John Wiley and Sons. New York.

Voet, D., and J. G. Voet. 1990. *Biochemistry*. John Wiley & Sons. New York.

Wolfe, S. L. 1993. *Molecular and cellular biology*. Wadsworth Publishing Company.

Review and Discussion Questions

1. Some evolutionists suggest that the first cells arose in clay sediments while others maintain that the first simple cells originated in water. Compare and contrast the evidence for each of these possible origins.

2. Why is the code that dictates the bonding arrangement of tRNA molecules along the mRNA molecule comprised of codons and anticodons of three nitrogenous bases? Why is a code based on one or two nitrogenous bases not feasible?

3. Describe how proteins are formed from amino acids.

4. Why is it more advantageous for protoplasm to be in colloid form rather than operate as a simple solution or suspension?

5. How does the fact that cell membranes are semipermeable affect the physiological rates of photosynthesis and respiration?

6. Use your knowledge of diffusion and osmosis to explain how plant roots absorb water and minerals from the environment.

7. List and describe the basic properties of at least five elements that are necessary for living organisms.

8. List and define at least five organic substances that can be defined as compounds and five substances that fit the definition of molecules. Now list five ions that are important to life.

9. What chemical properties of water make it so important to the life of the plant cell?

10. Differentiate between the primary, secondary and tertiary structure of a protein.

Plant Cells and Their Function

Chapter 3

Discovery of Cells
Types of Cells
Plant Cell Structures
    Cell Walls and Membranes
    Organelles
    Nucleus
Mitosis and Cell Division

The Discovery of Cells

One of the great advantages of the development of the microscope was the ability to see small living structures. Inanimate objects were also investigated. In 1665, an English scientist named Robert Hooke sliced a piece of cork, the bark of the cork oak, and examined it under a microscope. He saw a grid-like network of partitions and open spaces. He called the spaces **cells** because they reminded him of the small cells in which monks lived. For the next one hundred and fifty years, cells of plants and animals, having been isolated, were examined and described in detail.

> **The fact that all organisms are made of cells and substances produced by cells is called the cell principle. To this we add the fact that all cells come from pre-existing cells.**

The appreciation of cells as living structures and the fact that they are the basic units of all life was not formally realized until 1839 when Matthias Schleiden and Theodor Schwann, two German biologists, proposed the **cell theory**. The cell theory, in its simplest form, states that all living things are made of cells and substances produced by cells. Cells have been studied with microscopes and by biochemical techniques. Today, because of the electron microscope and other modern tools of molecular biology we know the ultrastructure of cells almost to the atomic level. Cells are the physical and chemical functioning units of plants and animals. All of the basic activities of living organisms such as reproduction, photosynthesis, respiration and metabolism occur within or between cells.

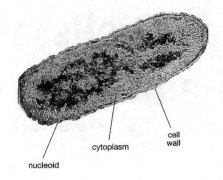

Figure 3–1 Comparison of prokaryotic and eukaryotic cells. *Source:* Teresa Audesirk and Gerald Audesirk (1999), p. 90.

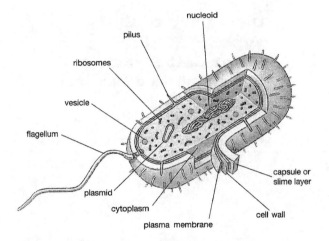

A Generalized Cell

A typical plant cell is bounded and protected by a rigid **cell wall** that encases the **protoplasm**. The protoplasm in turn is surrounded by a surface layer called the **plasma membrane**. Centrally located within the protoplasm is a large, spheroidal **nucleus**. Between the nucleus and the plasma membrane is the **cytoplasm**, in which a number of distinctive structures called **organelles** are located.

TYPES OF CELLS

There are two basic kinds of cells found in nature. All cells of plants, animals, fungi and algae contain a nucleus that houses and protects the chromosomes of DNA. Such cells are termed **eukaryotic** and the organisms which are made up of eukaryotic cells are called eukaryotes. Cells of many bacteria, cyanobacteria and archaebacteria lack a nucleus and are **prokaryotic**. Eukaryotic organisms are generally larger and more complex than prokaryotes and are considered evolutionarily more advanced.

Plant Cell Structures

CELL WALL

Cell walls are a unique feature of plant cells and are entirely lacking in animal cells. The protoplasm of plant cells is encased in a series of protective layers that are collectively

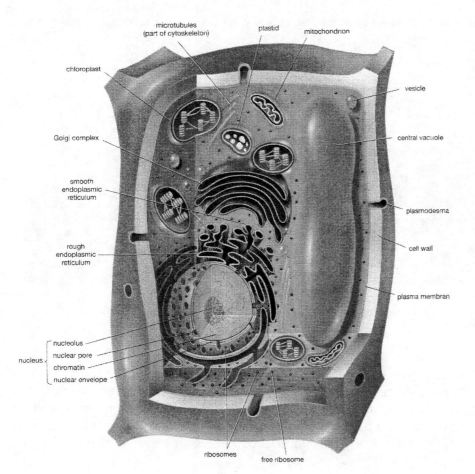

Figure 3–2 The structure of a generalized plant cell. *Source:* Teresa Audesirk and Gerald Audesirk (1999), p. 95.

called the cell wall. The cell wall is a semirigid structure that provides the framework, strength, and support for the cell within and also provides support for the plant in general. The cell wall of plant cells consists of a **primary layer** laid down next to the cells and a **middle lamella** which is the region between the primary walls of two adjacent cells. The middle lamella is made up mostly of the carbohydrate **pectin**. Long, fiber-like **cellulose** molecules are laid down on either side of the middle lamella. The cellulose molecules are grouped together in **microfibrils** which in turn are twisted together to form structures called **macrofibrils**. These macrofibrils are cemented together by pectin and constitute the main part of the cell wall. When a new cell wall is formed, a **primary cell wall** is laid down first, made up of the middle lamella and cellulose layers on either side of it. Afterwards, a **secondary cell wall** forms on either side of the primary cell wall. **Lignin**, another fibrous protein, may be impregnated in cell walls to add strength.

Most cell walls in plants contain small openings formed from minute tubules called **plasmodesmata** that extend through the cell walls from one cell to another. Plasmodesmata provide passageways for cells of a tissue to communicate and exchange materials; for example, the conduction of fluids and other dissolved substances from cell to cell usually occurs through the plasmodesmata. The filamentous plasmodesmata may also help bind cells together as the plant twists and turns in the wind.

Figure 3–3 Generalized structure of the cell walls of plant cells. *Source:* Teresa Audesirk and Gerald Audesirk (1999), p. 82.

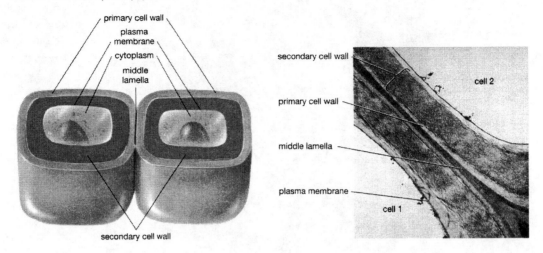

MEMBRANES

Located just inside the cell wall is the **cell membrane** or **plasma membrane**, about 10 nm thick, and comprised of two layers of phospholipids in which various proteins may be embedded. Because cell membranes are made up of two layers they are generally called double-unit membranes or simply **unit membrane**s. Membranes similar in composition and structure to the plasma membrane are found in several other areas of the cell, forming the surface of cellular structures such as the organelles and fashioning tubes or systems of tubes within the cytoplasm.

Plasma Membrane

The plasma membrane functions as a semipermeable membrane that helps regulate the movement of materials into and out of the cell, thereby controlling the chemical composition of the protoplasm. It basically acts as a traffic cop, permitting some substances to enter, some substances to leave, and retaining other substances. Substances may enter or leave cells through several basic transfer and diffusion processes.

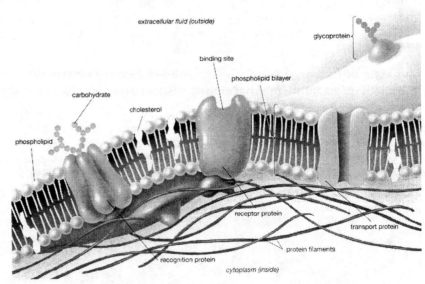

Figure 3–4 The fluid mosaic model of a cell membrane. *Source:* Teresa Audesirk and Gerald Audesirk (1999), p. 71.

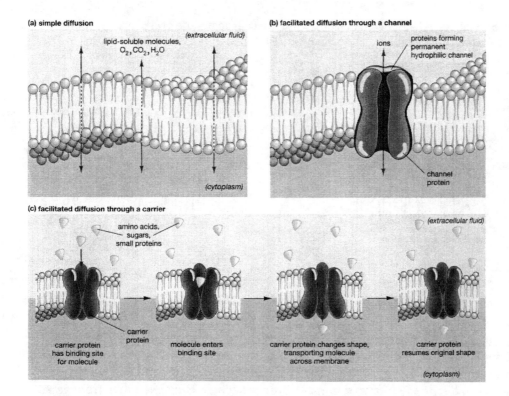

(a) simple diffusion

lipid-soluble molecules, O_2, CO_2, H_2O

(extracellular fluid)

(cytoplasm)

(b) facilitated diffusion through a channel

ions

proteins forming permanent hydrophilic channel

channel protein

(c) facilitated diffusion through a carrier

amino acids, sugars, small proteins

(extracellular fluid)

carrier protein

carrier protein has binding site for molecule

molecule enters binding site

carrier protein changes shape, transporting molecule across membrane

carrier protein resumes original shape

(cytoplasm)

Figure 3–5 How diffusion occurs through a cell membrane. *Source: Teresa Audesirk and Gerald Audesirk (1999), p. 75.*

Diffusion. Chemically, diffusion is the movement of a substance from an area of greater concentration to an area of lesser concentration. Ions and some small fat soluble chemical molecules can diffuse directly through the plasma membrane following a concentration gradient. Other ions and small chemical molecules can diffuse through minute pores in the membrane. Because of its lipid structure the plasma membrane is most permeable to hydrophobic chemicals such as fatty acids and glycerol molecules; most large molecules and hydrophilic chemicals must cross the membrane in other ways discussed below.

Facilitated Transport. Even with a favorable concentration gradient, many electrolytes and larger molecules cannot readily pass through the plasma membrane because they are physically too big to move through the membrane pores or are instead repelled by its physical structure. Such molecules are transported through the membrane with the help of specific proteins that form tube-like transmembrane channels within the plasma membrane itself. These proteins bind with substances and transfer them into the cell (or from the inside to the outside of the cell, in some cases). This type of transport is called facilitated diffusion because the transmembrane proteins help, or facilitate the movement of substances with a concentration gradient.

Active Transport. Cells require many molecules which must be pumped into or out of the cell against a concentration gradient. For example, cells tend to "hoard" needed minerals such as potassium, calcium and iron. Larger substances that the cell must transport across the membrane against concentration gradients include disaccharides and polysaccharide sugars, fatty acids, and amino acids from the surrounding extracellular fluids. Conversely, cells must void or excrete cellular waste chemicals such as uric acid molecules from the interior of the cell to the tissue fluid outside. Active transport may also involve the movement of secretory products such as hormones into or out of the cell.

Figure 3–6 A model of facilitated diffusion across the cell membrane of a plant cell. *Source:* Frederic H. Martini. *Fundamentals of Anatomy and Physiology* 3/e (1995), Prentice-Hall, p. 78.

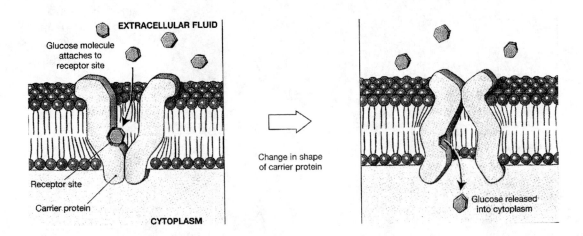

All of these kinds of molecules are usually transported through the membrane by complexing with membrane proteins which then deposit the molecules to the other side of the membrane. Because the substances are transported against a concentration gradient, energy is needed for this transfer process, which is called active transport.

In active transport, the substance to be moved first complexes with proteins in the membrane, then enzymes called permiases and translocases move the molecule through the membrane. In essence, the enzymes dissolve the membrane, move the molecule, and then reform the membrane. Once the substance is moved through the membrane the chemical complex it formed with membrane proteins is dissolved or broken, and the molecule is freed from the membrane.

Endocytosis and Exocytosis. Under certain conditions the plasma membrane may fuse with large organic molecules or with molecule carrying vesicles at the surface of the membrane. If the vesicles are released to the exterior the process is called exocytosis, and the substances represent secretory or excretory products. Endocytosis is essentially the opposite of exocytosis, in which the plasma membrane "captures" a molecule on its surface, invaginates and buds off a vesicle containing the captured molecule into the cytoplasmic interior of the cell.

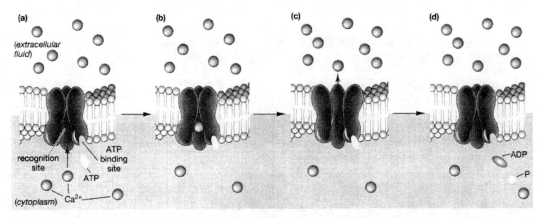

Figure 3–7 Active transport across a cell membrane. *Source:* Teresa Audesirk and Gerald Audesirk (1999), p. 78.

Figure 3–8 Endocytosis across a cell membrane. (a) pinocytosis occurs as a dimple deepens, drawing in fluid and pinching off internally (b) receptor mediated endocytosis in which a protein receptor binds with a substance and delivers it interiorly (c) phagocytosis. *Source:* Teresa Audesirk and Gerald Audesirk (1999), p. 75.

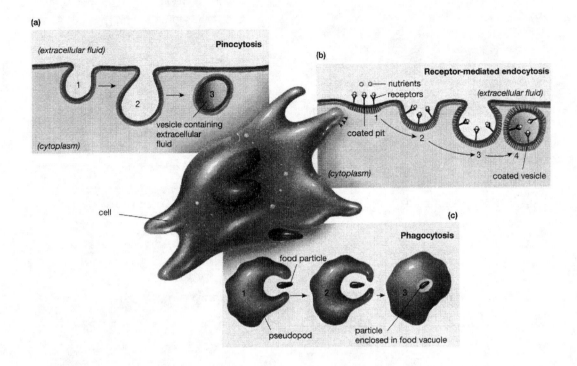

Cytoplasm

The fluid-filled space of the cell lying between the nucleus and the plasma membrane is the cytoplasm. Chemically, the cytoplasm is a mix of water in which many other substances such as minerals, inorganic and organic molecules may be found. Most of the cytoplasm appears as a clear fluid which is termed the **cytosol**.

Organelles

The larger structures in the cytoplasm are the **organelles**, which are the sites of many specific chemical events that occur within the cell. Organelles are in a sense, analogous to the organs of plants and animals. Cells are small and the organelles are even smaller with sizes ranging from 10 to 100 microns. The types of organelles vary greatly in size and structure. They also vary in function. We can imagine a cell as a bag of protoplasm with organelles suspended within it. A number of organelles are found in most plant cells.

Mitochondria. Among the most important organelles in cytoplasm are the cigar-shaped mitochondria. Mitochondria are the sites of aerobic (= oxygen consumption) cell respiration, where glucose and other hydrocarbons are systematically fragmented to produce cellular energy molecules called **ATP (adenosine triphosphate)**. The ATP molecules produced in the mitochondria are the energy currency of the cell and are used to power all of the cell's metabolic activities.

Systematically disassembling molecules of glucose and other hydrocarbons is a complicated chemical process requiring many enzymes operating in an exact sequence. A cross section of mitochondria reveals a series of inward membrane folds

Figure 3–9 A mitochondria, sectioned to show interior detail. *Source:* Frederic H. Martini. *Fundamentals of Anatomy and Physiology* 3/e (1995), Prentice-Hall, p. 87.

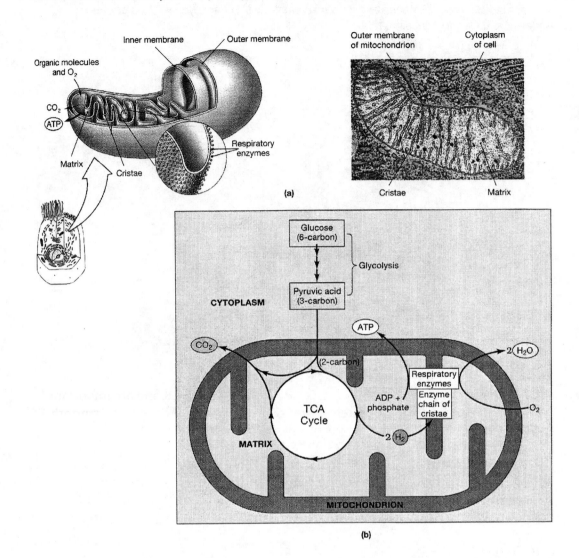

called **cristae** which hold the many enzymes required for respiration aligned in the proper sequence. Mitochondria are in constant motion and concentrate where energy is needed by the cell. Unlike most other cell organelles, mitochondria (and plastids also) have their own DNA molecules which direct the production of new mitochondria following cell division. Because they have their own genetic material, mitochondria are thought to represent the remains of primitive organisms that were incorporated into cells early in the evolution of eukaryotic cells and now exist in a kind of symbiotic (mutualistic) association with the remainder of the cell; the mitochondria provide the energy molecule for the cell in which they reside while the cells in turn provide nutrients and protection for the mitochondria.

Endoplasmic Reticulum. This organelle consists of a system of tubules and membranes that extend throughout much of the cytoplasm, the whole forming a network that is used for the transport of materials from one part of the cytoplasm to another. The endoplasmic reticulum may also function to help strengthen the cell and serve as a conduit to transport substances from one part of the cytoplasm to another.

Figure 3–10 The structure of the endoplasmic recticulum. *Source:* Teresa Audesirk and Gerald Audesirk (1999), p. 98.

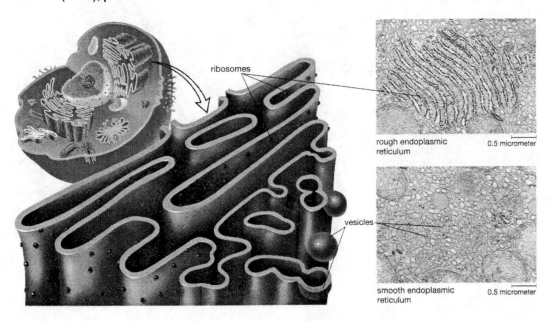

ribosomes

rough endoplasmic reticulum

0.5 micrometer

vesicles

smooth endoplasmic reticulum

0.5 micrometer

Two general types of endoplasmic reticulum (abbreviated **ER**) are recognized. Some ER have small granular-like organelles called ribosomes attached to their surface. These regions of the endoplasmic reticulum are called **rough ER** and are important for the formation and storage of proteins. Areas lacking ribosomes are called **smooth ER** and appear to be sites where lipids are assembled and secreted. The completed lipid is enveloped in the membranous wall of ER, which pinches off as a vesicle that carries the lipid to another part of the cell.

Ribosomes. These small organelles are made up of proteins complexed with ribosomal RNA which is produced in the nucleus. Most plant cell ribosomes are embedded in the rough ER and also in the cytoplasm, nucleus and chloroplasts. When separate from the ER they are often found in small clusters called **polysomes**. Ribosomes are where cells manufacture proteins and parts of proteins using messenger RNA molecules as

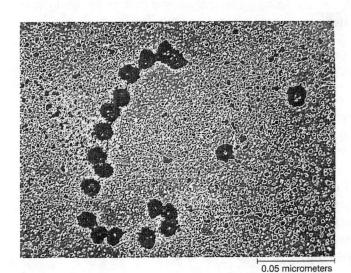

0.05 micrometers

Figure 3–11 A string of ribosomes in the cytoplasm. Most ribosomes are bound to the endoplasmic recticulum but some also occur within the cytoplasm. *Source:* Teresa Audesirk and Gerald Audesirk (1999), p. 97.

Figure 3–12 The dictyosome (golgi) complex. *Source:* Teresa Audesirk and Gerald Audesirk (1999), p. 99.

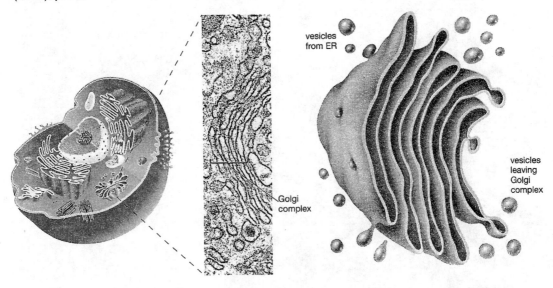

blueprints that direct the synthesis of a specific protein. Some proteins are released directly into the cytoplasm, but many are enclosed with the endoplasmic reticulum where they are either assembled or simply transported to other areas. Ribosomes are much more common in animal cells which require the synthesis of large numbers of proteins, but some plants, especially those of legumes (peas and beans are a rich source of protein) also have many ribosomes.

Dictyosomes. Also called Golgi bodies (especially in zoology textbooks), dictyosomes are a series of 4–8 convoluted tubes and membranes that occur in layers, rather like a stack of pancakes. The edges of the layers "bubble" outward to form numerous **vesicles**, which contain the secretory products of the cell. All plant cells contain dictyosomes but they are especially numerous in growing plant cells such as in the root tip of plants; these cells may hold several dozen dictyosomes which act to package and secrete cell products such as plant hormones. Dictyosomes are also the sites where complex carbohydrates (polysaccharides) are synthesized.

Plastids. Like cell walls, plastids are a distinctive and common feature of plant cells. They are also found in some protistans and fungi. Most plant cells have several kinds of plastids which have different functions.

Chloroplasts are the most conspicuous kinds of plastids. They contain the color pigment chlorophyll and are responsible for the distinctive green color of plants. Chloroplasts are the organelles in which photosynthesis takes place. During photosynthesis, the green chlorophyll pigments capture light energy and incorporate it into the manufacture of a molecule of sugar. The whole process is enzymatically directed.

Chloroplasts occur in many shapes from the corkscrew-like ribbons seen in cells like the green algae *Spirogyra* to the disc-shaped, football-shaped, round or oval structures commonly found in most plant cells. Chloroplasts are often one of the more numerous of cytoplasmic organelles, numbering between 75–125 chloroplasts per cell.

Like all organelles, chloroplasts have a double membrane forming their surface. The outer membrane is mainly phospholipid and is formed from endoplasmic reticulum while the much more extensive inner membrane is derived from the plasma

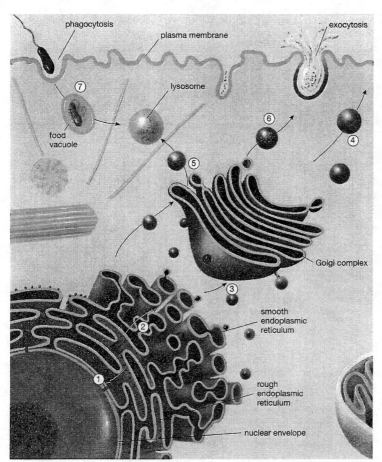

Figure 3–13 The relationship between the endoplasmic recticulum, vesicles, and the golgi complex. *Source:* Teresa Audesirk and Gerald Audesirk (1999), p. 100.

phagocytosis

plasma membrane

exocytosis

lysosome

food vacuole

Golgi complex

smooth endoplasmic reticulum

rough endoplasmic reticulum

nuclear envelope

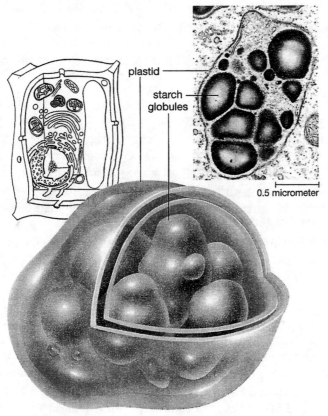

Figure 3–14 A generalized plastid. *Source:* Teresa Audesirk and Gerald Audesirk (1999), p. 104.

plastid

starch globules

0.5 micrometer

Figure 3–15 The detailed structure of a chloroplast. *Source:* Teresa Audesirk and Gerald Audesirk (1999), p. 104.

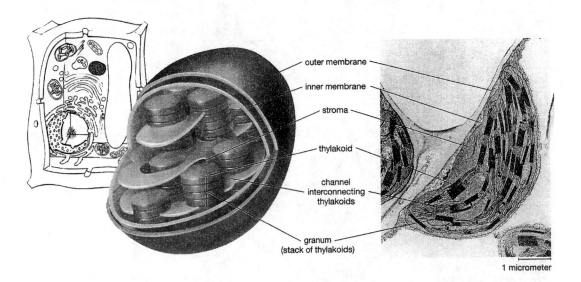

outer membrane
inner membrane
stroma
thylakoid
channel interconnecting thylakoids
granum (stack of thylakoids)

1 micrometer

membrane and is highly folded into the interior of the organelle. Attached to this inner membrane is yet another series of membranes called **thylakoids** that extend deep into the chloroplast. Thylakoids fold several times into coin-like stacks of membranes called **grana**, filled with pebble-like chlorophyll molecules, all embedded in a fluid-filled interior called **stroma**. This complex arrangement of the chloroplast interior is necessary to house the enormous number of enzymes involved in photosynthesis.

Like mitochondria, chloroplasts have their own circular strand of DNA for encoding genes that direct the reproduction of chloroplasts during cell division and provide the chemical blueprints to produce many of the enzymes necessary for photosynthesis. As in the case of mitochondria, chloroplasts are thought to have been independent organisms at one time eons ago, but were incorporated into, and exist in, a symbiotic relationship with cells.

Other Plant Plastids. Several other kinds of plastids may occur in plants cells. **Chromoplasts** are more angular in shape than chloroplasts, and probably develop from chloroplasts through internal changes. They are yellow, orange or red in color due to carotenoid pigments which they synthesize and store. A third type of plastid are called **leucoplasts**. These are large, colorless plastids that synthesize fats and other complex organic molecules. Leucoplasts that store oil are called **elaioplasts**. Elaioplasts are a common form of oil storage plastid in some of the protistan algae. Still other leucoplasts store protein and are called **proteoplasts**.

Still another type of leucoplasts specialize in storing starch and are called **amyloplasts**. Amyloplasts are numerous in roots of some types of plants such as potatoes (which is why potatoes are so starchy). They are also abundant in the endosperm tissue of seeds (which will provide nourishment for the germinating plant), and in root cap cells. Amyloplasts in root cap cells also function as gravity detectors and direct the growth of the root downward into the soil.

Microtubules and Microfilaments. Scattered through the cytoplasm are membranous tubes and rods of fibrous proteins called microtubules. **Microtubules** are unbranched, thin, hollow, tube-like structures of various lengths and 15–25 nanometers in diameter. They are found just inside the cell membrane where they control the

(a) The probable origin of mitochondria and chloroplasts

An anarobic, prokaryotic cell engulfs an aerobic bacterium. The bacterium is enclosed in a sac of the predatory cell's membrane. The resulting "proto-organelle" has a double membrane, one from the predator and one from the prey.

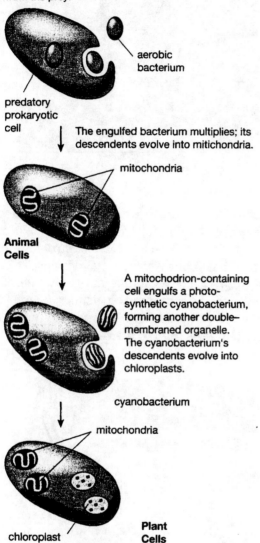

aerobic bacterium

predatory prokaryotic cell

The engulfed bacterium multiplies; its descendents evolve into mitichondria.

mitochondria

Animal Cells

A mitochodrion-containing cell engulfs a photosynthetic cyanobacterium, forming another double-membraned organelle. The cyanobacterium's descendents evolve into chloroplasts.

cyanobacterium

mitochondria

chloroplast

Plant Cells

Figure 3–16 The capture and subsequent symbiotic relationship of a chloroplast within a primitive cell. *Source:* Tom M. Graham (1997), p. 79.

addition of cellulose to the cell wall. Other microtubule complexes direct dictyosomes and their contents toward the cell membrane and aid the movement of flagella, and cilia. They also participate in cell division which will be discussed later.

Microfilaments often occur in bundles and play a role in cytoplasmic streaming and the movement of cells. This cytoplasmic streaming is called **cyclosis** and appears as though organelles are moving in a current of cytoplasm. This movement in cells is caused by the contraction of microfilaments and probably facilitates the exchange of material between parts of the cell. They may also help move materials from cell to cell. Both microtubules and microfilaments provide a flexible framework within cells and represent a kind of cytoskeleton.

Figure 3–17 Diagrammatic representation of the cytoskeleton of a cell. *Source:* Teresa Audesirk and Gerald Audesirk (1996), p. 97.

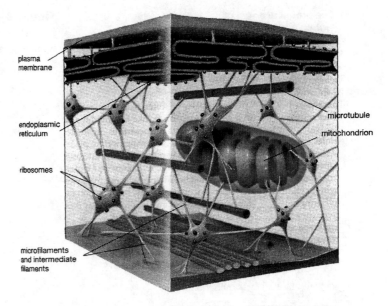

Some plant cells have elongated, thread-like microtubules called **flagella** on their surface. Structurally, flagella have an inner core of two microfilament strands around which a ring of 9 microfilaments is arranged. This is a so-called 9 + 2 structural plan. The flagella is anchored in the cytoplasm by a **basal body**, which may also assist in the whip-like rotation of the flagella. Flagella are most commonly found in mobile plants such as some algae where they constitute the main locomotory structures. Some plant cells may also have **cilia** which are shorter versions of flagella. Cilia may aid in locomotion or act as filters and are more common in animal than in plant cells.

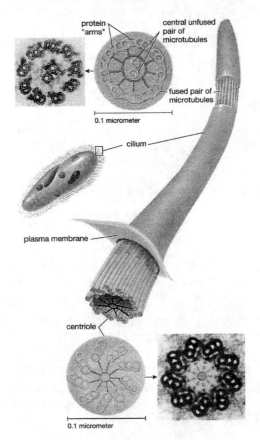

Figure 3–18 The structure of flagella and cilia. *Source:* Teresa Audesirk and Gerald Audesirk (1999), p. 106.

Vacuoles. When viewed under a microscope, the interior of many plant cells appears clear and almost empty. This is because most of the cell's interior is comprised of large, thin-walled organelles called vacuoles. Vacuoles are the largest distinctive structures in plant cells. Vacuoles function primarily as the cell's storage vaults. They store food and waste material. In young cells water filled vacuoles are small and fairly numerous and occupy only a small portion of the total interior volume of the cell. In mature plant cells, however, up to 90 percent of the cytoplasmic volume may be taken up by one or more central vacuoles bounded by membranes called **tonoplasts**. These membranes are similar in structure to that of the cell membrane.

Vacuoles are filled with a fluid called **cell sap** which is slightly acidic and helps maintain pressures inside the cell. The cell sap may contain water, dissolved salts, sugars, organic acids and small quantities of soluble proteins. They may also contain water-soluble pigments called anthocyanins. These form the colors red, blue or purple in flowers. Some vacuoles contain large crystals of waste.

Microbodies. Some plant cells may contain additional types of small, spherical organelles that are collectively called microbodies. Microbodies in seeds, for example, include **glyoxysomes**, which help fragment oils to yield fatty acids which can then be used for energy or as substrates for the enzymatic manufacturing of lipids, sugars and proteins needed for plant growth.

Peroxisomes are microbodies closely associated with chloroplasts and can be very numerous in green leaves. Peroxisomes have several enzymes that promote a key photosynthetic process called glycolate oxidation.

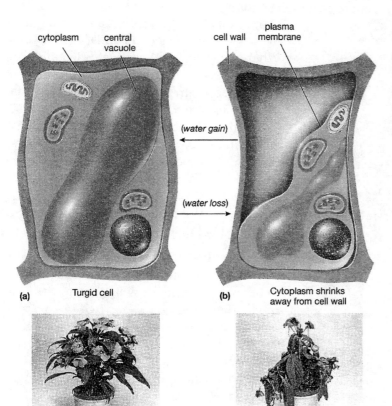

Figure 3–19 The central vacuole and its relationship to turgor pressure in plant cells. *Source:* Teresa Audesirk and Gerald Audesirk (1999), p. 102.

The major organelles and their functions include:

plasma membrane	protection, material flow
mitochondria	respiration
endoplasmic reticulum	transport, lipid synthesis
ribosomes	manufacture of enzymes
dictyosomes	packaging of cell products
chloroplasts	sites of photosynthesis
vacuoles	storage of water, minerals
nucleolus	mRNA synthesis

NUCLEUS

Most plant cells have a large, centrally located **nucleus** which contains chromatin. Chromatin is a thin, long, uncoiled DNA (deoxyribonucleic acid) molecule connected to beads of histone protein. The nucleus is surrounded and protected by a membrane called the **nuclear membrane** (also called the nuclear envelope), which is structurally similar to other cell membranes but often has somewhat larger pores in the membrane for the transfer of molecules from the cytoplasm to the nucleus and the reverse. The nuclear membrane may junction with the endoplasmic reticulum as well.

The interior of the nucleus is filled with nucleoplasm, a kind of protoplasm that is similar to cytoplasm but contains higher concentrations of substances used in the manufacture of the nucleic acids DNA and RNA. When the cell is not actively dividing, the DNA molecules are unwound (uncoiled) in the nucleoplasm and appear as long, thin, thread-like strands called **chromatin**. Thus exposed, the chemical blueprints along the DNA can be used to manufacture messenger RNA copies which, in turn, will migrate from the nucleus to the ribosomes to direct the manufacture of enzymes. This copying process usually takes place in a **nucleolus** discussed below.

Nucleolus. The nucleus of most cells often contains one or more of what appear to be miniature nuclei which are termed the **nucleolus**. The nucleolus is rich in enzymes that control the synthesis of RNA and has a large pool of nitrogenous bases. The nucleolus is the site where several kinds of RNA molecules including mRNA (messenger RNA), rRNA (ribosomal RNA), and tRNA (transfer RNA) are manufactured. The functions of these different types of RNA molecules will be presented in later chapters.

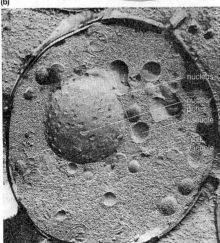

Figure 3–20 The nucleus of the cell; (a) generalized diagram (b) an electron micrograph of the nucleus of a yeast cell. *Source:* Teresa Audesirk and Gerald Audesirk (1999), p. 106.

Figure 3–21 Light micrograph of the chromosomes in the nucleus. *Source:* Teresa Audesirk and Gerald Audesirk (1999), p. 96.

Cell Division: Mitosis—A Basic Cell Function

One of the basic characteristics of life is that organisms have a life history. They are produced, grow to maturity, reproduce and then die. Cells also exhibit a kind of life cycle; they are produced, grow, mature, reproduce and then some die. At the cellular level this is called the **cell cycle**. Central to the life of cells (and of the multicellular organisms comprised of cells) is reproduction which always and invariably occurs only at the cellular level.

Cell reproduction is termed **cell replication**, or less commonly cell division or cell duplication. During cell division, a cell termed the **mother cell** divides into two **daughter cells**, each about half of the size of the mother cell. Each of the daughter cells then undergoes a period of growth until they are the size of the original mother cell. Note that "death" at the cellular level does not occur during cell reproduction, as the mother cell lives on in the daughter cells. The daughter cells may in turn undergo cell division.

Cell division is also the method by which plants (and other organisms) grow and repair themselves. Growth actually has two components; first, cells divide, thereby adding to the total number of cells and, therefore, the size of multicellular organisms. Second, following cell division each of the daughter cells may grow to maturity—-this also increases the size of the organism. For example the small, newly formed leaves of spring contain all of the cells that will make up the leaf throughout the summer. As the individual leaf cells grow, the leaf enlarges in size to that of the mature leaf in late summer.

The duplication of cells also enables plants to repair or replace damaged structures. When plant tissues are injured the cells surrounding the wound may spontaneously undergo cell division to seal off the wound, then produce new cells to replace the damaged or destroyed cells.

Mitotic cell division in higher plants takes place only in certain tissues called meristems. These are discussed more fully in the next chapter.

In lower plants and bacteria cell division occurs more-or-less continuously, given adequate food and optimum environmental conditions. In most higher plants however, active cell division is limited to specific times of the year and specific regions of the plant called **meristem tissue**. For example, roots and stems have meristem tissues that regularly undergo cell division to produce new cells which results in root and stem growth. Other areas of meristem tissue are found in a cylindrical band of tissue within the stem called the vascular cambium. The cell division of this layer of meristem tissue increases the thickness of the plant. Some woody and herbaceous plants have a fourth layer of meristem tissue, the cork cambium, which gives rise to the bark of shrubs and trees.

EVENTS IN CELL DIVISION

Cell division involves two separate but interrelated events, (1) the replication and sorting of chromosomes, and (2) the duplication and division of cytoplasm and cytoplasmic organelles. The duplication and sorting of chromosomal genetic material is called **mitosis** or **karyosis**, when referring to the production of normal plant cells and **meiosis** when reproductive cells (eggs and sperm) are manufactured. (Meiosis will be described in a later chapter). Near the end of mitosis the cytoplasm and certain of its organelles such as the mitochondria and plastids duplicate and are divided among the daughter cells in a process termed **cytokinesis**.

CELL DIVISION IN PROKARYOTES

In bacteria the genes are arranged along one or two simple, naked strands of DNA. When bacteria divide the DNA attaches to the cell wall, then enzymes make a copy of the DNA along its length. One part of the newly copied DNA strand also attaches to the wall of each of the new bacteria. Thus, when copying is completed the bacterial cell has two DNA strands the original and its copy attached to the cell wall at separate sites. The cell wall between the two DNA strands begins to invaginate, pushing them apart. When invagination is completed the walls fuse and two new bacterial cells have been formed, each with its own complete strand of DNA.

CELL DIVISION IN EUKARYOTES

Cell division in eukaryotes is considerably more complicated than in prokaryotes because of the larger amount of DNA present, which must be copied and allocated to the new daughter cells. Much of the time spent in eukaryotic cell division is consumed in correctly copying and reforming chromosomes.

CHROMOSOMES DURING CELL DIVISION

Compared to the simple DNA strand found in bacteria, eukaryotes have hundreds, perhaps thousands of genes along their DNA. To provide a structural strength and organization to the eukaryote DNA, it is packaged in a jacket of proteins. The combination of DNA and a protein jacket is called a chromosome, and it follows that chromosomes are the carriers of the genes.

Chromosomes are the DNA nucleic acids packaged in protein jackets. When chromosomes are unwound they are thin, threadlike and called chromatin. During cell division the chromatin winds and folds tightly around beads of protein, becoming shorter and thicker. Each chromatin strand is then called a chromatid. When they duplicate the two chromatids, called sister chromatids are joined together by the centromere. When the chromatids are released they are called chromosomes.

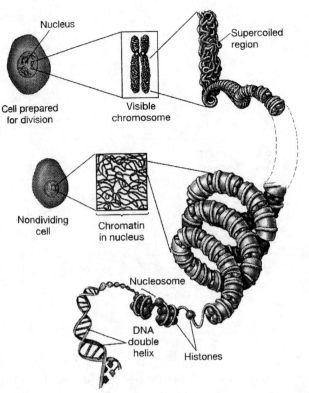

Figure 3–22 The structure of a chromosome. *Source*: Frederic H. Martini. *Fundamentals of Anatomy and Physiology* 3/e (1995), Prentice-Hall, p. 93.

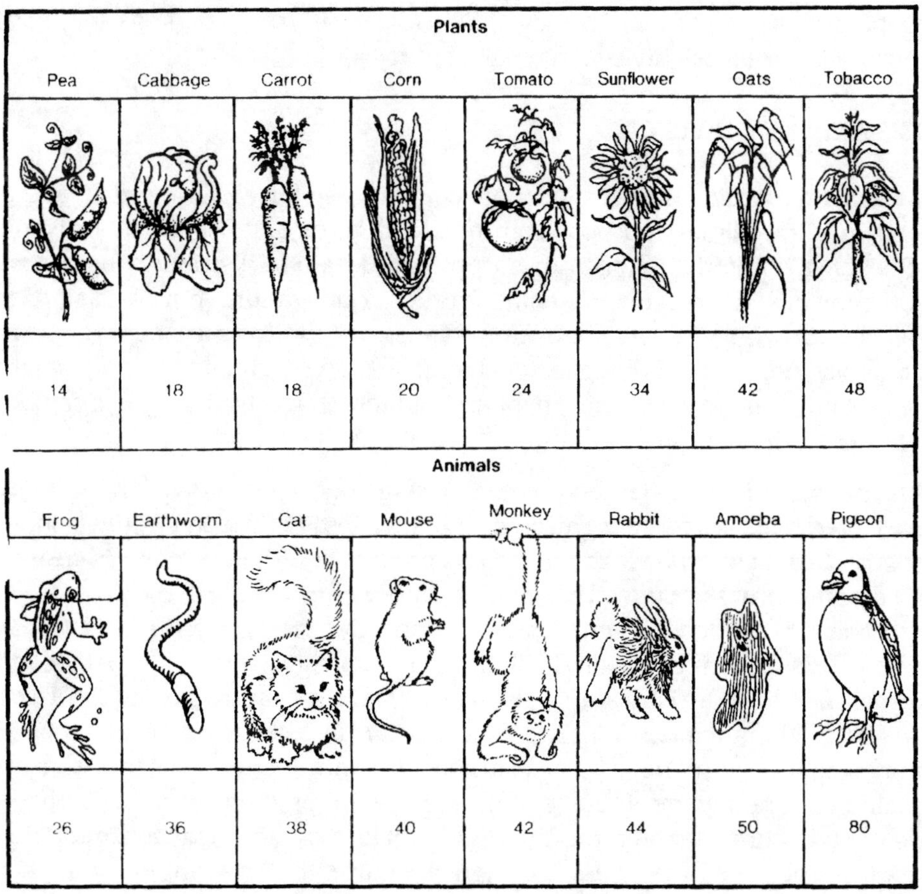

Plants							
Pea	Cabbage	Carrot	Corn	Tomato	Sunflower	Oats	Tobacco
14	18	18	20	24	34	42	48

Animals							
Frog	Earthworm	Cat	Mouse	Monkey	Rabbit	Amoeba	Pigeon
26	36	38	40	42	44	50	80

Figure 3–23 Chromosome numbers of various plants and animals. *Source:* Tom M. Graham (1997), p. 300.

Figure 3–24 Events in the cell cycle of duplication. *Source:* Teresa Audesirk and Gerald Audesirk (1999), p. 180.

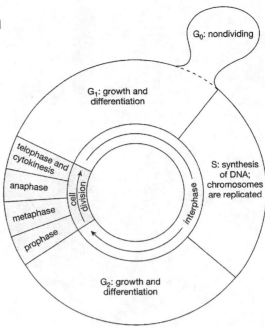

Each organism has a specific number of chromosomes, all of which must be copied correctly. Humans, for example have 46 chromosomes in all body cells with the exception of sex cells and red blood cells—-the latter extrude their nucleus and its chromosomes before they mature. The events involved in the copying and sorting of chromosomes during cell division are called mitosis.

MITOSIS AND CELL DIVISION

Mitosis has three basic functions, to produce new cells for growth, repair, and asexual reproduction. The primary purpose common to all three of these functions is to exactly copy the genetic material of the chromosomes and then to distribute one complete set to each of the new daughter cells arising from cell duplication. In most plants, cell division takes place within a 24–36 hour time span or less. Mitosis is a continuous process, but for convenience in describing events that take place we recognize five major stages, interphase, prophase, metaphase, anaphase and telophase. Dividing cells can be identified by their swollen nucleus and appearance of the chromosomes.

Interphase. Originally named the resting stage because no divisional activity could be seen, interphase is now recognized as the most active time in cell division; it is also the longest. During interphase the nucleus is present and the nucleolus is clearly visible but the chromosomes are uncoiled and cannot be seen.

Interphase is divided into three phases, Gap_1, Synthesis and Gap_2. G_1 (or Gap 1) is the time period following an initial cell division. During G_1 the cell is busy conducting its normal metabolic activities and also is involved in manufacturing DNA segments that will be used in the next cell division. If a cell is in cell cycle arrest it stops dividing and remains in G_1 permanently. For example all nonmeristem cells in plants are fated to remain permanently in this stage of interphase. In dividing cells the G_1 phase represents a period of growth and maturation. If a cell is going to divide again it enters the S (or synthesis) phase of interphase, during which time the long, thin, genetic segments of DNA comprising the chromatin are replicated. By the end of the S phase the cell contains two duplicate sets of chromatin (the uncoiled chromosomes), held together by a

Figure 3–25 The duplication of a DNA molecule. The original DNA molecule has been enzymatically unzipped along a portion of its length. New strands are being copied within the open strands. They will join to form duplicate DNA molecules. *Source:* Frederic H. Martini. *Fundamentals of Anatomy and Physiology* 3/e (1995), Prentice-Hall, p. 100.

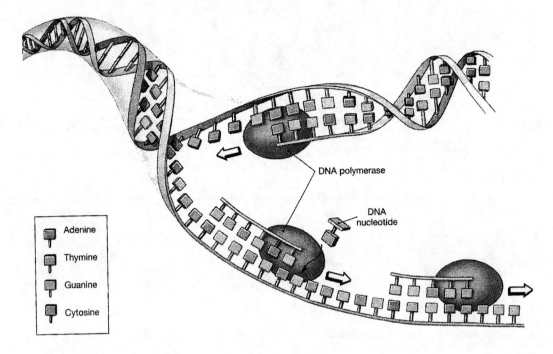

thread-like band of protein called the **centromere**. The S phase is followed by a G$_2$ (Gap 2) stage, in which the cell is manufacturing the necessary enzymes to catalyze the cell replication events that follow.

Towards the end of interphase, a **preprophase band** of microtubules develop just under the cell membrane. In most plants the band of microtubules become the fibers that orient and transport the chromosomes to the new daughter cells.

Prophase. Late in interphase or early in prophase the chromatin condenses and coils, becoming shorter and thicker. The chromatin is now visible, appearing as two dark strands called **chromatids** which are still attached together. The two chromatids, usually called **sister chromatids**, represent the halves of a duplicated pair of **chromosomes**, bearing the genes.

As prophase develops, the nucleolus disappears and the nuclear membrane is enzymatically dissolved. In some cells of animals, fungi, and algae, spindle fibers are formed from organelles called the **centrioles**. The centrioles migrate to opposite ends of the dividing cell, and somehow weave a system of protein microtubules that connect with each of the chromosomes. The whole apparatus of tubules is called a **spindle bundle**.

The microtubules of the spindle bundle attach to anchoring devices called **kinetochores**, a dense area located within each centromere. Centrioles are considered to be primitive structures that do not appear in higher plants where the spindle bundle is formed without the aid of centrioles. Prophase may take as little as 30-60 minutes to complete.

Metaphase. When prophase is completed the chromosomes of the cell are ready to be separated and distributed which occurs during the next stage in mitosis, called metaphase. Metaphase is generally short, normally taking only a few minutes to complete. In metaphase, the microtubules of the spindle bundle stretch from opposite ends

Figure 3–26 The cell cycle of events in the plant cell in mitosis. *Source:* Teresa Audesirk and Gerald Audesirk (1999), p. 182..

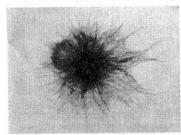

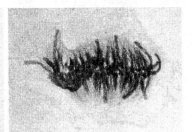

(a) **Interphase** in a cell of the endosperm (a food-storage organ in the seed) before mitosis begins: The chromosomes are in the thin, extended state and appear as a mass in the center of the cell. The microtubules extend outward from the nucleus to all parts of the cell.

(b) **Late prophase:** The chromosomes have condensed and attached to microtubules of the spindle fibers.

(c) **Metaphase:** The spindle fibers have pulled the chromosomes to the equator of the cell.

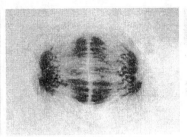

(d) **Anaphase:** The spindle fibers are moving one set of chromosomes to each pole of the cell.

(e) **Telophase:** The chromosomes have been gathered into two clusters, one at the site of each future nucleus.

(f) **Resumption of interphase:** The chromosomes are relaxing again into their extended state. The spindle fibers are disappearing, and the microtubules of the two daughter cells are rearranging into the interphase pattern.

of the cell to each of the sister chromatids (or from the centrioles to each of the chromosomes in algae and fungi, for example). By contractile movements, the spindles move each pair of sister chromatids to the cell center so that they are aligned in a metaphase plate. Towards the end of metaphase the centromeres duplicate and in the process the sister chromatids separate and are now generally referred to as the chromosomes.

Anaphase. After separating, the now single-stranded chromosomes separate further, migrating towards opposite ends of the cell. In plant cells that lack centrioles the microtubules somehow pull the chromosomes towards the opposite ends of the cell. Two theories suggest how the microtubules move the chromosomes. One suggestion is that microtubules in the cytoplasm between the migrating chromosomes absorb water and swell, thereby pushing the newly separated chromosomes away from one another and towards the sides of the cell. An alternate suggestion is that the spindle fibers shorten and contract to pull the chromosomes towards the sides of the cells. Possibly both processes are occurring at the same time. Near the end of anaphase, exactly half of the chromosomes are clustered on each side of the dividing cell. That is, a complete set of chromosomes is clustered at each end of the replicating cell. Anaphase takes about 20–30 minutes to complete. In many replicating cells cytokinesis, the replication of the organelles and other cell components other than the chromosomes, begins at this point.

Telophase. Early in telophase, new nuclear membranes begin to form and surround each of the two sets of chromosomes now clustered at opposite ends of the cell.

Figure 3–27 The events of cytokinesis in a plant cell. *Source:* Teresa Audesirk and Gerald Audesirk (1999), p. 184.

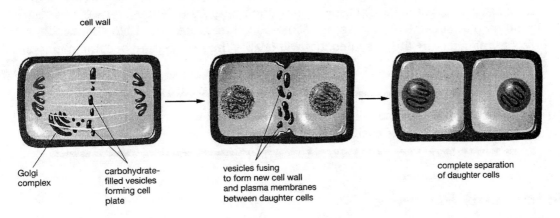

cell wall

Golgi complex

carbohydrate-filled vesicles forming cell plate

vesicles fusing to form new cell wall and plasma membranes between daughter cells

complete separation of daughter cells

As telophase continues one or more nucleoli are formed within the nucleus and the chromosomes again begin to unwind into long, thin strands of chromatin.

The spindle bundle dissolves and simultaneously a membrane shaped from micro-tubule fragments called a **phragmoplast** begins to assemble in the center of the dividing cell, where the metaphase plate was located at the completion of metaphase. In the phragmoplast, dictysomes produce vesicles which fuse to form a **cell plate**, which grows outward from the center to fuse with the cell wall. Cellulose is deposited along a middle lamella shared by each of the daughter cells to form a **primary wall**. With the completion of the new cell wall, the mother cell is split into two daughter cells, each about half the size of the original cell. Later, secondary cell walls develop as each of the daughter cells grows and matures. Each of the daughter cells contains a nucleus with exactly the same number of chromosomes as the original mother cell plus enough cytoplasm and cytoplasmic organelles to provide the basic machinery of the new cell.

Cytokinesis. Cytokinesis actually begins during telophase or earlier in some cells. During cytokinesis the mitochondria and chloroplasts of each of the daughter cells divide repeatedly, enlarging the populations of these two important organelles. Simultaneously, the cell is busy synthesizing enzymes to direct the manufacture of other organelles and cell structures.

Step-by-step summary of events in mitosis:

Interphase	DNA (the chromosomes) duplicate, chromatin coils
Prophase	nuclear membrane dissolves, spindle bundle forms
Metaphase	sister chromatids line up in center of cell
Anaphase	chromosomes migrate
Telophase	nuclear membrane forms around each cluster of chromosomes, cell plate forms, daughter cells are produced

DAUGHTER CELLS

Mitosis is now complete. Where there had originally been one cell there are now two daughter cells, each about half the size of the original cell prior to duplication. The daughter cells grow and carry on all the functions of normal cells until they also go through mitosis, if they are destined to do so (remember that in higher plants only cells of the meristem tissues undergo repeated cell divisions). The daughter cells are now in interphase again. As the daughter cells grow and mature they enter a new G_1 substage. Within the nucleus, the chromosomes again uncoil to expose the DNA chemical blueprints to manufacture the enzymes that will enable the new cells to become metabolically active components of the plant.

An acronym to remember the order of the stages of mitosis can be formed by taking the first letter of each stage, thus forming the pseudoword IPMAT

Key Words and Phrases

amyloplast
cell
cell wall
cell membrane
endoplasmic reticulum
chloroplast
nucleus
chromatid
sister chromatid
vacuole
mitosis/karyosis
prophase
telophase
daughter cells
cell plate

plastid
middle lamella
organelle
cytoplasm
ribosomes
chlorophyll
nuclear membrane
gene
centromere
prokaryote
cytokinesis
metaphase
centriole
phragmoplast

cytoplasmic streaming
Gap_1 and Gap_2 phases
Synthesis phase
mitochondria
golgi body
cyclosis
chromatin
chromosome
kinetochore
eukaryote
interphase
anaphase
spindle fibers
tonoplast

Selected References and Resources

Baker, N. R., and J. Barber. Eds. 1984. *Chloroplast biogenesis.* Elsevier Science Publishing Company. New York.

Karp, G. 1984. *Cell Biology.* 2nd. Edition. McGraw-Hill. New York.

Lodish, H., D. Baltimore, A. Berk, S. L. Zipursky, P. Matsudira, and J. Darnell. 1995. *Molecular Biology.* 2nd Edition. Scientific American Books. W. H. Freeman & Company. New York.

Murray, A., and T. Hunt. 1993. *The Cell Cycle. An Introduction.* Oxford University Press. New York.

Robinson, D. G. 1985. *Plant Membranes.* John Wiley & Sons. New York.

Stryer, L. 1988. *Biochemistry.* 3rd. Edition. W. H. Freeman & Company. San Francisco.

Wolfe, S. L. 1993. *Molecular and Cellular Biology.* Wadsworth Publishing Company. Belmont, California.

1. Draw and label the organelles and other structures of a typical plant cell.
2. Which of the cell organelles are responsible for the synthesis, assembly and final packaging of cell organic chemicals?
3. How are materials transported within the cytoplasm? Within the nucleus?
4. Describe the basic differences between prokaryotic and eukaryotic cells. What are the advantages of eukaryotic cells? Do prokaryotic cells have any functional advantages over eukaryotic cells?
5. What would happen to plants if they were to lose the following cell organelles: mitochondria, dictysomes, ribosomes, plasma membrane?
6. Why is it believed that DNA is replicated during interphase?
7. Years ago scientists suggested that the spindle fibers seen during mitosis actually represented either stress lines in the dividing cell or perhaps provided evidence for a magnetic field. Discuss both possibilities.
8. How do mitochondria and chloroplasts differ from all other cell organelles?
9. In comparing the number of chromosomes found in different plant species, for example, you may note that a fern can have 50 times as many chromosomes as does a giant sequoia. Is there any obvious relationship between the size and complexity of organisms and their number of chromosomes?
10. What are some of the functions of microtubules and microfilaments in cells?
11. What are the differences and similarities between chromatin, chromatids, and chromosomes?

Chapter 4

Plant Tissues

Meristematic Tissues
 Primary and Secondary Tissues
 Apical Meristems
 Intercalary Meristems
Non-Meristematic Tissues
 Simple Tissues
 Secretory Tissues
 Dermal Tissues
Complex Tissues
 Xylem
 Phloem
 Periderm

Plants are a very complex and diverse group of organisms numbering about 275,000 different species and belonging to at least four kingdoms: the monera, algae, fungi, and true plants. The true plants in turn can be divided into two basic groups, the **vascular plants**, so called because they have well developed tissues for conducting water, minerals, sugars, and other nutrients, and the **nonvascular plant**s, which lack specific internal conducting systems. Examples of nonvascular plants include the mosses and liverworts. Examples of vascular plants include the flowering plants and conifers.

Most of the world's plants are the vascular plants of which the most common and familiar are the seed bearing plants, the gymnosperms, exemplified by pines, spruces and firs, and the angiosperms, commonly called the flowering plants. The flowering plants number about 235,000 species and comprise the vast majority of all plants.

We will first study the different kinds of plants, which will establish the basis for discussing the structure and function of plant organs. We will concentrate on flowering plants for they provide excellent and often familiar examples of plant tissues and organs. It may appear to be approaching things backwards as flowering plants are the summit of plant evolution, but we have chosen to start here because they are the most important of all plants and those which most people know about.

Two Kinds of Flowering Plants

••••••••••••••••••••••••••••▼

All flowering plants produce flowers, roots, shoots, stems, and leaves, or modifications of these structures. Plant biologists recognize two basic kinds of these flowering plants, based on several evident structural differences in seeds, venation in leaves, number of flower parts and other features.

The seeds of flowering plants have tiny leaves on them called **cotyledons**. These seed leaves function to provide the plant with food until the adult leaves can form from

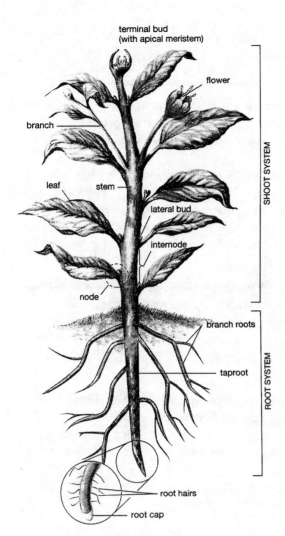

terminal bud
(with apical meristem)

flower

branch

leaf

stem

lateral bud

internode

node

SHOOT SYSTEM

branch roots

taproot

ROOT SYSTEM

root hairs

root cap

Figure 4–1 Growth organization of a typical vascular plant. *Source:* Teresa Audesirk and Gerald Audesirk (1999), p. 452.

the apical meristem. If there is one seed leaf on the seedling the plant is called a **mono-cotyledon** or simply a **monocot**. If there are two seed leaves on the seedling it is a **dicotyledon** or **dicot**. There are many other characteristics that separate dicots and monocots, a few of which we will discuss now. Monocots typically have elongate leaves with parallel veins and flower parts in threes. Examples of monocots include the grasses and lilies. Dicot leaves are typically broader and with netlike venation. The flower parts of dicots usually occur in fours or fives. Examples of dicots include most of the trees and shrubs such as the oaks, maples and hickories, the cacti, roses and sunflowers.

Plant Tissues

Regardless of whether they are monocots or dicots, all flowering plants are comprised of millions of cells that cooperatively interact to run the plant. These plant cells are grouped into distinct units or layers called tissues. **Tissues** are groups of cells that have a similar morphology and perform a common function. Most organs and other struc-tures of plants are comprised of several to many different kinds of tissues. Among the flowering plants, three basic tissue patterns can be found in stems and roots; (1) woody dicots, (2) herbaceous dicots, and (3) monocots.

primary tissues	**form the primary plant body**
secondary tissues	**form the woody secondary growth**

All of the billions of plant cells that comprise a tree or other flowering plant are produced by meristematic tissue. Depending on their life cycle, flowering plants are composed of one or two basic kinds of tissues; **primary tissue**, which forms the herbaceous plant structure and **secondary tissue**, which is woody growth produced in subsequent years. To understand this you must realize that angiosperms can be divided into three groups, based on life cycles.

Annuals. These are plants that complete their life cycle in one year and then die. The species lives on by producing seeds which develop into new plants the following year. Most vegetables that you plant in your garden are annuals, as are many flowers in your flower garden such as milkweeds, marigolds, dandelions, and petunias. A plant that lives for only one year will only consist of primary tissue produced by meristematic tissue during the growing season.

Biennials. Plants in this category require two years to complete their life cycle. Typically, biennials grow during the first year but do not mature and flower. At the end of the growing season they die back, but live through the winter in the form of hardy, persistent roots or basal rosettes of leaves. Growth during the second year is often aimed at producing a flowering stalk. Most biennials are also comprised entirely of primary tissue. Examples of biennials include bee balm, foxglove, forget-me-nots, and pansies.

Perennials. These are plants that live more than two years. During the first year of life their meristematic tissues produce the primary tissues making up the plant body. Every year thereafter new tissues are produced by secondary meristems and are called secondary tissues. Deciduous trees such as oak, maple, beech, and birch as well as evergreen trees such as hemlock and pines are considered perennial since they have secondary tissue. The most common and familiar example of secondary tissue produced by secondary meristems during subsequent years is wood. Some flowers such as tiger lilies, black-eyed susans, tulips, irises, violets, and daisies are also perennials. They do not produce any woody (secondary) tissue yet they can be included in the perennial grouping because they grow back year after year.

Although most of a plant is comprised of either primary or secondary tissues or both, these tissues do not contribute further growth of the plant, once formed. They remain mitotically inactive until their death—only meristematic tissues actively divide to produce further plant growth. We will further consider the relationships between meristems and primary and secondary plant tissues below.

MERISTEMATIC TISSUES

Meristematic tissues are plant tissues where cells divide and plant growth occurs. Unlike animals, growth in plants occurs only in these specific **meristem tissues**. Meristem tissues are comprised of cells that actively divide. Meristems occur in the tips of roots and in the stems of all plants and are responsible for the increase in root length and shoot length, respectively in the growing plant. All meristems are strategically important tissues that are protected by layers of cells. For example, the layers of cells that cover and protect the root meristem are called the **root cap** while the stem meristem tissues are protected by young leaves that partially envelop and protect them.

The relationship between meristematic tissues and **primary tissues** is as follows. When a plant develops from a seed, the first cells to arise form primary tissue. As the new plant develops there are two active areas of cell division—one at the very tip of the stem and another near the tip of the roots which are called **apical meristems**. This apical meristems of stems and roots is responsible for producing most of the plant growth.

Apical Meristems

The tip of each stem, also called a **shoot**, is where primary tissue actively divides to produce new cells, actively increasing the length of the shoot. This is the only active region of plant growth in the stems of first year and annual plants. The typical cell in these growth areas is small and resemble a six-sided box, with a large nucleus. The meristem cells either lack vacuoles or have very small vacuoles. As they mature they develop into three kinds of primary meristems, **ground meristem, protoderm,** and **procambium**.

The external layers of the apical meristem form a meristem tissue layer called the **protoderm**. This protoderm tissue will form protective, leaf-like covers around the apical meristem. The protoderm is also responsible for producing a layer on the outside of the plant called the epidermis. The epidermis is the "skin" of the plant and will be discussed later. These protoderm cells are the precursors of many other cells and tissues associated with the outer layer of the plant. Besides the epidermis, the protoderm tissues form **guard cells** of stomata, **nectar cells, hairs,** and any other cells which functionally operate on the surface of the plant.

The second meristem tissue layer produced by the cells of the apical meristem are found beneath the protoderm and are called the **ground meristem**. This tissue is also

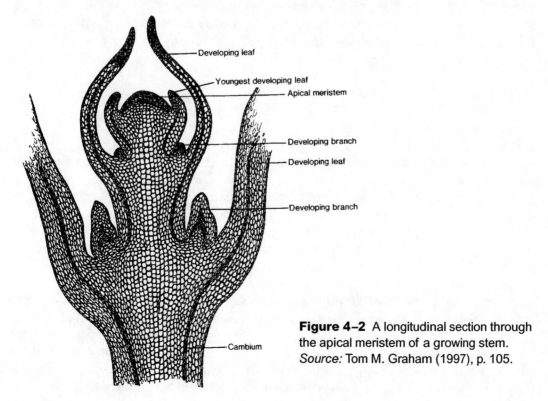

Developing leaf

Youngest developing leaf

Apical meristem

Developing branch

Developing leaf

Developing branch

Cambium

Figure 4–2 A longitudinal section through the apical meristem of a growing stem. *Source:* Tom M. Graham (1997), p. 105.

Table 4–1 Non-meristematic tissues derived from meristems.

Meristematic Tissue	Non-meristematic tissue formed from this meristematic tissue
Primary Tissue	
Protoderm	Epidermis
Ground Meristem	Parenchyma, collenchyma, sclerenchyma
Procambium	Primary xylem and primary phloem
Secondary Tissue	
Vascular Cambium	Secondary xylem and secondary phloem
Cork Cambium	Periderm (cork cells)

found in peripheral areas of the root. Ground meristem can form several tissue types; the most common tissue produced is **parenchyma**, which contains cells that are equipped with large vacuoles. Parenchyma cells have very thin walls. They are utilized by the plant for storage, support, and secretion of substances. When they are used for photosynthesis they are termed **chlorenchyma** cells because they contain chloroplasts.

The ground meristem can also produce **collenchyma** cells which are the primary cells used for strength and may be especially plentiful in areas where plants bend or are subjected to torsion, twisting, and bending stress. To resist this stress, the cell walls of collenchyma tend to be thickened at the corners which lend to added support. Lastly, the ground meristem produces **sclerenchyma** cells which contain tough fibers impregnated with lignin. Much of the sclerenchyma tissues of plants are dead when mature and function as walls or bulwarks that support and protect the plant.

The third tissue layer produced by apical meristems lies below and lateral to the apical meristem, consists of **procambium** tissue. The procambium forms vascular tissue in the plant. This vascular tissue is comprised of tissues called **xylem** and **phloem** which transport and distribute water and food throughout the plant. These vascular tissues produced by the procambium are called **primary xylem** and **primary phloem**. The procambium is also responsible for forming the veins that go into and out of leaves.

MERISTEMS AND SECONDARY TISSUES

In biannual and perennial plants, tissues produced by the meristems during the second and subsequent years of life are called **secondary tissues**. These contribute to the woodiness of some plants and typically comprise the bulk of the plant tissues throughout the life of the plant.

Secondary, or woody tissues are produced by lateral meristems that develop from the primary meristems, **cork cambium** and **vascular cambium**.

Both cork cambium and vascular cambium occur as thin, cylindrical layers of branching cells, lying just under the epidermis and run the length of stems and roots of perennials (and also in some herbaceous annuals). The mitotic activity of the cells in these two lateral meristems increases the girth of the plant. The inner layer of lateral meristem is called **vascular cambium**. It consists of individual self-perpetuating cells called **initials** which produce vascular tissue (xylem and phloem, for example) as their name implies. The inner layer of vascular cambium produces xylem cells while the outer layer produces phloem cells. Wood which forms most of the bulk (and trunk) of trees is actually xylem produced from the vascular cambium. Xylem and phloem produced by vascular cambium is called **secondary xylem** and **secondary phloem**.

vascular cambium	forms the new vascular tissues, the secondary or woody tissues after the plant has formed.
cork cambium	forms the periderm that replaces the epidermis

The outer layer of these lateral meristems produces another secondary meristematic tissue called **cork cambium**. Like vascular cambium, cork cambium is cylindrical and runs the length of a plant's stems and roots. It is located just outside of the vascular cambium and produces **cork cells** which form the bark of woody plants.

INTERCALARY MERISTEMS

Monocotyledons are mostly annuals (plants that have a life cycle of one year) such as the grasses and lilies. They have a special type of meristem growth area called **intercalary meristems**. These intercalary meristems are located at joint-like positions called **nodes** along the stems. Intercalary meristems are responsible for the growth of the monocot's length and girth. They are the tissues that promote the often rapid growth rate observed in many monocots such as grasses and corn. The location of intercalary meristems along the stem of the plant confers a special advantage on monocots. For example, if the tops of grasses are cut or grazed by herbivores the plant will continue to grow, because of the mitotic activity of undamaged intercalary meristems along the stem. By comparison, if the apical meristems of dicots are cut, diseased or die, the entire plant may die or its growth may be stopped or stunted.

Non-Meristematic Tissues

Non-meristematic tissues are derived from the meristems but do not replicate (i.e., do not undergo mitosis), although they otherwise remain functional cells until they die. They assume many specialized shapes and tasks. Some of these non-meristematic tissues are of only one kind of cells while others are mixed. Two basic kinds of non-meristematic

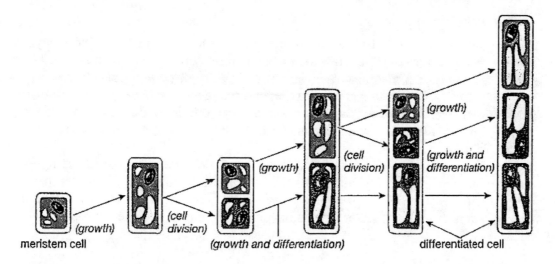

Figure 4–3 The growth and maturation of meristem cells in vascular plants. *Source:* Teresa Audesirk and Gerald Audesirk (1996), p. 500.

tissues occur in plants, **simple tissues** and **complex tissues**. Examples of these tissues are discussed below.

SIMPLE NON-MERISTEMATIC TISSUES

In simple tissues all the cells are of one type, that is, they have a similar shape and perform a similar function. They constitute some of the most important tissues found in plants.

Parenchyma Tissue

Parenchyma tissue is the most common of the plant's ground tissues and **parenchyma cells** are the most abundant plant cells. Parenchyma tissue is widespread in higher plants, forming much of the stems, roots, leaves, and fruits. Parenchyma cells are thin walled and spherical when new. At maturity the cells have flattened cell walls at points of contact with other cells. When parenchyma cells are tightly packed they can have up to fourteen sides. The cells of parenchyma tissue are characterized by having large vacuoles and may contain starch grains, oils, tannin, crystals and other secretions within. Parenchyma tissue functions primarily as storage tissue in many plants but the cells may also carry on photosynthesis and act as secretory tissue. Plant waste products called **ergastic inclusions** and food are stored in the large vacuoles in these cells. When spaces occur between cells of parenchyma tissue **(intercellular spaces)** as in water lilies, the trapped air helps the plant float. Unlike most kinds of tissue, parenchyma cells retain the ability to divide at maturity and help seal plant wounds and regenerate damaged or lost tissues. They also contribute to growth.

Some parenchyma tissue in plants is modified for other uses besides storage of food and wastes. Other parenchyma cells trap air which serves as a buffer or makes the plant more buoyant. Parenchyma cells that contain chloroplasts are important areas for photosynthesis and are called **chlorenchyma cells**. These cells are especially common in leaves near the epidermis.

Parenchyma cells are important to us because they are the cells that store starch for the plant. This stored food is why we eat plants. When we eat vegetables and fruits, the plant tissue that we are actually eating is parenchyma. Some parenchyma cells are very durable with some in cacti living to over 100 years.

Collenchyma Tissue

Another kind of ground tissue is comprised of **collenchyma** cells. Collenchyma cells are also long-lived cells. They resemble parenchyma cells, but have walls of uneven thickness with the thicker areas occurring at the corners. Collenchyma cells form the collenchyma tissue that lies just beneath the epidermis. The cells are elongate and have strong and pliable walls. They provide a firm but flexible support for growing organs such as leaves and flowers and also provide important layers of support for the mature plant.

The stringy strands of tissue along the length of a celery stalk are a good example of collenchyma tissue; they are the tissues that allow you to bend and twist the celery stalk, which then returns to its original shape when released. The long and flexible stems of plants and the stalks of flowers have large amounts of collenchyma tissue as well.

Figure 4–4 The structure of three primary types of ground tissues in plants, parenchyma, collenchyma, and sclerenchyma. *Source:* Teresa Audesirk and Gerald Audesirk (1999), p. 456.

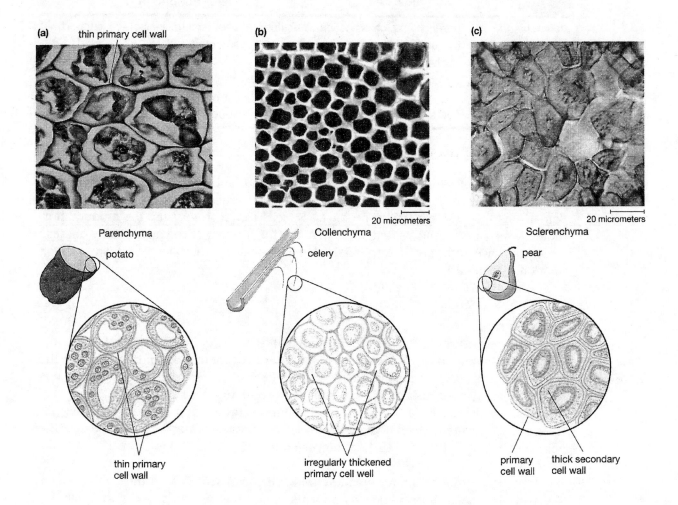

Sclerenchyma Tissue

Sclerenchyma cells are more widely scattered in plant tissue than are other kinds of tissue. They usually have thick, tough walls that are impregnated with lignin, creating a strong supporting structure. Cells of sclerenchyma tissues are dead at maturity but because of the strength of their cells walls, are able to support the plant. There are two kinds of sclerenchyma of interest to us. **Sclereids** are randomly distributed in other tissues. They are hexagonal cells in which the space between the cell walls is filled with lignin which extends out through the plasmodesmata in the cell walls. Sclereids form the seed coats of peanuts and other fruits. When we eat pears we feel a gritty sensation in the pear flesh. The cells that cause this are stone cells that support the structure of pear parenchyma tissue. Stone cells are examples of Sclereids.

Fibers are a second type of sclerenchyma tissue commonly found in plants. Fibers are elongate, tapered cells found associated with different tissues in roots, stems, leaves, and fruits. They are formed from cells that are longer than they are broad, with a tiny cavity or lumen in the center. Fibers are widely used in the manufacture of textile goods, rope, paper products and strong canvas. Plant fibers have been in use for over 10,000 years.

Table 4–2 Simple ground tissues and cell types and their functions.

Tissues	Cell Types	Major Functions
Parenchyma	parenchyma, chlorenchyma, lactifers, oil ducts, resin and gum ducts, epithelial cells	photosynthesis, storage, support, secretion
Collenchyma	collenchyma cells	photosynthesis, support, geotopic (gravity sensing)
Sclerenchyma	fibers and sclereids	support and protection

Secretory Tissues

Many kinds of parenchyma tissues secrete various substances produced within the cytoplasm. They may secrete plant products as nectar, oils, mucilage, latex, and resins. Sometimes they excrete waste products. Specialized secretory tissues produce hormones which are chemicals that are vital to the functioning of the plant. Many of these secretions have important commercial value and include things like pine resins, rubber, mint oil, and opium.

Dermal Tissues

Epidermis

The outermost layer of cells of all young plants is called the epidermis. It is flexible and can be modified in response to changing environmental conditions. Usually the epidermis consists of a single layer of cells. Unlike most external plant tissues, the epidermis typically does **not** contain chloroplasts as one might assume.

In a few plants such as orchids special **velamen roots** are produced by epidermis. Here the epidermis is several layers in thickness. Leaves of figs and members of the pepper family also typically have a thicker epidermis which helps protect the plant's interior tissues.

Most epidermal cells have **cutin**, a lipid substance secreted on the outer surface. The cutin is especially important as it forms the **cuticle** which is made with wax for protection. The thickness of the cuticle determines the amount of protection the plant has against desiccation. Cuticles are also resistant to bacteria and the invasion of the plant by other pathogens. Carnauba wax is a cuticle product from the leaves of the wax palm. It is used in high quality polishes.

Specialized Epidermal Structures. Epidermal cells are capable of producing other structures needed by the plant. For example, **root hairs** that often occur abundantly along the roots of plants are a simple extension of individual epidermal cells. They are vital to the survival of many plants because they increase the surface area of the root for the absorption of water and nutrients. The underside of the leaves of dicots and both leaf surfaces of many monocots have openings called **stomata**. On either side of the stomata are special epidermal cells called **guard cells** which control the opening and closing of the stoma to balance gas exchange and water content. The guard cells have cell walls with an uneven thickness. One side of the guard cell is thicker than the other which causes the cells to arc and push apart when absorbing water, thus creating an opening to allow gas and water exchange.

Gland cells are epidermal cells involved in the secretion of protective or aromatic substances. Groups of these cells are called **glands** and constitute a form of secretory tissue formed from epidermis.

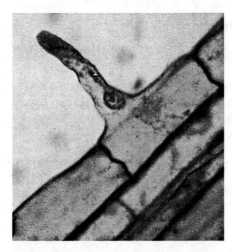

Figure 4–5 Section of onion root tip epidermis showing how a root hair is formed from a single epidermal cell. *Source:* Roy H. Saigo and Barbara W. Saigo. *Botany: Principles and Applications* (1983), Prentice-Hall, p. 130.

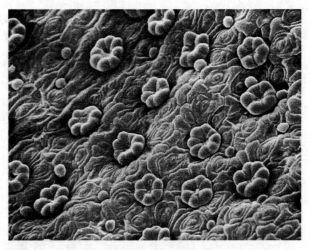

Figure 4–7 Scanning electron micrograph of the epidermis of ivy showing multicellular gland hairs and stomata. *Source:* Roy H. Saigo and Barbara W. Saigo. *Botany: Principles and Applications* (1983), Prentice-Hall, p. 130.

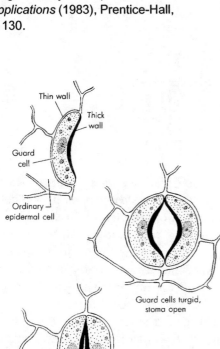

Figure 4–6 Stomatal cell anatomy and function. *Source:* Arthur W. Galston, Peter J. Davies and Ruth L. Satter. *The Life of the Green Plant* (1980), Prentice-Hall, p. 85.

Lastly, some plants are covered with hair-like growths called **plant hairs**. Plant hairs have many functions ranging from protection to ornamentation. They are also derived from one or more epidermal cells.

COMPLEX TISSUES

In advanced plants, like the conifers and the flowering plants, some tissues are formed from more than one kind of cell. These tissues are termed **complex tissues** and are primarily secondary tissues.

Xylem

One of the most important substances in a plant's environment necessary for survival is water. Water is normally absorbed by root hairs on the roots. Once it gets into the plant it is carried by special conduction tissue called **xylem**. Xylem is derived from procambium in annuals and from vascular cambium in perennials. Xylem is complex because it can form in several ways. The cells conducting water may be one of two kinds of xylem, **tracheids** or **vessel elements**. These cells are dead at maturity and the only structure involved in their functioning is the cell wall. Let's look at the two main xylem cells.

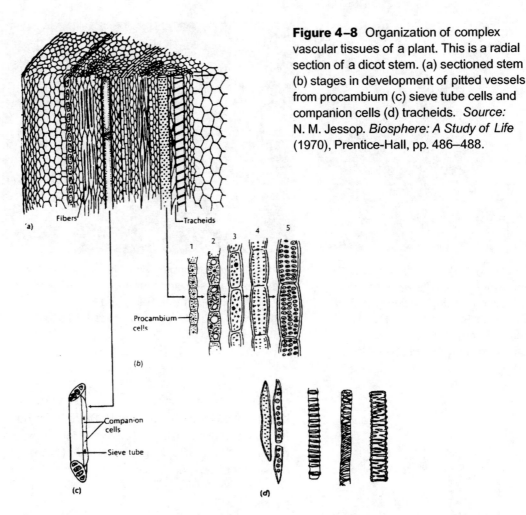

Figure 4–8 Organization of complex vascular tissues of a plant. This is a radial section of a dicot stem. (a) sectioned stem (b) stages in development of pitted vessels from procambium (c) sieve tube cells and companion cells (d) tracheids. *Source:* N. M. Jessop. *Biosphere: A Study of Life* (1970), Prentice-Hall, pp. 486–488.

Vessels are long tubes made up of individual cells called **vessel elements**. These cells are open at each end, with bar-like strips extending across the opening. The cells are joined end-to-end to form tubes which extend throughout the length of the plant.

Tracheids are also dead at maturity but are shaped differently than vessel elements. They are tapered at each end and have no large openings like the vessel elements. Tracheid cells are arranged end to end with the tapered ends overlapping. Where two or more tracheids connect there are small openings called **pits** present, which permit the movement of water from one tracheid to another. Tracheids may also have spiral thickenings in the walls. These look like coiled springs under the microscope. Conduction of water (and minerals carried in the water) through these cells of the xylem is normally from the roots up through the plant. Some xylem may also extend laterally to supply water and minerals of the outer tissues and leaves of plants.

Ray Cells also conduct water but are actually formed from parenchyma. Like parenchyma cells, ray cells may also store food, and are long-lived. Ray cells form in horizontal rows by special ray initials produced by the vascular cambium. In woody plants they radiate out from the center of the plant like the spokes of a wheel. This arrangement allows for the transport of food and water to areas that would not normally be supplied by the xylem and phloem arrangement in the plant.

Xylem cells, because they are mostly cell wall, are very strong and constitute much of the strength areas of plants. Wood of trees is mostly xylem. Hardwood trees such as oak and maple are formed from vessel elements. Softwood trees such as pines and hemlocks have their wood formed from tracheids. Many fiber products derived from

Figure 4–9 The structure of xylem. *Source:* Teresa Audesirk and Gerald Audesirk (1999), p. 457.

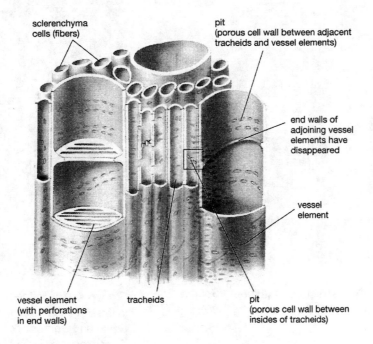

sclerenchyma cells (fibers)

pit (porous cell wall between adjacent tracheids and vessel elements)

end walls of adjoining vessel elements have disappeared

vessel element

vessel element (with perforations in end walls)

tracheids

pit (porous cell wall between insides of tracheids)

plants are made of xylem vessel elements that have been stripped out of the plant. Other fibers that we use to produce products are also made of sclerenchyma tissue. Sclerenchyma fibers are much stronger and more durable than those of xylem.

Phloem

Phloem conducts food in plants and is a different tissue than xylem in many ways. Like xylem, phloem is also derived from vascular cambium initials but whereas xylem cells are produced on the inside of the cambium layer, phloem cells are produced on the outside. Phloem cells also differ in that they function while still alive.

Phloem conducts food in the form of sugar and starches from the leaves and stems where the sugars are conducted to other parts of the plant for storage and for other uses. Unlike xylem, where conduction is mostly upwards, conduction in phloem is mostly downwards. Phloem is also a part of the rays made of parenchyma. These phloem rays parallel xylem rays in the plant. Phloem, as in xylem, may also consist partly or entirely of fibers which give added support since phloem structure is normally weak. Phloem is considered complex tissue because it is formed from two kinds of cells, **sieve-tube elements** and **companion cells**. Sieve tube cells are hollow and laid end-to-end forming long **sieve tubes** through which movement of substances occurs. The end walls of the sieve tube elements lack large openings but have many tiny pores through which cytoplasm extends. The ends with their pores are called **sieve plates**.

The living sieve-tube cells have no nuclei at maturity. Instead they are supported by **companion cells** which provide some nuclear control. In ferns and cone bearing trees we have sieve cells that resemble sieve tube cells but they overlap at their ends like tracheids rather than end-to-end like vessel elements and sieve tube elements. In these plants the sieve tube cells also lack nuclei and have adjacent cells called **albuminous cells** which function like companion cells.

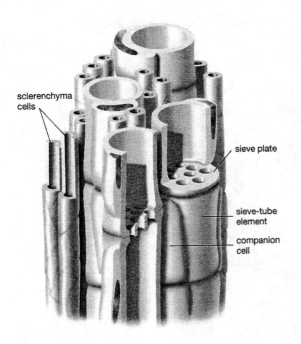

Figure 4–10 The structure of phloem. *Source:* Teresa Audesirk and Gerald Audesirk (1999), p. 457.

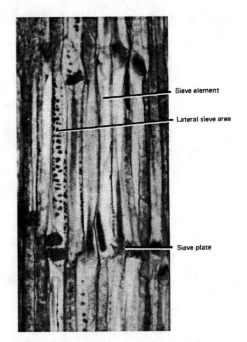

Figure 4–11 Phloem conducting cells in the Virginia creeper. *Source:* Roy H. Saigo and Barbara W. Saigo. *Botany: Principles and Applications.* Prentice-Hall. 1983, p 134.

Table 4–3 Summary of vascular tissues, cell types, and functions.

Tissues	Cell Types	Functions
Xylem	vessel members, tracheids, schlerenchyma cells, parenchyma, cells resin and gum cells	conduction of water and minerals, support and protection of conducting cells
Phloem	sieve tube members, companion cells, albuminous cells, fibers, sclereids, phloem parenchyma cells, resin and gum cells	conduction of sugars, hormones, other organic compounds support and protection of phloem conducting cells

Companion cells are scattered throughout the phloem bundle and are smaller than sieve tube cells. They are long and slender cells resembling fibers but their main function is to support the sieve tube or sieve cells, providing nuclear function to those cells.

Periderm

Periderm is another name for bark. In woody plants the periderm replaces epidermis. The periderm is a complex tissue since it consists of two kinds of cells. Both of which are derived from the same source. There is, under the bark, a layer of meristematic tissue called the cork cambium. The cork cambium forms cells called **cork cells** which at maturity are rectangular and box-like. They are dead at maturity but before dying they secrete **suberin** into the cell wall. This makes the cell waterproof, forming a

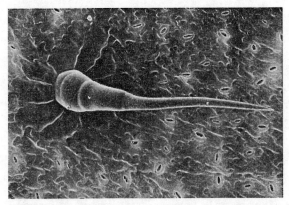

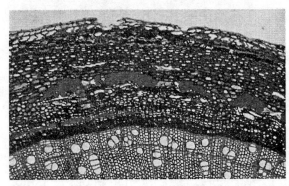

(a)

(b)

Figure 4–12 Dermal tissues of plants. (a) epidermis of a young root (b) the dense, waterproof covering of a woody stem. *Source:* Teresa Audesirk and Gerald Audesirk (1999), p. 456.

protective barrier on the outside of the plant. Some cork cambium has pockets of parenchyma cells that lack suberin. These pockets of cells protrude through the bark and appear on the surface of the periderm as **lenticels**. They function in gas exchange. Usually fissures in bark have lenticels at the base.

Key Words and Phrases

vascular plants	nonvascular plants	dicots
monocots	tissues	meristems
apical meristem	primary tissues	secondary tissues
annuals	biennials	perennial
root cap	shoots	stems
protoderm	epidermis	guard cells
nectar cells	hairs	periderm
cork cells	ground meristem	parenchyma
collenchyma	chlorenchyma	sclerenchyma
procambium	xylem	phloem
primary xylem	secondary xylem	primary phloem
secondary phloem	cork cambium	initials
vascular cambium	cork cells	nodes
intercalary meristems	simple tissues	ergastic inclusions
intercellular spaces	sclerenchyma cells	sclereids
fibers	hormones	secretory tissues
hormones	epidermis	cutin

cuticle
guard cells
vessel elements
sieve-tube elements
companion cells
lenticels

root hairs
plant hairs
tracheids
sieve tubes
albuminous cells

glands
complex tissues
ray cells
sieve plates
suberin

Selected References and Resources

Bold, H., C. Alexopoulos, and T. Delevoryas. 1980. *Morphology of Plants and Fungi*. 4th Edition. Harper & Row. New York.

Bracegirdle, B., and H. Miles. 1971. *An Atlas of Plant Structure*. 2 Volumes. Heinemann Education Books. London.

Core, H., W. Cote, and A. Day. 1979. *Wood Structure and Identification*. Syracuse University Press. Syracuse, New York.

Cutler, E. F., and K. L. Alvin. 1982. *The Plant Cuticle*. Academic Press. San Diego, California.

Esau, K. 1988. *Plant Anatomy*. 3rd. Edition. John Wiley & Sons. New York.

Mauseth, J. D. 1988. *Plant Anatomy*. Benjamin/Cummings Publishing Company. Menlo Park, California.

Roland, J. C., and R. Roland. 1981. *Atlas of Flowering Plants*. Longman Publishers, Inc. New York.

Review and Discussion Questions

1. Distinguish between meristems that produce primary tissues and meristems that produce secondary tissues.
2. Which meristems produce elongation of the plant and which produce an increase in the width or girth of the plant?
3. What cells and tissues provide strength and support for the plant? Which of these are flexible tissues and which contribute rigidity to the plant?
4. Why are some tissues called simple tissues while others are complex?

Plant Stems

Why Stems?

When a new plant emerges from the soil, a stem is the first thing we see. This little shoot is a beginning that will lead to trunks, leaves, flowers, and fruits. Plant stems are very useful in everyday life. Almost everything built of wood comes from stems. Stems, produced by meristems, are called **shoot systems** and usually grow erect. In ferns and some other plants they may grow horizontally under the ground.

External Structure of Stems

If we examine a woody twig we see a long, axial structure with leaves attached. The arrangement of the leaves along the stem is called **phyllotaxy**. When the leaves attach in a spiral around the twig the arrangement is termed **alternate**. The leaves may also occur in pairs, in which case their attachment pattern is **opposite**. In some cases the leaves arise from the stem in clusters of three or more and the attachment pattern is called **whorled**. The area where these leaves attach is called a **node**. The stem region between nodes is an **internode**. Thus a stem is a linear sequence of nodes and internodes. Each leaf is attached to the twig by a flattened blade called a **petiole**. The angle between the petiole attachment and the twig is called an **axil**. This is the place where new growth occurs. New growth in twigs may be in the form of buds in the axil, in which case they are called **axillary buds**. New growth also occurs at the tip of the twig, in which case they are **terminal buds**. Buds have a potential to become branches, leaves or flowers and are protected by bud scales which fall off in the spring as growth begins.

    Terminal buds, at the end of the twig, are like axillary buds except they are larger and their growth results in an increase in the length of the twig. Terminal buds are also equipped with bud scales which fall off when growth begins at the start of spring. As they are lost, they leave **terminal bud scars** around the base of the terminal bud. You can age a twig by counting the number of bud scale scar rings separated by internodes.

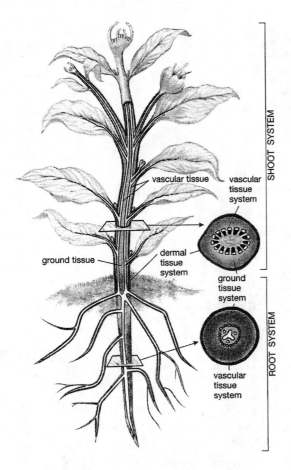

Figure 5–1 The structure of the stem and the root of a typical plant. *Source:* Teresa Audesirk and Gerald Audesirk (1999), p. 454.

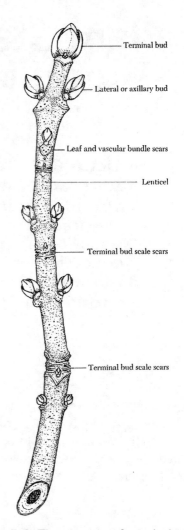

Figure 5–2 The structure of a typical twig. *Source:* Harold C. Bold and John W. LaClaire II. *The Plant Kingdom* (1987), p. 100.

Some leaves also have paired appendages called **stipules** at the base of the petiole. As the stipules fall off, they may also leave scars on the twig called **stipule scars**. In the fall of the year many plants with woody stems lose their leaves. These plants are called **deciduous** plants and after their leaves drop, their twigs are scattered with **leaf scars** that contain dormant axillary buds above them. An examination of a leaf scar shows **bundle scars** of the vascular tissue indicating the location of spicules, petioles and bud scars from a vascular bundle that entered the leaf during the previous year. The configuration of these leaf scars and bundle scars is used in keying woody plants to determine the species. In other words, the arrangement of these scars is unique to each kind of plant and can be used to identify each kind.

Growth and Development of Stems

If you remember the discussion of tissues in the last chapter you know that each stem forms from a shoot and each shoot has at its tip an apical meristem. This area of

Figure 5–3 The growth zone of a stem shown in longitudinal section. *Source:* N. M. Jessop. *Biosphere* (1970), Prentice-Hall, p. 165.

Figure 5–4 The major growth areas of a stem. *Source:* Tom M. Graham (1967), p. 105.

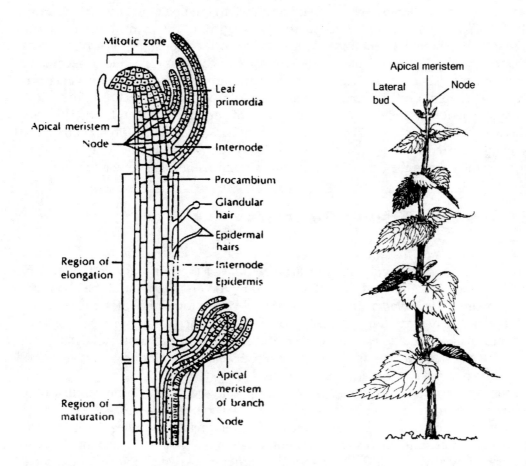

growth tissue is dormant until spring. It is located in the terminal bud and is surrounded by leaf primordia which is in turn covered by bud scales.

Each spring, these cells in the apical meristem undergo mitosis and develop into the three primary meristems which produce primary tissues: **protoderm, procambium** and **ground meristem**. The protoderm is outermost tissue and gives rise to the epidermis and cuticle. The procambium is internal to the protoderm and produces primary xylem and phloem cells.

Beneath the protoderm is the ground meristem which produces the cortex and pith. Located in the center of some stems, the pith is formed from large cells of parenchyma and is used for the storage of food. In most plants, pith parenchyma cells eventually break down leaving a space, or they may be crushed by other developing tissue. Most of the tissue in stems, located away from the center is called **cortex**. The cortex may be more extensive than pith but is eventually replaced also as both cortex and pith are primary tissue. In perennials the primary tissue is eventually replaced by secondary tissue. Both cortex and pith function to store food.

Leaf primordia develop on the surface of the stem and become mature leaves and buds. As the leaf primordia grow they produce a strand of xylem and phloem called a **leaf trace**. Xylem and phloem from the main vascular bundle branch off through the cortex and enter the leaf. In some plants like ferns there is an area above the leaf trace called a **leaf gap** where there is no conducting tissue. The possession of leaf gaps in vascular plants is an indication of an advanced plant.

In perennials there is a meristematic area called the **vascular cambium** beneath the bark. This is a layer of cells between the xylem and phloem from which both are derived. The combination of vascular cambium, xylem, and phloem is called the **cambium**. This is secondary tissue which increases the girth of the plant. It produces tracheids, vessel elements, fibers and if it runs deep to the meristem, it also produces secondary xylem. If found outside the meristem, cambium produces secondary phloem and companion cells. Outside of the cambium layer is a layer of **cork cambium**, or phellogen. Cork cambium is found only in woody plants. It produces cork cells impregnated with suberin. This combination of cork cambium and cork cells constitutes the **periderm** or bark. The main function of bark is to provide protection for the underlying cells and to prevent water loss or desiccation. Vascular cambium, phloem, and cork cambium are the only living tissues in the stems (trunks) of woody plants.

Kinds of Stems and Tissue Patterns

Stems are characterized by the interior arrangement of their primary and secondary tissue. The kinds of stems are best differentiated by the arrangement of their vascular tissues. In simple vascular plants the conductive tissue forms bundles called **steles** which are generally located in the middle of the stem. These steles are composed of xylem and phloem and often pith. The simplest vascular stele is a **protostele** which has a solid core of xylem surrounded by phloem. Protosteles are found in primitive vascular plants such as whisk ferns and club mosses.

In more advanced plants there is an area of pith in the center of the vascular bundle. This arrangement constitutes a **siphonostele** which occur in ferns. Most vascular plants have the simple vascular stele broken up into individual bundles. Each of these steles is called a **eustele**. In this arrangement, the original stele is divided into individual masses of xylem and phloem with vascular cambium between. Each of these separate sections of xylem and phloem cells is called a **vascular bundle**. This condition is found in most modern flowering plants. Since we are confining our discussion of stems to angiosperms we will concentrate on stems with eusteles.

Shoots of plants refers to the stems and leaves.

Remember in the last chapter we introduced the idea of plants with cotyledons, or seed leaves, and we stated that flowering plants develop from seeds with one (monocotyledon) or two (dicotyledon) seed leaves. Each of these plant types has different patterns of growth in their stems. We will compare them and note the similarities and differences. There are basically three patterns of stem growth that we can concern ourselves with: (1) herbaceous dicot stems (2) woody dicots, usually trees and shrubs, are perennials that form wood from secondary xylem, and (3) the monocots of soft tissues with little, if any, woody growth in most.

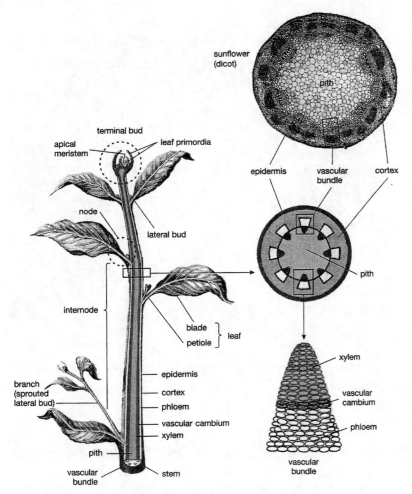

Figure 5–5 The structure of a young dicot stem. *Source:* Teresa Audesirk and Gerald Audesirk (1999), p. 461,

HERBACEOUS DICOTYLEDONOUS STEMS

Plants with herbaceous dicot stems are annuals and are generally composed of soft tissues. By soft tissues we mean that these annuals do not form wood. Some herbaceous dicots are perennial and may develop secondary tissue, especially in the roots. These perennial dicots usually have above ground tissues that die back in the fall; the plant survives by growing new tissue from the roots during the next spring and summer. In perennial herbaceous dicots, the roots contain secondary tissue but the stems are formed from primary tissue each year.

A cross section of an herbaceous dicotyledon stem shows a large area of **pith** in the middle which is formed from parenchyma cells. Outward from the pith, the plant has a distinct **cortex** containing the vascular tissue. The vascular bundles are widely separated within the cortex, as in the eustele pattern. Each eustele consists of three distinct layers. The layer closest to the pith consists of **primary xylem**. It is formed from a layer of **procambium** located in the middle of the vascular bundle. This procambium forms **primary phloem** towards the outside, or surface, of the bundle. The vascular bundles form a ring around the pith. This ring-like configuration is usually characteristic of eusteles and also of herbaceous dicot stems.

The eusteles are surrounded by more cortex which is topped by a layer of **collenchyma** cells with their thickened walls. Above the collenchyma cells is a layer of **chlorenchyma cells** (parenchyma cells with many chloroplasts), which lies just under

Figure 5–6 Cross section of a young dicot stem showing the ring of vascular bundles. *Source:* Roy H. Saigo and Barbara W Saigo. *Botany: Principles and Applications* (1990), p. 68.

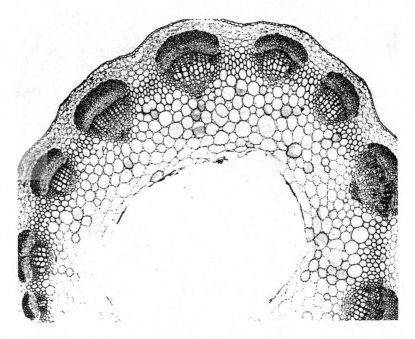

the surface of the plant. The outermost layers of the dicot stem are the **epidermis** and its layer of cutin-forming a **cuticle**.

Woody Dicotyledonous Stems

Woody dicots are common flowering trees and shrubs of our natural and modified landscapes. The stems of woody dicots are also similar in structure to the stems of cone bearing or evergreen trees such as pines, hemlocks and spruce. The early shoots (first year's growth) of both woody dicots and conifers plants resemble a siphonostele and contain a small amount of pith, primary xylem, and phloem. As these plants mature they develop a vascular cambium which produces secondary xylem **(wood)** and phloem. On the outside of the plant, a layer of cork cambium produces the periderm. The stems of woody dicots grow each year, producing a distinctive growth pattern. At the start of the second year of growth the vascular cambium forms and produces **secondary xylem** towards the inside, or interior of the stem. As the xylem is formed the new cells crush the primary xylem and pith of the first year. This second year's growth (and also growth in subsequent years) results in a yearly increase in the diameter of the stem. **Phloem** is produced on the outside of the **vascular cambium**. The **cork cambium** forms under the epidermis and produces **cork cells** which establish a **periderm**. Thus a thin bark is formed. In subsequent years secondary xylem and phloem continues to be formed outside of the previous year's growth. The result of this yearly growth is a distinctive series of **annual rings** clearly seen in the stems of most woody perennials. To a botanist, these annual rings can yield a lot of information about the climate, ecology, and well being of the plant during the past years of its life. For example, the number of annual rings tells the age of the tree.

Each annual ring is actually comprised of two segments. A close look at an annual ring reveals that one segment is comprised of many large vessel elements but few tracheids. This segment represents the secondary xylem that is produced early in the spring, when the plant is absorbing large amounts of water. This layer of the annual ring is called **spring wood**. As the season progresses the weather gets dryer and the vascular elements become fewer in number and smaller in size; there is a correspond-

Figure 5–7 Cross section of a young dicot stem showing early secondary growth. *Source:* Roy H. Saigo and Barbara W Saigo. *Botany: Principles and Applications* (1990), Prentice- Hall, p. 69.

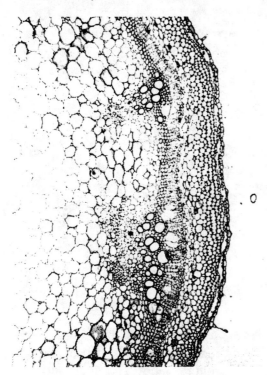

ing increase in the number of tracheids. The resulting xylem is called **summer wood**.

The combination of spring and summer wood appears as a distinct line, which is what we call an annual ring. Thus, an annual ring represents one year's growth. Yearly and seasonal differences in weather, especially rainfall produces larger or smaller, thicker or thinner annual rings. As a result, annular rings can tell us a lot about past climates as they contain a living record of wet and dry periods of each year, drought years and similar information. To get this information a tree does not have to be cut down. Botanists use a tool called an **increment borer** which is forced into the trunk like a drill. The borer removes a continuous strip of wood called a **core**. The core is a sample of the annual rings of the tree which can then be read and interpreted.

Wood. The vascular cambium that forms the annular rings produces more xylem than phloem. Furthermore, xylem cells have stronger and more rigid cell walls than phloem, so it follows that the bulk of a tree trunk is annual rings of xylem produced wood. A transverse section of the trunk of a tree or shrub shows an interior mostly of wood with several to many dark lines called **rays** radiating out from the center, across the annual rings. These rays are comprised of parenchyma cells, and may take the form of xylem rays or phloem rays. The parenchyma cells in rays live ten years or more and conduct nutrients and water laterally through the stem of the shrub or tree.

If you examine the cross section of a tree trunk, you will notice that the wood differs in color from area to area; there is usually an irregular region toward the middle of the trunk that is different in color than the surrounding wood. This is caused by the aging of the tree. As the tree ages, some cytoplasm of parenchyma cells around the vascular bundles grow into the pits in the walls of the xylem and phloem. Eventually this cytoplasm fills the cavity of the vessel elements. The protrusion of this cellular material is called a **tylose**. The formation of tyloses in xylem and phloem prevents the conduction of water and food. Resins, tannin, gums, and other plant materials begin to accumulate along with pigments. This changes the color of the wood to a darker material called **heartwood**. The lighter that surrounds the center of the stem is still comprised of living, functioning cells and is called **sapwood**. Heartwood eventually rots but since the living sapwood that surrounds the interior heartwood still supports the tree we end up with a hollow tree.

In addition to color differences in wood there is also a marked difference in hardness of the various kinds of woody dicots. In evergreen trees such as pines and hemlocks the main cellular components of wood are tracheids. These xylem elements form soft wood and hence evergreens are called **softwoods**. Softwood is a valuable timber which is extensively used for studs and supports such as 2x4 lumber and also in producing

Figure 5–8 Examples of secondary growth in a dicot stem. *Source:* Teresa Audesirk and Gerald Audesirk (1999), p. 463.

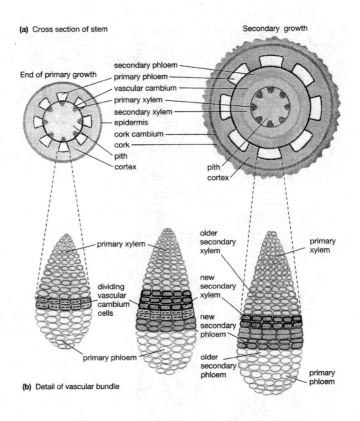

(a) Cross section of stem

End of primary growth

Secondary growth

secondary phloem
primary phloem
vascular cambium
primary xylem
secondary xylem
epidermis
cork cambium
cork
pith
cortex

pith
cortex

primary xylem

older secondary xylem

primary xylem

dividing vascular cambium cells

new secondary xylem

new secondary phloem

primary phloem

older secondary phloem

primary phloem

(b) Detail of vascular bundle

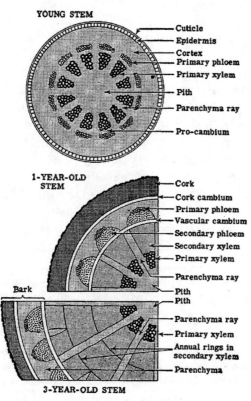

YOUNG STEM

Cuticle
Epidermis
Cortex
Primary phloem
Primary xylem
Pith
Parenchyma ray
Pro-cambium

1-YEAR-OLD STEM

Cork
Cork cambium
Primary phloem
Vascular cambium
Secondary phloem
Secondary xylem
Primary xylem
Parenchyma ray
Pith

Bark

Pith
Parenchyma ray
Primary xylem
Annual rings in secondary xylem
Parenchyma

3-YEAR-OLD STEM

Figure 5–9 Diagram showing typical features of the secondary growth of dicot stems. *Source:* Lorus J. Milne and Margery Milne. *Plant Life.* (1959), Prentice-Hall. p. 107.

plywood used in building houses. Softwoods such as pine are also used in making furniture and shelving and for decorative carving.

Many softwoods have **resin canals** scattered throughout the wood. These tube-like structures are lined with cells that excrete resin into the cavity. The resin is protective and antiseptic for the tree. Cedar trees have extensive systems of resin canals, which we harvest and convert into cedar linings for closets and cedar chests.

Resin is also especially important in some tropical flowering trees. The olibanum and myrrh trees are famous for producing frankincense and myrrh, which were highly prized by ancient civilizations because of the aromatic quality of the resin.

The xylem of deciduous trees consists mostly of vessel elements and fibers which provide additional strength and supportive structure for the tree. Because of its toughness, the wood of deciduous trees is called **hardwood** and the deciduous trees themselves are usually called hardwoods. Hardwood is more durable

Figure 5–10 Cross section of a four year old pine stem showing secondary growth. The openings in the wood are resin cavities. *Source:* Roy H. Saigo and Barbara W Saigo. *Botany: Principles and Applications* (1983), Prentice-Hall, p. 157.

than softwood and consequently is more desirable. It is used in the manufacture of furniture and tool implements such as the handles of hammers, axes and other tools. Maple, oak, chestnut and cherry are good examples of hardwood trees.

The outer layers of a woody dicot stem consist of **bark** or **periderm**. Actually bark is a complex tissue because it includes all of the tissues between the vascular cambium and the surface of the tree. Since the vascular cambium produces secondary xylem on the inside and secondary phloem on the outside, the phloem is actually considered to be part of the bark. The layer of phloem is usually called **inner bark**. The **outer bark** is **cork cambium** which produces the **cork cells**. The cells of phloem and cortex eventually are crushed by new cells produced by the cork cambium. This results in some alternating layers of crushed phloem and cork in the outer bark. The phloem layers nearest the cork cambium conduct sugars rich in food energy. As a result, the phloem layer is desirable as food by herbivores such as rabbits and por-

cupines. The sugars in phloem were also harvested for food by the American Indians. Today, we still gather the sugary sap as maple syrup.

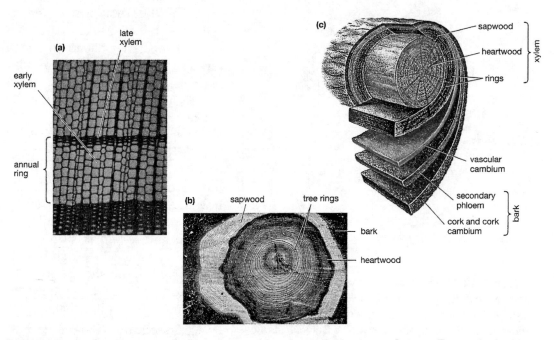

Figure 5–11 The formation of the inner core of a tree and tree rings. *Source:* Teresa Audesirk and Gerald Audesirk (1999), p. 464.

Another structure commonly found in the stems of some twenty families of herbaceous and woody flowering plants are **lactifers**. These are specialized cells or ducts that are common in the phloem and other tissue of the stem. They resemble vessels and form extensive branched networks to produce **latex**, a thick fluid, white to red-orange in color and consisting of gums, proteins, sugars, oils, salts, alkaloidal drugs, and enzymes. Latex in plants may help to close and heal wounds such as bark punctures and torn limbs. This latex is found in rubber trees, the opium poppy, milkweed, dandelions, and dogbanes.

MONOCOTYLEDONOUS STEMS

The monocots are common and widespread plants such as the grasses that develop from seedlings with a single seed leaf. Most monocots are smaller than the woody dicots such as trees and shrubs although some monocots, such as the palms, can achieve great size.

The stems of monocots differ from dicots in lacking vascular cambium and cork cambium. Thus there are no secondary vascular tissues or cork. Instead, monocot stems are covered and protected by epidermis. Furthermore, the xylem and phloem of monocots are derived from procambium and occur in discrete vascular bundles that are scattered throughout the stem, instead of forming distinctive rings, as in dicots. Each vascular bundle has xylem towards the center of the stem and the phloem towards the plant surface as in dicots.

Corn is a member of the grass family and its stem shows a typical configuration for a monocot. The stem is composed of parenchyma tissue called **ground tissue**. This ground tissue is continuous, rather than being divided into separate layers of cortex and pith. Scattered throughout the ground tissue are vascular bundles of **xylem** each consisting of two large vessels and several small vessels between. As xylem grows and matures, the first-formed xylem cells stretch, collapse and die, leaving an irregularly shaped air space toward the base of the vascular bundle. The remnants of xylem vessels are often present in this **air space**.

The **phloem** in these vascular bundles is comprised of sieve tubes and companion cells, and forms the tissue in the vascular bundle towards the surface of the stem. The entire vascular bundle of phloem and xylem is surrounded by parenchyma cells which form a protective **bundle sheath**. In most monocots, the vascular bundles are more numerous toward the stem surface than towards the middle. Note that the general configuration of the vessels in the monocot vas-

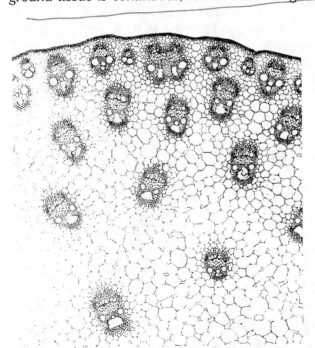

Figure 5–12 Cross section of a young monocot stem. Note that the vascular bundles are scattered through the matrix of ground parenchyma.
Source: Roy H. Saigo and Barbara W Saigo. *Botany: Principles and Applications* (1990), Prentice-Hall, p. 69.

Figure 5–13 The vascular bundles in a monocot stem. *Source:* Roy H. Saigo and Barbara W Saigo. *Botany: Principles and Applications* (1990), Prentice-Hall, p. 69.

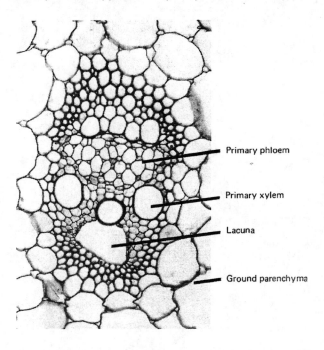

Primary phloem

Primary xylem

Lacuna

Ground parenchyma

cular bundles resembles a **"monkey face"** and is a useful diagnostic feature for identifying monocot vascular bundles within the stem.

The growth pattern of the stem in these annual monocots differs from that seen in dicots. For example in wheat, barley, rice, oats, and corn there is a layer of intercalary meristem at the base of the nodes in the stem. As a result growth occurs at the intercalary meristems resulting in rapid increases in stem length but not in girth.

Growth in palms is somewhat different from growth in other monocots. Palm trees are the largest monocots. They grow rather like dicot trees, producing a secondary "woody tissue" of sorts, because their parenchyma cells continue to divide and enlarge for support. However, palms do not develop true wood—rather, some primary tissue in palms acts like secondary tissue and performs the same function. The growth of secondary tissues in some household monocots can also be examined. For example, *Ti* plants and *Dracaena* also have a secondary meristem which develops as a cylinder that extends throughout the stem. This is not a true vascular cambium as it only produces parenchyma to the outside and vascular bundles to the inside. As with the condition in palms, the parenchyma gives a woody type of growth in the stem similar to dicots.

Lastly, we must think about those monkey face vascular bundles in a different way. We normally consider plant fibers to be made of fiber cells of sclerenchyma. Some monocots are used commercially for the production of fibers. For example, broom corn, *Mauritius* and *Manilla* hemps, and sisal are all fibers from stems and leaves of monocots. These are generally considered to be weak fiber products as the entire vascular bundles are scraped free of surrounding parenchyma cells by hand during their commercial preparation. These monocot fibers are basically made from xylem and are not as strong or durable as the dicot fibers comprised of sclerenchyma cells. The individual strands of fibers are wrapped around each other to construct a durable form of rope or twine.

Modified Stems

We indicated earlier that stems are mostly erect plant organs that can be separated into nodes and internodes. There are, in plants, many specialized stems that are not erect shoot systems and may not resemble the usual stem. Instead they may appear to be roots or leaves. However, these many specializations all have stem structure internally

Figure 5–14 Examples of modified stems. (a) stolons of the strawberry plant (b) rhizome of Iris (c) stages in the development of a potato tuber. *Source:* Harold C. Bold and John W. La Claire II. *The Plant Kingdom* (1990), Prentice-Hall, p. 101.

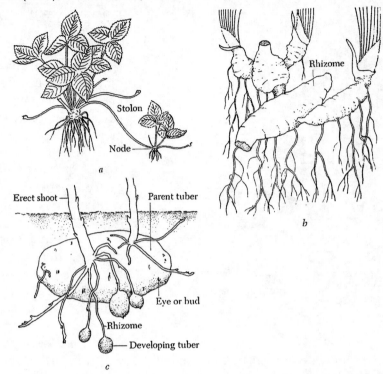

and many have nodes, internodes and axillary buds. For the most part these modified stems are functional storage organs of the plant.

RHIZOMES

Rhizomes are horizontal stems that grow below ground level usually arising from a lateral bud near the base of the main stem. They always occur near the surface of the soil. They superficially resemble roots, but they have scale-like leaves arising from the nodes and axillary buds. There may develop adventitious roots along the rhizome on the lower surface. Rhizomes are often thick fleshy food stores as in *Irises* or slender as in grasses and ferns.

STOLONS

Stolon systems are often called runners and are similar to rhizomes but are very slender. They grow above the ground and run along horizontally to the surface as in strawberries or are subterranean as in Kentucky bluegrass. Stolons are good explorers since their especially long internodes provide an excellent means of travel in search of a suitable micro habitat. New plants normally develop at the end of stolons and have the capability of surviving on their own should older parts of the plant die. In nurseries, many plants are propagated by cutting and planting the apical ends of stolons which thus grow into a new plant.

TUBERS

A tuber is actually a very short rhizome that is swollen with parenchyma cells filled with starch. Tubers usually form at the tip of an underground stem. After the tuber forms, the stolen between it and the parent plant may die, isolating the tuber to form a new plant. White or Irish potatoes are the best known examples of tubers. The eyes of a potato are nodes with axillary buds. In the axil of each eye can be found a rudimentary bud surrounded by scale-like leaves. If you cut up a potato so each piece has an eye, each section is capable of forming a new plant. Tubers are an effective form of food storage for the plant and ensure survival of the plant over winter by developing at depths that do not freeze or dry out. If a potato is found too close to the ground's surface some of the tuber's etiolated parenchyma cells will develop into chlorenchyma cells and begin to photosynthesize. If the green portion is ingested a person will become very sick.

BULBS

A bulb is essentially a large bud with a small stem at the lower end surrounded by numerous fleshy leaves. Adventitious roots grow from the bottom of the stem to form a complete plant. The leaves of the bulb store food. Good examples of bulbs include onions, lilies, hyacinths, and tulips. The structure of the bulb provides an excellent means of surviving the cold winter and the modified leaves act as a food reserve until above ground leaves photosynthesize to produce an adequate food supply.

CORMS

Corms resemble bulbs and are often mistaken for them. Unlike bulbs, which have a large mass of storage leaves surrounding a stem, corms are almost completely stem with a few papery scalelike leaves. Adventitious roots also form at the base of the stem as in bulbs. Corms differ from bulbs in that food is stored in the stem, rather than in leaves. Some plants that have corms are crocuses and gladioli. The function of a corm is also to escape the inclement weather of the winter and emerge in the spring. Corms, like bulbs, exhaust their food reserve until the shoot is developed enough to provide the necessary food.

CLADOPHYLLS

A cladophyll is a flattened stem that superficially resembles a large fleshy leaf. Cladophylls are also photosynthetic as well, which is why they are so often mistaken for true leaves. In the center of each cladophyll is located a node with small scale-like leaves and clusters of spines. Cladophylls are another reproductive strategy of some plants. The plant drops a cladophyll-like stem and it produces a new plant from the node. The feathery appearance of first year asparagus plants is due to numerous cladophylls. Also cladophylls are common in greenbriars, orchids and some cacti.

More Specialized Stems

Succulents. Succulent stems hold a special, mucilaginous tissue for water storage. The large and fat stems of arid dwelling Cactaceae of the world are adapted with large water storing parenchyma cells and a thick epidermis and cuticle to protect the plant from desiccation. The spines of cacti and some other succulents help keep rodents and other desert animals away from the water holding tissues in the cactus interior.

Spines/Thorns. There are many kinds of spines produced on stems of plants. Those of the honey locust tree (*Gleditsia triacanthos*) are actually complete stems in structure and are of importance in protecting the plant. On the other hand, spines of the black locust tree are at the base of leaves and actually represent stipules of those leaves. Spines and thorns are stiff, sharp pointed, woody structures usually occurring to prevent predation of the plant by herbivores. Thorns of roses (*Rosa*) and raspberry originate from the epidermis and are not true thorns but rather outgrowths called **prickles**.

Tendrils. Climbing plants develop holdfast mechanisms called tendrils which can be modified leaves or stems. Grape plants (Vitis), Boston Ivy and Virginia creeper (Parthenocissus) have modified stems that curl around objects and hold the plant in place. These curling organs, or tendrils, are true stems. The curling response that they exhibit is termed **thigmotropism** or **stereotropism** and is a direct response to the contact of the surface they encounter. Tendrils also appear in peas and cucumbers and are modified leaves rather than stems. In English Ivy tendrils also occur but are formed from adventitious roots.

Economics of Wood

Plant stems in the form of tree trunks represents the lumber that we harvest and use for an enormous variety of market demands. Most of this wood represents the secondary xylem. This wood is used for building material and other products such as paper. Approximately half of the weight of wood is water. Thus wood must be dried to a point where 10% or less of the weight is water. This drying process is called **seasoning**. If seasoning occurs too rapidly the wood will warp and split along xylem rays. Well seasoned wood is 60–75% cellulose and 15–25% lignin. There are also traces of gums, resins, oils, dyes, tannins, and starch that make up the rest of the bulk of the wood. The amounts of these traces determine the use of wood. Several other factors are also involved in the commercial value of wood and other lumber products.

The **density** of wood is the comparative weight per unit of volume. If one considers that the weight of an equivalent volume of water is 1, then wood will float if the density is less than one. In actuality most wood does float due to air in cells in the wood giving the wood a specific gravity of less than 1. The lightest wood is balsa which has a specific gravity of 0.12%. The heaviest wood is South American Ironwood and *Lignum Vitae* with a specific gravity of 1.25%. These last two woods are so strong, heavy and durable that they are substituted for metal in some manufacturing situations.

The **durability** of wood is its ability to withstand decay against organisms and insects for long periods of time. In general the less moisture in wood, the more durable it is. Also special other material such as tannins and oils help to increase the durability of particular woods. If the tannin content of wood is over 15%, a fallen log may survive on the forest floor for many years. The most durable American woods are cedar, catalpa, black locust, red mulberry, and Osage orange. Some of the least durable woods include cottonwood, willow, fur, and basswood.

Wood may also be graded by the quality of its hardness, porosity, strength, and texture. When trees are lumbered, soon after cutting they are transported to a sawmill where they are cut in various ways so as to provide the most material from the log. Also

Figure 5–15 Cutting boards for lumber. *Source:* Lorus J. Milne and Margery Milne. *Plant Life.* (1959), Prentice-Hall. p. 24.

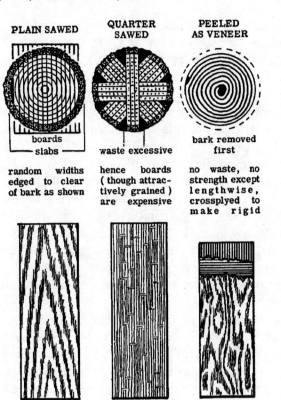

PLAIN SAWED

boards
slabs

random widths edged to clear of bark as shown

QUARTER SAWED

waste excessive

hence boards (though attractively grained) are expensive

PEELED AS VENEER

bark removed first

no waste, no strength except lengthwise, crossplyed to make rigid

certain cutting patterns produce wood of higher quality than others. High quality wood is judged by the beauty of the pattern that the sapwood and heartwood make and by how well the wood is seasoned. Logs may be cut longitudinally in one of two ways. A **quarter-sawed** log is cut along the radius of the log and shows annual rings in side view. These annual rings appear as longitudinal streaks and are very conspicuous. Because of the beautiful pattern produced, quarter sawed wood is expensive.

Tangentially sawed wood is cut perpendicular to the rays. As a result the annual rings appear as irregular bands of light and dark alternating streaks or patches with the ends of rays being visible as narrower vertical streaks. Tangentially sawed wood is often called **plain saw**ed or **slab cut**, and represents cheaper cuts of wood.

Some wood has numerous **knots**, such as knotty pine, and is considered desirable for the attractiveness of the knot patterns. Actually knots are the bases of lost branches that have been covered over by new annual rings as the tree increases in girth. The greatest concentration of knots is in the older part of a tree near the center.

Texture is another important physical consideration in valuing wood. Texture refers to the size and variation of wood cells, especially of vessels, fibers and sclereids. Oak wood has wide vessels and is coarse textured while the fine textured wood of sycamore has narrow vessels and thin rays. Mahogany and walnut produce medium textured wood.

The odor of wood is also an important consideration. The resinous aromas of pines and cedars are desirable for closets and similar cabinetry while the spicy smells of sandalwood and Spanish cedar increase the value of these woods. A few woods such as the viburnums have a fetid, unpleasant odor.

Some of the finest wood that is much in demand for furniture construction comes from the abnormal, wart-like growth on tree trunks called **burls**. Most often seen on older sugar maples, burls also grow on many other species as well. Burls may be caused by frost injury, bacterial or viral invasions or possibly insect damage. Whatever the cause, the cork cambium produces an irregular growth of wood to seal the damaged area, in the process creating the raised burl on the surface of the tree trunk. Burls produce highly figured wood such as burled walnut and burled mahogany.

Another strikingly beautiful wood pattern is found in **crotch** pieces. The crotch of a tree is where the main stem forks to produce two stems. Smaller crotches occur where branches fork from the main stem. Like burls, the wood sawn from tree crotches is highly figured and very desirable. Crotch mahogany, for example, is used for decorative table tops and for veneering of the best and most expensive furniture.

When wood has been cut and seasoned it can be used for the production of various products. In the U.S. half of all wood produced is used as lumber. Most of this wood is from softwoods and goes into the manufacture of studs and plywood for building houses. Sawdust and waste from sawmills is converted into particle board and pulp for paper manufacture. Most of the hardwood lumber goes into furniture making. One has to be careful when choosing expensive furniture as some wood is actually cheap soft-woods with a **veneer** of hardwood glued on the outside. This is a thin sheet of beautiful, highly decorative hardwood that makes the furniture look good. Expensive, well-made furniture uses hardwoods throughout the construction without the use of veneers.

In some areas of the United States softwood trees are grown specifically for the manufacture of pulp to make paper, synthetic fibers, plastics, and linoleum. Wood pulp is also used as a filler for ice cream and bread. Hardwoods can be used to manufacture wood alcohol and acetic acid. Other wood uses include the manufacture of charcoal, excelsior, cooperage (kegs, casks, and barrels), railroad ties, boxes and crates, musical instruments, bowling pins, tool handles, pilings, cellophane, and photographic film. Tree farms in some areas of the U.S. specialize in growing Christmas trees for the holiday market.

In developed countries most of the wood is cut for commercial uses. Unfortunately, in developing countries much of the wood is cut and used for fuel. In the U.S. 10 % of all wood is burned for fuel, but in Brazil 70 % is burned for fuel, mostly for cooking food but also to provide warmth. It is estimated that more than one third of the world's population depends on wood or wood products for heating and cooking and that each year 50 % of all wood used worldwide goes to provide fuel. Burning wood contributes to the greenhouse effect by adding pollutants to the atmosphere. Some fossil fuels such as coal actually represent the remains of woody remains of trees and other plants that have been compressed over millions of years under great extremes of pressures and heat into the fossil fuels that modern industry relies on for energy sources.

Key Words and Phrases

alternate phyllotaxy	opposite phyllotaxy	whorled phyllotaxy
node	internode	axillary bud
terminal bud	terminal bud scar	pith
cortex	stele	annual ring
spring wood	summer wood	heartwood
sapwood	bundle sheath	rhizomes
stolons	tubers	bulbs
corms	tendrils	thigmotropism
seasoning	petiole	axil
protoderm	procambium	pith
ground meristem	leaf trace	leaf primordia
leaf gap	vascular cambium	cork cambium
steles	protostele	siphonostele
eustele	vascular bundle	wood
primary phloem	primary xylem	cuticle

annual rings	core	tylose
sapwood	softwood	hardwood
resin canals	lactifers	latex
ground tissue	air space	stolon
cladophyll	succulent	spine
thorn	prickles	tendril

Selected References and Resources

Core, H. A., W. A. Cote, and A. C. Day. 1979. *Wood Structure and Identification*. 2nd Edition. Syracuse University Press. Syracuse, New York

Dickson, W. C. 2000. *Integrative Plant Anatomy*. Harcourt, Academic Press, Inc. San Diego and San Francisco

Esau, K. 1988. *Plant Anatomy*. 3rd. Edition. John Wiley & Sons. New York.

Hoadley, R. B. 1980. *Understanding Wood*. The Taunton Press. Newtown, Connecticut

Metcalfe, C. R., and L. Chalk. Eds. 1989. *Anatomy of the Dicotyledons*. 2 Volumes. Oxford University Press. New York.

Panshin, A. J., and C. De Zeeuw. 1980. *Textbook of Wood Technology*.

Zimmerman, M. H., and C. L. Brown. 1975. *Trees: Structure and Function*. Springer-Verlag. New York.

Review and Discussion Questions

1. Make a sketch and label the major features of the cross section of a monocot stem and a dicot stem.
2. How do rings form? Of what tissues are rings formed? How can you differentiate between the xylem and phloem of annual rings?
3. How do summer and spring wood differ?
4. From what parts of the tree stem (the trunk) are lumber products manufactured?
5. What are the major functions of stems? How do stems of aquatic plants differ from stems of terrestrial (land) plants?
6. What is the secondary growth of a stem? How does it resemble but differ from the primary growth of the stem?
7. What structures in the stem give it strength? Protection? Serve to transport water and nutrients?

Chapter 6

Roots

The appearance of roots in plants is a sign of evolutionary advancement and provides a major advantage for plant success. Roots developed early in the evolution of plants as they were needed to survive on land. Roots were needed by early land plants for two main reasons. First they **anchored** the plants in a fixed position in the soil. High winds exert a tremendous force on the plant body, but the flexible stem and tightly intertwined root system allows the plant to bend rather than blow over or be torn away.

Plant roots often form branching networks of plant tissue that constitute up to one-third of the dry weight of a plant. They usually extend no deeper than 10–15 feet, however, in some plants such as mesquite, they may extend down to 175 feet below the ground surface to available water and soil minerals.

Roots are not just anchors for the plant. Rather, their main function is to **absorb water and nutrients** from the soil and **conduct** it to the above ground structures of the plant. The vast majority of roots (and the rootlets that develop from main roots) are in the upper three feet of soil, where nutrients and water are most abundant.

Roots also function as a storage place for food that the plant has manufactured during the growing season. Starch, water, minerals, and other substances are stored in roots for future growth or as a reserve against periods of harsh environmental conditions. Finally, many plants can be propagated vegetatively by their roots.

Types of Roots

A root develops from that part of a seedling called a **radicle**. As the seed germinates one part of the seedling grows upward toward the sun producing the shoot while the other part of the seedling, the radicle grows downward into the soil. Roots are said to be **positively geotropic** which means that they always grow in the direction of gravity. For example, a plant suspended upside down will change the direction in which the roots are growing as well as the direction of the stem growth (cells in the stem are negatively geotropic). As the radicle continues to grow it has the potential to produce at least two kinds of root system types.

Figure 6–1 The two major types of root systems found in plants. (a) taproot (b) fibrous root system. *Source:* Tom M. Graham (1997), p. 105.

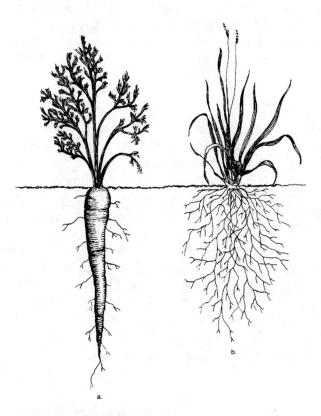

Taproots are root systems in which there is a single major root branch that grows deep into the soil. Taproots are sometimes called seminal roots because they begin to form in the embryo of the germinating seed. Branches of the taproot are called **lateral root** branches and are usually considerably smaller in size and minor in function. **Taproots** are common in plants that live in areas where water sources are deep, or in situations where the soil profile is such that roots can grow deeply into the soil. Taproots are also characteristic of many dicots. A familiar example of a taproot is a carrot.

Fibrous root systems are those in which there is not one central taproot but a whole network of similar-sized roots that spread out underground from the base of the plant. In this situation the roots are generally shallow in depth but cover a large area around a plant with the root system. This is a common root system in plants that live in arid regions such as deserts and grasslands where the survival of a plant depends upon gathering limited water resources and other nutrient resources from as large an area as possible. Monocots such as grasses and corn are good examples of plants with a fibrous root system. The roots of grasses, for example, are numerous and thickly intertwined which provides excellent anchorage from grazing animals. When you pull up a clump of grass, you will see that there are generally many roots attached along with a good portion of soil into which the roots intertwine and fasten.

A single rye plant may have as many as 15 million roots.

Adventitious roots are sometimes considered to be a third type of plant root. Adventitious roots develop from internodes near the base of the stem, where the stem transitions into the root. Corn plants and some aquatic plants such as mangrove may have hundreds or thousands of these adventitious roots. Because adventitious roots are typically slender and fiber-like they are often considered to be another kind of fibrous plant root rather than a third distinctive type of plant root.

Root Hairs. Almost all plant roots have additional modified epidermal cells called root hairs which enhance basic root function. In fact, the efficiency of a root system depends on the abundance of its root hair surface area and their distribution along the roots.

Anatomy of Roots

If we examine a growing root such as a taproot or the terminal end of a root in a fibrous root system, we find there are four specific regions or zones in that growing root. These areas of the growing root are derived from the embryonic tissue, which is the radicle of the seedling. The areas of the growing root are as follows.

THE ROOT CAP

All roots grow from the area just behind the outermost tip of the root. As a result the root tip must be pushed downwards (forced downwards) through the soil. To protect the root from the sheer stresses involved in growing downwards, the plant produces a cap-like mass of parenchyma cells called the **root cap** covering the growing tip of the root. The root cap consists of many, tightly packed cells containing dictyosomes filled with a slimy substance which lubricates the surface of the root as the cells containing it are crushed. These cells are continuously sloughed off and replaced.

The root cap also has within it a mechanism that provides the plant with a perception of gravity. Cells within the root cap contain **amyloplasts** which are plastids with starch grains. These amyloplasts collect on the sides of the rootcap facing in the direction of gravitational force. There are calcium ions in the amyloplasts which may control growth of the root cap by influencing the distribution of growth hormones in cells. The result of all this is that the cells grow toward the strongest pull of gravity, in other words they grow down. This is the positive geotropism that was discussed above.

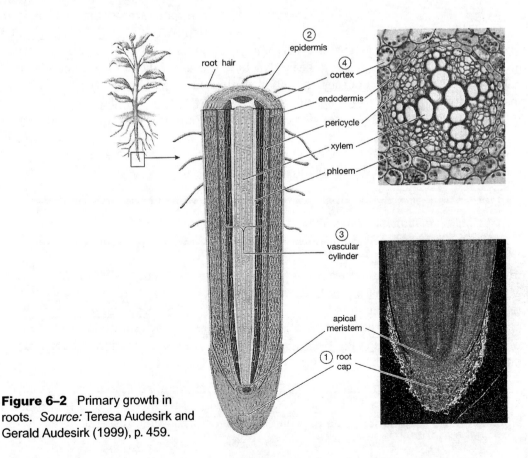

Figure 6–2 Primary growth in roots. *Source:* Teresa Audesirk and Gerald Audesirk (1999), p. 459.

THE REGION OF CELL DIVISION—ROOT APICAL MERISTEM

Within the center of the root tip, behind the root cap, is an area of apical meristem similar to that in a stem tip. This constitutes the region of cell division and here cells divide every 12–36 hours. Cell division is cyclic with most mitosis occurring at noon and midnight. The actively dividing cells are cuboidal in shape and have a large nucleus and few or no vacuoles in the cytoplasm. As in stems, this apical meristem of roots produces three distinct areas in the root. The outermost layer produced by the apical meristem is called the protoderm, which forms the epidermis of the root. Interior to the protoderm is a second layer of meristem called the ground meristem. The ground meristem produces parenchyma cells of the stem cortex. The third area of the root lies deep in the interior, where cells of the procambium produce a solid cylinder of vascular tissue in the center, which in turn produces primary xylem and phloem. A root pith is absent in dicots but present in many monocots.

THE REGION OF ELONGATION

Above the apical meristematic tissue (towards the stem rather than towards the earth) in the region of cell division lies an area of cells about one centimeter long. Here the cells elongate several times their original length. Each cell grows until it develops a large vacuole in the center of the cell, which occupies up to 90% of the cell volume. It is this elongating process of the cells that is responsible for pushing the root cap and the apical meristem through the soil. Some growth occurs in this area, which causes an increase in girth of the root, mostly from the production of secondary tissues. However, most growth in roots represents the elongation from the cells in this region. In most cases the root stays the same width throughout life.

THE REGION OF MATURATION

Behind or above this zone of elongation is a region of the root where the cells mature and specialize. This portion of the root is sometimes termed the **root hair zone.** Within this region the basic structure of the root is well established. In reality, this is the most functional region of the root because this is the area of the root that is actually absorbing nutriments and water from the soil. A section through this region of the root will reveal several specific distinctive structures.

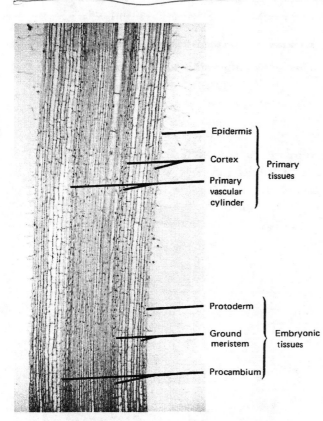

Epidermis

Cortex } Primary tissues

Primary vascular cylinder

Protoderm

Ground meristem } Embryonic tissues

Procambium

Figure 6–3 Development of embryonic tissues of roots. *Source:* Roy H. Saigo and Barbara W. Saigo. *Botany: Principles of Applications* (1990), Prentice-Hall, p. 59.

Epidermis

The outer covering of roots is initially a single layer of cells called the epidermis, which is similar to the epidermis of the stem. Like the stem, the epidermis is covered by a thin cuticle of suberin. The epidermis of roots often gives rise to lateral cellular extensions or extrusions called root hairs.

Root Hair Cells

Root hairs develop from cells of the epidermis, and are actually cytoplasmic extensions of these epidermal cells. They grow into the soil by apical extension of the tip of the cell rather than an elongation of the cell wall. Structurally, root hairs have only a thin layer of cellulose in their cell walls which are especially thin at the tip and therefore better able to absorb water and minerals. The outer wall of root hairs has a thin covering of mucilage which helps bind the root hair to the soil and also attracts bacteria and fungi. These organisms embed in the mucilaginous layer and by their metabolic activities release a variety of organic substances and minerals available which can then be absorbed by the root hair.

Root hairs adhere to soil particles where they come in intimate contact with water and nutriment molecules in the soil. In some plants there may be as many as 250,000 root hairs per square inch of root surface. Each root hair is less than one cm in length but the combination of hundreds of thousands of root hairs greatly increases the surface area of the root to promote effective absorption of water and minerals.

On actively growing roots, root hairs are being continuously produced at the rate of millions each day.

Unfortunately, root hairs are also very fragile. (When we transplant a plant, if we don't leave dirt with the roots and aren't careful not to disturb that dirt, we tear off or destroy the root hairs. Thus a transplanted plant cannot effectively absorb water and will wilt and die.) Without root hairs most plants would not be able to absorb even a fraction of the water and minerals needed to survive. In transplanting, we usually compensate for the loss of root function by pruning the top of the plant and shading and watering it to help it survive and grow new root hairs.

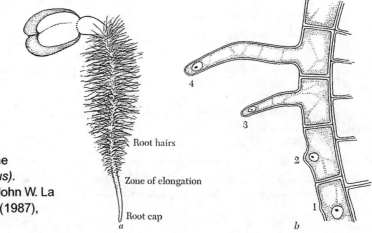

Root hairs

Zone of elongation

Root cap

a

4

3

2

1

b

Figure 6–4 Root hairs of the germinating radish *(Raphanus)*. *Source:* Harold C. Bold and John W. La Claire II. *The Plant Kingdom* (1987), Prentice-Hall, p. 110.

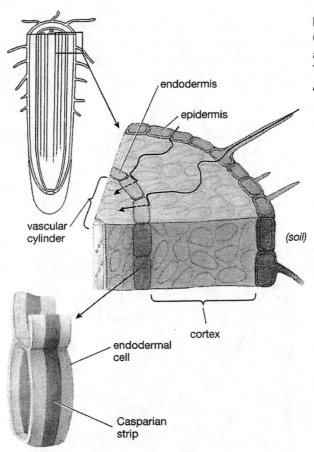

Figure 6–5 The role of the Casparian strip in water absorption by roots. *Source:* Teresa Audesirk and Gerald Audesirk (1999), p. 460.

endodermis

epidermis

vascular cylinder

(soil)

cortex

endodermal cell

Casparian strip

The root hair area is always just above the root cap near the end of the root. As a root elongates and continues to grow longer, the older root hairs die and the root cap moves farther away. The old area of growth eventually matures and the epidermis is replaced by periderm formed by secondary tissue. This area of the root then ceases its absorptive functions but continues to function as an anchor for the plant and to conduct fluid and nutrients from the lower extension of the root.

The Cortex

Interior to the epidermis and comprising the bulk of most roots is the cortex, which is made up mostly of parenchyma cells. The parenchyma cells of the cortex are the primary sites used for food storage. These parenchyma cells are similar to the parenchyma cells found in the plant stem, but they have a layer of **endodermis** cells at their inner boundary.

The endodermis is a ring of cells that is a single layer thick and is considered to be the interior layer of the cortex. Endodermis is typical of roots but is never found in stems. Endodermal cells have thickened cell walls with a coating of suberin covering all internal walls of the cells and forming what is termed **Casparian strips** around the radial and transverse walls of the cells. (If you were to imagine the cells in the arrangement of a smokestack the suberin would look like the mortar between the bricks.) Casparian strips form a barrier to the passage of water through cell walls. This barrier forces water to go through the cytoplasm of endodermal cells and into the interior core of the root where the xylem is located.

In some roots the epidermis, cortex, and endodermis are crushed and abraded as the root grows. In other roots the epidermis is preserved. Regardless of the root type, the inner cell walls become coated with suberin. Thin walled passage cells are scattered in small groups throughout the endodermis to help control the flow of water.

The Pericycle

Inside of the endodermis, deep in the interior of the root, is a cylinder of parenchyma cells, one to a few cells wide. This layer is called the pericycle and is very important as the cells here retain their ability to divide even when mature. The pericycle layer is responsible for producing the lateral branch roots which develop. Thus the pericycle is extremely important for development of fibrous root systems where

Figure 6–6 Cross section of a monocot root. *Source:* Roy H. Saigo and Barbara W. Saigo. *Botany: Principles of Applications* (1990), Prentice-Hall, p. 62.

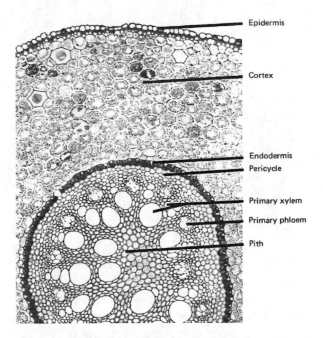

Epidermis

Cortex

Endodermis
Pericycle

Primary xylem
Primary phloem

Pith

Figure 6–7 Water movement through the cortex of roots. *Source:* Roy H. Saigo and Barbara W. Saigo. *Botany: Principles of Applications* (1990), Prentice-Hall, p. 62.

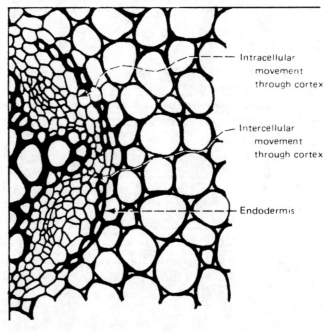

Intracellular movement through cortex

Intercellular movement through cortex

Endodermis

Figure 6–8 Initiation of growth of lateral roots. *Source:* Roy H. Saigo and Barbara W. Saigo. *Botany: Principles of Applications* (1990), Prentice-Hall, p. 63.

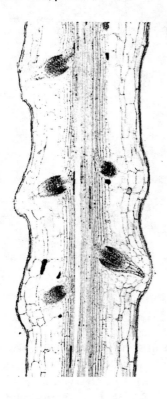

branching is a major component of the structure. In dicots the pericycle is actually part of the vascular cambium which develops here.

Primary Xylem

In roots, the primary xylem forms a solid core of "X"-shaped tissue in the center of most dicot and conifer roots. The xylem configuration in roots is somewhat different from the xylem structure and configuration in stems. Root xylem forms with two or four arms extending from the center to the pericycle. Where these xylem arms reach the pericycle, branch roots can form in the pericycle. In some dicots and in most monocots the primary xylem forms a cylinder surrounding pith parenchyma cells and lacks the "arms." These differences in the position and structure of root xylem make identifying monocots and dicots easy—just as it does in stems.

Primary Phloem

The phloem in roots consists of food conducting cells just as it does in stems. In roots, the phloem forms in the areas between the arms of primary xylem, next to the pericycle. As in stems the phloem is always outside the xylem (towards the exterior, or epidermis). Phloem is important in roots in many ways. It carries food downward from the leaves to feed the cells of the root. Many roots are important food storage areas for the plant. Thus the phloem is a delivery system for the food to be stored.

Lateral Roots

The pericycle also gives rise to lateral roots or branch roots. Lateral roots begin when one or more pericycle cells begin to divide and differentiate into a root apical meristem. This new meristem is the source of the lateral root growth which then resembles, in its general organization, the other roots and has the different regions of root growth. The lateral root continues to grow outwards, through the cortex and epidermis and penetrates into the soil. In larger and older roots, branch roots may also originate and grow from the root vascular cambium.

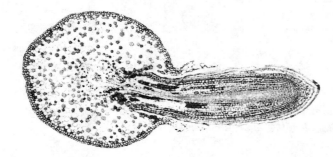

Figure 6–9 Cross section of a later root developing. *Source:* Roy H. Saigo and Barbara W. Saigo. *Botany: Principles of Applications* (1990), Prentice-Hall, p. 63.

Figure 6–10 Cross section of a woody root. *Source:* Roy H. Saigo and Barbara W. Saigo. *Botany: Principles of Applications* (1990), Prentice-Hall, p. 64

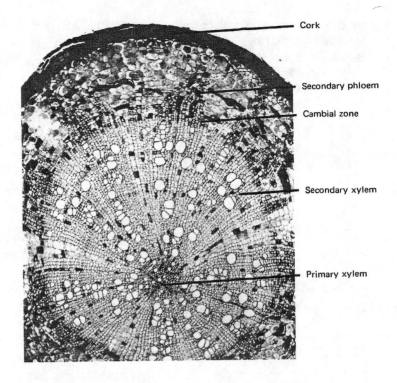

Cork

Secondary phloem

Cambial zone

Secondary xylem

Primary xylem

Vascular Cambium of Roots

In the roots of some woody dicots, herbaceous dicots and conifers, parts of the pericycle and parenchyma cells between the xylem arms form a layer of vascular cambium that produces secondary phloem to the outside and secondary xylem to the inside (as earlier noted in stems). This layer eventually forms concentric cylinders around the primary tissue in the middle which is later crushed out of existence. Thus older roots may resemble woody trees and shrubs in that they have wood. These woody roots function for support and as anchors for the plant. They are also usually closer to the surface than the roots that bear root hairs and aid in absorption.

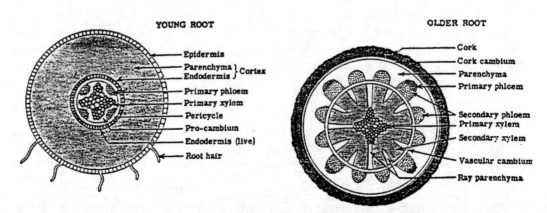

Figure 6–11 Development of root structures during the maturation of woody roots. *Source:* Lorus J. Milne and Margery Milne. *Plant Life* (1959), Prentice-Hall, p. 120.

Cork Cambium—Phellogen—of Roots

In older roots of woody plants, a layer in the pericycle gives rise to cork cambium which in turn produces cork tissue (periderm) or bark as in stems. Thus, the older roots of woody plants may have regions of heartwood, sapwood and annual rings just as in trunks of woody trees and shrubs. Monocot roots, like monocot stems, seldom have secondary meristems and secondary growth.

Specialized Roots

As we have seen in stems, root tissue has a potential to produce specialized modifications to increase absorption of water or minerals. These modifications may also be utilized for storage of water and food or for the propagation of new plants.

FOOD STORAGE ROOTS

In most plants roots are used to store food, but in some plants the roots have become specialized and enlarged to store large amounts of starch and other needed foodstuffs and nutrients. The sweet potato *(Ipomoea batatas)* and yam have additional cambial cells that develop in parts of the xylem of branch roots to produce extra parenchyma cells. These are the storage cells for starch and are also the tissues we eat. A similar situation is found in water hemlocks and dandelions. In some plants food is stored in both the root and stem. This situation exists in carrots, beets, turnips, and radishes where the food storage root is actually a combination of stem and root. Extensive carbohydrate storage occurs in a few biennials but is mostly found in perennials to provide a food reserve for the new shoots or flowers in the following spring. Annuals require little or no food storage capacity in their roots.

WATER STORAGE ROOTS

Examples of large, water-storage roots are found in the pumpkin family of plants. Usually water storage roots are found in plants growing in arid regions where water is scarce and plants must conserve water over long dry periods. The roots of the man-roots and calabazilla plants are good examples of this root storage capability. The plants remove and recycle this stored water when none can be obtained from the soil. The water storage cells of roots are similar to those food storage cells—the water is stored in large vacuoles in parenchyma cells.

PROPAGATIVE ROOTS

Some plants have adventitious buds along the roots that grow near the surface of the ground. These buds develop into aerial stems called suckers which have additional rootlets at the base. These suckers can be separated from the parent plant to propagate a new plant. Propagative roots are found in many common plants such as cherries, pears, horseradish, rice-paper plant, and Canada thistles.

PNEUMATOPHORES

Some swamp plants develop spongy roots that grow on the surface and absorb gases from the atmosphere. These specialized breathing roots are called Pneumatophores. They are found in such aquatic plants as black mangrove *(Avicennia nitida)* and the bald cypress *(Taxodium distichum)* and function to aerate the plants that develop in poorly drained soil or in soil covered by stagnant water.

AERIAL ROOTS

Some plants live on other plants and are thus above the ground with their roots entirely out of the soil. Plants with aerial roots are fairly common in tropical rain forests and are called epiphytes. Since light levels are so low at ground level due to the thickness of the rain forest vegetation many plants live in the canopies of the tall trees in an attempt to reach sufficient light. In orchids *(Epipactis)* there are velamen roots, which absorb gases and contaminants in the air. Aerial roots also are photosynthetic. In corn there are prop roots which help to maintain the erect posture of the corn plant. In the tropical banyan trees the roots form large props around the base of the tree for the same reason. As ivy grows up the side of a building, the plants produce adventitious roots which help the plant hold onto its precarious habitat. All of these are examples of roots that project from an above-ground stem.

CONTRACTILE ROOTS

In some herbaceous dicots and monocots there are roots that pull the plant deeper into the ground each year. Plants that overwinter as bulbs have contractile roots that continue to pull the bulb down into the ground until a stable area of temperature is reached. This condition also exists in dandelions. The contractions of the root tissue occur when parenchyma cells thicken and constrict causing xylem elements to spiral—like a corkscrew. The spiraling effect results in a shortened root.

BUTTRESS ROOTS

Also known as prop roots, buttress roots are commonly found in many tropical trees. Unlike the more typical taproots and fibrous roots, buttress roots grow laterally and outward from the plant to form large buttresses that provide stability for the tree. These roots look like they are a part of the trunk and contribute greatly to the woody portion of the base of the trunk. Corn plants, mangrove trees, and tropical fig trees are good examples of plants with buttress roots. Buttress roots are sometimes called prop roots. Buttress roots are especially important anchors for plants growing in thin soils and in areas where roots cannot or do not deeply penetrate into the soil or wetland substrate to anchor the plant.

PARASITIC ROOTS

Some plants lack chlorophyll and live as parasites, growing on other plants and animals. Members of the Kingdom Fungi are the best examples of these kinds of plants. Fungi have root-like projections called **haustoria** which develop along the body of the plant that is in contact with the host. The haustoria are parasitic roots that invade the outer tissues of the host and develop connections with the hosts' conduction tissue. In addition to the fungi, examples of parasitic plants are mistletoe *(Phoradendron)* and dodder *(Cuscuta)*.

MYCORRHIZAE

The parasitic root systems of plant parasites discussed above can sometimes benefit both parasite and host. In many cases the parasitic fungi are breaking down dead tissue and recycling the nutrients into the ecosystem. Furthermore, under certain conditions, parasitism is also beneficial. Many flowering plants have fungi associated with their roots. These fungi are called mycorrhizae and are in a mutualistic relationship with the flowering plant. In a condition of mutualism both fungi and flowering plant benefit and are dependent on each other. The fungus forms millions of thread-like strands around the root which penetrate into the cortex. The root of the flowering plant gives the fungus sugars and amino acids, and in the process the fungus helps the root absorb water and nutrients. These mycorrhizae have been found to be necessary for the survival of some flowering plants. They are particularly important in orchids and forest trees. Their main benefit is to help some plants live in areas where certain nutrients are scarce. Studies have shown that plants lacking the parasitic fungi eventually whither and die from lack of nutrients.

Scientists are also interested in and concerned about mycorrhizae because of the recent development of acid rain in our environment. It has been known for some time that acid rain from pollution decreases the pH of water systems and has many deleterious effects on plants and animals living in that environment. It has now been found that plants are impacted also as the mycorrhizae are especially sensitive to acid rain. When acid rain kills the mycorrhizae the plants associated with them also die. Forests in many areas of the world are under attack by acid rain for this reason. In Eastern Europe, where pollution was unchecked under the Communist governments, the forests are dying. The mycorrhizae systems have been severely damaged or completely destroyed.

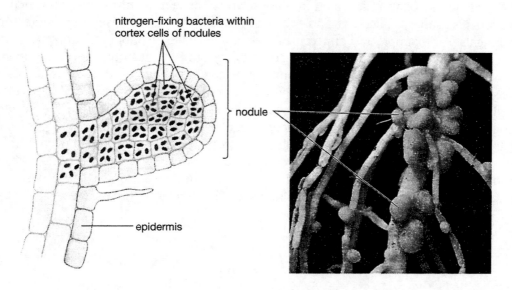

Figure 6–12 Photograph and diagram of root nodules. *Source:* Teresa Audesirk and Gerald Audesirk (1999), p. 471.

Root Nodules

Fungi are not the only organisms to be associated with plant roots. Bacteria also form a large population in the soil around plant roots. In one group of flowering plants called legumes (beans and peas, for example), there are swellings on roots which contain nitrogenous bacteria. These bacteria have the ability to trap nitrogen from the environment and make it available to the plant to use as needed. The nitrogen obtained by (or fixed by) these nodule bacteria represents a major supplement to the plant's nitrogen supply. Nitrogen is one of the critical nutriments needed by plants for growth and legumes seem to need more of it than other plants. As a result the root nodules with their bacterial cultures are extremely beneficial to the plant. When gardeners start peas and beans in the spring they inoculate each seed with the nitrogen fixing bacteria by immersing the seed in seed starter compound. This material can be bought at most garden shops and is actually dormant cysts of the bacteria. Thus the seed is planted with its own bacterial colonies and both develop together. The legume provides a place in the root tissue for the bacteria to live and the bacteria provides nitrogen. This is another case of mutualism.

Many other plants develop swellings on their roots as well. However, this is usually a pathological condition and may be caused by infections of disease organisms or roundworms. These conditions are harmful to the plant.

The Economics of Roots

Roots are a very important source of food for humans. Many plants with expanded storage roots are cultivated specifically for food. Most root crops are biannual plants that during the first year store food in a swollen taproot. The plant utilizes this stored food during the second year when it needs extra nutrients for the process of reproduction. Examples of storage root foods often used as food crops for humans include sugar beets, beets, turnips, rutabagas, parsnips, radishes, horseradishes, carrots, sweet potatoes, yams and, cassava (tapioca).

Some roots are also harvested for their flavors. These roots produce spices such as sassafras, sarsaparilla, licorice, and angelica. Other roots are also used to manufacture chemicals. For example, sweet potatoes are used to make alcohol in Japan. Fermentation of sweet potatoes and rice is the source for most of the alcoholic beverages in the orient. Some roots also produce pigments which can be used to produce dyes. Plants of the coffee family are used to make the colors red and brown in the dying of cloth. Lastly, many drugs have been developed from roots. These include aconite, ipecac, ginseng, gentian, and reserpine. Reserpine is widely used as a tranquilizer. Ipecac is especially important as it is a common substance in the medicine cabinets of parents of young children. Syrup of ipecac is given to induce vomiting in children who inadvertently ingest unknown or harmful substances. Another root product is the pesticide rotenone which is used to kill a variety of insects and small mammal pests.

Key Words and Phrases

radicle	taproot	fibrous root system
positively geotropic	root cap	apical meristem
region of elongation	region of maturation	root hair
endodermis	pericycle	primary phloem
primary xylem	vascular cambium	cork cambium
buttress roots	mycorrhizae	root nodules
lateral root	amyloplast	endodermis
Casparian stripp	neumatophores	cortex
phellogen	aerial roots	buttress roots

Selected References and Resources

Bold, H., C. Alexopoulos, and T. Delevoryas. 1980. *Morphology of Plants and Fungi*. 4th Edition. Harper & Row. New York.

Bracegirdle, B., and P. H. Miles. 1971. *An Atlas of Plant Structure*. 2 Volumes. Heinemann Educational Books. London.

Esau, K. 1988. *Plant Anatomy*. 3rd. Edition. John Wiley & Sons. New York.

Fahn, A. 1982. *Plant Anatomy*. 3rd. Edition. Pergamon Press. Elmsford, New York.

Russell, IR. S. 1977. *Plant Root Systems. Their Function and Interaction with the Soil*. McGraw-Hill Book Publishers. New York.

Torrey, J. G., and D. Clarkson. Eds. 1975. *The Development and Function of Roots*. Academic Press. San Diego, California.

Review and Discussion Questions

1. Sketch and label the features of a monocot root and a dicot root.
2. What tissues arise from the root meristem?
3. Describe the major kinds of tissues that occur in roots and their functions.
4. What are some of the modifications of roots?
5. Economically, what are some of the major uses of roots?
6. Describe the symbiotic relationships between plant roots and fungi and plant roots and bacteria.
7. Why are fibrous root systems more efficient in binding soil than taproots?
8. Why have plants chosen roots as their major storage organs rather than stems or leaves?

Leaves

Leaves have evolved to become the solar energy panels of plants. They function to absorb the kinetic energy of sunlight and transform it into the chemical energy of organic molecules through the process of photosynthesis. The leaves of most plants follow the sun through daylight hours by twisting on their petioles so as to always be at right angles to the incoming sunlight.

Leaves are also involved in the movement of water and minerals from the roots up through the stem. Water is evaporated from the small pores in the under surfaces of leaves called stoma by **transpiration**. Also called evapotranspiration, this process creates a suction which pulls a water column up through the xylem in an action rather similar to sucking on a soda straw. In some plants the resulting suction is so strong that it forces water out of **hydathodes** which are openings at the tip of leaf veins. Some substances such as monosodium glutamate can be collected from the water produced at hydathodes in plants. Some Leaves can also act as excretory organs as they produce waste which is deposited in the leaves which is then dumped when the leaves are shed.

Leaves are considered to be part of the shoot system of plants. They develop from special areas in the shoot buds called **primordia**. The primordia are special primary tissue that grow outward producing the parts of a leaf. At maturity a leaf consists of a stalk-like **petiole** which holds the leaf up and away from the stem and a flattened **blade** or **lamina**. At the base of each petiole there may be little leaflets called **stipules**. The leaves of grasses are divided into a basal sheath which encircles the stem and a long, narrow blade. Photosynthesis and related metabolic activities occur within the broad, flattened blade of the leaf. A network of **veins** (vascular bundles) transports water and minerals up to the cells of the leaf and the photosynthetically manufactured sugars down into the shoot and root. In flowering plants the vascular bundles arise in the stem and travel into the leaf. Where the vascular bundle diverges from the stem to the leaf there is a gap left in the stem vascular bundle. Such spaces are called **leaf gaps** and are characteristic of more advanced plants.

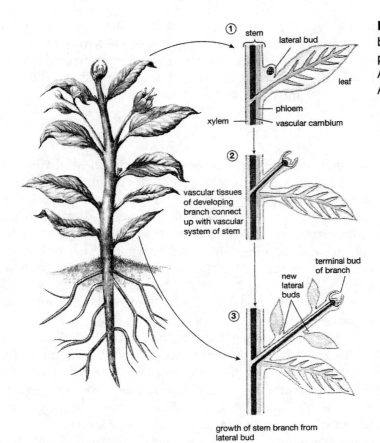

Figure 7–5 Formation of branches and leaves in plants. *Source:* Teresa Audesirk and Gerald Audesirk (1999), p. 462.

① stem
lateral bud
leaf
phloem
xylem
vascular cambium

② vascular tissues of developing branch connect up with vascular system of stem

③ new lateral buds
terminal bud of branch

growth of stem branch from lateral bud

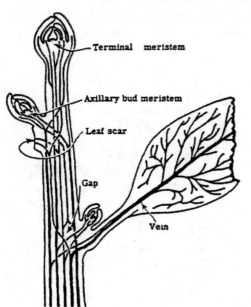

Figure 7–2 The origin and development of leaves. *Source:* Lorus J. Milne and Margery Milne. *Plant Life* (1959), Prentice-Hall, p. 72.

Terminal meristem
Axillary bud meristem
Leaf scar
Gap
Vein

Leaf Shape and Arrangement

The efficiency of leaves depends mostly on their form, arrangement on the stem, and their structure. If you examine plants with true leaves you will find that there are many different shapes and forms that leaves can take. In some cases the shape of leaves may even differ from place to place on the same plant—mulberry trees and sassafras provide good examples of how leaves may vary on a single plant. When looking at common plants like pine trees with simple needle-like leaves, or lilies with long strap-like leaves, or maple trees with broad flat leaves and intricate marginal shapes, or ferns with large finely divided fronds, you will notice that leaves have many shapes but that there are many kinds of decorations and colors as well.

PHYLLOTAXY

The study of the shape and arrangement of leaves on a stem is called **phyllotaxy**. Leaves are formed on stems in a spiral or alternate pattern. If the leaves form opposite each other at a single node the plant has an **opposite** leaf pattern. Plants with opposite leaves include many herbaceous plants such as mints and *Coleus,* and woody plants such as dogwoods, ashes, and maples. If the leaves arise at different nodes along the stem the pattern is called **alternate**. Oaks, elms, philodendrons, geraniums, beans, and roses are examples of plants with alternate leaf arrangements. If three or more leaves develop at the same node the pattern is **whorled**. In a whorled pattern the leaves are arranged in a circular pattern completely around the node. Plants with whorled leaves include *Catalpa, Auracaria,* and bedstraw.

Leaf shape also occurs in different patterns. If the leaf has an undivided blade, the leaf is considered **simple**. The leaves of the dogwood tree is a good example of this condition. They are also oppositely arranged. When the basic leaf lamina is divided into leaflets the leaf is called **compound**. Black locust, hickory, tree-of-heaven, and the ashes are trees that exemplify the compound condition. If the leaf stalk bearing paired leaflets is divided the leaf is **pinnately compound**, as seen in honey locust.

If the leaf is divided into leaflets which all attach at the same point at one end of the petiole (like the fingers attach to the palm) the leaf is **palmately compound**. Palmately compound leaves are found in such trees as Ohio buckeye and horse chestnut. Some plants such as the Kentucky coffee tree have **bipinnately** compound leaves. Here the

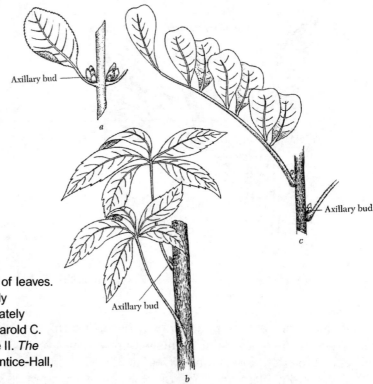

Figure 7–3 Arrangement of leaves. (a) simple leaf (b) palmately compound leaves (c) Pinnately compound leaf. *Source:* Harold C. Bold and John W. La Claire II. *The Plant Kingdom* (1987), Prentice-Hall, p. 114.

leaflets of compound leaves are further subdivided creating the complex pattern seen in fern fronds.

The shape of leaves is not the only factor to consider in separating leaves into type. Leaves develop distinct venation patterns as well. **Venation** is the arrangement of veins (the vascular bundles) within the leaf tissue. Veins form distinctive lines on the surface of leaves and can be used to separate leaves into several main configurations.

In many plants the leaf has a single main vein, the **midrib**, with secondary veins branching out from it. These leaves are called **pinnately veined** (or net-veined) and can be seen in oaks, birches, and elms. In other plants all the veins in a leaf are the same size and emerge from a common point on the petiole. Such veins are called **palmately veined**. Maples, for example, have palmately veined leaves.

Veins in leaves also may occur as dichotomously branching or parallel veined. **Dichotomously branching veins** are branches that emerge from other veins at angles to form a complex branching network over the entire surface of the leaf. This kind of vein pattern is characteristic of most dicots. The dichotomously branching condition usually is distinctive in that not all veins involved are of the same size. There is one group of plants called ginkgos that also have dichotomous venation. In this case the leaves do not have midribs and all the branching veins are equal in size.

In a large number of plants the veins branch palmately at the base of the leaf and form several parallel, unbranched, veins on the leaf surface. This condition is called **parallel venation** and is characteristic of most monocots.

The shape of leaf margins is also used to distinguish plant species. Leaf margins may be smooth or **entire** as seen in magnolia and catalpa leaves. Leaves with sharp, tooth-like edges are called **dentate** (e.g., American elm) while those with rounded teeth such as the leaves of basswood and big-toothed poplar are **crenate**.

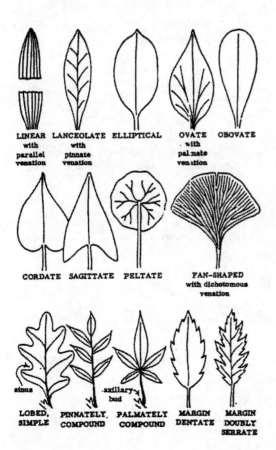

Figure 7–4 The forms of leaves, leaf margins, and venation. *Source:* Lorus J. Milne and Margery Milne, *Plant Life.* (1959), Prentice-Hall, p. 89.

Leaves of oaks and sassafras and many other plants have distinct invaginations called **lobes**. If the lobes extend towards the midrib such as seen in oak leaves the leaf is **pinnately lobed** but if the lobes extend outward from the base of the leaf (near the petiole) the leaf is **palmately lobed**. Maple leaves are a familiar example of palmately lobed leaves.

Leaves of some plants may also be distinctive in texture. Leaves of American elm and slippery elm have many hairs which produce a rough surface while leaves of dogwoods and most maples are hairless and have a smooth surface. Leaves of alders are thick and coarse compared to the thinner and finer leaves of plum or peach trees. The thick, fleshy leaves of many desert plants are termed **succulent**.

Leaf Anatomy

The primordia from which leaves develop contain primary tissue representing the major primary meristems. There is protoderm which produces the outer layer of the leaf, ground meristem which forms parenchyma and modified parenchyma of the leaf interior, and lastly, procambium which produces vascular tissue or veins of the leaf. A cross section through a leaf reveals several distinctive layers.

Epidermis

Leaf epidermis is the outer, single layer of cells covering the entire surface of the leaf which fit together like a jigsaw puzzle. It typically consists of flattened cells which have a waxy cuticle covering on their outer surface. Because the leaf is a double-sided structure there is an **upper epidermis** and a **lower epidermis**. These layers of epidermis form a relatively impenetrable layer that prevents entry of bacteria and fungi. The waxy coating also helps retard water loss.

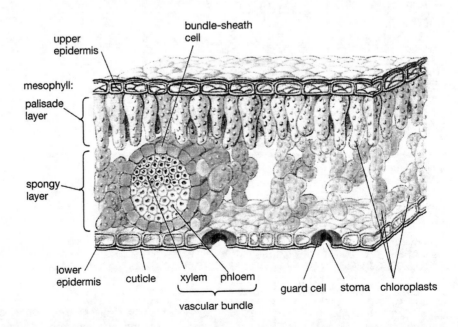

Figure 7–5 The structural organization of a typical dicot leaf. *Source:* Teresa Audesirk and Gerald Audesirk (1999), p. 465.

Figure 7–6 Stomata structure. *Source:* Teresa Audesirk and Gerald Audesirk (1999), p. 474.

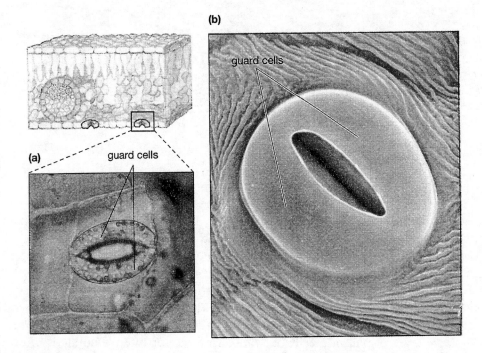

The lower epidermis of most plants contains minute pores called **stomata** which are openings into the leaf that permit gas exchange. The leaves of some monocots such as corn and alfalfa also have stomata on their upper surfaces. Aquatic plants that have submerged leaves lack stomata.

Stomata openings are controlled by a pair of specialized epidermal cells called **guard cells**, which basically surround the pore. The pair of guard cells and stomatal pore together constitute each **stoma** (stoma is the singular of stomata). Guard cells, which are the only epidermal cells with chloroplasts, function to open and close the pores in response to environmental conditions. In the morning, when sunlight strikes the leaf photosynthesis within the guard cells produces sugars which increase the osmotic potential of their cytoplasm. Following a concentration gradient, water enters from adjacent tissues, swelling the guard cells and causing the stomata to open. In the late afternoon and evening the leaves are increasingly shaded and photosynthesis in the guard cells ceases; the osmotic drops and water leaves the shrinking guard cells, causing the stomata to close again.

The leaf epidermis may also form other structures as well. Some leaves have specialized **glands** or **hairs** on the surface of the leaf. Leaf glands may be sessile or stalked and usually secrete sticky substances that make the leaf unpalatable or trigger an allergic reaction such as a rash. Leaf hairs may be sensory and can trigger movements such as the folding of the leaf in the Venus fly trap.

There are an average of 29,000 stomata per square centimeter on the underside of an apple leaf. The leaves of a large tree may have well over a billion stomata with a total area of several thousand square meters.

Figure 7–7
Organization seen in the cross section of a corn leaf. *Source: Roy H. Saigo and Barbara W. Saigo. Botany: Principles of Applications* (1990), Prentice-Hall, p. 80.

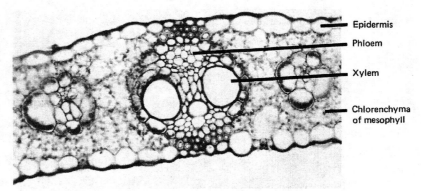

Epidermis

Phloem

Xylem

Chlorenchyma of mesophyll

LEAF MESOPHYLL

The interior of the leaf is called the mesophyll. It is comprised of several layers of parenchyma cells and is the main site of leaf photosynthesis.

Two layers of mesophyll are recognized. The upper mesophyll consists of one to several layers of columnar parenchyma cells and is termed the **palisade layer**. These cells have many chloroplasts and could be termed chlorenchyma cells (specialized parenchyma cells that contain chloroplasts). They are similar to photosynthetic chlorenchyma cells found in the cortex of herbaceous plant stems. Most plants have only a single layer of palisade cells but those in direct or intense sunlight often have three or four layers of palisade mesophyll.

Beneath the palisade layer is an area of irregularly shaped parenchyma cells called the **spongy mesophyll**. Unlike the highly structured palisade mesophyll, the cells of the spongy mesophyll are loosely aggregated with large **intercellular air spaces** between them that interconnect with the stomata openings in the lower epidermis. These air spaces facilitate the exchange of oxygen entering the stomata into the leaf interior and the diffusion of gas and water vapor from the leaf interior out into the air surrounding the leaf. The surfaces of mesophyll cells are generally moist. This moisture helps to maintain the pressure in the vacuoles of the cells. If moisture decreases because of too much water loss via transpiration, the mesophyll cells produce substances that shrink the guard cells and close the stomata. The leaves of monocots typically consists only of spongy mesophyll.

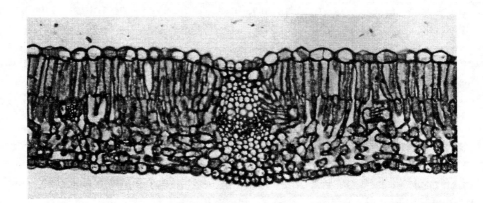

Figure 7–8 Cross section of the layers of a dicot leaf. *Source:* Roy H. Saigo and Barbara W. Saigo. *Botany: Principles of Applications* (1990), Prentice-Hall, p. 80.

Leaf Veins

All true leaves contain **veins** or **vascular bundles** scattered throughout the mesophyll. The vascular bundles are extensions of the procambium in the stem and consist of **xylem** and **phloem** surrounded by fibers called a **bundle sheath**. The vascular bundles are the visible leaf veins which form the skeleton of the leaf. They strengthen the leaf and also provide the "plumbing" of the mesophyll. Xylem brings water from roots and phloem redistributes food made by the mesophyll parenchyma. This food, in the form of starch or sugar, is transported in the phloem down into the stem and roots for storage.

In some monocots large, thin-walled **bulliform cells** occur on each side of the vascular bundles. The cells absorb water and swell, acting as a reservoir for the plant. If the plant dries the bulliform cells collapse, causing the leaf to fold or roll up and thus reducing the exposure of stomata to the air. This action greatly reduces water loss by the leaf.

Adaptations of Leaves

Plants have successfully invaded many kinds of terrestrial and aquatic environments, in part because of modifications of leaves and other plant structures that enable the plant to survive with local environmental conditions. Plants in deserts, for example, require different survival mechanisms and modifications compared to plants of tropical rain forests. Leaves have proven to be one of the most adaptable organs of plants. Leaves have been utilized in many ways by plants to enable them to survive different environmental conditions.

Shade Leaves and Sun Leaves

Sunlight conditions differ greatly across the leaves of plants. Upper leaves are exposed to full sunlight while lower leaves are partly or completely shaded. Compared to sun leaves, shaded leaves are larger but thinner with fewer chloroplasts. Their larger size helps intercept as much of sunlight filtering down through the foliage as possible. In contrast, sun leaves are smaller but thicker with numerous chloroplasts occurring in the palisade cells for photosynthesis. Leaves in direct sunlight may also have a thickened cuticle and fewer stomata to help reduce water loss.

Leaf Adaptations for Arid Conditions

The leaves of plants that live in deserts must function in photosynthesis but at the same time protect the plant from **desiccation** (drying out). Leaves of these plants are termed **xeromorphic** and have many adaptations. They are generally thick and leathery with stomata sunken below the surface of the leaf. Many plants develop leaves that store water, or they have discarded their leaves entirely to conserve water. In these plants photosynthesis occurs mainly in stems. Cacti are familiar examples of these kinds of desert plants. Other plants adapted to dry, xeric conditions have leaves with a dense, hairy epidermis. The hairs entrap and hold morning dew which is then absorbed by the plant. Still other desert plants have leaves equipped with a special layer of thick-walled cells called **hypodermis**, which also retards water loss. At least some desert plants avoid water loss through their leaves by turning the leaves at right angles to sunlight during the hottest hours of the day.

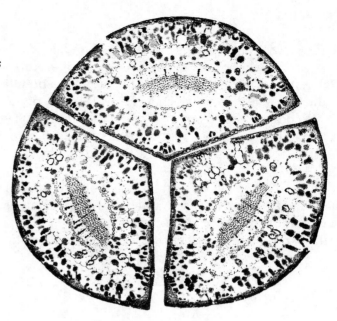

Figure 7–9 Cross section of a pine needle. *Source:* Roy H. Saigo and Barbara W. Saigo. *Botany: Principles of Applications* (1990), Prentice-Hall, p. 83.

LEAF ADAPTATIONS FOR AQUATIC ENVIRONMENTS

Aquatic plants are adapted to live in hydric habitats such as lakes, ponds, streams, and wetlands. For these plants, water is abundant rather than scarce so leaves must be adapted to withstand rather than conserve water. Plants such as water lilies have leaves with large intercellular air spaces that enable the leaves to float on the surface of the water where sunlight and oxygen is abundant. These leaves also have stomata located in the upper epidermis to facilitate gas exchange and a thick cuticle covering the rest of the leaf to prevent water entry.

Conversely, submerged aquatic plants such as waterweed *(Elodea)* and water milfoil have long, narrow leaves with a thin epidermis that permits rapid diffusion of gases into and out of the leaf.

Autumn Colors of Leaves

During spring and summer months, leaves produce food in the form of simple sugars. Some of this food is used for further plant growth and the propagation of flowers, fruits and seeds but much of it is stored in the roots. As summer draws to an end, trees and other perennials store more and more of the food produced in the leaves in their roots in preparation for next year's growth.

With the advent of autumn, a tree conserves its energy even more by cutting off the supply of water and other nutrients to the leaves in the layer of cells known as the abscission zone. Without water and nutrients leaves cannot continue to manufacture new chlorophyll. As the green pigment disappears, the leaves slowly acquire the colors of the hardier pigments that remain behind, such as the orange hues of the fatty pigments of carotenes, and the pale yellow of xanthophyll pigments. Not all the trees share the same autumn colors. Aspens, ashes, and sassafras turn a bright, golden yellow. Birches are paler yellow and most of the oaks first turn red, then fade to brown. The dry, earthy shades of many oak leaves are caused by tannins, which are brownish chemicals that oaks manufacture to protect their leaves against leaf-eating herbivores.

Some of the very best and brightest of leaf reds, rusts, and purple colors appear in maples, beeches, sumacs, and other trees and shrubs through a different process. Unlike most other plants, the leaves of these trees and shrubs retain a high sugar content through the autumn months. The bright autumn sunlight chemically transforms the leaf sugar into a reddish pigment called anthocyanin, which produces the brilliant reds and rusts we see in autumn forests. The most vibrant reds are also dependent on an abundant supply of bright sunlight during autumn's short days and cold, crisp nights. If the weather is rainy and cloudy the chemical transformation occurs too slowly and the leaves turn a faded shade of red and orange but fail to produce the brighter colors. Similarly, too much rain dulls the colors, as the pigments are quickly leached out of the leaves. Early frosts can also dull autumn colors by killing the leaves, which then slowly transform into dull and wrinkled wisps of brown.

Leaf Fall (Abscission)

Almost all plants shed their leaves at some time during the year. Even the needles of evergreens are periodically shed and replaced by new needles every year. In tropical and subtropical habitats leaf fall and the growth of new leaves is associated with periodic wet and dry seasons. In temperate regions of the world most flowering plants and some evergreens shed their leaves within a short period of time in late autumn. Plants that annually shed their leaves each autumn are called **deciduous**.

The shedding of leaves is termed **abscission**. Other plant structures such as fruits, floral remnants and sometimes twigs and branchlets may also be dropped at the same time. Abscission is a plant response to environmental changes in which the plant discards unneeded organs and other structures, generally just before the onset of inclement weather conditions such as the snow and ice of winter months.

Abscission occurs in a thin layer of parenchyma cells called the **abscission zone** which is located near the base of the leaf petiole. During the spring and summer growing season, auxins and other plant hormones produced by the leaf blade inhibit the growth of cells in the abscission zone. In autumn, the longer nights and colder temperatures inhibit the production of auxins, and the cells of the abscission zone resume growth, forming two distinct layers of cells. The cells growing nearest to the stem form the **protective layer**, which may be from one to several cells in thickness and coated with suberin. The thick suberin coating protects the stem after the leaf drops, preventing water loss and also preventing fungal or bacterial invasion.

On the blade side of the abscission zone a **separation layer** of cells develops. The cells of the separation layer divide, swell, and become gelatinous. As autumn progresses towards winter the cells of the separation layer die and start to decompose, further weakening the petiole.

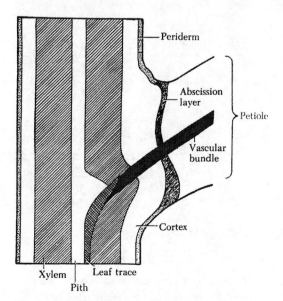

Figure 7–10 Abscission layer of deciduous leaves. *Source:* Harold C. Bold and John W. La Claire II. *The Plant Kingdom* (1987), Prentice-Hall, p. 117.

Eventually only a few strands of the tougher xylem are left to hold the leaf in place. Wind and rain eventually break these xylem strands and the leaf falls free.

Specialized Leaves

LEAVES AS SPINES

We have seen that spines can be produced by stems and as outgrowths from the epidermis. Spines protect leaves from leaf-eating herbivores. Spines of some plants also help combat water loss by reducing the surface area of leaves which is exposed to the air. Spines are common in many desert plants for both reasons.

Spines may be formed from leaves or from stipules of leaves. In some woody plants such as mesquite and black locust, stipules form spines that lie along the petiole of the leaf. In barberry plants the entire leaf becomes a spine. The thorns of roses and raspberry are not leaves, but develop from the epidermis of the stem.

LEAVES AS TENDRILS

Some leaves curl around structures as they grow. These modified leaves are called **tendrils**, or leaf tendrils, and help to hold the plant in place. Tendrils derived from leaves are found in peas, where the leaves are compound and the tendrils are the end leaflets. Tendrils function by rapid cell growth opposite the side making contact with the object to be encircled. The tendril grows in the form of a spring-like coil. If pressure is exerted on the opposite side of a tendril, coiling can be stimulated to reverse. When the final coil occurs, sclerenchyma cells develop in the area of contact to make the tendril strong and flexible. In plants like yellow vetch, the whole leaf is modified as a tendril. In this case photosynthesis is done by the leaf stipules. In some plants such as *Clematis*, the rachis of the compound leaves serves as a tendril.

Figure 7–11 Modification of leaves as prickles and spines as seen in wild currant.. *Source:* Roy H. Saigo and Barbara W. Saigo. *Botany: Principles of Applications* (1990), Prentice-Hall, p. 85.

LEAVES FOR STORAGE

Leaves modified to store water (succulent leaves) are common in desert plants. These storage leaves consist of many large, thin-walled parenchyma cells containing cytoplasmic vacuoles that swell with stored water. These leaves may even retain stored water for several weeks after being dropped by the plant. Leaves of onions and lily bulbs become fleshy with carbohydrates stored in their vacuoles. (Both lily bulbs and onions are actually stems surrounded by leaves).

Figure 7–12 Leaves modified as tendrils in grape. *Source:* Roy H. Saigo and Barbara W. Saigo. *Botany: Principles of Applications* (1990), Prentice-Hall, p. 84.

FLOWER POT LEAVES

The leaves of the Australasian plant *Dischidia* develop into vase-like pouches that become the home of ant colonies. The ants carry in soil and nitrogenous wastes from the outside. Water from stomata collects in these areas as well. This interior mix of soil and water allows adventitious roots to form from the same node as the leaf and to grow into the soil. Thus the leaf, by holding the soil, becomes a flower pot out of which the plant grows.

WINDOW LEAVES

Plants of the carpetweed family of the Kalahari Desert of South Africa have leaves shaped like ice cream cones that are buried in the sand. The only part of the plant exposed to the sun is a dime-sized end of the leaf. Protected by a thick epidermis and cuticle, the stomata form a transparent "window." Beneath the window are water storage cells and mesophyll with chloroplasts for photosynthesis. In this way, most of the plant remains buried within the soil and away from the wind which would dry the plant out.

LEAVES AS REPRODUCTIVE ORGANS

Some plants have leaves that produce new plants at their tips. In this kind of condition different generations of plants can be linked together. In plants like Walking Fern, air plants, Jade Plant and Christmas Cactus, new plants are formed by leaves dropping or breaking free and developing into new plants where they land. When the leaf lands on a suitable piece of soil it establishes adventitious roots and then a stem forms from the leaf tissue producing a new plant.

LEAVES AS FLOWERS

Floral leaves or bracts are specialized leaves at the base of flowers or flower stalks of many plants. A common example is the familiar Christmas plant, the Poinsettia (*Euphorbia pulcherrima*). The showy flower petals of Poinsettia are really leaves that enclose an almost inconspicuous flower. Similarly, the spectacularly colored "petals" of flowering dogwood are actually leaves. The flower-like leaves of these and similar plants increase the apparent size of the flower, making it more visible and attractive to pollinators.

Leaves of Carnivorous Plants

About 200 species of plants have special devices that trap and digest insects. Most of these plants occur in swampy areas and bogs of tropical and temperate forests. The soil of these habitats is often deficient in minerals such as nitrogen as well as other plant requirements. As an adaptation to living in these habitats, these carnivorous plants have developed sophisticated methods to catch insects which are then digested and their nitrogen and other nutrients absorbed. Most insect-trapping plants also have chlorophyll and are able to photosynthesize food. There are four basic kinds of insectivorous plants.

a. Sundews

Sundews *(Drosera)* are small plants with rounded leaf tips covered with 200 or more glandular hairs, each of which resembles miniature clubs. The tip of each club holds a clear drop of sticky fluid filled with digestive enzymes. The droplets sparkle in the sun attracting insects which land on them and get stuck. The sticky hairs react by bending inwards to further entrap the insect. Afterwards, enzymes in the droplets digest the insect within a few days. After digestion is completed the hairs return to normal, the leaf uncurls and the sundew plant is ready for its next victim.

b. Pitcher Plants

Pitcher plants *(Darlingtonia)* and cobra lilies have hollow, vase-like leaves that form a columnar tube to entrap insects and other arthropods. Glands located near the rim of the leafy tube secrete a nectar which attracts insects to the opening. Once inside, insects slide down the tube into a pool of watery digestive fluid at the base. Stiff down-

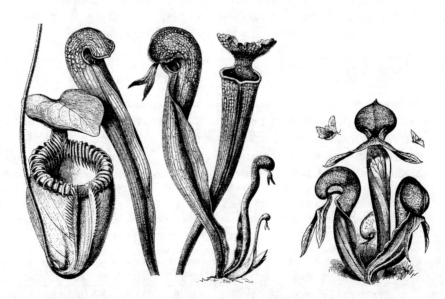

Figure 7–13 Pitcher plants represent modified leaves. *Source:* Jim Harter (1988), p. 92.

ward pointing hairs along the length of the tube interior keep the trapped insects from climbing back out. The trapped insects drown and are digested by enzymes in the water.

At least one animal has learned to take advantage of the carnivorous pitcher plant. Malaysian tree frogs lay their eggs in the vases of Asian pitcher plants to protect them from egg-eating insects. The eggs of these frogs, which contain substances that neutralize the digestive enzymes of the pitcher plant, hatch in safety and the young emerge to feed on the insects.

Due to over collecting, pitcher plants and some sundews are today on the endangered species list.

---

c. Venus Flytraps

Venus flytraps (*Dionaea muscipula*) are tiny plants that live in wet, boggy and swampy areas of North and South Carolina. The leaves of Venus flytraps are folded into two halves which are bordered by bar-like hairs. Tiny hairs on the leaves act as triggers. If touched by flies and other insects the triggers snap the two halves of the leaf closed to trap the insect inside. Once closed, the leaf secretes digestive enzymes which kill and dissolve the trapped insect.

d. The Bladderworts

Bladderworts are small, water-loving plants with finely dissected leaves that float in shallow water along the margins of lakes and streams. Near the base of each leaf is a stomach-shaped bladder with a trap door covering an opening at one end. Four stiff, curled hairs at the top of the trap door act as triggers. When an insect touches one of the hairs the trapdoor springs open, thereby allowing water to rush into the bladder and sweeping the insect in also. The door shuts behind and the insect is trapped.

Leaves as Commodities

Plant leaves are important commodities. They have both monetary and esthetic value. One of the most common and colorful uses of plant leaves is as landscape ornamentals that beautify our property and alter our external environment to adjust its usefulness for our needs.

Many plant leaves are used for food. For example, we eat leaves when we consume cabbage, parsley, celery, lettuce, spinach, and chard. Rhubarb is the petioles of the rhubarb leaf rather than the leaf, which is actually poisonous. Alfalfa leaves are ground up to make a curd which is high in protein. Now used as livestock and pet feed, the alfalfa curd is being tested for human consumption. If successful, it may provide cheap and common protein for many of the world's people, especially in poorer areas of the world where protein foods are in short supply.

Some leaves are processed to provide spices. The flavoring agents thyme, marjoram, oregano, tarragon, peppermint, spearmint, wintergreen, basil, dill, sage, and savory are all products extracted from leaves.

Leaves are also the source of innumerable products manufactured in one form or another. Some leaves have valuable pigments in them. These are made into dyes which are used to produce colors for cloth. Yellow dye comes from bearberry leaves, red from henna leaves and pale blue dyes are extracted from leaves of the blue ash.

Leaf fibers provide cordage such as manila hemp while Panama hats are woven using fibers from palm leaves. Similarly, cane chairs are made of the dried and interwoven leaves of rushes, cattails, and other aquatic plants.

Bowstrings come from the fibers of the Sansevieria plant.

Leaves of many plants are also important sources of oils. Petitgrain oil comes from leaves of orange trees while oil of citronella is an active agent in mosquito repellents. Oil of lavender is added to soaps while patchouli and lemon grass oils are often ingredients in some of the best, or at least the smelliest, perfumes. Eucalyptus oil, camphor, cajeput, and pennyroyal oils, all extracted from plant leaves, are used as ointments and liniments.

Many drugs, both legal and illegal, contain secretions produced by and extracted from leaves. Cocaine, for example, comes from the cocoa leaves of a South American plant while belladonna and atropine are both extracted from leaves of the deadly nightshade plant. Scopolamine, a tranquilizer, has also been isolated from nightshade leaves.

Many important medicinal drugs are also extracted from leaves. Digitalis, used in treating heart disease is produced in foxglove leaves. Lobeline sulphate, commonly used as a treatment in the attempt to stop smoking, is produced from leaves of lobelias. Aloe vera is an African plant whose leaves contain a juice used to treat skin burns. This material is so soothing to the skin that it is a common ingredient in many lotions, hand creams and soaps.

One of the most important cash crops in North America is the leaf of the tobacco plant. Approximately two billion pounds of this leaf are harvested annually and converted into cigarettes, cigars, and other forms of tobacco. Nearly 125,000 Americans die from lung cancer annually as a result of the use of this plant leaf. Although illegal, marijuana ranks as another important cash crop based on a plant leaf. The active component of marijuana, THC is produced in the leaves and hair secretions of the female flower.

Beverages such as teas are widely produced in many areas of the Orient and have a wide economic impact on many areas of the world. Another tea-like drink, mate, is made from leaves of the holly. Pulque and tequila both come from leaves of Agave. Absinthe liqueur is a product of leaves of wormwood.

Other leaf products include insecticides such as the secretion which is obtained from the leaves of the cockroach plant of Mexico. Secretions from the neem tree of India are also effective insect controls. A single drop may kill a hundred insects or more. Lastly, leaves produce waxes which are harvested for many human uses. Carnauba and caussu waxes are products of the tropical palms.

Key Words and Phrases

hydathodes	primordia	petiole
lamina	stipule	leaf gaps
phyllotaxy	simple leaf	compound leaf
pinnately compound	palmately compound	pinnately veined

palmately veined	parallel venation	epidermis
stomata	guard cells	mesophyll
spongy mesophyll	palisade layer	bulliform cells
xeromorphic	tendril	spine
insect trapping plants	carotenoid	abscission

Selected References and Resources

▼ ●

Addicott, F. T. 1982. *Abscission.* University of California Press. Berkeley, California.

Cutler, D. F. 1978. *Applied Plant Anatomy.* Longman, Inc. New York

Dale, J. E., and F. L. Milthorpe. Eds. 1983. *The Growth and Functioning of Leaves.* Cambridge University Press. New York.

Esau, K. 1965. *Plant Anatomy.* 2nd Edition. John Wiley and Sons. New York.

O'Brien, T. P., and M. E. McCully. 1969. *Plant Structure and Development.* The Macmillan Company. New York.

Ray, P. M. 1972. *The Living Plant.* 2nd Edition. Holt, Rinehart & Winston. New York.

Roth, I. 1984. *Stratification of Tropical Forests as Seen in Leaf Structure.* Kluwer Academic Publications. Norwell, Massachusetts.

Warlaw, C. W. 1968. *Morphogenesis in Plants. A Contemporary Study.* 2nd Edition. Methuen & Company. London.

Review and Discussion Questions

▼ ●

1. How do the colors of leaves indicate adaptation to different habitats? To different climates?
2. What modifications do needle and scale leaved plants show? What are the functions of these modifications?
3. Describe the process of leaf abscision that occurs during the fall.
4. Describe the special modifications that protect leaves.
5. What are some of the most common and most controversial uses of leaves of plants?

Chapter 8

Flowers, Fruits, and Seeds

Dicots and Monocots
Flower Structure
Fruits
Fleshy Fruits
Dry Fruits
Dispersal of Fruits
Seeds
Germination of Seeds

The success of any living organism can be measured by its ability to reproduce. If organisms do not leave offspring their genes will not be passed on to the next generation and their uniqueness will die with them. All organisms expend more energy during reproduction than in normal activities to insure the successful survival of the offspring. In plants, reproduction takes many forms with many variations in those forms. Almost all plants can reproduce asexually by propagation of leaves, stems, or roots but the offspring are genetically identical. Sexual reproduction solves this dilemma by combining genes from two different parental stock, thereby ensuring that descendants are genetically different. Simple plants such as mosses and ferns, sexually reproduce by gametes or spores and asexually by budding or fragmentation. Only flowering plants (the angiosperms) sexually reproduce by flowers. Seeds are produced deep within the flower.

All or part of the flower may form a protective covering of the seeds in the form of a fruit or vegetable. The flowers of flowering plants come in a seemingly endless variety of interesting shapes and colors and scents that attract specific pollinators such as insects, birds, and even bats. These pollinators transfer pollen (sperm) from one flower to another in exchange for nectar.

The largest of all flowers are produced by the *Rafflesia* plant from Indonesia. The flowers of this tropical rain forest plant may be more than a yard in diameter and weigh 20 pounds. In contrast, the flowers of grasses and other wind pollinated plants are small and inconspicuous as they have no need to attract pollinators. Some flowers are not always the showy blossoms that we generally imagine. There are some plants that have flowers that grow and bloom beneath the surface of the soil.

Dicot and Monocot Flowers

Approximately three quarters of all flowering plants are dicots. These include all the flowering trees and shrubs, and many herbaceous plants. The monocots include lilies,

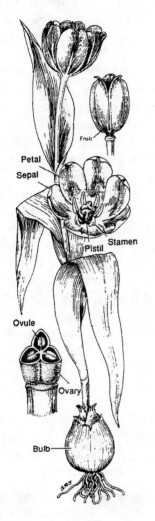

Figure 8–1 The tulip flower and plant. *Source:* Kent A. Vliet. *A Lab Manual for Integrated Principles of Biology* (1977), Simon and Schuster Custom Publishing, Figure 18-10, p. 183.

Petal
Sepal
Fruit
Pistil   Stamen
Ovule
Ovary
Bulb

Figure 8–2 The flowers of Norway maple. *Source:* Roy H. Saigo and Barbara W. Saigo. *Botany: Principles of Applications* (1990), Prentice-Hall, p. 32.

grasses, orchids, irises and palms. Monocots are thought to have been derived from dicots and represent a specialization and perhaps an advancement of the dicot structure.

We have already indicated that dicots are plants that form from a seedling with two cotyledons or seed leaves. Dicots are also distinctive in flower structure. All flowers consist of a series of whorls. In dicots, each whorl is made up of flower parts in 4's or 5's or in multiples of 4 or 5. The leaves of dicots are also distinctive with a network of dichotomous veins rather than parallel veins. Dicots, if they are woody, have vascular cambium and frequently cork cambium present. In the herbaceous dicot stems, the vascular bundles of the stem are in a ring. Lastly, in dicots, the male reproductive cells are carried in pollen grains with 3 apertures or openings.

In monocots the flower whorls consist of parts in 3's or in multiples of 3. The veins of monocot leaves seldom branch dichotomously but rather form a more-or-less parallel pattern. Even though palms may be woody, there is never vascular cambium or cork cambium in monocots.

Flower Structure

The sexual reproductive organ of a flowering plant is the **flower**. Flowers originate as a primordium that develops into a bud. The bud is actually a specialized branch at the tip of a stalk called a **peduncle**. This peduncle grows and swells to form a **receptacle**, from which all the rest of the flower is formed. Thus, the receptacle is the point at which the flower parts attach to the peduncle.

Flower parts typically occur in whorls which are specific in number for a particular species of plant. The basic flower has four sets of structures, the sepals, petals, stamens, and pistil. The outermost whorl of a flower normally consists of between three-to-five small green, leaf-like structures called **sepals**. The sepals of a flower may be separate or they may fuse together to form a **calyx**. The function of the sepals and calyx is to protect the flower while it is in the bud. Sepals are analogous to the bud scales of leaf primordia.

The second whorl of the flower consists of the **petals**, which collectively form a disc called the **corolla**. The petals are often large and showy structures to attract pollinators to the flower. Some petals have special markings that serve as "landing lights" or markers to guide pollinators into the flower interior. Other flowers have guide markers that are invisible to the human eye but capable of being seen by insects who can see in the ultraviolet range of light. The corolla may be reduced or lacking in flowers that are wind pollinated. The combination of the calyx and corolla is called a **perianth**.

Interior to the perianth are the reproductive structures of the flower. Some flowers may contain both male and female reproductive structures but many flowers have either male or female reproductive organs (they have only one sex). If the flower contains both female and male organs the plant is called **monoecious** (mon = one, ecious = house). If the flower includes only male or female organs the plant species is called **dioecious (di = two, ecious = houses)**. Dioecious species consist of separate male and female plants. Flowers of dioecious plants are called **imperfect** flowers because they lack the flower parts of the other sex. Flowers that contain only male organs are called **staminate** flowers while those with only female structures are called **pistillate** or **carpellate**.

MALE ORGANS OF FLOWERS

The male part of a flower consists of **stamens**, which attach to the receptacle around the base of the pistil. A flower may have several stamens or a single stamen. Each stamen consists of a slender elongated **filament** which supports a sac-like **anther** on the

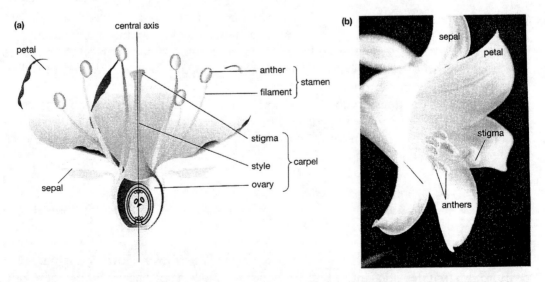

Figure 8–3 The anatomy of a complete flower. *Source:* Teresa Audesirk and Gerald Audesirk (1999), p. 487.

free end of it. The anther consists of sac-like chambers that produce, store, and finally release male reproductive cells called pollen. **Pollen grains** are the male gametes of flowers and contain **sperm**. When mature, the pollen is released through long slits that form on the anthers of most flowers.

FEMALE ORGANS OF FLOWERS

The female parts of the flower are represented by one to several vase-shaped **carpels** (= **vessels**), which are the dominant structures in the middle of the whorl of sepals and petals. Carpels, which are sometimes called **pistils**, may be folded lengthwise, resembling a rolled leaf from which they are evolutionarily derived. A flower may have a single carpal or contain several fused carpels. Each carpel has three distinct regions, a **stigma**, style and ovary. The most obvious is the stigma, which is a slight swelling at the top of the carpel. The stigma is often sticky and serves as the pollen receptor; it is here that the male gametes, in the form of pollen grains, are deposited by a pollinator (e.g., insects or wind). Beneath the stigma, the carpel narrows to form a long, slender, neck-like **style**. The style swells to form a swollen ovary at the base of the carpel, which in turn is attached to the peduncle.

The ovary may be composed of one to several internal divisions which are the **ovules**. **Simple** carpels have a single ovule while those with two or more are said to be **compound**. Inside the leaf-like or fleshy ovules are masses of tissue which produce eggs, the female gametes. Each egg is attached to the wall of the ovule by a placenta. Fertilization of the eggs occurs inside the ovule. The fertilized egg becomes the zygote while the surrounding ovule develop into a seed. In turn they are surrounded, protected, and nourished by the flesh of the ovary that later becomes all or part of the fruit.

TYPES OF FLOWERS

Flowers of different species vary in size, color, and arrangement of parts. Differences in flower arrangements are important aids in identifying and classifying flowers. Thus, flowers that have all typical floral structures such as sepals, petals, stamens, and pistils are termed complete flowers. If one or more of these features are lacking they are called **incomplete flowers**.

Flowers can also be grouped by the number of flowers that occur on each peduncle. As a general rule there is one flower per peduncle. However, in some plants clusters of flowers arise from a single peduncle to form an **inflorescence**.

Botanists recognize several types of floral inflorescenses which are important in identification of many flowering plants. If the individual flowers are carried on **pedicels** of equal length and arise from the same place on the pedicel the inflorescence is called an **umbel**. Parsnips, dill, carrots and other members of the family Umbelliferae are familiar examples of umbels. Highly branched inflorescences are termed **panicles** and are commonly seen in grasses. If the flowers arise as lateral branches from a main axis, the inflorescence is called a **raceme**. The catkins of a cottonwood tree are an example of a raceme. If the flowers are **sessile** along the main axis the inflorescence is a **spike**. A **cyme** is a flat-topped inflorescence in which the youngest flowers form the periphery and the oldest flowers are clustered at the center. If the central cluster consists of younger flowers the inflorescence is called a **corymb**.

Finally, the position of the ovary in relation to the receptacle is also used to classify flowers. If the sepals, petals, and stamens are attached to the receptacle beneath the ovary the flower is **hypogynous** and has a **superior ovary**. Conversely if the sepals, petals, and stamens are attached to the top of the ovary the flower is **epigynous** and

Figure 8–4 Types of floral inflorescence (a) spike (b) raceme (c) umbel (d) corymb (e) head.
Source: N. M. Jessop. *Biosphere: A Study of Life* (1970), Prentice-Hall. p. 523.

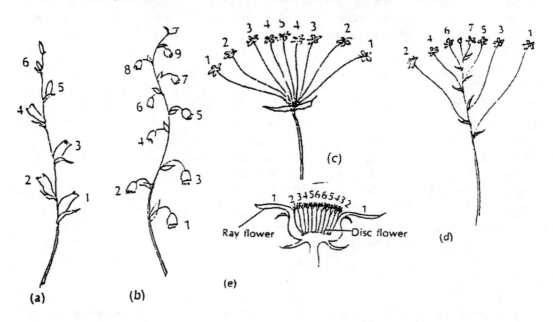

has an **inferior ovary**. The receptacle grows up around the ovary of epigynous flowers and the ovary appears to be buried completely within the whorls of petals and sepals. In a third type of ovary called **perigynous**, the floral parts emerge from the sides and the ovary is termed an **intermediate ovary**.

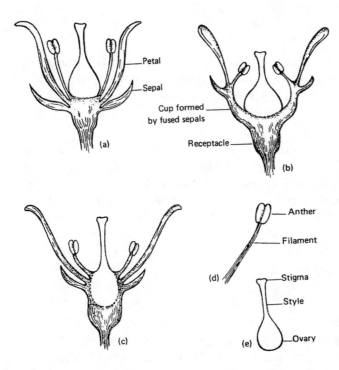

Figure 8–5 Anatomy of flowers based on position of ovary (a) superior ovary (b) superior ovary (c) inferior ovary (d and e) parts of stamen and pistil (carpel).
Source: Roy H. Saigo and Barbara W. Saigo. *Botany: Principles of Applications* (1990), Prentice-Hall, p. 32.

FLOWER STRUCTURE AND POLLINATION

Plants can be either **cross-pollinated** or **self-pollinated**. Plants that are dioecious and have imperfect flowers must be cross-pollinated. That is, pollen from the male flower of one plant must be transferred either by wind or insects or some other agent to the eggs in the ovary of the female flower on another plant.

Since both sexes are present in the flowers of monecious plants self-pollination may occur, in which pollen from the anthers is transferred to the stigma of the same flower. Cross-pollination also usually occurs, as pollen gametes from one flower of the plant are transferred to the stigma of another flower of the plant. Since cross-pollination, by definition, involves combination of genes from different individuals and is therefore more desirable some plants secrete chemicals which make it impossible for self-pollination to occur.

Fruits

The fruit is an ovary that has been fertilized, developed and matured. Some fruits include other floral parts such as the sepals and petals, as well. Fruits are noted for their dramatic growth as they ripen they greatly increase in volume. Consider, for example, the difference in size between an apple flower and the ripened apple which ultimately develops. Fruit growth begins with mitotic activity that produces an enormous increase in the number of cells making up the ovary wall. Later, these new cells expand as they mature. In some fruits growth is also due to an increase in spaces between cells which are filled with juices.

Fruits that contain seeds may be considered as delivery systems for the dispersal of those seeds. Many of the so-called vegetables that we eat, such as tomatoes, string beans, cucumbers and squashes as well as sweet fruits are actually examples of plant ovaries that have matured and are technically fruits. True vegetables, in contrast, consist of plant structures other than fruits such as stems (celery and potatoes), leaves (lettuce and cabbage), and roots (turnips, radishes, and carrots).

All fruits and vegetables arise from flowers and are found only in the flowering plants. To mature properly they must first be fertilized. If there is no fertilization, the fruit will wither and drop.

Pollen grains contain hormones that initiate fruit development. As seeds develop they produce hormones that are responsible for much of the growth observed in fruits. Seedless fruit can be produced artificially; growers spray the plant with plant hormones that "fool it" into reacting as though it were fertilized—and the ovary develops into a fruit. This is how seedless grapes and watermelons are produced. None of these seedless varieties are fertile however—that is, if you try to plant a seedless grape or watermelon it will not germinate and grow because the seeds inside have never been fertilized.

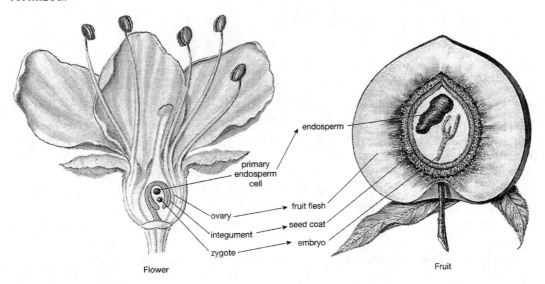

Figure 8–6 Development of the flower and seed. *Source:* Teresa Audesirk and Gerald Audesirk (1999), p. 495.

Figure 8-7 Types of fruits. *Source:* N. M. Jessop. *Biosphere: A Study of Life.* (1970), Prentice-Hall. p. 523–525.

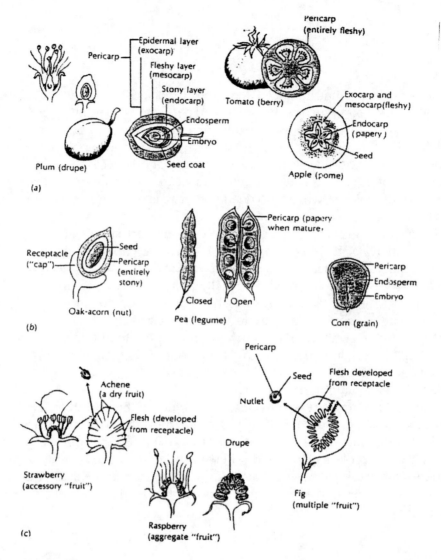

ANATOMY OF FRUIT

All fruits are built on the same anatomical plan. The ovary wall develops into a **pericarp** which consists of three specific regions. The **exocarp** is the outer covering, or skin, of the fruit. The interior of the fruit is the **endocarp**, which forms the boundary around the seed. The endocarp may be hard as in a peach pit or papery as in apples. Between the outer exocarp and the interior endocarp is an area called the **mesocarp**, which may or may not be fleshy. Both the exocarp and mesocarp form protective layers around the seeds of the endocarp. To understand fruit structure, consider the makeup of the peach. The interior of the peach, surrounding the seed, is a hard bony endocarp. The juicy reddish-yellow pulp of the peach is the mesocarp while the thin, fuzzy skin is the exocarp.

We must understand also that fruits may contain one seed, in which case there was one pistil in the flower with an ovary that was simple. There may also be multiple seeds in fruit. In this case the fruit may be produced from a single flower with more than one pistil, or a single pistil with a compound ovary or an inflorescence of flowers that has grown together. Let us look at some examples.

Fruits are generally classified on the basis of their pericarp into fleshy or dry fruits. In some fruits the mesocarp is fleshy or partially fleshy at maturity. In other fruits the mesocarp dries to become a hard covering. In this case the fruit is considered dry. Let us begin by looking at some kinds of fleshy fruits.

FLESHY FRUITS

There is a large assemblage of fruits that have a mesocarp or accessory tissue that contains fluid and concentrations of sugars to make the flesh tasty. Such fruits are called fleshy fruits.

Simple Fleshy Fruits

When a single flower with a single pistil is fertilized it produces a simple fleshy fruit. Not all simple fleshy fruits are the same. They differ because the single pistil may have a simple or compound ovary (containing a single or several ovules). Some simple fruits may also develop from floral structures other than ovaries. Some types of simple fleshy fruits include the following.

a. Drupes

Drupes are fruits that have a single seed enclosed by a hard stony endocarp forming a pit. They usually develop from flowers with superior ovaries and a single ovule within. The mesocarp is usually fleshy but not always, as in coconuts where it is a fibrous husk. Normal drupes, with a fleshy mesocarp, include apricots, cherries, peaches, plums, olives, and almonds.

b. Berry

A berry develops from a compound ovary which may contain one or more seeds. The pericarp is fleshy but it is often difficult to distinguish between the mesocarp and endocarp layers. There are three types of berries.

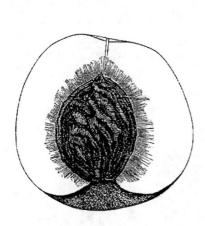

Figure 8–8 Example of a drupe. *Source:* Jim Harter (1988), p. 278.

Figure 8–9 Example of a berry. *Source:* Jim Harter (1988), p. 282.

1. True Berries. Normal true berries include single seeded forms such as avocados and dates, and multiple seeded forms such as tomatoes, grapes, persimmons, peppers and eggplants. They have a thin skin and a fleshy pericarp. Examples of berries include tomatoes, peppers, eggplants, dates, avocados, and grapes. There are many plants with "berry" in the name but they are not true berries. These include strawberries, raspberries and blackberries.

Some berries are derived from flowers with an inferior ovary so other parts of the flower contribute to the flesh of the fruit. These berries can be identified by some flower parts or scars persisting at the tip of the fruit. This situation exists in gooseberries, blueberries, cranberries, pomegranates and bananas.

2. Pepos. A pepo is a modified berry with an exocarp in the form of a thick rind which protects the tissue beneath. The mesocarp and endocarp combine to form the flesh of the fruit. The fruit develops from a flower with a single pistil and compound ovary. Examples of pepos include pumpkins, cucumbers, watermelons, squashes and cantaloupes.

3. Hesperidium. Hesperidia are modified berries with a leathery skin made up of the exocarp and mesocarp that contains aromatic oils. Within the fruit, outgrowths of the inner lining (the endocarp) of the ovary become sac-like and swollen with juice. All citrus fruits such as oranges, lemons, limes, grapefruit, tangerines and kumquats are hesperidia.

c. Pomes

Pomes are simple fleshy fruits in which the bulk of the flesh of the fruit comes from the enlarged receptacle that grows up around the ovary. Thus, a pome is actually mostly the receptacle which has become modified into a fruit. Inside the receptacle, the endocarp becomes papery or leathery and surrounds the seed. Pomes include apples, pears and quinces. In the apple, for example, the core is the ovary, the papery tissue in the middle is the endocarp, and the rest of the fruit is the receptacle.

Aggregate Fruits

Aggregate fruits develop from a single flower that has several to many pistils. Each individual pistil develops into tiny drupes or other fruitlets. As these little fruits mature, they remain clustered together. Aggregate fruits include many examples that are commonly called berries such as raspberries, blackberries, and strawberries. To illustrate this fruit further, blackberries consist of small drupes (druplets) clustered on a common receptacle.

In strawberries, the flower has a cone-shaped receptacle which becomes fleshy and red and each pistil develops into a kind of fruit that is called an achene—we will discuss

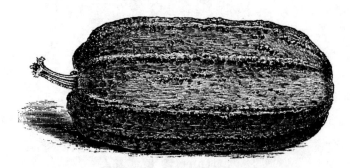

Figure 8–10 Example of a pepo. *Source*: Jim Harter (1988), p. 292.

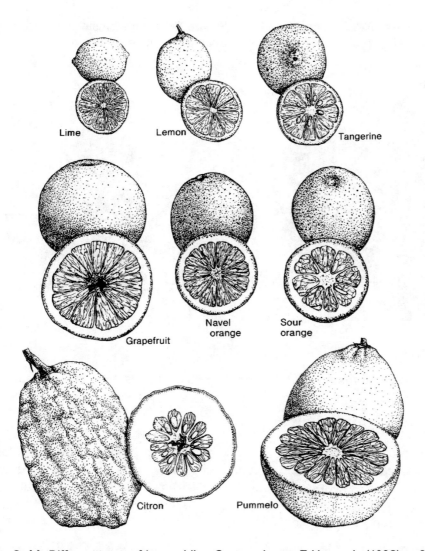

Lime

Lemon

Tangerine

Grapefruit

Navel
orange

Sour
orange

Citron

Pummelo

Figure 8–11 Different types of hesperidia. *Source:* James F. Hancock. (1992), p. 263.

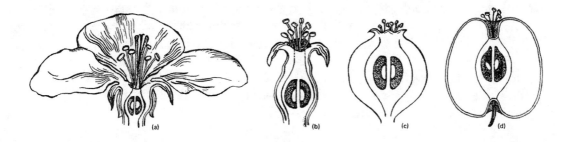

(a)

(b)

(c)

(d)

Figure 8–12 An apple becomes a pome. Diagrams show the inclusion of the apple flower into the apple fruit. *Source:* Roy H. Saigo and Barbara W. Saigo. *Botany: Principles of Applications* (1990), Prentice-Hall, p. 33.

Figure 8–13 An example of an aggregate fruit. *Source:* Jim Harter (1988), p. 281.

Figure 8–14 An example of a multiple fruit. *Source:* Jim Harter (1988), p. 284.

achenes later. While the strawberry is considered an aggregate fruit, it also incorporates part of the receptacle.

Multiple Fleshy Fruits

When several flowers of an inflorescence combine to produce one fruit structure we have what is called a multiple fruit. Each flower has its own receptacle but as the flowers mature, they grow together into a single fruit. That is, multiple fruits are a fusion of parts or all of several flowers. Examples of multiple fruits include the mulberries, figs, Osage oranges, and pineapples.

DRY FRUITS

Dry fruits are formed when the mesocarp and exocarp dry out and become hard or leathery. Dry fruits are usually separated by how they split at maturity to liberate the seed within or for that matter if they split at all.

Dry Fruits That Split At Maturity—Dehiscents

Many dry fruits have seams along one or both sides to enable the exocarp to open and liberate the seeds. Included in this group of dry fruits are the following.

a. Follicle
A follicle is a simple fruit or seed pod that splits open along one side or seam only, exposing seeds within. Some common examples of follicles include larkspur, columbine, milkweed, and peony.

b. Legume
Legume pods split open along two sutures on opposite sides of the pod. Common examples of legumes are found in peas, beans, garbanzo beans, lentils, carob, kudzu, and mesquite.

Figure 8–15 Examples of dry fruits.
Source: Lorus J. Milne and Margery Milne.
Plant Life (1959), Prentice-Hall. p. 185.

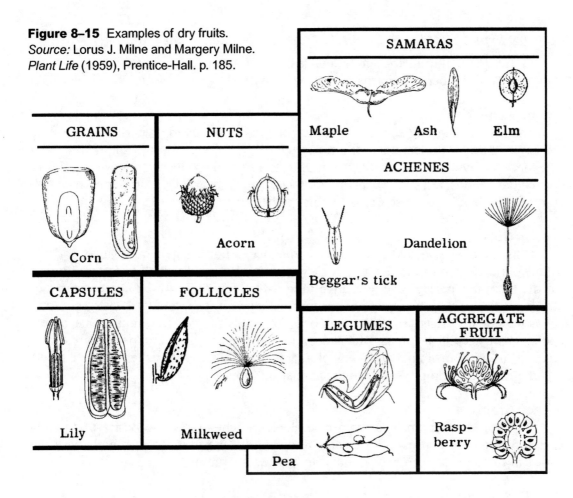

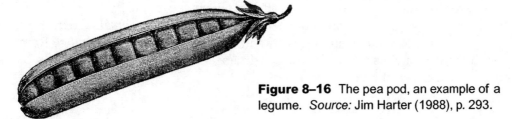

Figure 8–16 The pea pod, an example of a legume. *Source:* Jim Harter (1988), p. 293.

c. Siliques

Siliques are compound fruits with two carpels that separate when mature. Like legumes, the seed pod of siliques splits along two sides or seams. Siliques differ from legumes in that the seeds are carried on a central partition which is exposed when the two halves separate. The fruits which result from this splitting are called siliques. Siliques are most common among members of the mustard family, including broccoli, cabbage, radish, shepherd's purse, and watercress.

d. Capsule

Capsules are the most common of all dry fruits that split. Capsules consist of at least two carpals which split in various ways, including along partitions between carpals, or split through cavities in carpals. Others form a cap toward one end that pops off when mature. Some form a row of pores through which the seeds are shaken out as the capsule rattles in the wind. Capsules are found in irises, orchids, lilies, poppies, violets, rhododendrons, azaleas, and snapdragons.

Dry Fruits That Do Not Split At Maturity—Indehiscent fruits.

In this group of fruits the single seed is fused or attached to the pericarp to varying degrees. Thus the pericarp forms a shell over the fruit.

a. Achene

The achene is a single seed that is attached to the surrounding pericarp only at its base. The husk or pericarp is easily separated from the seed. Most of the members of the large family of Composite have complex flowers and produce achenes for fruits, of which dandelions and sunflowers are the most familiar examples. Some species of buttercups and buckwheat also produce fruits in the form of achenes.

b. Nuts

Nuts are single seeded fruits similar to achenes but are generally larger and the stony pericarp is much harder and thicker. All nuts also develop with a cluster of bracts at the base, technically called the **involucre**, which fuse to form the cup of acorns or the husk of a walnut. Examples of true nuts include acorns, hazelnuts, hickory nuts and chestnuts. Many fruits are called nuts but technically are not true nuts. For example peanuts are actually legumes, while coconuts, almonds, walnuts and pecans are examples of drupes. Brazil nuts are seeds of a large capsule and the cashew nut is a single seed of a peculiar drupe. Pistachio nuts are also drupes.

c. Grains

Also called a caryopsis, a grain resembles an achene, but the pericarp is tightly fused to the seed and cannot be separated from it. The fruits of all members of the grass family such as corn, wheat, oats, and barley, are grains.

d. Samara

Samaras are one or two-seeded fruits in which the pericarp around the seeds extends out in the form of wings or membranes to aid in dispersal. When the wind blows these winged seeds spin and twirl and can be carried some distance from the parent plant. Examples of these winged fruits are found in maples, ashes, elms, birches, and the tree-of-heaven.

Figure 8–17 A walnut. *Source:* Jim Harter (1988), p. 275.

e. Schizocarp

A schizocarp is a twin fruit unique to the parsley family. It is found in parsley, carrots, anise, caraway, and dill. A schizocarp is made of twin fruits that break into two one-seeded segments when dry.

Dispersal of Fruits and Seeds

Just as may flowers are colored and configured to attract pollinators, many fruits have developed methods to attract dispersers which carry the seeds away from the mother plant.

WIND DISPERSAL

Wind and other similar meteorological events are important dispersers of many kinds of fruits. Many fruits exhibit structures that enable them to be easily picked up and carried by wind. For example, the samara of maples causes the fruit to spin and be carried on the wind. In hop hornbeam seeds, the samara is an inflated sac to make the structure buoyant in even light winds. Fruits of many other plants have equally adaptable devices to take advantage of wind dispersal. The seeds of buttercups, sunflowers, milkweeds, and dandelions, for example, have plumes which act as parachute canopies that can float away on even the lightest of breezes. Similarly, seeds of willows are surrounded by woolly hairs that catch the wind and allow the seed to fly. Button snakeroot and Jerusalem sage fruits are round and can be rolled along the ground by wind. The seeds of orchids and heath plants are so tiny that they are easily picked up and blown away on windy days of late summer and autumn. In tumbleweeds the entire plant rolls along in the wind, scattering its seeds in the process.

ANIMAL DISPERSAL

Animals are good seed distributors by the very nature of their range of movement. The main reason a fruit is sweet and good smelling (or in some cases, very fowl smelling) is to attract animals to eat it. Many birds and mammals, in particular, are drawn to these brightly colored morsels and are large consumers of fruits. Because of the resistant endocarp, seeds may pass harmlessly through the digestive tract of the animal and are eventually deposited in feces which function to provide a rich source of fertilizer for the developing seed. Seeds that have a thick endocarp around them may actually require a processing trip through an animal's digestive tract to soften and thin the endocarp so the seed can germinate.

Some seeds do not need to be eaten but are rather picked up and carried on the animal as an attachment. Shorebirds carry seeds in the mud on their feet from place to place and help dispersal of many species of plants. Some seeds are gathered and stored in food caches by rodents such as field mice, chipmunks, and squirrels. Those seeds that are not eaten during the winter, may germinate next spring. Blue jays and woodpeckers carry seeds away to eat. Many are dropped and lost by the birds. These will also germinate if the conditions are correct.

Many fruits and seeds attach themselves to the host and are carried inadvertently. Plants like bedstraw, burr clover, twinflowers and flax are sticky to the touch or have hooks, barbs or bristles of one kind or another for attaching to animal fur. Some, such as bleeding hearts and trilliums, have oils that are attractive to ants. The ants seek them out and carry the seeds away.

Water Dispersal

Some fruits, as in sedges, contain trapped air so they float in water. Others have a waxy outer surface so they don't absorb water while floating. A heavy downpour of rain will cause floods and uproot plants on a stream bank. Another method of water dispersal is in the form of rain. Large raindrops may splash seeds out of opened capsules. Some seeds with thick spongy pericarps absorb water very slowly and are dispersed over salt water as in the case of the coconut palm. All of these are adaptations that allow water to influence the spread of seeds.

Other Dispersal Mechanisms

Some plants mechanically eject seeds from capsules by building up pressure with gas or water. When the pressure reaches a certain point the capsule explodes and the seeds are thrown considerable distances. This happens in witch hazel and some legumes. In manroots and some pumpkins, seeds are squirted out of the end of melon-like fruits. Humans are the best dispersers of seeds. Seeds are carried inadvertently and on purpose. Many edible plants have been carried by man across oceans and continents. This accounts for the wide variety of vegetables and fruits we find in supermarkets today. They didn't all grow here but instead have been imported from other areas of the world to suit our needs.

Seeds

The seed represents the fertilized embryo of a plant. Within what we call a seed is a developing seedling and stored food material that is used for its development. Seeds are the result of sexual reproduction and the fusing of sperm and egg. Angiosperm seeds are unique as they also have stored food material called **endosperm**. Endosperm is also the result of a fusion of sperm and other cells. Thus the angiosperm seed has a double fertilization process in its formation. We will discuss this double fertilization in some detail later.

To examine the structure of a seed we can use a kidney bean as a good example. The bean is elliptical with a concave side and a convex side. The concave side is called the **hilum** and has a white scar on it to indicate where the bean was attached to the ovary wall. Near the hilum may be seen a small opening called the **micropyle**, which is where pollen entered the ovule. If the bean were to be opened and the seedling exposed, there would be seen two **cotyledons**. These are actually the two halves of the bean. In beans they are food storage organs that function as seed leaves. The embryo is a tiny plant to which the cotyledons are attached. As the seedling germinates and grows, a shoot emerges. The tip of this shoot is called a **plumule** and it contains the apical meristem at one end of the embryo. Cotyledons are attached just below the plumule. The stem below the plumule can be divided into an **epicotyl**, the stem part above the cotyledons, and the **hypocotyl**, the stem part below the cotyledons. On the opposite end of the seedling the **radicle** is growing downward to form the root end of the new plant. It also contains an apical meristem. As indicated above, in some plants there is special tissue called endosperm to provide food for the developing embryo. In some seeds such as corn, the food storage is in separate tissue and cotyledons do not play a role. In our bean, the endosperm is in the cotyledons.

GERMINATION OF SEEDS

If a seed is dispersed and lands in a suitable place where there is sunlight, water and nutrients, the seed will **germinate**. The process of germination is controlled by many factors. Sometimes seeds are dormant for varying periods of time before they germinate.

Dormancy

Dormany is an adaption the that allows seeds to survive harsh climatic periods or other unfavorable environmental conditions. In other instances, seeds may be in a dormant state when they are dispersed. In many plants, dormancy is a necessary period of quiet before germination of the seed can begin. Dormancy is preparation time for germination and the end of dormancy is brought about by environmental, mechanical, or physiological factors or several of these factors combined.

In legumes, for example, the seeds have a thick seed coat that must be abraded by soil and rocks before the coat is thin enough to take up water. Seeds that fall to the ground in autumn will be subjected to alternate thawing and freezing through the winter. This will also result in movement of the rocks and soil that helps abrade the seed coat. Termed **scarification**, this natural scraping away of the seed surface activates the seed for germination.

Some substances in the seed coat may inhibit growth. These hormones are in the mesocarp and must be washed away before the seed is activated. This is a common

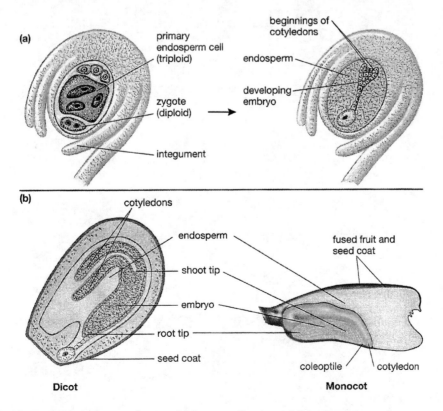

Figure 8–18 The development of a seed (a) generalized seed (b) comparison of a monocot and dicot seed. *Source:* Teresa Audesirk and Gerald Audesirk (1999), p. 496.

situation in desert plants. Fruits like apples, pears, and citrus fruits have inhibitors to keep seeds from germinating within the fruit. As the fruit rots, the flesh is washed away taking with it the inhibitors. The well-washed seeds can then germinate.

Holly seeds do not germinate until after the fruit has dropped and the embryo has developed completely with the aid of food from the endosperm, a condition called **after-ripening**.

Dormancy can also be broken by **stratification**, in which seeds experience a wet period of several weeks followed by cold temperatures. Seeds of many woody plants of temperate regions germinate following stratification.

Germination

Germination may occur immediately following dispersal or may follow dormancy. Germination depends on exposure of the seed to sufficient light conditions as well as a source of soil nutrients, water, and temperature. Light and water, or their absence, are often the most critical factors influencing seed germination.

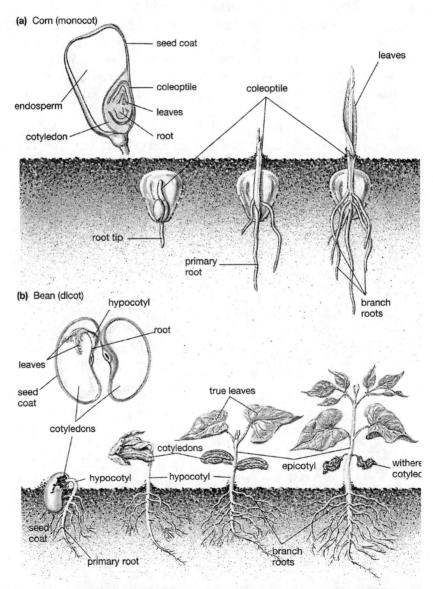

Figure 8–19 The germination of a seed (a) example of corn, a monocot seed (b) example of bean, a dicot seed. *Source:* Teresa Audesirk and Gerald Audesirk (1999), p. 498.

All seeds must take in water for growth and some seeds require enormous amounts —up to ten times their weight in water before they start to grow. This uptake of water, or **imbibition**, serves to rehydrate the enzymes in the protoplasm and start the chemistry of the cells of the seed. Anaerobic respiration may take place in seeds before germination but aerobic respiration begins after the splitting of the seed coat liberates the seed for further growth. Growth during germination requires enormous amounts of oxygen to sustain the rapid cell division and growth that occur during germination.

Longevity

Longevity, or the length of time a seed is viable and capable of germinating, varies greatly in plants. Seeds of the aquatic lotus plant have germinated after 1,000 years and arctic lupines have germinated after being frozen for 10,000 years or more in the tundra ice.

Generally, the viability of seeds varies greatly. The seeds of some plants such as willows, cottonwoods, orchids, and tea can survive only a few days or weeks, although their longevity can be extended by storage at low temperatures. Among common plants, members of the pumpkin family show some of the longest periods of seed viability. A familiar example of the importance of seed longevity and viability for humans is found on the packets of plant seeds. For example, seeds in stores are dated to indicate average usefulness. Each package has a date indicating when the seeds should give a high yield of germination. Each year after that fewer and fewer seeds will remain viable.

In some plants the embryo grows almost immediately following fertilization, hence there is no dormancy period and the longevity period is extremely short or nonexistent. This condition is called **vivipary** and is characteristic of the red mangrove. Seeds of red mangrove and similar plants must be discarded almost immediately after they are fertilized.

Key Words and Phrases

dicot	monocot	peduncle
receptacle	sepals	calyx
petal	inflorescence	gametes
pistil	stigma	style
superior ovary	egg	ovule
seed	imperfect flower	perfect flower
stamen	filament	anther
pollen grain	cross pollination	self pollination
fruit	pericarp	dehiscent seeds
indehiscent seeds	dispersal	endosperm
exocarp	cotyledon	radicle
longevity	vivipary	inferior ovary
wind dispersal	water dispersal	hilium
micropyle	plumule	hypocotyl
epicotyl	radicle	endocarp
mesocarp	simple fleshy fruit	drupe
berry	pepo	hesperidium
pome	aggregate fruit	multiple fruit

follicle	legume	silique
capsule	achene	nut
dry fruit	grain	samara

Selected References and Resources

Bewley, J. D., and M. Black. Eds. 1985. *Seeds: Physiology of Development and Germination*. Plenum Publishing Corporation. New York.

Duffus, C. M., and J. Slaughter. 1980. *Seeds and their Uses*. John Wiley and Sons. New York.

Holm, E. 1979. *The Biology of Flowers*. Penguin Books. New York.

D'Arcy, W. G., and R. C. Keating. 1996. *The Anther*. Cambridge University Press. New York.

Rudall, P. 1992. *Anatomy of Flowering Plants. An Introduction to Structure and Development*. 2nd. Edition. Cambridge University Press. New York.

Review and Discussion Questions

1. Which of the kinds of fruits are economically important as foods? As sources of fiber? As other products?
2. Morphologically and structurally, how does a flower become a fruit? Which parts of the flower become which parts of the fruit?
3. What are the four basic classes of fruits?
4. How are some fruits morphologically structured to facilitate dispersal by animals? By water? By air?
5. What is the advantage of dormancy. In what kinds of climates do we find the most numerous species that produce seeds with dormancy potential?

Water, Minerals, and Soil

Water is the magic ingredient of plants. It is the major component of plant cells, in which it comprises up to 90 percent of the volume of protoplasm. Water is also the avenue for the transport and distribution of foods, nutrients, and minerals throughout the body of the plant. Since all plant activities occur in water, through water, or by means of water, it is important for us to learn how water is absorbed, held, and moved through living plants. We will also examine the structure and composition of soils and how plants remove water and minerals from soils.

How Water and Minerals Move

In order to understand the absorption and flow of water and minerals in plants we must briefly review the basic physicochemical behavior of water and ions and how they each move from one location to another.

The movement of water and minerals is governed by simple processes. Basic to their movement is the fact that molecules and ions are in a constant state of agitation called **Brownian movement**, resulting from collisions at the atomic and molecular level. Brownian movement causes the diffusion of water and minerals from areas of greater concentration to areas of lesser concentration. Diffusion continues until the concentration of the substance is the same throughout the system, which is then in a state of equilibrium. Many chemicals needed by plants follow the basic rules of diffusion. For example, leaf cells require oxygen for cellular respiration. Since there is usually more oxygen in the air surrounding the leaves than in the leaf cells, oxygen diffuses from the air into the cells where it is consumed. Conversely, since there is often more carbon dioxide within the leaf cells, it diffuses outward into the air around the leaf.

Unfortunately, however, the movement of most minerals and other nutrients in plants involves water as a basic transport medium and is somewhat more complicated. Water is a **solvent**, which is a substance in which other materials may dissolve. Minerals, gases, and other nutrients dissolved or carried in the water are **solutes**. The movement of solutes such as minerals (usually in ion form) is regulated by concentration gradients, electrical charges, and the size of atoms and molecules that are affected by Brownian movement.

Like minerals, water moves by diffusion from its environment (the soil) where there is more water to areas (the plant) where there is less. Inside the plant, water moves across cell membranes following diffusion gradients in a process called **osmosis**. Most minerals are dissolved and carried in the water, so their movements and concentrations are closely tied with the movements of water.

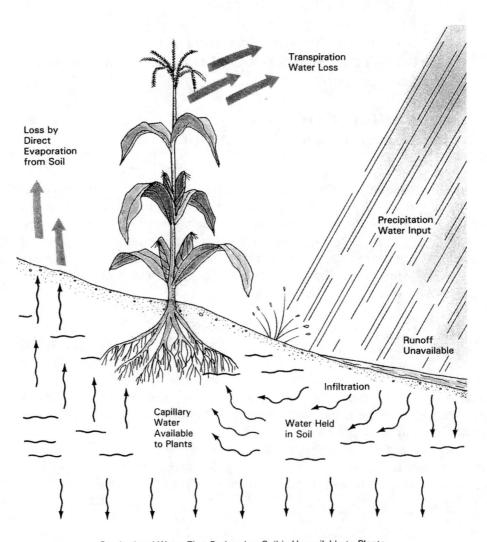

Gravitational Water That Drains thru Soil is Unavailable to Plants

Figure 9–1 The soil and water relationships of plants. *Source:* Bernard J. Nebel. *Environmental Science* (1990), Prentice-Hall, p. 159.

The Importance of Water to Plants

Water is an extremely important commodity in plants: more than 90 percent of the weight of young plant cells is water. Enzymes, proteins, and other chemicals are dissolved or carried in water in cells or in tissue water and almost all of the innumerable chemical reactions take place in water. Most water in plants is used to maintain turgor pressure which helps maintain cell shape and function, but some is also used in photosynthesis and other chemical events.

In plants, water moves freely from cell to cell in response to osmotic pressure gradients. If water is already in a cell, its presence can prevent more water from entering and further osmosis does not occur. The amount of water that a cell can hold is called the **osmotic potential**. Osmotic potential is important in plant cells because when water is absorbed into the cell, the cell wall reaches a point where it cannot expand any further and the cell becomes rigid or turgid. When this happens there is water pressure exerted on the cell walls to keep them stiff. This water pressure is called **turgor pressure** or **pressure potential**.

Water can also move out of cells in response to reduced osmotic pressures. If water diffuses out of a cell the turgor pressure is reduced because water leaves the cell

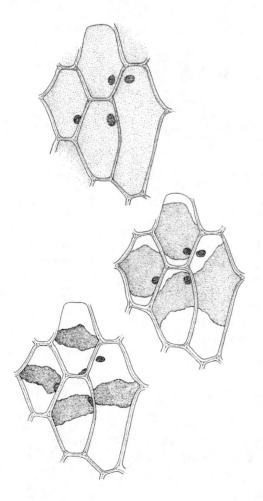

Figure 9–2 Changes in vacuoles of plant cells during plasmolysis (a) when the cell contains its normal water content (b) when the cell is in a sucrose solution some of the water leaves the cell and the cell membrane starts to shrink inwards, away from the cell wall (c) most of the water has moved out of the cell, the cell membrane has shrunken away from the cell wall and the cell is said to be plasmolyzed. *Source:* Roy H Saigo and Barbara Saigo. *Botany. Principles and Applications* (1983), Prentice-Hall, Figure 3–13, p. 41.

vacuoles and there is no longer enough water to keep the cells rigid. The cytoplasm shrinks away from the cell walls and they collapse inward in a process called **plasmolysis**. When the cell walls collapse the plant wilts.

The movement of water between cells and through the plant results from different osmotic pressures in different parts of the plant. Most plants need a constant supply of water to maintain cell shape and function. The amount of water that a plant needs is the **water potential**. The water potential is measured as a combination of the osmotic potential and the pressure potential.

Water Movement in Plants

Plants absorb water from the soil and, less frequently from moisture in the air. They lose some water through chemical reactions in cells (where water is chemically bonded with other molecules to form organic compounds, especially during photosynthesis, when water molecules are bound with carbon dioxide molecules to produce sugars.) However, plants lose most of their water through evaporation from leaf air spaces, open stomata, and the leaf surface. Smaller amounts are lost through the cuticle that covers the surface of the plant.

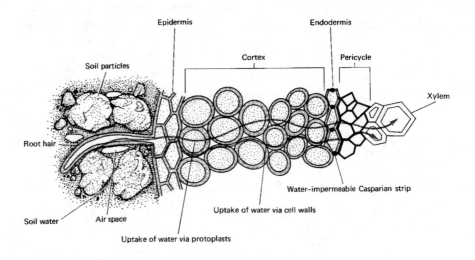

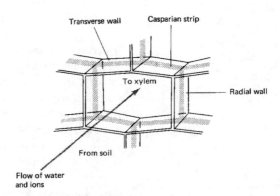

Figure 9–3 A summary of the mechanisms by which water moves out of the soil and into a plant. *Source:* Arthur W. Galston, Peter J. Davies, and Ruth L. Slater. *The Life of the Green Plant* (1980), Prentice-Hall. p. 148.

WATER ABSORPTION

Because water is continuously being lost through transpiration, through evaporation, and through metabolic activities, the plant needs to constantly replenish its water supply. Plants obtain most of their water through the millions of root hairs along the root. Following an osmotic gradient, water from the soil is absorbed into the root hairs and transferred into the cells of the root cortex. Still following an osmotic gradient, water is funneled into the endodermis and directed, by means of the waxy Casparian strips, into the root xylem. Once in the xylem, water is transported up through the stem and, via the vascular bundles, out into the leaves. In the leaves, water is transferred from the xylem into the mesophyll cells where some fraction of the water is tied up in chemical reactions such as photosynthesis. Most of the rest of the water escapes the leaf by transpiration through the open stomata or by evaporation through the leaf surfaces.

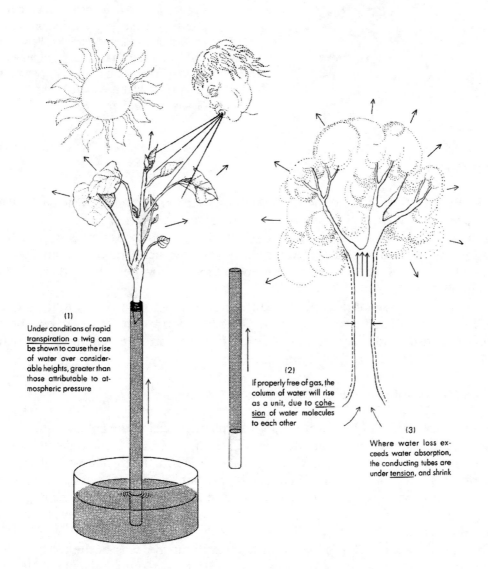

(1)
Under conditions of rapid transpiration a twig can be shown to cause the rise of water over considerable heights, greater than those attributable to atmospheric pressure

(2)
If properly free of gas, the column of water will rise as a unit, due to cohesion of water molecules to each other

(3)
Where water loss exceeds water absorption, the conducting tubes are under tension, and shrink

Figure 9–4 A general summary of how water rises in plants. *Source:* Arthur W. Galston, Peter J. Davies, and Ruth L. Slatter. *The Life of the Green Plant* (1980), Prentice-Hall, p. 159.

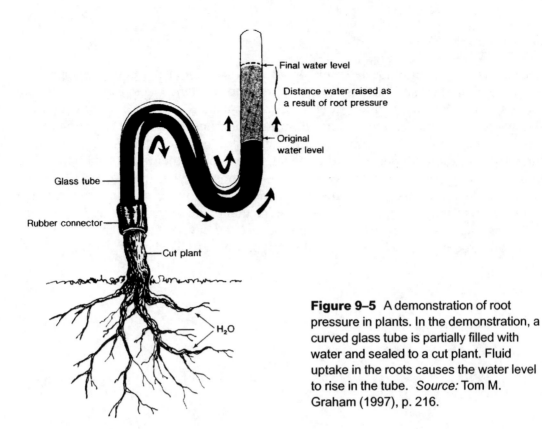

Glass tube

Rubber connector

Cut plant

Final water level

Distance water raised as
a result of root pressure

Original
water level

H₂O

Figure 9–5 A demonstration of root pressure in plants. In the demonstration, a curved glass tube is partially filled with water and sealed to a cut plant. Fluid uptake in the roots causes the water level to rise in the tube. *Source:* Tom M. Graham (1997), p. 216.

ROOT PRESSURE

Several factors contribute to the movement of water in the xylem. One such factor is **root pressure**. When a plant is pruned in the spring, water oozes from the cut stem. Water is rising as a result of root pressure, which is caused by water being absorbed by the roots in such quantities that water above is forced upward and eventually out the cut ends of the stems. Root pressure drops off in the summer when other factors are functioning.

Root pressure can at least partly explain how water is forced up into the stem, but root pressure isn't sufficient to get water up to the tops of the tallest trees. The most reasonable explanation for the movement of water from root xylem up through the stem to the leaves is called the **Cohesion-Tension Theory**.

COHESION-TENSION THEORY

Another explanation of how water moves in plants is called the cohesion-tension theory. According to this theory, as water evaporates from leaves the loss creates a pulling force on the water column below. Water molecules are electrically neutral but asymmetrically shaped so they are differently charged at each end—that is, they exhibit a polarity. This polarity causes water molecules to have a strong cohesive force, so they stick to each other and to the walls of the xylem vessels. As water evaporates from mesophyll cells in the leaf or as water is lost through the stomata, the cells develop lower water potential than adjacent cells throughout the cells of the xylem column. This produces a continuous pull or tension on the water column in the plant—from root to stem to leaves. This water tension is so strong that it can move water all the way from the roots to the top of a tree 300 feet or more in height. If the water column

Figure 9–6 The cohesion-tension theory of how water flows from the root to the leaf in plants. *Source:* Teresa Audesirk and Gerald Audesirk (1999), p. 472.

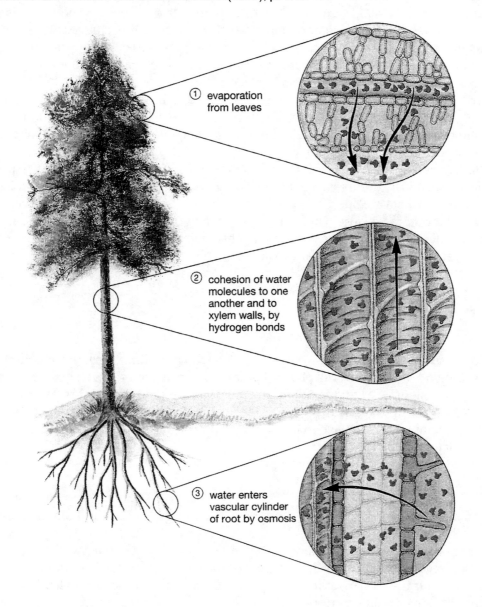

① evaporation from leaves

② cohesion of water molecules to one another and to xylem walls, by hydrogen bonds

③ water enters vascular cylinder of root by osmosis

breaks anywhere along the xylem, a gas bubble is introduced, breaking the continuous column of water in the xylem. This blocks further water movement until the plant repairs itself by absorption of more water.

BULK FLOW THEORY

A third factor that may contribute to water movement in plants is called the **bulk flow theory**. According to this idea, water and solutes in roots travel across the epidermis and cortex layers via cell walls until the water molecules reach the endodermis. Here the water is forced to cross the cytoplasm of the endodermal cells due to Casparian strips which form an impermeable layer between the cells. When the plant is actively transpiring, water may move by **bulk flow** instead of osmosis. Bulk flow is simply the rapid flow of water from an area of high water concentration to an area of low water potential.

Under some circumstances, water may also enter a plant through a process called **imbibition**. As we have learned earlier, the protoplasm of plant cells is a kind of colloidal suspension. Colloids are suspensions of materials that contain fine particles and large molecules like cellulose and starch which have electrical charges. These molecules attract water. Water molecules exhibit polarity in that they have different charges at each end. Because of this they are attracted to large organic molecules and become cohesive in that they stick to one another.

This process of colloids attracting water is called **imbibition** and is responsible for causing cells to swell to several times their normal size. Imbibition is important in the germination of seeds, as imbibition pressure can become forceful enough that germinating seeds can actually split rocks.

Regardless of how it is accomplished, the movement of water through plants occurs continuously during daylight hours when leaf cells are actively photosynthesizing and the stomata are open. It is slowed or stopped at night when the photosynthesis stops and the stomata close. This form of water movement is absolutely necessary for plant functioning, but water loss must be conserved as well and the plant has mechanisms that balance water use against water loss.

Water Loss in Plants

The process of water loss from stomata is called **transpiration**, or **evapotranspiration**. Transpiration is a very powerful physical process. A single corn plant transpires an average of four gallons of water a week through its surfaces. One acre of corn can transpire 350,000 gallons of water in a 100 day growing season. If we were to use as much water as a corn plant we would have to drink ten gallons of water a day just to maintain our water balance.

CONTROLS ON TRANSPIRATION RATES

Transpiration in plants is controlled by the activity of guard cells and stomata. Guard cells with elastic walls surround and encase the stomata. Each guard cell is shaped like a sausage-shaped balloon. The stomata open and close due to changes in turgor pressure in the guard cells. The stomata are closed when the turgor pressure is low and open when it is high. Changes in turgor pressure occur due to changes in light intensity, carbon dioxide, or water concentration.

The turgor pressure within the guard cells changes as osmosis and active transport occur between guard cells and the epidermal cells around them. During active transport there is an ion exchange and guard cells take up potassium ions and chloride ions from adjacent cells. Energy is expended by guard cells as they take up potassium ions. The uptake of potassium by the guard cells changes their osmotic pressure and results in the cells absorbing water, increasing the turgor pressure and causing the cells to swell. As the cells swell, the inner wall (the wall adjacent to the stomata opening) of each guard cell is thinner than the outer wall and will shrink inwards. This causes the stomata to open. When the guard cells release potassium ions, turgor pressure drops as water leaves the cell by osmosis. The guard cells collapse and the stomata close. The guard cells may continue to shrink and become partly plasmolyzed.

The stomata can also be chemically controlled by hormones. If the mesophyll cells of leaves are subject to water stress they produce a hormone called **abscisic acid**. Abscisic acid increases the loss of potassium ions from the guard cells and reduces

Figure 9–7 The opening and closing of stomata in leaves following turgor movements. *Source:* Tom M. Graham (1997), p. 185.

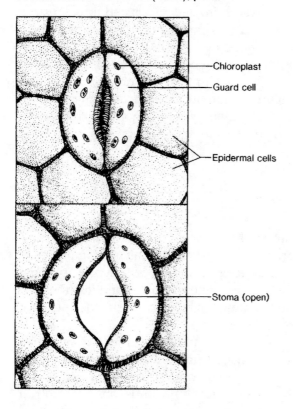

- Chloroplast
- Guard cell
- Epidermal cells
- Stoma (open)

their osmotic potential. Water leaves the guard cells and they collapse, closing the stomata. In contrast, if there is sufficient water, mesophyll cells don't secrete abscisic acid and the guard cells remain open.

The stomata of most plants open during the day and close at night. In some desert plants, however, the stomata may open during the night and close during the day to conserve water. Since sunlight heats up the surface of a plant and causes evaporation of water from open stomata, many desert plants take added precautions to avoid excessive water loss during the heat of the day. Instead, they open at night when cooler ambient temperatures reduce their rate of water loss. Some desert plants also have a special photosynthetic process called **CAM photosynthesis** in which the plant stores carbon dioxide chemically for use during the day while the stomata are closed.

Other desert plants protect against excessive water loss by having their stomata sunken in pores covered by epidermal hairs. Conversely, in the tropics some plants have stomata raised above the surface of the leaf to increase the transpiration rate. Water plants lack stomata on the submerged surfaces of their leaves.

Wind conditions, changes in humidity, and changes in temperature may also influence the activity of stomata. Water gradients in leaves may be affected by air currents sweeping away water molecules as they emerge from stomata in a kind of surface evaporation. Humidity may play a role as well. During periods of high humidity the air is saturated with water and this will reduce the rate of transpiration. On the other hand, low humidity will normally increase the transpiration rate. Temperature may also play

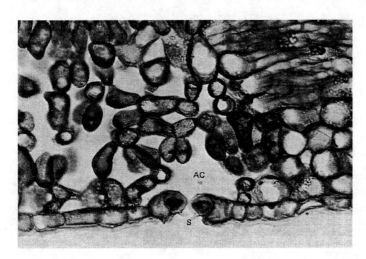

Figure 9–8 Cross section of a leaf with open stomata and interior air cavity. *Source:* Arthur W. Galston, Peter J. Davies, and Ruth L. Slatter. *The Life of the Green Plant* (1980), Prentice-Hall, p. 150.

a role as high temperatures increase the chemical activity of plant cells and raise the rate of transpiration while low temperatures decrease chemical activity and transpiration rates.

If a cool night follows a warm humid day, water droplets, produced through structures called **hydathodes**, form at the tips of veins in some plants. The loss of water in this fashion is called **guttation**. The water resembles dew but dew is from the condensation of water in the air, while guttated water is from root pressure. As guttated water evaporates, it leaves behind a residue of salt concentrates and organic substances which can be harvested. MSG (monosodium glutamate), the active ingredient in Accent, a flavor enhancer, is one such product obtained by guttation. In the tropics, guttated water from the taro plant is used by Polynesians to make poi.

Phloem Transport of Foods

Phloem vessels transport food and other nutrients in a solution of water from one part of the plant to another. During the summer months, most of the transport in phloem is from the leaves and stems, where food is produced, to the roots, where it is stored. Food and other nutrients produced in the leaves are also transported and distributed to the cells of leaves and roots for metabolism. In spring the reverse occurs; food stored in the roots is transported to the other tissues of the growing plant.

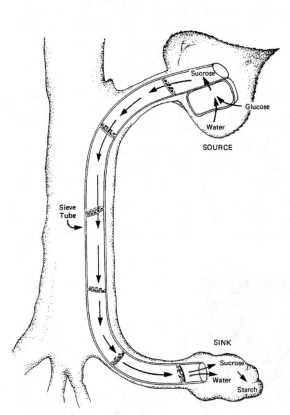

Figure 9–9 The pressure-flow hypothesis of phloem transport in plants. *Source:* Roy H. Saigo and Barbara W. Saigo. *Botany: Principles of Applications* (1990), Prentice-Hall, p. 89.

This transport of food in phloem is called **translocation**. Water is involved because water is a solvent. Since most organic compounds are insoluble in water, plants transport food and nutrients in simple, soluble forms. For example, most carbohydrates are converted into molecules of disaccharide sucrose and then transported in phloem. Insoluble proteins and fats are broken down into amino acids and fatty acids, respectively, before entering the phloem. Movement in phloem is up to 100 centimeters per hour which is much too rapid to be done by diffusion or cyclosis.

Exactly how food and other nutrients are transported in phloem is unclear, because it seems to vary with the accepted rules that substances diffuse from areas of greater concentration to areas of lesser concentration. For example, since sugars are manufactured in leaves there is usually more sugar in leaves than in the stem and in the root, where the sugar is to be transported. The answer is best explained by a theory called the **Pressure-Flow Hypothesis**.

Figure 9–10 Aphids feeding on the sugary fluid of phloem. *Source:* Teresa Audesirk and Gerald Audesirk (1999), p. 475.

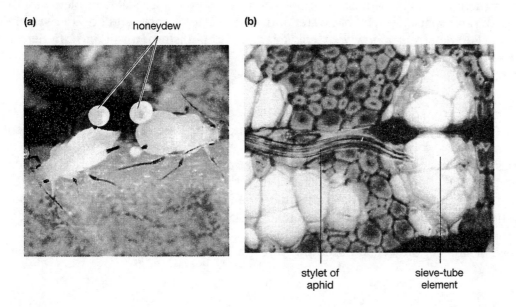

(a) honeydew

(b)

stylet of aphid   sieve-tube element

PRESSURE-FLOW HYPOTHESIS

According to this theory, food flows from a source where it is manufactured to a sink where food is utilized. A **sink** is a place where water is lost and the solute (in this case sugars and starch) are concentrated. Food in plants moves along concentration gradients based on water, with water going from its own area of high concentration to an area of low.

Active transport helps direct and accomplish this movement. Leaf cells actively transport sugars into the sieve tubes of phloem in the leaves. Increased concentrations of sugars in the leaf phloem cells raise the osmotic potential and water flows into the phloem from surrounding cells. This inflow of water helps "drive" the fluid through the sieve tubes toward the sink.

At the sink (e.g., the roots) cells actively transport the sugars from the phloem into the cells. As sugar is removed from the phloem tube at the sink, water also leaves, causing water pressure at the sink ends of sieve tubes to be lowered. This, in turn, continues the mass flow of sugars and other carbohydrates from source to sink. Following the delivery of sugars to cells of the sink, most of the water returns to the xylem where it is carried back to the leaves and eventually transpired.

Soil—The Source of Water and Nutrients

Soil is the uppermost part of the earth's crust that is dynamic and changing. Soil may be thin or up to hundreds of feet thick. Soil is usually a complex mixture of ingredients, including sand, rocks, pebbles, silt, clay, humus, dead leaves, twigs, clods of clay and organic matter, plant roots, small animals like ants, pill bugs, millipedes, earthworms and many microorganisms, such as bacteria, fungi, and soil protozoa.

SOIL STRUCTURE

The structure of soil is almost as important as its ingredients. Soil is tunneled by millions of **pore spaces** which hold water and air. The size of pores and how densely they are packed determines how well soil is aerated. In undisturbed soil one can detect a series of **horizons**. In a soil profile, the horizons illustrate different stages of soil development.

O Horizon

The uppermost layer of the soil is the O horizon. It contains surface litter of freshly fallen and partly decomposed plant materials, leaves, stems, twigs, flower and fruit parts, and other organic materials including decaying animal remains and animal exudate. Although the O horizon is typically thin it shows a decay gradient from top to bottom; leaves, twigs, dead animals and other organic material are constantly being added to the surface layer of the soil. As more layers of organic materials accumulate above them, these fragments of plants and animals decompose and intermix with dirt. As these decay and are decomposed they are gradually reduced to a consistent organic debris.

A Horizon

Immediately beneath the leaf litter horizon is the **A horizon**. This horizon consists of decomposing organic matter called humus, plant roots, minerals, and a wide variety of soil organisms. The A horizon is generally what we call topsoil and is the richest and most fertile layer. The A Horizon can be subdivided into several layers. The top part of the A Horizon is often darker in color than the other layers and contains most of the organic matter of the soil. This layer is called the **A1 layer**. The layers of the A horizon are the major zones of active decomposition. Bacteria, fungi, protozoa and other soil microorganisms decompose the organic matter of plant and animal remains. Towards the base of the A horizon—deep within the A2 layer—these materials will be more-or-less completely broken down into minerals such as calcium, magnesium, and phosphorous.

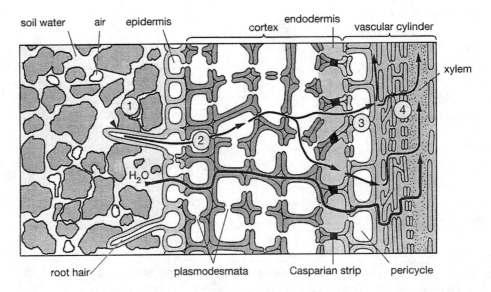

Figure 9–11 Mineral and water uptake by roots. *Source:* Teresa Audesirk and Gerald Audesirk (1999), p. 464.

As these minerals are released via decomposition they may be leached from the soil by the action of water. This typically occurs in the lowest layer of the A horizon, which is called the zone of leaching. Minerals that have been freed by decomposing of the organic material in the A horizon are leached out of this layer by the percolation of water down to the water table, leaving behind a featureless and rather infertile layer of soil. Some soil scientists make a distinction between the A horizon area of decomposition which they term the A horizon, and the area of leaching, which they call the **E horizon**.

B Horizon

Beneath the top soil of the A horizon (or E horizon) is the **B horizon**, or subsoil, containing more clay. Lighter in color, the B horizon can often be seen as a distinct grayish layer beneath the darker and richer organic layers of the A horizon. This is the soil one sees most commonly exposed in a new housing development where the top soil, or A horizon, has been stripped away leaving the B Horizon. Some topsoil will be returned and spread over the subsoil upon completion of the building.

The B horizon is area where the minerals leached from the A horizon are deposited. This is also the soil horizon into which most plant roots penetrate in order to absorb these now available minerals. The base of the B horizon grades into the parent material which is called the C horizon.

C Horizon

The **C Horizon** consists of unaltered rock and other debris. Depending on its geological history, parent material accumulates from the weathering of igneous rocks derived from volcanic activity. Fragments of rock are moved by glacial activity. Climate varies from place to place and weathering action varies accordingly. In deserts there is not much weathering by rain and the formation of soils is slow. In areas of high rainfall there may be good soils, especially if there is volcanic activity. Where the climate provides great temperature changes, rocks are cracked and broken apart by frost wedging.

R Horizon

Beneath the weathered rock and debris of the C horizon is the parent bedrock which is labeled the R horizon (R = regolith horizon). The R horizon is undisturbed except for fracturing but when exposed will weather to create the C horizon.

SOIL ORGANISMS

The soil is home to a variety and abundance of plants and animals and other organisms. Plants sink their roots into soil, thereby altering its structure and in some cases its texture. Their occurrence also helps trap wind-driven dirt and other debris, in the process building up soil. When they die, their roots and other structures add organic matter to soil. Larger animals burrow in soil, dig in soil, take refuge in soil, and otherwise transform it in various ways. The variety and abundance of soil animals also contribute importantly to soil formation, fertility, and function.

The comparative abundance and importance of soil organisms is shown in Table 9-1. Bacteria, fungi, and plants are, by weight, the most important soil organisms.

Figure 9–12 The relationship between plants and soils and soil nutrients. *Source:* Bernard J. Nebel. *Environmental Science* (1990), Prentice-Hall, p. 158.

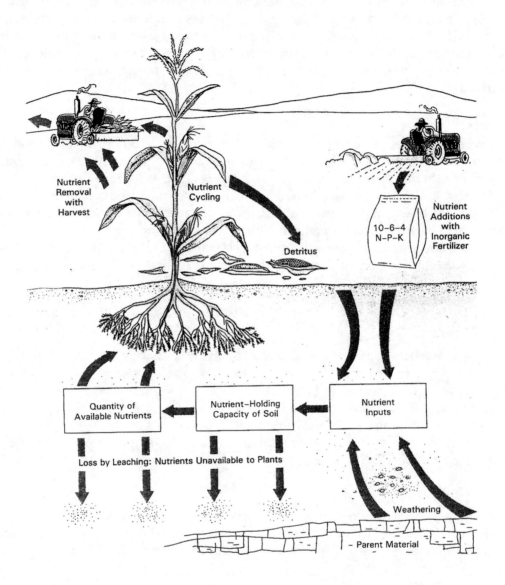

Table 9-1 Weight of soil organisms in an acre of fertile soil.

Organisms	Abundance by weight in pounds
Bacteria	2200
Fungi (molds, yeasts, club and true fungi)	2100
Animal protistans (the protozoa)	200
Soil algae	100
Worms (roundworms = nematodes, segmented worms = annelids)	650
Insects and other invertebrates	450

Animal activities also alter the structure, texture, and often the organic content of soil. Most of the smaller animals, fungi, bacteria and protozoa are found in the A horizon. These living organisms can be abundant in soil; for example, a handful of soil may hold several million bacteria along with assorted fungi and protozoa. By weight, soil microorganisms may comprise about one-thousandth of the weight of soil, or about 3 tons per acre. Bacteria, fungi, and soil protozoa are important decomposers of organic matter in soil. Roots of plants and all other organisms produce carbon dioxide which combines with water to produce carbonic acid. This weak acid dissolves minerals and helps to break down parent material. Animals also cultivate soil by their activities. Worms are especially important as they constantly turn the soil over. They also produce a vast amount of organic wastes which add to the nutrients in the soil. Finally, when plants and animals die their bodies decompose and add to the organic material in the soil.

SOIL COMPOSITION

If we analyze an average sample of topsoil we will find that it consists of about 25 percent air, 25 percent water, 48 percent minerals, and 2 percent organic matter. Soil in low wet areas has little oxygen and little microorganism activity. Wet soils accumulate unaltered organic material to the point were it may be up to 90% organic matter. This is rich loam which can be sold as highly priced topsoil. Except in legumes, almost all nitrogen for plants comes from decomposing organic matter. Decay also produces acids that break down minerals and consume available oxygen in the pore spaces. That is why a humus pile must be turned periodically - to replace oxygen that has been depleted by the decaying process.

SOIL QUALITY

Soil quality is influenced by the topography of the land. Steep slopes are subject to erosion by water or wind, leaving behind a barren and infertile landscape comprised mostly of rocks and other inorganic debris. Flat and poorly drained areas that accumulate water such as wetlands and ponds are normally not well oxygenated and have little animal variety. Without animals, decomposition is slowed and the soils are consequently infertile. The ideal topography is that which allows good drainage but not erosion. Well drained soils provide good substrates for plants to root and hold the soil. Organic matter accumulates and decomposers are abundant, creating soils of high quality and fertility.

SOIL TEXTURE

Both soil texture and mineral composition determine the ability of soil to be useful to plants. Soils containing sands and gravels are usually composed of many small particles bound together chemically or by a cementing matrix. **Silt** is a soil composed of particles that are mostly too small to be seen by the naked eye. These tiny particles, when dry, turn to a fine dust. **Clay** is soil that contains particles called **micelles**. These particles are sheetlike, negatively charged, and held together by chemical bonds. The electrical charges attract, exchange or retain positively charged ions. Clay is a plastic-like material because water adhering to the surface acts as a lubricant and makes it slippery.

Because of particle size and content, soil texture can vary greatly. Light soils have high sand and low clay content, while heavy soils have high clay content. Coarse textured soils do not hold much water and clay does not allow water to pass through.

The texture of soil is determined by the size and arrangement of soil particles. These soil particles are arranged into groups or **aggregates**. In sand and gravels there is little cohesion and not many aggregates. Agricultural soils have aggregates that stick together and thus hold many nutriments. In productive agricultural soils we have granular soils with pore spaces that occupy between 40–60% of the total volume of the soil. That is important as the pores contain vital air and water. In clay soils there are actually more pore spaces than sandy soils, but the pores are so small that water and air are restricted in movement. The sandy soils have large pores that drain by gravity. Water is replaced by air but this speeds nitrogen release and plants are unable to use the nitrogen up fast enough. Thus most nitrogen and other nutrients that occur in the soil may be lost in runoff.

Water is a major factor in the problem of runoff. Too much water leaches out minerals from the top layers of the soil. Waterlogged conditions slow the release of nitrogen and accelerate breakdown of nitrates present in the soil; as a result almost all nitrates are lost in runoff. To relate this in a practical way, houseplants frequently die because of too frequent and too much watering, thereby flushing the nutrients out of the soil before the plant has a chance to absorb them. Just a hint - don't water your plants until the surface of the soil is dry.

SOIL WATER

The water that is found in soil occurs in three forms. **Hygroscopic water** is water molecules that are physically bound to soil particles and unavailable for plant use. **Gravitational water** is the water which drains out of pore spaces after a rain. That is, gravitational water percolates down through the soil to the water table and is generally unavailable to plants. If there is too much runoff, gravitational water will leach away the nutrients. If there is poor drainage gravitational water collects in the upper layers of soil and causes waterlogging of soils. Water logged soils interfere with plant growth and are generally infertile. The third kind of water in the soil is called **capillary water**, which is the water that stays in the pore spaces and is most useful to plants. The chemical structure of the soil and the amount of organic matter within the soil also affect its ability to hold water.

After a rain or following irrigation, the gravitational water drains away by gravity. The water remaining is the **field capacity** of the soil, represented mostly by capillary water. This is controlled by the texture (its porosity) of the soil and its chemical structure. Plants can absorb water when the soil water holding capacity it is at or near field capacity level. As the soil dries, the water around each particle shrinks until it is unable to be tapped by the root. If more water is not added, eventually the plant wilts. Soil is then at the **permanent wilting point**. In clays, the permanent wilting point is reached when the water content drops below 15%. In sandy soils the permanent wilting point may be as low as 4%.

SOIL pH

The **pH** or hydrogen ion concentration of soil affects the soil and the plants growing in it. The pH scale ranges from 0 to 14. A pH of 7 is neutral while anything between 8–14 is considered basic or alkaline while a pH between 0 and 6 is acidic. Soil pH is affected by the interaction of water, soil organisms, and soil minerals. Soils that are too acid or too alkaline may be toxic to plant roots.

Acid soils contain large amounts of H^+ ions which are a byproduct of the chemical reaction between CO_2 and H_2O that produces carbonic acid as follows: CO_2 + H_2O

$\longrightarrow$ H_2CO_3 (carbonic acid) which then disassociates into H^+ and HCO_3^- ions. Acidic soils are common in areas where there is high rainfall and much leaching of minerals that would normally buffer the free hydrogen ions. Acidic soils inhibit the growth of nitrogen-fixing bacteria and other organisms useful to many plants. In addition, acidic soils are susceptible to heavy leaching of soil minerals such as calcium and potassium. We reduce acidity of soils by adding carbonates of calcium or magnesium in the spring of the year in a process called liming.

Alkaline soils form when salts of calcium, sodium, and magnesium accumulate and have high concentrations of OH^- ions. Soils high in sodium salts are especially toxic to plants and also have poor drainage, aeration, and low permeability. Alkaline soils with high concentrations of calcium carbonate are called black alkali and are common in the southwestern United States and similar desert regions across the earth where salts accumulate because of low rainfall. As the alkalinity of the soil increases, many minerals become chemically bound to soil particle and are unavailable to plants. Farmers and gardeners treat alkaline soils with applications of organic fertilizers high in phosphates which remove OH^- ions and thereby reduce alkalinity.

SOIL FERTILITY

The fertility of soil is determined by the dissolved nutrients found within. Oxygen is the most common element in view of the weight of all soil minerals. Other common elements include hydrogen, silicon, aluminum, iron, potassium, calcium, magnesium and sodium. Plant nutrients are stored in the form of ions and there are more in clay and top soil than in sand and silt.

Plant Nutrition

All living systems require minerals for healthy growth. Plants are no exceptions but rather have very specific mineral requirements. Of the 92 naturally occurring elements (minerals and non-metals), 46 have been found in plants and other living organisms. Some 20 or so are absolutely essential for most plants; they are used as building blocks for the numerous chemical molecules and compounds. The four most important elements required by plants include carbon, hydrogen, oxygen, and nitrogen. These are the basic atomic components found in all of the organic chemicals of plants. Plants obtain carbon and hydrogen from carbon dioxide or from water molecules. Oxygen is obtained from the air or from oxygen dissolved in water. Despite its abundance in the atmosphere, nitrogen is considerably more difficult for plants to obtain a suitable form. Most uptake is through nitrogen fixed by fungi or bacteria or in the form of nitrogen compounds in the soil.

MINERALS IMPORTANT TO PLANTS

At least 15 minerals are essential to plants. Most of these minerals are available to the plant in either ionized form or in organic substances in soil. Minerals that are required in comparatively large amounts, generally greater than a tenth of a percent (0.1 percent) by dry weight, are called **macronutrients**.

Table 9-2 Six of the most important essential elements in plants.

Element	Source	% composition by dry weight
Carbon	CO_2 in atmosphere and soil	45
Oxygen	O_2 or CO_2 from air or water, or directly from H_2O	45
Hydrogen	H_2O	6
Nitrogen	NO_3^- (nitrate) or NH_4^+ (ammonium) from soil, fungi, or nitrogen fixing bacteria	1.5–2
Potassium	soil or as ion dissolved in water	1.0–1.5
Calcium	soil or as ion dissolved in water column	0.5
Magnesium	soil or as ion dissolved in water	0.2
Phosphorus	H_2PO_4 or HPO_4^- in soils or in water column	0.2

The Macronutrients

Some of the macronutrients, such as nitrogen, phosphorous, and sulfur are additional chemical components of proteins or nucleic acids. A sampling of mineral elements and the role in plants is presented in Table 9-3. Most of the macronutrients function as key components in the molecular structure of DNA, chlorophyll, cytochromes, and other metabolically essential plant molecules or as components of enzymes.

Phosphorous, for example, is part of all DNA and RNA molecules as well as the energy molecule ATP. Phosphorus is also an essential ingredient in many plant processes including photosynthesis, respiration, flowering and fruiting, and in protein synthesis. Lack of phosphorus causes stunted growth and reduced yields. Gardeners add bone meal or superphosphate compounds to their garden soils to ensure that their flowers have sufficient phosphorous available.

Sulfur figures in the tertiary structure of proteins and in some amino acids. Because of its importance some plants such as onions and garlic hoard large quantities of sulfur in their roots. Sulfur is normally abundant in soils in the form of SO_4^- ions but may be lacking in alkaline soils. Sulfur deficiency in plants causes a yellow spotting of leaves and results in reduced growth and metabolic efficiency.

Potassium plays many roles in plants. It increases growth, especially of roots, acts as an enzyme activator, and stimulates the conversion of pyruvic acid which is an absolutely essential event in the aerobic respiration pathway that produces ATP. Potassium is also an osmotic ingredient necessary for guard cell functioning. Some of the deficiency symptoms of potassium include yellowing of leaves and restricted growth. Under extreme deficiencies stems are weakened and readily blown over in windstorms and rainstorms. Because of its importance to so many aspects of plant metabolism, potassium is a key component of most applied fertilizers, along with nitrogen and phosphorus.

Calcium is involved in altering the permeability of the plant cell membranes to several minerals, thereby permitting exchanges between cells and also in the uptake of minerals from the soil. It is also needed to assemble the spindle fibers that radiate from the chromosomes to the centrioles (the spindle bundle) during mitosis. Without calcium, cells cannot divide and further growth stops.

Magnesium is a central component of the chlorophyll molecule and absolutely necessary for molecular formation and for photosynthesis. The first signs of magnesium

Table 9-3 The functions of minerals in plants.

Nutrient	Function	Deficiency
Macronutrients		
Potassium	enzyme component in synthesis of sugars, starches, proteins	weak, wilting stalks and roots, mottling and curling leaves
Nitrogen	basic component of amino acids, nucleic acids, chlorophyll	growth stunted, yellowing and dying leaves
Calcium	component of middle lamella, promotes cell division,	death of terminal buds and reduced growth
Phosphorus	nucleic acid and ATP component,	stunted growth, reduced yields
Sulfur	maintain tertiary structure of proteins, vitamin component	weak stems and reduced growth with yellowing leaves
Magnesium	central component of chlorophyll molecule, enzyme component	chlorotic plants with drooping leaves
Micronutrients		
Chlorine	unit of photosynthesis pathway, also in root and shoot growth	wilting plants with bronzing, necrotic leaves
Copper	enzyme component	death of terminal buds and leaves, stunted growth
Iron	used in chlorophyll synthesis	leaf chlorosis
Boron	stimulates flowering and fruiting, turgor pressure and water movement	terminal buds, lateral branches and leaves die
Zinc	stimulates auxin, chlorophyll and enzyme synthesis	abnormal roots and bronzed leaves
Molybdenum	component of enzymes involved in nitrogen uptake and use in plant	pale, nitrogen deficient leaves become rolled and die
Manganese	coenzyme, as in chlorophyll synthesis	leaves whiten, die and fall off

deficiency are a yellowing or chlorosis of leaves which ultimately wilt and die. Magnesium is also an important activator of many plant enzymes.

The Micronutrients

Conversely, micronutrients are chemicals needed in lesser amounts, sometimes only in minute quantities. However, both micronutrients and macronutrients represent the basic chemical needs of plants. Their abundance and their distribution within an ecosystem directly affects the abundance and distribution of plant species that require them. Furthermore, if the soil or water supply of any macronutrients or micronutrients becomes depleted or absent, plants exhibit characteristic symptoms of **mineral deficiency**. These include decreased metabolism and growth because of the lack of sufficient numbers and kinds of enzymes needed and a general weakening of the plant. Serious deficiencies of even one plant nutrient may eventually lead to plant death. Some specific micronutrient needs are described in the following section.

Molybdenum and **boron** are important in nitrogen metabolism but the exact mode of their actions in plants remains unknown. The lack of sufficient boron causes browning and rot in apples and sugar beets, for example, and tissue decay.

Manganese is involved in the release of oxygen during photosynthesis. It apparently acts as a cofactor to stimulate the photolysis of water: $H_2O \longrightarrow 2H^+ + 2$ electrons $+ \frac{1}{2}$

O_2. A lack of manganese impairs photosynthesis and is first evidenced by the spotting of leaves, which turn pale and gray. Leaf loss follows and the defoliated plant dies.

Zinc and **Copper** are enzyme cofactors necessary for a variety of crucial metabolic events. Copper is needed for the conversion of nitrite to ammonium while zinc aids the formation of ammonium to nitrogen needed to synthesize amino acids. Deficiencies of either micronutrient result in stunted growth but lack of zinc is manifested by a spotting of interveinal areas and shorter internodes of twigs while copper deficiency causes a withering of shoot tips and leaf tips.

Iron is another micronutrient that functions as a cofactor in metabolically important enzymes. Iron is a component of many of the cytochromes which carry the hydrogen electrons during respiration. Lack of iron impairs this critical phase of ATP energy production. Iron also helps catalyze the synthesis of chlorophyll, another absolutely essential plant need. Because it is so critical, iron deficiency quickly shows up, first in the yellowing of leaves, then veins, and finally stems. Application of iron to soils in the form of iron chelates, iron sulfate, or iron citrate will quickly correct these symptoms.

Key Words and Phrases

diffusion	osmosis	solute
solvent	water potential	plasmolysis
imbibition	active transport	transpiration
root pressure	Cohesion-Tension theory	bulk flow
translocation	Pressure-Flow hypothesis	guttation
soil horizons	soil/silt/clay	hygroscopic water
gravitational water	capillary water	permanent wilting point

Selected References and Resources

Baker, D. A. 1990. *Transport of Photoassimilates.* Halsted Press. New York.

Donahue, R., and J. Miller. 1983. *Soils. An Introduction to Soils and Plant Growth.* Prentice-Hall. Englewood Cliffs, New Jersey.

Epstein, Emanuel. 1972. *Mineral Nutrition of Plants. Principles and Perspectives.* John Wiley and Sons. New York.

Kramer, P. 1983. *Water Relations of Plants.* Academic Press. San Diego, California.

Luettge, U., and N. Higinbotham. 1979. *Transport in Plants.* Springer-Verlag. New York.

Peel, A. J. 1974. *Transport of Nutrients in Plants.* John Wiley and Sons. New York.

Singer, M. J. 1986. *Soils.* Macmillian Publishing Company. New York.

Wardlaw, I. F., and J. B. Passioura. Eds. 1976. *Transport and Transfer Processes in Plants.* Academic Press. New York.

Zimmerman, M. H., and J. A. Milburn. Eds. 1976. *Transport in Plants: Phloem Transport.* Springer-Verlag. New York.

Review and Discussion Questions

1. Distinguish between macronutrients and micronutrient of plants.
2. How are minerals absorbed by plants? That is, how does the root structure and shoot structure and water flow contribute to water and mineral absorption and transportation in the plant?
3. Trace the path of a water molecule from the soil to the leaf surface.
4. Trace the path of a sugar molecule from the leaves to the root.
5. What climatic factors influence transpiration rates? What morphological and physiological mechanisms do plants use to control transpiration rates?
6. Describe the components and processes involved in soil formation.
7. Describe how field capacity and wilting coefficient relate to soil water.

Chapter 10

Photosynthesis and Respiration

Cell Energy Sources
Photosynthesis
    Components
    Light Reactions
    Dark Reactions
    Three-carbon Pathway
    Four-carbon Pathway
Respiration
    Glycolysis
    Krebs Citric Acid Cycle
    Electron Transport System
    ATP Molecules

Green plants are unique among all living things in being able to trap solar energy and convert it into the chemical energy of simple sugars and other carbohydrates. This chemical form of energy is then used by plants to power their activities and as energy and substrates to manufacture other tissues. Since plants are the only organisms with this capability, all animals are ultimately dependent on plants for their food as well. As a result, green plants form the base of almost all food chains in nature and are the ultimate source of energy for all ecosystems and the biosphere. The ability of plants to manufacture their own food separates them from animals and other organisms; plants and other organisms that manufacture their own food by means of photosynthesis are called **autotrophs** while organisms that consume other organisms as a source of energy are **heterotrophs**.

As we have learned before, all living cells require energy to survive and energy to reproduce, grow or do work. There are actually two processes that operate in plant cells that are used to produce energy and put it to work in cells. During **photosynthesis** plant cells use the energy of sunlight trapped by chlorophyll to combine carbon dioxide and water and make sugar, giving off oxygen as a by-product during the reaction. Plants (and other organisms) consume the sugar to produce energy for cellular work in a process called **oxidative respiration**. During respiration, the sugar molecule is metabolically fragmented, releasing its stored energy for work (powering enzyme reactions within the cell). Carbon dioxide and water are the by-product released.

Whether plants, animals, or bacteria, all living organisms require energy to survive. This energy is produced and consumed at the cellular level. The energy molecule used by all plant cells is called adenosine triphosphate (ATP). Chemically ATP consists of a molecule of adenine and ribose sugar to which are bonded three phosphate molecules.

ATP and other energy trapping molecules of cells are considered to be high energy phosphate compounds. They are made of adenine, glucose and phosphoric acid. The simplest compound in the system is adenine monophosphate (AMP), which has no high energy bonds. When free energy is present with phosphorous, AMP is changed to **adenine diphosphate (ADP)** which now has one high energy bond. A further addition of energy makes ADP into **adenine triphosphate (ATP)** which has 2 high energy phosphate bonds and is the storage form of energy in the cell. The process by which each phosphate molecule is added is called **phosphorylation**. In ATP, the third phosphate is

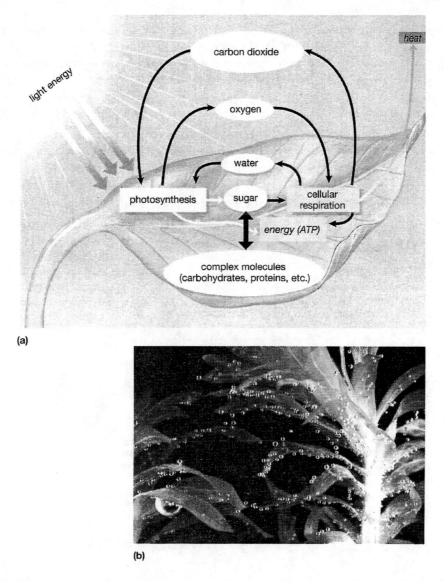

(a)

(b)

Figure 10–1 The relationships between photosynthesis and respiration. *Source:* Teresa Audesirk and Gerald Audesirk (1999), p. 112.

held by a high energy bond which, when broken, releases energy (about 7.3 kcal/mole) for cellular work. For example, ATP is formed by adding a phosphate molecule to ADP in the chemical reaction as follows:

$$ADP + P + energy \longrightarrow ATP$$

Should the cell need energy, the terminal phosphate of ATP is broken and the energy contained within that bond, equal to about 7.3 kcal/mole, is converted into useful work by the plant. At this point, ATP becomes ADP again and more energy from respiration must be used to reform (phosphorylate) ATP. In cells, ATP is formed from the systematic dismantling of molecules of glucose and other organic chemicals.

Photosynthesis

COMPONENTS

Photosynthesis is the single most important chemical reaction in the world. It is the sole means of supporting life as it produces oxygen and traps solar energy in the form of sugar. Despite the fact that there are tremendous numbers of land plants, much of photosynthesis occurs in the ocean. Photosynthesis is important to animals as well. It has been estimated that 40-50% of atmospheric oxygen, which is necessary for animal life, comes from this source.

By definition photosynthesis is the process whereby the cells of leaves, stems and other green parts of plants trap energy from sunlight and convert it through a series of steps into a chemical form of energy. The energy is stored in the form of sugar molecules which are produced by the interaction of carbon dioxide and water in a chloroplast in the presence of chlorophyll. In the process oxygen is released. Let us begin our discussion of photosynthesis by examining each of the active participants.

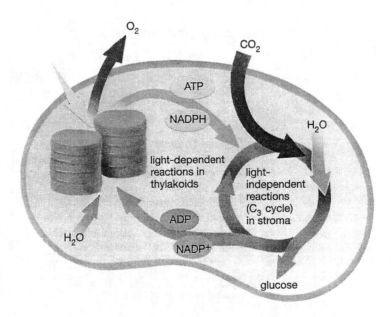

Figure 10–2 A summary of photosynthesis. *Source:* Teresa Audesirk and Gerald Audesirk (1999), p. 119.

$$6\ CO_2 + 6H_2O + \text{sunlight} \longrightarrow C_6H_{12}O_6 + 6\ O_2$$

1. Carbon Dioxide

The atmosphere that we breath is a mixture of gases. Analysis of air indicates that it contains about 79% nitrogen and 20% oxygen. The remaining 1% is a mixture of other gases including about 0.035% carbon dioxide. Carbon dioxide enters the plant by diffusion through the stomata and goes into solution in water and into mesophyll cells. Inside, it diffuses through the cytoplasm and eventually reaches the chloroplasts where it is consumed. The amount of carbon dioxide needed by plants is huge. It has been found that one acre of corn uses 11 tons of carbon dioxide per growing season. Although the demands for carbon dioxide are tremendous, there is a large reservoir of carbon dioxide in the ocean which constantly renews the supply in the atmosphere. Because of human activity, primarily the burning of fossil fuels for our industries and our transportation, atmospheric concentrations of carbon dioxide have been steadily increasing. While small increases may initially benefit plants, too much carbon dioxide can cause global warming, can precipitate the production of some kinds of smog, and is generally harmful to other components of ecosystems.

2. Water

Although water is vital to photosynthesis (which could not occur without it), less than 1 percent of all water absorbed by plants is consumed during photosynthesis; the other 99 percent is transpired or incorporated into plant structure. In photosynthesis, water is fragmented; the hydrogen atoms are incorporated in the sugar molecule produced and the oxygen is liberated and given off into the atmosphere to become atmospheric oxygen. If water is in short supply, it may limit the rate of photosynthesis in plants. If water is absent photosynthesis stops.

3. Light

Light reaches the earth in the form of waves or bursts of energy called photons. The shortest wavelengths of the electromagnetic spectrum are x-rays, while the longest are radio waves. Not quite half of the radiant energy that we call the electromagnetic spectrum occurs in the form of visible light. Visible light, when passed through a prism, breaks up into different wave lengths represented by different colors. The longest wave lengths are represented by red colors with violets being the shortest. Orange, yellow, green, blue, and indigo fall between.

Most of the light waves used in photosynthesis are on the extremes of the visible light spectrum such as the violet-blue and red-orange wavelengths. Chlorophyll and its associated pigments are able to capture and absorb the energy of these wavelengths and use it in photosynthesis. Some of the energy of light waves helps heat plant surfaces and is called **sensible heat production**. Light that is not used in photosynthesis and is not used in sensible heat production is reflected from plant surfaces. (Plants are green because their photosynthesis pigments absorb reds and blues, reflecting the unused green portion of light back into the atmosphere).

Photosynthesis varies with the duration and intensity of sunlight. Light changes with time of day, season of year, altitude, latitude and atmospheric conditions. In turn, the amount of photosynthesis that takes place varies with the availability and quality of light. While too little light stops or reduces photosynthesis, too much light is also detrimental to photosynthesis. Excess light causes photo-oxidation of chlorophyll, destroying

Figure 10–3 The chemical nature of light trapping molecules of photosynthesis. *Source:* N. M. Jessop. *Biosphere: A Study of Life* (1970), Prentice-Hall, p. 339.

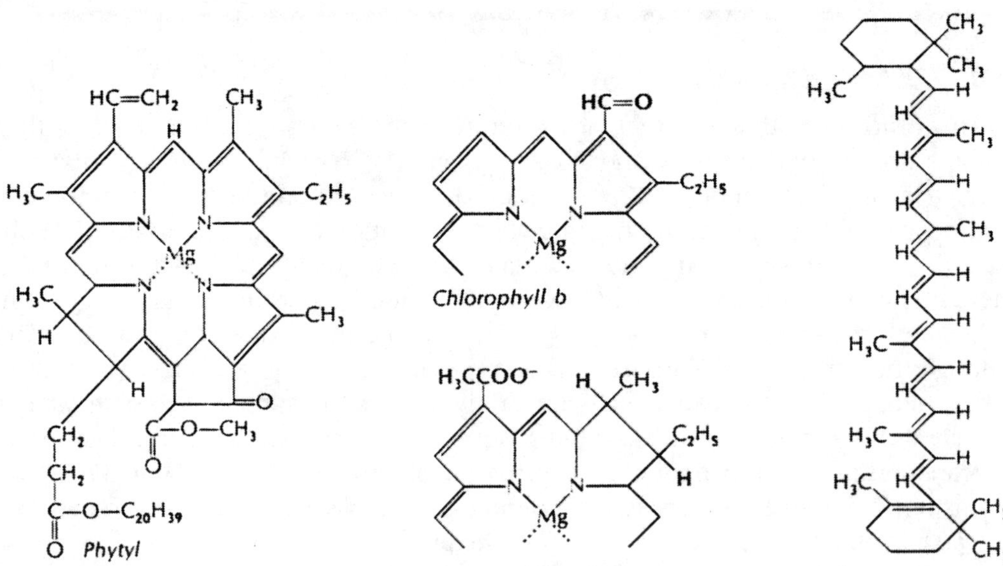

Chlorophyll a

Chlorophyll b

Bacteriochlorophyll

β-Carotene

the pigment and stopping further photosynthesis. Furthermore, too much light will cause an increase in transpiration causing the closing of stomata and hence a reduction of the amount of carbon dioxide entering the leaf.

4. Chlorophyll

Chlorophyll is a general term for several types of photosynthetic pigments that all contain one molecule of magnesium in their centers. Chlorophyll structure is similar to the heme structure in the vertebrate blood pigment called hemoglobin. Each chlorophyll molecule has a lipid tail that anchors the molecule to the walls of thylakoids in the chloroplasts.

The different kinds of chlorophylls are designated by letters and vary in chemical structure and color. These molecules are important as they determine the kinds of light a plant can use for photosynthesis. They also have morphological importance as the possession or absence of some kinds of chlorophyll indicates the relationships between different groups of plants.

Chlorophyll *a* is bluish green in color, and is the most common kind of chlorophyll found in plants. Approximately 75% of all chlorophyll is chlorophyll *a*.

Chlorophyll *b* is a yellowish green pigment and constitutes about 25% of chlorophyll in green plants. It is especially important in photosynthesis as chlorophyll *b* absorbs light and transfers the energy to chlorophyll *a*. Thus chlorophyll *b* enables plants to photosynthesize over a wider spectrum of light than just chlorophyll *a*. Some other chlorophylls such as *c, d* and *e* take the place of chlorophyll *b* in some algae. In each chloroplast of a cell there are between 250–400 chlorophyll molecules. These are grouped together in a light harvesting unit called a photosynthetic unit. Most of these are located in each grana of the chloroplast.

Carotenoids. Most plants have several other light absorbing pigments as well. These are collectively called carotenoids. Carotenes are the red, orange, and yellow pigments that are responsible for the colors of tomatoes, squashes, bananas, and avocados. Xanthophylls are yellower and browner versions of carotenes. Carotenes and

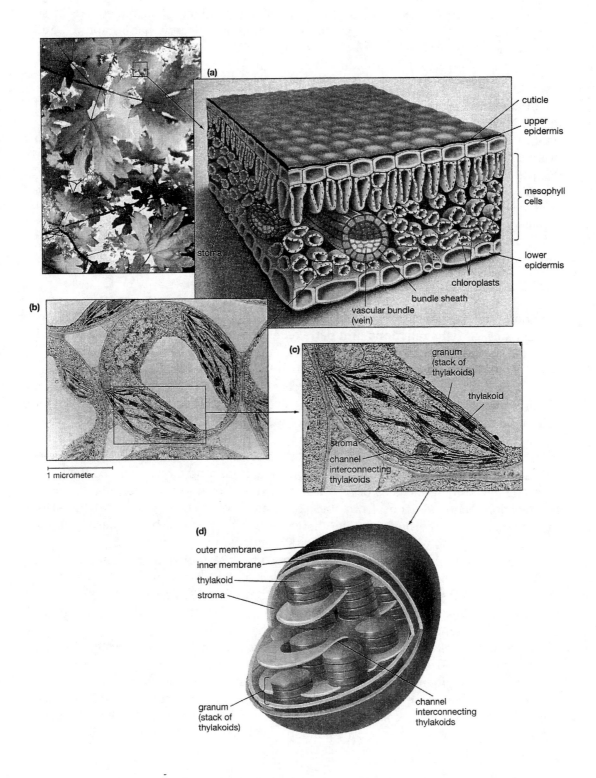

Figure 10–4 The structures involved in photosynthesis. *Source:* Teresa Audesirk and Gerald Audesirk (1999), p. 113.

xanthophylls are considered accessory pigments in photosynthesis. They assimilate light that chlorophyll cannot absorb, and transfer it to chlorophyll molecules. In so doing, these accessory pigments extend the range of light energy that is captured and used in photosynthesis.

5. The Chloroplasts

In green plants almost all photosynthesis takes place in the spongy mesophyll of leaves. These cells contain thousands of chloroplasts which are the organelles in which photosynthesis takes place. Chloroplasts are complex, multi-layered organelles that internally consist of thylakoids, grana, and stroma.

The **thylakoids** are the pigment-containing structures of the chloroplast. Each thylakoid consists of a series of several flattened membranes that form a pancake-like layered structure. Coin-like stacks of thylakoids called **grana** are immersed in the semiliquid **stroma** that fills the interior.

PROCESSES IN PHOTOSYNTHESIS

1. The Light Reactions

Photosynthesis involves two major kinds of chemical reactions, light-dependent reactions called **light reactions** and dark-dependent reactions called **dark reactions**. The light reactions take place in the thylakoids during daylight hours provided there is sufficient light of the proper wavelengths. The inputs into the light reaction include sunlight, water, and carbon dioxide. The products are ATP, NADPH, and oxygen.

In simplest terms the light reactions involve light waves striking chlorophyll molecules that are embedded in the thylakoids of the grana in chloroplasts. The light waves cause electrons to become excited which creates reactions that result in the conversion of light energy to chemical energy. In the process several things happen. Water molecules are split apart producing hydrogen ions, electrons, and oxygen gas. At the same time energy-storing molecules of ATP are created to provide energy for a later part of the reaction. Hydrogen ions from the split water are used to make NADPH + H + (hydrogenated nicotinamide adenine dinucleotide phosphate) which is also a stored energy molecule and will be used in the dark reactions.

Light is captured by two photosystems involving chlorophyll a and b and antenna pigments which function like an antenna to collect and transfer light energy to the reaction centers. **Photosystem I** has a light absorption peak of 700 nm (nanometers) and is called P_{700}. It consists of 250 molecules of chlorophyll a, smaller amounts of chlorophyll b plus carotenoid pigments. Light energy captured by the P_{700} pigments is transferred to an iron-sulfur complex that forms the reaction center of Photosystem I where the chemical transformations actually take place.

The second pigment system, **Photosystem II**, also consists of chlorophyll a and b—carotene molecules. A small amount of chlorophyll b, and one special reaction-center molecule of chlorophyll a called pigment 680 are involved. Pigment 680 is a primary electron acceptor of a molecule called pheophytin and this photosystem is symbolized as P_{680}.

Photolysis

The light reactions begin when light energy is used to split the water molecule. Technically, a photon of light strikes the P_{680} molecule and provides the energy to boost an electron out of place and into a higher energy level. This electron is picked up by a substance called pheophytin and then passed on to another compound, acceptor Q.

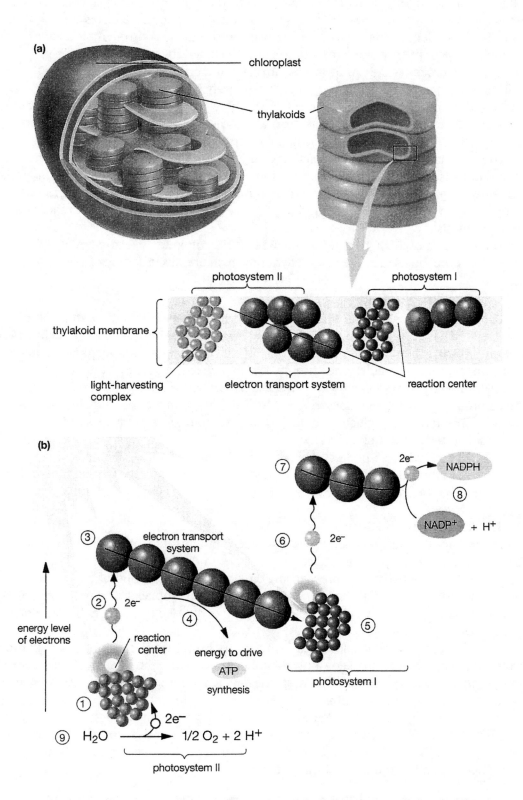

(a)

chloroplast

thylakoids

thylakoid membrane

photosystem II

photosystem I

light-harvesting complex

electron transport system

reaction center

(b)

energy level of electrons

electron transport system

reaction center

energy to drive ATP synthesis

photosystem I

photosystem II

⑦ 2e⁻ → NADPH

⑧ NADP⁺ + H⁺

⑥ 2e⁻

③

② 2e⁻

④

⑤

①

⑨ H_2O → 2e⁻ → 1/2 O_2 + 2 H^+

Figure 10–5 The light dependent reactions of photosynthesis. *Source:* Teresa Audesirk and Gerald Audesirk (1999), p. 116.

The electron lost by P_{680} is replaced by an electron from the water molecule. As water molecules are split to provide the necessary electrons, a molecule of oxygen and four protons are produced. The splitting of the water molecule is controlled by enzymes on the inside wall of the thylakoid membrane and the reaction is called **photolysis**.

A second process called **photophosphorylation**, occurs when the acceptor Q molecule releases that excited electron to an electron transport system that passes it on to a high energy storage molecule $NADPH + H+$. There are pigments called cytochromes and plastocyanin which pass the electron along the transport system. ATP molecules are formed from ADP molecules during the electron transport process.

The third process, **chemiosmosis**, is catalyzed by an enzyme located on the thylakoid membrane of the grana. This reaction splits water and results in a proton gradient being formed across the thylakoid membrane. The result of this is more energy being released and more ATP being formed which will support the dark reactions of photosynthesis.

The products of the light reaction include carbon dioxide, ATP, and $NADPH^+$ molecules. These will be used in the dark reactions which are discussed next.

2. The Dark Reactions

The dark reactions of photosynthesis take place outside of the grana, in the stroma, of the chloroplasts. Also called the Calvin-Benson Cycle, the dark reactions begin when carbon dioxide is added to a 5-carbon molecule called ribulose diphosphate to form a 6-carbon glucose molecule. The energy for this reaction is furnished by ATP and $NADPH^+$ molecules manufactured during the light reactions. Some of the glucose molecules produced by this reaction are used for cell energy in a process called **photorespiration**. The remaining glucose molecules are combined to produce starch which is then transported to the stems and roots.

The dark reaction of photosynthesis can take one of three distinctive pathways called the 3-carbon pathway, the 4-carbon pathway, and Crassulacean Acid Metabolism (CAM photosynthesis).

The Three Carbon Pathway

In order for the dark reaction to work, it needs energy. It takes the energy molecule ATP and the acceptor molecule called $NADPH^+$ from the light reaction and uses them to synthesize carbohydrates from carbon dioxide. A whole series of reactions, each mediated by an enzyme, takes place in the stroma of chloroplasts. The reactions in the Calvin-Benson Cycle involve carbon dioxide being converted to carbohydrates, along a **three carbon pathway**.

In the process, six molecules of carbon dioxide from the air combine with six molecules of a 5-carbon sugar called ribulose diphosphate under the control of an enzyme. This reaction produces six 6-carbon molecules which are immediately split into twelve stable glyceraldehyde 3-phosphate (GA3P) molecules. Ten of the twelve GA3P molecules are enzymatically rearranged to become six 5-carbon sugar molecules (ribulose diphosphate). The other two GA3P molecules are combined to form glucose, the ultimate product of photosynthesis. Glucose can further be modified to make starch, glucose, cellulose and all the other compounds needed by the cell.

The products of photosynthesis are used directly by the plant to store energy in the form of starch, make available the glucose molecule for cells and also make other needed compounds such as cellulose.

Figure 10–6 A summary of the chemical events of the Calvin-Bensen cycle of the dark reactions in photosynthesis. *Source:* Arthur W. Galston, Peter J. Davies, Ruth L. Slatter. *The Life of the Green Plant* (1980), Prentice-Hall. p. 99.

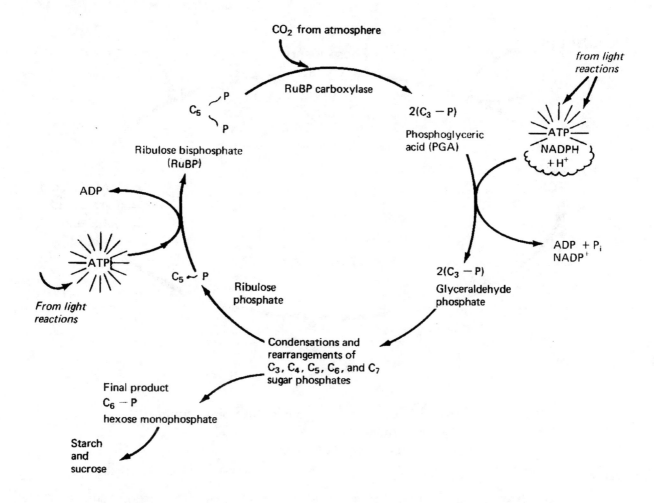

The Four-Carbon Pathway

Some plants use a **four-carbon pathway** (C_4) metabolic pathway instead of the three carbon pathway described above. Also called the Hatch-Slack metabolic pathway, after the plant scientists who discovered it, C_4 plants are named for the 4-carbon oxaloacetic acid molecule which holds (fixes) the carbon dioxide molecules until they can be shunted into the Calvin-Benson cycle of the dark reactions.

C_4 plants are mostly tropical but some familiar examples include corn, crabgrass, sugarcane, and sorghum. The leaves of these plants have a distinctive arrangement named **Kranz anatomy**, in which vascular bundles are surrounded by layers of mesophyll cells.

The mesophyll cells of C_4 plants fix carbon dioxide in the form of oxaloacetic acid which is then transported in a reduced form to bundle sheath cells until needed. During the intense sunlight of midday the stomata close to prevent transpiration water loss and carbon dioxide levels start to decrease. As carbon dioxide becomes depleted bundle cells convert their molecular stores into pyruvic acid and carbon dioxide. The pyruvic acid returns to meosphyll to regenerate phosphoenolpyruvate while the carbon dioxide is shunted into the Calvin-Benson cycle.

Figure 10–7 A brief summary of the chemical events in the four-carbon pathway of photosynthesis. *Source:* Roy H. Saigo and Barbara W. Saigo. *Botany: Principles of Applications* (1990), Prentice-Hall, p. 18.

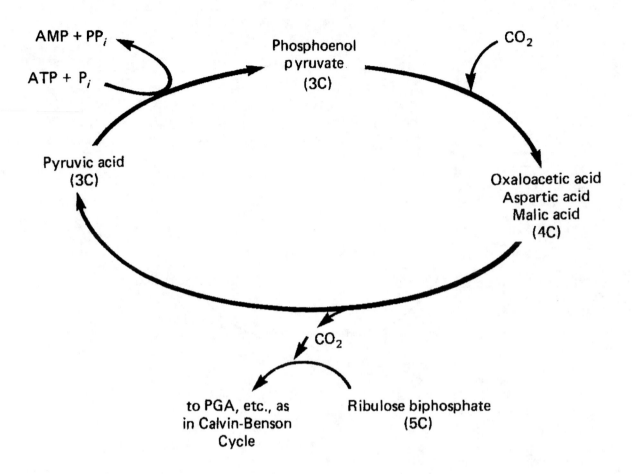

This method of storing carbon dioxide permits C_4 plants to function at higher temperatures than three carbon plants. They have photosynthetic rates that are two to three times higher than three carbon plants.

CAM Photosynthesis

A third variation of the Calvin-Benson Cycle occurs in some plants growing in high light situations such as many desert species. This process is called **CAM Photosynthesis** (crassulacean acid metabolism) and is found in twenty families of plants including cacti, stonecrops, orchids, bromeliads and many succulents. The plants in this group do not have well defined palisade layers in their leaves.

Chemically, CAM photosynthesis is similar to the four carbon cycle described above, except that stomata open at night to gather carbon dioxide which is converted to malic acid and stored in the vacuoles of chlorenchyma cells. During the day, malic acid is converted into carbon dioxide which can then be shunted directly into the Calvin-Bensen cycle.

This arrangement provides two advantages for these desert plants. First, since they gather and store carbon dioxide at night their stomata can remain closed during the dry, hot days, thereby considerably reducing water loss. And second, the stores of

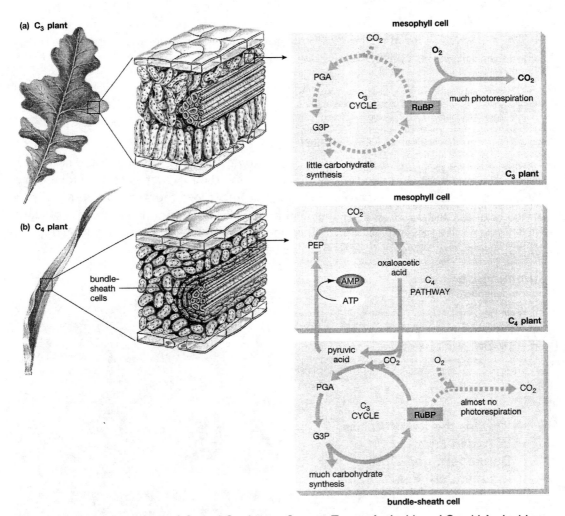

Figure 10–8 A comparison of C₃ and C₄ plants. *Source:* Teresa Audesirk and Gerald Audesirk (1999), p. 120.

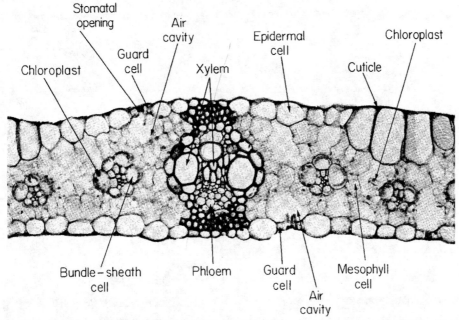

Figure 10–9 Cross section of a corn leaf, a plant that uses the four-carbon pathway. Note that the vascular bundles are tightly enclosed in a ring of protective tissue which isolates the carbon compounds. *Source:* Arthur W. Galston, Peter J. Davies, and Ruth Slatter. *The Life of the Green Plant* (1980), Prentice-Hall, p. 104.

malic acid provide an abundant carbon dioxide supply for photosynthesis each day since the stomata remain closed and admit little carbon dioxide.

Respiration

Photosynthesis is only half the process necessary for energy to be harvested and used. A plant traps sunlight to make sugars which are turned into starches or used for energy. When a plant uses the sugars to make energy it undergoes the same process that animals do. It performs oxidative respiration in its cells. Respiration is a process of using stored energy (sugar) and reclaiming that energy in small amounts so it can be trapped and stored in special molecules of adenine triphosphate (ATP).

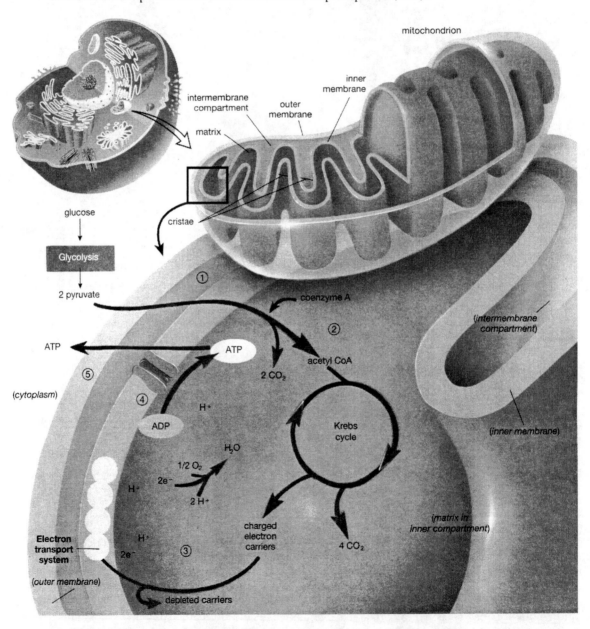

Figure 10–10 An overview of the events of cellular respiration. *Source:* Teresa Audesirk and Gerald Audesirk (1999), p. 132.

$$C_6H_{12}O_6 + O_2 \longrightarrow 6CO_2 + 6H_2O + energy$$

In simplest terms, respiration is an energy releasing process that takes place in all active cells twenty-four hours a day, regardless of whether photosynthesis is occurring or not. It starts in the cytoplasm and takes place in the mitochondria. In the process, sugar molecules are enzymatically fragmented to produce carbon dioxide, water, and energy. In aerobic organisms, oxygen is consumed in the process of respiration. Some bacteria and soil animals do not require oxygen input during respiration and are called **anaerobic organisms**. Bacteria and yeasts that obtain energy by **fermentation** are also anaerobes. Energy resulting from all three of these processes is stored in ATP molecules. Aerobic respiration involves three chemical events, glycolysis, the Kreb's citric acid cycle, and the electron transport system.

GLYCOLYSIS

Glycolysis is the first stage in cell respiration. It takes place in the cytoplasm adjacent to the mitochondria. In glycolysis, a molecule of the 6-carbon glucose is split into two 3- carbon molecules which are then enzymatically rearranged into two molecules of pyruvic acid. The fuel for glycolysis is always glucose. If starches and other glucose-containing polysaccharides are used they must first be broken down into disaccharides and then into glucose molecules.

In the first step of glycolysis, a glucose molecule is combined with phosphate to form glucose-6-phosphate by a process called phosphorylation. This reaction requires energy. The glucose-6-phosphate is graded through a series of reactions, until the final product of glycolysis, two 3-carbon molecules of pyruvic acid, is produced. At each stage in glycolysis, energy is required to make the reaction take place but more energy is liberated from the reactions than is used so there is a net energy gain by the cell. While the energy required to start glycolysis involves 2 ATP molecules, four molecules of ATP are ultimately recovered. As a result glycolysis produces two ATP molecules for the cell.

KREB'S CITRIC ACID CYCLE

The second stage in cell respiration is called the Kreb's Citric Acid cycle. Prior to entering the mitochondria, the 3-carbon pyruvic acid molecules produced in glycolysis are enzymatically changed into acetyl coenzyme A (a derivative of vitamin A) which is then shunted into the Kreb's citric acid cycle. The cycle consists of a series of enzymatic reactions which terminate in the complete fragmentation of the original glucose molecule.

Each of the reactions in the Kreb's Cycle is under the control of a dehydrogenase enzyme which strips hydrogen away from the molecule. The hydrogens are bound to carrier molecules called NAD and FAD, which become NADH and FADH. Four molecules of carbon dioxide are also released as a waste product. This is the carbon dioxide that plants give off as a waste product and animals such as humans breath out. Although energy is consumed at several stages during the Kreb's cycle there is a net gain of two ATP molecules. At the end of the Kreb's Citric Acid Cycle the glucose molecule has been disassembled. The hydrogen atoms are attached to carriers and the carbon and oxygen atoms form the carbon dioxide that is voided. The reduced NADH and FADH molecules are then shunted into the last stage in cell respiration called the electron transport system.

Figure 10–11 A summary of the chemical events of respiration. *Source:* Arthur W. Galston, Peter J. Davies, Ruth L. Slatter. *The Life of the Green Plant* (1980), Prentice-Hall, p. 123.

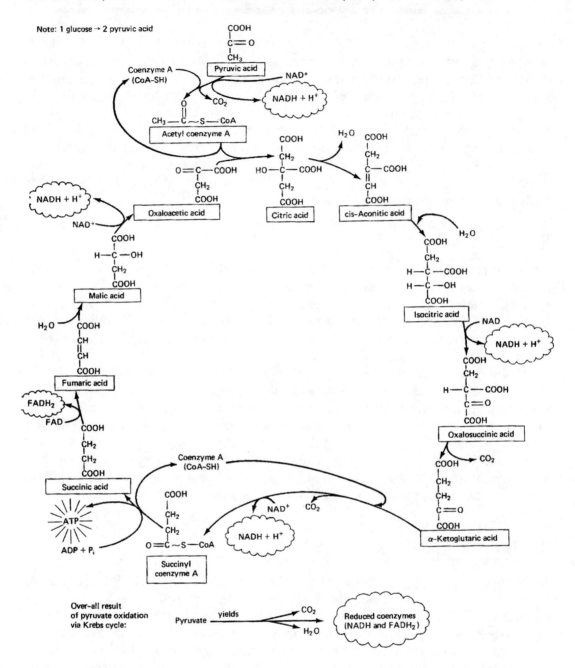

ELECTRON TRANSPORT CHAIN

During the electron transport system, the energy-rich NADH and FADH molecules are transferred along a series of enzymes called cytochromes and flavins, which are arranged along the cristae, deep inside the mitochondria. At several transfer steps energy is stripped from the hydrogen electrons and used to form molecules of ATP from ADP and P by the equation:

$$\text{ADP} + \text{P} + \text{energy} \longrightarrow \text{ATP}$$

Figure 10–12 The chemical events of the electron transport system. Note that the initial inputs are hydrogen atoms obtained from the Kreb's Citric Acid cycle. *Source:* Arthur W. Galston, Peter J. Davies, and Ruth Slatter. *The Life of the Green Plant* (1980), Prentice-Hall, p. 125.

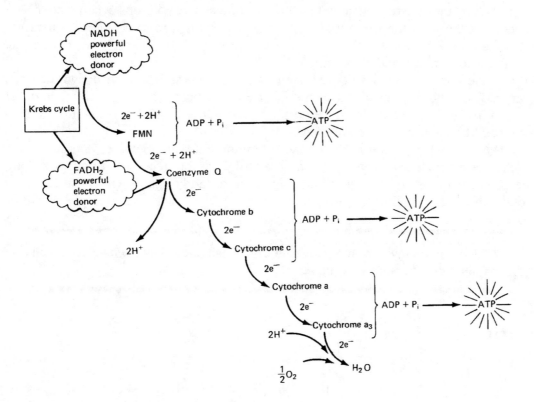

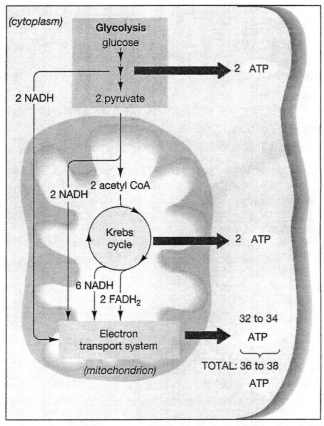

Figure 10–13 The energy harvest from a molecule of glucose. *Source:* Teresa Audesirk and Gerald Audesirk (1999), p. 138.

The energy that is used to attach ADP and P to form ATP comes from the oxidization of NADH and FADH to their reduced form, NAD and FAD. This energy is extracted by a technical chemical process called **chemiosmosis**. As the hydrogen protons are transferred along the electron carriers (the citric acid molecules) protons accumulate on the outside of the inner mitochondrial membrane. Following a concentration gradient, the protons diffuse back through the membrane, providing the energy that triggers ATP synthase to combine ADP and P into ATP.

In the end, the remaining hydrogen atoms are combined with oxygen to form water. Thus, the final products of the electron transport system are water and ATP energy molecules. (Note also that the final products of oxidative respiration include water, carbon dioxide and ATP molecules).

The final energy count obtained by respiration amounts to some 36 molecules of ATP for each molecule of glucose that enters the aerobic respiration pathway. Some bacteria are even more efficient and can obtain an additional 2 ATP molecules for a total of 38 ATP energy rich molecules obtained.

ATP is the energy currency molecule of the cell and is used whenever a cell needs energy to perform work.

Fermentation

Some bacteria and yeasts, and also some animals, use the process of fermentation to produce energy. Fermentation does not involve the use of oxygen so organisms that use this means of ATP production are anaerobic. Fermentation begins with glycolysis, in which glucose and organic molecules are converted to pyruvic acid. Carbon and oxygen molecules are then stripped off pyruvic acid to form carbon dioxide which is released as a waste product. Some of the hydrogen atoms are also stripped away to oxidize NAD into NADH which enters the production pathway for ATP. The remaining 2-carbon molecule is ethyl alcohol (C_2H_5OH). In some soil bacteria and intestinal bacteria the pyruvic acid is reduced to lactic acid and NADH rather than alcohol.

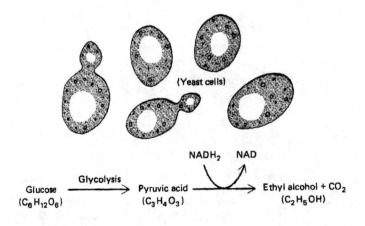

Figure 10–14 Anaerobic energy production in yeast. *Source:* Tom M. Graham (1997), p. 154.

Compared to aerobic respiration, fermentation is very inefficient. Anaerobes produce only 2-4 ATP molecules for every molecule of glucose consumed. The rest of the energy content remains untapped in the pyruvic acid, lactic acid, or alcohol molecules. This is why the alcohol that we drink is so high in calories (a calorie is a unit of energy). Cells can't stand much alcohol as it is toxic. As we indicated before, when the concentration of alcohol reaches 12%, most cells die. Yeast cells forming wine are no exception. Natural wine has only 12% alcohol as a result.

Factors Affecting Respiration Rate

In normal oxidative respiration, there are several factors that affect the rate of respiration. Temperature is important as warm temperatures have a tendency to increase the speed of chemical reactions. Thus in warm climates, oxidative respiration is faster. The sugars within are broken down to produce energy by the plant cells. We eat fruits and some vegetables because we like the sweet taste of sugar. If oxidative respiration is allowed to continue, the sugars are broken down and the taste of the crop changes. If we refrigerate the fruit or vegetable, the process is slowed down. High temperatures also deactivate the enzymes of the Kreb's Cycle, slowing or stopping respiration entirely.

Other factors affecting the rate of respiration include the availability of water and oxygen. Respiration needs water, and if water is in low amounts, respiration slows or stops. On the other hand, oxygen is also necessary for respiration. It is important when storing food to reduce oxygen by keeping the food in closed containers. This limiting of oxygen slows down the rate of respiration.

In large warehouses where fruits and vegetables are stored, it is a normal procedure to seal the building and pump in nitrogen gas to replace oxygen. By reducing the amount of oxygen present the rate of respiration is slowed and the amount of sugars broken down is less (this is what ripening is all about).

In large warehouses where fruits and vegetables are stored it is customary to seal the building and pump in nitrogen gas to replace oxygen. By reducing the amount of oxygen present, the rate of respiration is slowed and the amount of sugars in the fruits and vegetables that are broken down is decreased, thereby preventing over ripening and spoiling of fruit.

Metabolic Uses of Energy

Plants obtain and use energy through the complimentary events of photosynthesis and respiration. The ultimate result of these chemical events is that some of the kinetic energy of sunlight is stored in the potential energy of the chemical bonds of sugar. When energy is needed the chemical bonds are broken, and the energy is temporarily stored in ATP molecules, again in the form of potential energy. This ATP molecule is very special to the cell. It provides energy for chemical reactions for the synthesis of all the basic building blocks of the cells. When ATP molecules are split to yield energy for chemical reactions, some of the stored energy of the phosphate-ADP molecule

Figure 10–15 The input of various substances into the respiration cycles. *Source:* Teresa Audesirk and Gerald Audesirk (1999), p. 127.

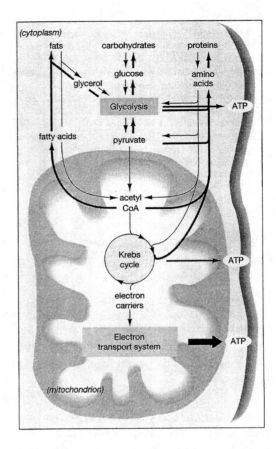

becomes kinetic energy to power the plants numerous activities and some of it can be incorporated as stored energy in the bonds of new organic molecules manufactured by the plants. ATP molecules are the ultimate, and the only source, of energy that the plant uses to produce its tissues, hormones, toxic substances, waxes, resins, and the many thousands of materials that plants produce in order to survive. Without this energy and the ability to store it until needed, plant functioning stops and the plant either becomes dormant or dies.

Key Words and Phrases

autotroph	heterotroph	photosynthesis
oxidative respiration	ATP	chlorophyll a
chlorophyll b	carotene	dark reaction
light reaction	Photosystem II	Photosystem I
NADPH	P_{700}	P_{680}
photolysis	Calvin-Benson Cycle	PGA
3 carbon pathway	4 carbon pathway	chemiosmosis
CAM photosynthesis	respiration	glycolysis
Kreb's Citric Acid Cycle	Electron Transport System	fermentation
aerobic respiration	anaerobic respiration	absorption

Selected References and Resources

Attridge, T. H. 1990. *Light and Plant Responses.* Cambridge University Press. New York.

Clayton, R. K. 1981. *Photosynthesis: Physical Mechanisms and Chemical Patterns.* Wiley Interscience. New York.

Fong, F. K. Ed. 1982. *Light Reaction Path of Photosynthesis.* Springer-Verlag. New York.

Gregory, R. P. 1989. *Photosynthesis.* Routledge, Chapman and Hall, Inc. New York.

Hall, D. O., and K. K. Rao. 1994. *Photosynthesis.* Fifth Edition. Cambridge University Press. New York.

Kirk, J. T. O. 1997. *Light and Photosynthesis in Aquatic Ecosystems.* 2nd Edition. Cambridge University Press. New York.

Raghavendra, A. S. 1997. *Photosynthesis. A Comprehensive Treatise.* Cambridge University Press. New York.

Raschi, A., and F. Miglietta, R. Tongnetti and P. Van Gardingen. 1997. *Plant Responses to Elevated CO$_2$.* Cambridge University Press. New York.

Zelitch, I. 1971. *Photosynthesis, Photorespiration, and Plant Productivity.* Academic Press. San Diego, California.

Zubay, G. 1983. *Biochemistry.* Addison-Wesley. Menlo Park, California.

Review and Discussion Questions

1. In terms of caloric content of the glucose molecule just how efficient is photosynthesis in converting light energy into chemical energy?

2. Why are plants green? Why do they absorb energy for photosynthesis only in a verynarrow band within the broad magnetic spectrum of sunlight?

3. How does the structure of mitochondria contribute and relate to the processes and enzymatic activities involved in respiration?

4. What are the inputs and products of each of the three stages of respiration?

5. What are the inputs and products of the two basic stages of photosynthesis?

6. Why might it be advantageous for plants to exhibit the CAM photosynthesis pathway? In what kinds of habitats do most CAM plants occur?

7. What is the electron and proton connection between hydrogen and the making of an ATP molecule?

8. How would you determine whether a red or purple leaf had chlorophyll and carried on photosynthesis?

9. How is water both used and produced in the process of photosynthesis?

10. Discuss the differences between the three energy producing processes, respiration, fermentation and digestion.

Chapter 11

• • • • • • • • • • • • • • • ▶ • ▶ • ▶   Plant Growth

Plant Hormones
>   Auxins
>   Gibberillins
>   Cytokinins
>   Abscisic Acid
>   Ethylene

Taxes and Other Movements

Photoperiodism

In plants and animals growth is an increase in the number of cells and this increase requires the process of mitosis. In plants, growth may be **determinate** meaning the plant grows until it develops to a certain size and then stops or its growth may be a type called **indeterminate** in that it continues to grow as long as it lives.

All plants begin life as a single fertilized cell. With the mitotic production of more cells, the plant develops groups of cells which differentiate into tissues. Tissues form organs and other plant structures comprised of specialized cells that perform specific functions. The process of growth therefore involves the continuous production and differentiation of new cells. The control of growth and differentiation of cells into tissues, of tissues into organs and other plant structures is under the direction of genes, chromosomes, and hormones.

A **hormone** is a chemical substance that is produced in one place and is then circulated in the plant in phloem and xylem fluids to act on cells and tissues in another area. Even in small amounts hormones have a profound impact on growth and development. Most plant hormones stimulate certain plant activities such as growth but a few are inhibitory. Often two or more plant hormones work together to stimulate or enhance a particular activity. Examples of plant hormones include auxins, cytokinins, gibberellins, ethylene, and abscisic acid. Many of these hormones have been put to work by humankind to control the processes of growth, development, and ripening that occur in plants.

Plant Hormones

• ▼

As we have seen earlier, the thousands of metabolic steps in plants are controlled by enzymes which are manufactured by cells under the direction of genes. Genes also direct the production of hormones by cells. These chemical substances are transported to another part of the plant where they produce specific effects. Vitamins are also often involved. Vitamins are organic compounds produced by the plant and are necessary for the growth and well-being of the plant. They work as activators for enzymes or as precursors for other activities. Both hormones and vitamins are growth regulating sub-

Figure 11–1 Darwin's experiments to determine how plants respond to light stimuli. *Source:* Teresa Audesirk and Gerald Audesirk (1999), p. 506.

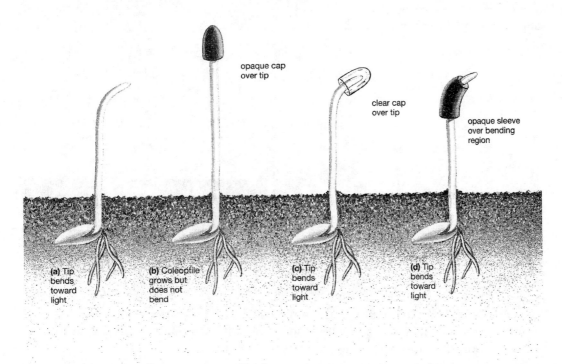

stances; some stimulate growth and others inhibit growth. Plant growth is a balance between simulator and inhibitor hormones. The plant hormones have been divided into several major types.

AUXINS

Auxins were the first plant hormones to be discovered. The name auxin is a Greek word meaning "to increase". Three major groups of auxins are known. All of them promote or inhibit growth depending upon the concentration of the auxin. From these, other synthetic auxins have been developed.

The plant synthesizes auxins from amino acids in the cytoplasm of the cell. Auxins are produced primarily in the apical meristem, buds, young leaves, and other actively growing young parts of the plant. When auxins are produced, the reaction of the cells is determined by concentrations of the auxin, location of the cell and other factors. The same concentration of auxins that promotes shoot growth may inhibit root growth. Auxins may stimulate the enlargement of a cell, but at the same time may also trigger the production of different hormones causing an opposite effect. Many monocots are less sensitive to auxins than dicots and their shoots are less sensitive to auxin stimulation than the roots. High concentrations of auxins will kill plant tissue and as a result, auxins can be used as weed killers.

The movement of auxins from cells where it is produced to other areas of the plant requires ATP to provide energy and involves active transport. The movement of auxins is polar in that they flow away from the production source and usually travel downward from the stem tip. They are not carried through phloem but proceed from cell to cell in the parenchyma that supports the phloem.

The chief role of most auxins in plants is to stimulate growth; auxins cause cell elongation in most tissues, promote mitotic cell division in the vascular cambium,

Figure 11–2 How coleoptiles bend towards a light source. *Source:* Teresa Audesirk and Gerald Audesirk (1999), p. 507.

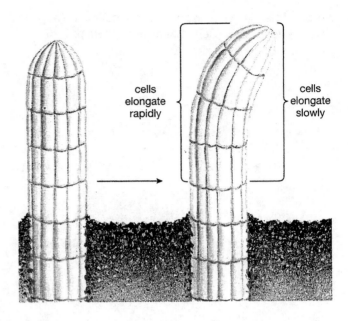

cells elongate rapidly

cells elongate slowly

increase cell differentiation in stem tissue, and promote growth and development of fruits. Auxins also retard the loss of ripening fruit and leaf fall.

Auxins and cytokinins are chiefly responsible for establishing **apical dominance**. Auxins produced by the apical meristem stimulate cell division and elongation of the shoot but inhibit growth and development of lateral buds. Since auxins are produced in apical meristems their concentrations are usually highest at the tip of the shoot and decrease progressively toward the base of the plant. Because of this concentration gradient, smaller branches are produced at the top of the stem and progressively larger branches grow towards the base, resulting in the conical shape of many trees such as the pines, spruces, and firs.

a. Indoleacetic acid (IAA) is one of only a few active auxins. IAA stimulates the formation of roots on any plant organ. IAA has been prepared synthetically and is widely used today as rooting powder in nurseries. When plants are to be propagated from cuttings, the fresh cut stem is dipped in rooting powder and inserted into the soil. The rooting powder containing IAA causes the growth of roots in the area that it was applied. Fruit growers spray fruit trees with IAA to promote uniform flowering and fruit set. There is great advantage to this. In situations where the fruit needs to be harvested all at the same time, IAA insures that the fruit all ripen together. Fruit growers also spray fruit with IAA to prevent the formation of abscission layers to prevent premature fruit drop. Keeping all the fruit on the tree allows fruit to be picked without bruising by dropping to the ground. IAA may also be applied to flowers before pollination to create seedless fruit. The IAA starts the growth of the pericarp before the seeds have formed and thus we can eat seedless grapes and watermelon. Selective applications of IAA can also control the number of fruits that mature and their shape. In some markets, only select fruit brings a high price. The fruit grower selects only a few flowers per tree to treat with IAA. This results in a smaller fruit yield but the fruits produced are much larger due to the tree putting its entire effort into the production of just that small number.

b. PAA or phenylacetic acid is more abundant than IAA is but is less active. In some situations PAA is substituted for IAA where a more controlled use is needed.

c. **4-chloro IAA or 4-chloro-indoleacetic acid** is an important auxin used in germinating legume seeds, and may be a part of the mix used to make starting powder for peas and beans.

Agent Orange is a synthetic auxin used as a defoliant during the Vietnam war.

---

d. **Synthetic Auxins-2,4-D; 2,4,5-T; 2,4,5-TP** are auxins synthesized in the laboratory and used as herbicides or weed killers. When they are sprayed in low concentrations, they kill weeds. Most are harmless to humans but 2,4,5-T has been banned in the United States. These two synthetic auxins received great notoriety in the post Vietnam War era as the controversial herbicide Agent Orange. This auxin is actually a 1-to-1 mixture of both 2,4,5-T and 2,4-D auxins. Actually the two synthetic auxins are relatively safe to use but the 2,4,5-T contains a carcinogen called **dioxin** which is a contaminant produced in tiny amounts during the manufacture of the auxin. Dioxin has been implicated in causing birth defects, leukemia, miscarriages, and liver and lung disease. There is also a concern about lawn maintenance programs by professional lawn maintainers. The introduction of improperly applied synthetic auxins to lawns and golf courses, for example, may endanger water supplies where runoff affects wells and reservoirs. Cases have been reported of dogs developing tumors on their feet caused by running on treated lawns and some children that run barefoot have become sick from exposure.

GIBBERELLINS

There are seventy or more compounds of gibberellins that have been isolated from seeds, especially dicots and fungi. Gibberellins probably also occur in algae, mosses or ferns, although they have not yet been identified in these other plants. The respiratory compound acetyl coenzyme A is a metabolic precursor of gibberellins.

In plants, gibberellins increase growth rates and are stronger than auxins alone. However, auxins must also be present for gibberellins to act at maximum strength. Monocots and dicots react but conifers and other evergreens show little effect from the application of gibberellins. Gibberellins act on stems but have no effect on roots. Thus, they can be used to stimulate the growth of commercial flowers such as long-stemmed roses. Gibberellins can also bring about the formation of flowers and stimulate the emergence of seeds and buds from dormancy. Following germination, gibberellins continue to stimulate growth and development of embryos and seedlings.

By the judicious use of gibberellins, horticulturalists can keep plants in a dormant state while they are shipped over long distances. Upon reaching their destination, the dormant plants are activated by an application of gibberellins. Gibberellins can also cause plants to start growing at lower temperatures. When gibberellins are sprayed on lawns, the grass turns green a few weeks earlier in the spring. This is very important for greens keepers of golf courses.

Gibberellins are important in producing seedless grapes and increasing the size of fruit. When sprayed with a dilute solution of gibberellin very early in fruit development, the clusters may reach two to three times their normal size. Gibberellins are also used to lengthen the internodes between fruit so growing fruit is spaced farther apart. This allows better air circulation and less susceptibility to fungus infections. Also, gibberellins can be sprayed on oranges and other fruits that ripen quickly in summer heat to delay the aging of the fruits' skin. By the judicious application of gibberellins, fruit can be shipped long distances and remain ripe without spoiling. Sprays of gibberellins also increases the shelf life of the fruit once it reaches the store.

CYTOKININS

Like auxins and gibberellins, cytokinins are plant hormones that promote cell division. There are several kinds known and all are structured like the organic base adenine found in nucleic acids. Cytokinins are found in meristems and in other developing tissues, especially in young fruit. They cause the enlargement of cells and the differentiation of tissues. They promote the development of chloroplasts, and stimulate the development of cotyledons in seedlings. Cytokinins can also delay the aging of leaves.

Cytokinin may be sprayed on lettuce and other vegetables to extend their shelf life.

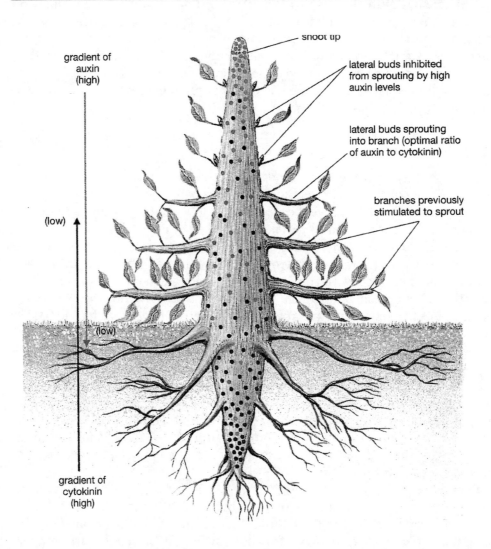

Figure 11–3 The interacting roles of auxin and cytokinin in shaping a plant. *Source:* Teresa Audesirk and Gerald Audesirk (1999), p. 512.

Cytokinins are used to prolong the life of vegetables in storage, which allows supermarkets to more effectively distribute fresh fruit and reduce waste by over-ripening or spoilage of fruits on the store shelves.

Synthetic forms of cytokinins are used to regulate the height of ornamental shrubs and keep harvested mushrooms fresh. They may also be used to shorten straw length in wheat so the plants are closer to the ground and don't blow over as easily in the wind. They are also used by florists to lengthen the shelf life of cut flowers. Many times a small packet of powder will accompany fresh cut flowers in which the person receiving them can add the powder to water and "feed" the flowers small amounts of cytokinin.

ABSCISIC ACID OR ABA

Abscisic acid is synthesized in the plastids of cells from carotenoid pigments. It is produced in leaves and in the root cap. Highest concentrations are found in the abscission zone of the petioles in plants and it may be especially abundant in fleshy fruits where it prevents seeds from germinating while the fruit is still on the plant. Abscisic acid is also common in dormant tissues and promotes dormancy in plants by preventing the synthesis of enzymes necessary for germination.

Abscisic acid almost universally inhibits cell growth. When applied to active plant buds the leaf primordia form bud scales and the bud becomes dormant. It is also used to treat nursery plants that are shipped long distances; their growth is inhibited so they stand less chance of damage in the dormant state.

The hormonal effects of abscisic acid can be reversed by the application of gibberellins as indicated above. Abscisic acid also helps leaves respond to excess water loss because it is the material produced by mesophyll cells as they dry. One of the most important roles of abscisic acid is to help control stomata closing. When leaves wilt, abscisic acid is produced in greater amounts and directly interferes with the transport or retention of potassium ions. This causes the guard cells to lose water and collapse, causing the stomata to close. When water returns, abscisic acid is metabolically broken down and the guard cells absorb water, causing them to swell and open the stomata.

Abscisic acid is also essential during the leaf fall or leaf shedding that occurs in most deciduous trees in autumn. When light levels and temperatures decrease during the fall, higher levels of abscisic acid are produced in the petiole of the leaf. These eventually result in leaf fall. The high levels of abscisic acid are maintained throughout the winter but with the return of spring the levels gradually decrease as the amounts of gibberellins, auxins and cytokinin rise.

ETHYLENE

Ethylene is a gas that is naturally produced by fruits, flowers, seeds, leaves, and roots. Several fungi and some bacteria also produce large amounts of ethylene. The production of ethylene gas usually occurs after a plant is bruised or cut, although the addition of auxins will also cause a release of the gas.

Ethylene is involved in a plant response called **thigmomorphogenesis**, which is a reduction in the elongation of stems subjected to mechanical stress such as wind or contact. Small amounts of ethylene gas stimulate more to be produced, thereby enabling the plant to rapidly respond to a wound or a stress. However, excess production of ethylene can cause flowers to wilt or plants to die. Households heated with natural gas sometimes have problems with raising and maintaining house plants as ethylene gas is a component of natural gas and a small leak in the house's heating system can introduce enough ethylene gas into the atmosphere to kill the plants or to cause damage to them.

Commercially, ethylene is used to ripen harvested green fruits such as lemons, bananas, mangoes, honeydew melons, and to cause citrus fruit to produce its normal fruit color. In the ripening process, fruits naturally release large amounts of ethylene gas during the respiratory process of changing stored energy into soluble sugars. Pears and peaches are also ripened with ethylene gas. Many fruits are shipped in an unripened state and are stored in warehouses until delivery to local grocery stores. To prepare these fruits for market, the warehouse is pumped full of ethylene gas. In a few days the fruit is ripe and ready for sale. Ethylene gas can also be used to control the sprouting of potatoes and the flowering of pineapples. Pumpkin growers use it to produce more female flowers on their plants. In nurseries it can be used to thicken the trunks of small trees in the nursery stock.

To speed the ripening of fruits at home enclose the fruit in a plastic bag so all the ethylene gas naturally produced by the fruit is concentrated and not allowed to diffuse away.

How Plant Hormones Interact

Plant hormones are chemical messengers that are produced in a tissue and then carried to some other areas where they cause an action. One important result of hormone influence is the establishment of **apical dominance** or the suppression of growth of axillary or lateral buds brought about by an auxin-like inhibitor. Apical dominance is strong in trees with a conical shape such as pines and conifers. It is weak in trees with stronger branching toward the top which produces a crown. This condition exists in ash, elms, willows, maples and oaks. The removal of a terminal bud causes axillary buds to develop, so this tells us that the inhibitor is in the terminal bud. This is important information to the gardener. When a gardener prunes plants he/she removes the terminal buds and forces axillary buds to grow. By pruning tall spindly plants we can force them to branch more fully and produce a larger crown.

Another major interaction between hormones and plant tissue is that of **senescence**, which is a breakdown of cell components and membranes that eventually leads to the death of the cell. Leaves of deciduous trees die back each fall and drop through the process of abscission. Even in conifers and other evergreens there is a gradual exchange of leaves. Plant parts age because there may be an aging factor. It is known that abscisic acid and ethylene promote aging whereas auxins, gibberellins and cytokinin delay the process.

There are other hormonal interactions as well. When a seed germinates, the seedling develops roots and shoots. The regulation of this may be controlled by a combination of auxins and cytokinin. For example, living pith cells of tobacco will enlarge due to auxins, but will not divide unless cytokinins are present. By varying the amounts of cytokinin we can cause pith cells to differentiate into roots or buds from which stems can be produced.

Despite the fact that plants appear stationary, time-lapse photography shows that plants are capable of movements although these movements are typically very slow and almost imperceptible. **Growth movements** in plants result from varying growth rates in different parts of an organ. These movements are seen principally in young parts of plants and are very slow. It takes up to two hours after a stimulus has been applied for a reaction to occur. The stimuli that cause growth movements are either internal or external but most plant movements are directed by or at least influenced by plant hormones.

INTERNAL STIMULI—HORMONAL ACTION

Growth movements that result primarily from internal stimuli are caused by hormonal action which causes differential growth. There are at least five specific growth movements that are considered hormone induced. **Helical** or **spiraling movements** are the common twisting motions seen in young plants as they grow. In this condition, the young plant twists in a spiral as the shoot reaches for the sun. This is due to differential growth at various points in the shoot caused by hormones.

Some plants exhibit **nodding movements** as they grow. This condition is similar to helical movement except that the plant oscillates from side to side. This growth pattern is common in the legume family. Nodding movement is not restricted to the shoot but also is seen in roots. Here it facilitates the progress of the growing plant tip through the soil.

Plants that climb are equipped with tendrils from stems or leaves. The tendrils exhibit **twining movements** as they grow. Twining movements are stimulated both internally and externally. The stems of these climbing plants elongate in differing places on the stem to cause a visible spiraling growth. In tendril twining, coiling is initiated by contact of cells with something hard. This results in the elongation of cells on the side opposite the contact, causing the tendril to bend toward the object in contact. This contact is an external stimulus while growth of cells opposite the contact is the result of an internal stimulus. The twining has been found to be caused by auxins in some plants and ethylene in others.

The **contraction movements** of roots have been previously noted in our discussion of root structure and function. The **contraction movements** of roots result in a kind of "pulling" action that drives the plant deeper into the ground. Contraction movements are common in plants that have bulbs. In surface-generating seeds that produce bulbs 4-6 inches below ground level, the temperature at ground level determines how much contraction the roots will make. When the bulb reaches the right depth underground where day-night temperatures are the same, contraction movements stop.

Some plants exhibit **nastic movements**, which are actions of flattened plant organs such as leaves or flower petals. These flat organs bend up and down as cells grow alternately on the top and bottom of their structure. These movements are nondirectional movements as they are not influenced by external stimuli such as sunlight. Such movement without orientation or external stimuli are called nastic movements. In some plants, such as tulips, the flowers open and close in response to light and temperature. This is due to changes in turgor pressure and is controlled by the circadian rhythms of the plant. Such changes in position are caused by external stimuli and are not affected by hormones. They are tropisms, to be discussed next.

Figure 11–4 Early experiments demonstrating the growth of roots and shoots in response to plant hormones. *Source:* Lorus J. Milne and Margery Milne. *Plant Life* (1959), Prentice-Hall. p. 89.

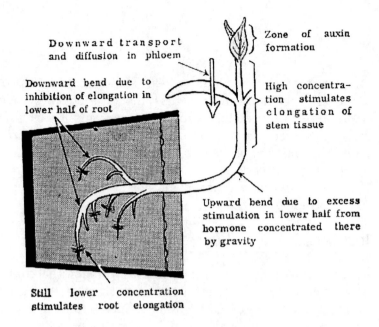

Downward transport and diffusion in phloem

Zone of auxin formation

Downward bend due to inhibition of elongation in lower half of root

High concentration stimulates elongation of stem tissue

Upward bend due to excess stimulation in lower half from hormone concentrated there by gravity

Still lower concentration stimulates root elongation

The sensitive plant *(Mimosa pudica)* and the Venus Flytrap *(Dionaea muscipula)* both display nastic movements in that their leaf movements are not related to differential growth.

External Stimuli—Turgor Pressure, Hormones, and Tropisms

External stimuli also have a major effect on the growth and movement of plants. These actions result in permanent, directed movements resulting from external stimuli, and are referred to as **tropisms**. They are achieved through changes in turgor pressure of cells and groups of cells that cause movement in the plant.

Tropisms are named for the stimulus that causes them. For example, **phototropism** is the most common tropism in nature. Photo refers to light, thus phototropism is a response to light. **Positive phototropism** is growth toward light, while negative **phototropism** is growth away from light. Leaves may twist on petioles to become perpendicular to the light source. Some leaves are sun tracking in that they follow the light source as it moves. Such leaves are called **heliotropic**. Actually phototropism is a term applied to a growth response. The leaves twisting on petioles are exhibiting phototorsion as no growth is involved.

Growth toward light is promoted by auxins migrating to the darker side (the shaded side) of a plant stem and stimulating growth on that side, bending the plant toward the light. Active transport allows auxins to migrate against the diffusion gradient eventually reaching the cells on the dark side. Thus phototropism involves turgor pressure which creates temporary movement as in phototorsion, while hormonal activity with auxins creates a more permanent growth.

Another common tropism involves gravity. We have discussed earlier that roots have a gravity sense and have the ability to grow downward. This is because they exhibit **gravitropism** or are said to be positively geotropic. Gravitropism refers to plant growth responses stimulated by gravity. Primary roots of plants are positively gravitropic while side branches are negatively gravitropic. Roots perceive gravity through the movement of starch grains in cells in the root cap called **statoliths**. Statoliths are

Figure 11–5 Circadian clock of pinnae movements that twist leaves to orient them towards sunlight. *Source:* Arthur W. Galston, Peter J. Davies and Ruth Slater. *The Life of the Green Plant* (1980), Prentice-Hall, p. 309.

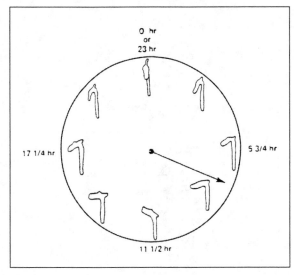

equipped with amyloplasts in which auxins and abscisic acid interact in such a way as to stimulate growth. Calcium ions are also involved as they collect on the bottom of amyloplasts and may be the actual agent to indicate where gravity is the strongest.

Plants are involved in other tropisms as well. For example **thigmotropism** is a response to solid objects. Roots grow around stones and tendrils of climbing vines coil around solid objects. **Hydrotropism** involves growth towards water. This may not be a true tropism as water is necessary for life; however hydrotropic action is important in roots. **Chemotropism** is a response to chemicals, while **thermotropism** is a response to temperature. **Traumotropism** is a response to wounding often characterized by the release of ethylene gas, and **electrotropism** is a response to electricity. Most plants avoid dark and are thus negatively **skototropic**. Some plants need high oxygen environments and are positively **aerotropic**. **Geomagnetotropism** is a response to magnetic forces.

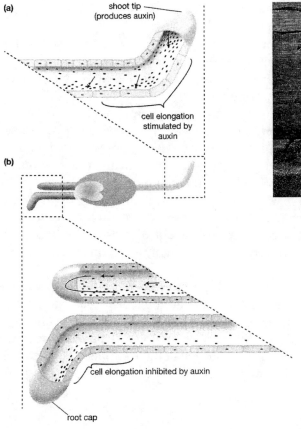

(a) shoot tip (produces auxin)

cell elongation stimulated by auxin

(b)

cell elongation inhibited by auxin

root cap

Figure 11–6 The gravitropism mechanisms of shoot and root response to gravity. *Source:* Teresa Audesirk and Gerald Audesirk (1999), p. 510.

Figure 11–7 Sleep movements in the monkey pod tree. Daytime leaves are at left, nighttime leaves are at right. Sleep movements are regulated by changes in turgor pressures in cells located in the base of leaves. *Source:* Slater. *Journal of General Physiology* 64: pp. 413–430.

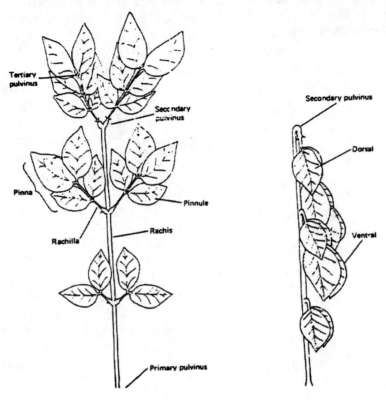

Specific Turgor Movements

Some movements in plants result from changes in internal water pressures alone. Such changes in turgor pressure affect cells of normal parenchyma tissue of the cortex or special swellings called **pulvini** located at the base of leaves. These changes in turgor pressure result mainly in phototorsion described above.

However, not all turgor movements are examples of phototorsion. There are also some plants that exhibit **sleep movements**, such as leaves or flower petals folding as though going to sleep. The folding takes place in regular daily cycles with folding occurring at dusk and unfolding at dawn. These dark-light cycles are called **circadian rhythms**. They are apparently controlled internally but can be altered by changing the length of the photoperiod.

The movements of specific plant structures are produced by turgor pressure with changes being caused by the passage of water in and out of cells at the base of the leaves and petals. Bioluminescence, the production of light, in dinoflagellate algae, is also a kind of circadian rhythm.

Changes in turgor pressure are also involved in **water conservation movements**. In the leaves of many monocots such as grasses there are bulliform cells that lie in the epidermis below parallel-lengthwise grooves in each leaf. When water is scarce, bulliform cells lose turgor pressure and the leaf rolls up or folds. This leaf movement reduces transpiration up to 90-95 % because the stomata on the surface of the leaf have become buried in the folded or rolled leaf and are no longer exposed for evaporation of water.

Figure 11–8 Soybean stems exhibiting negative geotropism, bending away from the pull of gravity. *Source:* E. Webber in Tom M. Graham (1997), p. 185.

Turgor pressure may also be involved in **contact movements**. When some plants are touched there are sudden turgor changes caused by electrical charges released by cells upon contact, or as a result of variation in light or temperature. These changes usually cause contraction movements that involve one or more plant structures or the entire plant. For example, plants that trap insects such as bladderworts and Venus fly traps exhibit sudden contact movements. The sensitive plant, mimosa, has well-developed swellings (pulvini) at the base of each leaf. When the plant is stimulated by touch, heat, or wind potassium ions migrate from half of the pulvini parenchyma cells to the other half. This results in the loss of cellular turgor pressure and a rapid folding of the leaf.

Many flowers and leaves also exhibit contact movements or contact responses. Stamens and pistils move in response to the touch of pollinators. In the African sausage tree, the pistil is two-lobed. As pollen lands on the pistil, the two lobes move inward to force the pollen downward. Stamens of barberry and moss rose snap inward suddenly upon contact to shake pollen over insect pollinators. Conversely, many species of orchids have contact traps to ensure that pollen gets on insects which will then be agents of pollination for the species, carrying the pollen to another orchid. Some of these are trap door-like structures in the flower and involve contact movements to operate.

Taxes and Other Movements

Just as a tropism is the response of a part of a plant to a stimulus, **taxes** are movements involving the entire plant or its reproductive cells and organs. Taxes do not occur among flowering plants but they are common in single-celled plants such as algae or bacteria. Many of these plants swim by moving flagella in response to a stimulus. Furthermore, the reproductive cells of many of these organisms also move by flagella or

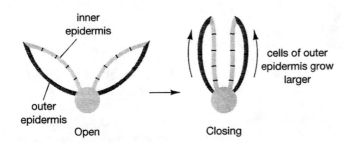

Figure 11–9 Response of the leaves of Venus flytrap to touch. *Source:* Teresa Audesirk and Gerald Audesirk (1999), p. 518.

other locomotory structures. Movement of the cells or organisms may be towards or away from the source of the stimulus.

Stimuli that cause taxes and other movements include chemicals, light, oxygen, and gravitational fields. Taxes are named for the stimulus just as tropisms discussed previously are named for the specific stimulus. Thus taxes which are responses to chemicals are called chemotaxis, those responses to light are called phototaxic, to air are aerotaxic, and to currents are rheotaxic.

There are other movements that occur in plants that are neither caused by hormones nor changes in turgor pressure. For example, slime molds flow, algae glide over each other and diatoms expel water in a jet-propelled movement caused by the contraction of cell fibrils. Dehydration movements, or wilting of plants, is due mainly to physical forces. When turgor pressure drops, gravity takes over and the plant moves downward. Dehydration causes fruits and seed pods to coil up and/or split. In some plants, the expulsion of seeds is due to gas buildup or other physical means. Imbibition, or the uptake of water, causes the seeds of plants to swell and split open.

Phytochromes

Phytochromes are pale blue, proteinaceous pigments that are found in all higher plants. Most phytochromes are associated with the absorption of light. Very small amounts are produced by meristematic tissues. Phytochromes occur in two stable forms, P-red or P-far red, depending on the light spectrum each absorbs. When one form of phytochrome absorbs light, it is converted to the other form. Thus phytochrome-red and phytochrome-far red are always alternating between one form or the other.

Phytochromes are involved in plant development, photoperiodism, changes in plastids, production of anthocyanin pigments, and the detection of shading by other plants. They also affect the germination of seeds, and cause seeds to germinate in the dark. P-red changing to P-far red triggers the production of ethylene gas, causing a seedling to straighten up. Also phytochromes cause seedlings in shade to grow out from under the shade and seek the sun.

PLANT PHOTOPERIODISM

Photoperiodism is the response of plants to the amount of daylight hours. The length of the photoperiod is related to the onset of flowering in plants. The **critical length** of

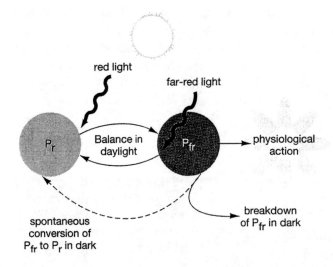

Figure 11–10 Response of the light sensitive pigment phytochrome to red light. *Source:* Teresa Audesirk and Gerald Audesirk (1999), p. 514.

the photoperiod is about 12–14 hours. This means the plant is most productive when it receives about 12–14 hours of sunlight. In this condition the plant can do all the things necessary for survival and at the same time reproduce.

Not all plants are adapted to a photoperiod of 12–14 hour light periods. Some are **short-day plants**, in that the plants will not flower unless the photoperiod is shorter than the critical length. Included in this group are plants that bloom in the fall of the year such as asters, chrysanthemums, dahlias, goldenrods, poinsettias, ragweeds, sorghum, and salvias. Some spring flowering plants are also short-day plants, as they are stimulated by the short days and long nights of spring. Strawberries and violets are spring short-day plants. **Long-day plants** are typically summer flowering plants which bloom when the photoperiod is longer than the critical period. Examples of long-day plants include garden beets, larkspur, lettuce, potatoes, spinach, and wheat. Usually these plants flower in mid-summer.

Short and long-day plants are not the only alternatives. Some species are **intermediate-day plants** that will not flower if days are too short or long. These are late spring or early fall plants. Some plants are **day-neutral plants**. They are primarily tropical plants that will flower under any length of photoperiod so long as they have received a

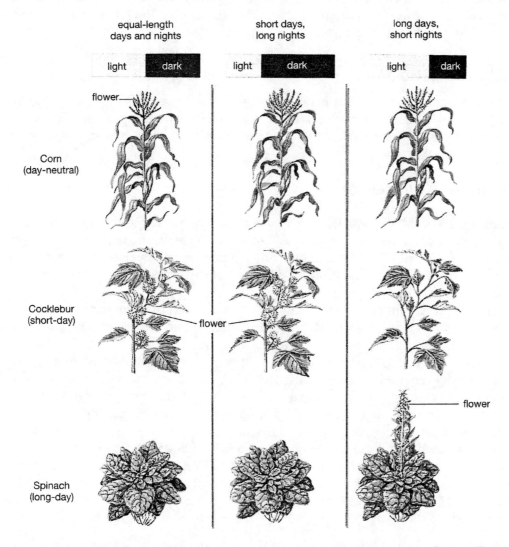

Figure 11–11 The response of flowering plants to daylight and night length. *Source:* Teresa Audesirk and Gerald Audesirk (1999), p. 513.

minimum amount of sunlight. There are also many temperate plants that are day neutral as well. For example, garden beans, calendulas, carnations, cyclamens, cotton, nasturtiums, roses, snapdragons, sunflowers, tomatoes and dandelions are all day neutral.

Photoperiodism is important to most plants. Some species are so sensitive that even one-half hour difference in light duration will determine whether the plant blooms or not. Some plants can be grown in northern or southern climates but will only bloom in the South. Photoperiodism is used in nurseries to raise ornamentals such as poinsettias and chrysanthemums for holidays like Christmas and Mother's Day. The length of artificial light is controlled to force the plant into blooming at a specific time.

Other Plant Responses

FLORIGEN

Florigen is a compound that may be found in leaves that are the most sensitive to photoperiodism. Florigen is thought to be a flowering hormone that is transmitted to meristems where flower buds are produced. The existence of florigen is only hypothesized as it has not actually been isolated.

TEMPERATURE AND GROWTH

Each species has an optimum temperature for growth and that level may vary throughout the life of the plant. Thermoperiodism is a process whereby plants grow better when the temperature is not constant. Young plants develop best at one temperature and adults at another.

DORMANCY AND QUIESCENCE

Dormancy is a period of inactivity during which normal metabolic activities are minimal or stilled. In plants, dormancy has been observed in seeds, bulbs, buds, and other plant organs. Dormancy is influenced by many environmental and internal events, and even when environmental requirements of temperature, water or day length are met internal factors may keep the plant dormant.

Dormancy is important as many plants require a period of dormancy for survival. During this period some tissue development is completed and the seed is prepared for germination. Dormancy must not be confused with quiescence.

Quiescence is a state in which a seed cannot germinate unless environmental conditions normally required for growth are present. Quiescence cannot be disrupted in nature but can be in the nursery. There are many factors that affect quiescence: germination of seeds is primarily determined by temperature, moisture, photoperiod, thickness of seed coat, enzymes, and the presence or absence of growth inhibitors. Quiescence in seeds can be disrupted by a process called **stratification**. In this situation seeds are refrigerated and kept moist for several weeks. This fools the seeds into reacting as though they had been through a winter and wet spring period. They then germinate and grow normally as long as suitable conditions are kept in the greenhouse or where they are transplanted.

Key Words and Phrases

hormone	auxins	IAA or indoleacetic acid
gibberellins	cytokinin	abscisic acid or ABA
ethylene	apical dominance	growth movements
spiral movements	nodding movements	twining movements
contraction movements	nastic movements	tropisms
phototropism	gravitropism	taxes
photoperiodism	critical length	dormancy

Selected References and Resources

Bopp, M. 1985. *Plant Growth Substances.* Springer-Verlag. New York.

Boss, W. F., and J. D. Morre. Eds. 1988. *Second Messengers in Plant Growth and Development.* Alan R. Liss, Inc. New York.

Davies, P. J. Ed. 1987. *Plant Hormones and Their Role in Plant Growth and Development.* Martinus Nijhoff. Dordrecht, Netherlands.

Einset, J. W. 1988. *Plant Growth and Development.* John Wiley and Sons. New York.

Jacobs, W. P. 1979. *Plant Hormones and Plant Development.* Cambridge University Press. New York.

King, J. 1997. *Reaching for the Sun. How Plants Work.* Cambridge University Press. New York.

Nickell, L. G. 1981. *Plant Growth Regulators. Agricultural Uses.* Springer-Verlag. New York.

Thimann, K. V. 1977. *Hormone Action in the Whole Life of Plants.* University of Massachusetts Press. Amherst, Massachusetts.

Wareing, P. F., and I. D. Phillips. 1981. *The Control of Growth and Differentiation in Plants.* 3rd. Edition. Pergamon Press, Inc. New York.

Weaver, R. J. 1972. *Plant Growth Substances in Agriculture.* W. H. Freeman and Company. San Francisco, California

Review and Discussion Questions

1. What are growth hormones? What are growth regulators? How are the two similar and different in their origin and mode of operation?

2. Use information from this and the chapter on photosynthesis and respiration to describe the mechanism of growth stimulating hormones versus photosynthesis inhibiting hormones.

3. How do roots and stems respond to gravity and sunlight?

4. Which are the major hormones of plant growth that induce flowering and the timing of flowering?

5. Discuss how short day and long day plants respond to extrinsic and intrinsic factors.

6. What are day neutral plants? What factors determine their growth and flowering?

7. How do gardeners and greenhouses get plants to germinate, grow and flower at almost any time of year?
8. Make a list of common short day, long day and day neutral plants that grow naturally in the fields and woodlands of Connecticut.

Life Cycles of Plants

Chapter 12

Meiosis
Stages in Meiosis
Meiosis compared to Mitosis
Significance of Meiosis
Plant Life Cycles

Like all organisms, plants must reproduce to perpetuate the species. Reproduction can occur in one of two basic ways, asexually or sexually. As its name implies, **asexual reproduction** takes place without sex. **Budding** is a common type of asexual reproduction in plants. In the process of forming a bud, mitotic growth takes place in specific locations along the plant (e.g., along the stem). When the bud is sufficiently mature, it is discarded, either through action of the plant or because of wind or other meteorological activity. The bud takes root or otherwise germinates and becomes another plant. Budding is a common form of asexual reproduction in many species of bacteria and protistans. Another common form of asexual reproduction called **binary fission** is seen in *Euglena*. In binary fission, a single *Euglena* basically splits in two lengthwise, resulting in two new Euglena which then undergo a period of growth.

In contrast, **sexual reproduction** in plants involves the production of different sex cells, or **gametes**, either by the same plant or by different plants of the same species. One plant produces female gametes and the other produces male gametes. Sexual reproduction is completed when the gametes unite to form a **zygote**, which is the first stage of a new individual. For example, in flowering plants, male flowers produce gametes **(sperm)** in the form of **pollen**, which **fertilizes** (or pollinates) the ovary containing the female gametes **(eggs)**. The fertilized eggs along with surrounding parts of the embryo develop as **seeds**. Through various mechanisms, seeds are dispersed from the parent plant, germinate and grow into new individuals.

Sexual reproduction results in the production of individuals that have new genetic combinations, since they are comprised of chromosomes inherited from each parent. For example, the male pollen contained a complete set of chromosomes obtained from the male plant and the female egg contained another set contributed by the female plant. Since the seeds resulted from the union of pollen and eggs, each new plant that develops from a seed contains two complete sets of chromosomes, one set obtained from each parent plant. This means that the genetic makeup of the new plants are similar to, but also different from, either of the parent plants. This new genetic variability that results from the recombination of chromosomes is a basic function of sexual reproduction. It serves to increase the variability in the plant population.

As in the parent plants, all of the cells (except the sex cells) of the new plants will have two complete sets of chromosomes, one set inherited from each parent. This

Figure 12–1 Budding as a form of asexual reproduction in prokaryotic cells (1 and 2) circular DNA duplicates (3) cell elongates (4) invagination of the cell membrane (5) the parent cell has divided into two daughter cells, all without sexual reproduction. *Source:* Teresa Audesirk and Gerald Audesirk (1999), p. 178.

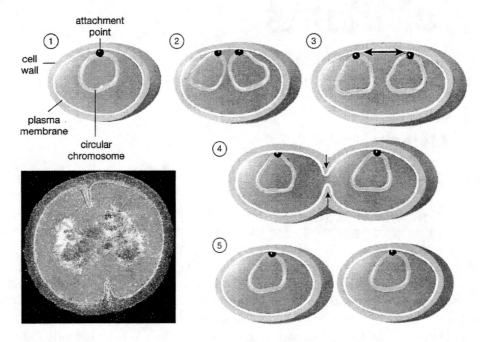

condition is called **diploid (also represented as 2n)**, and is common in higher plants and animals. In contrast, sex cells such as pollen and eggs contain a single set of chromosomes which is termed **haploid (n)**.

The genetic events of sexual reproduction can also be broadly outlined using humans as a familiar example. All of the cells of humans except sex cells contain 46 chromosomes. These include one set of 23 chromosomes that were contributed in the egg and another set of 23 chromosomes which came from the sperm. The union of sperm and egg produced a zygote (you!) consisting of 46 chromosomes. Therefore, your genetic makeup of chromosomes is similar to, but also different from, each of your parents. Furthermore, all of your body cells are diploid with the exception of your sex cells; sperm and eggs each contain a single set of chromosomes and are haploid.

Because they have two sets of chromosomes in most of their cells, diploid organisms face a unique challenge when reproducing. If all cells contained 46 chromosomes, then the union of eggs and sperm would produce humans with 92 chromosomes in each of their cells. If they reproduced, their offspring would contain 92 + 92 chromosomes and so forth. Very shortly, the offspring would be just one big ball of chromosomes! Since this situation obviously cannot occur, sex cells in diploid organisms must undergo a special process of cell division called **meiosis,** in which chromosomes are duplicated and then precisely allocated so that each sex cell receives one complete set of chromosomes (n).

Gametes (sex cells) are haploid (n) in number and when joined form a zygote (fertilized egg) that is diploid (2n). Meiosis produces sex cells that are haploid (n) again.

Meiosis is a special kind of cell division that only occurs in the production of sex cells which are called **gametes**. Eggs and sperm are examples of gametes. In all organisms, meiosis takes place only in certain, limited regions such as the sex organs or in special sex cells. Like mitosis, the goal of meiosis is to produce new cells containing chromosomes. However, each of the daughter cells resulting from mitosis contained exactly the same number of chromosomes as the parent cell. In contrast, each of the sex cells resulting from meiosis contain exactly one-half the number of chromosomes as the original diploid cells.

Meiosis differs from mitosis in having two sequential divisions which result in four haploid cells, each with one-half the chromosome complement of the original cell. As in mitosis, the events of meiosis can be divided into separate stages or phases. Since meiosis goes through two complete sequences of stages seen in mitosis it takes considerably longer to complete. While mitosis in most organisms takes less than 24 hours to complete, meiosis may take two or more weeks to manufacture sex cells.

The process of meiosis can be divided into two separate divisions, the first is represented as **meiosis I** while the second is **meiosis II**. The first division reduces the number of chromosomes and is called reduction division. The second division equally distributes chromosomes among the sex cells and is called equation division.

As in mitosis, the events of meiosis can be subdivided into separate stages or phases which have the same names as those originally described for mitosis, interphase, prophase, metaphase, anaphase, and telophase. Because there are two divisions, these stages are identified for each division as, for example, prophase I, metaphase I, and so forth for meiosis I and prophase II, metaphase II, and so forth for meiosis II.

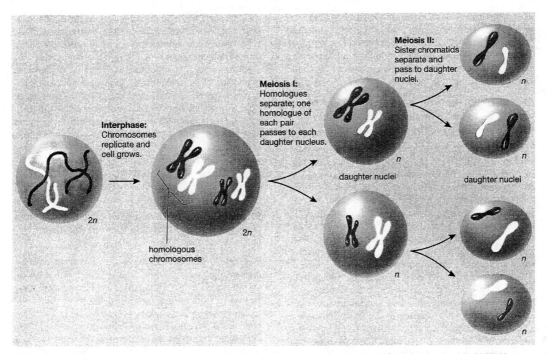

Figure 12–2 An overview of meiosis. *Source:* Teresa Audesirk and Gerald Audesirk (1999), p. 188.

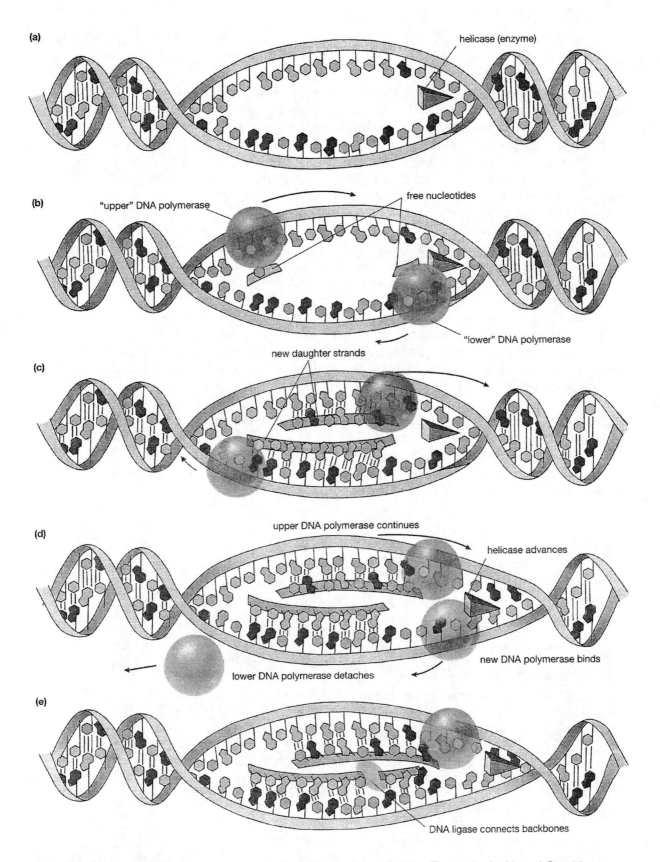

(a)
helicase (enzyme)

(b)
"upper" DNA polymerase
free nucleotides
"lower" DNA polymerase

new daughter strands

(c)

(d)
upper DNA polymerase continues
helicase advances
new DNA polymerase binds
lower DNA polymerase detaches

(e)
DNA ligase connects backbones

Figure 12–3 How the DNA chromosomes duplicate themselves. *Source:* Teresa Audesirk and Gerald Audesirk (1999), p. 462.

The first events of meiosis involve the duplication of chromosomes. Prior to the first stage in meiosis, all of the chromosomes have been duplicated and the chromosome and its copy (called chromatids) are held together by centromeres.

MEIOSIS I

In meiosis the cells go through the same stages that were described in mitosis, however, different things happen to the chromosomes involved.

Prophase I

The first stage of meiosis I is prophase I. At the beginning of this stage, the chromosomes coil, becoming shorter and thicker and are soon visible. Shortly into this stage, the nuclear envelope and nucleolus disappear, and the chromosomes migrate towards the center of the cell. During this migration the chromosomes form **homologous pairs**, which are loosely held together along their length in a kind of stitching process between each chromosome and its homologue. This process of pairing of the homologous chromosomes is called synapse.

To illustrate the nature of homologous chromosomes we will again use humans as an example. Recall that human cells consist of two complete sets of chromosomes, one set inherited from each parent. Each of the chromosomes of a set contains all of the genes necessary for the numerous body functions and activities. The genes that catalog all of these functions (and are also the units of heredity) are located at exact sites on chromosomes and each chromosome carries its own set of genes. When homologous chromosomes pair, the chromosome that contains a specific complement of genes (and was inherited from one parent) pairs with the chromosome that contains the same genes that was contributed by the other parent.

The pairing of homologous chromosomes during prophase results in the alignment of four sets of chromatids (two chromatids in each of the paired homologous). Therefore, the paired homologous chromosomes are called **tetrads** ("tetra" means four = 4 chromatids). At this time, the four chromatids are in close proximity to each other and in some cases they interact to form a **chiasmata**. Chiasmata are places where the adjacent chromatids lie across each other and form x-shaped areas. These chiasmata are actually areas where the chromatids exchange genetic material in a process called crossing over.

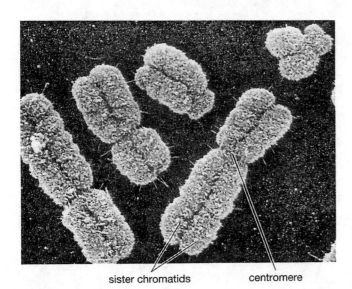

sister chromatids   centromere

Figure 12–4 A scanning electron micrograph of duplicated chromosomes held together by their centromeres. *Source:* Teresa Audesirk and Gerald Audesirk (1999), p. 179.

Crossing over takes place when parts of the adjacent chromatids intertwine, fragment and reform, in the process, genetic material is switched from one chromosome to another. When crossing over occurs, genetic material is exchanged between homologous chromosomes. This process creates new combinations of genes which can then be transmitted to offspring. Crossing over process is important in evolution as well, as the newly created variations can be the basis of evolutionary change, although they mostly account for the differences between individuals in each species rather than major changes that could create new species. Following chromatid formation, spindle fibers develop and attach to the centromeres of the chromosomes and to the poles of the cell.

Metaphase I

In metaphase the homologous pairs of chromosomes are aligned in the center of the cell and the spindle bundle is complete. Generally, metaphase is a brief event in meiosis, and shortly thereafter anaphase begins. Metaphase of meiosis I differs from metaphase of mitosis in that homologous pairs are centrally aligned in meiosis. To illustrate, during metaphase of human cells undergoing mitosis, 46 pairs of chromosomes will be lined up in the center of the cell, each pair consisting of the original chromosome and its copy, held together by the centromere. In contrast, during metaphase I of meiosis in human production of sex cells, 23 tetrads will be lined up in the center of the cell—each tetrad consisting of the two homologous chromosomes and their copies.

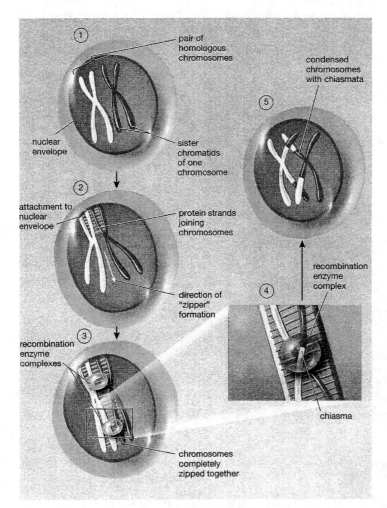

Figure 12–5 The mechanism of crossing over. *Source:* Teresa Audesirk and Gerald Audesirk (1999), p. 190.

Anaphase I

Anaphase I of meiosis is a divisional process. During anaphase I, the homologous chromosomes separate and one chromosome and its copy from each homologous pair migrates from the equatorial plate to one pole of the cell. There is a major difference between mitosis and meiosis at this stage. In mitosis, each chromatid of a chromosome migrates. Thus each chromosome is split into chromatid halves. In meiosis the entire chromosome (the two chromatids still bound by their centromere) migrates. In this case, chromosomes are not split apart, instead individual chromosomes of homologous pairs are separated.

Telophase I

Telophase completes the first division of meiosis. During telophase, the chromosomes arrive at the opposite ends of the dividing cell and nuclear membranes begin to form around each of the two chromosome sets, just as seen in mitosis. The cell wall invaginates and two daughter cells are produced. Again, as in mitosis, each of the daughter cells contains a complete set of chromosomes. That is, each daughter cell is still diploid with respect to its number of chromosomes. Thus, in humans, the daughter cells at this stage of meiosis would still contain 46 chromosomes, or two complete sets.

Interkinesis

The cells resulting from meiosis I next enter a quiet period called interkinesis before starting meiosis II. Usually, the chromosomes unwind and become chromatin within the nucleus. Typically, this interkinesis interlude between meiotic divisions is short, and the meiosis again resumes through several stages called meiosis II.

MEIOSIS II

Two sex cells result at the end of meiosis I, each of which are diploid and contain two complete sets of chromosomes. If this process were mitosis, the cells would then go into interphase and either enter a period of growth and development or immediately resume DNA replication during the S stage. Meiosis differs from mitosis in that there is no duplication of DNA at the end of division I—instead, the two sex cells from meiosis each start dividing again almost immediately.

Prophase II

At the start of prophase II we now have two diploid sex cells (each with one-half the chromosome number of the original cell that began meiosis in prophase I. Prophase II begins with the coiling and thickening of chromatin which again become visible as pairs of chromatids, still held together by a centromere. The stage is now set for the equational division of meiosis II.

Events in prophase II parallel those of prophase I. The nuclear membranes disappear (they are enzymatically reabsorbed), spindle fibers are formed, and the chromatid pairs begin migrating towards the center of the cell.

Metaphase II

Again, the pairs of chromatids align themselves on the equatorial plate of the dividing cell. Strands of fibrils from the spindle bundle attach to each of the chromatids at their centromeres. This configuration is now identical to that of mitosis.

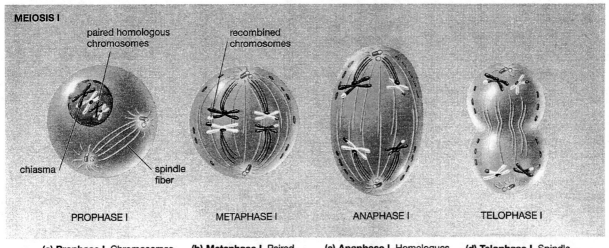

MEIOSIS I

paired homologous
chromosomes

recombined
chromosomes

chiasma

spindle
fiber

PROPHASE I   METAPHASE I   ANAPHASE I   TELOPHASE I

(a) Prophase I. Chromosomes thicken and condense. Homologous chromosomes come together in pairs, and chiasmata occur as chromatids of homologues exchange parts. The nuclear envelope disintegrates, and spindle fibers form.

(b) Metaphase I. Paired homologous chromosomes line up along the equator of the cell. One homologue of each pair faces each pole of the cell. Both chromatids become attached to spindle fibers at their kinetochores (in red).

(c) Anaphase I. Homologues separate, one member of each pair going to each pole of the cell. Sister chromatids do not separate.

(d) Telophase I. Spindle fibers disappear. Two clusters of chromosomes have formed, each containing one member of each pair of homologues. The daughter nuclei are therefore haploid. Cytokinesis commonly occurs at this stage. There is little or no interphase between meiosis I and meiosis II.

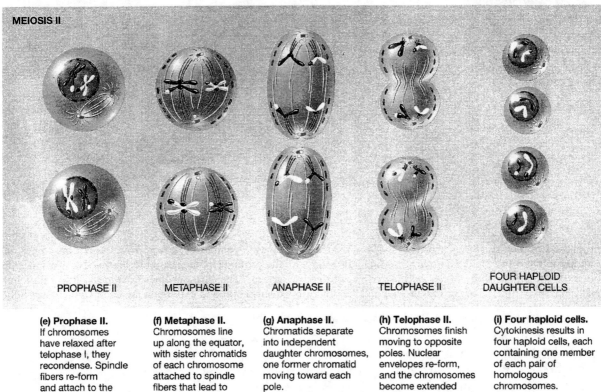

MEIOSIS II

PROPHASE II   METAPHASE II   ANAPHASE II   TELOPHASE II   FOUR HAPLOID DAUGHTER CELLS

(e) Prophase II. If chromosomes have relaxed after telophase I, they recondense. Spindle fibers re-form and attach to the sister chromatids.

(f) Metaphase II. Chromosomes line up along the equator, with sister chromatids of each chromosome attached to spindle fibers that lead to opposite poles.

(g) Anaphase II. Chromatids separate into independent daughter chromosomes, one former chromatid moving toward each pole.

(h) Telophase II. Chromosomes finish moving to opposite poles. Nuclear envelopes re-form, and the chromosomes become extended again.

(i) Four haploid cells. Cytokinesis results in four haploid cells, each containing one member of each pair of homologous chromosomes.

Figure 12–6 A summary of the stages of meiosis. *Source:* Teresa Audesirk and Gerald Audesirk (1999), p. 189.

Anaphase II

The centromeres fragment and each set of chromatids (now called chromosomes) migrates to the opposite poles of the cell. Exactly how they are pulled across the cell towards the poles is somewhat of a mystery. One theory suggests that the spindle fibers "reel" them in, but other plant biologists believe that the spindle fibers shorten, thereby pulling the chromosomes along. However it is accomplished, by the end of anaphase II a set of chromosomes are clustered at each pole of the cell.

Telophase II

This final stage in meiosis results in the splitting of the dividing cell through the middle, producing two new cells. In telophase II, the cell walls invaginate and draw towards one another until they fuse. At the same time, nuclear membranes form around the chromosomes and nuclear structures such as the nucleolus reappear. Inside the nucleus, the chromosomes lengthen and become thinner, unwinding to form the chromatin network.

Since two cells entered meiosis II, the final result of meiosis is the production of four sex cells, each with half the number of chromosomes as the original cell. That is, each of the sex cells are haploid. Referring to humans again, each of the four sperm resulting from meiosis now has one complete set of 23 chromosomes. Thus, in the production of sperm (and human eggs also) we go from one original diploid cell containing two complete sets of chromosomes to four haploid cells each of which contains a single set of chromosomes.

In higher plants the four haploid cells resulting from meiosis are called meiospores. They further develop into cells or tissues that become or produce gametes. Gametes are sex cells that are haploid. When two gametes combine they produce a diploid zygote and the cycle of reproduction is complete.

Differences between Meiosis and Mitosis

The events of cell division observed in meiosis are similar to, but also different from, those seen in mitosis. The primary difference, of course, is that meiosis results in four haploid cells—the sex cells—while mitosis results in duplicate diploid cells. The second basic difference is that mitosis consists of a single cell division while meiosis consists of two cycles of cell division, meiosis I and meiosis II. Again, the first division in meiosis is usually called reduction division because the total number of chromosomes allotted to the two new cells is reduced by half; the second is called equational division because each of the four cells that result receives the same complement of chromosomes.

The Significance of Meiotic (Sexual) Reproduction

Cell replication by mitosis inevitably produces cells that are exactly like the original cell. After all, the same chromosomes and genes of the original cell are being duplicated and therefore the genetic makeup of the original and replicated cells will be the same genetically. In contrast, sexual reproduction dramatically increases genetic variation of the population. Consider that the egg produced during meiosis contains a complete set of chromosomes of one plant while the sperm contains a complete chromosome set produced by another plant. When egg and sperm unite the new plant contains genetic material from two different parents, thereby resulting in an individual that is genetically similar to, but also different from each of the parent plants. This combination of two sets of chromosomes (the egg and sperm) is called **genetic recombination** and contributes genetic variation to a population. Furthermore, since there are two metaphase events during meiosis (metaphase I and metaphase II) the potential for crossing-over exchanges between homologous chromosomes is twice enhanced, thereby increasing genetic variability of the plant population still further. It is this genetic variability that can result from meiotic events and from recombination that is the real secret of **sex**, for genetic variability increases the chances of survival of populations, especially in changing environments. Asexual reproduction, however, retains an adaptive advantage for populations if the environment is stable. This is probably the reason why so many plants can, when needed, employ both sexual and asexual reproductive strategies.

In sexual reproduction the gamete cells (egg and sperm) produced during meiosis combine to produce a new individual that contains a genetic mix derived from both parents. The new individual will therefore be similar to, but also different from either parent. Furthermore, because the potential for crossing-over during the metaphase I and metaphase II stages of meiosis is high, the progeny will likely inherit an even greater genetic variation.

Plant Life Cycles

Plants exhibit a variety of life cycles, ranging from simple to complex. Basically, the lower plants such as bacteria and algae exhibit the simplest life cycles while the more advanced plants such as the flowering plants have considerably more complex life cycles.

In simple plants reproduction is often asexual and the normal cells of individuals do not have homologous pairs of chromosomes. As a result, they are haploid cells. Reproduction is vegetative and mitosis is the primary reproductive process in the simplest of plants.

In more complex plants there have developed homologous pairs of chromosomes and so at least some cells are diploid. This has resulted in the development of sexual reproduction. Each plant may have some cells that are haploid and others that are diploid. In most animals, haploid cells are only gametes (sex cells) but this is not generally true in plants. Most plants above the grade of bacteria and algae have developed a complex life cycle called **alternation of generations**, which involves an alteration between haploid and diploid life stages. This means that one generation of a species is haploid, and the offspring it produces become the next generation which is diploid. The plants of the diploid generation in turn produce a haploid generation, and so forth. The generation that is formed from diploid cells is called the **sporophyte generation**, while the haploid generation that follows is called the **gametophyte generation**.

The sporophyte generation develops from a diploid (2n) zygote. At maturity, the sporophyte plant produces spore mother cells (2n meiocytes), each of which undergoes meiosis to produce four haploid (n) cells (gametes). The haploid spores develop into plants of the gametophyte generation. At maturity, these gametophyte plants form sex organs and produce haploid gametes. However, when these gametes unite, they form a diploid zygote which grows into the sporophyte plant. To summarize the steps in alternation of generation, meiosis occurs in the sporophyte generation to produce

Figure 12–7 The three major types of life cycles that occur in organisms. *Source:* Teresa Audesirk and Gerald Audesirk (1999), p. 193.

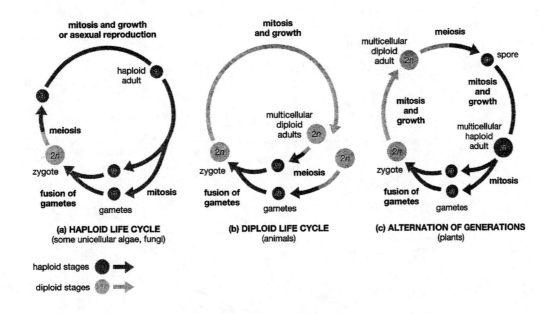

the gametophyte generation and mitosis occurs in the gametophyte generation to produce gametes that will become the sporophyte plant.

The diploid sporophyte generation always produces haploid spores which give rise to the haploid gametophyte generation. The two haploid gametes fuse to give rise to the diploid sporophyte generation again.

In lower and simpler plants the gametophyte generation is usually the dominant generation and the sporophytes grow on (and depend on) the mature gametophytes for support and nourishment. That is, the "leafy" plants that we see are gametophytes while the egg capsules that grow at the ends of leaves and stems of these leafy plants represent the comparatively brief sporophyte generation.

As plants become more complex in structure there is a gradual change from the gametophyte stage being the dominant stage in the life cycle to the sporophyte stage being dominant. For example, most algae that we see are haploid plants. What we view as an algae is actually the gametophyte stage of the life cycle and is haploid. When an alga reproduces, two haploid algal sex cells combine to form a diploid zygote, which represents the sporophyte stage in the life cycle. However, rather than growing into a mature diploid algae, the zygote undergoes meiosis to produce haploid cells which start new algal colonies. Thus in algae the haploid or gametophyte stage in the life cycle is dominant because the plant spends most of its life in that stage. In contrast, the diploid sporophyte stage is a brief transition from one gametophyte generation to another.

We can compare this to the life cycle of a tree or any of the other higher plants. In its life cycle, the tree is actually the sporophyte (2n) generation and all of its cells, except its sex cells, are diploid. The sex cells contained within the flowers of the tree produce gametes (pollen and eggs) by meiosis. These gametes represent the gametophyte (n) generation of the plant. These unite to form the zygote which will eventually

Figure 12–8 Alternation of gametophyte generations with sporophyte generations in higher plants. *Source:* Roy H. Saigo and Barbara W. Saigo. *Botany: Principles of Applications* (1990), Prentice-Hall, p. 30.

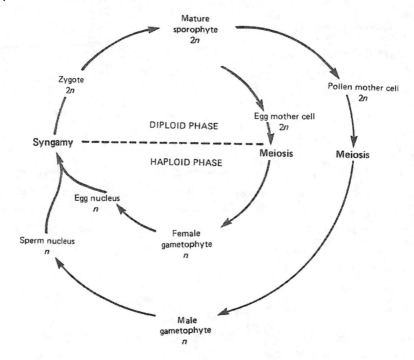

grow into the next generation of trees, all of which are sporophytes and diploid. Thus, in trees, as in almost all higher plants, the visible, leafy plant is a sporophyte and the dominant generation. In comparison, the gametophyte generation consists of sex cells produced in sex organs supported by the sporophyte.

The story of this change in life cycle stage dominance is the essence of describing plant evolution. Later in this book we will go on a tour of the plant groups and we will see a gradual change from a dominant gametophyte generation to a dominant sporophyte generation. In the meantime there are specific rules that can be used to identify which part of the life cycle is gametophyte or sporophyte.

Key Facts to Remember

1. The cells of the gametophyte generation are usually haploid.
2. The final result of the gametophyte generation is the production of sex cells called gametophytes.
3. The union of gametophyte sex cells produces a diploid sporophyte generation.
4. The sporophyte generation produces haploid spores through meiosis from spore mother cells.
5. Therefore the change from the sporophyte generation to the haploid generation is preceded by meiosis.
6. The change from the gametophyte generation to the sporophyte generation occurs by fertilization.

Key Words and Phrases

asexual reproduction
mitosis
division II
crossing over
sporophyte generation

sexual reproduction
meiosis
homologous pair
alternations of generations
gametophyte generation

gametes
division I
chiasmata

Selected References and Resources

Grant, V. 1975. *Genetics of Flowering Plants.* Columbia University Press. New York.

Klug, W. S. 1991. *Concepts of Genetics.* 3rd. Edition. Macmillan Publishing Company. New York.

Mitchison, J. 1972. *Biology of the Cell Cycle.* Cambridge University Press. New York.

Prescot, D. 1976. *Reproduction of Eukaryotic Cells.* Academic Press. New York.

Russell, P. J. 1992. *Genetics.* 3rd. Edition. Harper/Collins. New York.

Strickberger, M. 1985. *Genetics.* 3rd. Edition. Macmillan Publishing Company. New York.

Review and Discussion Questions

1. Trace the number of chromosomes in each of the stages of meiosis. What is the basic accomplishment of meiosis as far as the genetic variation is concerned?
2. How does meiosis differ from mitosis in terms of the number of divisions and the number of chromosomes that each of the daughter cells ends up with?
3. What advantages, if any, do plants that have life cycles with alternation of generations have over organisms that do not exhibit this pattern?
4. Are the gametophytes always a separate generation represented by separate individual organisms? Are the sporophytes?
5. Why is meiosis necessary in the life cycle of organisms that reproduce by sex.
6. If meiosis is so complicated, what are its advantages to the species?
7. Some years ago some botanists proposed that the term "alternation of phases" be substituted for "alternation of generations." Discuss this.

Plant Genetics

The branch of science that deals with inheritance is called **genetics.** Genetics is the study of genes, how they occur, how they are expressed, and how they are transmitted from parents to offspring. Another name for the science of genetics is heredity, which refers to how offspring inherit and express the genes and genetic traits that they carry in the chromosomes inherited from their parents.

Before the discovery of genetics, people believed that heredity was a form of blending inheritance. In other words offspring were the combined characteristics of the two parents, just as one combines two liquids. According to this early idea of heredity, the characteristics of the two parents were completely mixed in the offspring and could not be separated again. For example, if red roses were crossed with white roses all of the seeds would give rise to pink roses. Furthermore, all of the pink roses would produce pink roses as well. Apparently, no one noticed that when pink roses are crossed they gave rise to red and white roses as well as pink roses!

The modern science of genetics (or heredity) began nearly 150 years ago with the studies conducted by an obscure Austrian monk named **Gregor Mendel.** Like other scientists of his time, Mendel was interested in learning how characteristics of parents are transmitted to, and expressed in, their offspring. In studying heredity, Mendel chose to work with common garden peas. His results provided our first clear understanding of the basic laws of genetics. His experiments also finally disproved the idea of blending inheritance and replaced it with our modern ideas of inheritance. Unfortunately, Mendel's discoveries were published in a small Austrian scientific journal and were overlooked until the turn of the last century when several scientists simultaneously rediscovered the laws of genetics. While searching the published scientific literature, they came across Mendel's earlier work on genetics and very properly gave him credit for discovering the basic laws of genetics.

To illustrate some of the basic ideas, terminology, and laws of genetics, we will review Mendel's pioneering studies of garden peas (*Pisium sativa*). Mendel was fortunate to choose the garden pea plant for his experiments because they reproduce in an uncomplicated way and their genetics is relatively simple and easy to follow. Garden pea plants are self-fertilizing but can also be artificially cross-fertilized.

Mendel's classic experiments illustrate the methods scientists use to investigate problems. Mendel hypothesized that all of the visible traits of garden peas such as height and flower color were produced by inheritable factors. Mendel called these factors "**unit factors**" or simply "factors" because he could not actually see what material was involved. (We now know that these inheritable factors are **genes)**. To discover how the unit factors were inherited and expressed, Mendel studied seven easily identifiable traits of pea plants such as height, flower color, and the shape of the seed pods (Table 13-1).

Mendel began by obtaining **true-breeding** stocks of pea plants for each of the traits. For example, true-breeding tall pea plants always produced tall offspring while pure-breeding stocks of dwarf pea plants always produced dwarf offspring. Mendel studied the inheritance of one trait at a time, then he examined how two different traits such as height and flower color were inherited together. Mendel made large numbers of experimental crosses and kept careful records of his results. He then crossed the offspring of the first generation to produce subsequent generations, again keeping careful numerical tallies.

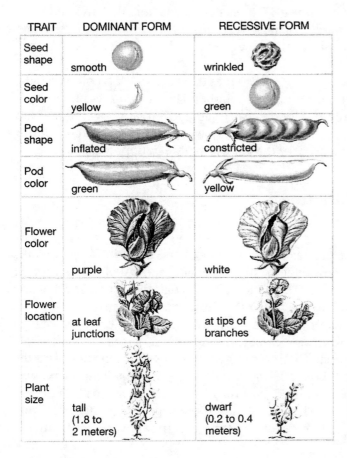

TRAIT	DOMINANT FORM	RECESSIVE FORM
Seed shape	smooth	wrinkled
Seed color	yellow	green
Pod shape	inflated	constricted
Pod color	green	yellow
Flower color	purple	white
Flower location	at leaf junctions	at tips of branches
Plant size	tall (1.8 to 2 meters)	dwarf (0.2 to 0.4 meters)

Figure 13–1 Some of the traits of pea plants that Gregor Mendel studied. *Source:* Teresa Audesirk and Gerald Audesirk (1999), p. 207.

Table 13-1 Results of Mendel's experiments.

Trait	Dominant	Recessive	F_2 progeny Dominant	F_2 progeny Recessive
plant height	tall	dwarf	787	287
flower color	red	white	705	224
seed form	round	wrinkled	5474	1850
seed color	yellow	green	6022	2001
flower site	axil	terminal	621	207
pod form	inflated	tight	882	299
pod color	green	yellow	428	152

After several years of investigations and hundreds of experiments Mendel was able to establish several basic facts about inheritance. First, he confirmed his initial premise that traits such as flower color and pea plant height were transmitted from generation to generation in the form of discrete units that he termed unit factors. Furthermore, these units maintained their distinctive identity rather than blending or disappearing. From these results, he formulated the first law of genetics, which states that units remain separate entities. This fact is called the **Law of Segregation** or the **Law of Unit Factor Inheritance**.

Mendel also noticed that not all of the unit factors were equal in how they were expressed in the offspring that inherit them. Some factors always appeared in offspring when two different true-breeding lines of pea plants were crossed but others were only expressed when the "stronger" factor was not present. Mendel called the factors that always appeared in the offspring **dominant.** He termed the factors that showed up in the offspring only when the dominant genes were absent as **recessive**. From this, Mendel suggested that the **Law of Dominance** described the difference between strong and weak factors.

From his experiments Mendel also discovered that unit factors which produced different traits were inherited separately from one another. He termed this phenomena the **Law of Independent Assortment**. Mendel was unable to explain how the unit factors assorted independently in offspring. Today we know that these factors sort during meiosis, when the chromosomes that carry the genes migrate to opposite poles.

Unit Factors, Genes, and Alleles

Mendel called the inheritable substances which produced the traits in his pea plants unit factors because he had no knowledge of the molecular biology of genes or their function (which is not surprising, since the science of molecular biology was still nearly 100 years away in the future). Today, we know that all traits are controlled by genes which are, in turn, carried on the chromosomes. During reproduction, each parent contributes a gene for each trait so offspring actually end up with a pair of genes for each trait, one inherited from each parent. The pair of genes is called a **genotype** and the genes are **alleles** of one another. If both alleles are alike the genotype is **homozygous**; if the alleles differ the genotype is termed **heterozygous**. The alleles of a genotype interact to produce a visible trait, which is called the **phenotype**. The concepts, terminology, and methods of genetics can be further illustrated in monohybrid and dihybrid crosses.

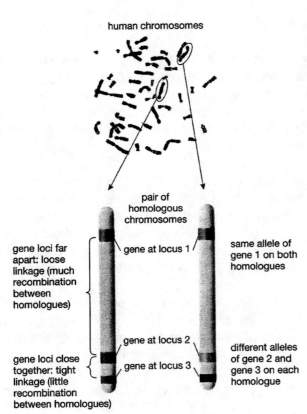

human chromosomes

Figure 13–2 The relationships between alleles, genes, and the chromosomes on which they are carried. *Source:* Teresa Audesirk and Gerald Audesirk (1999), p. 203.

pair of homologous chromosomes

gene loci far apart: loose linkage (much recombination between homologues)

gene at locus 1

same allele of gene 1 on both homologues

gene at locus 2

gene at locus 3

gene loci close together: tight linkage (little recombination between homologues)

different alleles of gene 2 and gene 3 on each homologue

Terms Used in Genetics

Alleles	The alternate forms of a gene
Gene	Section of chromosome that controls a trait
Chromosome	DNA which contains many discrete segments called genes
Locus	The position, or location, of a gene on a chromosome
Genotype	The genes carried on the chromosomes
Phenotype	What the organism looks like, the expression of the genes in the physical appearance of the organism
Dominant Gene	Gene that is always expressed
Recessive Gene	Gene that is masked if a dominant gene is present
Homozygous	Having the same alleles for a trait (AA)
Heterozygous	Having different alleles for a trait (Aa)

A Monohybrid Cross

A monohybrid cross follows the inheritance of a single trait. In one of his first experiments with monohybrid crosses, Mendel crossed true-breeding tall pea plants with true-breeding dwarf pea plants. He called them true-breeding or pure-breeding because all of the progeny of the tall pea plants were tall and the progeny of the dwarf pea plants were always dwarf. Mendel found that all of the first generation of pea plants resulting from this cross were tall. Mendel carefully self-fertilized several plants of the first generation and found that three-fourths of the second generation produced were tall and one-fourth were dwarf.

To describe and evaluate these results, Mendel devised a kind of "convenient shorthand" that we still use today. He designated the first letter of the dominant trait as the symbol used in referring to the genes. In his crosses Mendel discovered that tall genes are dominant over dwarf genes in pea plants so he designated the gene that produced tall pea plants as T while the gene of the dwarf pea plants was symbolized as t. Mendel was also the first to capitalize the dominant gene (T) and indicate the recessive gene in lower case (t).

Mendel realized that the parental stock of pea plants carried a pair of genes for height (as well as every other trait). He therefore designated the pair of gene pairs by the tall pea plants as TT (they, in turn, had inherited one of each of the (T) genes from each of their parents.) The genotype of the dwarf pea plants that produced only dwarf offspring is tt. When the true breeding tall pea plants (TT) were crossed with true breeding dwarf pea plants (tt) their offspring inherited one gene from each parent for this particular trait (pea plant height).

The original pea plants, the parents are designated as the **P** or **parental generation**. To find the results of this cross, we must first determine the genes that can be contributed to the offspring by each parent pea plant. When the parent tall pea plants meiotically produce female gametes (eggs) or male gametes (pollen or sperm) each gamete will carry a dominant gene (T) for height. Similarly, each of the eggs or pollen gametes produced by the parent dwarf pea plant will carry a recessive gene (t). When the male gamete carrying its gene for pea plant height fertilizes the female gamete with its gene the offspring inherit a Tt pair of genes that interact to control height. Since the gene pair includes a dominant gene (T) all pea plants of the first generation (called the **F$_1$** or **first filial** generation) will be tall.

To describe this monohybrid cross in modern genetics terms, we are crossing a homozygous dominant tall pea plant (TT) with a homozygous recessive dwarf pea plant that has a tt genotype. The F$_1$ progeny have a heterozygous Tt genotype and their phenotype is tall. No matter how many first generation offspring plants are produced in this pea plant cross, they will all have exactly the same genotype (Tt) and all of them will exhibit the tall phenotype. We should also note that their Tt genotype consists of two alternate expressions of a gene which are **alleles** of one another; that is, T is an allele of t.

To Mendel, it seemed as though the factor that produced dwarf pea plants had been lost, since it did not appear in any plants of the F$_1$ generation. To test this possibility, Mendel cross-fertilized members of the first generation of pea plants to see what would happen in the second generation, which in genetics is called the **F$_2$ generation.**

To examine this cross, we must again consider how the alleles in the genotype will be assorted during the production of the gametes. The F$_1$ generation pea plants being crossed have the same genotype (Tt) and both will produce two kinds of gametes, one with the T allele and another with the t allele. If an egg with the T allele is fertilized by pollen carrying the t allele the resulting F$_2$ pea plants will have the genotype Tt for the height. Conversely, if an egg carrying a t allele unites with a pollen carrying a t allele, the offspring will have the genotype tt. Furthermore, a pollen carrying the T allele can unite with an egg carrying another T allele to produce a TT genotype. Thus, three different combinations of alleles can be inherited in the second generation of pea plants.

To keep track of how the alleles are inherited in the second generation we use a **Punnet square**, which is a series of cells arranged in a grid. The number of cells in a Punnet square is determined by multiplying the number of different gametes that each pea plant can produce. The construction of a Punnet square for the pea plant monohybrid cross is shown as follows:

Example of a Monohybrid Cross
T = tall pea plants
t = dwarf pea plants

The parent or P generation contributes the following genotypes to the offspring:

TT pure-breeding tall pea plants
tt pure-breeding dwarf pea plants

The genotype of one F_1 pea plant Tt
The genotype of the other F_1 pea plant Tt

To set up a Punnet Square, place the alleles genes that can be transmitted by the first plant to the offspring on the first column while the genes transmitted by the other parent are placed in the left outer column as shown below:

	T	t
T		
t		

Now, fill in the cells in the table by taking the column and row letter and adding them to each cell respectively. These will be the genotypes inherited by the offspring. To illustrate:

	T	t
T	TT	Tt
t	Tt	tt

The completed Punnet square reveals that F_2 pea plants can inherit one of three possible genotypes TT or Tt or tt. The Punnet Square also indicates that F_2 offspring will have twice the chance to inherit the Tt genotype as they do either TT or tt. The genotype ratio that occurs in the F_2 generation is 1:2:1, that is 1/4 TT, 1/2 Tt or 1/4 tt. Since the tall allele T is dominant over the recessive allele t, the F_2 offspring will be 3/4 tall pea plants and 1/4 dwarf pea plants.

To describe these results in genetics terms, 1/4 of the F_2 generation may inherit a homozygous dominant genotype *(TT)*, 1/2 a heterozygous genotype *(Tt)*, and 1/4 a homozygous recessive genotype *(tt)*. These represent statistical possibilities that can be inherited by the offspring. For example, chances are that 75 percent of the F_2 generation will be tall and 25 percent will be dwarf. That is, if there were 1000 pea plants produced in the F_2 generation, the chances are that 750 of them will be tall and 250 will be dwarf. Conversely, if only one pea plant was produced in the F_2 generation, there is a 75 percent chance that it would be tall and a 25 percent chance that it would be dwarf.

Testing Unknown Genotypes—The Backcross

The plant geneticist has no way of knowing if the tall F_2 pea plants have a homozygous dominant (TT) or heterozygous (Tt) genotype. To find out, the researcher crosses true-breeding second generation (F_2) individuals that exhibit the dominant trait, with true-breeding individuals that only exhibit the recessive trait. This kind of cross is called a **backcross** or **test cross** and is commonly used to confirm the genotypes of progeny, or other unknown individuals.

For example, we can test tall F_2 pea plants that we think are heterozygous *(Tt)* by back crossing them with true-breeding dwarf pea plants that have a *tt* genotype. Progeny resulting from this back cross are 1/2 tall pea plants and 1/2 dwarf pea plants, thereby confirming the heterozygous *(Tt)* genotype of the tall pea plant stock used in this back cross. The Punnet square for this back cross is set up as follows:

	T	*t*
t	*Tt*	*tt*
t	*Tt*	*tt*

As a further check, we can back cross *Tt* pea plants with pure-breeding tall pea plants *(TT)*. In this back cross 1/2 of the progeny will have a *TT* genotype and 1/2 will have a *Tt* genotype. Phenotypically, all will be tall pea plants. Results from back crosses further confirm Mendel's law of segregation, since it was obvious that the allele (t) for dwarf pea plants had neither blended nor become lost in subsequent generations of pea plants.

A Dihybrid Cross

A monohybrid cross illustrates how a pair of genes (= alleles) that produce a particular trait is transmitted, inherited, and expressed in offspring. A cross in which we follow the inheritance patterns of two pairs of genes that produce two traits is called a **dihybrid cross**. For an example of a dihybrid cross we will again return to Mendel and his garden peas. In another of his many experiments with garden peas, Mendel crossed pure-breeding strains of garden peas that produced round and yellow pea seeds with another strain of pure-breeding peas that produced wrinkled and green pea seeds. He found that all of the peas of the F_1 generation had round and yellow pea seeds. Mendel planted seeds of the F_1 generation and self-fertilized their flowers to produce an F_2 generation of 556 pea plants. Of these, 315 plants had round and yellow seed seeds, 101 were wrinkled and yellow, 108 were round and green, and 32 had wrinkled and green pea seeds.

We can interpret these results by using our "genetic shorthand" and Punnet square. In this dihybrid cross we are following the inheritance of two traits, seed color (green or yellow), and seed texture (wrinkled or round). Since all of the F_1 pea plants were phenotypically yellow and round these must be the dominant alleles while the alleles for wrinkled and green must be recessive.

Example of a Dihybrid Cross

R = round pea seeds
r = wrinkled pea seeds

Y = yellow pea seeds
y = green pea seeds

Therefore, the genotype of the parent strain with round and yellow pea seeds must be *RRYY* while the genotype of the parent strain with wrinkled and green seeds is *rryy*. Note that we are now dealing with two sets of alleles; interaction of the *Rr* pair determines the shape of the seed (one trait) while the *Yy* pair determines the color of the seed coat (a different trait).

Next, we must consider the genetic makeup of the gametes that each of the parent pea plants can contribute to their F_1 generation offspring. The pea plants with round and yellow seeds have an *RRYY* genotype and can only contribute pollen or eggs with *RY* alleles. The parent pea plants with wrinkled and green pea seeds have an *rryy* genotype and can only contribute pollen or eggs with *ry* alleles. Therefore, all of the F_1 progeny resulting from this cross will have an *RrYy* genotype and all will produce round and yellow seeds. That is, it doesn't matter whether 10 or 100 or 1000 pea plants are produced in the F_1 generation, as they will all have the same pea seed color and shape.

The inheritance of seed color and shape in the F_2 generation is determined by crossing two F_1 generation pea plants. Each can contribute one of several possibilities to the allele makeup of the gametes: *RY, Ry, rY,* or *ry*. To see how these gametes are transmitted and inherited from the F_1 parents to their F_2 offspring, we again set up a Punnet square. This time the Punnet square consists of four rows and four columns and 16 cells. The Punnet Square is set up as follows:

	RY	*Ry*	*rY*	*ry*
RY				
Ry				
rY				
ry				

Again, take the row and column letters to fill in the cells.

	RY	*Ry*	*rY*	*ry*
RY	*RRYY*	*RRYy*	*RrYY*	*RrYy*
Ry	*RRYy*	*RRyy*	*RrYy*	*Rryy*
rY	*RrYY*	*RrYy*	*rrYY*	*rrYy*
ry	*RrYy*	*Rryy*	*rrYy*	*rryy*

As can be seen, there are several genotypes in the 16 different cells but some of the genotypes result in the same phenotype. An examination of these genotypes reveals that four kinds of phenotypes are possible in the F$_2$ generation; round and yellow, wrinkled and yellow, round and green, and wrinkled and green. The Punnet square also shows that the expected genetic ratios of these phenotypes is 9:3:3:1. That is, the chances are that 9/16 of the F$_2$ pea plants will have round and yellow seeds, 3/16 will have round and green seeds, 3/16 will have wrinkled and yellow seeds, and 1/16 will have wrinkled and green seeds.

Thus, if 10 or 100 or 1000 pea plants were produced in the F$_2$ generation the laws of genetics and statistical probability tells us that 9/16 of them will have round and yellow seeds. If only one pea plant was produced in the F$_2$ generation the chances that it would have round and yellow seeds are still 9 out of 16. Conversely, the chance that the single pea plant would have wrinkled and green seeds is only one in sixteen.

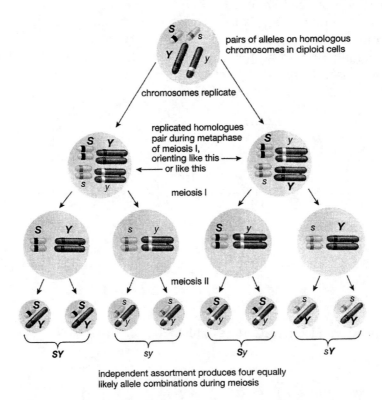

Figure 13–3 An example of independent assortment of alleles in a dihybrid cross. *Source:* Teresa Audesirk and Gerald Audesirk (1999), p. 209.

The expected genetic ratios in a dihybrid cross involving dominant and recessive alleles for each trait are also confirmed in Mendel's observed results which are very close to the predicted genetic ratios of a dihybrid cross.

$$315/556 = 56.6\% \text{ round and yellow seeds}$$
$$101/556 = 18.2\% \text{ wrinkled and yellow seeds}$$
$$108/556 = 19.4\% \text{ round and green seeds}$$
$$33/556 = 5.9\% \text{ wrinkled and green seeds}$$

Mendel also noted that the two traits—-seed color and texture—-appeared in different combinations in the F_2 progeny. From this, he formulated a second fundamental law of genetics, called the **Law of Independent Assortment**, which points out that the alleles for different traits are inherited independently of one another in offspring. That is, alleles are not linked together and do not blend, but rather remain separate and assort randomly in the genetic makeup of the egg or pollen. (If alleles did not assort independently, then pea plants would always produce yellow and round seeds or wrinkled and green seeds).

The Law of Independent Assortment only holds true if the alleles for each trait are carried on different chromosomes. Mendel was fortunate because the alleles for seed color are carried on a different chromosome than the alleles for seed texture. For many traits, however, alleles are carried on the same chromosome and are inherited together. Since Mendel's studies, many variations in genetic inheritance have been found.

Modern Genetics

Not all genetic crosses are as clear-cut as the monohybrid and dihybrid examples that we have presented, nor are they as clear-cut. Often genotypic information is not known or is incompletely known or the genetic cross is complicated by many other factors that influence the ways in which genes are inherited and expressed.

INCOMPLETE DOMINANCE

Many inheritable traits in plants consist of dominant and recessive alleles. In some however, neither allele is totally dominant. Rather, both are equally expressed in the progeny which appear to be a blend of the parents. Genetic crosses in which neither allele is dominant are examples of **incomplete dominance** and the alleles are **codominant**.

The flowers of plants called four o'clocks provide a good example of incomplete dominance. The flowers of four o'clocks are either red, white or pink. The trait for flower color in four o'clocks is determined by a single pair of alleles. We can designate the alleles of pure-breeding four o'clocks that always have red flowers as *RR*. The alleles of four o'clocks that always produce white flowers are *rr*. If pure breeding red flowered four o'clocks are crossed with pure-breeding white flowered four o'clocks, all of the F_1 progeny inherit an *Rr* genotype and all have pink flowers. The pink flowers result because both alleles are being expressed equally. That is, when seen with a microscope the flowers are actually a mix of red and white pigments that appear pink. Neither allele is dominant but neither allele is recessive either.

The results of this cross seems to show that the alleles blended in the offspring. To test this possibility, two of the pink-flowered plants of the F_1 generation are self-fertilized to produce the F_2 generation. Again, a Punnet square can be set up for this cross as follows:

	R	r
R	RR	Rr
r	Rr	rr

Inspection of Punnet square results reveals that the expected genotype ratios in the F_2 generation of four o'clocks are 1/4 RR, 1/2 Rr and 1/4 rr. The F_2 phenotypic ratios are 1/4 red flowered, 1/2 pink flowered and 1/4 white flowered. To confirm that the pink flowered four o'clocks are heterozygous, we can backcross them with pure breeding white flowered four o'clocks. This backcross results in 1/2 white flowered and 1/2 pink flowered four o'clocks. Similarly, a backcross of pink flowered four o'clocks with red flowered four o'clocks will produce 1/2 red flowered progeny and 1/2 pink flowered progeny. Results offer further confirmation of Mendel's law that alleles remain separate rather than blending.

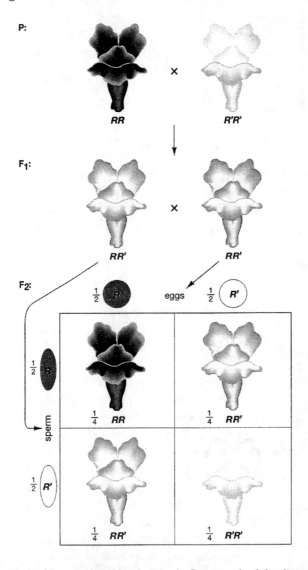

Figure 13–4 An example of incomplete dominance in flower color inheritance of snapdragons. *Source:* Teresa Audesirk and Gerald Audesirk (1999), p. 212.

MULTIPLE GENE INHERITANCE

Many traits in plants are controlled by one set of genes, as seen in previous examples. Some traits are, however, controlled by two or more pairs of genes. The inheritance of traits that are produced by interactions of two or more gene sets is called **multiple gene inheritance**.

The color of wheat grain provides an example of multiple gene inheritance in plants. Wheat grains are deep red, red, light red, pink, or white in color. The color of the grain is produced by the interaction of two pairs of genes controlling for a single trait, wheat grain color.

To illustrate the inheritance of grain color we will cross a pure-breeding wheat plant that produces only deep red grains with a pure-breeding wheat plant that produces only white grain. The genotype that produces the deep red color can be designated $R_1R_1R_2R_2$ while we will designate the genotype of the white grain plants as $r_1r_1r_2r_2$. Note that in this case, we are using two gene sets (as also seen in dihybrid crosses), but now the two gene sets control for a single trait (grain color) rather than two different traits, as in the dihybrid cross.

The F_1 progeny resulting from this cross all have the genotype $R_1r_1R_2r_2$ and are all intermediate red in color. This is because the alleles for grain color in wheat show incomplete dominance, so the F_1 hybrids have a combination of both deep red and white grain colors which interact to produce an intermediate red grain color.

As in previous examples, we self-fertilize members of the F_1 generation to determine grain color inheritance in the F_2 generation. Each of the F_1 plants can produce R_1R_2, R_1r_2, r_1R_2, r_1r_2 gamete combinations and the Punnet square is set up as follows:

	R_1R_2	R_1r_2	r_1R_2	r_1r_2
R_1R_2	$R_2R_1R_2R_2$	$R_1R_1R_2r_2$	$R_1r_1R_2R_2$	$R_1r_1R_2r_2$
R_1r_2	$R_1R_1R_2r_2$	$R_1R_1r_2r_2$	$R_1r_1R_2r_2$	$R_1r_1r_2r_2$
r_1R_2	$R_1R_1r_2R_2$	$R_1r_1R_2r_2$	$r_1r_1R_2R_2$	$r_1r_1R_2r_2$
r_1r_2	$R_1r_1R_2r_2$	$R_1r_1r_2r_2$	$r_1R_1r_2r_2$	$r_1r_1r_2r_2$

While the Punnet square shows that many different genotypes can be inherited in second generation of wheat plants, only five phenotypes will result. To translate the genotypes into phenotypes, assume that a dominant gene (designated by a capital letter) adds one degree of pigment color to wheat grains. Thus, one of the 16 inheritable genotypes consists of all dominant genes ($R_1R_1R_2R_2$) and wheat plants that inherit this genotype are deep red. F_2 wheat plants that inherit genotypes with three dominant genes (e.g., $R_1R_1R_2r_2$, $r_1R_1R_2R_2$) are red, genotypes consisting of half dominant and half recessive genes (e.g., $R_1r_1R_2r_2$, $r_1r_1R_2R_2$) are intermediate and produce intermediate red grain color while genotypes with a single dominant gene (e.g., $R_1r_1r_2r_2$, $r_1r_1r_2R_2$) are pink in color. One of the 16 possible genotypes ($r_1r_1r_2r_2$) is comprised only of recessive genes and produces white grain. Note that throughout our analysis of this example of multiple gene inheritance, it doesn't matter if the dominant alleles inherited are R_1 or R_2 but rather how many are present, as both R_1 and R_2 increase pigment content of grain.

PENETRANCE

Some traits do not always appear in some organisms, even though the dominant allele is present in their genotype. For example, all of the F_1 generation of garden pea plants with the genotype Tt described in the monohybrid cross should be tall. If we observe an F_1 population from this cross in which 90 % of the pea plants are tall and 10 % are dwarf, this indicates that the penetrance of the dominant allele for tall T was incomplete.

EXPRESSIVITY

Expressivity refers to how much a dominant allele is exhibited in the phenotype. To illustrate this concept, some of the tall pea plants in the F_1 generation discussed above may be quite tall, others above average in tallness, and some shorter. This variation in height is a reflection of **Expressivity** of the dominant allele T in the phenotype. The more a dominant gene is expressed in the phenotype (i.e., the closer the F_1 pea plants are to all being of equal tallness), the greater the Expressivity of the allele.

ENVIRONMENTAL EFFECTS

Genes operate within the organism to create a phenotype. The phenotype is normally produced by genes directing protein synthesis to create enzymes to perform a function. The action of the gene is thus buried deep within the organism. The only outward expression of the gene is the visible phenotype.

The genetic development of many traits is dependent both on the interaction of the alleles that produce them and on environmental conditions. Deprivation or superabundance of resources including nutrients needed for growth or special minerals needed for development can produce varied phenotypic expressions of a particular trait, even if a dominant allele is present for that trait. Similarly, exposure to extreme conditions such as excess water, high temperatures or the reverse may restrict or enhance the development of many structures, especially in plants. For example, the white water buttercup is a small, aquatic representative of buttercups that grows partially submerged in shallow water along the edges of ponds and wetlands. Water buttercup has two distinctive types of leaves: its underwater leaves are finely dissected, while its emergent leaves are broader and more typically plant-like. This phenotypic variation shows that the gene that produces leaves in the water buttercup is responding to different environments. This ability of a plant to produce variation in response to an environment is called **phenotypic plasticity**.

LINKED GENES

The genes that are transmitted from generation to generation are carried on chromosomes. Plant chromosomes typically carry dozens and sometimes hundreds of genes, each located at discrete places along the length of the chromosome. The actual position of a gene on a chromosome is called its locus. Since the chromosome is the unit of inheritance, all of the genes that are located on the chromosome will be inherited as a unit and are called **linked genes**. Furthermore, since linked genes are inherited together, linkage invalidates Mendel's Law of Independent Assortment, which applies only to genes carried on different chromosomes.

Because genes carried on a chromosome are inherited together linkage decreases genetic variability that can be inherited by the progeny. In some cases gene linkage can be useful because it provides the genetic mechanism to ensure that an important link-

Figure 13–5 An example of crossing over in which there is an exchange of dominant (wide bar) alleles and recessive (narrow bar) alleles. As a result of crossing over, reproductive cells carry a new and different assortment of genes. *Source:* Tom M. Graham (1997), p. 318.

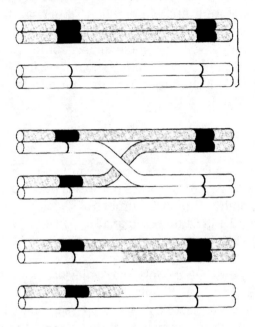

CROSSING-OVER

age group will be inherited together to perform some vital function for the plant.

Linked genes and linkage groups can be broken up by the phenomena termed **crossing- over**. Recall that during meiosis the homologous chromosomes line up in pairs in the center of the dividing cell at metaphase. At this time the alleles are lined up opposite one another on their respective chromosomes. In many species, segments of the homologous chromosomes bend and twist around each other, sometimes spontaneously breaking and reforming. This frequently results in gene bearing segments of one chromosome switching with the same gene bearing segments of its homolog. This event is called crossing-over. Since the reformed chromosomes will assort randomly and independently in the production of the gametes, crossing over serves to increase the amount of variation that can be transmitted to the offspring. Furthermore, the frequency of crossing-over can be used as a measure of how close or how far apart genes are on a chromosome. The further that two alleles are apart on a chromosome, the less frequent that cross-overs will result in a reformed chromosome carrying both alleles. Crossing-over is also considered a good test of whether two traits are controlled by a single gene or by two different genes.

Detecting Linkage and Crossing Over

The occurrence of linked genes can often be detected in a back cross against pure-breeding parents. Consider the results displayed in the following Punnet square of the F_2 cross of garden peas with blue flowers and long grains with red flowers that have

	bl
BL	BbLl (blue-long) 43.7%
Bl	Bbll (blue-round) 6.3%
bL	bbLl (red-long) 6.3%
bl	bbll (red-round) 43.7%

round pollen grains. Since blue flowers and long pollen grains are dominant we would expect a typical dihybrid cross ratios but the results don't meet expectations.

However, these results can be understood by realizing that the high number of blue-long (BbLl) and red-round (bbll) genotypes indicate that the alleles for blue-long and red-round are carried on the same chromosome and are inherited together rather than being independently assorted. We can be fairly certain of this because if the alleles for these two traits were not linked the proportions would be 9:3:3:1 as we would expect in a typical dihybrid test cross.

But what about the small numbers of blue-round (Bbll) and red-long (bbLl) garden peas that appear in the results. Surprisingly, this is once again best explained by linkage. If the alleles are carried on the same chromosome we would expect some crossing-over to occur and this is exactly what is indicated by the Punnet square results. The fact that the incidence of crossing-over is low indicates that the different alleles are located close together on the chromosome.

CYTOPLASMIC INHERITANCE

Some plant characteristics are inherited as a result of genes located in cytoplasmic organelles, rather than caused by genes carried on chromosomes in the cell nucleus. In plants, for example, both plastids and mitochondria contain a number of genes located in unique, circular chromosomes that are found within these organelles. The genes on these chromosomes produce enzymes needed for the metabolic activities of the organelles.

Unlike genes carried on nuclear chromosomes the cytoplasmic genes are not randomly assorted in the production of gametes. Since the cytoplasm of the male gamete (the sperm or pollen) does not enter the egg, no cytoplasmic genes are passed on to the zygote, so all progeny inherit the genetic makeup of the plastid and mitochondria of the female's cytoplasm. For that reason, cytoplasmic genes normally do not vary from generation to generation and therefore do not follow Mendelian inheritance patterns.

Genetic Variations in Plants

WHAT IS VARIATION?

Variation refers to the different types and different degrees of types of traits that occur in plants and other organisms. In any given species of plants (or any other organisms) no two individuals are exactly alike. All of the individuals are somewhat similar but all are somewhat different as well. These differences are the result of the interaction of many different genes. Collectively, they ensure that plant species populations retain a certain amount of variation. The variation of a population is called the gene pool and is a measure of the adaptability of the population to environmental changes. As we will discuss in the chapter on evolution, the phenotypic variations of a plant population provide the raw material for speciation in evolution.

CONTINUOUS AND DISCRETE VARIATION

All of the traits that we have studied so far in plants are examples of discrete variation. Discrete variation refers to the presence or absence of a phenotype. This means that either the plant does or does not exhibit the trait. For example, either the garden pea plant had green seed pods or it had yellow seed pods. Similarly, either the pea plant was tall or it was dwarf. Many traits of plants exhibit continuous variation along what is termed a bell-shaped curve. For example, in many plants (other than garden pea plants) height is controlled by the interaction of several genes. Thus, the individuals of a species may range over a whole series of heights. To illustrate this concept more closely, if the height of a plant species can range from 1–2 meters in height and if height is controlled by several genes then progeny can be 1 meter tall, or 1.1 meters tall, or 1.15 meters tall, or 1.2 meters tall, and so forth.

CAUSES OF VARIATION

Genetic Recombination

The most important source of variation within a population is due to genetic recombination. Genetic recombination refers to the union of eggs and sperm, each carrying their randomly assorted chromosomes containing their assortment of alleles. The recombination that results produces—in all cases—organisms that are similar to, but different from, the parents.

Mutation

The second basic source of genetic variation in a species population originates with mutations. Mutations are changes in the structure of the genes at the chromosome level or changes in the structure of chromosomes that carry the genes. While mutations often produce dramatic phenotypic changes, the great majority are harmful (deleterious) and are discarded within a few generations.

Two basic kinds of mutations are recognized, point mutations and chromosomal aberrations. **Point mutations** occur at a point along a DNA strand, and usually involve substitution of an incorrect nitrogenous base. For example, the correct nitrogenous base pairing along the DNA molecule of the chromosome are always adenine-thymine (A–T) or cytosine-guanine (C–G). If an incorrect base is substituted (e.g., A–G) the chromosome segment carries a point mutation.

Chromosomal aberrations are mutations that involve the alteration of all or parts of a chromosome, or sometimes alterations of sets of chromosomes. Several types of chromosomal aberrations may result during crossing-over. For example, during some crossing-over events the chromosome fragments don't realign correctly; one chromosome ends up with two copies of an allele instead of one while the homolog chromosome ends up missing the allele entirely. The chromosome carrying the extra copy of the allele has a **duplication** while the chromosome missing the allele carries a **deletion**. Deletions may also occur if a chromosome fragments and one or more of the fragments does not reconnect to the chromosome strand. If the gamete (egg or sperm) with the chromosome bearing a duplication unites with a normal gamete the resulting individual has three instead of two copies of a particular allele. Conversely, if the chromosome with the deletion unites with a normal gamete the new organism has one instead of two copies of a gene. Either type of mutation is often deleterious. In yet another type of chromosomal aberration the fragments become turned around, then fuse together. This rearrangement of genes along a chromosome is called an **inversion**. Finally, the fragments of one chromosome may fuse with a nonhomologous chromosome, resulting in a chromosomal aberration called a **translocation**.

Chromosomal mutations can also result when pairs of homologous chromosomes fail to separate during meiosis; both homologs then migrate to one side and are incorporated in the gamete. If this gamete unites with a normal gamete the resulting individual will have three instead of two copies of a particular chromosome, a condition called **trisomy**. Down's syndrome in humans is an excellent example of the trisomy condition; the cells of all Down's syndrome individuals carry three instead of two copies of chromosome 21 (trisomy 21). This means that all of their cells (except red blood cells) have 47 chromosomes instead of the normal complement of 46 chromosomes that are in your cells. Another mutation that may result from the incorrect sorting of chromosomes results in a zygote with more than two complete sets of chromosomes, a condition called **polyploidy.** In plants (but not in animals) polyploidy sometimes results in much larger than normal growth and some of the giant vegetables gardeners are so fond of are the result of polyploidy.

Population Genetics

Population genetics is the study of how gene frequencies change over time and what causes these changes. Actually, in the absence of environmental change or mutation, the frequencies of alleles that comprise the population's gene pool remain stable. For example, if we survey the proportion of dominant genes to recessive genes in a normally interbreeding population in which mating is random and genetic drift and mutation are not important, we find that the percentages of each allele remain constant over time. This is to say that if neither allele is selected for or against by environmental factors, both remain in the population, regardless of whether they are dominant or recessive. This constancy of allele frequencies in populations is named the **Hardy-Weinberg Law** after the two scientists who independently discovered it. Under normal circumstances genes do not change and thus there is no evolution. When changes in gene frequencies do occur, it is an indication that evolutionary forces are at work. This means that evolution, at its most basic level, can be defined as any change in the frequency of a gene.

How Genes Work

ONE GENE—ONE ENZYME HYPOTHESIS

Genes are segments of chromosomes. As there are tens of thousands of genes and generally only a few chromosomes, each chromosome carries hundreds and sometimes thousands of genes located along their length. Each of the genes along the chromosome consists of a specific sequence of nitrogenous bases that provide, in chemical form, a blueprint that specifies the manufacturing of a particular protein enzyme or part of a protein enzyme. Generally, the sequence from gene to enzyme works like this: Chromosome—Gene—messenger RNA—ribosome—enzyme—activity. Exactly how the gene is "turned on" to produce the protein enzyme is called the Operon Theory.

THE OPERON THEORY

The interplay of genes produces the traits that we observe in the phenotype of an individual. It was originally thought that gene structure was just a segment on a DNA molecule and the sequence of organic bases stored information for constructing a substance. Today it is known that individual genes are just structural units of operating systems called **operons.**

Figure 13–6 A giant chromosome. The darker stained material is RNA being transcribed. *Source:* Teresa Audesirk and Gerald Audesirk (1999), p. 170.

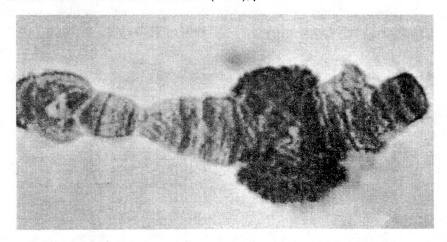

Within a cell is all the genetic information needed to metabolize, grow and reproduce, and this information is carried on the DNA molecules. If this were the case, all the cell needs is a supply of glucose for energy and inorganic molecules for building blocks. For the average cell, however, as many as 600–800 enzymes must be produced to accomplish the various reactions. Some enzymes, such as those needed for respiration, are present all the time but many are produced only when they are needed. The big question has always been asked, how does the cell know when to start producing an enzyme which will enable the production of a needed product, or how does a cell know when to stop producing a particular substance? A model was proposed by Jacob-Monod called the operon theory of gene regulation to account for this ability of the cell. It has been found that there are three places on a DNA molecule which are responsible for gene action. These include a regulator gene, an operator gene and one or more structural genes.

The operon system works something like this. A product activates the **repressor gene** when combined with the product and produces a repressor molecule which turns the **operator gene** off. On the other hand, the presence of a substrate acts as the inducer, and combines with the repressor molecule and turns the repressor off. Hence

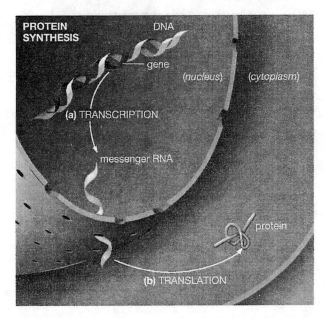

Figure 13-7. From gene to RNA to protein synthesis. *Source:* Teresa Audesirk and Gerald Audesirk (1999), p. 170.

the operator gene will not be repressed and will signal the **structural gene** to produce proteins.

The importance of all this is that gene action is much more complex than originally thought. There is a whole series of genes operating together in a linkage group to produce one result. This also illustrates the fragility of the system. Any change in any part of the system results in a malfunction of the gene.

Plant Breeding

Humans have used plant breeding techniques for millennia to develop the modern grains and other crops that we use for food from their ancestral wild plants. In fact, almost all of our crops or ornamentals have been produced by cross-breeding or hybridizing strains of wild-type stock with favorable characteristics.

Similarly, long before the concepts of genetics were discovered, horticulturalists cross-bred strains to produce the many colorful varieties of flowers, fruits and shrubs. They also hybridized strains to produce horticultural varieties of plants that are especially adapted for special habitats.

Today, botanists are constantly exploring for new strains and hybrids of plants to interbreed for food, drugs, paper products, wood products and for hundreds of other

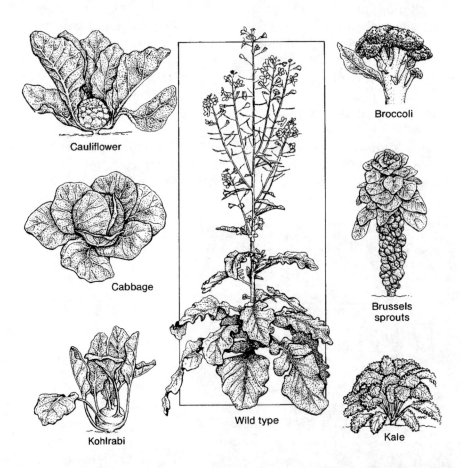

Figure 13–8 The varieties of cultivated plants that have been hybridized from the original wild type in the center. *Source:* James F. Hancock. *Plant Evolution and the Origin of Crop Species.* (1992), Figure 11.3, p. 269.

possible uses. Plant breeding can also be used to identify and select the best characteristics of plants to improve crop yields, develop novel sources of fibers and other plant-derived textiles, and extract useful medicines. This is one reason why the loss of tropical rain forests is so tragic. There are many plants in the tropical rain forests of the world that are lost forever without ever having been tested for their potential usefulness as sources of food or medicines. Such losses are potentially dangerous to us because we will never know what we have lost.

Plant breeders use a variety of methods for developing strains or new hybrid plants besides finding new ones. Old plants can be cross-bred with other known varieties to produce **hybrids.** Known varieties can be altered genetically in the laboratory by **polyploidy,** or deliberately induced **mutations.** The intelligent use of either or both of these processes of plant breeding can yield highly desirable strains.

Hybridization is the process whereby different varieties of plants are crossed to produce a plant with hybrid vigor. Hybrid vigor is a situation that develops in which the resulting plant is especially successful and a high producer of crops. Usually hybrid vigor occurs only in the F_1 generation and the effect of hybrid vigor disappears in the F_2. Most corn crops grown in America are F_1 hybrids. Each year the farmers buy F_1 seeds to plant. They produce very successful plants with good tasting corn. Unfortunately, these plants are normally sterile or have a low fertility. As a result the seed they produce cannot be used the following year, so the farmer must buy more. This planned obsolescence in corn is not the result of industry design but the natural result of non homologous chromosomes from two different parents not operating well together; this is called **hybrid breakdown.**

When desirable characteristics are found in a plant, **inbreeding** of the parent stock is used to reinforce the good characteristics. Plants are bred to develop resistance to disease. For example, wheat used to be decimated by the black stem rust, a fungal disease. Modern wheat is not attacked because a strain that had a resistance to the rust was located and its qualities were introduced into the modern strains of wheat.

Sometimes chromosomes can be manipulated in the laboratory to create changes in plants. **Polyploidy** is a process whereby plants are deliberately changed by causing chromosome sets to become duplicated. This is done by treating plant cells with a chemical called colchicine, during mitosis. The chemical breaks down the spindle fibers and the chromosomes do not separate. Yet at the next interphase they duplicate themselves to produce plants with extra sets of chromosomes. A normal diploid plant is 2n, but triploids (3n), tetraploids (4n), hexaploids (6n), and octoploids (8n) can be artificially made. After polyploidy occurs, the resulting plants can be hybridized to produce allopolyploids, in which polyploidy of two different plants can be combined. Another form of polyploidy mutation involves crosses between polyploidy plants of the same species and is called autopolyploidy. Hybrids produced in this process are usually sterile.

An examination of the chromosome numbers of plants in nature shows a large number of them are part of polyploidy complexes. In these complexes the chromosome numbers are all multiples of the parent species chromosome number. For example the parent plant may have 10 pairs of chromosomes while others may show 20, 40, 80, 160 etc. Thus the fact that polyploidy occurs naturally is a major factor in producing the great diversity among plants. It has been estimated that approximately half of all dicots and monocots are polyploids.

Polyploidy is therefore a kind of **mutation** that can be usefully employed in genetic engineering of plants. Mutations are changes in the structure of a gene. This changes the function of that gene and may cause a change in the phenotype of the plant. Where single genes are involved in mutations, we are speaking of a micromutation. When polyploidy or chromosomes become units of a mutation we are dealing with a macromutation. Mutations are usually harmful as the genetic information is changed and produces nonfunctional genetic nonsense. When this occurs the plant is badly affected. Occasionally a mutation can be very useful. Such mutations are the ultimate source of variations in natural populations and are the basis for evolutionary change.

TISSUE CULTURE

The culturing of plant cells in artificial containers is called tissue culture. The cultured cells can be manipulated using a variety of experimental techniques. Genes can be inserted and removed or their locus changed in a process called **genetic engineering**. Hybridization of desired strains can also be performed through **protoplast fusion,** a process in which cell walls are digested away leaving naked protoplasts which can be fused, creating hybrid cells. In another process called cloning, meristem cells are separated and cultured and thus become the source of large numbers of plants started from these cells. In **cloning**, all the individuals produced from a culture will be identical as they all came from the same cell and have the same genetic material.

The benefits of plant tissue culture can be numerous. For example, plant tissues can be subject to a wide variety of harsh environmental conditions such as excessive heat, cold, light radiation, diseases or pollutants. Tissues that survive given conditions can then be used to breed new strains and varieties of plants able to grow under these conditions. In a similar manner, tissues can be exposed to disease organisms or pests, and those with the most resistant abilities selected to produce disease-free strains of crops. Most of the corn and wheat varieties grown in the United States, for example, have been developed from tissue cultures which are resistant to fungal infections.

Plant Genetics and the Green Revolution

Some of the most spectacular successes resulting from plant breeding have been realized in the production of high yield varieties of a number of important food crops. Using plant genetics and plant breeding, researchers have been able to breed new strains of rice and wheat that grow so rapidly that two crops may be harvested each year instead of the traditional single crop. Experiments in Mexico, for example, produced strains of corn that yielded kernels with high concentrations of lysine and other amino acids which are uncommon in most foods.

For example, **Norman Borlaug** won the Nobel Prize in 1970 for developing new strains of wheat in Mexico. Borlaug is considered to be the father of the **Green Revolution**. Most of the farmlands of Mexico are in the highlands, where the soils are barren and comparatively infertile. For much of its history, food production in Mexico has been insufficient to meet the needs of its people. Even though it is a wheat growing country, Mexico could not grow enough wheat to feed its population. The Mexican government asked Norman Borlaug to help. He used plant breeding techniques to develop special varieties of wheat that would grow in the Mexican climate and turned Mexico from a wheat importer to being self sufficient. He established the groundwork to use science to improve food production throughout the world. His ideas helped in the development of high yielding crops that have the potential of feeding the world's hungry masses. Unfortunately, the green revolution has been a double-edged sword. It has stimulated the mass cultivation of crops that has destroyed the ecology in some areas. The cheap production of food is causing a lowering of prices which hurts the farmer. In many areas of the United States, farms are being abandoned due to the inability of

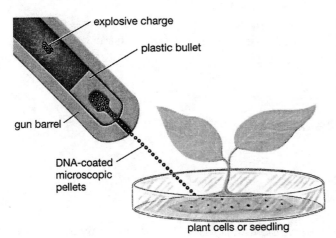

explosive charge

plastic bullet

gun barrel

DNA-coated
microscopic
pellets

plant cells or seedling

Figure 13–9 Genetic engineering illustrated by inserting genes into plant cells. *Source:* Teresa Audesirk and Gerald Audesirk (1999), p. 239.

farmers to earn a living. Traditional farming has become an agribusiness with large corporations applying economies of profit and loss to farming.

GENETIC ENGINEERING OF NEW VARIETIES

The genetic engineering of plants is a relatively new but extremely important science. Genetic engineering holds great potential and many promises for the development of new crops to satisfy not only demands for basic foodstuffs to feed the world's growing populations but also has led to the development of genetically engineered strains that can yield important dietary substances and supplements. Genetic engineering works by inserting one or two genes into a species in order to make that species more productive, have greater resistance to disease, or incorporate higher concentrations of certain substances in tissues. For example, genetic engineering by Monsanto Food Corporation scientists has incorporated traits to produce canola plants high in unsaturated fatty acids. In another experiment, scientists at the Swiss Institute of Technology in Zurich added two daffodil genes and one bacterium gene to produce a strain called golden rice in provitamin A (a beta-carotene). In Mexico, scientists have spliced genes into staple strains of corn and rice to help these new strains grow in tropical soils high in aluminum and other toxic minerals.

Plant geneticists are now exploring the use of plants as vehicles for the production of natural vaccines to guard us against everything from tooth decay to AIDS, cholera, and other life threatening infections, all through the use of genetic engineering.

Key Words and Phrases

Gregor Mendel	gene	dominant gene
recessive gene	genotype	phenotype
homozygous	heterozygous	allele
law of dominance	monohybrid cross	testcross
Law of Segregation	locus	Punnet Square
Law of Independent Assortment	F_1 Generation	F_2 Generation
test cross	backcross	codominance
incomplete dominance	linkage	mutation
Hardy-Weinberg Law	operons	hybrid

repressor gene　　　　　　operator gene　　　　　　structural gene
hybridization　　　　　　　Green Revolution　　　　tissue culture
genetic engineering　　　　cloning　　　　　　　　　polyploidy
protoplast fusion　　　　　inbreeding

Selected References and Resources

Berg, P., and M. Singer. 1992. *Dealing with Genes: The Language of Heredity.* Carolina Publications.

Dunn, L. 1965. *A Short History of Genetics.* McGraw-Hill. New York.

Evans, L. T. 1993. *Crop Evolution, Adaptation and Yield.* Cambridge University Press. New York.

Harten, a. M. Van. 1997. *Mutation Breeding.* Cambridge University Press. New York.

Hartwell, L. H., L. Hood, M. Goldberg, A. Reynolds, L. Silver, and R. Veres. 2000. Genetics. From Genes to Genomes. McGraw Hill. New York.

Hartl, D. L., and E. W. Jones. 1999. *Essential Genetics.* Jones and Bartlett Publishers. Boston, Massachusetts.

Holden, J. 1993. *Genes, Crops, and the Environment.* Cambridge University Press. New York.

Itis, H. 1966. *Life of Mendel.* Haffner Publishing. New York.

Klug, W. S., and M. R. Cummings. *1995 Concepts of Genetics.* 4th Edition. Charles E. Merrill Publishing Company. Columbus, Ohio.

Lewin, B. 2000. *Genes VIII.* 6th Edition. Oxford. New York and London.

Peters, J. 1969. *Classic Papers in Genetics.* Prentice-Hall. Englewood Cliffs, New Jersey.

Schaum's Outline Series. 1991. Theory and Problems of Genetics.

Singer, C. 1962. *A History of Biology to about the year 1900.* Abelard-Schuman Publishing Company. New York.

Stern, C., and E. Sherwood. Editors. 1976. *The Origins of Genetics.* W. H. Freeman and Company. San Francisco.

Review and Discussion Questions

1. Why does linkage present a problem to plant breeders and others who are trying to develop new plants and select for desirable plant characteristics?

2. In Jimson weeds, purple flower (P) is dominant over white flower (p) plants and spiny pods (S) over smooth (s). Assume that the pairs of alleles are not linked and that we are crossing true breeding Jimson weeds with purple flowers and spiny pods with true breeding Jimson weeds with white flowers and smooth pods. Answer the following questions:
   (a) what are the genotypes of the parent plants?
   (b) what are the genotypes of the F_1 generation?
   (c) what are the phenotypes of the F_1 generation?
   (d) set up a Punnet square to show the genotypes of the F_2 generation.
   (e) what are the genotype ratios of the F_2 generation?

3. In violets the gene for blue petals is dominant over the gene for yellow petals. The gene for large violet flowers is dominant over the gene for small flowers. A violet with yellow petals and large flowers was crossed with a violet that had blue petals

and small flowers. The F_1 generation was composed of the following assortment of individuals:

51 violets with yellow petals, large flowers
47 violets with yellow petals, small flowers
52 violets with blue petals, large flowers
44 violets with blue petals, small flowers.

What were the genotypes of the parent generation? How can you determine this? Is this an example of a monohybrid or dihybrid cross?

4. In violets the allele for tall is dominant over the allele for short. If we cross a heterozygous tall violet with a dwarf violet, what proportion of the F_1 generation can be expected to be tall?

5. If we cross two tall heterozygous violets what kinds and ratios of phenotypes can we expect in the F_1 generation?

6. Why do polypoidy plants tend to be larger, have larger flowers and bear larger fruits or vegetables?

7. If one gene has alleles A or a and another gene has alleles B or b, what kinds of gametes (eggs or sperm) can be produced by each of the following genotypes:
   (a) AABB
   (b) AaBb
   (c) aaBb
   (d) aaBB

8. How many different kinds of gametes can be produced by the following:
   (a) AABBCC
   (b) AaBbCc
   (c) AaBbCC
   (d) AaBBCC

9. Discuss the role of genetics in establishing the Green Revolution.

10. What types of genetic inheritance produce the following genotype ratios?

   55: 2: 2: 48
   1: 2: 1
   9: 3: 3: 1
   1: 67 :1
   50: 50
   1: 4: 6: 4: 1
   15: 1
   3: 1

Chapter 14

Evolution

History of Evolutionary Theory
The Modern Synthesis of Evolution
Evidence For Evolution

Evolution has been one of the most controversial topics in science for the past 400 years. One of the problems with evolution has always been the direct conflict with organized religion. This conflict stems from their opposing views on how life came into being—whether it was divine orchestration by a supernatural being or a result of chance occurrence. On this topic people will always be polarized. Significant evidence has been found to support the theory of evolution, yet research at the Institute of Creation Research in California has produced astonishing scientific evidence to support the theory of creation. It should be noted that the theory of evolution and the theory of creation are just that—they are **theories** that have been advanced to explain how life came into being and the interrelationships among organisms.

In this chapter the theory of evolution will be discussed in an attempt to explain the interrelationships and diversity of plant life. Evolution, by definition, is the gradual process by which modern species of plants and animals are derived directly or indirectly from species of earlier times and that these lines of descent stem originally from a common simple unicellular ancestry. Many times the word evolution is used synonymously with change.

Figure 14–1 A swamp forest of the carboniferous period of geologic time. The trees in this ancient forest are actually tree ferns and giant club mosses. *Source:* Teresa Audesirk and Gerald Audesirk (1999), p. 322.

The origin and evolution of plant and animal species in one form or another is not a new concept. Early Egyptian, Babylonian, and Greek philosophers speculated the origins and changeability of life. Thales, Epicurus, and the natural historian **Aristotle** proposed many versions of what is today called evolution. Of these, the writings of Aristotle had the most influence on early ideas. Aristotle suggested that life evolved in a particular way; from the simple to the more complex, and from imperfect to perfect. To Aristotle, the plants and animals that he studied and catalogued in a "ladder of nature," represented a continuum and each plant and animal that we see today was specially created in its present form. Aristotle's idea was called the **fixity of species**. The early Christian Church adopted the Aristotle doctrine which formed the basis of church dogma. This divine creation concept still exists today in all translations of the bible and in the beliefs of the more fundamentalistic Christian sects. Many other religions accept their own version of divine creation.

In spite of early church dogma, speculations about evolution were renewed during the Middle Ages when fossils were discovered. Leonardo da Vinci correctly identified these fossils as the remains of plants and animals that had previously existed but had become extinct in past ages. This led to the theory of **catastrophism**, which suggested that life was periodically destroyed by floods and other natural catastrophes and then was replaced by new acts of special creation.

It was not until the late 1700's that the idea that species can change (or evolve) and have changed in the past was formulated. In 1780, the French naturalist, **Comte de Buffon** proposed that species are not permanent but rather change gradually over time. Buffon used the fossil record available at the time to trace the history of life on earth. **Erasmus Darwin**, the grandfather of Charles Darwin, also developed a number of theories about evolutionary change. In 1800, he proposed that species evolve in response to changes in their environment. He also felt that species could change during their life and that they could pass these traits on to their offspring. This type of evolution is called the **inheritance of acquired characters**.

This concept of accumulating changes and passing them along to their offspring was also of considerable interest to **Jean Baptiste Lamark**, a French zoologist. In 1809, Lamark published a theory of evolution centering on the "use and disuse of organs" that was to become the basis for **Lamarkinism**. Like Erasmus Darwin before him, Lamark felt that traits acquired during the life of an organism could be passed on to later generations. Lamark further extended this theory by proposing that new organisms (new species) could result from accumulations of these acquired characteristics. In Lamark's view, structures that are developed during the lifetime of the individual can be passed on to their offspring. Conversely, if an organism stops using an organ or body part it is eventually discarded, or retained as a **vestigial** organ. Thus, in the Lamarkian view, giraffes grew their long necks by stretching them to reach into the tops of trees for leaves which they eat. For example, the ancestors of modern giraffes had short necks. As the trees grew taller, each generation of giraffes stretched their necks longer and longer to reach into the tops of trees. These "acquired stretched necks" were passed on to the next generation of giraffes as inherited characteristics. Through many successful generations of "neck stretching giraffes" modern giraffes acquired their long necks. (Since modern giraffes already have long necks, there is no need to stretch them any further, so we can't find any evidence of continuing giraffe evolution, at least with respect to their necks). Lamark's ideas of evolution were widely discussed among the scientists of that time. Even today we occasionally read of some evolutionary event being described as Lamarkian.

Because they had no other method to explain evolution, many scientists of Lamark's time accepted Lamark's theory that organisms evolved by the inheritance of acquired characters. One such believer was **Charles Darwin**, the grandson of Erasmus Darwin. Charles Darwin was sent to the University of Edinburgh to study medicine. He did not show an aptitude for the profession and his parents decided to transfer him to Cambridge University to study for the ministry. While at Cambridge he made friends with members of the faculty who were interested in natural sciences. He spent much time in the field collecting beetles and hunting. After graduation in 1831, his influential friends helped him to obtain a position as the ship's naturalist on board the HMS *Beagle*, a British naval ship that was about to depart on a five year expedition to explore and chart the world's seas and coastlines.

During his travels, Charles Darwin amassed a tremendous number of specimens and a large amount of data about the flora and fauna of the world. While the ship charted coastlines and harbors, he was allowed to leave and go inland to explore and collect. When Darwin returned home in 1836 he married his cousin, Emma Wedgewood (of the Wedgewood potteries) and settled in a country estate south of London. He spent the rest of his life studying and writing about the specimens and data he had discovered and collected on the expedition and about the observations of natural history he had made during those five years.

Figure 14–2 Lamark's theory of use and disuse illustrated with giraffes. According to Lamark, modern giraffes developed their long necks because their ancestors had to stretch their necks longer and longer to get at leaves that were higher and higher in the tree tops. The long necks that they developed by stretching them were transmitted to their offspring. *Source:* Tom. M. Graham (1997), p. 404.

Darwin was intrigued by the idea of evolutionary inheritance of acquired characters proposed by his grandfather. He was also aware of the gradual but continual changes in the earth's crust over time that were detailed in one of the first textbooks of geology called *Principles of Geology*, published in 1837 by his friend, the geologist Sir Charles Lyell. Reading the book and reflecting on the observations he had made during his travels gave him the idea that evolutionary change in species is gradual, just as changes in the earth's geologic history are also gradual. Furthermore, the time scale of the geological changes in the earth that were proposed by Lyell provided sufficient time for the evolution of life to occur—instead of the earth being created some 4000 years ago, as specified in the bible, geology suggested that the earth was millions of years old. For Darwin, this long geological time scale provided the millions of years during which speciation, so necessary for evolution, could occur.

Darwin needed evidence to develop his ideas about evolution. During the *Beagle's* voyage around the world, Darwin visited the Galapagos Islands which are located on the equator in the Pacific Ocean. There he noted that the giant tortoises, iguana lizards and finches of the islands differed slightly in form, and sometimes in behavior, from island to island but that each kind of animal had clearly (or so it seemed) arisen from a single ancestor. This gave Darwin the germ of an idea that was to become known as natural selection.

Because of his work on the expedition, and his writings afterward, Darwin developed a reputation as a careful and prolific researcher. It became known in scientific circles that he was interested in the evolutionary changes in plants and animals. Darwin began to write a book about his ideas concerning evolutionary change. At the same time another young naturalist, **Alfred Russell Wallace**, was collecting specimens in the islands of what are now Indonesia. Wallace developed malaria while in the jungles and during his period of recovery, he thought about how organisms change in time. Wallace wrote a summary of his ideas about evolutionary change in a letter to Darwin. When Wallace's letter arrived, Darwin was in the middle of writing his own book on how evolution takes place in natural populations. Wallace's letter came as a shock because his ideas concerning how species change were very similar to those being proposed by Darwin. The two scientists had independently arrived at the same conclusions from different observations each had conducted on opposite sides of the world. Their ideas were published as a jointly authored paper read before the Linnaean Society of London.

Darwin hurriedly finished a rough draft of a book summarizing his own ideas about evolution. Published on November 4, 1859, Darwin's book was entitled ***"On The Origin of Species by Natural Selection"***. The book proved to be a "best seller" and the first edition sold out the first day. *The Origin* provided the first clear insight into how plants and animals can evolve through time. In many ways this is one of the most significant books written in modern science. Darwin (and Wallace) proposed that species change through an interactive process with the environment called natural selection. His theory of natural selection was based on several major ideas.

First, Darwin noted that the members of species differ from one another. That is, the species population exhibits variability. While this is most obvious to the human population around us (the height of humans varies along a continuum from very tall to very short), but all populations exhibit this variability. This variability is centered in the genes and can be transmitted from parent to offspring.

Second, Darwin noticed all species have the capacity to produce far more offspring than can survive. For example, plants manufacture billions of pollen grains yet produce only thousands of seeds. A single bacteria can produce, if unchecked, millions of decendents within a few days. This capacity for reproduction is evident in all species of plants and animals.

Third, Darwin realized that despite this capacity for reproduction, no organism has as yet taken over the earth. Instead, in each species population, many individuals are produced but only a few live long enough to themselves reproduce. Conditions and resources act to limit the number of individuals that live. Since all life is in competition, there is a constant **struggle for existence**.

Fourth, this constant competition for resources means that only the most fit organisms i.e., those individuals that can exploit the resources of their environment most effectively, survive while those that are less fit die. Darwin termed this the **survival of the fittest**. Survival of the fittest is a synonym for natural selection.

Fifth, he proposed that the variations that made the organisms successful enough to survive may be passed on to the next generation through inheritance.

Darwin called his theory natural selection because nature did the selecting! That is, the environment was the final arbiter of good and bad variations. Good variations were retained in the population while bad variations were discarded. Of course, organisms had something to do with this. Organisms that had the good (adaptive) variations in their genetic make-up survived and reproduced while organisms that lacked this adaptive variations died.

Lastly, Darwin felt that accumulations of these advantageous variations make the new species or changed populations more successful than the older species. To summarize, organisms that inherit successful variations from their parents are better able to

Figure 14–3 Darwin's concept of how giraffes got their long necks. According to Darwin's theory of natural selection, as trees got taller, natural selection would favor giraffes with longer necks. They survived while short-necked giraffes would die because they couldn't reach into trees and feed. This natural selection continued through many generations of giraffes, resulting in the long-necked giraffes of today. *Source:* Tom. M. Graham (1997), p. 408.

exploit their environment than those that did not. These inherited variations give them an advantage in the further struggle for existence. Thus, organisms with the most successful variations have a greater chance of surviving long enough to reproduce and leave offspring that carry their efficient genes. The result is that a population of organisms gradually changes toward forms that have accumulated the most fit variations. This change is the basis for the theory of evolution and the mechanism is natural selection.

Darwin could not provide a satisfactory explanation for the mechanism controlling the inheritance of adaptive variations. That is, Darwin knew nothing about genes controlling phenotypes and how genes are passed from generation to generation. To complicate Darwin's lack of information, most variations created in plants and animals by artificial hybridization are **not** inherited. For example, many people pierce their earlobes in order to wear earrings, but this variation does not appear in our offspring.

Unknown to Darwin, Mendel had discovered the genetic mechanisms on which natural selection actually works.

The Modern Synthesis

Since the time of Darwin, there has been a union of Darwin's concept of natural selection as the driving force in evolution and modern genetics. This new concept of evolution is called **neodarwinism** or the **modern synthesis**. In essence, the modern synthesis accepts the basic tenants of Darwinian theory of evolution by natural selection and combines them with the laws of genetics to explain how organisms inherit the genetic variability on which evolution works.

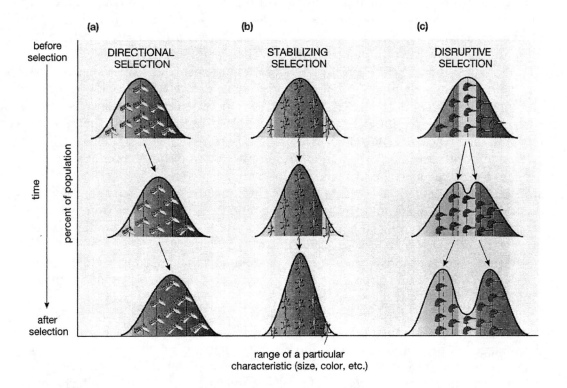

Figure 14–4 Three possible ways in which natural selection affects populations over time. *Source:* Teresa Audesirk and Gerald Audesirk (1999), p. 283.

MECHANISMS OF CHANGE

All sexually reproducing populations have a normal range of genetic variation in their population and such variations account for the phenotypic differences that we observe when we look at each other. This variation in appearance is partly the result of independent sorting of genes and chromosomes during meiosis and partly caused by recombinations of genetic material in the offspring. The variations are important in evolution because they sometimes result in adaptive combinations that increase the fitness of the organism to its environment. If the environment of the organism changes, or if enough genetic variations accumulate in a subpopulation, new species may result.

Changes acquired during genetic recombinations may also be supplemented by **mutations.** It was not until the early 1900's that the idea of mutations was firmly established. Two basic types of mutations are known. Changes in the structure of genes are called **point mutations**, because they occur at a particular point along the sequence of nitrogenous bases on the DNA molecule. Since the sequence represents the chemically coded instructions for the production of a specific protein, any changes in the blueprint will produce a different protein. These mutations are caused by a variety of factors ranging from radiation to accidents occurring during DNA replication in sex cells. The most important aspect of these variations is that they have a new affect on the population.

Those variations that result from gene or organic base pairing changes are called **micromutations**. The micro prefix implies that the mutation has a minor effect on the individual. Micromutations are important as they create changes in individuals that are usually not radical enough to endanger the organism's ability to survive. On the other hand, **macromutations** are changes in whole chromosomes or sets of chromosomes. Macro means large and the affect of macromutations is that the major changes either make the organism superior or inferior immediately. This is a make it or break it situation with the organism surviving or dying as a result of a massive change in the chromosome compliment. In the last chapter we discussed **polyploidy**. Polyploidy is a kind of macromutation. It produces plants that are different immediately. If these new forms can find a way to reproduce they have a good chance to be successful.

Macromutations do not necessarily involve entire sets of chromosomes. In some cases a macromutation involves a single homologous pair or two homologous pairs of chromosomes. Occasionally, crossing over occurs between non-homologous pairs of chromosomes. The resulting chromosomes are called **translocations**. The new chromosomes are varied and the genes on them have been rearranged to produce different effects. In some cases normal crossing over between homologous chromosomes may result in a gene sequence being reversed. This reversal of gene order is called an **inversion**. Sometimes in normal crossing over the chromosome is stretched and one gene is duplicated. Such **duplications** result in new variations also. In crossing over, one whole section of a chromosome can become detached and lost. The genes on that segment are lost forever. Such gene loss is called a **deletion**.

Regardless of the kinds of mutations, it is mutations that are considered the source of all variations in natural populations of organisms. It is upon these variations that the theory of evolutionary processes operate.

The most important process to support the theory of evolution is **natural selection**. When variations occur, they may be neutral, beneficial or harmful to the organism. If the mutation is neutral or beneficial the organism has a good chance to survive long enough to reproduce and pass the variation on to the next generation. The more beneficial the variation is, the greater the chance of survival. Should a variation be harmful, this does not necessarily mean the plant is doomed to die, but it does mean there is a

Figure 14–5 How species can arise through polyploidy. *Source:* Teresa Audesirk and Gerald Audesirk (1999), p. 300.

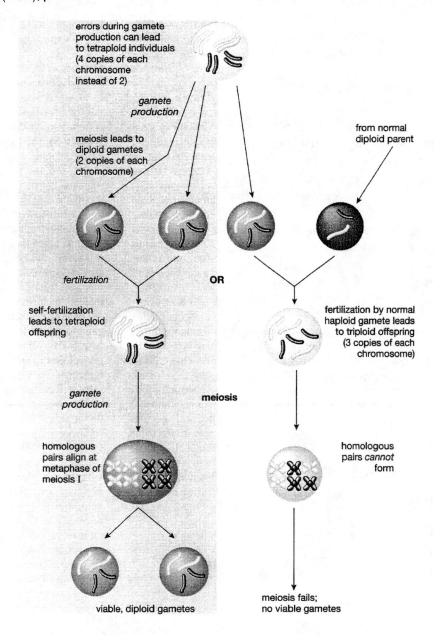

smaller statistical chance of survival long enough to reproduce. The majority of mutations are harmful or neutral.

SPECIATION

As organisms accumulate mutations and gene combinations they become different from their ancestors. At some point, these differences prevent interbreeding and a population splits into two separate species, each with its own gene pool. This process of evolving new species is called **speciation**. Speciation often occurs during an evolutionary and ecological process called **adaptive radiation**. When the first individuals reach a new area not previously inhabited they gradually occupy most of the new habitats that are found. In time, the selection of genetic differences enabled them to become more efficient at exploiting certain habitats, resulting in a series of new species. For example, during the late Cretaceous and early Tertiary geological periods, a few marsupials reached the island continent of Australia. Over millions of years, these marsupials underwent an adaptive radiation, gradually evolving into the diverse marsupial fauna that now occupies most of the ecological habitats of Australia.

MECHANISMS OF SPECIATION

Genetic Drift. When mutations and their variations occur in an individual of a large mainland population, the effect is most often lost when the varied individual breeds with a normal individual. Thus mutations are most prevalent in small isolated populations such as those on the Galapagos islands. Here there is a small number of individuals and a mutation in a small population has a major effect. Due to chance, such a variation may become very common in the island population. The chance gain or loss of variations in small isolated populations is called **genetic drift**. Accidents occur in all populations and the accidental death of a small segment of an island population may create a situation where a characteristic was originally controlled by a pair of heterozygous alleles. The loss of some individuals may create a population where that character is now controlled by a homozygous gene allele. When this happens all the individuals have the same genes for a characteristic. That characteristic then becomes standard for that population and is one of the population's identifying characteristics.

Gene Flow. Another factor in creating variation is **gene flow**. Gene flow is essentially the physical movement of alleles throughout a population. Many plants are wind

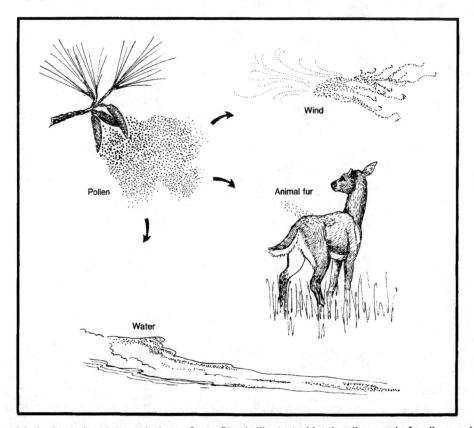

Figure 14–6 Gene flow in populations. Gene flow is illustrated by the dispersal of pollen grains over long distances to other pine woodlands through the action of wind, water, and animals. *Source:* Tom. M. Graham (1997), p. 416.

pollinated. As the wind blows pollen, it is often carried farther than normal until it fertilizes plants of the same species that have been isolated in different populations. The introduction of genes from a distant population into another population is called gene flow. The effect of gene flow on the new population can be good as it introduces new variations into that population and gives new opportunities to change. It may also be harmful to the new population as too much gene flow can introduce so many genes from the old population that it makes the new population more like the old population, thus destroying the new population's uniqueness.

Hybridization is another evolutionary process. Most plants are reproductively isolated from each other by gene combinations that prevent the fertilization of eggs of one species by the sperm of another. Occasionally accidents occur and hybrids do form. Hybridization may be good or bad depending on the outcome. Hybrids are good because they produce new variations and new plants for nature to test. If they are healthy plants and can find a place in the ecosystem, they may prosper and form new species. Most often, hybrids are bad because they are inferior plants and soon are eliminated through competition with the parent plants. Also hybrids have a major problem with reproduction. Most hybrids are sterile or develop sterility in the F_2 generation. The result is that most hybrids are a waste of gametes for plants as they come to no good end.

Isolation. Regardless of all the evolutionary processes at work, the key to successful evolution is **isolation**. Plants, in order to survive, either as hybrids, or simply as forms with unique variations must become isolated from the parent stock. If they are not isolated they end up interbreeding with the parent population and their uniqueness is diluted or destroyed. Isolation takes at least three forms. Isolation may be spatial or **geographic**. This means the new population is separated from the parent stock by distance. A unique plant may be carried to a distant island by water currents and end up as an isolated population. Isolation may be **ecological**. A group of unique plants may end up in an ecological situation different from the parents, in which case the plants are isolated by lifestyle and requirements from the environment. The most important isolating factor is reproductive.

Reproductive isolation means the new and old plants cannot interbreed. This is the ultimate form of isolation and is one of the main criteria for forming new species. Most flowering plants have evolved by polyploidy which has the advantage of creating immediate reproductive isolation on the new individuals. Thus the uniqueness is preserved and can be tested by natural selection without dilution from interbreeding with the parent stock. One of the fastest ways to develop reproductive isolation is to become self-fertilizing. This strategy occurs in many plants with unique variations. Plants which breed with themselves guarantee no dilution from the parent stock.

Evolutionary Rates

Darwin believed that evolutionary processes are slow and that natural selection acts over a long period of time. Under normal circumstances the changes in a population are very gradual and the evolutionary appearance of new species may take thousands of years. In the slow version of speciation, changes are governed by micromutations and take a long time to accumulate.

Some evolutionary events are not thought to occur like this however. In the 1980's two paleontologists, Eldridge and Gould proposed the theory of **Punctuated Equilibrium**

Figure 14–7 Two ways in which isolation can work to produce new species. *Source:* Teresa Audesirk and Gerald Audesirk (1999), p. 297.

which suggests that sometimes speciation can occur very rapidly. The theory of punctuated equilibrium attempts to explain rapid shifts in evolutionary trends sometimes seen in the fossil record. Eldridge and Gould observed that many populations of organisms change rapidly in the space of a few generations. Most biologists agree that this happens but no one has proposed the mechanisms that cause this to occur. It has been suggested that macromutations can be very successful and create new organisms very quickly. No better example of this exists than in flowering plants where the macromutation process of polyploidy has affected over half of all groups. Flowering plant evolution has been very rapid and polyploidy is the reason.

The consensus of opinion today is that punctuated equilibrium probably works under certain circumstances such as rapid changes in the environment and that these changes can result in the relatively rapid appearance of new species in response to these changes. Gradual change is also at work with natural selection creating the evolutionary force to fine tune a population to fit better into an available ecological niche. Thus the two processes may work together. Punctuated equilibrium creates the new species while natural selection continues to modify it, making it more adaptable to its new environment.

Kinds of Evolution

Regardless of the formative process, populations are theorized to evolve in one of four directions. Most evolution is viewed as **progressive**, in that a population is acted upon by natural selection, resulting in the population becoming more and more adapted to the existing environment. This progressive evolution results in the entire population changing gradually.

A second view is that evolution can also be **divergent**. If there are vacant ecological niches, some individuals may be sufficiently adapted to invade and exploit it. Regardless of how the new population may have formed, it can survive if it is isolated from the parent stock and is adaptable to a new environmental condition. Through natural selection, this new population may separate from the parent stock. The new population will diverge because it occupies an environment different from that of the parents. In some cases there may be a population of organisms that occupies many ecological niches. In this case, each niche may provide some ecological isolation for its population different from the occupants of other niches. Natural selection will provide organisms that become better and better adapted to the available niches they occupy. Thus each population diverges away from the original type.

In some cases two very different and unrelated populations may compete to occupy the same niche. As these two populations adapt their characteristics **converge** toward the best adaptations necessary to survive in that niche. Thus the two populations become more and more alike. Convergent evolution usually results in one population being successful and the other becoming extinct. Sometimes convergent evolution is not complete and both competing populations develop to a point and then stop. Instead they evolve **parallel** to each other. More commonly two populations from the same parent stock begin to diverge and then stop for some reason. They have become separated to a certain degree but not very far and then develop in parallel to each other. Parallel evolution allows two potentially competing populations to avoid competition with each other and at the same time occupy niches similar to each other.

Evidence for Evolution

Fossil Record. Fossils are one of the best, most reliable, and most familiar of the various proofs that evolution of organisms has occurred. Fossils are the remains of organisms that lived in past ages of the earth's history but are no longer present. Fossils are remains or traces of long dead organisms. They may be bones, impressions, tracks, and other physical remains but most commonly fossils are casts, either naturally or artificially produced. By the systematic accumulation of fossils we can—in many cases—obtain the **fossil record** of a particular species or group of species and trace its evolution through time. First, the fossil record proves the existence of organisms that lived in the past and shows their similarity to modern life forms. Fossils provide evidence between links of major groups. For example, from the fossil record we can trace the origin and early evolution of birds and mammals from reptiles, which took place over 140 million years ago. In some cases, such as the horse, we have an almost complete fossil history of the animal, from its earliest beginnings to its present form. We can see changes and in come cases measure rates of change. Fossils also provide evidence for divergent, convergent, and parallel forms of evolution.

Embryology is the study of the embryonic development of an organism. In embryology, we examine the developmental stages of a life form from the fertilization of the egg to the birth or germination of that form. Embryology suggests that organisms develop in a series of progressively more complex stages. These stages correspond to many of the evolutionary steps that have been described for living things. For example, stages in the development of the seed of a flowering plant represent early life stages of more primitive plants.

Comparative Anatomy is a science that compares the anatomical features of different kinds of organisms. Comparative anatomy is a basic tool used in the classification of organisms. In evolutionary studies, structures of different organisms or groups of organisms are compared to determine the degree of similarity and differences that exists between them. The more similarities that are found, the closer the relationship between the groups is considered to be.

Vestigial organs are organs or structures (e.g., muscles in animals) that occur but have no known function or no useful function. Many structures in plants have lost their usefulness; their retention suggests that their usefulness has only recently been lost, and they will probably be discarded in time. The evolutionary relationships of plants that retain vestigial organs can be construed by comparing them with plants in which the organ is still functional.

Comparative physiology and **biochemistry** are sciences that compare the molecular and chemical structures of organisms. For example, by comparing similarities and differences in the DNA of different groups of plants we can often determine their evolutionary history and relationships.

Plant distribution gives us clues as to where groups of plants originated and the pathways they took to spread. The most ancient representatives of a group are considered to be those closest to the **center of origin**. A center of origin is identified by determining where the biggest population of a relic species of a plant group is located. The area with the most plants of that species is the center of origin. Plants gradually spread outward from the center of origin to other habitats and other areas of the world. The distribution patterns of plants are dependent upon the ability of plants to travel. As we

Figure 14–8 Fossil evidence for evolution is well illustrated by horse fossils, which span a time period of nearly 50 million years. *Source:* Teresa Audesirk and Gerald Audesirk (1999), p. 263.

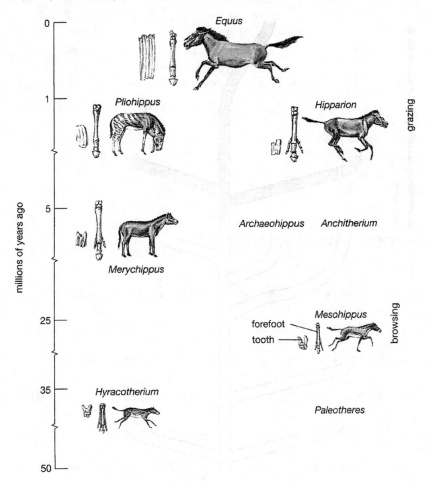

have indicated earlier, plants have developed many means of dispersal by wind, animals and water. The more successful these dispersal methods, the more dispersed plants have become. Also widely dispersed plants indicate that they are generally older than less dispersed ones.

Evidence from Recent History. Lastly, we can sometimes find **historical evidences** of evolutionary change in modern plants. Humankind has used plants for many purposes for thousands of years. We have altered many kinds of plants through selective breeding to improve their usefulness to us. The fact that we can take wild plants and alter them by controlled breeding is an indication of (artificial) selection in action—humans have taken the place of natural selection and replaced it with artificial selection. In spite of human intervention, natural selection still prevails and when crop and garden plants go untended they revert back to the wild type.

Key Words and Phrases

theory	evolution	fixity of species
Lamarkinism	Charles Darwin	natural selection
Neodarwinism	Aristotle	Buffon

punctuated equilibrium
mutations
translocation
deletion
hybridization
reproductive isolation
divergent evolution
embryology
comparative physiology
struggle for existence
inheritance of acquired characteristics
production of excessive offspring
survival of fittest

fixity of species
micromutations
inversion
genetic drift
geographic isolation
progressive evolution
convergent evolution
comparative anatomy
Alfred Russell Wallace

Erasmus Darwin
macromutations
duplication
gene flow
ecological isolation
gene pool
parallel evolution
vestigial organs

Selected References and Resources

Brandon, R. N. 1996. *Concepts and Methods in Evolutionary Biology*. Cambridge University Press. New York.

Briggs, D., and S. M. Walters. 1997. *Plant Variation and Evolution*. Cambridge University Press. New York.

Cowen, R. 2000. *History of Life*. Blackwell Science. Malden, Massachusetts and Oxford, England.

Darwin, C. 1859. *On the Origin of Species*. John Murray. London.

Desmond, A., and J. Moore. 1992. *Darwin*. Warner Books. New York.

Donovan, S. K. (Ed.). 1991. *The Process of Fossilization*. Columbia University Press. New York.

Givnish, T. J., and K. J. Sytsma. 1997. *Molecular Evolution and Adaptive Radiation*. Cambridge University Press. New York.

Hoffmann, A. A., and P. A. Parsons. 1991. *Evolutionary Genetics and Environmental Stress*. Oxford University Press. New York.

Lack, D. 1974. *Darwin's Finches*. Cambridge University Press. England.

Pielou, E. C. 1991. *After the Ice Age: the Return of Life to Glaciated North America*. University of Chicago Press. Chicago.

Ridley, M. 1993. *Evolution*. Blackwell Scientific Publications. Oxford.

Sober, E. (Ed.) 1984. *The Nature of Selection*. MIT Press. Cambridge, Massachusetts.

Stebbins, G. 1966. *Processes of Organic Evolution*. Prentice-Hall Inc., Englewood Cliffs, New Jersey.

Stewart, W. N., and G. W. Rothwell. 1993. *Paleobotany and the Evolution of Plants*. 2nd. Edition. Cambridge University Press. New York.

Williams-Ellis. 1977. *Darwin's Moon*. Blackie. London and Edinburgh.

Review and Discussion Questions

1. The discussion of evolution has proved controversial ever since its inception. Discuss some of the fears and misconceptions about evolution.
2. How has the Darwinian theory of natural selection evolved to the present day version?

3. What do we mean by the evolution of a new species? How does this differ from the new varieties that are produced by horticulturalists?
4. What can you find about plants that seems to support or detract from the theory of evolution?
5. Trace the evolutionary history of plants through the geologic ages.
6. What are the basic causes of evolution?
7. Relate the genetic concepts of genes and variation learned in the last chapter to Darwin's theory of natural selection.
8. What is the significance of sexual selection and evolution? Does it tend to increase or decrease the rate of evolution?
9. Which is more important, mutation or environmental changes, in hastening the evolution of new plants? Explain your answer fully.

Chapter 15

Plant Taxonomy

History of Classification Systems
The Species Concept
How and Why Species Are Named
Taxonomic Categories and Hierarchies
Kingdoms of Life

Taxonomy, also commonly known as **systematics** is the science of sorting, cataloging and labeling. In this complex world we are confronted by a vast panorama of plants and animals that may include upwards of five million species.

How does one keep from being overwhelmed by the earth's diversity? We must classify things into groups with similar characteristics and provide a systematic inventory of all the components of nature. This systematic sorting enables us to identify the various kinds of organisms and study their history and relationships to other organisms.

History of Classification Systems

Originally the need to classify organisms arose from a desire to collect information about and list all the known kinds of plants and animals. The attempt to name and classify plants and animals began with the Greek scientists such as Theophrastus and Aristotle. Theophrastus (370–285 B.C.) tried to classify all plants on the basis of their longevity and form of growth. He grouped all known plants into herbs, shrubs, under story trees, and mature trees. Aristotle improved and expanded this classification sys-

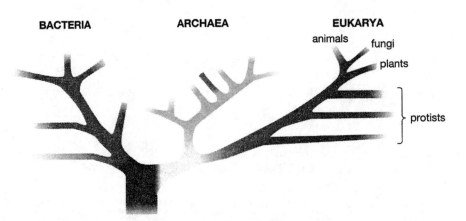

Figure 15–1 The evolutionary tree of life. The bacteria and the archaea are both monerans. All other organisms are eukarya. Viruses are not included in this tree of life. *Source:* Teresa Audesirk and Gerald Audesirk (1999), p. 344.

tem, listing all known forms of plants and commenting about their relationships or **phylogeny**.

The classification system proposed by Theophrastus and Aristotle stayed in use with very little modification until the early 1700's, when the French scientist Tournefort made another attempt at establishing a meaningful taxonomy of plants. He divided all flowering plants into trees and herbs which were further separated into herbs that had flowers with separate petals and herbs that had flowers with united petals. An English botanist, John Ray, expanded the taxonomic treatment of flowers still further, recognizing the differences between dicots and monocots and eventually recognizing and naming 18,000 species of flowering plants. Today, we recognize over 375,000 kinds of plants and probably 1.5 million animals. Each year, some 5,000 new plants and 10,000 more animals are added to the lists. This need to sort out and classify led to scientists who specialized in collecting, accumulating, and publishing lists and descriptions of the known forms of life. One of the major problems these botanists faced was how to name a new species that they discovered. This led directly to the development of binomial nomenclature which was first proposed by the Swedish naturalist Carolus Linnaeus (1707–1778).

DEVELOPMENT OF BINOMIAL NOMENCLATURE

By the middle ages, the name for each plant (and other known organisms) consisted of long and involved descriptions written in Latin, based on the features that best helped to identify each plant and animal. As more and more organisms were discovered and added to the list, it proved too cumbersome to refer to an organism by its 12-word-long description. Furthermore, this method of referring to organisms did little to show how species were related to one another.

Carl von Linne, a Swedish naturalist, known better by the Latinized form of his name, **Carolus Linnaeus,** solved the dilemma of how to deal with all these organisms and give them meaningful names. Linnaeus assigned a unique scientific name to each known species consisting of two names, a genus name and a species name. Thus for example, the species name for humans is *Homo sapiens; Homo* is the genus name and sapiens is the species name. The practice of assigning two names to each plant and animal species is called the **Binomial System of Nomenclature,** and is still used in science today. Basically, the science of plant taxonomy dates from the time of Linnaeus to today.

The Species Concept

A **species** is the basic unit of taxonomy. Species are populations of organisms that have common morphological and physiological characteristics that are unique to that population. Also species are characterized by reproductive isolation. This means they can breed within their species population but not with organisms outside the population. Thus individuals of a species can only breed with other members of that particular species. Put another way, different species cannot interbreed, except under very unusual conditions.

Scientists must be able to do more than just recognize species. They must classify them and assign names to them so they can be formally studied. In order to assign a name to a newly discovered species population, plant taxonomists must link the new species to those forms that are most closely related to them. In general, this means that other populations may share a common ancestry. Once relationships have been established, a scientific name can be assigned and the populations' relationships recorded in a taxonomic hierarchy. The relationships between organisms is called a **phylogeny**. A phylogeny is a sort of family tree.

HOW AND WHY SPECIES ARE NAMED

Almost all organisms have two kinds of names. Since most people are not scientists and are not fluent in the Latin language of the science of taxonomy, **common names** are provided for the organism. Unfortunately, common names often vary from place to place. Not only are there geographic changes for the common name but as we cross international borders the common names that are given to a particular species may change in language as well. For example, one of the most common weeds of lawns and gardens in the United States is a small, inconspicuous plant called common plantain. In New England it is also sometimes known as broad-leafed plantain. Common plantain occurs throughout North America and much of Europe and has many local names. For example, in different parts of North America common plantain might be called Dutchman's britches, colicweed, Indian boys and girls, and little blue stagger. Between North America and England there are at least 46 common names for the same plant. Furthermore, in Europe, the French have eleven names for plantain, the Dutch have seventy five common names and the prolific Germans have no fewer than 106 names for this plant—all for a single species. This profusion of local common names makes any formal scientific comparison and discussion of broad leafed plantain very confusing.

Linnaeus solved this problem of confusing common names in 1758 with the publication of the 10th edition of *Systemae Natura* which was an update of his earlier book, *Species Plantarum,* published in 1753. In these works, Linnaeus attempted to recognize and name all of the known plants and animals of the world. Throughout the *Systemae Natura,* Linnaeus used binomial scientific names to denote all of the known species. To Linnaeus and other scientists, the scientific name recognizes that a unique population of organisms is a species. He decided to cut the twelve word Latin description down to two words, hence the name binomial, and make these not only descriptive but also show relationships as well. His scientific names not only applied a unique genus-species combination name for each organism, it also gives information about who the species is related to by the genus name. Scientific names are today used world-wide, and whenever a species is referred to in the literature, it is always first identified by its scientific name. This binomial standard permits scientists of different countries and different languages to identify, compare and discuss any particular species. A typical scientific name would look something like the following:

Mentha spicata **Linnaeus.**

In the above combination we have the scientific name of a plant called the spearmint. The **genus** name *(Mentha)* is first and is always capitalized. The genus name is common to all the scientific names for close relatives of the spearmint. The **species** name, *spicata,* is unique to this one kind of plant. Notice that it is written in lower case letters and both genus and species are italicized. Scientific names are special and they must be set off by italics to show they are different from other kinds of names. If scientific names are written or typed they are normally underlined. The last part of the name, Linnaeus, is the name of the scientist who first assigned this name to the particular species of plant or animal. That is, he is the name giver and the discoverer of that particular species. The **author's name** is capitalized but is never in italics or underlined. In most references, the author's name generally is omitted. Lastly, the genus and species names are usually Latin or Greek roots and of a descriptive nature; they usually refer to a unique feature of the new species. In the above case *mentha* is Latin for mint, while *spicata* is a Latin word meaning spiny, a condition found on spearmint leaves. So the scientific name for spearmint means a mint with spines. This kind of scientific name is **descriptive or anatomical**. It describes a unique morphological condition for the plant. Some scientific names are **geographical** in nature. For example, *Fraxinus americana* is the scientific name for a tree called the white ash. The species name *americana* is geographic in nature. It indicates that this tree is a *Fraxinus* from the Western Hemisphere. Occasionally scientific names may be **commemorative** in nature. In this case, the scientific name includes the name of an honored scientist who did considerable research in some aspect of that plant group. Another science worker honored that individual by using his or her name as a part of the scientific name. For example, the ornamental herbaceous dicot with brightly variegated leaves is *Coleus blumei*. The species name was chosen to honor a botanist named Blume. Even though Blume is a proper name, because it is used as part of a species name it is not generally capitalized.

The binomial system of nomenclature was quite adequate for the needs of the past century. However more and more new kinds of organisms continue to be discovered. It has been found that although the species is the basic unit of taxonomy, there may be

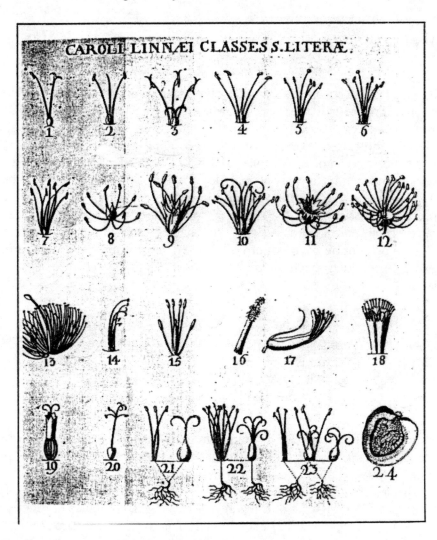

Figure 15–2 A page from the 10th edition of Systema Natura by Linnaeus. *Source:* N. M. Jessop. *Biosphere. A Study of Life.* (1970), Prentice-Hall, p. 65.

distinctive subdivisions of a population that can vary enough to be recognized and describe separately. **Subspecies or varieties** are portions of species populations that have become isolated from the main population and have developed considerable uniqueness. They lack reproductive isolation but are still recognizable as being different from the main group of organisms. Very often, subspecies and varieties are the precursors of future species. Because subspecies or variety names are needed, the binomial system of nomenclature has been expanded to become a **trinomial system of nomenclature.** To go back to our original example of a scientific name, we can expand the binomial for spearmint into a trinomial by adding a subspecies name between the species and author names. The trinomial name for an organism looks like this.

Mentha spicata spicata Linnaeus

The trinomial name above consists, in order, of the genus name, species name, and subspecies name. Note that the subspecies name is written in italics and lower case as is the species name. As with the species name, the subspecies name usually refers to some distinctive feature of the group, or perhaps its geographic locality, or is named to honor its discoverer. Like all scientific names, the discoverer of the subspecies gets to name it.

Taxonomic Hierarchies

The genus, species and subspecies are part of a larger taxonomic hierarchy. This means that taxonomic groups like species can be lumped into larger groups which can be placed into even larger groups until an ultimate grouping of all similar species is achieved. As we indicated before, subspecies belong to species, species belong to genera, genera belong to families, families belong to orders, orders belong to classes, classes belong to divisions and divisions belong to kingdoms. This complex nesting of relationships is expressed as a **taxonomic hierarchy** in which the largest, most inclusive grouping is at the top and the smallest, most specific grouping is at the bottom. Taxonomic hierarchies are statements of phylogeny as they indicate relationships. As an example we present here a taxonomic hierarchy for the sugar maple, a familiar and widespread tree found throughout much of the deciduous forests of eastern North America.

Kingdom Plantae
Division Anthophyta
Class Dicotyledonae
Order Floriferae
Family Acericeae
Genus *Acer*
Species *saccharum* Marsh. sugar maple

The **species** name, *saccharum* is unique and stands at the bottom as the ultimate subdivision of this taxonomic hierarchy. That means it is the smallest subdivision that can be made. It belongs to the **Genus** *Acer* by virtue of specific characteristics it shares with other species of that genus. All *Acer* are placed in the **Family** Acericeae. This family would contain all the maples of the genus *Acer* as well as maples of other genera as well. The family Acericeae is one of several families to share the **Order** Floriferae. All the plants of the order Floriferae have specific characteristics in common. The order Floriferae is one of several orders within the **Class** Dicotyledonae which includes all the plants that have seedlings with two cotyledons or seed leaves. The Class Dicotyledonae is placed with the Class Monocotyledonae within the **Division** Anthophyta or flowering plants. The division Anthophyta is one of several plant divisions sharing the **Kingdom** Plantae, including all green plants with vascular tissue. Each of these steps of the hierarchy is called a **taxon**. Plants are grouped into taxons by matching their morphological characteristics and if possible studying their evolutionary histories.

The assigning of plants to taxa is based on several major principles of morphological comparisons. When we compare structures between two different organisms we are looking for homologies and analogies. Homologies are structures that have a common ancestry as indicated by structure and may or may not have a common function. For example, the trunk of a pine tree and the trunk of a maple share many similarities and are thus homologous and have the same function. They hold the tree upright. At the same time we can compare the stolon of a strawberry and a potato. We find they are also homologous as they have common structures such as nodes and internodes with the nodes having buds. But here they do not have the same function. The stolon is a runner, extending the plant out over the ground while the potato is an underground stem for storage of food. The more homologies plants share, the more closely they are related.

Analogies are structures that have little anatomy in common yet they always have the same function. For example we have sweet potatoes and white potatoes. An investigation of structure indicates that the sweet potato is a storage root, while the white potato is an underground stem. Both have the same function of storing food. Because these structures have little in common, they are indications of distant rather than close relationships. We can also use data from embryology, physiology, and molecular biology to determine taxonomic relationships.

Kingdoms of Life

Originally all living organisms were placed into two major groups. Animals were placed in the Animal Kingdom while plants were relegated to the Plant Kingdom. Most botanists of the 19th and 20th centuries further divided the plant kingdom into four basic groups: **thallophyta**, which included the algae and fungi, **bryophyta**, which included the liverworts and mosses, the **pteridophyta** which included the club mosses, horsetails, and ferns, and the **spermophyta**, into which the gymnosperms and angiosperms were placed. Bacteria were either included with algae or placed in a separate grouping as were animals.

It was long recognized, however, that organisms did not really fit into these neat little categories. This led to the five kingdom approach to classifying all living organisms. This is important to us since the organisms we call plants or plant-like are represented in four of them.

The most primitive group is the **Kingdom Monera** which includes organisms that are unicellular and lack a well defined cell nucleus. Organisms in the Moneran kingdom include bacteria and blue-green algae. These two broad groups are considered to be related because they are both prokaryotes. The viruses are also placed with the Monerans, partly for lack of a better place to put them.

The next group of organisms is placed in the **Kingdom Protista.** Protistans are fairly simple organisms, sometimes called simple plants, which are generally unicellular or colonial organisms. They differ from monerans in being eukaryotic (they have a well developed nucleus). The Kingdom Protista includes several animal groups collectively

Figure 15–3 A detailed look at the tree of life. *Source:* Teresa Audesirk and Gerald Audesirk (1999), p. 345.

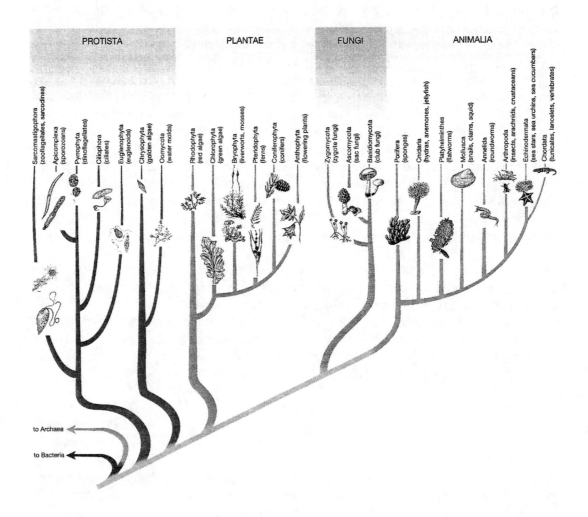

known as the protozoa as well as sponges. Plant biologists study the algae, diatoms and desmids which are also placed in this kingdom.

Fungi are plants that lack chlorophyll and absorb food in solution from other organisms. Most exist as parasites on other plants or on animals. All of the fungi along with slime molds are placed in the **Kingdom Fungi** and constitute a very distinctive grouping of plants.

Organisms that possess chlorophyll *a* and *b*, and can manufacture their own food through photosynthesis, and have vascular tissue are placed in the **Kingdom Plantae**. Plantae are the true green plants (sometimes called the higher plants) and include the mosses and ferns, conifers and flowering plants.

Lastly, all of the multicellular organisms that have to obtain food from other sources (the heterotrophs) are called animals and are placed in the Kingdom Animalia. These are the organisms that are studied in zoology courses.

Table 15-1 Some of the basic characteristics of organisms.

Kingdom	Type of Cell	Cell Number	Type of Nutrition
Viruses	noncellular	—	parasitic
Monera	prokaryotic	unicellular, filamentous	parasitic, absorption, photosynthesis
Protista	eukaryotic	unicellular, filamentous, colonial	photosynthesis, absorption, ingestion
Fungi	eukaryotic	unicellular, multicellular	absorption
Plantae	eukaryotic	multicellular	photosynthesis
Animalia	eukaryotic	multicellular	ingestion

In the final series of chapters in this textbook we will look at the variety of viruses, bacteria, fungi and plants. We will start at the beginning with the Kingdom Monera which consists of the bacteria. We include the viruses in this next chapter as well.

Key Words and Phrases

taxonomy	phylogeny	Carrolus Linnaeus
binomial nomenclature	genus	species
scientific name	common name	taxonomic hierarchy
Kingdom	Division	Class
Order	Family	Genus
Species	Monera	Protista
Fungi	Systematics	taxon
subspecies	trinomial system	

Selected Readings and References

Bold, H. C., and M. J. Wynne. 1985. *Introduction to the Algae: Structure and Reproduction.* 2nd Ed. Prentice-Hall. Englewood Cliffs, N.J.

Cronquist, A. 1981. *Integrated System of Classification of Flowering Plants.* Columbia University Press. New York, New York.

Gledhill, D. 1993. *The Names of Plants.* 2nd Edition. Cambridge University Press. New York.

Grant, W. F. (Ed.) 1984. *Plant Biosystematics.* Academic Press. New York.

Heywood, V. H. 1978. *Flowering Plants of the World.* Mayflower Publishers. New York.

Henning, W. 1966. *Phylogenetic Systematics.* University of Illinois Press. Urbana, Illinois.

Homes, S. 1983. *Outline of Plant Classification.* Longman Publishers. New York.

International Code of Botanical Nomenclature. 1978. Twelfth International Botanical Congress. Leningrad, Russia.

Margulus, L., and K. V. Schwartz. 1982. *Five Kingdoms: An Illustrated Guide to the Phyla of Life on Earth.* W. H. Freeman and Company. San Francisco.

Radford, A. E., R. J. Bandoni, J. R. Maze, G. E. Rouse, W. B. Schofield, and J. R. Stein. *Nonvascular Plants: An Evolutionary Approach.* Wadsworth Publishers. Belmont, California.

Walters, S. M. 1997. *Common Families of Flowering Plants.* Cambridge University Press. New York.

Wiley, E. O. 1981. *Phylogenetics: The Theory and Practice of Phylogenetic Systematics.* John Wiley & Sons. New York.

Wilson, E. O. 1992. *The Diversity of Life.* Harvard University Press. Cambridge, Massachusetts.

Review and Discussion Questions

1. Review, discuss and compare the advantages and disadvantages of the two kingdom approach to classification with the five kingdom method.
2. How are species related to subspecies related to varieties related to horticultural-species?
3. Use your knowledge of taxonomy and reference books to classify completely the following:
   (a) Red Oak tree
   (b) Maidenhair Fern
   (c) Red Algae
   (d) Sphagnum Moss
   (e) White Pine
4. Why is the life history and the structure of plants more important to taxonomists than size and color in identifying relationships among plants?
5. Look up a taxonomic key used in the identification of a plant group. How is it constructed? Why is it called a dichotomous key?
6. Species are considered to be natural entities but higher levels are artificial groupings. Discuss why this is so.
7. What are the interrelationships among classification, taxonomy and evolution?

Plant Ecology

The science that deals with the study of living things in relation to their environment is called **ecology**. People have always been interested in the ecology of plants and other organisms. Prehistoric societies that lived by gathering plants and hunting animals for food depended on their knowledge of how plants and animals lived and where they could be found and harvested. Now, as our population numbers in the billions of people we are even more vitally concerned with the practical aspects of ecology—what environments, for example, are best to maximize the growth and harvesting of our crops or how many salmon can we harvest without harming the salmon population by over fishing. This renewed interest in our natural environment has resulted in ecology being a central science today, in which the effects of pollutants and populations on plants and the landscape are studied and analyzed.

Populations, Communities, and Ecosystems

Like genetics, ecology has its own terminology. Ecology is concerned with how organisms interact with their environment individually, as units of populations, and as larger ecological units as well. Individuals, of course, exist by themselves, adapting to local conditions and extracting nutrients, and interacting with other organisms in their environment.

Populations. In a broader ecological sense, however, each individual is a functional member of a species population. A population is a group of individuals of the same species that interact with one another and live within the same species population range. Populations may consist of subpopulations occupying local habitats while the whole population is called a metapopulation. To illustrate this concept, consider the familiar cattails that grow in marshes and other wetland habitats. Almost every marsh has its own local population of cattails which comprise a subpopulation of the entire North American cattail population, the metapopulation.

Interactions at the population level may take the form of **competition** for available resources (water, food, shelter, mates), courtship and **reproduction**, territoriality and other events that occur at the population level. While a population is made up of individuals, its characteristics are derived from all of the members. Some specific population properties include density (how many plants there are in a given area), dispersion (how the plants are distributed), age distribution (e.g., the number of seedlings, saplings, immature and mature adults), growth (increasing or decreasing numbers of the plant species population), and regulation (what conditions and resources limit growth of the plant population). Populations are an integral and also a convenient unit of study for plant ecologists.

Community. When all the species populations of plants occurring in a given area are considered together, they form a unit called a **plant community**. Animals are also present and the sum total of plants and animals in a given area is a **biotic community**. A community can be studied and described in terms of the species populations that comprise it and their interactions with one another. For example, a wetland community of plants might include species populations of cattails, reedgrass, arrowheads, arrow arrum, water lillies, spatterdock, and many other aquatic species that occupy the wetland habitat. Animal components of this wetland community might include dragonflies, damselflies, spiders, frogs, water snakes, red-winged blackbirds, wood ducks, muskrats and beavers. Interactions that occur at the community level of ecology include predator-prey relationships, host-parasite relationships, and interspecific competition for resources. Plants not only interact with animals, but also interact with other plants. For example, many plant populations found in communities produce chemicals that inhibit the growth of other plants. Other examples of community level plant-to-plant relationships include symbiotic, such as mycorrhizal fungi and lichens. An interesting example of a plant-to-animal-to-plant relationships is seen in acacia trees and ants. Acacia trees have large, hollow thorns on their stems. Ants live in the thorns and feed on sugars produced by the tree. The ants repay their acacia host by attacking and destroying vines and other plants that touch the tree, thereby saving it from being overtopped and killed by strangler vines. As with populations, communities can be described and compared by specific, community level characteristics such as diversity (how many species of plants and animals occur), spacing (how species populations are spatially oriented towards one another), aspection (seasonal appearance and metabolism), nutrient cycling, and energy production and flow (photosynthesis and respiration).

Ecosystems. The interaction of members of a species community with their physical environment is called an **ecosystem**. Ecosystems include both the abiotic and biotic factors of the environment considered together. Abiotic factors are the conditions and resources that organisms must adapt to and exist with in an ecosystem. Examples of conditions include light, relative humidity, and temperature in terrestrial habitats and salinity, water flow, and water velocity in aquatic ecosystems. Resources are abiotic features that are required by the organisms of the ecosystem. Unlike conditions, resources are extracted and consumed; examples of resources for plants include water, light, soil space, and minerals.

The biotic factors in ecosystems are the plants and animals. Plants are the **producers** in the system, as they photosynthetically consume some solar energy and convert some of it into the chemical energy of sugars. Animals and decomposers are the **consumers** in ecosystems. The relationships between energy production by the plant producers and energy consumption by the consumers is called a **food chain** when linear and a **food web** if all of the organisms are considered.

Ecosystems can be large or small; they can vary from a tropical rain forest ecosystem that covers thousands of square miles to a puddle less than a foot in diameter. Like the tropical rain forest, the puddle contains its own temporary collection of plants and animals (phytoplankton and zooplankton), their decomposers (bacteria and fungi in the puddle), conditions (depth, water temperature), and resources (water, nutrients that fall into the puddle). The ecological study of larger ecosystems such as the tropical rain forest are, however, more frequently considered at the biome level.

Biomes. Large, contiguous units of ecosystems that have a similar species composition and growth form (physiognomy) are called biomes. The study of biomes includes the study of the resources and conditions that dictate the range and limits of the biome. Examples of the world's biomes will be described later in this chapter.

Biosphere. All of the biomes of the world, considered together, are called the biosphere, or less commonly, an **ecosphere**. The biosphere represents the range of life on earth. It considers the plants and animals of the soil (the lithosphere), the water (hydrosphere), and the air (atmosphere).

Organisms in Ecosystems

Species Habitat. The habitat is the place where a species occurs. We can also say that the habitat is the address of an organism—it is where we go to find it. Some species such as crabgrass or plantain occur in many different habitats, ranging from desert to forest to tundra. Other species, however, occupy only very specific habitats. For example, saguaro cactus are found only in the dry, arid habitats of the Southwest deserts of North America.

Species Niche. The niche is the role of a species in its habitat. Each species is morphologically, physiologically, and behaviorally adapted to exploit a habitat or a portion of a habitat differently and more effectively than any other species. Species are differently adapted to the range of environmental conditions such as temperature, moisture, and relative humidity. In addition, species extract resources (water, food and shelter) from their environment in very different ways from other species. The sum total of these adaptations for living in a habitat and for extracting resources differently from all other species define the niche. In any given habitat, no two species can occupy the same niche at the same time. If both species are present at the same time, then one species will be driven to extinction.

Ecological Processes

ENERGY PRODUCTION AND FLOW

Plants and animals of ecosystems "run" on the energy of sunlight. During photosynthesis, plants chemically convert a small portion of this sunlight energy into organic biomass, in effect, converting the kinetic energy of sunlight into the potential energy of organic molecules that comprise plant tissue. This plant-produced biomass is the sole source of energy that supports all of the vast assemblage of life on earth.

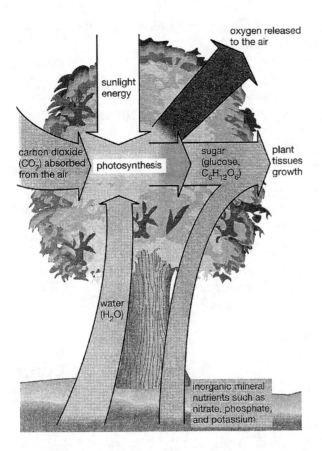

Figure 16–1 The flow of energy in the primary productivity of ecosystems. *Source:* Teresa Audesirk and Gerald Audesirk (1999), p. 837.

Green plants are the **primary producers** of an ecosystem, converting about one percent of the total sunlight into plant tissue. The biomass that green plants produce is called **gross primary productivity** and represents the total available energy to support all of the organisms of a particular ecosystem. Plants consume some of this biomass for their own energy requirements such as growth and reproduction. The remainder, generally about 30-60% of the plant biomass produced, is called **net primary productivity** and represents the energy supply initially available for the consumers of an ecosystem, the animals and decomposers.

Energy in the form of plant tissue is transferred to animals when **primary consumers** such as cows, grasshoppers, and other **herbivores** eat plants. The primary consumers digest, assimilate, and transform some of the plant tissue into herbivore tissue, which is called **secondary productivity**. They use the remainder to power their own activities such as growth, reproduction, and finding more plants to eat. In turn, herbivores are the energy source for **secondary consumers**, the **carnivores**, which eat them and transform some of their tissue into carnivore tissue, using the rest for their energy needs. A weasel eating a mouse or an accipiter taking a robin are examples of secondary consumers. A third group of secondary consumers eat both plants and animals and are called **omnivores**. Humans, pigs, and rats are familiar examples of omnivores. When plants and animals die their remains are returned to the soil on land and the substrate of aquatic habitats where organisms such as bacteria, fungi, and protozoa feed and decompose their bodies. Collectively, these organisms of decomposition are called **decomposers** or **detritivores** which obtain nutrients and energy from the organic tissues. In metabolically breaking down the plant and animal remains decomposers release the nutrients (minerals and organic compounds) into the soil which can then be absorbed and reincorporated in new plant tissues. Bacteria and fungi are the most

Figure 16–2 Examples of food chains in ecosystems (a) a simple terrestrial food chain (b) a marine food chain. *Source:* Teresa Audesirk and Gerald Audesirk (1999), p. 839.

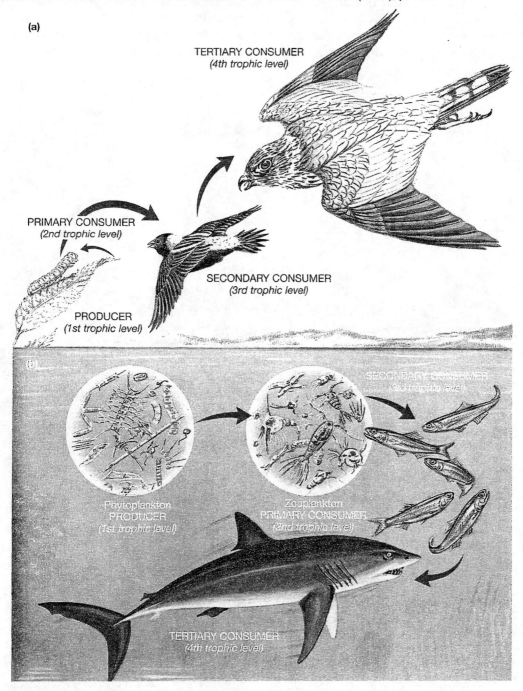

common decomposers but earthworms, nematodes, soil insects, and even vultures provide examples of the different kinds of decomposers. Although seemingly unimportant, detritivores play a significant role in ecosystem functioning. If not for their decomposer activities, all of the nutrients of an ecosystem would soon be tied up in the dead bodies of plants and animals, and none would be available to support new growth or new life.

Each level in the transfer of energy from primary producers through the different types of consumers (herbivores, carnivores, decomposers) in an ecosystem is called a **trophic level**. As a general rule, about 90 % of the energy is lost from one trophic level to a higher trophic level, either because it cannot be injested and assimilated by organisms at the next level or because the energy is consumed and transformed into heat energy which radiates out of the ecosystem and ultimately out of the biosphere and back into space. Thus, energy in ecosystems is produced by primary consumers and flows to upper trophic levels. It cannot be reclaimed or recycled, unlike the other major abiotic components of ecosystems, the minerals.

Figure 16–3 An example of a community food web. *Source:* Teresa Audesirk and Gerald Audesirk (1999), p. 840.

Figure 16–4 A comparison of the productivity of the various ecosystems of the world. The numbers represent net primary productivity, in grams of organic matter per square meter per year. *Source:* Teresa Audesirk and Gerald Audesirk (1999), p. 838.

NUTRIENT CYCLING IN ECOSYSTEMS

In addition to energy, all plants require nutrients for their physiological needs. These nutrients are obtained from the environment, usually in the form of minerals from the soil or gases or water vapor. Nutrients that are extracted from the environment are incorporated in plant tissue. When animals consume plants they digest, absorb, and retain these nutrients, generally in the form of animal tissues. When plants and animals die and are decomposed by the various detritivores the nutrients are liberated in the soil or in the air. In this form they can be absorbed by plants and once again incorporated in plant tissue. This continuous exchange of nutrients from the abiotic portion of the environment into the biotic and back to the abiotic is termed **nutrient cycling** or **biogeochemical cycling**.

Plants play a conspicuous role in nutrient cycling as they can absorb the nutrients from the environment and retain them in plant tissue. Ecologists recognize two distinct types of nutrient cycling, gaseous and sedimentary.

Gaseous Nutrient Cycles

Examples of nutrients that exhibit a gaseous nutrient cycle include oxygen, carbon dioxide, nitrogen, and water. The major abiotic reservoir for all of these nutrients is either the atmosphere, oceans, or both.

Hydrological Cycle

The movement of water provides a familiar example of how a gaseous nutrient cycles between the abiotic and biotic compartments of an ecosystem. Driven by solar energy, water cycles from the abiotic environment to the biotic and back again. Water is available to plants primarily as soil water and less commonly as water vapor. Much of the water that plants absorb drives the transpiration process and is quickly returned to the atmosphere in the form of water vapor that evaporates from the stomata. Some, however, is transformed into plant tissue during the dark reactions of photosynthesis. Once in the biotic spectrum, plant tissue is consumed by animals which retain the

Figure 16–5 The hydrological cycle. *Source:* Teresa Audesirk and Gerald Audesirk (1999), p. 848.

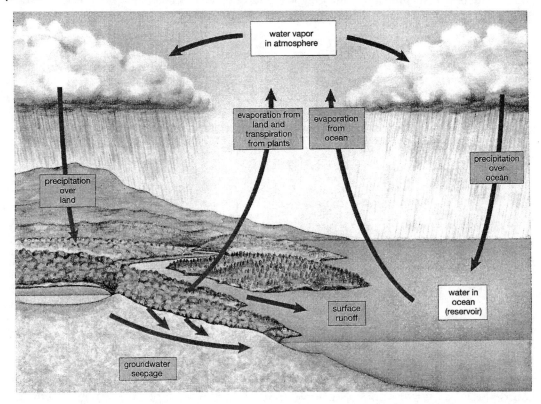

Figure 16–6 The cycling of nitrogen from its reservoir in the atmosphere through the biosphere and back. *Source:* Teresa Audesirk and Gerald Audesirk (1999), p. 846.

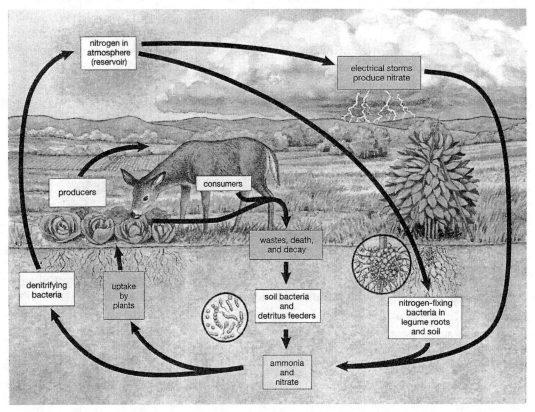

organic component for their own tissues. During the electron transport system of respiration the hydrogen atoms are again united with oxygen and water is formed and released, either through excretion or by evaporation back into the atmosphere to complete the hydrological cycle.

Nitrogen Cycle

The cycling of nitrogen transfers this critically needed element from the abiotic to the biotic. Despite its abundance in the atmosphere, nitrogen gas cannot be directly used, but must be converted into biological useable forms by nitrogen-fixing organisms such as fungi and bacteria which live in soil or in the root nodules of legumes and other plants. Nitrogen fixing organisms can enzymatically extract nitrogen (N_2) from the air and convert it into ammonia (NH_3) which dissolves in soil water to ammonium (NH_4^+). Plants can absorb ammonium or ammonia ions and incorporate them into proteins, nucleic acids, and other nitrogen-containing molecules. When animals eat plants they retain nitrogen-containing molecules for their own proteins and nucleic acids. Nitrogen is returned to the environment when plants and animals die and their bodies decompose, liberating the nitrogen in the form of ammonia which is chemically transformed into nitrate by denitrifying bacteria. Still other bacteria consume and ultimately convert the nitrate back into gaseous nitrogen in a process called **denitrification**, thereby completing the nitrogen cycle.

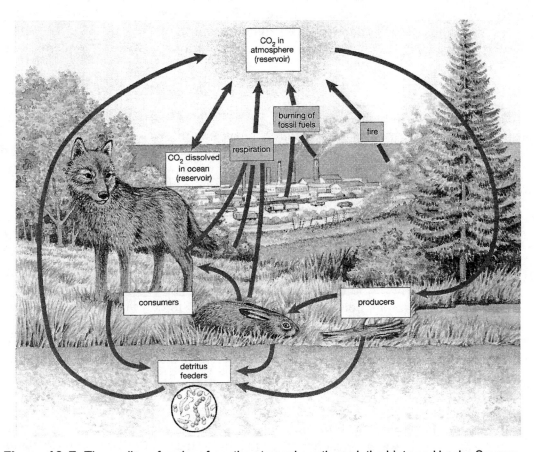

Figure 16–7 The cycling of carbon from the atmosphere through the biota and back. *Source:* Teresa Audesirk and Gerald Audesirk (1999), p. 845.

The Carbon Cycle

In the abiotic portion of ecosystems, carbon occurs mainly as carbon dioxide. The major abiotic reservoirs of carbon dioxide are the atmosphere, oceans, and soils. During photosynthesis, plants convert some carbon dioxide (along with water) into sugars and other organic molecules. Some of the sugars comprise plant tissues. Others are used during respiration, releasing the carbon dioxide back into the atmosphere and completing the carbon cycle. Similarly, some of the plant tissue eaten by animals is converted into animal tissues which retain the carbon. Like plants, when animals respire they consume carbon- containing organic tissue, releasing the carbon back into the abiotic spectrum in the form of carbon dioxide.

Carbon also sometimes accumulates and is retained for many years in the biotic spectrum as wood. When woody plants die and decompose the carbon is again released as carbon dioxide. Over geologic time, an enormous amount of carbon was buried as woody organic litter and transformed by heat and pressure into peat, coal, and petroleum deposits. When these fossil fuels are burned the carbon is once again released into the atmosphere as carbon dioxide.

Sedimentary Nutrient Cycles

The soils and rocks of the earth represent the abiotic reservoirs of nutrients that exhibit sedimentary biogeochemical cycles. Soil minerals such as calcium, potassium, and iron are all examples which cycle from the abiotic soils and rocks to the biotic and back again in sedimentary biogeochemical cycles. In order to be absorbed and incorporated in biotic tissue the minerals must first be released by **weathering**. During weathering exposed rock containing the minerals is fragmented by wind and rain, freezing and thawing. Fragmented particles are then further weathered by chemical or biotic action or both.

Calcium Cycling

Calcium is a key ingredient in the cell walls of plants and also contributes to the proper functioning of many plant and animal enzymes and related physiological activities. In nature calcium is most often found in the abiotic form of limestone and other calcium-containing rocks such as gypsum and marble. When limestone is exposed to water calcium is released by the following weathering reaction:

$$CaCO_3 + H_2O \longrightarrow Ca^+ + H^+ + HCO_3^-$$

Weathering releases calcium ions which can then be taken into plants with absorbed water. Calcium ions not absorbed may be carried away when water containing the ions is leached from the soil to enter nearby streams and transported through aquatic ecosystems, ultimately to the oceans where they percolate to the bottom and again become part of the abiotic portion of the environment. In contrast, the calcium ions taken up by plants become part of plant tissue which, when consumed, is retained in animal tissue where it is transferred to higher trophic levels. When animals die and their tissues decompose the calcium ions are again released and returned to the abiotic spectrum of the environment.

The Phosphorus Cycle

Phosphorus is a critically needed mineral that is normally found in small amounts in rocks. Weathering releases phosphorus as the phosphate (PO_4^{-3}) ion which plants absorb directly from the soil or water. Animals retain and incorporate the phosphate in proteins and nucleic acids of their own tissues. Following their death, bacteria and fungi

Figure 16–8 The phosphorous cycle. The cycle begins when phosphorous dissolves from rocks and enters the biota. It can be retained in terrestrial systems or leached and transported to aquatic systems. *Source:* Teresa Audesirk and Gerald Audesirk (1999), p. 847.

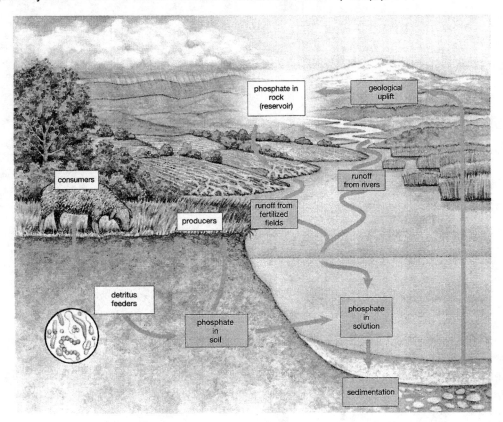

decompose the plants and animals and convert the phosphate-containing tissues back into phosphate ions which are released into the soil or water to complete the cycle.

Phosphate ions not taken up by plants may be leached from local ecosystems to enter rivers and streams. Plants in these aquatic habitats such as algae and aquatic hydrophytes absorb the phosphate which is retained in their tissues and those of aquatic animals that consume them.

Some phosphate is eventually transported to oceans where marine algae and animals again claim and retain it as part of their tissues. As they die and decompose however, phosphate ions not immediately absorbed may slowly settle to the ocean floor and become trapped in sediments. In this abiotic form, phosphorus is unavailable for either terrestrial or aquatic ecosystems for millions of years until geological events of mountain building occur, raising the sea floor and exposing the phosphorus-containing sediments to weathering processes again.

SUCCESSION IN ECOSYSTEMS

If a Connecticut woodland is logged, burned, or otherwise removed and the area abandoned an ecological process called succession begins. Within a year or two the bare area is colonized by a succession of weeds such as milkweed, vetch, crabgrass and other familiar weeds of old fields. In a few years the weedy field is replaced by orchard grass, bluestem, foxtail, and other grasses and resembles a western grassland. In a few more years shrubs such as cedar or sumac or seedlings of cherry, birch, and Russian

Figure 16–9 An example of primary succession from bare rock to a climax forest of spruce and fir. *Source:* Teresa Audesirk and Gerald Audesirk (1999), p. 827.

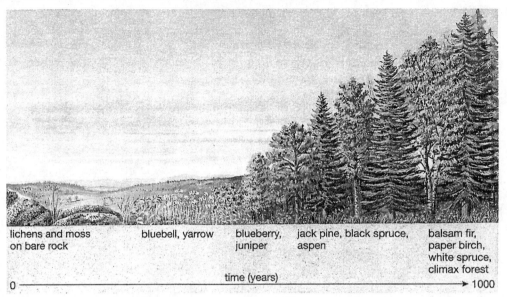

lichens and moss on bare rock | bluebell, yarrow | blueberry, juniper | jack pine, black spruce, aspen | balsam fir, paper birch, white spruce, climax forest

time (years)

0 ————————————————————→ 1000

olive take root, converting the grassland into a shrub covered field. Two or three years later seedlings colonize the shrub field, converting it into a woodland of birch, beech, cherry, and maple saplings that, when grown, produce a stable deciduous woodland community which represents the **climax community**. Ecological succession ceases with the production of the stable, self-perpetuating habitat.

Succession can by defined as the process whereby plant communities evolve to the point where they can reproduce themselves indefinitely, in the existing environment. If there was a volcano eruption, in Connecticut, the lava and ash would cover everything, killing all the plants and animals. The lava would eventually be broken down to form soil by lichens and bacteria which would have invaded the area from out of the ecosystem. These organism would be replaced or joined by shrubs and grasses to be replaced later by softwoods, which ultimately would be replaced by hardwoods. Each stage in this process is called a **sere**, and the final sere, which continues indefinitely as long as environment stays the same, is the **climax** vegetation.

Succession varies from place to place depending upon the climate. We chose Connecticut as an example, because here succession can be complete with hardwoods forming the climax. In many environments some of the seral stages listed above are the climax vegetation. For example the Great Plains have grasses for the climax vegetation. Major factors driving plant succession are the availability of water and the regional and local temperatures. Thus, deciduous woodlands develop in cool, wet areas where precipitation averages 50-60 inches each year and the summers are mild with long growing seasons. If much of the precipitation falls as snow and summers are shorter and cooler succession ceases with the development of a climax community of conifers, such as the great pine, spruce, and fir forests of Canada and Alaska. For example, in most of Eastern Canada, water is available but much of it is frozen for long periods of the year. Thus the climax vegetation there is softwoods such as evergreen forests. These plants have the best adaptations to that kind of environment. Conversely, if summers are mild but rainfall is less, averaging about 40 inches of rainfall and snowfall

Figure 16–10 An example of secondary succession from a plowed field to an oak and hickory woodland. *Source:* Teresa Audesirk and Gerald Audesirk (1999), p. 827.

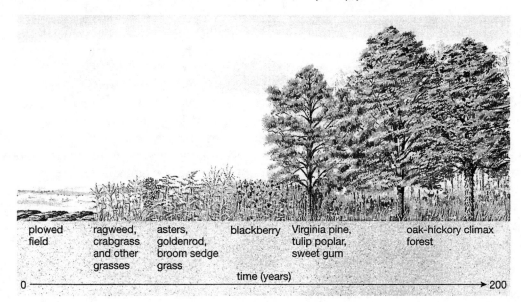

| plowed field | ragweed, crabgrass and other grasses | asters, goldenrod, broom sedge grass | blackberry | Virginia pine, tulip poplar, sweet gum | oak-hickory climax forest |

time (years)

0 ───► 200

each year, grasslands develop. In hot, dry areas with sparse moisture but high evaporation rates succession is brief, culminating in a desert climax community in areas where temperatures are high and in a tundra habitat in low temperature locales.

The succession we introduced above begins with **primary succession**. In primary succession the environment has to be made before plants can become established. **Secondary succession** occurs more rapidly than primary succession as the soil is already conditioned and primary species of plants may be nearby. Secondary succession generally follows human disturbance or forest fires etc.

Xerosere. In a xerosere, succession begins with bare rocks and lava being attacked by lichens, which become established and build up the soil. These are eventually replaced by more advanced plants until a climax community of plants and animals develops.

Hydrosere. A hydrosere is succession in aquatic habitats such as ponds, lakes and marshes. A hydrosere often begins around the margins of a pond, as seeds or other propagules of plants are carried in on muddy feet of waterfowl, blown in by winds, or floated in by water currents. Succession begins as the algae, duckweeds, water lilies, cattails, and other emergent aquatic vascular plants colonize the bottom muck or the wave-washed shoreline. Grass-like sedges become established along the margins of the bodies of water and gradually the margins of the body of water begins to shrink. As the land becomes less marshy, it is invaded by conifers which help to produce more soil. Finally the conifers are replaced by hardwoods. This process may take thousands of years.

Fire and Humans in Ecosystems

Fire ecology is a normal phenomenon caused by lightning. It is important as many conifers cannot germinate or release spores without fire. Fires generally benefit ecology of all regions as they reduce underbrush and return nutrients to the soil.

Humans also have a major effect on ecosystems. As the human **population increases**, this causes a major impact in many ways. There is a need for support goods such as food, clothing and building materials. We clear land, destroy habitat, and pollute. This is a wasteful approach to ecosystem usage and we need to limit our impact on the ecosystem. One of the most important recent initiatives for doing this is the program to **recycle**. By recycling we take less from the ecosystem and since we recycle, we pollute less.

Humans have many effects on the ecosystem. For example the burning of fossil fuels has created what is called the **Greenhouse Effect**. We have created a global rise in temperature due to the accumulation of carbon dioxide in the atmosphere. This excess carbon dioxide permits radiation to reach the earth's surface, heating us up.

These levels of carbon dioxide have increased over the past 30,000 years. We are burning fossil fuels and deforesting major regions of the world. In the last 25 years, the atmosphere has become 0.7 degrees warmer and the surface temperature of the earth has risen about 1.5 degrees on average. This seems like a small amount but the earth was only 7 degrees F colder during the last Ice Age. In the next 50 years, temperatures may rise enough to melt the polar ice caps, to cause high ocean levels inundating 7,000 square miles of the United States alone. This will also cause major changes in climate.

Another human activity contributing to environmental change is **methane production**. Swamps and wetlands are natural sources of methane from anaerobic bacteria.

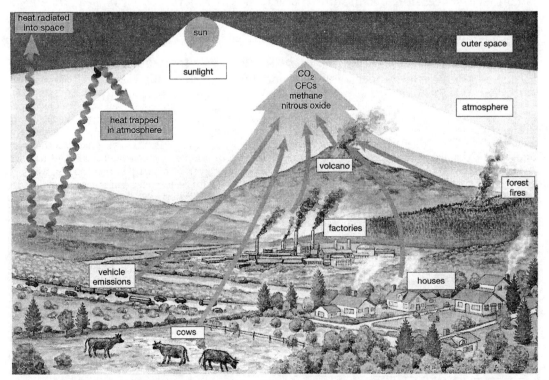

Figure 16–11 Human intervention in the natural landscapes of the world. *Source:* Teresa Audesirk and Gerald Audesirk (1999), p. 852.

Part of the observed increase in methane concentrations in the atmosphere is caused by animals, but much can be blamed on human activity. For example, termites exude methane as a by-product of their metabolism. Vastly increased termite populations living in the recently cleared tropical rain forest areas add significant amounts of methane to the atmosphere each year. Whether this trend is caused by industrial additions of methane and other pollutants to the atmosphere is unknown. What is known is that human interference has been a major factor in causing it and the atmospheric concentrations of many substances are being altered by the inadvertent introduction of chlorofluorocarbons used in refrigeration. These molecularly light-weight compounds quickly make their way by diffusion into the upper atmosphere where they interact with sunlight to form compounds that destroy ozone. **Ozone** is a natural barrier to ultraviolet radiation which in turn, is a mutagenic agent that alters DNA and other nucleic acids. For example, we expect a rise in skin cancer because of the increased ultraviolet radiation at the surface of the earth.

One of the most important human impacts has been in the production of **acid rain**. Acid rain is a residue from burning fossil fuels, which release sulfur and nitrogen compounds into the atmosphere. Sunlight and rain bring about chemical reactions to convert these residues to nitric acid and sulfuric acid. These acids combine with rain to form acid rain. Changes in the pH of the soil and the ecosystem occur as a result. Many forests are dying as a result, because the acid rain kills the mycorrhizae fungal systems around their roots. These mycorrhizae are necessary for the life of the tree. Acid rain is also destroying the aquatic life of lakes and ponds throughout the northeastern United States. Over 200 lakes in the Adirondacks of upstate New York are devoid of life because of their high acid levels which have been directly caused by acid rain.

Lastly, when we pollute directly or indirectly we contaminate the **water supply** for both us and other living things. Pollution from toxic materials to spraying of pesticides, combustion of fossil fuels, garden and farm fertilizers are all forms of pollutants that eventually find their way into the water table. No matter what we put into the soil, someone somewhere ends up drinking it.

Biomes of the World

Biomes are large subcontinental regions based on vegetation zones and moisture and climax vegetation. In essence, a biome is a giant subcontinental ecosystem limited by climate but exhibiting a uniformity of growth patterns. Biomes are named and described on the basis of their dominant plant or animal growth and growth form. Biomes are larger and more inclusive ecological units than ecosystems and communities. For example, three primary grasslands occur in North America, the short-grass grassland of Kansas and Colorado, the mid-grass grassland of Nebraska and Oklahoma, and the tall grass prairie of Illinois and Iowa. Each of these grass-dominated areas can be considered ecosystems but collectively, they comprise the grassland biome. Two broad categories of global biomes are recognized, terrestrial and aquatic.

TERRESTRIAL BIOMES

Tundra

The tundra biome occurs in a broad belt across Eurasia and North America, occupying the region north of the tree line but south of the areas of perpetual ice and snow

Figure 16–12 The relationships between elevation and temperature in determining the distribution of the biomes of the world. *Source:* Teresa Audesirk and Gerald Audesirk (1999), p. 863.

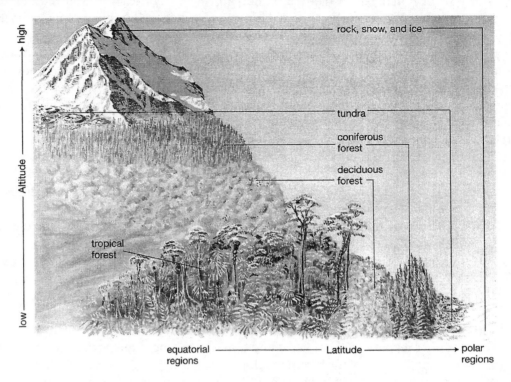

Figure 16–13 The interacting effects of rainfall and temperature in determining the types of natural habitats. *Source:* Teresa Audesirk and Gerald Audesirk (1999), p. 866.

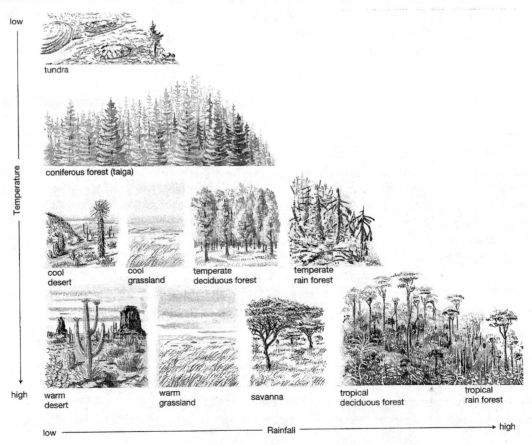

of the polar icecap. Small areas of tundra are also found in a few of the islands off the coast of South America and near Antarctica. A form of tundra, often called alpine tundra, occurs in the higher mountain elevations above the tree line.

Climatically, the tundra biome is marked by short, cool, and often wet summers followed by long winters of intense cold and snow. The long, sustained cold temperatures are not much different from North Dakota, for example, but it is cold for much of the year, making for a short growing season generally less than 90 days. Days are extremely short in midwinter but in the brief summers there is continuous sunlight, giving rise to the descriptor "land of the midnight sun."

Annual precipitation is relatively low, generally no more than 10-15 inches of rainfall or snowfall per year but evaporation rates are low because of the low temperatures. Therefore, snowfall is likely to remain covering the ground for much of the year.

Because of the extremely low temperatures **permafrost**—the presence of ice just a few feet beneath the surface—is present throughout the year and dictates drainage patterns and soil formation and thickness. Consequently, much of the tundra soil is shallow and often waterlogged. In the summer months the upper levels of the soil will thaw but the permafrost layer is always there. Many tundra lakes and ponds form in summer because water cannot drain through the subsurface layer of ice but instead accumulates in slight depressions.

The climax vegetation of tundra consists of sedges, grasses, lichens, fungi, mosses, small perennials and low growing shrubs, especially willows and heaths. Despite the severity of its climate and the shortness of its growing season, the tundra has an interesting and diverse fauna. Larger residents include a variety of mammal herbivores such as moose, musk ox, and caribou (called reindeer in the old world). The variety of small and medium sized herbivores includes chipmunks and ground squirrels, marmots, hares and cottontails, and lemmings. Some of the characteristic mammal predators of the tundra include the polar bear, grizzly, black bear, Arctic fox, and wolf. Native birds are much more limited, but include the snowy owl and ptarmigan. Summer faunas are enormously enriched by the return of mammal and avian migrants and the seasonal abundance of many dipterous insects such as flies, midges, and mosquitos. The innumerable shallow

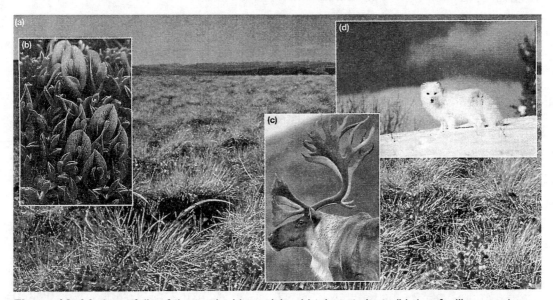

Figure 16–14 A portfolio of the tundra biome (a) cold-tolerant plants (b) dwarf willows, sedges, and cold-adapted windflowers (c) reindeer (d) arctic fox. *Source:* Teresa Audesirk and Gerald Audesirk (1999), p. 877.

ponds and lakes that dot the tundra in summer are optimal breeding locales for dipterans which in turn form food for a variety of nesting geese, ducks, sandpipers, gulls, and other shorebirds. For these birds, abundant food resources and long daylight hours for foraging provide optimum nesting conditions and the tundra is one of the world's premier breeding grounds for waterfowl and waterbirds.

Coniferous Forest

Dominated by conifers, this biome typically occurs in a broad belt across the northern continents just south of the tundra but north of the deciduous woodlands of the East and the grassland biomes of the Midwest and West. Smaller areas of coniferous forest occur southward along high mountain ranges just below the alpine tundra, where it is called the montane coniferous forest.

Over much of its length, a transition area called the **taiga** lies between the tundra and the coniferous forest biome. Climate conditions of the taiga are intermediate between tundra and coniferous forest biomes and plants are a mix of both biomes. The taiga is marked by growths of stunted and dwarf-like evergreens. In high mountain areas, the taiga can be recognized by the elphinwood growth of low, twisted evergreens that can be found above the tree line and just below the meadow-like alpine tundra.

Climatically, the coniferous forest biome is characterized by 30–40 inches of annual precipitation, much in the form of winter snows. Temperatures are cool in summer and cold in winter. This biome is sometimes called the microthermal snow forest because of the cold, snowy winters. Water is unavailable for much of the winter because it occurs only in the frozen state. During this time, plants are generally metabolically dormant. The soil is shallow like the tundra but differs in that the permafrost is absent from most of it. The growing season ranges from about 90 plus days along the border with the taiga to over 250 days along the southern edge of this biome.

The climax vegetation consists of vast conifer forests of spruces, firs, pines, and other conifers. Often huge areas are dominated by only one or two species of trees. Some animals of the coniferous forest biome include moose, black bear, snowshoe rabbit, red squirrel, northern flying squirrel, porcupine and spruce grouse. There are a few water snakes and some salamanders and frogs as well.

Temperate Forests

Called temperate forests or temperate deciduous forests, this biome occurs throughout most of the eastern United States and central and northern Europe. Belts of temperature forests are also found in India and China, northeastern Australia and in temperate regions of South America. Temperate rain forests are sometimes considered to belong to this biome type (but sometimes they are placed in a separate biome category).

Climatically, temperate forests have moderate to seasonally heavy rainfall but lighter winter snows than found in coniferous forest biomes. Precipitation generally averages about 60 inches annually, with about 5–10 percent of this occurring as snowfall. Winters are cold but summers are warm and often hot and humid, especially along the southern edge. The growing season ranges between about 300 days in the north to about 365 days. Soils are relatively shallow and are easily eroded and soon exhausted under agriculture. The rocky glacial tills of New England are a perfect example of this kind of soil.

The climax vegetation of temperate forests consists of mixed forests of deciduous trees such as oaks, chestnuts, maples, hickories, and beech. Conifers, especially pines often comprise part of the temperate forest, either occurring in its climax or as distinctive successional stages. Most temperate forests are deciduous; growth occurs during summer months but in autumn the trees shed their leaves and remain dormant throughout winter before renewing growth in spring. These temperate forests are usually called temperate deciduous forests.

Historically, temperate forests have been the biome in which the western civilization developed and as a consequence, nearly all the original forests have been destroyed and the present forests represent second or third growth. Much of the land today is occupied by farms, cities or industries.

Animal life of temperate forests is much more diverse and abundant than in coniferous forest biomes. Large, permanent mammals include deer, squirrels such as the gray squirrel, fox squirrel, and southern flying squirrel, raccoons, and chipmunks. In summer, the fauna is enriched by the return of neotropical migrants including the warblers and other songbirds. Woodpeckers, owls, hawks, thrushes, vireos, and sparrows can also be abundant and widespread animal components. Reptiles and amphibians occur throughout this biome including the copperhead and rattlesnake.

Grasslands

Grasslands occur on all continents of the world in the warmer, and often in the drier continental interior. Large expanses of grasslands are found in North America (prairie), South America (the pampas), central and southern Africa (veld) and Eastern Europe and Asia (steppes). Tropical grassland biomes in which scattered trees intrude are called savanna. Grasslands are dominated by grasses but other herbaceous plants, especially wildflowers, provide a common seasonal mix and are often quite abundant and varied.

Grassland biomes have a continental climate. Temperatures are cool to cold in winter and mild to very hot in summer. Annual precipitation is generally low, ranging

Figure 16–15 The life of the grassland biome (a) the grassland landscape (b) pronghorn antelope (c) prairie dogs (d) buffalo (e) coneflowers. *Source:* Teresa Audesirk and Gerald Audesirk (1999), p. 873.

between 15–30 inches of rain and snow per year. The soil is deep, rich and agricultural in nature. Climax vegetation includes many kinds of grasses becoming increasingly shorter as one travels west. Most of the grassland biomes of the world are home to (or have been home to) the enormous herds of mammals. The grasslands of the Serengetti in Africa support the huge populations of wildebeest, zebra, antelopes, water buffalo, elephants, and many other large, herbivorous mammals. Their predators, the lions, hyaenas, jackals, and hunting dogs are in attendance. Common animals of North American grassland biomes include pronghorn antelope, American bison, ground squirrels, prairie dogs, pocket gophers, prairie chickens, horned larks, several kinds of reptiles including prairie rattlesnakes and gopher snakes.

Chaparral

Also called the Mediterranean biome, the chaparral biome is intermediate in climate between that of coniferous forest and desert biomes. Chaparral typically occurs in the middle latitudes of the various parts of the world. Good examples of chaparral biome are found in western North America, especially in southern California and northwestern Mexico, in parts of Chile, South Africa, Australia, and, of course, along the Mediterranean in southern Europe.

Climatically, chaparral winters can be cool temperatures but summers are hot, dry and desert-like. Precipitation generally averages between 15-30 inches annually, mostly in the form of rain.

Plants of the chaparral are typically low growing woody shrubs and grasses over-topped by evergreens such as cedars, junipers, and pines and scrubby growths of oak and maples. Many chaparral plants are usually fire-adapted, able to withstand low intensity fires. Seeds of others germinate and grow quickly following fires. Animals are usually visitors from adjacent biomes. Large herbivores that frequent chaparral may include the mule deer in the Intermountain West, peccary in the Southwest, a variety of seed and fruit-eating birds and rodents, snakes and an occasional lizard.

Deserts

Deserts occur on all continents of the world. Examples of the world's greatest deserts include the Great Basin Desert of the Intermountain United States, the Sonora, Mohave, and Chihuahuan deserts of the southwestern United States, the Atacama desert along the western edge of South America, the Namib desert of southwestern Africa, the great Sahara desert and Arabian deserts to the north, and the Gobi desert in central and eastern Asia. All of these desert biomes are dry regions that typically receive less than 10 inches of precipitation annually. Winters range from warm to cool, especially in the upper deserts but summers are typically hot to very hot and dry. Lack of moisture prevents adequate soil development and desert soils are mostly clay with very little humus. For plants they are shallow and infertile. Very often, the soils contain salt or alkaline substances or minerals in inhospitable concentrations.

The climax vegetation of desert biomes contains shrubs and cactus resistant to dryness, creosote, bush, cholla, ironwood, ocotillo, brittle-brush and mesquite. All these plants have a thick cuticle or succulent leaves that help conserve water. Many desert plants are closely tied to seasonality of rainfall, germinating, growing, and flowering within a brief three or four week period during the rainy season and then enduring the dry season as resistant seeds, spores, or other structures.

Many desert plants have also adapted to the high light intensities constant throughout much of the year through Crassulacean acid metabolism, thereby eliminating the need for stomata to be open during the hot, dry, days.

Figure 16–16 The desert biome (a) desert landscape (b) sagebrush, cacti (c) prickly pear cactus and brittle bush, (d) kangaroo rat. *Source:* Teresa Audesirk and Gerald Audesirk (1999), p. 870.

To avoid the hot, dry, and sunny days most animal components of desert biomes are nocturnal or crespudcular (active during the twilight hours of dawn and dusk). Some familiar animals that have adapted to desert habitats include, lizards such as the chuckwalla and horned toads, snakes, pocket mice, kangaroo rats and even predators such as the kit fox and mountain lion.

Tropical Rain Forests

The tropical areas of the world include many biomes such as deserts, savannahs, tropical dry forests, tropical wet forests and tropical deciduous forests. Of these, tropical rain forest biomes are the best known for their richness of species. In land area, tropical rain forests comprise just 7 percent of the terrestrial biomes but nearly 90 percent of all plant and animal species are found in this biome.

Most tropical rain forests occur between the Tropics of Capricorn and Cancer. The best examples include the Amazonian rain forests of South America, the rain forests of the Congo basin in central Africa and the rain forests of India and Southeast Asia.

Because they are located near the equator, tropical rain forests experience almost equal day and night length of 12 hours for most of the year. This results in fairly uniform temperatures that average about 75–95°F which vary little from day to night. Precipitation is high, often over 500 inches of rainfall each year. Most tropical rain forests have no dry season but others, particularly further north or south, have both wet and dry seasons. Although rainfall is abundant and plant life diverse the soils beneath tropical rain forests are generally shallow and infertile with little leaf litter accumulation and almost no humus formation. Nutrients released by decomposition are either quickly absorbed by plants or leached out of the soil by the heavy rainfall. Tropical soils are, in fact, so poor that traditional agriculture easily exhausts and erodes soils within a few years. Often the soil is red or yellow in color and is only productive in regions where there is volcanic action. Abundant rainfall and sunlight provide for a growing season throughout the year.

The climax vegetation varies with the rainfall, but is typically dominated by broad-leaved trees forming a dense, multi-layered canopy. Tropical rain forests are noted for their great diversity of trees, vines and all kinds of flowering plants. Plant competition for available light has evolutionarily resulted in an impressive array of **epiphytes** such as orchids, air plants, and bromeliads which grow on other plants.

Animals are also diverse and abundant. Many kinds of primates and numerous other tree-dwelling mammals, birds and reptiles are found here. Bats have their greatest diversity in the tropics and many flowers are bat pollinated rather than insect or wind pollinated which is more commonly seen in other biomes. The tropics are also noted for their amazingly varied insect fauna. A single acre of tropical rain forest may hold hundreds of species of trees, shrubs, and flowers but thousands of species of insects.

The future of tropical rain forests looks bleak. During the 1960's, Brazil tried to convert its enormous Amazonian rain forest into large farms, hydroelectric plants and mines. This development proved a disaster. Forests were cleared, rivers filled with silt and animals killed or driven away before the ambitious project was dropped. However, in other areas of the world tropical rain forest biomes are still subject to similar devastation. Logging, agribusinesses, clearing for pastures, and clearing for towns and villages still pose a threat to large areas of tropical rain forest biome around the world each year.

Savanna

These biomes of subtropical areas are floristically dominated by scattered, park-like trees over an under story of grasses. Examples of savanna ecosystems are found in central and southern Africa, parts of subtropical South America, and Australia. Climatically, savanna biomes are transition zones between tropical rain forests and grasslands. They typically have three primary seasons, warm and wet, cool and dry, and hot and dry. Fires also are an important controlling aspect of this biome, preventing the establishment, spread, and replacement of the savanna trees by a forest of trees.

Savannas are noted for their high primary productivity of grasses and other vegetation which support a vast and diverse assemblage of grazing herbivores such as the great herds of antelopes, wildebeests, zebras, elephants, and giraffes in African savannas and the kangaroos of Australian savannas. Other animal inhabitants of savannas are the predators that live on the herds such as lions, leopards, and cheetahs.

AQUATIC HABITATS

Marine

The marine biome is the largest and most diverse of the world's biomes. Oceans cover nearly 71 percent of the earth's surface and range in depth from shallow shorelines to over 26,000 feet. Bays, estuaries, shallow seas, coastal areas, upwelling areas, and deep pelagic areas all testify to the varied habitats that are found in the marine biome.

Climatically, the marine biome experiences the greatest extremes of temperatures, sunlight, salinity, and concentrations of oxygen and other nutrients. Plant and animal diversity and distribution in the marine biome is limited to areas with adequate productivity and nutrient availability. Plant life is dominated by algae and seaweeds while dominant animal life consists primarily of fishes and mammals and a range of invertebrates.

Freshwater

Freshwater habitats such as lakes, ponds, wetlands, and rivers are found scattered in most terrestrial landscapes. They are water biomes set amidst terrestrial biomes. Like the marine biome, freshwater biomes vary tremendously in size, distribution, and nutrient concentrations.

Plant life is varied but generally consists of phytoplankton, aquatic mosses and algae, and aquatic vascular plants such as cattails, bulrushes, reedgrasses and a variety of flowering plants. Animal life is dominated by aquatic invertebrates and fishes. Freshwater biomes are also important to the animal life of adjacent terrestrial biomes which depend on them for water.

Key Words and Phrases

▼ •

population	community	ecosystem
taiga	grassland	desert
montane forest	tropical rain forest	deciduous forest
succession	xerosere	seral stage
sere	hydrosere	climax
upwelling areas	tundra	biosphere
ecosphere	niche	greenhouse effect
methane	ozone	acid rain
coniferous forest	temperate forest	population
chaparral	marine	freshwater

Selected References and Resources

▼ •

Agren, G. I., and E. Bosatta. 1997. *Theoretical Ecosystem Ecology*. Cambridge University Press. New York.

Barbour, M. G. 1987. *Terrestrial Plant Ecology*. 2nd. Edition. Benjamin/Cummings Publishing Company. Menlo Park.

Barbour, M. G., and W. D. Billings. 1988. *North American Terrestrial Vegetation*. Cambridge University Press. New York and London.

Bazzaz, F. A. 1996. *Plants in Changing Environments. Linking Physiological, Population, and Community Ecology*. Cambridge University Press. New York.

Begon, M., J. L. Harper and C. R. Townsend. 1996. *Ecology. Individuals, Populations and Communities*. Blackwell Scientific Publications. Boston and London.

Brewer, R. 1994. *The Science of Ecology*. 2nd Edition. Saunders College Publishing. Philadelphia.

Frankel, O. H., A. H. D. Brown, and J. J. Burdon. 1995. *The Conservation of Plant Biodiversity*. Cambridge University Press. New York.

Hastings, A. 1997. *Population biology. Concepts and Models*. Springer-Verlag Company. New York.

Huston, M. A. 1994. *Biological Diversity*. Cambridge University Press. New York.

Johnson, E. A. 1992. *Fire and Vegetation Dynamics*. Cambridge University Press. New York.

Lincoln, R. J., G. A. Boxshall, and P. F. Clark. 1997. *A Dictionary of Ecology, Evolution, and Systematics*. Cambridge University Press. New York.

Peterken, G. 1996. *Natural Woodlands*. Cambridge University Press. New York.

Richards, P. W. 1996. *The Tropical Rain Forest*. Cambridge University Press. New York.

Shugart, H. H. 1997. *Terrestrial Ecosystems in Changing Environments*. Cambridge University Press. New York.

Smith, R. L. 2000. *Ecology and Field Biology*. 5th Edition. Harper and Row. Englewood Cliffs, New Jersey.

Smith, T. M, H. H. Shugart and F. I. Woodward. 1997. *Plant Functional Types. Their Relevance to Ecosystem Properties and Global Change*. Cambridge University Press. New York.

Socolow, R., C. Andrews, F. Berkhout, and V. Thomas. 1995. *Industrial Ecology and Global Change*. Cambridge University Press. New York.

Walker, B., and W. Steffen. 1996. *Global Change and Terrestrial Ecosystems*. Cambridge University Press. New York.

Whelan, R. J. 1995. *The Ecology of Fire*. Cambridge University Press. New York.

Wilson, E. O. 1975. *Sociobiology. The New Synthesis*. Belknap Press. Cambridge.

Wilson, E. O. 1988. *Biodiversity*. W. H. Freeman and Company. San Francisco.

Review and Discussion Questions

1. Why are wetlands sometimes called the interface between freshwater biomes and terrestrial biomes.
2. What are the basic causes of desert biomes of the world?
3. How do fires and animals influence grassland biomes? Is there any difference in the impact of naturally caused fires and human caused fires on these and other biomes?
4. Which are the most common and widespread of the world's land biomes? Which are the least common and restricted in distribution?
5. What is the difference between a community, ecosystem and biome?
6. Compare and contrast the climate and growth features of tundra and desert biomes.
7. How do ecosystems repair themselves?
8. Describe the structure and typical animal components of tropical rain forest biomes.
9. How does climate, especially rainfall, dictate the types and distribution of terrestrial biomes?

Monera: Bacteria and Viruses

Chapter 17

Bacteria Cells and Function
Types of Bacteria
    Archaeobacteria
    True Bacteria
    Blue-Green Bacteria
Viruses
Viruses and Genetic Engineering

The Kingdom Monera includes the archaebacteria, the true bacteria and blue-green bacteria. The viruses are also usually included for discussion and comparison but they are not bacteria and are probably not even closely related to the bacteria, although this is uncertain.

Despite the fact that the Monera are small and primitive organisms, they have great economic impact on us and are functionally important organisms in natural environments. Many bacteria and viruses have been a bane on humans, as they are the cause of a variety of infections and pathologies. Most bacteria, however, are harmless but surprisingly important organisms in natural ecosystems. For example, along with fungi and some protozoa, the bacteria are the most important detritivores of the soil and water environment, decomposing the organic remains of plants and animals and releasing their minerals back into the environment.

Bacteria, especially the blue-green bacteria, share a number of characteristics with plants and are worthy of study in botany. The members of the Kingdom Monera have several distinctive characteristics. Unlike plants the monerans are prokaryotes—they lack nuclear membranes to house and protect their DNA. Furthermore, their DNA nucleic acids are represented by a single strand, or two strands of DNA, called a **nucleoid**. This nucleoid forms a loop in bacteria and functions much as a chromosome would. In addition to their nucleoid DNA bacteria also have small DNA bodies called **plasmids** in their cytoplasm.

The cytoplasm of monerans is more homogenous than in advanced plants. They lack membrane-bound organelles such as golgi bodies, endoplasmic reticulum, mitochondria or plastids but the bacterial membrane performs some of these organelle functions.

Bacterial cells may occur in a gelatinous matrix or in chain-like strings of cells called filaments. In these forms, each cell is completely independent. Some bacteria and blue-green bacteria are motile with a flagella or a pair of flagella.

Figure 17–1 The relative sizes of bacteria and other microorganisms. *Source:* Teresa Audesirk and Gerald Audesirk (1999), p. 352.

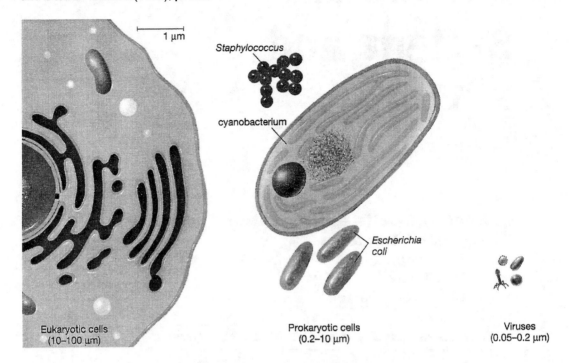

Bacteria satisfy their nutritional requirements by the absorption of food directly through their cell walls. Some monerans are **chemosynthetic** in that they manufacture food from chemicals in their surroundings. The more advanced monerans including the photosynthetic bacteria and the blue-green bacteria use photosynthesis to produce their food. Structurally, the blue-green bacteria are very similar to true bacteria except that they contain a blue-green chlorophyll.

Bacterial reproduction is either asexual, sexual, or involves the partial exchange of DNA. Most reproduction is asexual, with individual cells undergoing a form of mitosis called binary fission. Genetic recombinations occur in some bacteria by the formation of miniature tubes called **pili** that form between adjacent bacterial cells. The pili form channels within which DNA fragments are transferred from bacteria to bacteria. This process is sometimes called **bacterial conjugation**.

Characteristics of Bacteria

Although bacteria are generally the world's smallest living organisms, they are also the most abundant. A single handful of soil may contain a million or more individual bacteria. Bacteria represent the earth's earliest and in some ways the simplest forms of life. As a group, they have been around for a long time; fossils of bacteria have been found in rocks estimated to be 3.5 to 3.7 billion years old. These finds are important as the first eukaryotic cells are thought to be only 1.3 billion years old.

About 2,500 species of bacteria are known today. They are found in all types of environments, living in soil, water, air, and other organisms as well. Surprisingly, about 90 percent of all bacteria species are harmless or useful to us. However, the other 10 percent are responsible for causing many serious diseases of humans, other animals, and plants.

Figure 17–2 Generalized structure of a bacteria. *Source:* Roy H. Saigo and Barbara Saigo. *Botany: Principles and Applications* (1983), Prentice-Hall, p. 30.

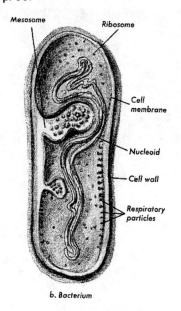

b. Bacterium

THE BACTERIAL CELL

The typical bacterium is a single-celled organism encased within a cell wall. It lacks a central nucleus and most other cell organs. Bacteria do have ribosomes for protein synthesis but these are about half the size of ribosomes that are found in the eukaryotic cells of higher plants and animals. The DNA nucleic acid occurs as a single naked strand curled in ring-like form called a nucleoid. Nucleoids are usually attached at one point to the plasma membrane. Bacteria also have between 30 and 40 small rings of DNA which are called plasmids. These plasmids are found in the cytoplasm and replicate separately from the nucleoid. This suggests that plasmids were originally separate organisms that were somehow incorporated into the bacterial system and now function as internal symbionts.

The cell wall of bacteria helps maintain their shape and provides rigid protection. Unlike cell walls of plants which are comprised mostly of cellulose, the bacterial cell wall contains peptidoglycans, which are large molecules of amino acids cross-linked to polysaccharides. Antibiotics like penicillin work by inhibiting cell wall formation and repair, thereby destroying the bacterial cell.

Bacteria exhibit a modified form (or perhaps a more primitive form) of mitosis. During bacterial replication, the nucleoid and plasmids duplicate themselves. Then, each of the two nucleiods and about one-half of the plastids migrate to opposite ends of the cell. The plasma membrane and cell wall pinch inward to form a cell wall, separating the dividing cell into the two new daughter cells. This asexual process of reproduction is called **binary fission** and under ideal conditions will take place every 10-20 minutes. Interestingly, both of the daughter cells produced in this division are equal in age (one is not older than the other). Thus, bacteria are immortal in a sense, as there is no such thing as an old bacteria cell.

Most bacteria lack true sexual reproduction, but some species exchange genetic material through a process called **conjugation**. In conjugation part of the DNA strand is transferred from one bacterium to another through a **pilus** or conjugation tube. This conjugation tube forms when two compatible

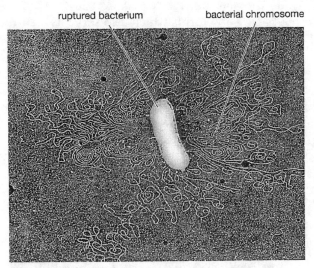

ruptured bacterium   bacterial chromosome

Figure 17–3 The bacterial chromosome. The 3 micrometer bacterial cell was ruptured to pull out and show its chromosome. *Source:* Teresa Audesirk and Gerald Audesirk (1999), p. 177.

Figure 17–4 Binary fission in bacteria. *Source:* Teresa Audesirk and Gerald Audesirk (1999), p. 359.

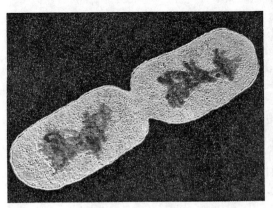

Figure 17–5 Conjugation mating in bacteria. Genetic material is exchanged between the bacteria through the hollow connecting tube which is called a pilus. *Source:* Teresa Audesirk and Gerald Audesirk (1999), p. 359.

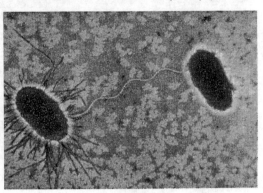

bacteria come into close contact with each other. The cell wall of one of the two bacteria evaginates (grows outwards) towards its partner and merges with it. When the tube is complete the DNA segment migrates through the tube to the recipient cell. Inside, it merges with and becomes part of the recipient cell's nucleoid, now enlarged and varied by the newly transferred genetic material.

Another process of genetic transfer called **transformation** may occur in some bacteria. In this process, a living bacterial cell picks up fragments of DNA released by fragmented dead cells and incorporates the fragments into its own nucleoid. The absorbed DNA increases the genetic variability of the bacterial cell. New characteristics may result from the interactions of the original genetic material with the newly acquired genetic material. Viruses exhibit a similar method of obtaining genetic material in a process called **transduction**. In **transduction,** fragments of DNA are carried from one cell to another by a virus—note that in this method of genetic transfer, the cell operates to transfer the genetic material rather than the virus itself. The virus is just a delivery system.

All bacteria are microscopic. They average only two or three microns in diameter and up to 60 microns in length. As a result, they are difficult to see, even with a compound microscope. Bacteria occur in three basic body forms which also serve as a simple method for recognizing and classifying them. **Cocci** bacteria are round, elliptical or spheroid in shape (singular coccus). Rod shaped bacteria are called **bacilli** (singular bacillus). The third bacterial form, called **spirilla,** are greatly elongated coils and are often corkscrew shaped. Spiral bacteria are often twisted in the form of a helix or spiral.

In addition to their basic body shape, all bacteria can be further classified by the presence of pigments and the development of slimy or gummy capsule-like sheaths around their cells. Some bacteria may also have hair-like or bud-like appendages called **pili** while others have a thick, internal wall called an **endospore**. In addition, some filamentous

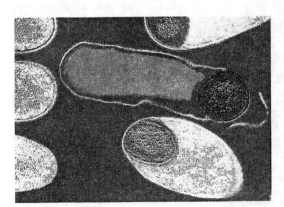

Figure 17–6 Spores protect bacteria during unfavorable environmental conditions. *Source:* Teresa Audesirk and Gerald Audesirk (1999), p. 359.

Figure 17–7 The three typical bacterial shapes (a) spherical or cocci (b) rod-shaped or bacilli (c) spirilla. *Source:* Teresa Audesirk and Gerald Audesirk (1999), p. 357.

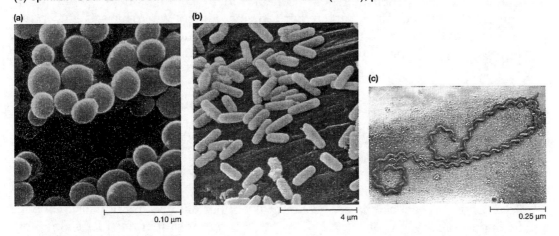

(a) 0.10 µm   (b) 4 µm   (c) 0.25 µm

bacteria have slender flagella that slowly rotate, propelling them through the medium in a spiraling glide. Some bacteria are non-motile for much of their life. The tube-like pili found in some bacteria serve as attachment structures that enable the bacteria to remain fastened in place to a suitable substrate.

Microbiologists can also separate bacteria into two broad groups based on their reaction to laboratory stains. A common laboratory technique is to apply Gram's stain (named for a Danish physician Hans Christian Gram who was instrumental in developing the science of bacteriology). In a gram stain test, a dye of crystal violet and iodine is added to a culture. Bacteria are designated as Gram positive if they retain the purple dye or Gram negative if they do not retain the purple dye.

CLASSIFICATION OF BACTERIA

Subkingdom Archaebacteriophytinea
Division Archaebacteria: The Ancient Bacteria

As their name implies, the **Archaebacteria** are thought to be the most primitive of the bacteria. They are so different from other bacteria, in fact, that some scientists believe that the archaebacteria should be placed in their own kingdom. Basically, they differ from other bacteria in several ways: in their metabolism, in the unique structure of their RNA molecules, in lacking muramic acid in their walls, and in the production of distinctive lipids. They are usually divided today into three groups.

Methane Bacteria

The most diverse group of archaebacteria are the methane bacteria. These are anaerobic (without oxygen) organisms that live in the mud of swamps and marshes, in the mud and murky debris of ocean floors, hot springs, lake sediments, animal intestines, sewage treatment plants and other areas in which free oxygen is not available. Methane bacteria are so-named because they generate methane gas from carbon dioxide and hydrogen. Also known as swamp gas, methane forms the major part of the atmospheres of the planets Jupiter, Saturn, Uranus and Neptune.

Salt Bacteria

Represented by *Halobacterium*, the salt bacteria are another ancient group that today are mostly confined to life in shallow salt water evaporation ponds common in parts of the western United States. When abundant, salt bacteria can give these ponds a distinctive red color. Their metabolism enables them to thrive under conditions of extreme salinity. In fact, salt bacteria require an environment where the salt concentration is almost at the saturation/crystallization point. Salt bacteria carry on simple photosynthesis using a red pigment called **bacterial rhodopsin.**

Sulpholobus Bacteria

The last group of primitive bacteria are the **Sulpholobus Bacteria**, which occur in the very high temperatures of sulfur hot springs. They thrive at temperatures ranging from 80 degrees C (176 degrees F) to 100 degrees C. The pH in these hots springs is also very acidic, being around 2.

Economic Importance of the Ancient Bacteria

Some of the archaebacteria are economically important because of their methane producing abilities. Some day, methane may become an important fuel source for engine or heating fuel and methane producing bacteria may be extensively used to manufacture the gas. Methane is cheap to produce and can be made from manure or other waste products that have been "worked on" by methane bacteria. The sludge that is left after the production of methane also makes an excellent fertilizer. Methane bacteria are currently used for fuel production in Italy, France and India. In the United States, methane is used as a source of hydrogen gas, which is needed in the commercial preparation of ammonia.

Methane gas is also used as a fuel source for water treatment plants. The methane gas produced by sewage is captured and used to run the equipment needed for purifying the water.

Subkingdom Eubacteriophytinea
Division Eubacteriophyta

The *Eubacteria* or "true bacteria" are bacteria that have muramic acid in their cell walls. The majority of *Eubacteria* are heterotrophic or parasitic but a few are autotrophic. The blue-green bacteria (formerly known as the blue-green algae) are also placed with the true bacteria. Two classes of true bacteria are recognized.

Class Eubacteriae: The True Bacteria

The Eubacteriae are unpigmented, purple and green sulfur bacteria. Most are saprobes, absorbing food directly from their environment. Some species are soil organisms which, along with soil fungi, are responsible for the decay and recycling of all types of organic matter. Some are parasitic, living in or on living organisms and depending on them for food. Many of these parasitic forms are responsible for serious diseases in humans and other animals. A few species of Eubacteria are autotrophs; like plants, they are photosynthesizers that produce food from carbon dioxide and water using sunlight as the energy source. Bacterial photosynthesis differs from that of plants as they do so without producing oxygen. Instead of chlorophyll, bacteria use another pigment called bacteriochlorophyll. In the process they substitute hydrogen sulfide for water which is why no oxygen is released in the process.

Still other true bacteria are classed as **chemoautotrophic;** they obtain their cellular energy by chemically fragmenting methane, hydrogen sulfide, and ferric iron. Some of the most important of these chemosynthesizers are the nitrogen-fixing bacteria, which fix biologically usable nitrogen.

Many plants rely on nitrogen-fixing bacteria to supply them with a vital source of nitrogen that is otherwise lacking in soil or present in very low concentrations.

Economic Importance of True Bacteria. Along with fungi, bacteria take organic waste such as spoiled or discarded food, manure, leaves, grass clippings and other organic waste and turn it into compost—a rich source of organic material used as fertilizer. Composting is very important to organic gardeners. Anyone can create a compost pile since no starter bacterial culture is needed. The naturally occurring bacteria in the normal yard environment will do. During the decay process, the bacteria generate heat and increase in numbers tremendously. If the organic material is kept moist and periodically turned to aerate it, the decay process will be even faster. The result of composting is that the old trash and cuttings from the garden are broken down and recycled. The result is compost—a rich, soil-like material that has good water holding capability and good particle size for aerating the soil. Thus compost is a good soil conditioner.

When one thinks of bacteria one most often thinks of **disease**. This is unfortunate since most true bacteria are not disease-causing agents. However, some species cause serious diseases of plants and animals including humans. Bacterial diseases of plants cost American farmers $4 billion dollars each year. These include bacterial diseases of many trunk crops such as pears, potatoes, tomatoes, squash, melons, carrots, citrus, cabbage, and cotton. Huge food losses also occur annually as a result of bacterial spoilage of agricultural products.

Bacterial diseases of humans cause enormous suffering and misery and millions of dollars in lost wages and medical bills. Bacteria enter the human body through several avenues. One common access is from the air. Every time someone coughs, sneezes or speaks loudly, they produce an invisible spray of saliva droplets containing bacteria. The fluid around these bacteria quickly evaporates but the bacteria cling to protein flakes that were also expectorated. These bacteria become airborne and through normal breathing enter our respiratory tracts. Once inside, they cross through the lungs to enter the body's circulatory system which transports them to tissues and organ systems from there. Most of us have a natural resistance to such bacteria but when our resistance is low we can get such diseases as whooping cough, meningitis, pneumonia, strep throat, diphtheria, and many others. Even our pets can be infected with bacteria. Birds, such as parrots, carry the disease psittacosis which is caused by inhaling microscopic bacteria called *chlamydias*. These *chlamydias* are an energy parasite as they cannot manufacture their own ATP and must extract energy from the cells of their host (the infected individual).

Legionnaire's disease is caused by a bacterium that lives in small amounts of water in air conditioning systems. It can be transmitted throughout an entire building by airborne particles that are blown through the air conditioning ducts.

Bacteria can also gain access to the body through the ingestion of contaminated food and drink. Bacterial infections caused by eating contaminated food is a widespread problem, especially in less developed countries of the world. However, even in the United States foods that have been inadvertently contaminated are periodically recalled from supermarket shelves. Within the last year, hamburger, cider, and chicken products have all been recalled because of well documented bacterial contamination.

Figure 17–8 Examples of harmful bacteria that cause various diseases and disorders of humans. *Source:* Lorus J. Milne and Margery Milne. *Plant Life.* (1959), Prentice-Hall, p. 116.

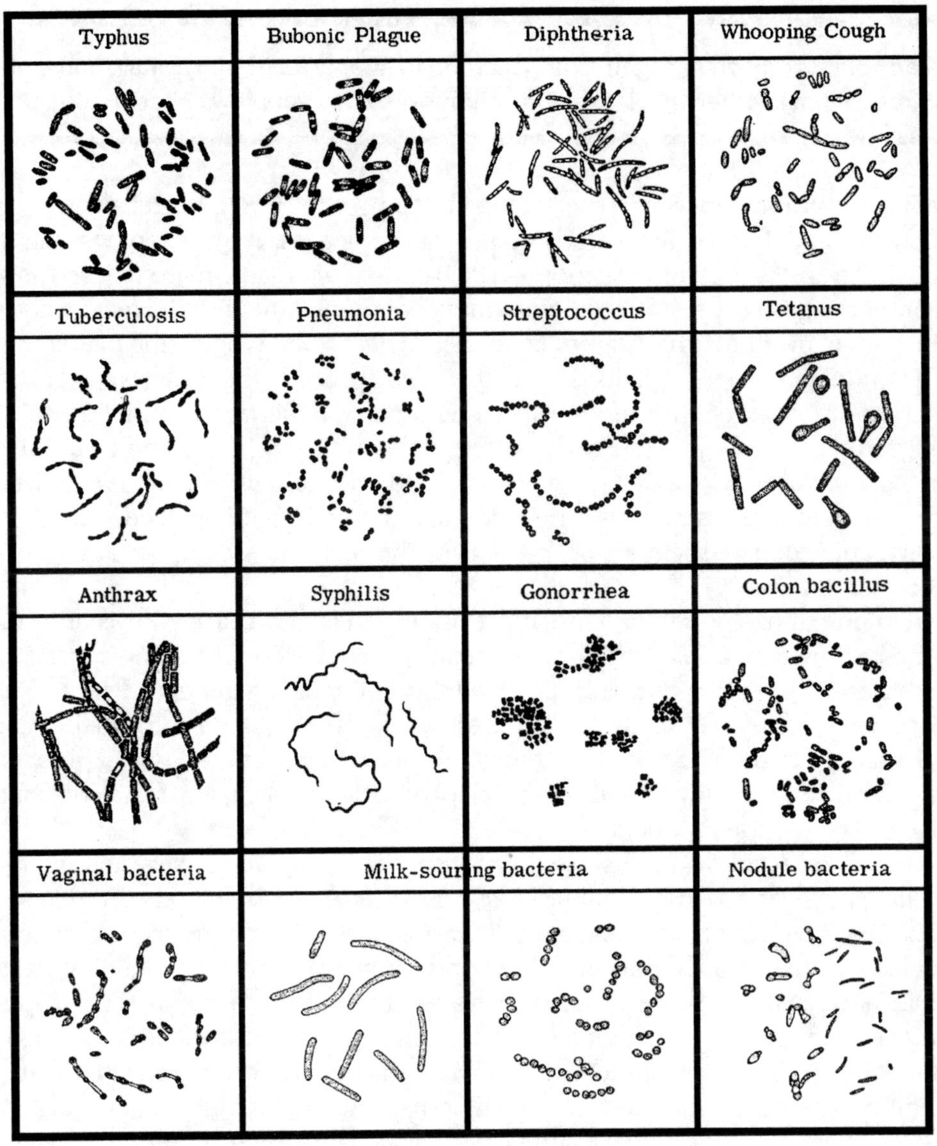

Typhus	Bubonic Plague	Diphtheria	Whooping Cough
Tuberculosis	Pneumonia	Streptococcus	Tetanus
Anthrax	Syphilis	Gonorrhea	Colon bacillus
Vaginal bacteria	Milk-souring bacteria		Nodule bacteria

In many areas, open sewers and unsanitary toilet conditions cause the transmission of water borne bacterial diseases such as cholera, dysentery, and food poisoning such as *Salmonella*. *Salmonella* multiply rapidly in improperly stored foods such as raw chicken, shellfish and eggs. Once ingested, the bacteria multiply in the intestinal tract and can be passed with urine. Health standards suggest that restaurant workers wash their hands after visiting a bathroom because they may contaminate their food. Many states, including Connecticut, have state laws requiring this.

Clostridium botulinum is a food poisoning bacterium that causes botulism. Here the condition is not a form of infection by the organism but the poisoning effect of the food by strong toxins that are produced by the bacterium feeding on the food. If food is not properly cooked, canned or bottled, the botulism bacteria can survive and produce toxins that, when in our system, are often lethal. Botulism bacteria produce an extremely toxic waste, and eating even a small amount of it can kill large numbers of people.

Soil bacteria produce spores which are heat resistant and can contaminate dirty food. The key to avoiding food poisoning is to be sure the food preparers are clean and the food is thoroughly washed before eating. Also food must be properly cooked and refrigerated to destroy or retard the growth of bacteria. Home canning techniques must be followed strictly in order to ensure the destruction of deadly bacteria. If home canned foods are not heated long enough some bacteria may survive and constitute a health hazard. Conversely, heating them too long may kill some of the "good" bacteria and allow the "bad" bacteria to multiply. A summary of the basic techniques for preventing bacterial contamination of food are:

1. Reduce or eliminate moisture in stored food (the moisture is a natural medium for bacterial growth).
2. Store food in an acidic or slightly acidic pH to reduce bacterial reproduction.
3. Expose foods to high temperatures prior to storage to kill bacteria.
4. Irradiate food to kill bacteria and bacterial spores prior to storage.
5. Store foods at low temperature.
6. Store treated food in sealed containers to prevent bacterial access.

Food in cans that are dented and bulge should not be eaten since this is a characteristic sign of the presence of botulism-causing bacteria. The toxins from these bacteria are so powerful that even small amounts could kill millions of people.

Other bacteria gain access to the body through direct contact. Most of the sexually transmitted diseases are caused by bacteria. Examples include syphilis and gonorrhea. Other diseases such as anthrax and brucellosis enter the body through the skin or mucous membranes. Anthrax is a disease of cattle and other farm animals. It is transmitted to workers in the tanning industry where they handle hides and wool. Brucellosis is also a disease from farm animals and is transmitted by contaminated milk. It is sometimes called undulant fever and is characterized by a daily rise and fall of temperature associated with the cyclic release of the toxins by the bacteria.

Other bacteria that live in the soil enter the body through **wounds**. The tetanus or "lockjaw" bacteria is a common soil organism. Puncture wounds caused by stepping on dirty nails and other sharp devices introduces the tetanus bacteria deep into the body. Once inside, it produces toxins that are extremely powerful. Tetanus is easily controlled by immunizations that are developed from an attenuated horse serum. Some soil bacteria can cause a disease called gas gangrene. These bacterium respire anaerobically in the body and basically destroy tissues while emitting damaging gases, hence their name. If untreated, a serious infection by gas gangrene bacteria can result in the loss of a limb.

Lastly, many bacteria gain access to the human body through the **bites of insects and other organisms**. If an organism transmits a disease-causing organism to a different host, the organism is called a **vector**. Many of the most feared and deadly of human diseases are caused by bacteria that are transmitted by vectors. For example, bubonic plague (black death) and tularemia are transmitted by fleas, deer flies, ticks, or lice. Of these, the most famous—and historically the most deadly—is bubonic plague, which is transmitted by fleas of rats and other rodents. Throughout recorded history, periodic visitation of plagues resulted in catastrophic "die off" of thousands, hundreds of thousands, and millions of people. The populations of Thebes, Athens, Rome,

Vienna, and other early cities suffered and survived many plague years. The most potent plague years were in the late Middle Ages, when nearly a third of the European population succumbed to the bacterial disease. Bubonic plague is still found today in the United States in ground squirrel populations and other rodents as well.

Tularemia is primarily a disease of animals but is transmitted to humans by ticks or deer flies. It is an occupational hazard of meat handlers who may obtain it through cuts in their hands. Ticks, lice and fleas also transmit **rickettsias** (tiny bacteria from eukaryotic cells).

Pleuropneumonias are tiny bacteria and have no cell wall. They are found in many plants, hot springs and in the respiratory tracts of animals and humans. They are the only prokaryotes that are known to be resistant to penicillin. Lyme disease, common in this area, is from a bacterium carried by deer ticks. It causes arthritis-like symptoms and was named after an outbreak occurred in Lyme, Connecticut in 1975.

We cannot discuss disease from bacteria without talking about **Robert Koch**. Koch was a German physician who became interested in bacteria and made the study of them his life's work. Koch is considered to be the "father of bacteriology" because he organized the study of bacteria into a science. During his research, Koch developed a technique to determine which bacteria were responsible for causing a specific disease. This technique or set of rules is known as **Koch's Postulates**. Koch also investigated anthrax and tuberculosis in the 1890's and formulated rules for isolating disease organisms.

Koch's postulates revolve around four basic ideas that are still applicable today. First, the microorganism must be present in all stages of the disease. Second, the microorganism must be isolated in pure culture from the victims. Third, when the microorganism from the pure culture is injected into a susceptible host organism it must produce the same disease in the new host. Lastly, the microorganism must be isolated from an experimentally infected host and grown in the pure culture for comparison with that of the original culture.

Koch's Postulates
1. the microorganism must be present to cause the disease.
2. the microorganism must be isolated in pure cultures from the victims.
3. the microorganism must produce the disease when injected into another individual.
4. isolate the same microorganism from an experimentally infected victim.

While some bacteria cause diseases, decay, and other problems that are the bane of humans, most bacteria neither benefit nor harm us and some are even very useful to humans. For example, we spray insecticides on plant crops to control crop pests. There is another way besides using toxic sprays to eliminate crop pests; we can use **biological controls**. *Bacillus thuringiensis* (BT) is a bacterium available in garden shops as a spray or powder. Placed on plants, it kills caterpillars and worms, including peach tree borer, European corn borers, bollworms, cabbage worms and loopers, tomato and fruit hornworms, tent caterpillars, fall webworms, leaf miners, alfalfa caterpillars, and leaf rollers. It is sold as a mass-produced, stable, moist dust containing millions of spores of the bacterium. It is harmless to humans, birds, earthworms or any living creatures (other than moth or butterfly larvae, of course). When the caterpillar ingests the bacterial spores they develop into the bacillus which multiply in the digestive tract and paralyze the gut of the worm. The crop pest usually dies as a result of ingestion in 2-4 days. Another variety, *Bacillus thuringiensis* (var. *israelensis*) (BTI) is used for the control of mosquitoes. It attacks only the mosquito larvae. Similarly, the annual, late summer outbreaks of Japanese beetles can be controlled by application of a bacterial power containing *Bacillus popilliae* which is specific to this beetle.

Other bacteria have important uses in the service of humans. Some are used in the cleanup of oil spills, sewage treatment plants, and toxic waste dumps, for example. *Pseudomonas capacia* is used to decompose oil spills. More benefits from bacteria are being developed using genetic engineering techniques. Bacteria also play a major role in the dairy industry as cultures in the production of buttermilk, acidophilus milk, yogurt, sour cream, kefir and cheese. Whey, the watery part of milk left in cheese production, is used in the manufacture of lactic acid. Lactic acid from lactate bacteria is also used in the textile industry, in the preparation of laundry products, leather tanning, and in the treatment of calcium and iron deficiencies.

We eat cultures of bacteria when we eat yogurt, sour cream and cheese.

Lactobacillus acidophilus is a common bacteria in the flora that lives in the human digestive tract. It aids in the digestion of milk products, is known to reduce cancer risk, and helps in the reduction of cholesterol levels. It is also used to eliminate female yeast infections of the vagina.

Bacteria are cultured in vats and used to manufacture chemicals such as acetone, butyl alcohol, dextran, sorbose, citric acid, some vitamins and medicinal preparations. Bacteria are also used to cure vanilla pods, cocoa beans, coffee and black tea. They are used in the production of vinegar, sauerkraut and dill pickles. Fibers from linen cloth are separated from flax stems by bacterial action. Green plant material is fermented in silos providing food for livestock through the action of bacteria. Lastly, bacteria producing the amino acid, glutamic acid, is used to produce monosodium glutamate (MSG), a common food ingredient.

Class Cyanobacteriae: The Blue-Green Bacteria

The cyanobacteriae or blue-green bacteria were formally known as the blue-green algae. They are different from true algae as they are prokaryotic while all of the green algae are eukaryotes. Blue-green bacteria possess chlorophyll *a* which is also found in green plants. This accounts for the large amounts of oxygen produced when they photosynthesize and they are a major source of atmospheric oxygen. Many blue-green bacteria may also have phycocyanin (a blue pigment sometimes called phycobilin), phycoerythrin (a red pigment), and carotenoids (red, yellow and orange pigments which function as antenna pigments to help gather light energy for photosynthesis). Their distinctive blue-green color is caused by the combination of chlorophyll and phycocyanin pigments.

The blue-green bacteria are the only organisms that can fix nitrogen and produce oxygen at the same time. The cells produce a nitrogenous food reserve called cyanophycin. They also produce and store carbohydrates and lipids. The blue-green bacteria lack flagella but move by rotating on their longitudinal axis, which gives them a forward gliding motion. When found in nature, blue-green bacteria often occur in chains or hairlike filaments. Some make irregular, spherical, or plate like colonies held together by gelatinous sheaths. These sheaths may be colorless or pigmented with shades of yellow, red, brown, green, blue, violet or blue-black.

Blue-green bacteria are found in a wide variety of habitats including soil, water, moist surfaces, and in root nodules of plants. They are even common in temporary

Figure 17–9 Examples of filamentous blue-green bacteria (a) *Oscillatoria* (b) a *Spirulina* (c) *Nostoc* (d) *Anabaena* with the thick-walled dormant spore called an akinete. *Source:* Harold C. Bold and John W. La Claire II. *The Plant Kingdom* (1987), Prentice-Hall, p. 22.

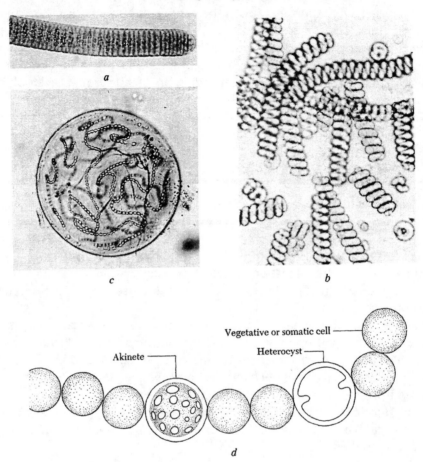

pools and ditches. They are often very abundant in fresh water habitats and may sometimes cause algae blooms. They also can be found living in the hot springs in Yellowstone National Park where they deposit calcium carbonate in the form of travertine rock.

Blue-green bacteria are among the first invaders of newly formed habitats. For example, they are found on new lava deposits around volcanoes and in newly opened fissures along deep sea volcanic ridges and mounts. They are even found in tiny fissures in desert rocks. Some blue-green bacteria occur in jungle soils and on the shells of turtles and snails. Others live as symbionts with amoebae, protozoans, diatoms, sea anemones, fungi and the roots of tropical cycads. Some species form a symbiotic relationship with algae to form lichens.

Reproduction in blue-green bacteria is mostly asexual. New cells form through fission or fragmentation. In *Nostoc* and *Anabaena*, which form chains, fragmentation occurs in special larger cells called **heterocysts**. These cells are also sites of nitrogen fixation from the air. These two genera may also produce thick walled cells called **akinetes** which resist freezing and other adverse conditions. Some can lie dormant for up to 80 years. Sexual reproduction is not known to occur in the blue-green bacteria although genetic recombination has been observed in some groups. Blue-green bacteria lack gametes and meiosis has not yet been observed in the group.

Some blue-green bacteria have chloroplasts within them. Other blue-green bacteria may live in the cells of other organisms and develop a symbiotic relationship. When

Figure 17-10 An electron micrograph of a section of *Oscillatoria*. *Source:* Teresa Audesirk and Gerald Audesirk (1999), p. 361.

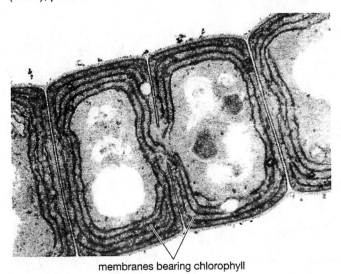

membranes bearing chlorophyll

blue-green bacteria are living in another cell they usually lack a cell wall and function as chloroplasts. When the eukaryotic host cell divides, so do the chloroplasts. Some scientists speculate that the chloroplast of living green plants may have developed from an initial symbiotic relationship with ancient blue-green bacteria.

Fossils suggest that the earliest forms of blue-green bacteria date from 3.5 to 3.7 billion years ago. Early forms closely resemble the modern forms. It is theorized that somewhere around 3 billion years the blue-green bacteria began to produce oxygen as a by-product of photosynthesis. Over billions of years, the photosynthesis activity of blue-green bacteria transformed the early atmosphere (which lacked free oxygen) into the modern atmosphere in which oxygen plays such an important role for all higher plants and all animals. Not incidentally, the accumulation of oxygen in the upper atmosphere produced the high altitude ozone layer as a by-product. This layer—so critically endangered now—helps shield animals and terrestrial plants from damaging ultraviolet radiation.

Economic Importance of Blue-Green Bacteria. Ecologically, blue-green bacteria are the photosynthetic organisms at the base of many food chains, especially in freshwater and marine habitats. They store energy in the form of sugar and are utilized by filter feeders. During the warm months of the year blue-green bacteria can temporarily become abundant and form floating mats of algal scum (called pond scum) that so often cover quiet waters of ponds and wetlands in late summer. The sudden increase of these blue-green bacteria populations results in what is termed an **algal bloom**. Algal and bacterial blooms result in massive die-offs of plant and animal populations because the huge blue-green bacterial populations consume all of the available oxygen in the water, so other organisms die from lack of oxygen, or asphyxiation. During a bloom, the water frequently smells bad and tastes bad because of the rapid accumulation of decomposing organic material. As the organisms decay they produce toxins which contaminate the water. Livestock that drink the water may be poisoned. As the blue-green bacteria die and decay further they eliminate oxygen in the water and other aquatic organisms die. In reservoirs and other human water supplies, large populations of blue-green bacteria clog filters, corrode steel and concrete structures, and cause a natural softening of water. They produce odors and discoloration which sometimes make water unpalatable. Water companies control populations of blue-green bacteria by adding copper sulfate to the water. For example, in almost every summer water quality control specialists of local water companies and the State Department of Environmental Protection add copper sulfate to the surface waters of Lake Zoar in the Naugatuck Valley to prevent the build-up of blue-green bacteria populations.

Over 40 species of blue-green bacteria can fix nitrogen directly from the air. This is important as nitrogen is the most common gas in the atmosphere and most nitrogen in rice paddies in Southeast Asia is from blue-green bacteria. Thus rice can be grown and no fertilizer is needed.

Class Prochlorobacteriae

The Prochlorobacteria were first discovered in 1976 from cells living on an animal called the sea squirt. They have chlorophyll *a* and *b*, but apparently lack accessory pigments found in other blue-green bacteria. Instead they have accessory pigments called carotenoids, which are also found in higher plants. The thylakoids of their plastids are double-layered as in higher plants, instead of single-layered as in other blue-greens bacteria. The relationships of these bacteria to other bacteria is unclear, but it has been suggested that they are similar to higher plants as they have the same combinations of chloroplast pigments.

The Viruses

Just before the turn of the last century, smallpox was a common and often lethal disease of humans. At times virulent and at other times dormant, it was carried everywhere by explorers and seamen. The accidental introduction of smallpox in Australia, Africa, and especially in the New World caused a massive die-off of natives, who had no natural exposure to, or immunity from, the disease. Smallpox was especially deadly to the American Indians; the tribes that first encountered the European settlers and explorers were hardest hit. Some 80–90 percent of the Incas and Aztecs of South America and as many as 70–80 percent of the coastal tribes of North America died within a few years of the European settlement of New England and the Atlantic Coast.

In fact, it wasn't until the turn of the last century that smallpox was finally eliminated in the United States due to vaccinations. Following this success, a world-wide program of inoculations has succeeded in ridding humans of this once feared disease.

Vaccination involves the introduction of a weakened form of the disease agent to stimulate the body to produce antibodies. Vaccinations were first performed by William Jenner in 1796 using cowpox from milkmaids. Cowpox was similar to smallpox and immunity to cowpox also gave immunity to smallpox. Smallpox is almost eliminated today as a threat to health. Unfortunately, its place has been taken by another virus that causes AIDS.

The actual placement of viruses among living systems is a matter of conjecture. Viruses have many characteristics that make them unique and their consideration as a living organism is controversial.

Table 17-1 Summary of the classification of the bacteria and viruses.

Taxonomic Group	Respiratory Pigments	Mode of Nutrition
Archaebacteria	bacteriorhodopsin	chemosynthetic, photosynthetic
Eubacteria	bacteriochlorophyll,	parasitic, photosynthetic, chemosynthetic, saprobic
Blue-green Bacteria	chlorophyll a, phycocyanin hycocyanin, phycoerythrin	photosynthetic, chemosynthetic, saprobic
Viruses	none	parasitic

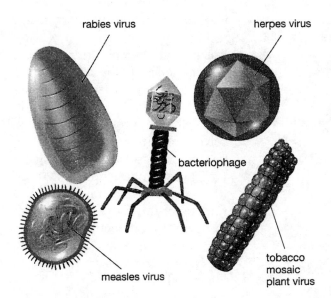

rabies virus

herpes virus

bacteriophage

measles virus

tobacco mosaic plant virus

Figure 17–11 The shape and basic structure of viruses. *Source:* Teresa Audesirk and Gerald Audesirk (1999), p. 353.

A single teaspoon of seawater contains 1 billion viruses.

In size, viruses are almost always considerably smaller than bacteria. Viruses that can pass through a porcelain filter that normally stops bacteria are called **filterable viruses**. These include viruses which cause smallpox, rabies, measles, mumps, chickenpox, polio, yellow fever, influenza, fever blisters, warts, herpes, AIDS, and the common cold. Some viruses of plants include viral mosaics of tobacco, alfalfa, and leaf curl of cotton and sugar beets. The most common symptoms of viral infections of plants include necrosis of tissue which may become evident as color changes, spotting or blotching. Viral infections of plants may also develop tumors and other unusual growths. Most plant viruses are host specific and only attack one species or a related group of plants. They can be transported from plant to plant by air, water, or insects such as aphids, leafhoppers, and other insects which feed on plant fluids.

To be classed as a virus the object must have the following features: first, it lacks a complete cellular structure; second, it does not grow by increasing in size or dividing; third, it does not respond to external stimuli; fourth, it cannot move on its own; and fifth, it is unable to carry on independent metabolism.

Viruses are widespread and extremely abundant. A single teaspoon of seawater may contain over one billion viruses. Most viruses are the size of large molecules, having a diameter of 15–300 nanometers. The entire organism that we class as a virus consists of a nucleic acid core surrounded by a protein coat. Due to the structure of the protein coat, there may be up to 20 sides, so they resemble miniature geodesic domes. Some have distinguishable head and tail regions. The nucleic acid core is either DNA or RNA but never both.

Viruses can be separated into two groups on the basis of the makeup of the nucleic acid core. They are further separated according to size and shape, nature of protein coats and the number of identical structural units in the core.

Viruses attack virtually every kind of living organism known. There are even specialized viruses called **bacteriophages**, that attack bacteria. These are the viruses with both head and tail-like structures. They also have six spider-like legs that hold them in place. Viruses differ from all living organisms in their reproduction. A virus is essentially an

Figure 17–12 Viruses invading a bacterium. *Source:* Teresa Audesirk and Gerald Audesirk (1999), p. 353.

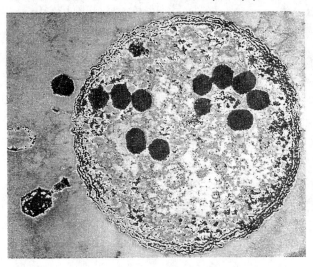

Figure 17–13 How viruses transfer genes from one host to another. *Source:* Teresa Audesirk and Gerald Audesirk (1999), p. 232.

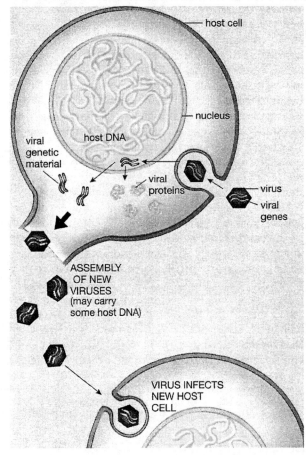

inert object (not even an organism, technically) until it gets into a living cell. It can **only** replicate in the host cell. It attaches to the cell by means of its filamentous legs and penetrates to the interior. Once inside the cell, the protein sheath dissolves and the core of DNA or RNA becomes associated with the nucleic acids of the host cell. These new nucleic acids take over the nucleus of the host cell and direct the cell to manufacture new virus structures. Eventually the host cell dies and the viruses are released to infect other cells. Some viruses such as the influenza virus and the AIDS virus mutate very rapidly, so new vaccines must be produced every year. Many forms of cancer may be caused by viruses. As cells are invaded by the virus, the cell produces an interferon which causes the cell to produce protein that prevents viral reproduction.

Needless to say, viruses can be very dangerous to the human population. The viruses that cause flu and colds produce loss of work time that is enormous. Childhood diseases like chickenpox, measles and mumps are all viral in nature. In the tropics, the viral disease known as yellow fever has been the fear of explorers and colonists alike. Today, viruses such as infectious hepatitis, Guillain-Barre Syndrome and Epstein Barr viral diseases are carried by everyone. These viruses sit in our tissues waiting for the proper stimulus to cause them to activate. There is considerable evidence that they may be triggered by aspirin used in young children.

Humankind's newest plague, the AIDS virus, HIV-1 and HIV-2 has spread all over the world and is constantly mutating which complicates the research in finding a cure.

The origin of these simple organisms (if they can be called organisms!) is unknown. Some botanists think that viruses were the first organisms or at least resemble the first

Figure 17–14 The life history of a virus. *Source:* Teresa Audesirk and Gerald Audesirk (1999), p. 354.

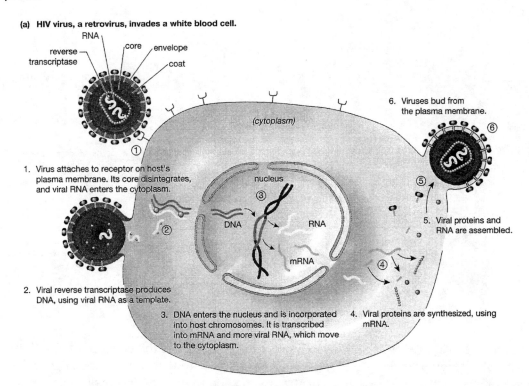

(a) **HIV virus, a retrovirus, invades a white blood cell.**

RNA

reverse transcriptase

core envelope

coat

(cytoplasm)

6. Viruses bud from the plasma membrane.

⑥

1. Virus attaches to receptor on host's plasma membrane. Its core disintegrates, and viral RNA enters the cytoplasm.

nucleus

③

⑤

①

②

DNA RNA

5. Viral proteins and RNA are assembled.

mRNA

④

2. Viral reverse transcriptase produces DNA, using viral RNA as a template.

3. DNA enters the nucleus and is incorporated into host chromosomes. It is transcribed into mRNA and more viral RNA, which move to the cytoplasm.

4. Viral proteins are synthesized, using mRNA.

organisms because they are so primitive and sit right on the boundary between life and nonlife. Other scientists think that the evolutionary origin of viruses is fairly recent, as all of them are obligate endoparasites: they can neither live nor reproduce on their own.

Viruses and Genetic Engineering

For many scientists, monerans are the organisms of choice for laboratory experiments. They are simple organisms which can easily be cultivated in large numbers. As a result they have been the subject of much **genetic engineering**, the artificial introduction of DNA into bacteria to change their characteristics. Genetic engineering is also called gene splicing and begins with the isolation of plasmid DNA from a bacteria. The DNA molecule is broken up into separate genes or groups of genes by special enzymes called restriction enzymes. The resulting DNA fragments are then mixed with repair enzymes and injected into another bacterium which absorbs the new genes and functions in a new way under the influence of the new genes or combination of genes.

Some genes are natural bacterium genes and others are taken from other organisms or synthesized in the laboratory. Bacteria, so changed, are used to manufacture compounds such as insulin. Viruses can also be doctored and used to inject genes into bacteria.

Genetic engineering has been the source of considerable controversy ever since its development. The problems are twofold. Is it ethical to manufacture organisms using human genes or advanced animal cells? How far will scientists go with the gene splicing techniques? Will they be used in an attempt to create favorable offspring? These are ethical and moral questions that need to be addressed. The other problems center on

Figure 17–15 How genetic recombination works in bacteria. New combinations or inserted genes figure in genetic engineering. *Source:* Teresa Audesirk and Gerald Audesirk (1999), p. 231.

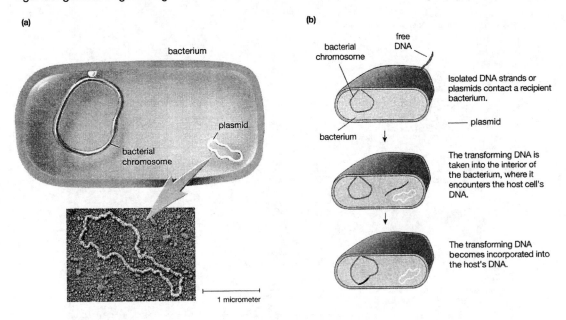

what happens if a genetically doctored organism escapes into the ecosystem. Can it be harmful? Are we producing a super germ? The answer to these questions is probably not, but scientists are under legal constraints to keep their experiments under control and must receive government and legal permission before releasing anything into the environment.

Key Words and Phrases

prokaryotes
binary fission
transduction
compost
Robert Koch
algae bloom
genetic engineering
pilus
conjugation
methane bacteria
sulphologus bacteria
Class Eubacteriae
contamination
Prochlorobacteriae

nucleoid
transformation
Archaebacteria
pathogen
Koch's Postulates
virus
plasmids
spirilla
transduction
salt bacteria
saprophytic
disease
vector
bacteriophage

AIDS

Eubacteria
transmission
cyanobacteria
vaccinations
bacteria
bacilli
heterocyst
bacteriophage
chemoautotrophic
Clostridium
akinetes

Selected References and Resources

Atlas, R. M. 1997. *Principles of Microbiology*. 2nd. Edition. Wm. C. Brown, Publishers. Dubuque, Iowa.

Bos, L. 1982. *Introduction to Plant Virology.* Longman. New York.

Carr, N. G., and B. A. Whitton. Eds. 1982. *The Biology of Cyanobacteria.* University of California Press. Berkeley, California.

Gibbs, A. J., and B. D. Harrison. 1979. *Plant Virology: the Principles.* John Wiley and Sons. New York.

Joklik, W. 1988. *Virology. Appleton and Lange.* East Norwalk, Connecticut.

Smith, K. M. 1978. *Plant Viruses.* 6th Edition. A Halsted Press Book. Chapman and Hall. London.

Starr, M. P., H. Stolp, H. G. Truper, A. Balows, and H. G. Schlegel. Eds. 1981. *The Prokaryotes. A Handbook of Habitats, Isolation, and Identification of Bacteria.* Springer-Verlag. New York.

Stolp, H. 1988. *Microbial Ecology.* Cambridge University Press. New York.

Tortora, G. J., B. R. Funke, and C. L. Case. 1998. *Microbiology. An Introduction.* Addison Wesley Longman, Inc. New York.

Van Demark, P. J., and B. L. Batzing. 1987. *The Microbes. An Introduction to the Nature and Importance.* Benjamin/Cummings Publishing Company, Inc. Menlo Park, California.

Volk, W. A., D. C. Benjamin, R. J. Kadner, and J. T. Parsons. 1991. *Essentials of Medical Microbiology.* 4th Edition. J. B. Lippincott Company. Philadelphia.

Review and Discussion Questions

1. Why are viruses considered by many to be nonliving, as opposed to living organisms?
2. What characteristics distinguish bacteria from viruses?
3. What characteristics distinguish the bacteria from the blue-green bacteria?
4. Provide examples and life histories of bacteria that are spread by wind, food, animals, water.
5. How do the composting bacteria work? Are they the only bacteria that are beneficial to humans? What is their importance in natural ecosystems of the world?
6. Name some common diseases that are caused by viruses.
7. Describe how viruses work. That is, how they obtain nutrients, live and reproduce. Why is it usually possible to develop effective vaccines against bacterial infections but very difficult to find vaccines against viral diseases?
8. Discuss Pasteur's principles of health and causes of disease based on his work with bacteria.
9. Why are bacteria usually placed in a separate group and not included with plants or animals?
10. Why is it so difficult for us to find cures for diseases such as AIDS? What is it about the AIDS virus that precludes finding a vaccine?

11. What are the causes and modes of the following diseases:
    (a) Typhoid Fever
    (b) Measles
    (c) Chicken Pox
    (d) Cholera
    (e) Common cold
    (f) Diptheria
    (g) Typhus
    (i) food poisoning
    (j) rabies

Chapter 18

Kingdom Protista: The Algae

Golden Brown Algae
Green Algae
Brown Algae
Red Algae
Economic Uses of the Algae

According to the theory of evolution less than one billion years ago all living organisms were confined to the world's oceans. The salt water provided protection from water loss (desiccation), ultraviolet radiation and fluctuations in temperature. Food was abundant and the nutrients from which more food could be manufactured were readily available in sea water.

The first land plants arose only about 400 million years ago when some ancient species of green algae successfully made the transition to land. These primitive unicellular and colonial plants gave rise to all modern land plants.

As land and water plants, green algae transformed the early atmosphere. Prior to the algae, the atmosphere consisted primarily of hydrogen and nitrogen—very little free oxygen was available. Algae and photosynthetic bacteria (and much later, modern plants as well) pumped oxygen into the atmosphere as a by-product of photosynthesis and were responsible for creating the comparatively high levels of free oxygen found in the atmosphere today. Furthermore, the high atmospheric conversion of some of this oxygen into ozone created the chemical blanket that shields organisms from ultraviolet radiation.

Green algae have been implicated as the ancestors of land plants for many reasons. Most importantly, green algae have a lignin-like material that is similar to the lignin found in most land plants. Lignin is important because it strengthens the cell walls of plants; the stronger walls provide erect stems necessary for land plants.

Green algae and the other forms of algae are placed in a separate kingdom, the Protista. The protista also include the smallest and simplest animals, the protozoa, such as *Euglena, Amoeba* and *Paramecium*. Some, such as *Euglena*, have features that are a combination of both plants and animals, and are studied in both botany and zoology courses.

The members of the Kingdom Protista all share the following features. They all possess eukaryotic cells, which means that their cells have a well-developed nucleus. Protistan species include unicellular and colonial species. A colonial form is a group of single organisms that grow together and function as one. Protistan nutrition is varied

Figure 18–1 Two types of reproduction in the protistans (a) binary fission in *Paramecium* (b) genetic material being exchanged across a cytoplasmic bridge in *Euplotes*. *Source:* Teresa Audesirk and Gerald Audesirk (1999), p. 364.

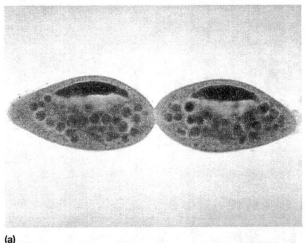

(a)

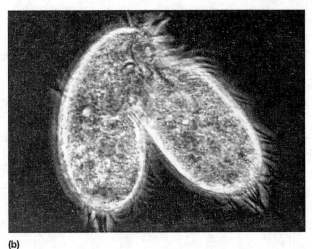

(b)

but all algae are photosynthetic and are thus autotrophic, while protozoa ingest food and are heterotrophic. Some protistans, such as the *Euglena*, both produce their own food in plant fashion and obtain food from the environment like animals.

Protistans vary in the complexity of their life cycles, but in most, reproduction is asexual by binary fission or budding. Sexual reproduction exists in several forms. Many protista are mobile but others are immobile or have limited powers of movement. In all, the reproductive gametes are mobile.

The Algae

The algae are like advanced plants in many ways but they lack true leaves or flowers. Although algae are water plants and require moisture for survival and reproduction, they have invaded a variety of terrestrial habitats with varying degrees of success.

Algae are classified by the kinds of photosynthetic pigments they contain. Chlorophyll is the main photosynthetic pigment but it exists in several varieties. The kinds of chlorophyll are designated by lower case letters such as *a, b, c* and so forth. All true algae have **chlorophyll *a***, a characteristic they share with land plants. Some algae are also categorized by the way they store food. We have come to think of stored food as sugar or starch. In algae the storage forms are sometimes starch but often are different chemical substances. Six divisions of algae are recognized.

DIVISION CHRYSOPHYTA—THE GOLDEN BROWN ALGAE

About 6,000 kinds of golden brown algae are known. They are all microscopic and many species are not well known to non-biologists. In form, color, and shape, the golden brown algae are some of the most beautiful algae known. They are united as a group by their specialized pigments, method of storing food, and certain cell characteristics. Some golden brown algae produce a resting cell stage called a **statospore,** which resembles a miniature bottle complete with a cork. Four classes of Chrysophyta are recognized. Of these, only the diatoms are economically important.

Class Bacillariophyceae

This class includes the diatoms, which are the most important economically of all the Chrysophyta. Diatoms are unicellular golden brown algae that inhabit both fresh and salt water in huge numbers. They are especially abundant in the colder marine climates of the world—in the northern and southern seas. Diatoms also dominate the algal flora of damp cliffs, the bark of trees, and the bare soil or sides of buildings. There are more than 5,600 species of diatoms. Structurally, they all look like little glass boxes consisting of two halves: one half of the rigid cell walls overlaps the other half, like a petri dish and its lid.

Most marine diatoms are circular in appearance but freshwater forms are fusiform. About 95 percent of the cell walls are comprised of silica, which are deposited on a framework of pectin. The cell walls have tiny designs that collectively make an intricate pattern of ridges, depressions, and holes on the surface of the diatom.

Most diatom cells have several to many chloroplasts. In most, the chloroplasts contain chlorophyll *a* along with accessory pigments such as chlorophyll *c* and chlorophyll *c2*. Diatoms also contain **fucoxanthin**, a brownish pigment which makes the chloroplasts look golden brown in color. The diatoms store their food reserves as oils, fats or in the form of a carbohydrate called **chrysolaminarin**. Despite their simplicity, many diatoms are capable of movement by means of tiny fibrils along their surface that take up and expel water in a jet-like stream. Many freshwater forms move back and forth in response to various environmental stimuli.

Diatoms reproduce asexually in a process called binary fission. The diploid diatom cell undergoes mitosis to enlarge, then splits into two halves, each of which will become a separate diatom. In reproduciton, the two halves first produce identical copies, then the cell wall separates; daughter cells remain in each half of the separated diatom. Each new copy (daughter half) fits inside one of the original halves of the diatom, producing two new diatoms, each a mix of old and new. This form of asexual reproduction usually occurs for a number of generations with the cells of each succeeding generation getting smaller and smaller. Sexual reproduction occurs when one of these small diatoms undergoes meiosis, producing 4 gametes which escape through the cell wall and swim about or are carried in water currents. These gametes fuse with other gametes to form zygotes called **auxospores**. The auxospores grow rapidly until they are the size of the original diatoms, then manufacture the cell walls that protect them but also prevent further growth.

Figure 18–2 Examples of diatoms (a) *Navicula* (b) *Coscinodiscus* (c) *Triceratium. Source:* Harold C. Bold and John W. La Claire II. *The Plant Kingdom* (1987), Prentice-Hall, p. 58.

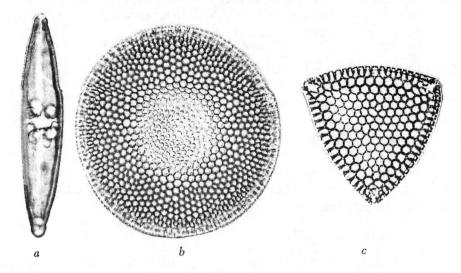

a b c

DIVISION PYRROPHYTA—THE DINOFLAGELLATES

In structure, the dinoflagellates are somewhat like armored spaceships. Some are smooth but others have rib-like supports for their shells. The dinoflagellate shell is formed from external plates of cellulose which are distributed under the plasma membrane of the cell. Dinoflagellates have two flagella attached near each other in two adjacent intersecting grooves. One flagellum acts as a rudder as it trails behind the cell. The second flagellum propels the cell in a spinning motion.

Internally most dinoflagellate cells have two or more disc-shaped chloroplasts which include brown pigments along with chlorophyll *a* and chlorophyll *c2*. Almost half of the dinoflagellates are heterotrophs that ingest food particles. Some have an eyespot, or **stigma**, which is an organelle that gives the organism information about the direction of the sun. All dinoflagellates have a unique nucleus with a chromosome that remains condensed and clearly visible throughout the life of the cell. These chromosomes contain up to 40 percent more DNA than is found in human cells. The food manufactured by dinoflagellates is stored as starch in the cytoplasm.

Dinoflagellates are found in most fresh and salt water habitats. The red tide is a marine phenomenon that results when the dinoflagellates increase rapidly to the extent that they are so numerous that they cause the water to appear reddish brown.

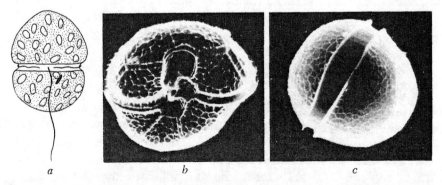

a b c

Figure 18–3 Examples of dinoflagellates (a) *Gymnodinium* (b and c) *Peridinium* covered with plates of cellulose. *Source:* Harold C. Bold and John W. La Claire II. *The Plant Kingdom* (1987), Prentice-Hall, p. 60.

This biological spectacle is caused primarily by *Gonyaulax* and *Gymnodinium* which produce a strong toxin that kills fish. These same toxins are ingested by shellfish and if they are in turn eaten by humans they can paralyze the nervous system. Red tides are sometimes a major problem for the fishing and shellfish industry. Fish caught and shellfish collected during a red tide cannot be sold as they are poisonous to humans.

Some dinoflagellates exhibit bioluminescence or the ability to produce biological or cold light. They are responsible for the luminescence that occurs on waves and the surface of the sea at night.

Reproduction in dinoflagellates is asexual and occurs by simple cell division. Sexual reproduction does occur, but it is rare.

DIVISION EUGLENOPHYTA—THE EUGLENOIDS

On farms and ranches water from rain collects into little pools that trap the organic sewage from livestock and other farm animals. We create the same environment by building sewage treatment plants into which we dump human organic wastes. Both farm pond and sewage treatment plants contain large amounts of organic wastes and make ideal breeding habitats for Euglenophyte. These unique little algae make a rich bloom, which accounts for the pungent odor of contaminated pools. There are up to 750 species of euglenoids. The most common member of this division is *Euglena*, a spindle-shaped cell with a flexible plasma membrane which gives it the ability to move and change shape like an animal. Beneath the plasma membrane are spiral strips parallel to each other that travel around the cell. These strips and membrane are called a **pellicle**.

The pellicle is slightly rigid and capable of changing shape and is partly responsible for the movement of euglenoids. There is also a single **flagellum** with numerous tiny hairs on one side of the algae which pulls the cell through the water. There is a second, very short flagellum located within a space called a **reservoir**, near the base of the large flagellum.

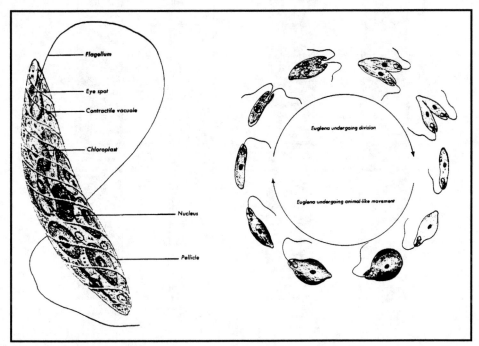

Figure 18–4 *Euglena,* structure on left, life cycle on right. *Source:* Elliott and Outka. *Zoology* (1976), Prentice-Hall.

About one-third of the euglenoids absorb food through a **gullet** or groove for food ingestion. The other members of this group have chloroplasts and manufacture their own food like true plants. Since some euglenoids are heterotrophs and others are autotrophs, they are generally classified as both plants and animals.

Other structural distinctions of most euglonophytes include the red **eyespot** which is located in the cytoplasm near the base of the flagellum. As in dinoflagellates, the eyespot provides a sort of visual information that allows the organism to distinguish various degrees of light and dark and the location of a light source. During photosynthesis, the eyespot enables a *Euglena* to orient towards sunlight and maximize interception of light by its chloroplasts. The organic molecules manufactured during photosynthesis are stored as starch in distinctive **paramylon bodies**, which are numerous in the cytoplasm. Most reproduction in euglenoids is asexual. A reproducing *Eugena* divides lengthwise down the length of the cell in longitudinal fission. Following reproduction, each of the daughter *Euglena* undergoes a period of growth. Sexual reproduction in the group has never been confirmed. In times of food scarcity, euglenoids can digest their chloroplasts. When food again becomes abundant they manufacture new chloroplasts.

DIVISION CHLOROPHYTA—THE GREEN ALGAE

The green algae number more than 7,500 species and constitute the largest division of algae. Some green algae are unicellular while others are colonial, forming plate-like, thread-like, net-like colonies, tube-like or hollow balls that are often comprised of hundreds or thousands of individuals, all living together.

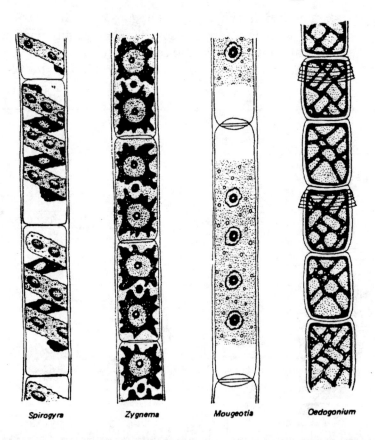

Spirogyra   Zygnema   Mougeotia   Oedogonium

Figure 18–5 Examples of the variability of chloroplast shapes and size in green algae. *Source:* Rushforth. *The Plant Kingdom* (1976), Prentice-Hall, p. 130.

Green algae vary widely in size. Some, such as sea lettuce, are large seaweeds, while others are minute and some are microscopic. Some unicellular forms grow in green patches on tree bark or in the hair or skin of jungle animals such as sloths. Green algae also inhabit snowbanks, flatworms, and sponges. A few species even grow on the backs of turtles and other slow moving animals. However, the vast majority of green algae are found in freshwater and marine aquatic habitats. Almost every puddle contains a sampling of green algae and they are often especially numerous and diverse in freshwater habitats as wetlands, ponds, lakes, and in the quiet reaches of streams.

In marine habitats, the green algae are the important element of **plankton**, the layer of tiny organisms that float just under the surface of the ocean. Green algae and other members of the plankton form the base of the food chain of living organisms in most of the world's oceans.

As in higher plants, the cells of green algae all contain chlorophyll *a* and *b*. Like vascular plants, they store food in chloroplasts in the form of starch.

Both asexual and sexual reproduction occur in green algae.

The life history and development of green algae is complex, but it can be best illustrated by examining four different forms. Each form shows a different stage of complexity in this important group.

a. Chlamydomonas

Chlamydomonas is a common algae found in quiet freshwater pools. It has been around a long time, and its remote fossil ancestors date from nearly 1 billion years ago. It lives as a unicellular life form with an oval cell consisting of a cellulose wall. *Chlamydomonas* move by means of a pair of whip-like **flagella.** Two **vacuoles** at the base of the flagella regulate water flow into and out of the cell. A single huge, cup-shaped **chloroplast** (which partially obscures the centrally located **nucleus**) is the most distinctive feature of the *Chlamydomonas* cell. The chloroplast contains two **pyrenoids** containing

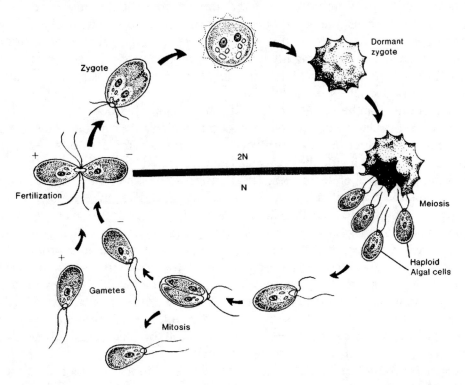

Figure 18–6 The life cycle of *Chlamydomonas*. *Source:* Tom M. Graham. *Biology* (1997), p. 352.

enzymes for the synthesis of starch. Most cells have a red **eyespot** on the chloroplast near the base of the flagella.

Chlamydomonas has a comparatively simple life history cycle that seems to represent an early stage in the development of green algae.

In *Chlamydomonas* asexual reproduction is most commonly observed. At the start of asexual reproduction, the flagella degenerate and fall off and the nucleus divides by mitosis. As reproduction continues, the entire cell is transformed into two identical bodies held within the original cell wall. As the new cells develop, mitosis may occur repeatedly, producing some 32 tiny daughter cells before the cellulose wall ruptures. All of the daughter cells are **haploid.** Asexual reproduction is completed when the daughter cells develop flagella and escape through the cell wall and swim away. Each daughter cell is a new *Chlamydomonas* that grows until mature, than initiates its own asexual reproduction events.

Sexual reproduction in *Chlamydomonas* is infrequently observed and poorly understood. Sexual reproduction begins when many cells congregate together. Pairs of cells within this mass are attracted to each other by reactions in the flagella and function as **gametes.** As they pair, the cell walls break down and the cytoplasm and nuclei of the two *Chlamydomonas* combine to form a **zygote**, which is diploid (2n). The diploid zygote may remain dormant for months, but eventually undergoes **meiosis,** producing four **zoospores** which swim away and become adult haploid algae. Although this is a very simple life cycle, it represents, for the first time, **alternation of generations** between haploid and diploid life stages that is a common feature of sexual reproduction in higher plants.

b. Ulothrix

Ulothrix is green algae that is often common on dead twigs, rocks and other debris in colder freshwater ponds, lakes, and streams. *Ulothrix* has a thread-like body form and its name is derived from the Greek and means wooly hair. *Ulothrix* is colonial, and consists of several cells that grow together to form the **colony.** Each colony consists of a single row of cylindrical cells attached end-to-end to form a thread or **filament.** The basal cell of each filament is slightly larger than the others and functions as a **holdfast.**

Each cell of the *Ulothrix* colony includes a central nucleus surrounded by a wide **chloroplast** shaped like a partially completed bracelet. The chloroplasts have one or more **pyrenoids** for the storage of starch. The colonial filaments increase in size as more cells mitotically divide. All cells except the holdfast are capable of cell division.

Asexual reproduction in *Ulothrix* occurs when the cytoplasm of a cell appears to clump and condense inside the cell wall. The condensed cytoplasm mitotically divides and becomes a series of **zoospores.** This division stage resembles *Chlamydomonas*, in that each of the zoospores has a contractile vacuole and an eyespot. Each of the *Ulothrix* zoospores have four flagella instead of the two seen in *Chlamydomonas*. Following its formation, zoospores escape through pores in the cell membrane. Each zoospore swims away in search of suitable habitats. They settle on submerged objects such as rocks and other debris. Once attached, the zoospore sheds its flagella and divides. One of the two daughter cells becomes the holdfast of the new filament and the other continues to divide to form the new colony. Some cells of the original colony exhibit a different mode of asexual reproduction. These produce nonflagellated zoospores which are released when the cell wall breaks down. They are called **alanospores** and float away to form new filaments.

Sexual reproduction in *Ulothrix* occurs when a cell in the filament divides by mitosis. The division continues in the cell until it forms up to 64 zoospore-like cells, each

Figure 18–7 Structure and reproduction in *Ulothrix*, a filamentous green algae (a) mature vegetative plant (b) zoospore formation (c) zoospore (d) development of zoospore into young filament. *Source: Harold C. Bold and John W. La Claire II. The Plant Kingdom* (1987), Prentice-Hall, p. 39.

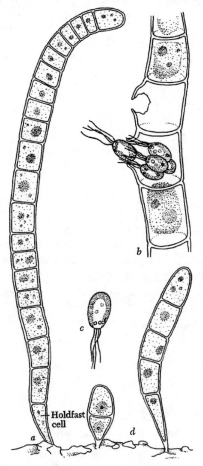

with two flagella. When the **zoospores** are liberated, they function as **gametes.** Zoospores from different colonies unite to form **zygotes.** Typically, the zygotes will form thick walls and enter a period of dormancy. During this time the zygote undergoes **meiosis** giving rise to haploid zoospores which will in turn give rise to new colonial filaments. In this form of sexual reproduction both of the zoospores (which function as gametes) are identical in size and appearance. This condition is called **isogamy.** If the gametes are unequal in size, as in *Chlamydomonas*, the conditon is called **anisogamy.** If the gametes are distinctly different in size, structure, and behavior (e.g., the female gamete is stationary and the male gamete swims freely in search of the female) this condition is called **oogamy.** In *Ulothrix*, zygotes are the only diploid cells in the life cycle. All other cells are haploid.

c. Spirogyra

Spirogyra is a common algae of freshwater habitats, often forming floating mats in quiet areas of water. It is sometimes called "water silk" because of its smooth, glossy green and glistening appearance. Like *Ulothrix*, *Spirogyra* often forms long colonies which consist of unbranched filaments containing hundreds and sometimes thousands of cells joined end-to-end. Each cell in the colony contains prominent ribbon-shaped chloroplasts embedded with evenly spaced pyrenoids.

Both sexual and asexual reproduction occurs. **Asexual** reproduction usually occurs by **fragmentation** of the spirogyra filament. The filaments simply break into pieces and float away, growing into new filaments that, in turn, will grow and fragment or undergo sexual reproduction.

Sexual reproduction in *Spirogyra* is by a process called **conjugation.** *Spirogyra* can be found in dense floating mats and the long filaments come into close contact with each other. Sexual reproduction involves an interchange of genetic material between filaments. Since the cells in the filaments are not actually male or female gametes, they are designated as a + or - mating filament. In mating, individual cells of adjacent filaments form extensions that grow towards a cell from the complimentary filament. These extensions meet and fuse to form **conjugation tubes.** Condensed cell protoplasts in each of the cells function as **gametes.** The protoplast from one filament migrates through the tube to the cell of the adjacent filament where it fuses with that cell. This kind of sexual reproduction, called conjugation, results in the formation of a **zygote.** The zygote develops thick walls and remains dormant for a period of time. Generally, *Spirogyra* overwinters as these resistant zygotes. In spring, or when environmental conditions improve, the

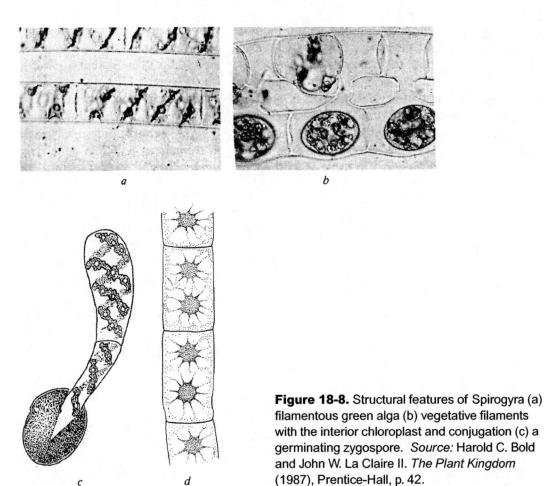

Figure 18-8. Structural features of Spirogyra (a) filamentous green alga (b) vegetative filaments with the interior chloroplast and conjugation (c) a germinating zygospore. *Source:* Harold C. Bold and John W. La Claire II. *The Plant Kingdom* (1987), Prentice-Hall, p. 42.

zygote undergoes meiosis to produce four haploid cells. Three of the haploid cells disintegrate but the fourth gives rise to a new filament.

The life cycle of *Spirogyra* shows several advanced features compared to other algae. First, conjugation is achieved by non-swimming gametes. Second, while both gametes are similar in size (isogamy) they differ in behavior. One moves and one is stationary, which is reminiscent of more advanced forms in which male gametes move and female gametes are stationary, a condition called **oogamy**. In essence, the *Spirogyra* life cycle has fallen into a familiar pattern of haploid cells forming gametes which in turn produce zygotes. The zygotes are diploid in the amount of nuclear material and undergo meiosis to produce haploid cells. Most growth occurs in the haploid or **gametophyte** generation. The zygote or **sporophyte** generation is often long-lived and is specialized as a resistant stage for the species to survive the winter.

d. Oedogonium

This advanced green algae is commonly found growing on aquatic flowering plants and other algae. *Oedogonium* are colonies with a filamentous form that may attach themselves onto other plants for use as support. *Oedogonium* and other organisms that attach to plants and animals without actually parasitizing them are called **epiphytes**.

Each filament of *Oedogonium* has a **basal cell** which forms a holdfast and a **terminal cell** which is rounded. The remaining cells in the filament are cylindrical in shape and are attached end-to-end. Each cell contains a large net-like chloroplast which rolls and forms a tube around each protoplast like a woven basket. Pyrenoids occur at the intersections within the netlike pattern of the chloroplasts.

Figure 18–9 Structure and reproduction of *Oedogonium* (a) formation of zoospores (b) female with oogonium containing egg (c) male plant liberating sperm from antheridia. *Source:* Harold C. Bold and John W. La Claire II. *The Plant Kingdom* (1987), Prentice-Hall, p. 40.

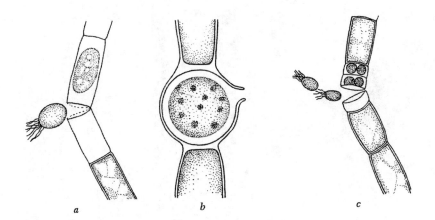

a   b   c

Two forms of asexual reproduction may occur in *Oedogonium*. During winter months, Odegonium asexually produces thick-walled cells called **akinetes**, which survive the winter as dormant, well protected cells. A more common form of asexual reproduction involves the production of zoospores in cells at the tips of filaments; each zoospore may develop about 120 small flagella which collectively form a fringe around the cell concentrating towards one end. After the zoospore escapes from the filament it eventually settles and forms a new filament.

Plants that display oogamy as a form of sexual reproduction are considered "more advanced" because their reproductive methods are more complex. In the same respect, plants that exhibit sexual over asexual reproduction are also viewed as more advanced.

Sexual reproduction in *Oedogonium* occurs when short, box-like cells called **antheridia** are formed in the filaments. These special cells live alongside ordinary vegetative cells but represent the male reproductive cells of *Oedogonium*. Each antheridium produces a pair of motile gametes which function as sperm. These male gametes are like zoospores but smaller. Other cells in the filament become round and swollen. These rounded cells are called **oogonia** and their contents become **eggs**. When the development of these specialized male and female cells is completed, a pore forms in the cell wall of the oogonium through which a free swimming sperm enters. Inside the oogonia, the sperm unites with the egg to form a zygote. Zygotes may remain dormant for a year or more, but eventually undergo meiosis to produce four zoospores, each of which is capable of developing into a new filament. This kind of sexual reproduction, in which one gamete is larger and stationary, is called **oogamy**.

Because of their relative sexual sophistication (at least in the world of green algae) *Oedogonium* are sometimes considered to be the most advanced of the green algae. For the first time we have specialized cells producing gametes. This development of antheridia and oogonia represents a further division of labor within the colony. Secondly, the development of oogamy establishes a pattern of sexual reproduction that is standard in advanced plants and animals. Lastly, we have essentially the same kind of

Figure 18–10 Examples of desmids (a) *Cosmarium* (b) cell division of *Cosmarium* (c) *Closterium* (d) conjugation between two *Closterium*. *Source:* Harold C. Bold and John W. La Claire II. *The Plant Kingdom* (1987), Prentice-Hall, p. 42.

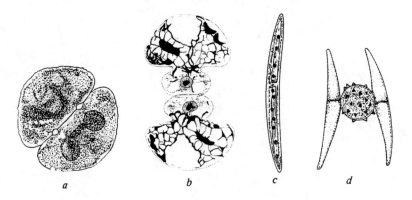

a   b   c   d

life cycle we had in all the green algae. The haploid cells form the filaments and the diploid cells are the zygotes. These same zygotes may form weather resistant growth forms adapted for surviving the winter.

e. More Green Algae

As indicated before, the green algae are a large and complex group. There are many other varieties and colony shapes besides the four examples given above.

Chlorella is a common form of green algae widely used in research. *Chlorella* is very hardy algae and is favored as a food source for future space travelers. Spaceships of the 21st century may carry tanks of *Chlorella* for food and also to produce oxygen.

Desmids are another group of about 2,500 species of green algae. Highly variable in shape, desmids form crescents, ellipticals, and star-shaped cells. All desmids are unicellular, free floating forms. They reproduce asexually by conjugation. One small spectacular green algae is called *Acetabularia*, or mermaid's wine glass. This is a marine algae consisting of a single huge cell shaped like a mushroom. Each cell is about one-quarter inch long. *Acetabularia* are used in scientific experiments to determine the effect of the nucleus on the size and shape of a cell.

Volvox is a common and interesting colonial form of green algae. The colony consists of a hollow ball of cells. Each cell contains chloroplasts and two flagella, which lie on the outside of the ball. The ball-shaped colony moves by beating flagella. Although the flagella beat individually their movements act to propel the entire *Volvox* sphere. *Volvox* colonies number from a few hundred to several thousand cells. Reproduction is sexual or asexual. Daughter colonies form inside the colony and are released when the parent colony breaks up.

Ulva or sea lettuce is a multicellular seaweed with flattened crinkly-edged green blades attaining lengths of a yard or more. The blades are haploid or diploid and are anchored to rocks by means of a holdfast. The diploid blades produce spores that develop into haploid blades bearing gamete-forming cells. The gametes from haploid blades fuse in pairs, forming zygotes and grow into the diploid blades.

Cladophora are branched, filamentous green algae that are found in both fresh and salt water. The cells are multinucleate, which means that each cell contains more than one nucleus.

Figure 18–11 The life cycle of *Volvox*. *Source:* Rushforth. *The Plant Kingdom* (1976), Prentice-Hall, p. 206.

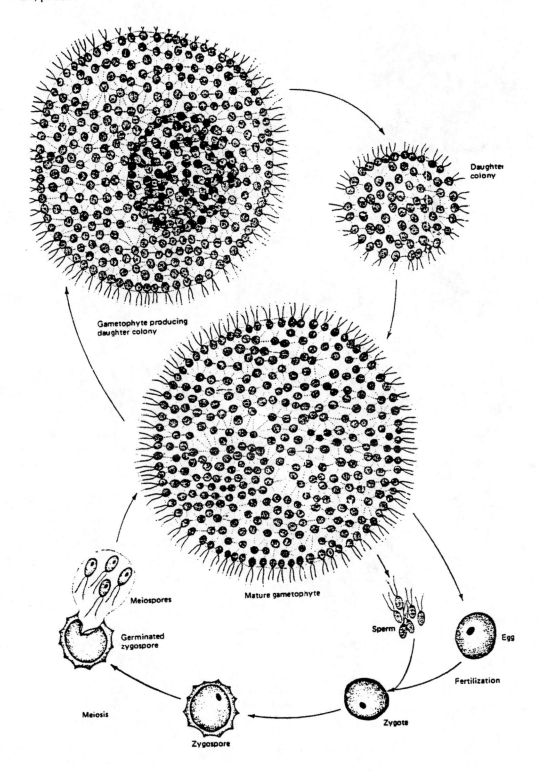

Daughter colony

Gametophyte producing daughter colony

Mature gametophyte

Meiospores

Germinated zygospore

Sperm

Egg

Fertilization

Meiosis

Zygospore

Zygote

Figure 18–12 The life cycle of *Ulva*, a large marine green alga. *Source:* Teresa Audesirk and Gerald Audesirk (1999), p. 394.

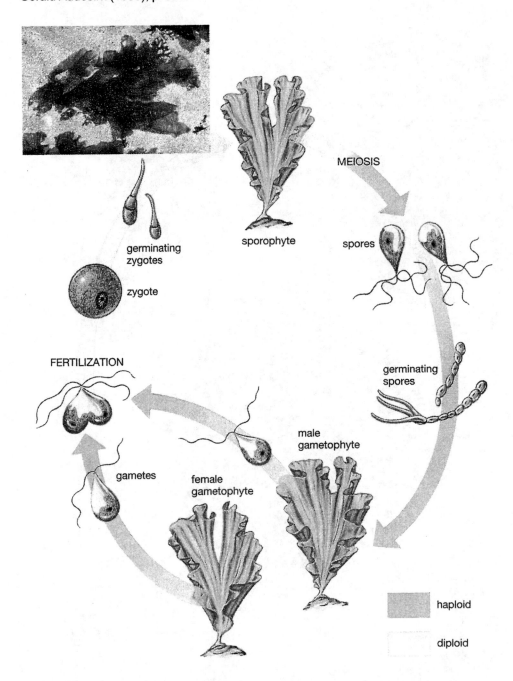

Stonewarts are green algae that resemble small calcium-encrusted horsetail plants. They reproduce sexually by oogamy and sometimes are placed in a separate plant division because the antherida are multicellular, a condition also seen in advanced plants.

DIVISION PHAEOPHYTA—THE BROWN ALGAE

Brown algae actually range from brown to olive color in appearance. They number about 1,500–2,000 species. Most brown algae are multicellular seaweeds, and some are quite large in size. Unlike the earlier groups of algae studied so far, none of the

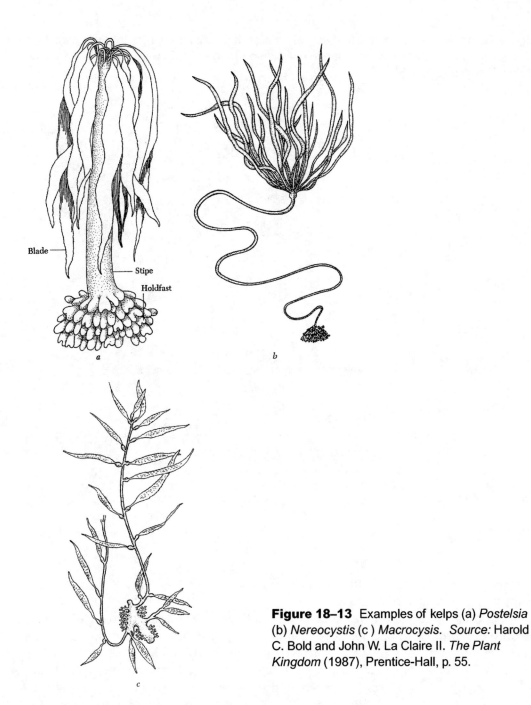

Labels on image (a): Blade, Stipe, Holdfast

Figure 18–13 Examples of kelps (a) *Postelsia* (b) *Nereocystis* (c) *Macrocystis. Source:* Harold C. Bold and John W. La Claire II. *The Plant Kingdom* (1987), Prentice-Hall, p. 55.

brown algae are unicellular or colonial. Four species are found in fresh water but all the rest are seaweeds. Most live in shallow waters of the colder oceans in the northern and southern reaches of the Atlantic and Pacific.

Perhaps the most extraordinary of the brown algae is the giant kelp, which average 100 feet in length. One kelp plant was measured at 710 feet long, which is a record for any single living organism. Kelp are fairly common along the wave drenched shorelines of many of the world's oceans. They attach to rocks and other debris in shallow water by a **holdfast organ** which resembles a fibrous root system. The kelp body that grows out of the holdfast is called a **stipe**. This long stipe consists of a hollow stalk with a meristem at the base where the blades are formed. **Blades** are the oldest part of the plant and resemble the leaves of higher plants. Some kelp have gas filled floats called **bladders** which are located near the base. The gas inside the bladder contains about 10

Figure 18–14 The structure and life cycle of *Laminaria* (a) the sporophyte (b) male gametophyte (c) a female gametophyte. *Source:* Harold C. Bold and John W. La Claire II. *The Plant Kingdom* (1987), Prentice-Hall, p. 54.

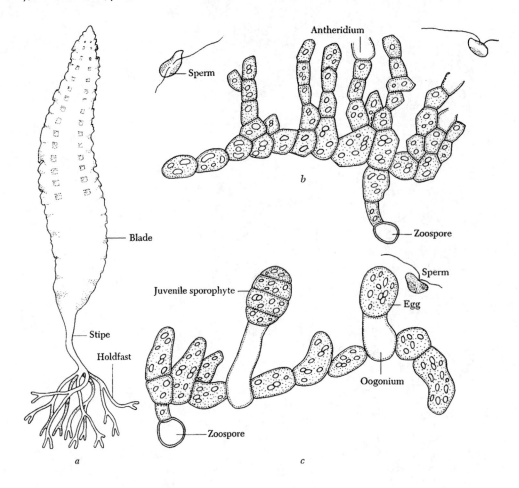

percent carbon monoxide, which is normally a toxic substance to life, but in this case helps the kelp to float in the waves.

Kelp cells contain many photosynthetic pigments; brown pigments (called **fucoxanthin)** predominate, but chlorophyll *a* and chlorophyll *c* are also common. Food is primarily stored in the form of a starch called **laminarin**. **Algin** (alginic acid) is found in or on the cell walls of kelp and forms up to 40 percent of their dry weight. We will discuss the importance of algin later. The reproductive cells of kelp also differ in having two flagella inserted, one on each side, instead of both at one end. In kelp, the reproductive cells are the only motile cells in the life cycle. As in most brown algae, kelp reproduces asexually by fragmentation. However, some brown algae may also produce **aplanospores**.

The Sargasso Sea is named for the common brown algae, *Sargassum.*

Sexual reproduction in the brown algae differs from that of other algae. In *Fucus*, the common rockweed, there are separate male and female body forms. These body forms are called **thalli** and are like flattened multicellular unorganized structures. They

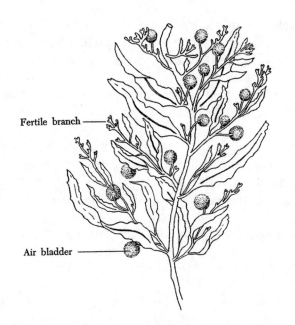

Figure 18–15 The brown alga *Sargassum*. *Source:* Harold C. Bold and John W. La Claire II. *The Plant Kingdom* (1987), Prentice-Hall, p. 57.

Fertile branch

Air bladder

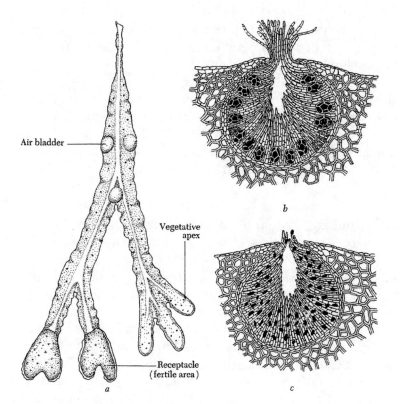

Air bladder

Vegetative apex

Receptacle (fertile area)

a

b

c

d

Figure 18–16 The life cycle of the rock alga *Fucus* (a) the plant (b) oogonial conceptacles, each with eight eggs (c) antherdia section (d) antheredia with sperm. *Source:* Harold C. Bold and John W. La Claire II. *The Plant Kingdom* (1987), Prentice-Hall, p. 56.

have puffy swellings, called **receptacles** located at the tips of each thallus. The surface of a receptacle has pores opening into chambers called **conceptacles,** which contain gamete forming bodies. Eight eggs are produced in each oogonium as a result of a single diploid nucleus undergoing meiosis followed by mitosis. Male gametangia (antheridia) undergo three mitotic divisions following meiosis, eventually producing a total of 64 sperm from the original cell. Both eggs and sperm are released into the water to produce zygotes.

The brown algae represent a major advancement for plants. For the first time we have **multicellular plants** instead of colonies. Unlike other algae, cells, when separated from each other cannot survive independently; this shows the complexity of multicellular brown algae and their specialization at the cellular level. We also see, for the first time, sexual differences in body form. Male and female thalli produce a condition called **sexual dimorphism**. This means that each sex looks different from the other.

DIVISION RHODOPHYTA—THE RED ALGAE

About 5,000 species of red algae are known. The vast majority are seaweeds which occur in deeper waters than brown algae. A number of species occur in the depths of the pantropic seas of the world. Some species are also found on rocks in intertidal zones where they are exposed at low tide. A few red algae are unicellular but most forms are multicellular filaments so tightly packed that they form blades or branching segments. Some red algae develop feathery appearing structures.

The chloroplasts contain **chlorophyll a** and d, and a distinctive red pigment obtained from **phycobilins** that is closely related to those in cyanobacteria. Food is stored in the form of **Floridian starch**. Some red algae also produce **agar**. Red algae have complex life cycles involving three different types of body structures. Meiosis occurs on a body form called a tetrasporophyte. Gametes are formed on separate male and female thalli. All cells are nonmotile and carried by water.

Polysiphonia

Polysiphonia is a feathery red algae common in marine waters. It contains three kinds of thalli—a male gametophyte, female gametophyte, and **tetrasporophyte**. All three of these thalli are finely branched and identical in appearance. The male sex structures (spermatangia) of *Polysiphonia* resemble clusters of grapes. Each spermatangium is released from its branch and functions as a nonmotile male gamete. The female sex structure is called a **carpogonia.** It is produced on a female thallus and consists of a large single cell with a neck-like structure called a **tricogyne**. There is a single nucleus at the base of the cell which functions as an egg. If male spermatangia brush against a carpogonia, the trichogyne breaks down, allowing the nucleus of the spermatangium to migrate to the egg nucleus, which unite to form a zygote. The zygote develops into a cluster of club-like carposporangia toward the base of an urn-shaped body or **cystocarp**, formed around the carposporangium by the female gametophyte thallus.

During asexual reproduction, diploid spores called **carpospores** are produced and released into the ocean currents. When they lodge in a crevasse, they germinate and grow into a new organism called a **tetrasporophyte**. This produces a tetrasporangium which undergoes meiosis giving rise to four haploid tetraspores. When these germinate, they develop into male or female gametophytes.

This complex life cycle illustrates why the red algae are considered to be the most advanced of the algae. This does not mean, however, that they are closely related to

Figure 18–17 Life cycle of the red alga *Polysiphonia.* *Source:* N. M. Jessop. *Biosphere: A Study of Life* (1970), Prentice-Hall, p. 867.

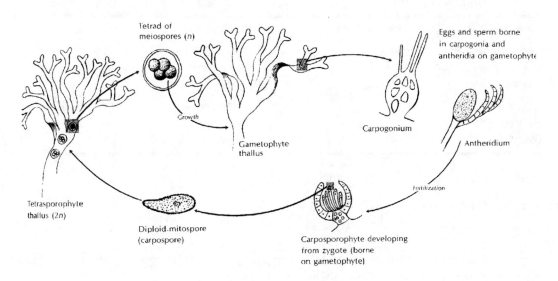

Table 18-1 A classification of the protistans.

Division	Examples	Pigments	Form
Chrysophyta	golden-brown algae	chlorophyll a,c, fucoxanthin	unicellular
Pyrrophya	dinoflagellates	chlorophyll a,c	unicellular
Euglenophyta	euglenas, amoebas	chlorophyll a	
Chlorophyta	green algae	chlorophyll a,b	unicellular, multicellular
Phaeophyta	brown algae	chlorophyll a,c, fucoxanthin	multicellular
Rhodophyta	red algae	chlorophyll a,d, phycobilin	multicellular

land plants, but rather that they, along with the brown algae, represent structural specializations that parallel the conditions of land plants in some ways. When one examines structure, photosynthetic pigments, and other factors, it is the green algae that represent the closest relative to land plants.

Considering the Classification of Algae

Traditionally, the term algae signified and symbolized simple plants or plant-like organisms. Actually, the classification of the "algae" is by no means certain, as some botanists consider the green, red, and brown algae to belong to the Kingdom Plantae but others consider them to be larger and more advanced protistans, as we have presented in this book. A summary of the organisms tagged "algae" is presented in Table 18-2.

Table 18-2 Summary of Algal Classification.

Common Name	Division	Kingdom
Blue-green algae (blue-green bacteria)	Cyanobacteria	Monera
Golden-brown algae, diatoms	Chrysophyta	Protista
Euglenoids *(Euglena, Volvox)*	Euglenophyta	
Dinoflagellates	Pyrrophyta	
Green algae	Chlorophyta	Protista/Plantae
Brown algae	Phaeophyta	
Red Algae	Rhodophyta	

Economic Importance of Algae

Algae are a large and economically important group of organisms. Below are listed some of the more important ways that we use algae.

Diatoms are valuable because they produce diatomaceous earth and oils.

Diatoms produce oil as a food reserve which can be converted into **cod-liver oil.** Diatoms are also harvested to provide oils rich in vitamins and minerals for human consumption. When diatoms die, they collect as ooze on the ocean floor where they form deposits hundreds of feet thick. Geologic deposits of this diatom remains have been raised above the ocean surface by geologic action and are mined as **diatomaceous earth**. The powdery diatomaceous earth has a high melting point and is insoluble in most acids. Diatomaceous earth is used in filtration devices so important in many industries. It is also the primary component in swimming pool filters, in silver and metal polish, as an ingredient in toothpaste, in light reflecting paint, and as insulation around blast furnaces and boilers. It is also used in the manufacture of panels for prefabricated housing.

Algin is obtained from the cell walls of kelp and other brown algae. It is used in the manufacture of a wide variety of products such as ice cream, salad dressing, beer, jelly beans, latex paint, penicillin suspensions, paper, textiles, toothpaste, ceramics, and floor polish. In ice cream and other frozen desserts, algin controls the development of ice crystals, so the food has a longer shelf life in supermarkets. Algin is also used to help regulate water penetration into porous surfaces. Among its many uses as a water regulator and retardant, algin is used to stabilize any kind of suspension, such as milk shakes.

In many areas of the world algae are also harvested and used as a source of **minerals** and **food,** and in food preparations. Kelp, a brown algae, is harvested and processed to produce iodine, nitrogen, and potassium. Kelp can also be ground up and used as fertilizer. In Northern Europe it serves as livestock feed. Many oriental cultures harvest marine algae to augment local food supplies and also as a food additive and as a readily available source of many organic chemicals. In Japan, for example, algae is used to produce acetic acid. The Japanese also harvest a red algae called nori, which is dried into sheets and eaten as the outer covering on sushi. Nori is also added to soups and eaten with rice. Irish moss is another red algae that is harvested for food. Irish moss also serves as a bulking laxative, in cosmetics, and in pharmaceutical preparations. A mucilaginous substance called carrageenan is extracted from Irish moss and used as a thickening agent in chocolate milk and in other dairy products. *Funori* is a red algae used as laundry starch, an adhesive in hair dressings, and in some water based paints.

Agar is extracted from a species of red algae called *Gelidium*. Agar is used around the world as culture medium for bacteria. It provides a neutral base on which bacteria can grow. Growth rate of bacteria can be controlled by adding specific ingredients to the agar culture. Agar is also a culture medium for cloning plants and growing animal cells. Agar is used to make drug capsules and is an agent in bakery products to retain moisture. It is also a base for cosmetics and an agent in gelatin desserts.

Scientists are testing a variety of algae, especially red algae for drugs and other chemicals that might prove valuable in the treatment of diseases. Medically, algae is used in preparations for controlling diarrhea, expulsion of worms from the human digestive tract, in cancer treatments, and as insecticides.

Key Words and Phrases

Division Chrysophyta
Division Pyrrophyta
Division Euglenophyta
Division Chlorophyta
Division Phaeophyta
pellicle
gullet
zoospores
sporophyte
stipe
anisogamy
conjugation tube
receptacle
agar
diatomaceous earth
fucoxanthin
thalli
phycobilins

Class Bacillariophyceae
dinoflagellates
Euglena
golden-brown algae
brown algae
flagellum
paramylon bodies
alternation of generations
filament
blade
oogamy
conceptacle
sexual dimorphism
oogonia
Chlamydomonas
laminarin

diatoms
algae
Volvox
red tide
eyespot
reservoir
pyrenoids
ametophyte
holdfast
isogamy
akinetes
Spirogyra
Oedogonium
antheridium
bladders
aplanospores

Selected References and Resources

Abbott, I. A., and E. Y. Dawson. 1978. *How to know the Seaweeds.* 2nd Edition. Wm. C. Brown Company. Dubuque, Iowa.

Becker, E. W. Ed. 1985. *Production and use of Microalgae.* Lubrecht and Cramer. Forestburgh, New York.

Becker, E. W. 1994. *Microalgae. Biotechnology and Microbiology.* Cambridge University Press. New York.

Bold, H. C., and M. J. Wynne. 1985. *Introduction to the Algae.* Prentice-Hall. Englewood Cliffs, New Jersey.

Buetow, D.E. Ed. 1968-1989. *The Biology of Euglena. General Biology and Ultrastructure.* 4 Volumes. Academic Press. San Diego, California.

Chapman, V. J., and D. J. Chapman. 1980. *Seaweeds and their Uses.* Chapman and Hall. London.

Cox, E. R. Ed. 1980. *Phytoflagellates.* Elsevier/North Holland. New York.

Darley, W. M. 1982. *Algal Biology. A Physiological Approach.* Blackwall Scientific. Oxford.

Dawes, C. J. 1981. *Marine Botany.* Wiley Interscience. New York.

Dring, M. J. 1983. *The Biology of Marine Plants.* Edward Arnold. Baltimore, Maryland.

Goff, L. J. 1983. *Algal Symbiosis. A Continuum of Interaction Strategies.* Cambridge University Press. London.

Irvine, D., and D. M. John, Eds. 1985. *Systematics of the Algae.* Academic Press. San Diego, California.

Kirk, D. L. 1997. *Volvox. Molecular Genetic Origins of Multicellularity and Cellular Differentiation.* Cambridge University Press. New York.

Lee, R. E. 1989. *Phycology.* 2nd. Edition. Cambridge University Press. New York.

Lobban, C. S., and P. J. Harrison. 1994. *Seaweed Ecology and Physiology.* Cambridge University Press. New York.

Round, F. E. 1984. *The Ecology of Algae.* Cambridge University Press. New York.

Sandgren, C. D., J. P. Smol, and J. Kristiansen. 1995. *Chrysophyte Algae. Ecology, Phylogeny, and Development.* Cambridge University Press. New York.

van den Hoek, C., D. Mann, and H. M. Jahns. 1996. *Algae. An Introduction to Phycology.* Cambridge University Press. New York.

Smith, G. M. 1950. *Freshwater Algae of the United States.* McGraw-Hill Book Company. New York.

Sze, P. 1986. *A Biology of the Algae.* Wm C. Brown, Publishers. Dubuque, Iowa.

Review and Discussion Questions

1. What characteristics distinguish the algae from the bacteria? Which group of bacteria do the algae most closely resemble?
2. What algae are beneficial to humans? Which are harmful?
3. Why are some of the algae such as *Volvox* and *Euglena* also studied in zoology-courses?
4. What are the most advanced of the algae? The most primitive? Defend your answers.
5. List at least four reasons why diatoms are important to humans.
6. Compare the life cycle of *Oedogonium* with that of *Ulothrix*. Which is considered to be the more primitive organism?
7. Why is the term protista usually substituted for the term algae? Which is considered to be the scientifically more valid term for the group as a whole?
8. In what habitats do the protistans occur? In what habitats do the algae occur?
9. What are the characteristics that are used to separate the major groups of algae? Of protistans?

The Fungi

Chapter 19

◄ ▪ ▪ ▪ ▶ ▪ ▪ ◀ ▪ ▪ ▪ ▪ ▪ ▪ ▪ ▪ ▪ ▪

The fungi have an image problem! We have a very low opinion of fungi and unfortunately we don't realize that they are the important decomposer organisms that break down organic materials and recycle the nutrients they contain. Fungi are also harnessed in many ways for the service of humankind. Some fungi are our sources of penicillin and other antibiotics. Common fungi of the beaches, such as *Corollospora martima*, may be the answer to cleaning up oil spills. Many foods such as cheeses and milk products are produced with the assistance of fungi. Furthermore, we eat many species of fungi. However, besides being helpful to us they can also cause huge losses in food spoilage and disease.

About 100,000 species of fungi are known, but several hundred new species are discovered each year, mostly from the tropics. Very possibly another 200,000 fungi species have yet to be discovered.

Fungi range in complexity from simple, single-celled organisms to large and complex multicellular mushrooms. Most fungi produce an intertwined mass of threads called **hyphae**, which tend to branch freely or fuse together. A mass of these hyphae is called a **mycelium**. These mycelia thrive in a wide variety of conditions. Fungi can reproduce sexually and asexually. Most species produce prolific numbers of spores,

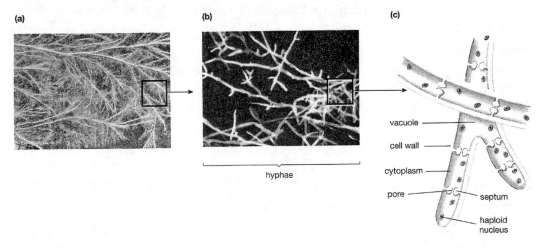

Figure 19–1 The body features of a typical fungus (a) a fungal mycelium (b and c) enlarged to show the hyphae. *Source:* Teresa Audesirk and Gerald Audesirk (1999), p. 378.

which are widely broadcast in the air as vegetative bodies called spores. Spores of fungi are everywhere and form a common contaminant in household dust.

Characteristics of Fungi

• ▼

The relation of fungi to other living organisms is unclear. As a group, they share some common features with prokaryotes, but most higher fungi appear to have many characteristics in common with green plants. At least one rather remarkable group, the slime molds behave more like protozoans of the Kingdom Protista. Most plant biologists believe that the fungi are a heterogenous group of organisms which share a few characteristics in common. In fact, the four major types of fungi are usually thought to represent different lineages that evolved from four separate protistan ancestral families.

Although a highly varied group, all fungi have one thing in common: unlike green plants, they lack chloroplasts and cannot manufacture their own food by photosynthesis. Instead, they are heterotrophic, absorbing food directly from the environment or from plant and animal hosts. Fungi that absorb organic materials from their environment are called **saprobes**. Those that absorb nutrients from organisms are termed **parasites**. Some fungi have feeding habits that are reminiscent of animals. In all cases, fungi feed by secreting digestive enzymes into the host or into the organic matter, then absorb the digested nutrients. Ringworm, athlete's foot, powdery mildew, and black bread mold are some familiar examples of fungi feeding on humans and other animals and organic substances.

In reality fungi occupy a middle ground between plants and animals in the world's ecosystems. The four major groups of fungi include the following:

Slime Molds are the most primitive fungi. They lack cell walls and consist of multinucleate masses of protoplasm called **plasmodia**. Slime molds are unique among fungi (and most other plants) in being able to move about like animals. Like amoeba, slime molds flow (or creep, or ooze!) over damp leaves, branches, or soil debris. During their reproductive phase slime molds become stationary and produce sporangia containing thousands of globular spores.

Chytrids are unicellular fungi with motile cells that have a single flagellum anchored towards the posterior end, or base, of the fungi. Chytrids have few features in common with other fungi and their relationships are uncertain. Chytrids are small and highly specialized little plants.

Water Molds resemble brown algae from which they are thought to be evolutionarily derived. They produce the same kinds of eggs, have cellulose in their cell walls, are predominantly diploid in their life cycle, and have zoospores that move by means of two flagella. In size and shape, water molds range from single spherical cells to branching thread-like hyphae.

True Fungi are filamentous masses of cells called **hyphae**. They have cell walls impregnated with chitin. The true fungi exhibit a variety of methods of sexual reproduction. Food is absorbed through cell walls and broken down by enzymes secreted to the outside of the cells.

Table 19-1 A classification of the fungi.

Taxonomic Group	Examples	Distinctive Characteristics
Myxomycotinae	slime molds	amoeba-like, lack cell walls
Chytridomycitineae	chytrids	unicellular, gametes with flagella
Mastigomycotineae	water molds	zoospores with two flagella
Eucomycotineae Zygomycota	coenocytic true fungi	reproduce via club-shaped gametangia fuse to form zygote
Eucomycotineae Eumycota	sac, club, imperfect fungi	basidium with perforated cell walls, spores produced in asci

Subkingdom Myxomycotinae—The Slime Molds

The 500 or so species of slime molds have spores just about everywhere in our environment. A typical slime mold is an organism that lives on the forest floor and has a body made of a protoplasmic mass called a **plasmodium**. Plasmodia can be of various colors—yellow, orange, blue, violet or black. Slime molds frequently attract our attention by their bright coloration in an otherwise drab woodland floor environment. A few slime molds are colorless.

Typically, slime molds thrive in old damp forest debris, under logs, on old shelf or bracket fungi, on older mushrooms and in moist areas where dead organic debris is abundant. Slime molds creep across the debris at a rate of one inch per hour, feeding on bacteria and other organic particles. Although containing many diploid nuclei, cell walls are lacking. The nuclei divide simultaneously, resulting in rapid growth; a plasmodium may increase 25 times in size in one week.

If food is lacking a plasmodium becomes immobile and converts to a **sporangium**. A sporangium is an upright growth that emerges from the surface of the plasmodium and contains minute, one-celled **spores**. Individual sporangia may form on stalks, or a plasmodium may form a single sporangium. The spores are dispersed through a jumbled mass of threads called a **capillitium**. Each spore that is formed consists of a single nucleus surrounded by a little cytoplasm and a cell wall. Meiosis takes place within the spore, producing four nuclei, following which three of the four resulting nuclei degenerate. When a spore germinates it produces an amoeboid-like cell called a **myxamoebae**. If the myxamoebae have flagella they are called **swarm cells**. Swarm cells may feed on bacteria before functioning as gametes. To complete the life cycle, two swarm cells fuse to form a zygote, which develops into the plasmodium of a new slime mold.

There are two kinds of slime molds in nature. Most regular slime molds have a true plasmodium as described above. A second group, the **cellular slime molds**, do not produce a true plasmodia. Instead there are individual amoeba-like cells that feed independently, dividing and producing new cells from time to time. When the population reaches a certain size they stop feeding and clump together in a **pseudoplasmodium**, which looks and crawls like a garden slug. This is transformed into sporangia-like masses of spores during reproduction.

ECONOMICS OF SLIME MOLDS

Because of their animal-like behavior, slime molds are uniquely interesting and also ecologically important. Like bacteria, they function as decomposers. Some slime molds

Figure 19–2 The life cycle of a cellular slime mold. *Source:* Teresa Audesirk and Gerald Audesirk (1999), p. 367.

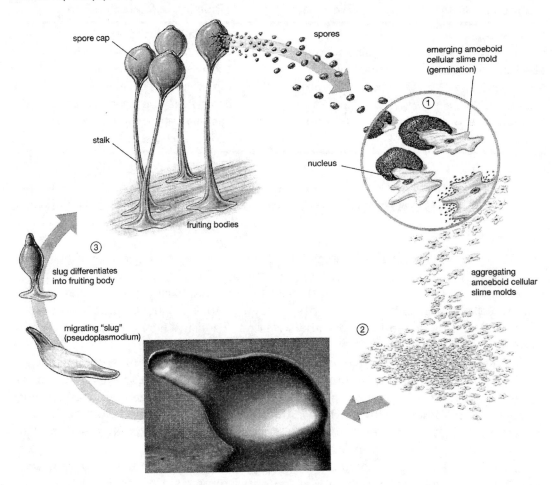

help to control bacterial populations of woodlands. A few are economically detrimental. One form attacks cabbages, another causes a powdery scab on potatoes, and a third is a disease of watercress.

Subkingdom Chytridomycitineae — The Chytrids

The chytrids are a small group of unicellular fungi. They are found on dead leaves, flowers, old onion bulb scales, and other organic debris. If we immerse an onion in water for a few days, chytrids will appear on its surface. Chytrids are unicellular and are the simplest of fungi. They function as parasites of aquatic flowering plants, other aquatic fungi, and algae. Most chytrids are colorless spherical cells with branching threads called **rhizoids** at one end. Some may have short **hyphae** that are multinucleate. Occasionally, the hyphae become **mycelia**, and when they do, there are no cross walls between the cells. This multinucleate condition is called **coenocytic**. In some, cell walls may be formed from cellulose along with chitin.

Most chytrids reproduce asexually, developing **zoospores** within the spherical cell. Each zoospore has a single flagellum. Some chytrids develop sexually by means of the fusion of two motile gametes with haploid nuclei or by the union of two nonmotile cells

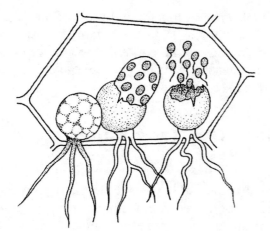

Figure 19–3 A chytrid growing in the leaf of an aquatic plant. *Source:* Harold C. Bold and John W. La Claire II. *The Plant Kingdom* (1987), Prentice-Hall, p. 249.

whose diploid zygote nucleus undergoes meiosis. The resulting zygote becomes a resting spore waiting for better environmental conditions.

The fact that chytrids have flagella and are unicellular are unique characteristics of this group of fungi. This condition resembles similar situations in animal-like protistans, and for that reason some experts feel chytrids are developed from protozoa. They have little or no economic importance.

Subkingdom Mastigomycotineae—The Water Molds

Water molds are a varied group of fungi. Some are parasites on aquatic and terrestrial plants but most parasitize aquatic algae and animals. The cottony growths that occur on aquaria fish where bruises and cuts develop are familiar examples of water molds.

In form, the diploid **hyphae** of water molds may branch repeatedly to form large **coenocytic mycelia.** Water molds may reproduce asexually or sexually. During asexual reproduction, the tips of some hyphae are separated by cross walls. Several biflagellated **zoospores** are produced in these. The zoospores emerge through a terminal pore in the hypha to form new water mold mycelia.

Sexual reproduction involves sex organs called oogonia and antheridia which form on side branches of the hyphae under the influence of hormones. The cells that produce eggs are called **oogonia** while sperm producing cells are **antheridia.** The mycelium of water molds is diploid and meiosis takes place in the sex organs. Haploid sperm swim to the oogonia and there fuse with the haploid eggs to form diploid **zygotes.** Following fertilization, the zygote secretes a thick, protective wall and enters a resting state. In spring, or when environmental conditions improve, it dissolves the wall and forms a new mycelium.

WATER MOLD ECONOMICS

Water molds cause serious diseases of aquaria fish and some plants. The **downy mildew of grapes** is a commercial pest of vineries. Downy mildew grows in the dew and develops on grape leaves, eventually killing the leaf and ultimately the vine. In the 19th century, downy mildew threatened the French wine industry until it was learned that it could be controlled by Bordeaux mixture (copper sulfate and lime).

Another important species of water mold causes **late blight**, a disease that rots potatoes and tomatoes. Late blight was responsible for the Irish potato famine of 1846.

During the 1800's potatoes were a staple crop in Ireland and most of the population depended on this single food source. Beginning in 1845, cool, damp growing seasons fostered the spread of late blight which wiped out the entire potato crop of Ireland for several years. Without their basic food, at least one million people starved and several million more migrated to North America to escape the famine.

Subkingdom Eucomycotineae—The True Fungi

The true fungi are plants that lack motile cells and have chitin in their cell walls. They are the vast majority of all fungi and are of great economic importance. The true fungi are a varied group that includes the coenocytic fungi, sac fungi, and club fungi. Another group of fungi often included with the true fungi are called the "imperfect fungi." They are an artificial group in which the life cycle is incompletely known.

DIVISION ZYGOMYCOTA—THE COENOCYTIC TRUE FUNGI

The zygomycota differ from other true fungi by their method of sexual reproduction. Most consist of an extensively branched haploid mycelium. During reproduction, club-shaped gametangia fuse to form a zygote, which, as in water molds, forms a thick-walled resting stage. Upon emerging, the zygote develops into a mycelium. In asexual reproduction, stalks grow upwards from the mycelium and terminate in spore-producing sporangia.

The coenocytic true fungi are mostly saprobes that feed on plants, especially decaying vegetables and other plant debris. A few are parasites of insects such as the common house fly. Probably the best known of the true fungi are the black bread molds. Originally, black bread molds were common before we learned to prevent their development by using preservatives. Today preservatives have a bad name and there is a tendency to eliminate all non natural material from food. Because we have removed the preservatives, the bread molds are making a comeback.

Black Bread Mold spores are very common and can be found on seemingly clean surfaces everywhere.

The black bread mold, or *Rhizopus*, has spores that are exceedingly common. When a spore lands, it germinates and produces a **coenocytic mycelium**. Since the mycelium lacks cell walls the nuclei and surrounding cytoplasm form a common mass. Within the mycelium, some hyphae called **sporangiospores** grow upwards to produce globe-shaped **sporangia** at their tips. Many black **spores** are formed within. When released, they blow away and form new mycelia. Black bread mold can also reproduce sexually by **conjugation**. In conjugation, the hypha of one strain encounters hypha of another. They develop multinucleate cell. Nuclei of the two strains of hyphae fuse together to make that cell. A thick, ornamented wall develops around the zygote, forming a **zygospore** which is eventually freed. The zygospore may lie dormant for a long time. Eventually the wall cracks or is dissolved, and one or more sporangiophores with sporangia at their tips grow out. During the period of dormancy meiosis has occurred and many black spores are formed. These are then liberated and the cycle starts again.

Figure 19-4 The life cycle of black bread mold. *Source:* Teresa Audesirk and Gerald Audesirk (1999), p. 381.

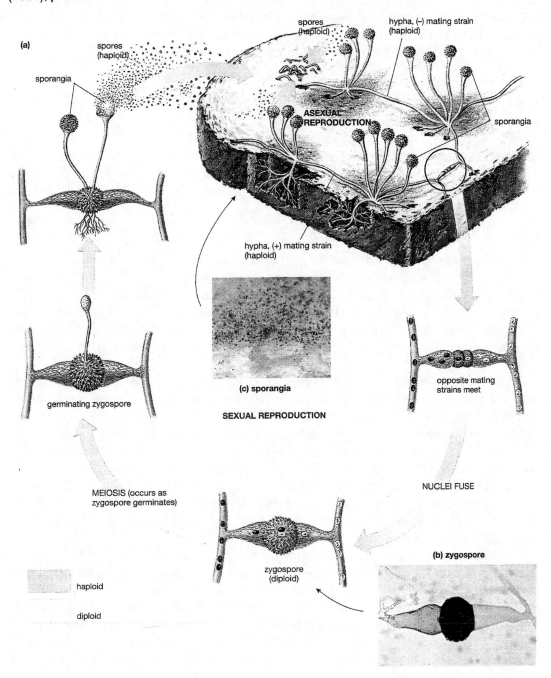

Another coenocytic fungus, *Pilobolus*, lives on dung and forcibly shoots spores out of its sporangia for distances of 20 feet or more. The spores adhere to grass and are eaten by animals. They pass through the animal's digestive tract and emerge in dung where they germinate to start the cycle again.

COENOCYTIC FUNGI ECONOMICS

The coenocytic fungi are important in some local economies where some species are used in the preparation of foods. In Indonesia, for example, a species of bread mold is used to make a food called tempeh, which consists of skinless soybeans that are boiled and then inoculated with a bread mold and allowed to sit for 24 hours. The tempeh is fried, roasted or diced for soup. Bread molds are also used to make a Chinese cheese called sufu. Some species are used in the preparation of birth control pills and anesthetics, while others are involved in making alcohols. Still other true fungi are used as meat tenderizers and to give margarine its distinctive yellow color.

Division Eumycota—The Sac, Club and Imperfect Fungi

Although distinctive in appearance and in some cases different in certain aspects of their life history, all of the eumycota are fungi that have well developed cell walls between nuclei.

CLASS ASCOMYCETES—THE SAC FUNGI

The sac fungi are so called because they produce spores in sac-like cells called **asci.** The 20,000 species of sac fungi include the yeasts, powdery mildews, brown fruit rots, ergot, morels, microscopic parasites of insects, and canned fruit fungi. Yeasts are the simplest of the sac fungi. All yeasts are single-celled organisms that reproduce asexually by budding. Most of the more advanced sac fungi produce hyphae but individual cells are segregated by cell walls between them. Many species are of great economic importance.

Truffles are prune-like fungi that grow underground around oak trees. In size, they may reach 4 inches in diameter and have a distinctive aroma. Natives use pigs to detect truffles, which are considered a gourmet delicacy. In the United States truffles sell for $200 a pound. Truffles are actually the reproductive bodies of sac fungi.

In truffles and most other sac fungi, asexual reproduction is by spores that are produced externally—that is, outside a sporangium. These external spores are called **conidia** and they occur either singly or in chains at tips of hyphae called **conidiophores.** In yeasts, asexual reproduction is generally by **budding.** Budding is like an unequal form of binary fission. The parent cell grows a small "bud" from its side, which eventually is freed and becomes a separate organism.

In sexual reproduction, sac fungi forms reproductive sacs called **asci.** When hyphae of two sexes become associated, male **antheridia**, which produce sperm, are formed on one hypha, while female **ascogonia**, which produce eggs, form on another hyphae. Male nuclei migrate into the ascogonium and pair with the female nuclei but do not fuse. Instead, new hyphae (ascogenous hyphae) each of whose cells contains one male and one female nucleus, grow from the ascogonium. The cells divide in a unique way so each cell has one male and one female nucleus. At maturity, pairs of nuclei unite and tubular asci develop into a layer called the **hymenium** which lies on the surface of a sac or cup-like growth called an **ascocarp**. It is the ascocarp that gives the sac fungi their name.

The united cells form a diploid zygote which undergoes meiosis and produces four haploid nuclei. These, in turn, divide mitotically to form eight nuclei in each ascus. Each of the nuclei becomes **ascospores.** Thousands of ascospores are packed together in the ascocarp which may be cup-shaped, flask-shaped or completely enclosed. When jarred the ascocarps look like they are producing a fine smoke as they release the microscopic spores. The spores germinate and produce hyphae and the cycle starts all over again.

Figure 19–5 The life cycle of a sac fungi. *Source:* N. M. Jessop. *Biosphere. A Study of Life.* (1970), Prentice-Hall, p. 857.

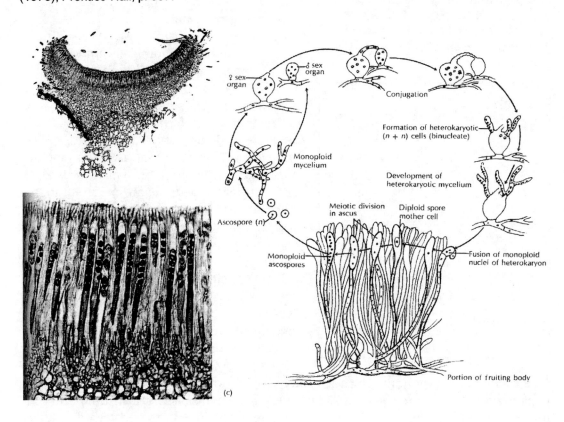

(c)

Economics of the Sac Fungi

Many species of sac fungi are considered to be important and desirable gourmet foods. Others are important food sources. Morels, which grow around the base of pine trees, are considered by some as the world's most tasty mushrooms and truffles are also a prized gourmet food. (Actually, neither morels nor truffles are true mushrooms, which are club fungi). Some people are allergic to these fungi and may die from eating them.

Some species of sac fungi cause serious diseases of plants, animals, and humans. *Ergot* is an important disease caused by sac fungi that has been a bane ever since humans started to cultivate cereal grains. *Ergot* fungi infect wheat, rye and other cereal grains. While *ergot* can cause serious damage to crops, it also causes a disease called St. Antony's Fire in people who eat grains contaminated by the *ergot* fungus. *Ergot* produces serious neurological disorders in humans, often leading to nervous hysteria, convulsions, and death. Another form of *ergot* disease causes gangrene limbs which often wither and fall off in the later stages of the pathology. During the Middle Ages, outbreaks of ergotism were common in Europe. The hysteria and other strange behaviors exhibited by people infected with ergotism may have led to the belief in witches that was so prevalent and widespread during that period of history. There is evidence that the Salem witch trials may have been caused by eating improperly stored grain. Today, *ergot* is used as a source of drugs for various medical uses. For example, in small doses, *ergot* fungus derivatives are useful in stimulating contractions in childbirth and in controlling migraine headaches. *Ergot* is also the source of the hallucinogenic drug, lysergic acid diethylamide (LSD). *Ergot* can be dangerous to cattle and other livestock, which

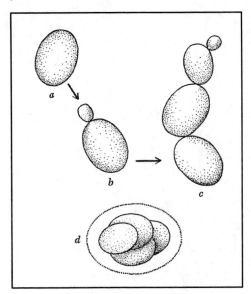

Figure 19–6 Brewer's yeast cells (a through c) highly magnified and budding 9d) Ascus with ascospores. *Source:* Harold C. Bold and John W. La Claire II. *The Plant Kingdom* (1987), Prentice-Hall, p. 255.

may feed on contaminated grains. In cattle it causes sickness and abortions of calves, and in severe cases, death.

Despite their simplicity, yeasts rank among the most economically important of the sac fungi. Yeasts are used in the preparation of baked goods and alcohol. The enzymes that yeast cells manufacture are used to promote fermentation of alcohols, raise bread dough, and flavor wines, beers, and ciders. Yeasts are also used to manufacture drugs like ephedrine which is used to treat asthma. Ephedrine, an important ingredient of medicines such as nose drops, is obtained from yeast cultures. Yeast is also a rich source of vitamin B and is used in the production of glycerol for explosives. Yeast is rich in protein and yeast preparations have been used as food additives in the feed of livestock. Another enzyme of yeast called invertase is used in softening the center of chocolate candies after the chocolate coating has been applied.

Several other important diseases result from infestation by sac fungi. Of these, perhaps the best known are chestnut blight and Dutch elm disease. At the turn of the century, the American chestnut tree was a valuable timber tree of the eastern deciduous forest. Its importance was celebrated in song and poems. "Under the spreading chestnut tree, the village smithy worked" is a line once memorized by every student of American literature while "chestnuts roasting on an open fire" is a popular stanza still sung at yuletide festivals. Yet, few, if any, of today's students and singers know or have seen a chestnut tree. The demise of the chestnut tree can be traced to the late 1800's, when a Long Island farmer imported several chestnut trees from Asia for his island estate. Unknown to him, the Asian chestnut trees also carried chestnut blight. The blight soon spread into nearby New York and Connecticut, and by 1917 throughout the whole of the eastern United States. Within a few years all of the once common and widespread chestnut trees had been destroyed throughout the range by the blight. In the 1940's and 1950's another blight devastated the American elm tree. Sometimes called the Dutch elm disease, this sac fungi was inadvertently imported from Europe sometime in the early years of this century. It spread slowly at first, but by mid-century caused the loss of most of America's elm trees. For example, New Haven was nicknamed the "elm city" because its streets were lined with tall, stately elms. The arrival of Dutch elm disease killed the city's elms and its nickname.

CLASS BASIDIOMYCETES—THE CLUB FUNGI

The club fungi include stink horns and mushrooms, toadstools, puffballs, earth stars, shelf or bracket rusts, smuts, jelly fungi, and birds' nest fungi. They are called club fungi because in sexual reproduction, the plant produces spores at the tips of swollen hyphae that resemble baseball bats or clubs. These are called **basidia**. Hyphae are divided into individual cells and each cell has either one or two nuclei. Cross walls of hyphae have a central pore surrounded by swellings and covered by a cap. The cap

Figure 19–7 A powdery mildew. Ascocarp with appendages and detail of single ascus. *Source:* Harold C. Bold and John W. La Claire II. *The Plant Kingdom* (1987), Prentice-Hall, p. 258.

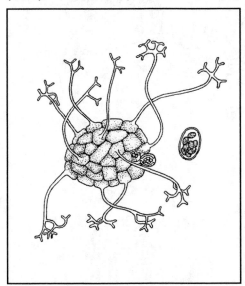

keeps the nuclei apart but allows for cytoplasmic exchange.

Asexual reproduction occurs less frequently in club fungi than in other kinds of fungi. When it does occur, it is mainly by the production of **conidia**, as in sac fungi. A few species produce buds, and a few have hyphae that fragment to produce new individuals.

Sexual reproduction in the club fungi occurs when a spore lands on a suitable substrate. It germinates and produces a mycelium just beneath the surface of the ground. The hyphae of the mycelium are divided into cells each of which contains a single haploid nucleus and is called **monokaryotic hyphae**. They form monokaryotic mycelia that often occur in four mating types, designated by numbers 1,2,3 and 4. Types 1,3 or 2,4 are able to mate with each other. If compatible mating types are brought together, the cells of each mycelium will unite, forming a new mycelium with cells having two nuclei which is then called a **dikaryotic mycelia**. The dikaryotic mycelia usually have little walled-off bypass loops, called **clamp connections,** between the cells on the surface of the hyphae. These develop as a result of a unique type of mitosis that ensures

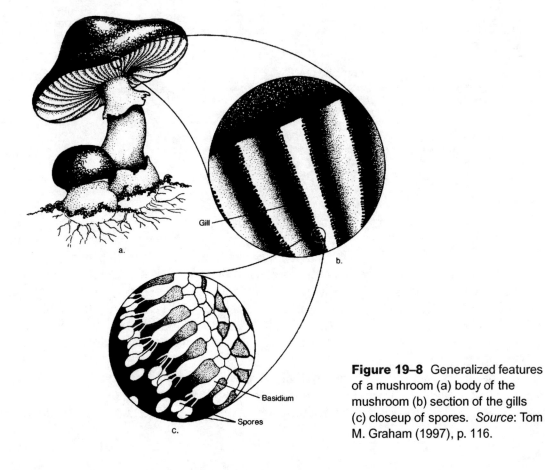

Gill

Basidium

Spores

a.

b.

c.

Figure 19–8 Generalized features of a mushroom (a) body of the mushroom (b) section of the gills (c) closeup of spores. *Source*: Tom M. Graham (1997), p. 116.

Figure 19–9 Life cycle of a typical mushroom. *Source:* Teresa Audesirk and Gerald Audesirk (1999), p. 384.

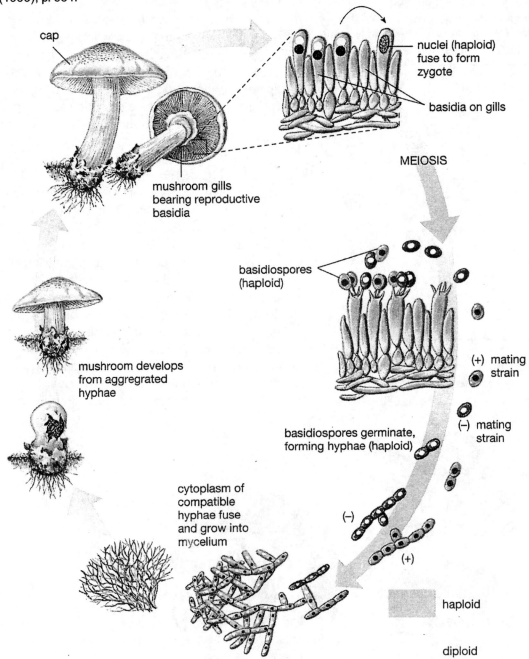

cap

nuclei (haploid) fuse to form zygote

basidia on gills

mushroom gills bearing reproductive basidia

MEIOSIS

basidiospores (haploid)

(+) mating strain

(−) mating strain

mushroom develops from aggregrated hyphae

basidiospores germinate, forming hyphae (haploid)

(−)

(+)

cytoplasm of compatible hyphae fuse and grow into mycelium

haploid

diploid

that each cell will have one nucleus of the original mating type. When the cell at the tip of the dikaryotic hypha is ready to divide, a small looping protuberance appears on the side of the cell and starts to grow backward, bending over itself. As it does so one of the complimentary nuclei migrates into it and both nuclei then undergo mitosis simultaneously. The protuberance fuses back to the cell and a transverse wall forms across it between the daughter nuclei.

Another cross wall forms in the original cell just above the point where the bypass loop has united with it. It forms between the two daughter nuclei of the second original nucleus. When the process has been completed, the hyphae ends up with two cells, each of which has one of the two kinds of nuclei and a walled off clamp connection to one side.

These dikaryotic mycelia may become dense and form a solid mass called a **button**. This button pushes to the surface and expands to form a **basidiocarp** or **mushroom**. Most mushrooms have a **cap** and **stalk**. Some have an **annulus** on the stalk and **gills** in the cap. Gills contain **basidia** at right angles to the flat surface of the gill. As each basidium matures two nuclei unite and undergo meiosis. Four nuclei result to become **basidiospores**. They have tiny pegs (sterigmata) which serve as stalks for the basidiospores. We can use the cap to make a spore print for identification. In nature some of the basidiospores repeat the reproductive cycle. Often dikaryotic mycelia radiate out in an ever expanding circle to make fairy rings.

There are a wide variety of club fungi found in nature. Shelf or bracket fungi grow out horizontally from bark or dead wood. Puffballs produce spores in parchment-like membranes or basidiocarps. They are usually edible and can grow up to 4 ft. in diameter. They are essentially mushrooms that lack a stalk. Thus the cap rests on the ground. Earth stars are like puffballs but they have a ring of appendages at their base that looks like a set of woody petals around a flower. Birds' nest fungus grow on wood or manure. They form nest-like cavities in which basidiospores form in the "eggs". Each "egg" may have a sticky thread attached and when raindrops fall on the nest the "eggs" are splashed out with the sticky thread catching on surrounding vegetation and whipping the "egg" around so that spores are well distributed.

The **smuts** are parasitic club fungi that damage corn, wheat, rye, and other grain crops. They have a mycelium that grows between the cells of the host, absorbing nutriments and stimulating cells to grow and divide, forming tumors on the corn or other grain. They eventually break open to release millions of tiny black spores.

Some smuts affect only the flowering head, while others infect the whole plant. **Rusts** are parasites that attack a wide variety of plants. Some exist on only one species while others require two or more hosts. Black stem rust of wheat has plagued farmers all over the world since wheat was first cultivated. More than 300 species of wheat rust are known. They require two hosts, the common barberry plant and wheat to complete their life cycle. The white pine blister rust parasitizes three hosts during different stages of its life cycle; its basidiospores affect pine trees, and when they germinate other spores are produced that affect currants and gooseberry bushes. An apple rust uses cedar trees as an alternate host and a poplar leaf spot rust depends on larch or tamarack as an alternate host.

Club Fungi Economics

Club fungi have a reputation for being poisonous. Actually there are about 25,000 species of club fungi, and only 75 are known to be poisonous. Unfortunately, many of the poisonous species are common and often hard to distinguish from harmless mushrooms. Many edible forms of mushrooms cause illness when consumed with alcohol. Accidentally eating a mushroom called death's angel causes about 90 percent of all fatalities from club fungi. Within 6-24 hours after eating this mushroom, the person experiences severe stomach ache, blurred vision, and violent vomiting which, if untreated, leads to death.

Harvesting mushrooms should never be done by an amateur since many of the poisonous species look nearly identical to the edible species.

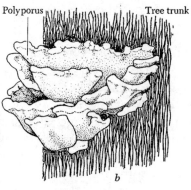

Figure 19–10
Examples of basidiomycota (a) a puffball (b) a shelf fungus. *Source:* Harold C. Bold and John W. La Claire II. *The Plant Kingdom* (1987), Prentice-Hall, p. 261.

There are many old wives' tales about mushrooms. For example, according to folklore, if a silver coin turns black while being cooked with mushrooms, the fungi are poisonous. This is not true. It is also believed that edible species can be peeled while poisonous species cannot be peeled. Again this is not true. Some people believe that poisonous mushrooms occur only in the fall or early spring. This idea is equally false. Some believe that all mushrooms eaten by snails or beetles must be safe. This is not true, as many animals that eat mushrooms have enzymes that allow them to eat what would normally be toxic to us. Other people believe that all purplish colored mushrooms are poisonous. This is also false. It is known that some poisonous mushrooms cause hallucinations and were used in the Mayan civilization. Some hallucinogenic mushrooms are still popular in Central America and teonanacatl (Gods' flesh) is used in rituals and other religious events. Mystics and other visionaries still use fly agaric mushrooms in Russia and India to induce hallucinations and colorful visions.

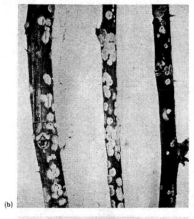
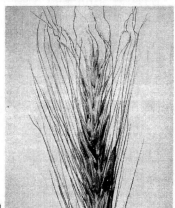

Figure 19–11
Examples of plant smuts (a) blackened grains of oats (b) smuts produce ulcer-like lesions of stems (c and d) ergot disease on rye and wheat. *Source:* Roy H. Saigo and Barbara Saigo. *Botany. Principles and Applications.* (1983), Prentice-Hall, p. 244.

Figure 19–12 Life cycle of the wheat rust (a) part of infected wheat plant (b) germinate and (c) infect other wheat plants (d through g) spores germinate to form basidiospores which infect barberry (h) spores being released from barberry leaf to infect wheat plant again. *Source:* Harold C. Bold and John W. La Claire II. *The Plant Kingdom* (1987), Prentice-Hall, p. 262.

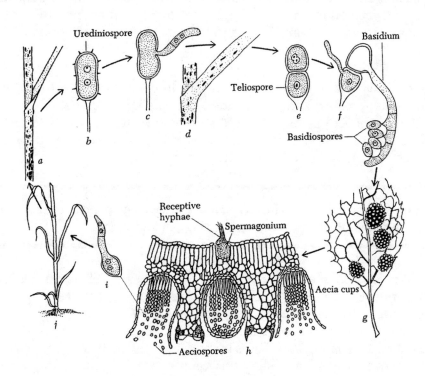

The food value of club fungi is somewhat limited as more than 90 percent of mushroom tissue is water. Despite this, some of the most nutritious mushrooms are the black forest or shiitake mushrooms of China and Japan. These grow on oak logs and are now cultured in the northwestern United States. Shiitake is rich in phosphorus, calcium and iron. The flesh contains lots of vitamin B, D_2 (ergosterol), and vitamin C. These mushrooms also contain high amounts of the nucleic acid RNA, which is reputed to retard the aging process. Another compound in shiitake called lentinacin lowers human cholesterol levels. Shiitake spores are natural antiviral spores that have been used in the treatment of influenza and polio viruses. Lastly, extracts from the shiitake spores cause animal cells to produce interferon, which is used to fight a variety of viral infections.

Club mushrooms have been cultivated since ancient times. In the United States we cultivate *Agaricus bisporus* in basements, caves and abandoned mines. Large operations use windowless warehouses that grow this mushroom on compost made of straw and horse or chicken manure. This fertile mix is pasteurized before use so the danger of disease is minimized. *Agaricus* is the common white mushroom that is widely sold in cans and grocery stores. Most of you have probably encountered it on pizza and in spaghetti sauce.

CLASS DEUTEROMYCETES—THE IMPERFECT FUNGI

The imperfect fungi include all of the fungi species that lack a sexual stage, or in which a sexual stage has not yet been identified. Since we lack information on their life cycle these fungi are called imperfect fungi and are grouped together. Obviously the imperfect fungi is an artificial group as all these organisms probably belong in another taxonomic group.

Whatever their relationships, the imperfect fungi include many well known fungi that are economically important. They reproduce by conidia and some parasitize protozoans and nematodes. Some of the more bizarre imperfect fungi have nematode trapping loops that entrap nematodes and other small worms and eventually squeeze them to death as they feed on them. Other imperfect fungi live in ant nests where the ants actually cultivate them by adding leaves and other plant debris for their nourishment.

Imperfect Fungi Economics

The best known example of an economically important imperfect fungi is *Penicillium* molds which produce antibiotics widely used to fight bacterial infections. Some imperfect fungi produce "smelly cheeses" such as blue, Camembert, Roquefort, Gorgonzola, and Stilton. Their enzymes break down the fat and protein in the milk which gives these cheese their distinctive odor and flavor.

The drug cyclosporine is produced by an imperfect fungi found in the soil and is used to suppress the immune system after organ transplants.

Aspergillus is used to produce many products such as dyes, indelible black ink, artificial flavorings, perfume substances, chlorine, alcohols, plastics, toothpaste, soap and the silvering of mirrors. It is also used to make soy sauce by fermenting soy beans. Miso, a flavoring used in the Orient, is made by fermenting soybeans, salt and rice with *Aspergillus*. The same genus also causes human diseases, such as infections of the respiratory tract and ears. A different genus causes "athletes' foot", ringworm, white piedra (a disease of beard and mustache) and tropical diseases of the hands and feet that cause limbs to swell to grotesque proportions. "Valley Fever" in the dryer areas of the United States is caused by inhaled spores that produce lesions in the upper respiratory tract and lungs. One form of imperfect fungi is used for pest control of scale insects in Florida. Another fungus may be used to control water hyacinths in the future.

Figure 19-13. The imperfect fungus *Penicillium* growing on an orange. *Source:* Teresa Audesirk and Gerald Audesirk (1999), p. 385.

Lichens are actually a symbiotic association of a fungus and algae mixed in a spongy body called a **thallus**. A thallus is a non-vascular plant body with no true roots, stems or leaves. Together, the fungus and symbiotic partner range in size from less than an inch to giants that may reach over six feet in diameter. Through photosynthesis, the algae provides the food while the fungus is the supportive and protective partner. The fungus also absorbs water and minerals for both itself and the algae..

There are about 25,000 kinds of lichens known throughout the world. The algae symbiont is a green algae, or a blue-green bacteria, or in some cases both. Some species of algae occur in several kinds of lichens but the species of fungus in each lichen is always different. The vast majority of the fungi involved are sac fungi but some are club fungi. They can be separated and cultured without the algae in an attempt to identify the species. The algae can be found in nature as a free agent but the fungus rarely occurs in nature without the algae.

Lichens grow slowly and can live for several thousand years. The oldest lichen found was estimated to be about 4,500 years old. Lichens are very tolerant of severe environmental conditions, and most are especially resistant to extreme heat and cold. They can live on bare rocks in the blazing heat of the desert and also in permafrost regions. Lichens have the ability to survive due to a gelatinous substance in the thallus of the fungus. This enables them to withstand loss of most of their body water (up to 98 percent) without dying. Although lichens are very hardy in some respects they are very sensitive to pollution and tend to disappear completely in industrial areas.

In structure, a lichen thallus consists of three or four layers of cells or hyphae. At the surface is a protective layer called the **upper cortex**. Hyphae are so compressed in the thallus that they resemble parenchyma and it is here that the gelatinous layer is located. Just below the upper cortex is the algal layer with the algae. Below this layer is a **medulla** formed from loosely packed hyphae for food storage. Below the medulla is a **lower cortex** similar to the upper cortex but thinner and has anchoring rhizomes to hold it to the substrate.

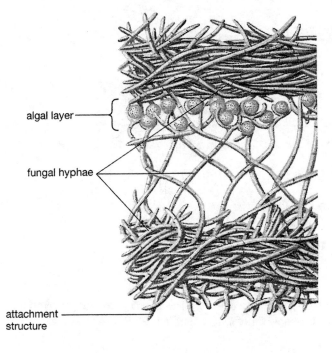

algal layer

fungal hyphae

attachment structure

Figure 19–14 The structure of a lichen. *Source:* Teresa Audesirk and Gerald Audesirk (1999), p. 385.

Lichens occur in several kinds of growth forms. The **crustose** lichens are attached to the substrate over the entire lower surface. Thus they form a tightly adhered crust over the surface of many rocks. **Foliose** lichens are a leaf-like thallus which overlaps others. They are weakly attached to the substrate, and the edges are frequently crinkly or divided into lobes resembling leaves (hence the name foliage/foliose). Lastly, **fruticose** lichens look like miniature upright shrubs or may hang down from branches. The thalli are branched and cylindrical in form.

Lichens reproduce sexually when the fungus symbiont undergoes sexual reproduction. In about one-third of the lichens, small powdery clusters of hyphae and algae called **soredia** are formed and pinched off from the thallus in a set pattern as they are grown. They are scattered by wind and rain. The fungus produces ascocarps as in other sac fungi, except spores are continually being produced. Algae produce by fission.

Lichen extracts are used as a perfume for scented soaps.

LICHEN ECONOMICS

Lichens are food for many animals, reindeer, caribou, and sheep. They are also important food supplements for humans. In some cultures, lichens are common ingredients in soups and laxatives. Some have antibiotic properties and one type is even used to treat tuberculosis. Others are used in the manufacture of salves for cuts and burns. They were a major source of dyes in the past and are still used in that fashion to a minor degree. Their use as dye was especially prevalent with Greeks, Romans and Native Americans.

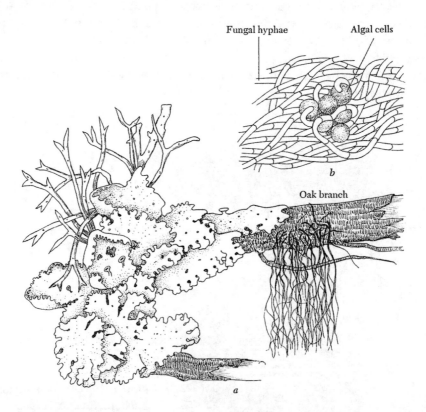

Figure 19–15 Lichens (a) on an oak branch (b) alga cells of a lichen within the fungal hyphae. *Source:* Harold C. Bold and John W. La Claire II. *The Plant Kingdom* (1987), Prentice-Hall, p. 265.

Lichens are still used to manufacture Scottish tweeds and litmus paper. A major use for lichens today is as scenery in model railroads and architectural models.

Key Words and Phrases

hyphae	mycelium	slime molds
plasmodium	thallus	rusts
coenocytic	antheridia	gametangia
sac fungi	club fungi	imperfect fungi
budding	ascocarp	ascospores
basidia	dikaryotic	clamp connections
cap	stalk	annulus
gills	lichens	smuts
crustose body type	foliose body type	fruticose body type
water molds	chytrids	true fungi
sporangium	spores	capillitium
myxamoeba	swarm cells	zoospores
pseudoplasmodium	rhizoids	zygospore
conidiospores	conidia	asci
hymenium	budding	
monokaryotic hyphae	dikaryotic mycelia	

Selected References and Resources

Ainsworth, G. C., and C. Bisby. 1983. *Dictionary of the Fungi*. 7th. Edition. Lubrecht and Cramer. Forestburg, New York.

Allen, M. F. 1991. *The Ecology of Mycorrhizae*. Cambridge University Press. New York.

Bold, H. C., C. J. Alexopoulos, and T. Delevoryas. 1987. Morphology of Plants and Fungi. 5th Edition. Harper and Row. New York.

Chiu, S., and D. Moore. 1996. *Patterns in Fungal Development*. Cambridge University Press. New York.

Courtenay, B., and H. H. Burdsall, Jr. 1984. *A Field Guide to Mushrooms and their Relatives*. Van Nostrand Reinhold. New York.

Deacon, J. W. 1984. *Introduction to Modern Mycology*. 2nd. Edition. Blackwall Scientific Publications. Menlo Park, California.

Deverall, B. J. 1969. *Fungal Parasitism*. Institute of Biology Study Number 17. Edward Arnold. London.

Frankland, J. C., N. Magan, and G. M. Gadd. 1996. *Fungi and Environmental Change*. Cambridge University Press. New York.

Griffin, D. H. 1981. *Fungal Parasitism*. Wiley. New York.

Hale, M. E. 1983. *The Biology of Lichens*. Edward Arnold. London.

Jennings, D. H. 1995. *The Physiology of Fungal Nutrition*. Cambridge University Press. New York.

Miller, O.K., Jr., and D. F. Farr. 1985. *An Index of the Common Fungi of North America*. Lubrecht and Cramer. Forestburgh, New York.

Moore-Landecker, E. 1982. *Fundamentals of the Fungi*. 2nd Edition. Prentice-Hall. Englewood Cliffs, New Jersey.

Nash, T. H. 1996. *Lichen Biology*. Cambridge University Press. New York.

Rinaldi, A., and V. Tyndalo. 1974. *The Complete Book of Mushrooms*. Crown Publishers. New York.

Sutton, B. C. 1996. *A Century of Mycology*. Cambridge University Press. New York.

Webster, J. 1980. *Introduction to the Fungi*. 2nd Edition. Cambridge University Press. New York.

Review and Discussion Questions

1. Name the basic divisions of fungi and their characteristics.
2. How do fungi reproduce sexually? How do they reproduce asexually?
3. Describe the life cycle of a club fungi, distinguishing between haploid and diploid states.
4. Why do we consider a lichen to be an excellent example of symbiosis? What other examples of symbiosis have we seen in the plant kingdom so far?
5. Why are the bacteria and algae so different that they are not included in the same kingdom with the fungi? Why are the plants also in a different kingdom? The animals?
6. Exactly how do most of the fungi obtain their food? What are the physiological processes involved?
7. Define the following terms: ascus, ascospore, ascocarp, basidiospore.
8. What is the economic value of the lichens to humans?
9. What is the economic value of the fungi to humans?
10. Describe the life cycle of wheat rust.

Chapter 20

Nonvascular Plants: The Bryophytes

Liverworts
> *Marchantia*—A Typical Liverwort

Hornworts

Mosses

Economic Importance of the Bryophytes

Land plants first appeared nearly 400 million years ago. The earliest land plants known included two distinctive groups, the bryophytes and the vascular plants. Simple representatives of both of these early groups are similar in many respects to green algae, indicating their evolutionary ties with both them and the monerans.

Like the green algae, both bryophytes and vascular plants have pigments such as chlorophyll *a* and *b*, and the carotenoids. Like algae, they also stored food in the form of starch. The cellulose in their cell walls is similar, as is the development of phragmoplasts and cell plates.

The early evolution of land plants was facilitated by the development of several important adaptations for a terrestrial existence including (1) an outer cuticle for protection against desiccation in air, (2) numerous stomata for gas exchange in tissues, leaves, and stems to regulate air and water vapor flow, (3) one or more protective layers of sterile cells surrounding and protecting the reproductive cells, and (4) an embryo that develops deep within the safety of the tissues of the gametophyte. These last two features are perhaps the most significant and innovative adaptations for terrestrial plants. That the new embryo is retained within parent tissues dramatically increases its chances of survival. In contrast, reproduction in algae, fungi and bacteria results in the release of an unprotected zygote which is far more vulnerable to injury, predation, and desiccation.

Members of the Kingdom Plantae also have a greater structural organization and diversity than found in Monera, Fungi, and Algae. They have specialized tissues for photosynthesis, conduction, support, anchorage, and protection. Sexual reproduction is the primary method of reproduction. In contrast, asexual reproduction is much more limited in scope than in protistans and monerans. In most advanced groups the sporophyte generation is dominant, but in some of the more primitive land plants the gametophyte is retained as the dominant, leafy structure.

Early in their evolution, two basic lines of land plants developed; the bryophytes and the vascular plants. The bryophytes are considered the most primitive members of the plant kingdom. They lack vascular tissues such as xylem and phloem and are

Figure 20–1 A generalized life cycle of the bryophytes exemplified by moss. *Source:* Tom M. Graham (1997), p. 355.

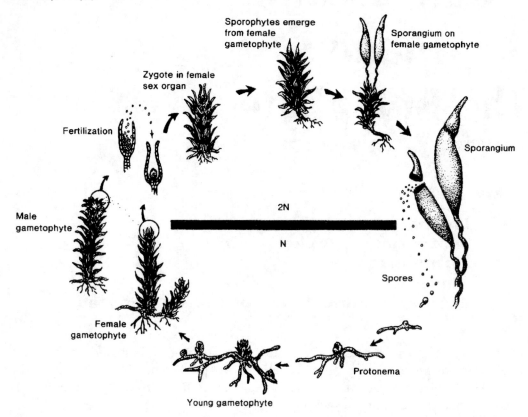

classes as nonvascular plants. In contrast, all higher plants such as the club mosses, ferns, conifers and flowering plants have xylem and phloem vascular tissues and are therefore classed as vascular plants.

Introduction to the Bryophyta

The bryophytes number about 16,000 species of mostly small plants, including the mosses, hornworts, and liverworts. Although widely distributed on a global scale, most bryophytes are ecologically limited to wetter habitats such as marshes, bogs, edges of ponds and other wetlands as they require some form of water such as droplets of rain or dew to facilitate reproduction. All bryophytes can reproduce by **oogamy** and thus the water serves as a medium for the sperm to swim through to reach the egg. In addition to lacking vascular tissue, bryophytes also lack true roots, stems or leaves, although they may have leaf-like, stem-like, and root-like organs which perform the same functions. Because bryophytes lack vascular tissue they are limited in size, and most are only a few centimeters tall. Although bryophytes are generally found in cool, shaded, and moist habitats many of them can withstand long periods in desiccation by becoming quiescent or in the form of resistant structures.

The life cycle of bryophytes includes an **alternation of generation**. The haploid **gametophyte** is the dominant stage in the life cycle. In bryophytes, as in higher plants, the gametophyte is derived from the germination of a spore and gives rise at maturity to the formation of male and female gametes. Both male and female gametophytes may be on the same plant in some species, but in others there are separate male and female plants.

In bryophytes, the male sex organ is called an **antheridium** and consists of several protective layers of cells surrounding a central mass of sex cells that give rise to sperm. The sperm are liberated with the disintegration of the antheridial walls.

The female sex organ, called the **archegonium,** is a vase-shaped structure that contains a single egg located within the base or **venter**. When water is present, the sperm swim from the antheridium and enter the canal-like neck of the archegonium to fertilize the egg. Chemical secretions produced by the archegonium help guide the sperm to the egg. When the sperm and egg gametes unite, a diploid **zygote** is formed. The zygote represents the first stage of the sporophyte generation, which grows as a stalk rising above the gametophyte plant. The sporophyte acts as a kind of parasite on the gametophyte plant, using it for support and as a source of nutrients. Cells towards the apex of the sporophyte stalk undergo meiosis to produce haploid spores which disperse in water at maturation. The haploid spores germinate to give rise to the comparatively prominent gametophyte green plant.

The bryophytes are sometimes called the amphibians of the plant world. Like frogs and toads, which can live on land but must return to water to reproduce, bryophytes must live only in wetlands and moist areas, as their flagellated sperm need water to swim to the egg during reproduction.

Mosses are the best known and most common of the bryophytes. *Sphagnum* moss, also called bog or **peat moss**, is one of the most economically important bryophytes, and also one of the most common and widespread species. *Sphagnum* moss is a transitional non-vascular plant that forms the green covering on damp banks, trees, and shaded logs. It often grows in thick, floating mats on quiet water and along the edges of wetlands, ponds, and lakes. Hardy and wide-ranging, *Sphagnum* mosses have been found from sea level to high mountain elevations. A few species are very restricted; some only grow on reindeer bones and antlers, or on the backs of large tropical insects for example. All *Sphagnum* mosses have mycorrhizal fungi associated with their rhizoids in a symbiotic relationship. This moss can grow so thick and intertwined that it can support the weight of an animal or small person. It was originally used for bandages in World War I as it has antiseptic properties.

Class Hepaticae — Liverworts

Liverworts are interesting small plants generally less than one 20 cm in size. They commonly grow in wetlands and along the edges of ponds. Liverworts are sometimes plentiful in bogs, along small brooks and creeks, and a few species live on the open water surface.

Liverworts comprise the second largest group of bryophytes and include about 8,000 known species. Two broad groups of liverworts include the broadly flattened liverworts represented by *Marchantia* and the leafy liverworts such as *Porella*. We will discuss the life cycle and characteristics of liverworts using *Marchantia*, a typical representative of this group.

Figure 20–2 Vegetative structure of *Porella,* a leafy liverwort (a) female plant with dehiscent sporophytes (b) closeup view of same (c) male plant. *Source:* Harold C. Bold and John W. La Claire II. *The Plant Kingdom* (1987), Prentice-Hall, p. 79.

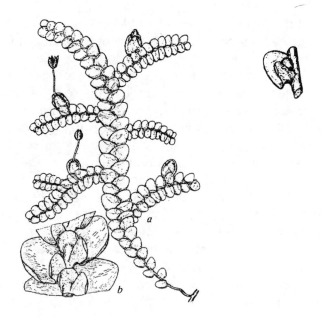

MARCHANTIA—A TYPICAL LIVERWORT

Marchantia is a common plant found along stream banks and in areas where there is constant high humidity, such as in fog zones. This liverwort can also often be found in the damp soil in fire-burned areas.

Like all liverworts, *Marchantia* has a thin, flattened, green lobate body called a **thallus**, which develops directly from spores. The thallus has a smooth, rather leaf-like upper surface and underneath develops rootlike **rhizoids** for anchorage. The liverwort thallus is about 30 cells thick at the center and tapers to about 10 cells thick at the margins. The thallus forks dichotomously as it grows and each branch has a notch at the apex with a central groove behind it. Meristematic cells located at the notches add new growth while older tissues behind the meristem decay. The surface of the thallus is divided into polygonal **segments** which outline chambers deep within the thallus. Each thallus segment has a small **pore** opening into the interior of the chamber below.

A cross section through one of these **chambers** reveals substrate **parenchyma cells** which are used to store food. Between the layers of parenchyma cells and the lower epidermis are branching rows of **chlorenchyma cells** along with aerenchyma cells. The

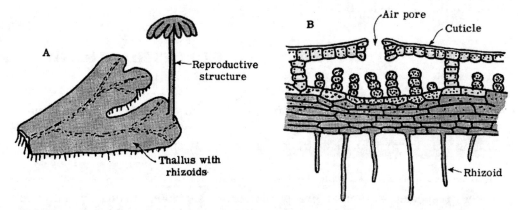

Figure 20–3 Details of the structure of a liverwort (a) thallus with rhizoids and reproductive structures (b) cross section of thallus. *Source:* Lorus J. Milne and Margery Milne. *Plant Life* (1959), Prentice-Hall, p. 141.

Figure 20-4 Details of the liverwort *Marchantia* (a) female plant with archegoniophores (b) male plant with antheridiophore and gemma cup (c) detail of antheridiophore showing antheridia (d) portion of archegoniophore showing the archegonia (e) egg and sperm in archegonium at time of fertilization. *Source:* Harold C. Bold and John W. La Claire II. *The Plant Kingdom* (1987), Prentice-Hall, p. 78.

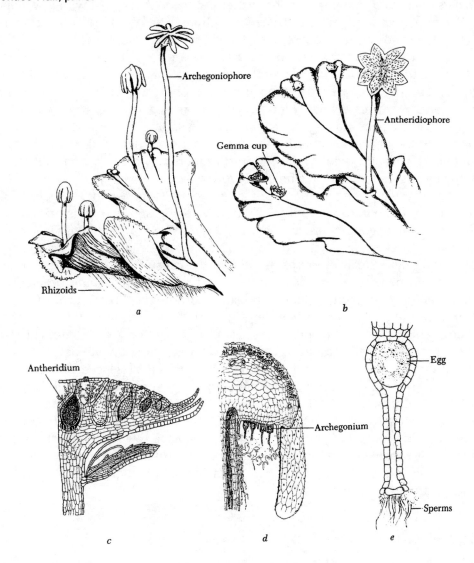

aerenchyma provide large spaces which form air chambers. The whole area opens to the exterior by a pore that remains open all the time.

MARCHANTIA LIFE CYCLE

Marchantia may reproduce asexually or sexually. When reproducing asexually certain cells on the surface of the thallus mitotically divide to produce small groups of cells called **gemmae.** The gemmae are individual disc-like structures that are retained in small **gemmae cups** on the surface of the thallus. Raindrops dislodge the gemmae and throw them outwards, a yard or more away from the original thallus. Following this unique form of dispersal, the gemmae grows into a new thallus. An alternate form of asexual reproduction may occur when the older thallus dies and the scattered fragments of its surviving tissue each develop into a separate thallus.

Sexual reproduction occurs when the thallus develops highly specialized **gametangia**. Male and female gametangia are produced on separate thalli called **gametophytes**. The individual gametangia are produced on the end of a stalk called a **gametophore**. These gametophores resemble umbrellas on slender stalks rising from a central groove in the thallus. The male gametangium or **antheridiophore** is disc-like with a scalloped margin. The female counterpart, the **archegoniophore,** resembles the hub and spokes of a wagon wheel and are more deeply lobed than the antheridiophore.

Sperm producing organs called **antheridia** grow in the interior of the anteridiophore. Each antheridia contains rows of **sperm** just beneath the upper surface. **Archegonia**, form on the underside of the archegoniophore and are vase-like in shape. Each archegonia produces a single female **egg**. The archegonia are arranged in rows that hang with their necks facing down beneath the spokes of the archegoniophore. Raindrops wash the flagellated sperm from the antheridia. They land on the archegonia of another thallus and swim to the egg. Fertilization may actually occur before the stalks of the archegoniophores have finished growing.

Fertilization results in the formation of a **zygote** which grows into a multicellular embryo called an immature **sporophyte**. This developing sporophyte is anchored in the tissues of the archegoniophore by means of a knob-like **foot** and hangs suspended by a stalk called a **seta**. The main structure of the archegonium which contains the immature sporophyte is called a **capsule**. Within the capsule are **spore mother cells** that will undergo meiosis. Some of these cells will remain diploid and develop into elaters. **Elaters** are elongated structures sensitive to humidity. They turn, twist, and untwist in response to changes in humidity. Their actions push the spores out of the sporangium, which serves to disperse spores. The growing zygote is encased in an outer layer of cells called the **calyptra**, which grows from gametophyte tissue. This is a thin sterile protective sheath that is discarded as the spores are released. **Spores** are liberated and travel by wind currents. When they find fertile ground they will germinate producing new gametophyte thalli.

Not all liverworts are like *Marchantia* in structure. Some leafy liverworts are common in tropical jungles and fog belts. Leafy liverworts have two rows of partially overlapping thalli. The thalli have folds and lobes on them and form little water traps that animals can drink out of. In some cases these thalli may function like the pitchers of pitcher plants and trap insects.

Class Anthocerotae — The Hornworts

The hornworts represent a much smaller group of bryophytes than the liverworts, numbering only about 100 species. Many species are common and widespread. Most hornworts live on or in moist soil that is shaded by grasses and herbs. Structurally, hornworts resemble liverworts but have a larger, more slender stem-like sporophyte rising from the thallus. The slender sporophyte resembles a miniature cow horn, hence the name given to this group.

Hornworts also differ from liverworts in having a single large chloroplast in each cell and pyrenoids which store starches. The prominent sporophyte has a central column of sterile tissue called the **columella**. A spore capsule develops at the apex of the sporophyte. At maturity, the capsule dehisces into two halves, exposing **tetrads of spores**. Each spore contains coiled **elater** cells which launch the spores outward.

The hornwort thallus is similar to that of liverworts and is also comprised of gametophyte tissue. The thallus has numerous pores and cavities filled with **mucilage** grow-

Figure 20–5 A typical hornwort. *Source:* Harold C. Bold and John W. La Claire II. *The Plant Kingdom* (1987), Prentice-Hall, p. 80.

ing on its surface. The mucilage filled cavities hold colonies of nitrogen-fixing blue-green algae such as *Nostoc* which live in a symbiotic relationship with the hornworts. Extending beneath each thallus are filamentous **rhizoids** which anchor the hornwort and absorb water and minerals from the substrate.

Hornworts reproduce asexually by fragmentation or separation of individual lobes from the thallus. Sexual reproduction is more complex and differs somewhat from that seen in the liverworts. During sexual reproduction, **archegonia** and **antheridia** are produced in rows lying just beneath the surface of the gametophyte. Some plants are dioecious (both male and female sex cells) and others are monoecious (possessing only male or female sex cells). Following fertilization, the **zygote** develops into a sporophyte that remains attached to the upper thallus, as in liverworts.

The sporophytes have numerous stomata and no setae. A **meristem** above the **foot** of the sporophyte continually increases the length of the sporophyte from the base. As growth occurs, spore mother cells surrounding a central rod-like axis in the sporophyte horn split into two or three ribbon-like segments, releasing spores. The segments continue to peel back and release spores as long as the meristem continues to produce new tissue.

Class Musci — The Mosses

The word "moss" is a common name and is often misused to refer to lichens, red algae, and flowering plants like Spanish moss and club mosses. The true mosses constitute the largest and most diverse group of bryophytes, and number about 15,000 different species. *Sphagnum* and some other true mosses have specialized tissue called **hydroids** located in the center of the stem-like plant for the conduction of water and minerals. Around the hydroids are a system of food conducting cells called **leptoids**. Because there is no vascular tissue, *Sphagnum* is soft and pliable. It is used by many birds in their nests. Like liverworts, the life cycle of mosses includes an alternation of generations. The leafy plant stage that we commonly see is part of the haploid gametophyte generation and produces gametes. The sporophyte stage in which spores are produced is represented by a capsule located on a stalk called a **seta** which grows out of the tip of the gametophyte. The peat mosses include *Sphagnum* which has already been discussed. A smaller group includes the rock mosses which exhibit an encrusting growth pattern.

The moss gametophyte thallus differs from other bryophytes in having leaf-like projections from the stem. These differ from true leaves as they have no mesophyll, stomata or veins. The blades have a midrib and their cells contain lens-shaped chloroplasts. Although they are not true leaves they function like leaves as they produce food for the plant and represent an evolutionary developmental stage towards the formation of true leaves. In peat mosses the leaves have large water storage cells within and green photosynthetic cells between the storage cells. The moss leaf-like structures are

Figure 20–6 Females (a) and male plants of the moss plant *Polytrichum*. *Source:* Harold C. Bold and John W. La Claire II. *The Plant Kingdom* (1987), Prentice-Hall, p. 84.

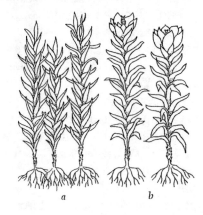

arranged in three rows and appear to spiral along the axis.

The axis is stem-like but has no xylem or phloem. Instead, there is a column of **hydroids** at the center. These are special cells in which the water travels in the cells on the outside of the central stele by capillary action. Because the capillary action created by the hydroid system is not very strong, the mosses are never more than 3 inches high, since the water cannot be carried above this height.

Asexual eproduction in mosses occurs by fragmentation as in other bryophytes. All parts of the moss can vegetatively reproduce. Sexual reproduction begins with the formation of multicellular gametangia at the apex of each leafy shoot of the gametophyte. Both male and female gametangia are produced on the same plant. The archegonia is vase-like in shape and projects upward from the base of the expanded gametophyte tip. Cells on the underside of the archegonium form a structure called a **venter** in which there is a cavity where a single egg cell is developed. The area above the cavity is called a **neck**, and may taper toward the tip. Within the long neck is a narrow **canal**. Many archegonia are produced at the same time with sterile filaments called **paraphyses**

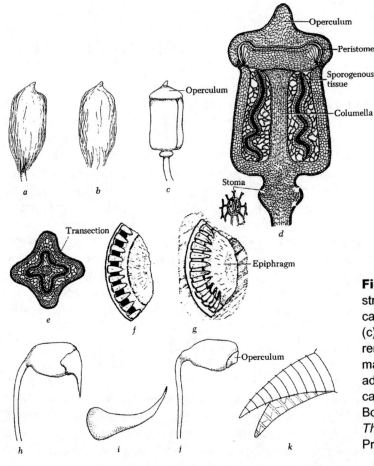

Figure 20–7 The capsule structure of a moss (a and b) capsule covered with calyptra (c) capsule with calyptra removed (d) section of maturing capsule (e through k) additional details of maturing capsule. *Source:* Harold C. Bold and John W. La Claire II. *The Plant Kingdom* (1987), Prentice-Hall, p. 89.

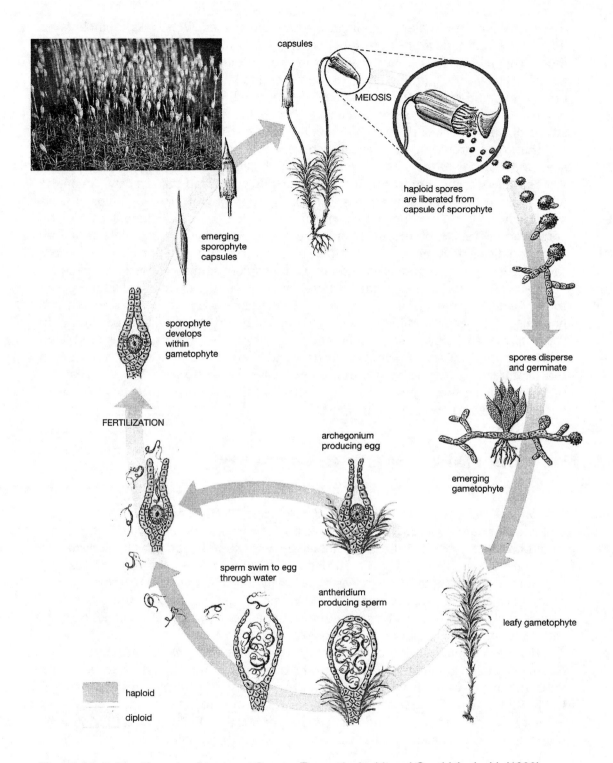

capsules

MEIOSIS

haploid spores
are liberated from
capsule of sporophyte

emerging
sporophyte
capsules

spores disperse
and germinate

sporophyte
develops
within
gametophyte

FERTILIZATION

emerging
gametophyte

archegonium
producing egg

sperm swim to egg
through water

antheridium
producing sperm

leafy gametophyte

haploid

diploid

Figure 20–8 The life cycle of a moss. *Source:* Teresa Audesirk and Gerald Audesirk (1999), p. 398.

between them. The male gametangia are sausage-shaped with walls a single layer thick. These antheridia are born on short stalks and also have paraphyses between them. The internal tissue forms coil-shaped sperm cells. Masses of sperm are forced out of the top as the antheridium takes up water and swells. The internal sperm mass breaks up and these flagellated cells are attracted to the archegonia. The archegonia have produced sugars, proteins and acids which guide the sperm to the egg. A sperm swims down the neck of the venter and unites with the egg to form a zygote.

The zygote grows rapidly into an embryo which breaks down the archegonial tissues and attaches to the stem by a swollen knob-like foot. The embryo continues to grow as a developing sporophyte. It forms a **capsule** with a cap called a **calyptra** on the top. When the sporophyte is mature, cells of the sporophyte carry on photosynthesis but depend on the gametophyte for some of its food. It is parasitic in nature just like the corresponding stage of the liverwort. The mature sporophyte capsule has a tiny rimmed lid called an **operculum** located under the calyptra. In the capsule are spore mother cells undergoing meiosis and producing haploid spores. These spores are produced by the millions. They escape through openings in the capsule, called the **peristome**. Encircling the peristome is a row of peristome teeth which are sensitive to humidity. Changes in humidity result in the opening and closing of the peristome. In some species the capsule splits open and no peristome is present. Spores are blown away in the wind. They land on the substrate and if conditions are correct, a fine green tubular thread of cells called the **protonema** will develop from each spore. Leaf-like buds form along the length of the protonema and they develop rhizoids at the base. Each grows into a new leafy gametophyte.

Economic Importance of the Bryophytes

Bryophytes are important pioneers and colonizers of bare areas and become soil builders. They are important in the colonization of barren areas during ecology succession. Bryophytes are often the first plants to appear when the land has been disturbed and the previous plant life has been destroyed. When it rains, bryophytes soak up moisture, retaining it and then releasing it slowly into the soil. Through this process, bryophytes also help reduce flooding and erosion. They are also an important food source in alpine and arctic areas, where they are a dietary staple of reindeer, caribou, moose, lemmings, and ground squirrels.

The most economically important bryophytes are *Sphagnum*, the peat mosses. Because they have numerous large water holding cells in the leaflets, they can retain vast amounts of water. For example, about two pounds of peat moss can absorb and hold 55 lbs of water! Nurseries and gardeners use bryophytes as soil conditioners. They exhibit a natural acidity and when mixed with the soil they inhibit bacterial and fungal growth. Peat deposits are locally common in the northern half of the world and are

Table 20-1 A classification of the bryophytes.

Class	Representative Examples	Typical characteristics
Hepaticae	liverworts	lack a filamentous stage
Anthocerotae	hornworts	archegonia embedded in thallus
Musci	mosses	have a filamentous stage

mined for the peat, which is burned for fuel. Peat is also a component used in the curing process for malt whiskey.

Key Words and Phrases

peristome	protonema	thallus
rhizoids	columella	capsule
elator	operculum	calyptra
operculum	foot	neck
paraphysis	hydroids	leptoids
archegonia	antheredia	alternation of generations

Selected References and Resources

Bold, H. C., C. J. Alexopoulos, and T. Delevoryas. 1987. *Morphology of Plants and Fungi.* 5th Edition. Harper & Row. New York.

Clarke, G. C. S., and J. G. Duckett. Eds. 1980. *Bryophyte Systematics.* Academic Press. San Diego, California.

Crum, H. A., and L. E. Anderson. 1981. *Mosses of Eastern North America.* Columbia University Press. New York.

Richardson, D. H. S. 1981. *The Biology of Mosses.* Wiley. New York.

Schuster, R. M. 1974. *The Hepaticae and Anthocerotae of North America.* 4 Volumes. Columbia University Press. New York.

Smith, A. J. Ed. 1982. *Bryophyte Ecology.* Routledge, Chapman, and Hall. New York.

Vitt, D. H., and S. R. Gradstein. 1983. *Compendium of Bryology.* Lubrecht and Cramer. Forestburgh, New York.

Watson, E. V. 1971. *The Structure and Life of Bryophytes.* Hutchinson University Library.

Review and Discussion Questions

1. Describe the key features that permitted the invasion of land by the early plants.
2. What features suggest that the bryophytes as a group are the most primitive members of the plant kingdom?
3. What are the similarities and differences between the bryophytes and the algae? Why do we think that they are descendants of the algae?
4. Why are mosses relatively unimportant as terrestrial plants, especially in inland and semiarid areas?
5. How do mosses spread and colonize new areas?
6. Why are bryophytes typically small and confined to cool and wet habitats?

Chapter 21

Lower Vascular Plants

Whisk Ferns
Club Mosses and Quillworts
Horsetails and Scouring Rushes
Ferns
Lower Vascular Plants in the Fossil Record

We have seen that bryophytes are a group of relatively small nonvascular plants forming the basic structures of the land plants that were to follow. Bryophytes lacked true leaves, stems, roots, vascular bundles, and large size. Beginning in Silurian times, the invasion of land by plants greatly accelerated. Not only did a number of vascular plants appear, but many were larger and structurally more advanced than the bryophytes.

With the development of vascular tissue provided the conducting mechanism that enabled plants such as flowers, trees and shrubs to flourish. In order for these terrestrial plants to attain great size and become upright, they needed stems and leaves in order to increase the leafy surface area available for photosynthesis. They also needed a conduction system for water and food since the bryophyte hydroids could not efficiently conduct large amounts of fluid very high (thus effectively limiting the size that the bryophytes could attain).

As their name implies the vascular plants are so-called because they have vascular conducting tissues, the xylem and phloem. This efficient conduction system allowed plants to achieve larger size as water could be carried higher against the pull of gravity. Large plants also require efficient roots for anchoring the plant and for the absorption of water and nutriments. With the evolutionary appearance of these structures in the early vascular plants, all of the necessary requirements for living in terrestrial environments were fulfilled, and the first vascular plants thrived and radiated out to occupy many terrestrial niches. Although they can survive in varying environments, all of the lower vascular plants have one thing in common; they reproduce by spores. None of the members of this group produce seeds, a major advancement which we will see becomes characteristic of the higher vascular plants.

The lower vascular plants first appeared about 400 million years ago, long before the age of the dinosaurs. Their descendants survive today in the form of the whisk ferns, horsetails, and ferns. Unlike bryophytes in which the gametophyte stage is the dominant and conspicuous plant, in all of the vascular plants the sporophyte stage is the dominant form.

Figure 21–1 A generalized life cycle of the lower vascular plants showing alternation between the haploid gametophyte generation and the diploid sporophyte generation. Source: Tom M. Graham (1997), p. 356.

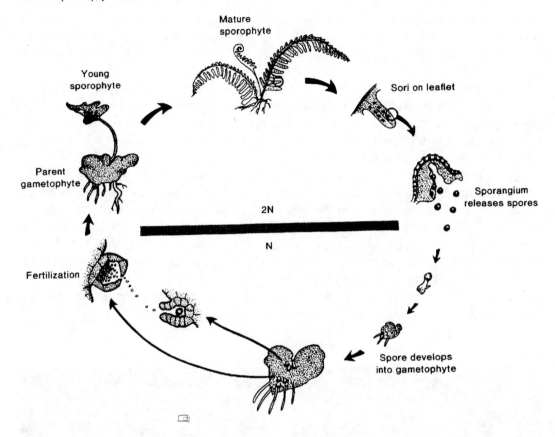

Seed and Nonseed Vascular Plants

Taxonomically, vascular plants are subdivided into major groups according to the type of propagule that they produce. Nonseed vascular plants such as the ferns produce spores. In contrast, seed vascular plants such as the gymnosperms and flowering plants reproduce using seeds.

Also called the lower vascular plants, the ferns and their allies are the subject of this chapter. They are subdivided into four major groups on the basis of the type of spores that they produce.

Whisk ferns, horsetails, a few club mosses and some ferns are called **homosporous** nonvascular plants because they produce only one kind of spore in a single sporangium. Once produced, the spore cells divide into bisexual gametophytes that contain both the male antheridia and the female archegonia.

In contrast, most of the club mosses, ferns and all of the vascular seed plants produce two distinct kinds of spores and are called **heterosporous**. The two kinds of spores produced are microspores, which develop into male gametophytes, and much larger megaspores, which become the female gametes.

Division Psilophyta—The Whisk Ferns

The whisk ferns exist today as a small group of vascular plants but they are believed to have been the dominant plants on land during the Silurian and Devonian ages of about 350 million years ago when some reached tree size and formed extensive woodlands and forests of whisk ferns.

The life cycle of whisk ferns is reversed from that seen in bryophytes. In mosses, the sporophyte is restricted to a capsule, parasitically growing on the thallus of the gametophyte. In contrast, in whisk ferns the sporophyte is the dominant stage in the life cycle; the gametophyte is still a separate stage, but is usually small, short-lived and rather insignificant in appearance.

The whisk ferns are the simplest of all vascular plants. The sporophyte has neither true leaves nor roots but consists of stems and rhizomes that fork evenly around the stem. They are found primarily in the tropical and subtropical regions of the world. In the United States whisk ferns are mostly limited to the southern tier along the Gulf Coast, from Florida across Louisiana and into Texas, Arizona and Hawaii. Whisk ferns are also extensively cultivated in Japan where they are harvested to make tatami mats. A close relative, *Tmesipteris*, is from Australia.

The extensive fossil record of the Psilophytes group of whisk ferns dates from the Silurian and Devonian times. Organisms like *Rhynia* and *Zosterophyllum* represent the

Figure 21–2 Examples of seedless vascular plants (a) club mosses (b) scouring rushes (c) ferns. *Source:* Teresa Audesirk and Gerald Audesirk (1999), p. 400.

Figure 21–3 Cross section of the stem of a whisk fern (a) general cross section (b) magnified stele in center. *Source:* Harold C. Bold and John W. La Claire II. *The Plant Kingdom* (1987), Prentice-Hall, p. 122.

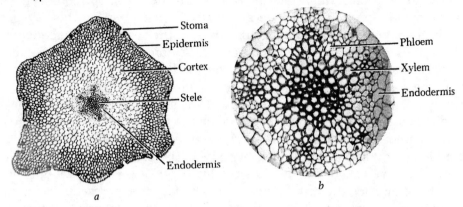

earliest vascular land plants known. They were like the modern *Psilotum* in form, but the fossil record ends and a huge 400 million year gap exists between them and the modern forms. One of the great mysteries of paleobotany is what happened to Psilophytes. They had an extensive fossil record in the lower Paleozoic Era and then nothing! Yet today there are but a few living species.

Once of the most common whisk ferns today, *Psilotum*, has a body form consisting of a simple green upright **stem** arising from **rhizomes** and covered with **stomata**. Within the stem is an undifferentiated **protostele** with **primary xylem** and **phloem**. **Cortex** appears around the outside of the protostele. The stems may be branching and are about one foot in length. They arise from underground stems or rhizomes with short rhizoids on them. The rhizomes and rhizoids have the same internal structure as the upright stems. Although leaves are lacking in the whisk ferns, the stems have small bumps, called **enations**, over their surface. The purpose of these may be to increase the surface area of the stem for photosynthesis. The vascular stele is a central column

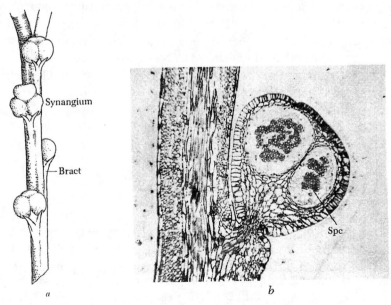

Figure 21–4 Whisk fern stem with synangia (a) stem (b) micrograph of a synangium with sporocytes in the center. *Source:* Harold C. Bold and John W. La Claire II. *The Plant Kingdom* (1987), Prentice-Hall, p. 123.

of xylem surrounded by phloem. The xylem may be a simple column or star-shaped in outline. This plant represents the **sporophyte**.

Reproduction occurs when the tips of the branches develop reproductive bodies called sporangia. **Sporangia** may be solitary but most often are fused together in groups of three. Within the sporangia are **spore mother cells** that undergo meiosis to produce **spores**. When the spores are mature, they are released from the sporangia. They are dispersed by wind and when they land on the proper substrate will germinate slowly in the soil. The resulting haploid plant is a **gametophyte** which arises from the spore. It is colorless and grows in or just under the soil. Gametophytes are shaped like tiny dog bones and are **saprobic**, meaning they obtain nutriments from fungi in the soil. As the gametophyte slowly grows, **archegonia** and **antheridia** develop on it. These will produce sperm and eggs as in the bryophytes. Fertilization occurs when liberated sperm swim to an archegonium and fuses with an egg. The resulting **zygote** produces a rhizome and grows upright stems. The zygote is diploid and represents the first stage of the sporophyte generation. This sporophyte will continue to grow upright, forming stems with sporangia on their tips and the cycle starts all over again.

Division Lycophyta— The Club Mosses and Quillworts

Unlike the whisk ferns, the club mosses and quillworts have true leaves. Because of these leaves, they are considered to be more advanced than the psilophytes. The tiny leaves of lycophyta are called **microphylls** and, like more advanced leaves seen in flowering plants, are capable of photosynthesis. Each microphyll has a single vein with no leaf trace into the stem.

With some 950 known species, the lycophytes are a larger and more diverse group than the whisk ferns. They are uncommon but widespread plants, occurring in suitable habitats over much of the globe. They are most abundant in the tropics and wet temperate areas. During the Devonian and Carboniferous periods some of the lycophytes were huge trees nearly one hundred feet in height. They formed dense swamps which, over millions of years, have been transformed into large coal deposits. The most common of these fossil forms included *Lepidodendron*, whose remains are found in most of the world's coal deposits that date from the Paleozoic.

The club mosses are the best known and most widespread of the lycophyta, and include two local and fairly common plants, *Lycopodium* and *Selaginella*.

LYCOPODIUM—GROUND PINES

Also known as princess pine, this club moss was one of the most common and widespread club mosses in Connecticut's woodlands. Ground pines comprise a group of low growing plants on the forest floor that resemble tiny evergreen trees. Unfortunately, they have greatly declined in abundance due to over collecting and habitat destruction.

In structure the ground pines and other club mosses have a **sporophyte** consisting of either simple or branched **stems** up to one foot in height. In some tropical forms the sporophyte may be five feet or more in height. The stems arise from **rhizomes** and have **microphylls** whorled or in a tight spiral around the stem. The rhizomes have **adventitious roots** on them which provide for absorption of nutrients and water.

Figure 21–5 The club moss *Lycopodium* (a) leafy plant (b) detail showing sporophylls (c) enlargement of sporophyll. *Source:* Harold C. Bold and John W. La Claire II. *The Plant Kingdom* (1987), Prentice-Hall, p. 128.

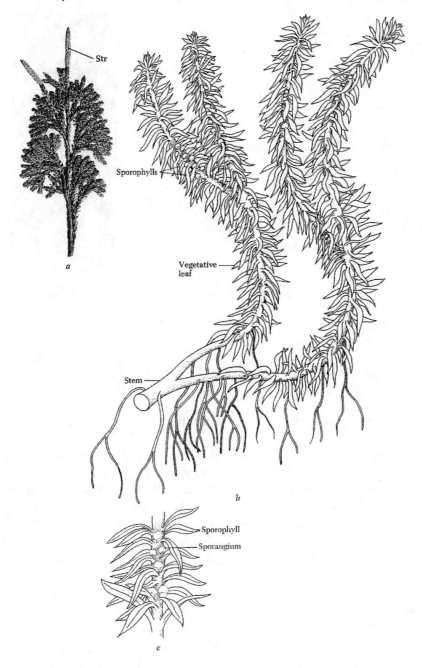

Reproduction in club mosses occurs when the sporophyte produces bean-shaped **sporangia** on sporophylls. The **sporophylls** are modified leaves that have become specialized for holding the sporangia. As in leaves, the sporophylls are whorled around the stems. In most species they are clustered into cone-like structures called **strobili.** Within the stobili, **spore mother cells** undergo meiosis to produce haploid **spores.** It is important to note that all the spores produced are the same size. This condition is called **homosporous.** When mature, the spores are liberated and carried away by wind currents. Spores that land on a suitable substrate germinate and produce a **gametophyte.** The gametophyte looks like a little carrot with most of the body developing in

Figure 21–6 Growth aspects of club moss. *Source:* Harold C. Bold and John W. La Claire II. *The Plant Kingdom* (1987), Prentice-Hall, p. 130

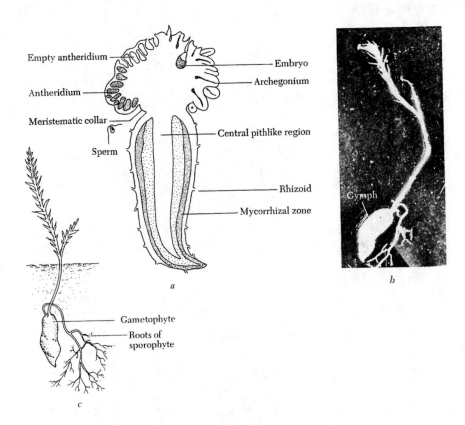

the ground. Some gametophytes develop on the surface of the ground or on mycorrhizal fungi.

Gametophytes may live for several years. They produce **archegonia** and **antheridia** on the same plant. As in whisk ferns, the antheridia and archegonia of club mosses produce gametes. The **sperm** swim to the archegonia and fertilize **eggs**. A diploid **zygote** results from this fertilization and develops into a rhizome called a **foot**. The sporophyte **stem** emerges from the rhizome and grows **leaves**. These eventually form into a mature plant. Some club mosses may also reproduce asexually by forming small **bulbils**, which are a kind of growth produced in the axils of the leaves. Bulbils may separate and form new sporophytes directly.

SELAGINELLA—SPIKE MOSSES

As in the club mosses, spike mosses typically form low, evergreen-like growths on woodland floors. They number some 700 species and are world-wide in distribution. Most spike mosses occur in wetter terrestrial habitats—along damp stream banks and in damp woodlands. *Selaginella* is the largest and best known of the two major genera of spike mosses. Spike mosses differ from club ferns in having leaves with a tiny tongue-like appendage called a **ligule** on the upper surface near the base. They are also **heterosporous**, which means they produce two kinds of spores.

During sexual reproduction, **sporangia** are produced on **sporophylls**. There are two kinds of sporangia which produce two kinds of spores. Some sporangia, called **microsporangia**, form small spores called **microspores**. Other sporangia, called **megasporangia**, produce larger spores called **megaspores**. Four megaspores are pro-

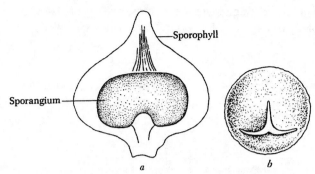

Figure 21-7. Sporophyll and sporangium of *Lycopodium. Source:* Harold C. Bold and John W. La Claire II. *The Plant Kingdom* (1987), Prentice-Hall, p. 129.

duced by each megasporangium. Each microspore develops into a male gametophyte while the megaspores develop into female gametophytes. (This differs from the life cycle of the club mosses, in which gametophytes produce both archegonia and antheridia).

In spike mosses, the heterosporous condition produces separate male and female gametophyte plants. This condition is called **dioecious**. Male gametophytes have antheridia and produce sperm which swim to female gametophytes with archegonia and fertilize the eggs. **Zygotes** form as in club mosses, but now only on the female gametophytes. A **sporophyte** grows from the zygote and represents the plant we see on the forest floor.

ISOETES—QUILLWORTS

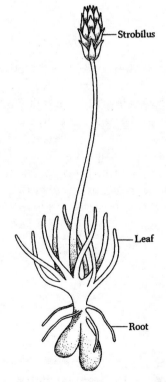

The quillworts are represented by about 60 species, all in the genus *Isoetes*. They live where they can be partially submerged in water for at least the growing and reproductive season of the year. Quillworts have tiny leaves that are spoon-shaped at the base and are arranged in a tight spiral on their stubby stems. Spines called **ligules** are present and located at the leaf bases. The rhizome of quillworts has vascular cambium and

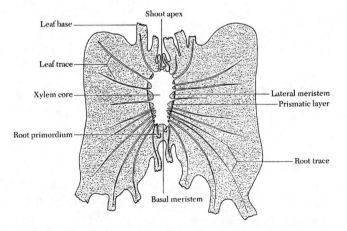

Figure 21–8 Leafy spike moss *Phylloglossum drummondi* with strobilus. *Source:* Harold C. Bold and John W. La Claire II. *The Plant Kingdom* (1987), Prentice-Hall, p. 127.

Figure 21–9 Developing the quillwort *Isoetes. Source:* Harold C. Bold and John W. La Claire II. *The Plant Kingdom* (1987), Prentice-Hall, p. 139.

Figure 21–10 Detail of the microsporangium and megasporangium of the quillwort *Isoetes*.
Source: Harold C. Bold and John W. La Claire II. *The Plant Kingdom* (1987), Prentice-Hall, p. 140.

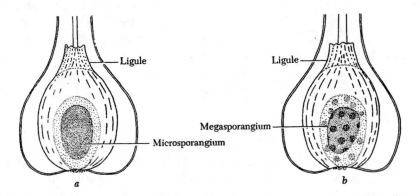

may live many years, becoming woody in older plants. Most quillworts are small plants with stem lengths up to four inches high.

Quillworts have a reproductive cycle similar to the club mosses in that they exhibit an alternation of generations between the sporophyte generation and the gametophyte generation. Like the spike mosses, they are also heterosporous. The sporangia are produced at the base of the leaves and the spores produce male and female gametophytes which in turn produce gametes. The eggs in the archegonia on the female gametophytes are fertilized to produce zygotes. The zygotes then grow into the new sporophyte.

ECONOMICS OF THE LYCOPHYTES

Ancient relatives of club mosses and ground pines were the dominant trees of the Devonian and Carboniferous forests and formed the huge coal swamps that we mine today. The largest of these ancient lycopods were tree-like, standing 100 feet tall with trunks nearly three feet in diameter. Quillworts first appear in the fossil record in the Cretaceous. They are very much like modern forms.

Most of the modern forms of lycopods are of little economic importance. At one time the spores were collected in huge numbers and used as flash powder and as an additive in some medicines. Locally, ground pines are used ornamentally for indoor Christmas decorations. The collection of "Princess Pine" for this use has contributed to the loss of many stands of *Lycopodium* and has driven this plant onto the endangered plant species list.

Division Sphenophyta—
The Horsetails and Scouring Rushes

The horsetails and scouring rushes represent another ancient group of plants that dominated the terrestrial landscape hundreds of millions of years ago in Devonian and Carboniferous times. Their ancestors formed huge forests that covered much of the early terrestrial landscape.

All modern horsetails and scouring rushes have a distinctive sporophyte with ribbed stems containing silica deposits and whorled scale-like microphylls that lack chlorophyll. The silica deposits make the stems useful as an abrasive and this accounts

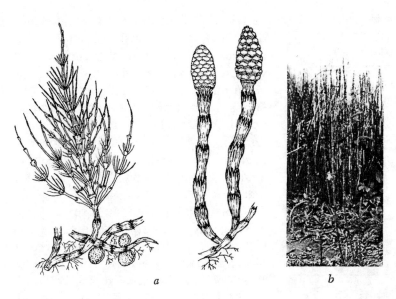

Figure 21-11 Scouring rush (a) vegetative plant (b) detail of strobiliferous branches (c) growth. *Source:* Harold C. Bold and John W. La Claire II. *The Plant Kingdom* (1987), Prentice-Hall, p. 142.

a

b

for the name scouring rush. Early settlers traveling westward used scouring rushes for cleaning their pots and pans.

Today, the horsetails and scouring rushes number about 25 species scattered throughout all the continents of the world. They can be large plants, commonly growing up to 4 feet tall. A few species may reach 15 feet in height.

SPHENOPHYTA—THE HORSETAILS

The early horsetails of the Carboniferous period were huge plants (for those times), nearly 50 feet in height. They grew in large stands with tree ferns and other early tree-like plants. Their remains form the coal swamps that date from this time. The surviving horsetails are a smaller and less diverse group.

The common horsetail, *Equisetum* is a widespread and familiar representative of this group. In structure, an *Equisetum* **sporophyte** has **stems** that are **ribbed** and exhibit well defined **nodes** and **internodes**, with numerous **stomata** in the grooves between the ribs. In cross section, a stem has **pith** in the center that breaks down at maturity, leaving a **central cavity**. Thus, mature stems are light and hollow, which makes them flexible. Surrounding the pith are rings of smaller canals. The inner ring consists of **carinal canals** which lie directly opposite the ribs. These canals represent vascular bundles with

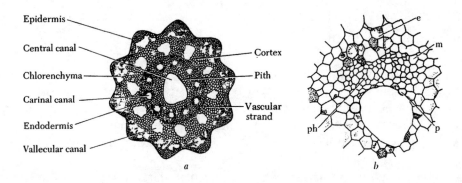

a

b

Figure 21-12 Cross section of horsetail *(Equisetum arvense)* (a) stem section (b) vascular strand. *Source:* Harold C. Bold and John W. La Claire II. *The Plant Kingdom* (1987), Prentice-Hall, p. 143.

Figure 21–13 Reproduction in horsetails (a) spore sacs in strobili (b) coiled arms of a spore (c) spores with arms extended (d) gametophyte developing from a spore. *Source:* Lorus Milne and Margery Milne. *Plant Life* (1959), Prentice-Hall, p. 148.

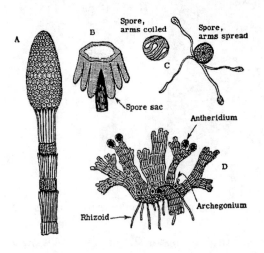

each having a patch of xylem located interiorly and phloem on the outside of the bundle. The outer ring of tissue contains **vallecula canals** which contain air and are arranged between ribs of the stem. Stems form from horizontal **rhizomes** which are stem-like in structure. *Equisetum* also develops **adventitious roots** that provide additional support and surface area for the absorption of water and minerals.

Horsetails can reproduce sexually and asexually. If stems and rhizomes are broken up by a storm, each fragment is capable of producing new sporophyte plants. This is a kind of **asexual reproduction**.

Sexual reproduction in horsetails begins in spring, when special stems grow from rhizomes. These stems develop **sporophytes.** In horsetails, the sporophytes are grouped into strobili in the form of cones on their tips. The outer surface of each **strobilus** looks as if it is covered with hexagonal plates giving it the appearance of the surface of a honeycomb. Each hexagon is the top of a **sporangiophore** which contains between five and ten **sporangia** that are attached to the inner surface of the rim.

Equisetum are **homosporous**, which means that each plant has only one type of sporangiophore and strobilus. The **spores** are distinctive in having four ribbon-like elaters at one pole. As the spore is carried on the wind, the **elaters** act like wings that aid in dispersal. When the airborne spores encounter a humid air pocket (such as along stream banks or around pond and wetland edges) the elaters coil around the spore, reducing its aerial buoyancy and it drops to the ground.

After the spore germinates, it produces a small, lobed **gametophyte** with rhizoids that anchor it to the ground. About half the gametophytes are male and the other half female. After a month or so the female gametophytes become bisexual, producing only antheridia from then on. Sperm are produced in antheridia. Rainfall or splashing water explosively eject the sperm, which then swim to nearby archegonia and fertilize the eggs. The union of eggs and sperm produces the zygotes which then grow into one or more sporophytes.

Economics of Horsetails

Some native peoples occasionally harvest horsetails for food or as feed for livestock. As food, especially in salads, horsetails can be surprisingly tender and tasty, especially after the outer layers of silica have been removed. Medically, horsetails have been used for their mild diuretic effect. Traditionally, horsetails have been used mostly as a cleansing or scouring agent for polishing brass, hardwood furniture, flooring, and, of course, for scouring pots and pans.

The many synthetic abrasives in use today have largely replaced the harvest of horsetails for scouring jobs. Undoubtedly, the greatest economic contribution of horsetails is a legacy of their distant ancestors, which formed the huge coal swamps of the

Carboniferous. The Appalachian coal deposits of Pennsylvania and West Virginia are evidence of the great numbers of giant horsetails that lived in Carboniferous times.

Division Pterophyta—The Ferns

Ferns are the most widespread and successful of the lower vascular plants, numbering some 11,000 species. They are often common throughout many of the world's ecological habitats, but reach their greatest abundance and diversity in cooler and damper locales. Most ferns are small or medium-sized plants but a few of today's species may each reach 80 feet in height.

The ferns differ from the other lower vascular plants by their leaves. Whisk ferns, club mosses and the other lower vascular plants previously discussed have microphylls but the sporophytes of ferns produce larger leaves called **megaphylls**. In addition to being considerably larger, fern leaves have more than one vein and a leaf trace is usually associated with a **leaf gap**. A leaf gap is a break in the vascular bundle that originally went to the limb. As the trunk expands through growth, leaf gaps occur. The occurrence of leaf gaps is considered to be a sign of advancement as leaf gaps are found in all higher plants. The veins are often large and much divided.

The most distinctive feature of the fern sporophyte is the megaphyll. Each leaf is called a **frond** and its **petiole** forms a central structure called a **rachis** which contains **pinnules** extending out from its sides. Pinnules may be further divided to produce a bipinnate configuration. In some ferns and in first year sporophytes the leaves may be much simpler than those described above.

Reproduction in ferns is characterized by **homosporous** sporophytes and monoecious gametophytes. The **sporophyte** is the conspicuous part of the fern life cycle as it is in all vascular land plants—it is what we see when we look at a fern. The sporophyte consists of **fronds**, a **stem** in the form of a **rhizome**, and **adventitious roots**. When fronds first appear each spring they are tightly coiled at their ends and are called **croziers** or **fiddle heads**. The name fiddle head is derived from the appearance of the young fronds which look much like the end of a fiddle. The sporophyte fiddle heads unroll and expand outwards to form pinnae which are attached to a midrib or rachis.

When ferns mature, **sporangia** form on the undersurface of the leaflet, or pinnae, usually in groups. These collections of sporangia are called **sori**. In some ferns they are protected by flaps of tissue called **indusia**, which cover the sori like miniature, upside down umbrellas. The

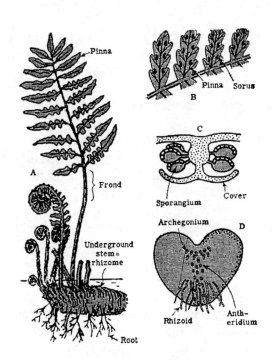

Figure 21–14 Details of fern structures (a) mature plant (b) leaf section showing the sorus (c) cross section at sora (d) developing thallus. *Source:* Lorus Milne and Margery Milne. *Plant Life* (1959), Prentice-Hall, p. 149.

Figure 21–15 A tree fern from the West Indies. *Source:* Harold C. Bold and John W. La Claire II. *The Plant Kingdom* (1987), Prentice-Hall, p. 150.

a   *b*

sporangia consist of rows of cells arranged along one end of the sorus called an **annulus**. As turgor pressure changes in the cells of the annulus, the weaker cells rupture, opening the sporangium and throwing the spores out. Before that happens, **spore mother cells** undergo meiosis in the sporangia, producing either 48 or 64 **spores** in each sporangium. The spores are carried by wind to wet habitats where they germinate and produce prothalli.

The **prothallus** of a fern is a small, green, heart-shaped structure that represents the **gametophyte** stage in the fern life cycle. The prothallus resembles a liverwort in appearance. Most prothalli are one cell thick except towards their middle where **rhizoids** are produced on the lower surface. **Antheridia** form near the base of the prothallus while **archegonia** are produced closer to the notch of the prothallus.

Sperm and eggs produced by the gametophyte stage unite to form a **zygote** which forms into a sporophyte on the prothallus. This new or **first year sporophyte** has small, simple leaves the first season but grows the larger leaves typical of ferns in the following year.

The development of a first year sporophyte is a new feature in plants and is not observed in the more primitive of the lower vascular plants. Up until this point, all plants completed the life cycle in one growing season. In contrast, ferns have a prolonged life cycle taking at least three years to produce a mature sexually reproducing plant.

Ferns are considered to be among the most ancient of land plants. The earliest ferns, found in the Silurian and Devonian periods, are intermediate between whisk ferns and modern ferns in appearance. Ferns were especially numerous and widespread in the Carboniferous, as fern fossils of many kinds are common in coal seams. Some paleobotanists call the Carboniferous the "Age of Ferns" because they were so diverse and abundant at this time.

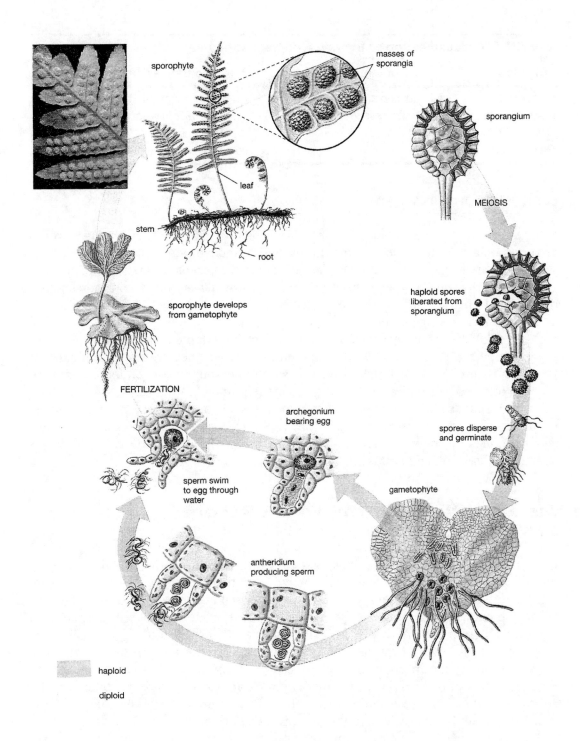

Figure 21–16 The life cycle of a fern. *Source:* Teresa Audesirk and Gerald Audesirk (1999), p. 401.

Table 21-1 A classification of the nonseed tracheophytes.

Division	Examples	Representative Characteristics
Lycophyta	club mosses and quill worts	simple leaves in spirals around stem
Sphenophyta	horsetails and scouring rushes	simple leaves in whorls around stem
Psilophyta	whisk ferns	lack true leaves
Pterophyta	ferns	complex leaves forming fronds

ECONOMICS OF FERNS

Ferns are familiar plants of field, wetland and woodland habitats. They are also favored as ornamentals. Many species make hardy and attractive house plants. The bark of some ferns makes an ideal substrate for germination of seeds of flowering plants. For example, *Anthurium*, a showy flowering plant of Hawaii, is grown commercially on native tree ferns. Orchid and bromiliad growers also may use fern bark and rhizomes as a mulch for growing plants.

Fern fiddle heads are occasionally gathered for food and can sometimes be found in local supermarkets, especially during the spring when they are most abundant. In Japan and New Zealand, bracken fern is sometimes cultivated for food. However, bracken fern has been shown to contain carcinogens and cause stomach tumors in animals. The Japanese, who often eat this fern in salads and as a delicacy, have the highest incidence of stomach cancer in the world. In the tropics some species of ferns have also been used in the preparation of tribal medicines. Fronds of the larger ferns are sometimes used to thatch roofs.

Lower Vascular Plants in the Fossil Record

One of the things that we have tried to stress in this chapter is the idea that many of these lower vascular plants have an extensive fossil record. In fact, most groups were much more diverse and widespread hundreds of millions of years ago than they are today. We know most of these early vascular plants from their fossil remains. Perhaps we should digress and briefly discuss plant fossils and their importance. A **fossil** is any trace of past life. It can be a part of an actual plant or just an imprint, or chemical residue. In order for an organism to be fossilized three things must occur. First, the organism must have hard parts or something resistant to be fossilized. Apparently the cuticle of land plants is resistant enough to fulfill this criterion. Secondly, there must be growth or death in an area where the organism will not be destroyed by predation. If, when it dies, it is eaten, it cannot form a complete fossil. Lastly, there must be a quick burial so that organic decay and scavengers have a limited time and impact on the remains. Quick burial not only gets the plant out of view from organisms that might eat it, but it also gets it out of the air so the aerobic bacteria of decay cannot act efficiently.

When plant fossils are formed they make remains in several ways. The most common types of fossils are **molds** and **casts** or **compressions** and **imprints**. In this situation there is a replacement of the original plant material, leaving a mold of the outside shape of the plant. The interior organic material is replaced by silt and becomes a model of the original. This is a kind of fossil called a cast. Compressions are plant remains that have been crushed by the weight of rock and soil above, resulting in a flat-

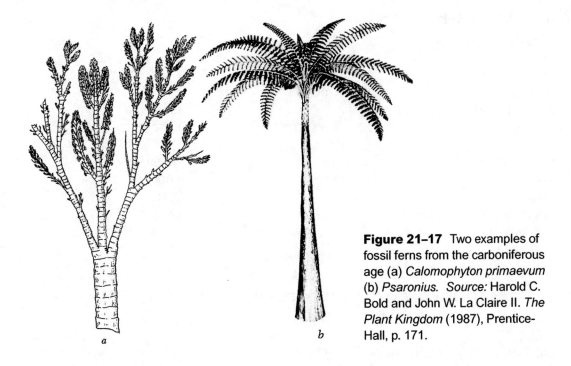

Figure 21–17 Two examples of fossil ferns from the carboniferous age (a) *Calomophyton primaevum* (b) *Psaronius. Source:* Harold C. Bold and John W. La Claire II. *The Plant Kingdom* (1987), Prentice-Hall, p. 171.

tened remnant. If the weight is heavy enough, the remains are heated to the point where all organic volatiles are boiled off, leaving a carbon smear behind. This type of fossil is called **carbonization**. Sometimes material is pressed into the mud and removed, leaving an outlined shape of the original, an imprint. A fossil imprint of a leaf is like a footprint.

The most valuable plant fossils are formed by **petrifaction**. The process of petrifaction occurs under conditions where groundwater percolates slowly down through the earth, towards the water table. As it seeps through the buried plant material (which will become the fossils) the minerals in the groundwater replace the organic constituents of the plant, resulting in a molecule-by-molecule replacement of the original plant. The resulting specimen is made of calcium, silicon dioxide and other minerals. These petrified fossils are especially valuable because they contain fine details and even cellular structure in their record. They can be thin-sectioned and cut into microscope slides to show fine details.

Some plant fossils are found indirectly. For example, **coprolites** are the fossilized dung of animals. An examination of this fossil dung sometimes reveals pollen and other remains of ancient plants and plant material left from the animal's last meal. Such fossils often yield information about the diet of the animal, the existence and structure of the plants that were consumed as food. They can also provide data about the climate of the area at the time the plant (and animal) fossil was formed.

Lastly, there can occasionally be **unaltered** fossils. These are plant remains that are unchanged and have been preserved in some special way. For example, plants that are buried by massive snowstorms or avalanches may be found intact centuries later when the glacier melts. Some of our best evidence for plant life during the Ice Ages actually comes from the stomachs of herbivorous mammals such as wooly mammoth, which were killed and buried beneath snows and ice shortly after their last meal. Analysis of their stomach contents reveals flowers, leaves, and twigs of plants that comprised their tundra habitat of 10,000 years ago.

Key Words and Phrases

Psilophyta
strobilus
heterosporous
Lycophyta
megaphylls
rachis
sorus
fossil
compression
petrification
coal forests

enations
homosporous
ligule
Sphenophyta
frond
pinnules
indusum
mold
imprint
coprolites

microphylls
bulbils
dioecious
elaters
petiole
fiddle head
annulus
cast
carbonization
unaltered fossils

Selected References and Resources

Bir, S. S. 1908. *Pteridophyta. Some Aspects of their Structure and Morphology*. Scholarly Publications. Houston, Texas.

Cobb, B. 1975. *A Field Guide to the Ferns and their related Families*. Peterson Field Guide Series. Houghton-Mifflin. Boston, Massachusetts.

Jermy, A. C., J. A. Crabbe, and B. A. Thomas. Eds. 1984. *The Phylogeny and Classification of Ferns*. Lubrecht and Cramer. Forestburgh, New York.

Lellinger, D. B. 1985. *A Field Manual of the Ferns and Fern Allies of the United States* and Canada. Smithsonian Institute Press. Washington, D. C.

Raghaven, V. 1989. *Developmental Biology of Fern Gametophytes*. Cambridge University Press. New York.

Sporne, K. R. 1975. *The Morphology of Pteridophytes. The Structure of Ferns and Allied Plants*. Humanities Press. Atlantic Highlands, New Jersey.

Taylor, T. N. 1981. *An Introduction to Fossil Plant Biology*. McGraw-Hill. New York.

Tryon, R., and A. Tryon. 1982. *Ferns and Allied Plants with special Reference to Tropical America*. Springer-Verlag. New York.

Review and Discussion Questions

1. Describe the structure and biota of the ancient coal forests.
2. What are the kinds of coal that are mined and used for energy? Are they all derived from fossil plants?
3. How are plants (and animals) fossilized? How were the coal plants transformed into coal?
4. Why are the lycopods considered to be more advanced than the bryophytes? How are they better adapted to terrestrial habitats than the bryophytes?
5. Which are the most advanced of the lower plants? Why?
6. What are economic uses of the lower plants?
7. Why is the quillwort included in this chapter with the ferns? Why are the club mosses included in this chapter and not grouped with our earlier discussion of the true mosses?

Chapter 22

The Gymnosperms

The Conifers
The Cycads
The Gnetatums
Economic Importance of the Gymnosperms

The gymnosperms and the angiosperms are seed bearing vascular plants. The first seed bearing plants appear in the fossil record in the Devonian Period of about 250 million years ago. The appearance of seeds was an adaptive innovation in the evolution of land plants. A seed is a plant embryo which develops from the zygote. It is part of the sporophyte generation that is protected by a seed coat. Each seed carries its own supply of food called **endosperm**, to nourish the growing embryo. The embryo and the seed may be able to lie dormant for long time periods, thereby escaping unsatisfactory environmental conditions. The comparatively long-term survival value of seeds was of major importance in the evolutionary success of the seed plants.

The first seed plants were fern-like in appearance and bore seeds on the ends of their fronds. These seed ferns were the probable ancestors of the gymnosperms. The word gymnosperm means "naked seeds", and refers to the exposed nature of the seeds borne on the sporophylls. In comparison, the seeds of flowering plants, which will be discussed in the next chapter, are entirely enclosed within an ovary or fruit. Gymnosperms boast the distinction of being the largest terrestrial organisms and also the oldest living plants on earth. The California redwoods and giant Douglas firs of the Pacific Northwest may reach heights of several hundred feet and diameters of several dozens of feet, both far larger than any other terrestrial plant (or animal). Both California redwoods and Douglas firs may be over a thousand years old. The longevity record, however, is held by another gymnosperm of western North America called the bristlecone pine. Some of these pines, which are native only to the arid and semiarid mountain regions of western Nevada and California, have been estimated at 4,900 years old.

Unlike ferns and the other seedless vascular plants discussed in the previous chapter, in gymnosperm, the sporophyte generation is dominant and the gametophyte generation consists of reproductive structures carried parasitically on the sporophyte. Reproduction is generally sexual. In sexual reproduction, the female sporophylls are almost always spirally arranged in female strobili, called cones, which develop on the sporophyte. The smaller male strobili, also in cones, produce pollen. The female gametophyte generation is produced within an ovule containing a fleshy, nutritive diploid layer, called the **nucellus**, that is itself encased in one or more layers of diploid tissue. These outer layers constitute an integument, which becomes the seed coat after fertilization, during the development of the embryo. So a seed, by definition, is a plant embryo encased in a series of integuments of diploid tissue.

Figure 22–1 A comparison of methods for bearing seeds (a) flowering plants (b) seed enclosed in pod (c) cross section of tomato fruit with enclosed seeds (d) seed cone of pine (e) close up of pine seed. *Source:* Harold C. Bold and John W. La Claire II. *The Plant Kingdom* (1987), Prentice-Hall, p. 176.

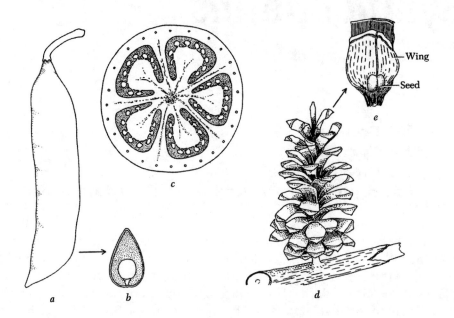

In gymnosperms, the sporophytes are normally trees or shrubs and the gametophyte is reduced—even more so than seen in the ferns. The gametophyte is not free living, but is a part of the sporophyte cone structure. There are four major groups of gymnosperms living today; the conifers, ginkos, cycads, and gnetophytes. The most widespread, diverse, and economically important of the gymnosperms are undoubtedly the conifers.

Characteristics of Gymnosperms

In gymnosperms the green plant represents the dominant diploid sporophyte generation. The gametophyte generation is a transitory reproductive stage attached to and totally dependent upon the sporophyte for support and nutrition. The female gametophyte produces an egg which is enveloped in nutritive tissue. The male gametophyte produces pollen which is wind dispersed. Following fertilization the diploid seed develops in cones. The seed represents the beginning of the next sporophyte generation. The gymnosperms include the conifers, cycads, ginkos, and gnetophytes.

Division Coniferophyta—The Conifers

Although familiar and widespread components of natural and human landscapes, the conifers are actually a relatively small group of plants; only 575 species have been identified. However, they are of enormous economic importance as the conifers include pines, firs, spruces, hemlocks, redwoods, larches, dawn redwoods, and cedars.

Figure 22–2 A comparison of seeds of the two major groups of seed plants, the pines (a) and flowering plants (b). *Source:* Teresa Audesirk and Gerald Audesirk (1999), p. 402.

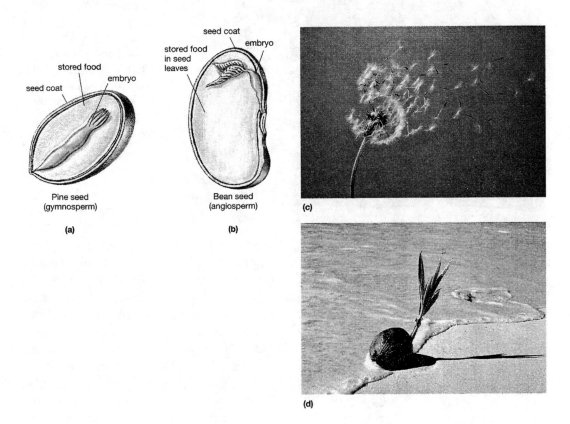

Collectively these conifers represent the softwoods from which lumber and paper and hundreds of other wood products are produced.

The first conifers appeared in the Late Carboniferous and probably were instrumental in replacing the dense stands of Lepidodendron and horsetails that had dominated the world's terrestrial forests up to that time.

PINUS—THE PINES

In structure, the pine is a tree or shrub with needlelike or scale leaves arranged in clusters or bundles numbering from 2–8 needles per cluster. Each cluster of needles forms a flexible cylindrical rod. Members of the genus *Pinus* are the largest and most widespread of the pines. Species of *Pinus* include the lodgepole pine, white, slash, pitch, Norway, and red pines. In some areas, these form the extensive, homogenous coniferous forests of the northern hemisphere. Only one species of pine occurs south of the equator.

Most pines grow best in colder regions of the world where the topsoil is frozen for a part of the year and water is difficult to obtain. Other species such as slash pine and pitch pine grow well in dry, sandy conditions. The ability of pines to tolerate these environmental extremes lies in the adaptive nature of the pine needle. All pine needles are covered by a thick "skin" which consists of several layers. The outer layer, the **epidermis**, of the pine needle is covered by a thick **cuticle** that retards water loss. Like all higher plants, pines and other conifers have stomata for gas exchange. However, in pines the stomata are sunken into the epidermis. This prevents water loss but still provides sufficient surface

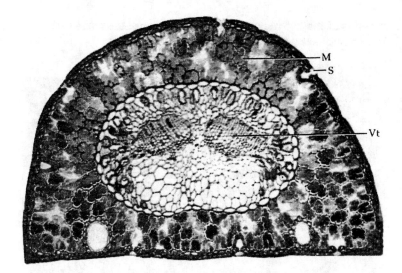

Figure 22–3 Cross section of pine needle showing the thick cuticle, sunken stomata (S), and interior vascular tissue (Vt). *Source:* Harold C. Bold and John W. La Claire II. *The Plant Kingdom* (1987), Prentice-Hall, p. 189.

area for gas exchange. In the interior of the pine needle, the mesophyll cells lack air spaces and are covered and protected by another protective layer called the **endodermis**.

The vascular bundles are found deep within the innermost layer of the needle, the **hypodermis**. This combination of thick cuticle, sunken stomata and several layers help pine leaves conserve water much more efficiently than other plants and is a major factor in their ability to grow in generally dry and otherwise inhospitable habitats.

In addition to conserving water, pine needles also carry their own insecticides. Resin canals occur in the mesophyll of needles and often in other parts of the pine as well. Resin, secreted by the canals, is aromatic and antiseptic, it prevents the development of fungi and acts as a deterrent to insects.

The xylem of pines and other conifers consists only of tracheids; there are no thick-walled vessel elements or fibers. Because of this, conifers are called "softwoods" in contrast to the "hardwoods" that are found in angiosperm trees and shrubs. Since softwoods are more easily worked than hardwoods, the softwoods of pines are a favorite medium for certain types of construction.

The phloem lacks companion cells but other cells, called **albuminous cells**, apparently perform the same function. Conifer roots usually grow in symbiotic association with mycorrhizal fungi. In this relationship, the mycorrhizae help the pine absorb water and minerals while the pine provides support and, through photosynthesis, produces

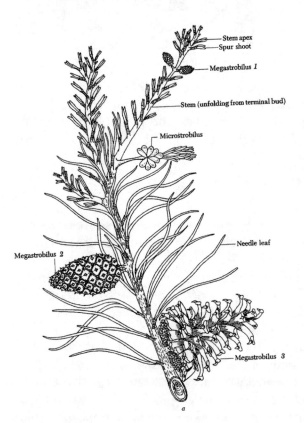

Figure 22–4 Pine branch showing megastrobilus and other features *Source:* Harold C. Bold and John W. La Claire II. *The Plant Kingdom* (1987), Prentice-Hall, p. 186.

(Figure 22–5 The developing structures of a pine pollen grain. *Source:* Harold C. Bold and John W. La Claire II. *The Plant Kingdom* (1987), Prentice-Hall, p. 189.

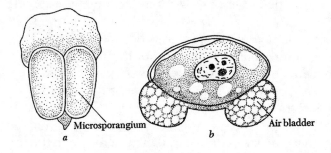

organic molecules needed by the mycorrhizae. If pines are deprived of their mycorhizzae they will generally die or grow slowly.

Sexual reproduction in pines occurs in the green plant, the sporophyte. Conifers produce two kinds of cones. The male cones contain **microsporangia** that develop in pairs towards the bases of the scales of the cone. In turn, the scales of the cone are arranged in a spiral or in whorls around a central axis, the whole forming a strobilus or male cone. Each spring, the microspore mother cells of the male cone undergo meiosis and develop into four haploid microspores which become pollen grains. Each pollen grain consists of four cells and a pair of external air sacs. We will follow their future later.

Female cones (also called strobili), are larger in size than male cones. They develop in the upper canopy while the male cones develop along the lower branches. This adaptive measure helps ensure that pine trees pollinate other trees rather than self-pollinate. (If male cones were in the upper branches, their pollen would drift down and pollinate the female cones in the lower branches of the same tree).

Structurally, each female cone is made up of scales with megasporangia on them. Megaspores are produced in the megasporangia located within ovules of the female cones. The ovules occur in pairs at the base of each scale of the immature female cones. They are larger and more complex than their male counterpart. Each ovule consists of a megasporangium within a multicellular nutritive tissue, the **nuceuus**. This, in turn, is surrounded by a thick, multi-layered **integument**. A channel called a **micropyle**

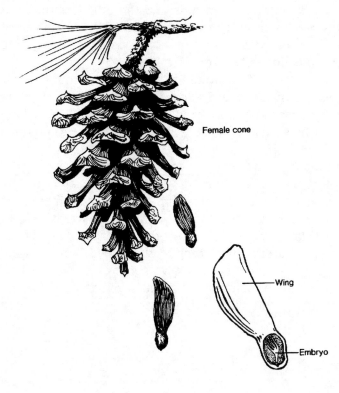

Female cone

Wing

Embryo

Figure 22–6 The female cone of a pine showing dispersal of the winged seeds. *Source:* Tom M. Graham (1997) p. 107.

traverses the integument toward the center of the cone. One of the integument layers later becomes the seed coat of the seed. A single megaspore mother cell within the nuceuus of each ovule undergoes meiosis to produce a row of large megaspores. All but one of these megaspores degenerates. The survivor grows and becomes the female gametophyte.

Over several months, the female gametophyte produces between two and six archegonia, each of which becomes differentiated at the end of the micropyle. Each archegonium contains a single egg. Female cones take at least two seasons to mature. During the first spring, the scales of the cone spread apart, to serve as natural traps for the wind blown pollen. Pollen grains carried by the wind sift down between the scales and adhere to sticky drops of fluid called pollen drops, which exude from the end of the micropyle. As the pollen drop evaporates, pollen is drawn into the micropyle to the top of the nucellus, where the female egg awaits it. Following the capture of the pollen, the scales of the female cone close, trapping the pollen inside and protecting the developing ovule.

Pollen is trapped and held by sticky pollen drops. The pollen is subsequently drawn into the micropyle to fertilize the egg within. About a month after pollination, meiosis occurs and female megaspores are formed.

The pollen grains develop a pollen tube which slowly digests its way through the nucellus to the area where the archegonia will form. As the pollen tube grows, two of the four original pollen cells enter it. One cell, the generative cell, divides and forms two cells; one is called a **sterile cell** and the other is a **spermatogenous cell**. The spermatogenous cell divides to produce sperm. The sterile cell (sometimes called the tube cell) directs the growth of the pollen tube. The pollen tube and its sperm represent the male gametophyte of the plant. Separate antheridium, as such, is not formed in pines or in other conifers. The female (gametophyte will slowly develop for a year or more following pollination. Inside, the archegonium is slowly maturing.

About 15 months following pollination the growing pollen tube reaches the archegonium which is by now mature. Sperm in the pollen tube unite with the egg, forming a zygote. The remaining cells in the pollen tube and the other sperm soon degenerate. Each zygote develops into an embryo. As the embryo develops, a layer of the integument hardens to form the seed coat. A thin membranous layer of the cone scale grows outward and is transformed into a wing on each seed.

The wings of the pine seed provides aerodynamic lift, twirling and soaring, and thereby aiding seed dispersal away from the tree. Squirrels, chipmunks and gophers may aid in seed dispersal by opening cones or by burying them in caches. They, along with other rodents will eat most of the seeds but those that escape survive to produce new trees.

In some species such as the lodgepole pine, jack pine and knobcone pines, the cones may remain closed for years holding the fully developed seeds safely inside. They open only after being scorched by a severe forest fire. This unusual method is actually an important ecological adaptation to areas that are periodically swept by fires. For example, when fire destroys an old growth conifer forest the cones are shut tight to protect the seeds within from the fire. After being scorched, they slowly cool and the scales open to release the seeds, which may be widely blown about over the now barren landscape. The seeds quickly become buried in the loose ash covering the ground. They will be the first plants to germinate and will eventually replace the fire-destroyed forest.

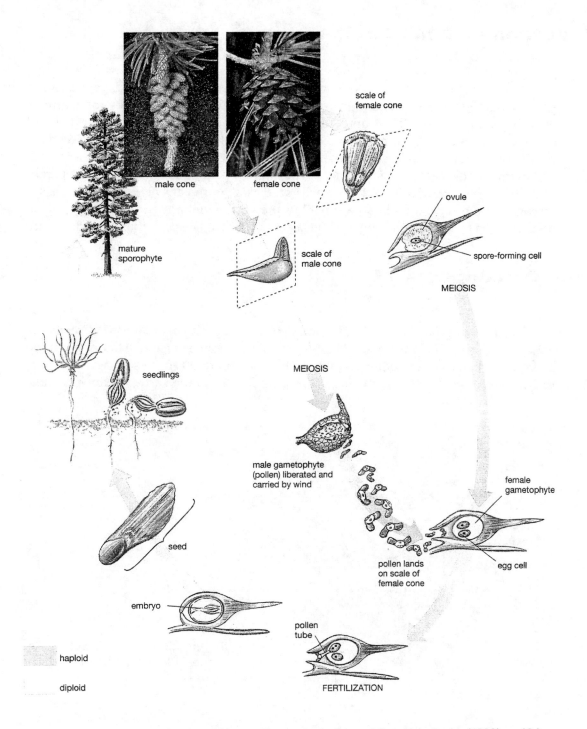

Figure 22–7 Life cycle of a pine. *Source:* Teresa Audesirk and Gerald Audesirk (1999), p. 404.

Reproduction in Other Conifers

All conifers exhibit the same cycle of reproductive events described above. Some species, however, exhibit variations on this reproductive theme. In yews, for example, the ovary is encased in a fleshy and nutritious covering called an **aril**. The nutritious aril attracts birds and small mammals, mostly rodents, which eat the seeds. Many seeds of conifers are activated only after passing through the digestive tract of animals. Birds and mammals also act as dispersal agents in spreading the seeds away from the parent tree. In this and other species, the thick seed coat is mostly digested as it passes through the digestive tract of an animal but the seed is unharmed. Following defecation, the seed is deposited, along with fertilizer that will aid its germination and growth.

Division Cycadophyta — The Cycads

The cycads represent a very ancient stock of relic gymnosperms that were diverse and abundant during the Mesozoic. Many cycads probably served as important food sources for dinosaurs and other animals of that era. About 90 species of cycads survive today, all confined to the tropical and subtropical regions of the earth. Cycads resemble

Figure 22–8 A cycad. *Source:* Jim Harter (1988), p. 87

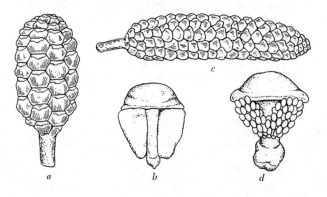

Figure 22–9 Strobili and sporophylls of the cycad *Zamia*. *Source:* Harold C. Bold and John W. La Claire II. *The Plant Kingdom* (1987), Prentice-Hall, p. 179.

Figure 22–10 Development of the male gametophyte (a) pollen grain (b) mature male gametophyte with its components. *Source:* Lorus J. Milne and Margery Milne, *Plant Life.* (1959), Prentice-Hall, p. 180.

Figure 22–11 Ovule of the cycad *Zamia* at time of fertilization. *Source:* Lorus J. Milne and Margery Milne, *Plant Life.* (1959), Prentice-Hall, p. 181.

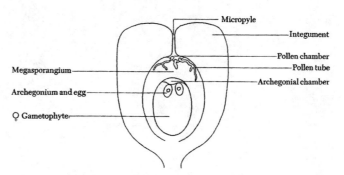

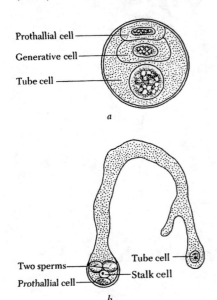

palm trees in having palm-like leaves but differ in their slow growth and in having seed-bearing cones like other gymnosperms. In form, cycads have unbranched trunks that may be 50 feet in height, with a crown of large, pinnately divided leaves.

The cycad life cycle is similar to that seen in conifers, but cycad gametophytes produce flagellated sperm instead of pollen to fertilize the eggs. The plants are dioecious and bear both male and female cones. In the more northern areas of the United States, such as in Connecticut, cycads are houseplant ornamentals or planted as landscape ornamentals or in botanical gardens. In warmer climates, cycads are more commonly grown as landscape ornamentals.

Division Ginkgophyta—The Ginkgos

Like the cycads, ginkos were once common and widespread, especially during the Age of Dinosaurs. Today, however, the ginkos are represented by a single living species, *Ginkgo biloba*, commonly called the ginko tree. Ginko trees have fan-shaped leaves and seeds with fleshy coverings. The ginko is also known as the maidenhair tree because its leaves resemble the pinnae of the maidenhair fern. Ginko leaves lack a midrib or prominent veins. Unlike most pines, there are separate male and female ginko trees.

The ginko life cycle is similar to that of cycads. The ginko is said to have lived so long that it no longer has any enemies. Ginkos are noted for their tolerance of air pollutants, especially vehicle emissions. Because of their hardiness and lack of natural enemies ginkos are widely planted in cities, parks and other open space as landscape ornamentals.

Although ginkos make an attractive landscape ornamental, female trees exude a nauseating odor during sexual reproduction. This stems from the fact that ginko seeds are enclosed in a very smelly, fleshy coating. The smell of the female flower attracts carrion flies which normally lay their eggs in decaying flesh. These carrion flies are drawn to the ginko and serve as pollinators. Since only female ginkos give off this odor, male ginko trees are preferred in residential and city plantings.

Figure 22–12 Leaves and sexual organs of Ginkgo. *Source:* Harold C. Bold and John W. La Claire II. *The Plant Kingdom* (1987), Prentice-Hall, p. 184.

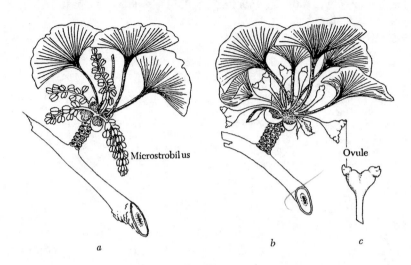

Microstrobilus

Ovule

a   *b*   *c*

Division Gnetophyta—The Ephedras, Welwitschia

The gnetophytes are a small group of mostly desert plants numbering about 70–75 species. They range widely over the deserts and semiarid habitats of western North America and Eurasia. The gnetophytes are unique among the gymnosperms in having wood with xylem vessel elements as well as tracheids. The gnetophytes include three basic groups of plants, the Ephedras, Gnetum and Welwitschia.

Ephedras represent the only American variety of petophytes. Ephedras are shrubby plants that are fairly common in western deserts such as the Great Basin Desert. Their light green stems carry on most of the photosynthesis for the plant. Some plants are dioecious, but others are monoecious.

The green stems of Ephedra can be boiled to produce a stimulating drink which is sometimes called Brigham's Tea, named after the Mormon leader, Brigham Young. An important medicinal extract derived from this plant is ephedrine, a drug widely used in the treatment of asthma.

Unlike other gymnosperms, the Gnetums are vine-like and have broad leaves similar to flowering plants. Gnetums occur in the tropics of South America, Africa and Southeast Asia.

Perhaps the most unusual gnetophyte is Welwitschia, which is found in the Namib and Mossamedes deserts of southwestern Africa. Also known as the century plant because they are reputed to live for about a hundred years, Welwitschia carries on CAM photosynthesis and have stomata that open only at night. The plants survive in the harshest deserts, drawing their moisture from dew and condensate from fog.

Structurally, Welwitschia consists of an oversized taproot from which arises a short, cup-shaped stem that bears the cones and a single pair of leaves. In older plants, the stem develops a crusty, bark-like covering on its surface. The wide, strap-like leaves have a belt of meristem at their base and grow more or less continuously, splitting repeatedly along their length. Eventually, the plants look like a scraggly pile of eaves. Male and female cones are produced on separate plants and emerge from axils of the two leaves.

Figure 22–13 The century plant *(Welwitschia mirabilis).* *Source:* Harold C. Bold and John W. La Claire II. *The Plant Kingdom* (1987), Prentice-Hall, p. 198.

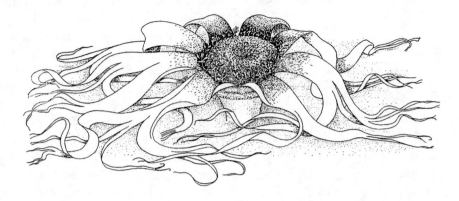

Table 22-1 A classification of the major groups of gymnosperms.

Division	Representative	Characteristics
Cycadophyta	cycads	fern-like leaves, seeds in strobili
Ginkgophyta	gingkos	deciduous with fan-shaped leaves
Gnetophyta	gnetophytes	vascular tissues for vessels
Coniferophyta	pines, spruces, cedars	seeds in cones, needle-like leaves

Gymnosperms as Commodities

Gymnosperms rank second only to angiosperms in their economic importance. Undoubtedly, the most important group are the conifers which supply the great bulk of softwoods for commercial and residential construction, furniture, and paper products. Plywood, formers, studs, planks, particle board, and other commercially important wood products are manufactured from conifers. A variety of wood and paper dyes are extracted from conifers such as hemlock.

On a local scale, some conifers are eaten for food, as the inner bark and seeds are nutritious. Since the colonial period, conifers such as white pine were used for the masts of sailing ships. The abundance of pines in the New World helped the United States to become a great seafaring nation during the age of sailing ships.

Another important product of conifers is the resin produced in the resin canals of the trees. From this material, turpentine and paint thinners are made. The collection of resin and other aromatic substances synthesized by conifers form the basis for the production of incense that is used in various religious and mystic ceremonies and rituals. Juice from the berry of the dwarf juniper is used to flavor gin and other alcoholic beverages. Wood, paper products, resin and turpentine are the most important commercial products obtained from conifers.

Conifers are also the major source of wood which is used in the production of paper. Newsprint is manufactured from stands of southern pine, slash pine, and yellow pine plantations grown especially for that purpose. Many conifers end up as ornamentals such as Christmas trees. Many areas of the Midwest, New England and southern Canada are the sites of large tree farms where trees are grown specifically for use in the

Figure 22–14 A fossil gymnosperm.
Source: Harold C. Bold and John W. La Claire II. *The Plant Kingdom* (1987), Prentice-Hall, p. 200.

Christmas trade as trees, wreaths, grave blankets, and other decorations. Many species of conifers are raised in nurseries for use as landscape ornamentals.

Conifers grow rapidly and make excellent decorative ornamentals as well as shelter, hedgerows, and other landscaping plants. Conifers are occasionally planted in rows to mark property boundaries or along the northern or windward side of the property where they form excellent windbreaks during the winter and living fences throughout the year. Some conifers have been especially bred to be dwarf varieties and these are sold for foundation trees for planting close to the house.

Lastly, conifers are also an important source of drugs used to fight cancer and other debilitating and life-threatening diseases. A powerful new cancer drug called taxol is derived from the bark of the Pacific yew. This tree is not very plentiful and recently the drug was synthesized in the laboratory. Taxol has been found to have a specific effect on tumors of female sex organs, in particular, ovaries, and breasts. Taxol may be the new hope for conquering breast cancer.

Key Words and Phrases

Gingko	conifer	pine
Cycad	resin	resin canals
Ephedra	Pacific Yew	needles
scales	fascicle	nucellus
megaspore mother cell	seed coat	microspore mother cell
integument	strobili	pollen drops
gymnosperm	Welwitschia	Bristlecone pine
pollen drops	wing	generative cell
tube cell		

Selected References and Resources

Allen, M. F. 1991. *The Ecology of Mycorrhizae.* Cambridge University Press. New York.

Beck, C. B. 1988. *Origin and Evolution of Gymnosperms.* Columbia University Press. New York.

Krussman, G. 1985. *Manual of Cultivated Conifers.* Timber Press. Portland, Oregon.

Singh, H. 1978. *Embryology of Gymnosperms.* Lubrecht and Cramer. Forestburgh, New York.

Spome, K. R. 1967. *Morphology of Gymnosperms. The Structure and Evolution of Primitive Seed Plants.* Humanities Press, Inc. Atlantic New Jersey.

Review and Discussion Questions

1. Why are female cones located in the top branches of conifers while male cones are located in the bottom branches?
2. How are the gymnosperms more evolutionarily advanced compared to the ferns and horsetails?
3. Why are pines and other conifers frequently planted around reservoirs? At the edges of property? As ornamentals?
4. Structurally, why are pines called softwoods? Discuss the economic importance of pines.
6. How does the global ecological distribution of pines and other conifers relate to global climatic conditions?
7. Explain why the seed plants have become the most successful and widespread plants on earth.

Chapter 23
• • • • • • • • • • • • • • • • • • ▶ • • ▶ ▶ • •

The Flowering Plants

Characteristics of Flowering Plants
Evolution of Flowering Plants
Reproduction of Flowering Plants
    Pollination and Fertilization
    Strategies for Success
Varieties of Flowering Plants
    Class Dicotyledonae—The Dicots
    Class Monocotyledonae—The Monocots

Angiosperms are the flowering plants. They number over 240,000 species and constitute the largest, most successful, and most widespread of the natural grouping of vascular plants. Species of angiosperms are found in wetlands, along waterways, around the edges of lakes and ponds, and along coastal marshes and marine shorelines. They occur in—and are often the dominant species of—just about every terrestrial habitat and are also important vascular components of freshwater aquatic habitats as well.

The word **angiosperm** means seed vessel, and refers to the fact that angiosperm seeds are carried within a container, the ovary. The ovary that carries a seed resembles a rolled leaf with the seeds on its margins turned inside out. Similar structures can be found in some fossil seed ferns, suggesting that these are the most likely ancestors of the modern flowering plants. (If that seed fern ancestor had its seeds rolled into a ball on the frond, an angiosperm ovary would result.) To systematic botanists, these structural similarities indicate that flowering plants are evolutionarily derived from seed ferns and that flowers are actually modified leaves. The long period of evolutionary transition from gymnosperms to angiosperms is most evident when comparing the flat and leaf-like sporophylls of seed ferns with the most primitive flowers found in *Magnolia* and buttercups. *Magnolia* flowers have long receptacles with spirally arranged flower parts that are separate. Flower parts are not differentiated into sepals and petals. Such flowers are strongly reminiscent of seed fern sporophylls.

The seeds of flowering plants develop from ovules and are part of an ovary that ultimately forms a fruit. The fact that seeds of flowering plants are encased and protected clearly differentiates them from the gymnosperms, in which the naked and exposed seeds are on cones or strobili.

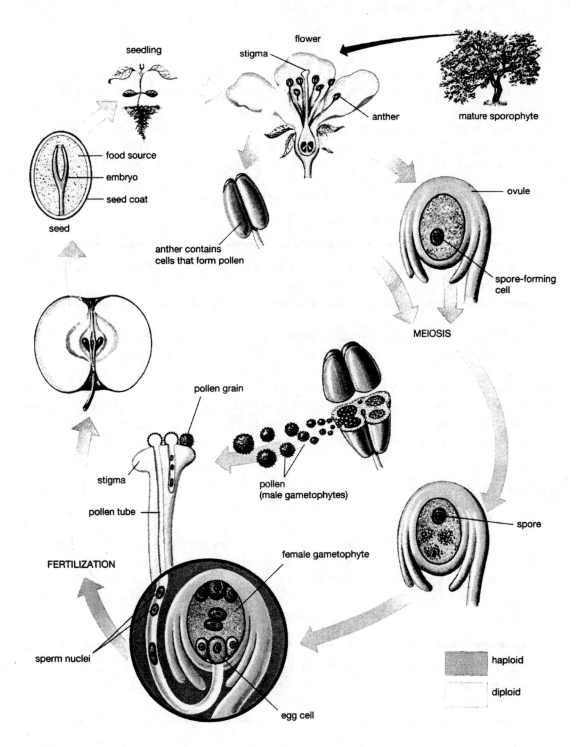

Figure 23–1 The life cycle of a flowering plant. *Source:* Teresa Audesirk and Gerald Audesirk (1999), p. 406.

Characteristics of Flowering Plants

Angiosperms are flowering and seed bearing plants in which the diploid sporophyte generation is the dominant green plant while the haploid gametophyte generation is retained as dependent reproductive tissue on the sporophyte and limited to the development of the male and female gametes. The gametes occur in two different sized forms, microspores and megaspores; thus, flowering plants are heterosporous. The seeds are enclosed in an ovary which in most flowering plants becomes a ripened fruit. The fruit provides nourishment for the germinating seed and may also aid in dispersal by attracting animals. Pollination is achieved mostly by animal agents and meteorological events such as wind, rain, or snow although some aquatic species depend on water currents for pollen and seed (or fruit) dispersal.

Angiosperms are flowering and seed bearing plants in which the green plant represents the dominant sporophyte generation.

Photosynthesis in angiosperms is accomplished by organized clusters of chloroplasts arranged in leaf patterns that maximize exposure to sunlight and enhance photosynthesis. Movement of gases across leaf-air interfaces is closely regulated by stomatal control. The xylem and phloem vessels are well developed and tightly organized, with several new supporting cells that enhance transfer efficiency of water, minerals, and dissolved sugars. Roots and stems (and less commonly leaves) may serve as storage reservoirs for water and starches.

Evolution of Flowering Plants

Fossils reveal that the first flowering plants appeared during the Late Jurassic period of about 130 million years ago, in the middle of the Age of the Dinosaurs. Flowering plants underwent an extensive adaptive radiation and developed in great profusion during the Cretaceous Era. By the start of the Cenozoic, about 65 million years ago, flowering plants were the dominant forms of plant life throughout the world.

Famed dinosaur paleontologist Robert Bakker has proposed that the rise of the flowering plants was instrumental in the demise of the dinosaurs, who were less efficient than the mammals in exploiting this new food supply.

During the Jurassic, the earliest flowers were spirally arranged and radially symmetrical. The pistil was formed by a blade or a leaf-like structure with ovules along its edges, rolling inward and fusing along the margins. This kind of fertile blade is called a **carpel**. Eventually the separate carpels of primitive flowers fused together to form the compound pistil found in modern angiosperms.

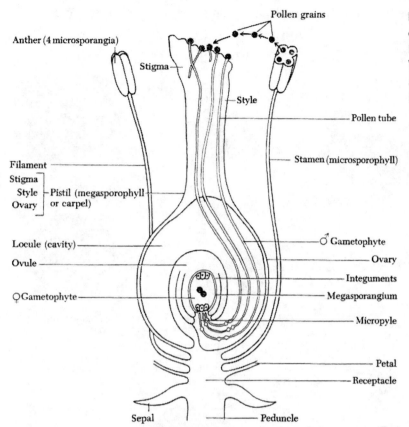

Figure 23–2 The parts of a flower. *Source:* Harold C. Bold and John W. La Claire II. *The Plant Kingdom* (1987), Prentice-Hall, p. 206.

Labels in figure:
Pollen grains
Anther (4 microsporangia)
Stigma
Style
Pollen tube
Stamen (microsporophyll)
Filament
Stigma
Style — Pistil (megasporophyll or carpel)
Ovary
Locule (cavity)
Ovule
♂ Gametophyte
Ovary
Integuments
Megasporangium
♀ Gametophyte
Micropyle
Petal
Receptacle
Sepal
Peduncle

Reproduction in Flowering Plants

Sexual reproduction begins with the production of male and female gametophytes. In angiosperms, the development of female gametophytes, borne on the sporophyte green plant, is complex. While the flower is developing on the bud, a diploid **megaspore mother cell** differentiates in the **ovule**. This cell undergoes meiosis to produce four haploid **megaspores**. Three of the megaspores degenerate but the fourth undergoes mitosis and enlarges. As the cell grows, its two haploid nuclei divide again, resulting in four nuclei, which divide yet again to produce eight haploid nuclei in the cell. By this time, the reproductive cell has grown to many times its original size. The two outer layers of cells of the ovule undergo differentiation to become **integuments**, which will ultimately form the seed coat. As these integuments develop, they leave a small opening, the **micropyle** at one end.

The eight haploid nuclei of the megaspore are divided into two groups of four at each end of the cell. One nucleus of each group, called the **polar nucleus,** migrates toward the center of the cell. The two migrating nuclei meet in the center and fuse to form a diploid nucleus. Cell walls begin to form around the remaining cells of the megaspore. In the group of cells closest to the micropyle, one will function as the **egg**. The remaining two, called **synergids,** either degenerate or are destroyed by the pollen tube. At the other end of the ovule are the remaining three cells (of the original group of four), called **antipodals**. They have no function and will later also degenerate. The surviving megaspore containing the seven or eight nuclei is called an **embryo sac** and constitutes the **female gametophyte**.

Figure 23–3 Pollen development in flowering plants. *Source:* Teresa Audesirk and Gerald Audesirk (1999), p. 492.

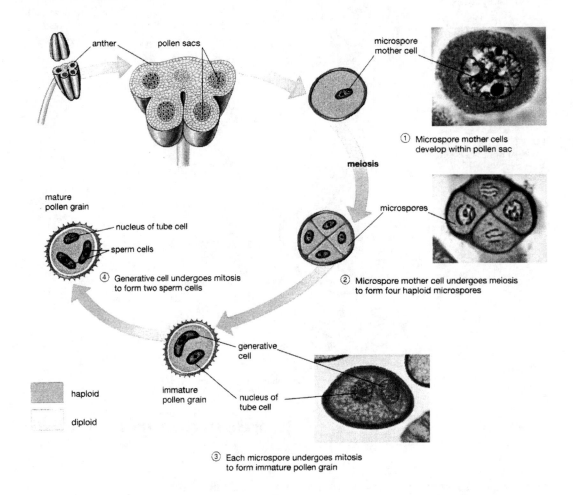

The male gametophyte is formed in much the same manner, but with some significant differences. In angiosperms, male gametophyte formation occurs in the **anthers**. As the anthers mature, four chambers of tissue become distinguishable within the main mass of cells. These chambers are the **pollen sacs** and are lined with nutritive cells called **tapetals** which can be seen in cross sections of anthers. Each of these four chambers contains diploid **microspore mother cells**. The mother cells undergo meiosis, producing four **microspores**. Following meiosis several things occur in rapid succession. First, the nucleus in each microspore divides once. Secondly, the members of each quartet of microspores separate from one another. Thirdly, a two-layered wall, which is often finely sculptured, develops around each microspore. When this event is completed, the microspores have been transformed into **pollen grains**.

POLLINATION AND FERTILIZATION

Although often used interchangeably to refer to the fertilization of an egg, pollination and fertilization have different scientific meanings. **Pollination** is the transfer of pollen grains from the anther of one flower to the stigma of a different flower. **Fertilization** is the union of a sperm produced by the anther and an egg produced by the megaspore. Fertilization usually (but not always) follows pollination but in many flowering plants it may not take place for days or weeks or months after pollination has occurred. Most

Figure 23–4 Development of the female gametophyte in flowering plants. *Source:* Teresa Audesirk and Gerald Audesirk (1999), p. 493.

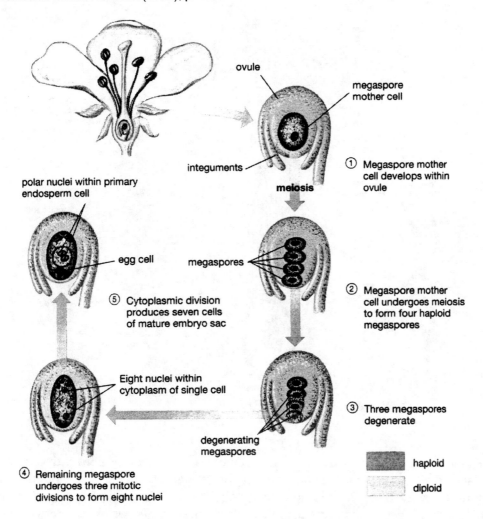

flowers are pollinated by the action of insects, wind, water, birds, bats, small rodents, or gravity.

Pollination is the transfer of the male gametophyte to the female gametophyte. Fertilization is the union of the sperm and egg nuclei within each of the gametophytes.

Pollination is a precisely controlled event. The outer layer of the pollen grain wall is called an **exine.** It contains substances that will produce chemical reactions when it comes in contact with the stigma of a flower. When the pollen grain is from another plant of the same species and if conditions are right, the cytoplasm of the pollen grain absorbs material from the stigma and swells to form a tube that penetrates through one of the apertures of the pollen grain. However, if the pollen grain was produced by the same plant, chemicals produced by the stigma inactivate further development of the pollen. This process helps avoid self-fertilization.

Figure 23–5 Events during the pollination and fertilization of a flower. *Source:* Teresa Audesirk and Gerald Audesirk (1999), p. 494.

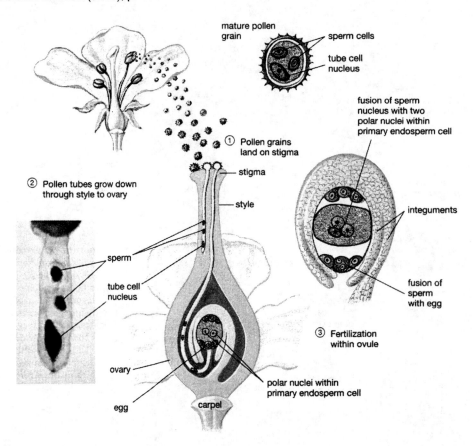

Pollen grains contain two small nuclei. One of the nuclei, the **generative nucleus**, will later divide, producing two sperms. The remaining nucleus, called the **tube nucleus**, is involved in the formation of the pollen tube. This swelling is the pollen tube, which grows between cells of the stigma and style until it reaches the micropyle. As the tube grows, the contents of the pollen grain are discharged into the tube. The tube nucleus remains at the tip of the pollen tube. The generative nucleus enters the pollen tube and mitotically divides, producing two sperms in the process. This germinated pollen grain and its pollen tube constitute the **male gametophyte**. When the pollen tube reaches the embryo sac, it destroys the synergid cells and discharges the two sperm into the sac. One sperm unites with the egg, while the second sperm fuses with the polar nuclei of the megaspore, producing a 3n or triploid endosperm nucleus. The union of the two sperm with their separate partners is called a **double fertilization**, an event which is unique to angiosperms.

In some monocots such as corn and other cereal grains, the endosperm forms much of the seed. For example, the endosperm is what we actually consume when we eat corn. In most dicots the endosperm is used up by the embryo that develops from the zygote so the endosperm has disappeared by the time the seed coat is hard. The result of these fertilization events is that the ovule has become a **seed** and the ovary has become a **fruit**. This complex reproductive process occurs in about 70 percent of flowering plants. The other 30 percent exhibit variations in which the embryo sac has from four to sixteen nuclei or cells at maturity and the endosperm may be 5n, 9n or even 15n.

Figure 23–6 Development of the seed. *Source:* Teresa Audesirk and Gerald Audesirk (1999), p. 496.

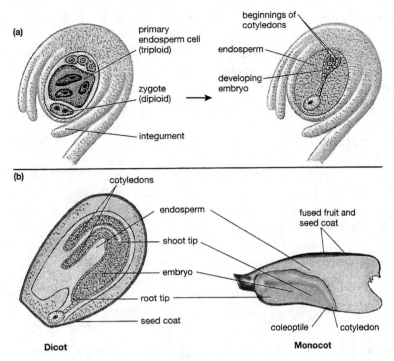

For example, in lilies, when the megaspore mother cell undergoes meiosis, all four of the haploid nuclei remain functional; three of them unite to form a 3n nucleus while the fourth nuclei remains haploid (n). The 3n nucleus divides twice by mitosis, forming two 3n nuclei in the first division and four 3n nuclei in the second. The haploid megaspore nucleus also divides in the same way, forming four haploid nuclei. At the same time the embryo sac also develops. During this time the embryo sac is also developing. It will ultimately contain eight nuclei of which four are 3n nuclei and four are haploid nuclei. One polar nucleus in the embryo sac is 3n, the other is haploid. Fertilization by haploid sperm occurs and a 5n endosperm results.

Some Deviations—Apomixis and Parthenocarpy

Apomixis is a process whereby the plant produces seeds from tissue other than the embryo. In *Poa*, a common and widespread genus of grass that includes Bermuda grass, almost 98 percent of the seeds produced are apomixic. In these grasses, the seeds are derived from the wall of the ovule rather than by sexual reproduction. This strange situation seems to have evolved as an evolutionary stratagem to maintain the genetic variability of the *Poa* species.

By way of explanation, consider that grasses typically live in dry or semiarid conditions where the environment is stable and usually has remained unchanged for millions of years. As long as environmental conditions remain the same there is no need for evolutionary variation in the individuals that comprise the *Poa* population. However, if the grassland environment changes, genetic variation provides a pool of adaptations that may prove beneficial in a new environment. As long as the environment remains the same, *Poa* produces seeds from sterile tissue and all of the individuals of the population are genetically similar. Genetic insurance is provided by the other 2 percent of *Poa* population in which seeds are produced by normal sexual reproduction. These members of the population carry the genetic insurance in the form of genetic variation.

The variations of these members may enable the grass to adapt to a changing environment, should the need arise.

Parthenocarpy. An embryo may develop directly from a diploid (2n) nutritive cell. Or alternately, in some plants another cell of the ovule instead of the zygote may develop into the seed. Seeds produced in this manner represent vegetative rather than sexual reproduction. Fruits that develop from ovaries having unfertilized eggs are called **parthenocarpic**. Such fruits are seedless and are found in varieties of bananas, naval oranges, and varieties of figs and grapes.

STRATEGIES OF POLLINATION

Almost all of the flowering plants depend on pollination agents for the transfer of the pollen from the male to the female gametophyte. Because of this, a key feature in the evolution of flowering plants has been the precise shaping of flower structure and color to ensure pollination by animals or certain meteorological conditions. In many instances, the size, color, and shape of the flowers provide clues as to how they are pollinated. For example, the small, almost inconspicuous flowers of grasses are almost all wind pollinated. To facilitate pollination by the wind the flowers are located high on the plant, where they will most likely intercept wind driven pollen. Since large, showy petals and sepals might act as a wall, lessening the chance of pollination they are generally discarded or severely reduced.

Conversely, flowers pollinated by animal agents are usually large and conspicuous, often very brightly colored and boldly marked. Many of them exude odors or nectaries as animal attractants. The use of animals as agents of pollen transfer has been marked by a long coevolution that resulted from a series of mutual benefits obtained by both the flowering plant and its pollinator. The flowering plants benefit because the animal transfers the pollen more surely and effectively than the vagaries of wind and water could do. Since animal pollinators are more effective dispersers of pollen, the flowering plants that use pollinators can reduce their production of metabolically expensive pollen and flowers. (The pollinators act as a kind of insurance policy). The pollinators benefit from the relationship as well; pollen is an important food source which is rich in high-energy carbohydrates. In temperate regions of the world many insects such as bees, flies, butterflies, moths, and beetles serve as the primary pollinators of flowering plants. Non-insect pollinators include hummingbirds and small rodents. Insects are also important pollinators in the tropics but some species of bats are pollinators of flowers that grow high in the canopy of the tropical rain forest. In both tropics and temperate regions, bees are generally the most important pollinators of flowering plants.

The colors and markings commonly seen in many flowers act as signal flags to attract specific kinds of insects which associate the flowers with food. Flower structure may also be an adaptation for animal vectors. For example, the lower, lip-like petals seen in some flowers such as snapdragons are actually landing platforms for insects. After landing, the insect is guided through a narrow floral chamber to obtain the nectar. This tunnel travel helps ensure that the insect will come in contact with the sticky pollen which adheres to their legs.

Flowers that are pollinated by bats and hummingbirds are often brightly colored—usually red—and tubular. Since red appears black to insects, they will generally overlook tubular flowers but the reds provide a signal to hummingbirds, which, like humans, can see color. For hummingbirds, the elongate tube flowers provide perfect feeding stations that exclude other organisms from this energy rich food source.

Some markings of flowers are invisible to us as they appear only in ultraviolet light. They attract the many species of insects that can "see" ultraviolet light. The paler yellow and white flowers of many cacti and other desert succulents are often pollinated by moths and bats which are active at night. For these night flyers, the large, light-colored flowers are as conspicuous as beacons in the desert night. Most "night flowers" remain closed during the day, opening at dusk for the night flying animal vectors which will visit them.

Orchids have evolved several interesting strategies to attract pollinators. Some orchid flowers are shaped like female insects; males arrive and try to mate with the female-like flower, thereby pollinating it in the process. Some orchids also produce special pollen sacs that stick to the legs or abdomen of insects and are transported to the next flower by them. Other orchid flowers lead the insect in a pool of intoxicating fluid through which it must swim to escape. In the process, the insect pollinates the flower.

STRATEGIES FOR SUCCESS

Several features of angiosperms contributed to their ecological success and made them the dominant plants of all of the earth's ecosystems, a position they have maintained over the past 100 million years or so. First, the coevolution of flowers and their pollinating agents, insects, birds, rodents, bats, and other mammals helped ensure a more effective pollination mechanism for transferring the sperm to the egg. Second, the multiple nuclei of pollen grains, especially the tube nuclei which interacted with the female gametophyte, actually facilitate the final transfer of the male sperm and also function to prevent pollination by another species. Third, the endosperm nourishment carried with the seed contributes to its germination and initial growth—both critical times in the life of a new plant. Fourth, by enclosing a seed in a nutritive coat (the fruit), many flowering plants attract effective dispersal agents in the birds and mammals that eat the fruit and ultimately disperse the seeds. For others, the development of aerial structures on the seed such as wings or parachutes has markedly enhanced dispersal.

The Varieties of Flowering Plants

The angiosperms are a huge group, and as one might expect, they exhibit a great variety of form. They range in size from the duckweeds, which are tiny plants that float on the surface of ponds, to the huge hickories and maples of the deciduous forests of the world.

Angiosperms constitute the Division Anthophyta which is divided into two great subclasses, the dicots and the monocots.

Taxonomically, the flowering plants are also the most diverse of all plants. They number more than three hundred families divided into two major classes, the **Monocotyledonae** (monocots) and **Dicotyledonae** (dicots). We have chosen just a few of the most representative families to give you an overview of the variety of these plants and their importance.

Figure 23–7 A comparison of the basic characteristics of dicots and monocots. *Source:* Teresa Audesirk and Gerald Audesirk (1999), p. 453.

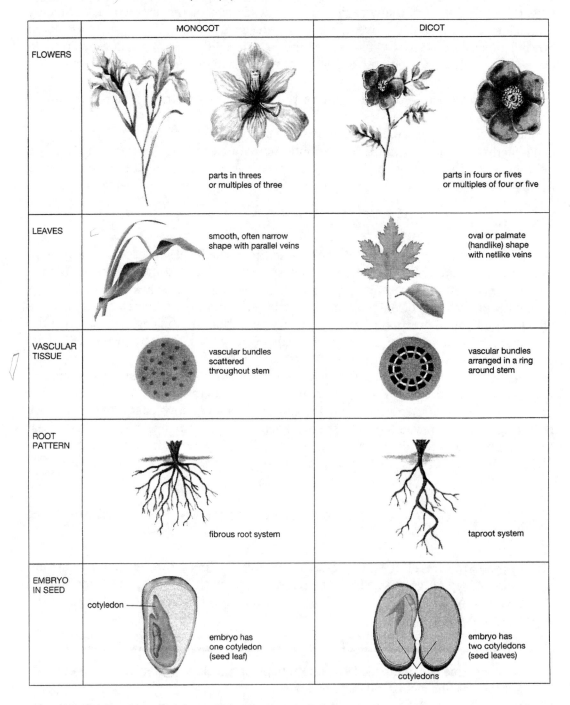

CLASS DICOTYLEDONAE—THE DICOTS

The dicots are the most diverse class of flowering plants and include a much larger number of families and species than found in the monocots. Some authorities suggest that there are at least 200,000 species of dicots. Familiar examples of dicots include the magnolias, fruit trees, roses and their allies, mustards, nightshades, melons and pumpkins, cacti, peas, beans and other legumes. Most of the larger tree groups are also dicots such as the beeches, birches, oaks, maples, and hickories. As their name implies,

Figure 23–8 The columbine *Aquilegia vulgaris,* a member of the buttercup family. *Source:* Jim Harter (1988), p. 210.

Figure 23–9 Structure of the bellflower (a) stem and flower (b) single flower (c) cross section of flower (d) transection of compound ovary. *Source:* Harold C. Bold and John W. La Claire II. *The Plant Kingdom* (1987), Prentice-Hall, p. 236.

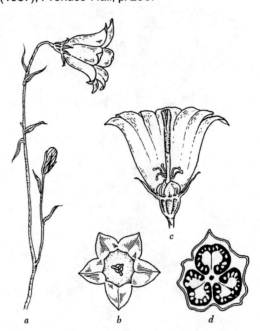

the dicots are so-called because their seed embryos have two cotyledons. In addition, the leaves generally have reticulate (net) venation and the vascular bundles in the stem occur in a single ring. Flower parts usually occur in sets of five or multiples of five although some have flower parts in sets of four (or multiples of four) and a few have flower parts in sets of three.

Family Ranunculaceae—The Buttercups. This is a very primitive family of flowering plants. The flowers have numerous stamens and pistils with the petals being variable in number. The ovary is superior. There are approximately 1500 species concentrated in north temperate and Arctic regions of the world. They are herbaceous in nature and include buttercups, columbines, larkspurs, anemones, monkshood and *Clematis*. Most members of this family are slightly poisonous and many folk medicines are made from them.

Family Lauraceae—The Laurels. The flowers of laurels lack petals but the six sepals are sometimes petal-like. The stamens occur in three or four whorls, each whorl consisting of three petals. The ovary is superior. There are over 1,000 species of laurels, with most being tropical with aromatic leaves. Many spices and foods are from this family, including cinnamon, cassia, camphor, sassafras, sweet bay and avocados.

Family Papaveraceae—The Poppys. These are herbaceous plants of the temperate and subtropical regions north of the equator. They have numerous stamens but only one pistil. A milky or colored sap is produced in the rhizomes. Plants like the Opium Poppy, produce opium and several derivatives used as drugs and analgesics such as morphine, codeine, papaverine, noscapine and heroin.

Family Brassicaceae—The Mustards. In this family the four petals of the flowers are in the form of a cross. The flowers also have four sepals, four nectar glands and six

Figure 23-10 The blue Himalaya poppy. *Source:* Jim Harter (1988), p. 198.

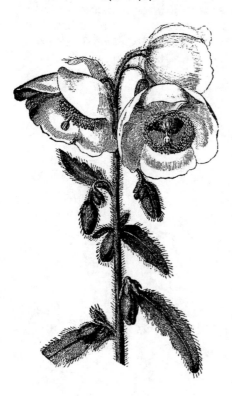

Figure 23-11 The mustard flower Brassica (a) the flower (b) a single flower (c) cross section of the ovary (d) fruits. *Source:* Harold C. Bold and John W. La Claire II. *The Plant Kingdom* (1987), Prentice-Hall, p. 232.

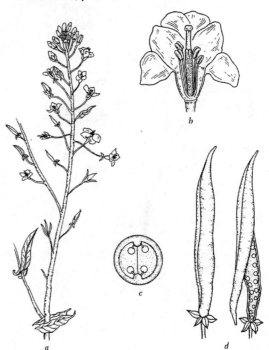

stamens. All mustards produce siliques as fruits—they are the only family to do so. There are about 2,500 species of these herbs widely distributed mostly throughout temperate and cooler regions of the world. This family supplies many of the common vegetables including, cabbage, cauliflower, Brussels sprouts, broccoli, radish, kohlrabi, turnip, horseradish, watercress and rutabaga. The family also includes many hardy weeds of fields, roadsides and waste areas.

Family Rosaceae—The Roses. This is a cosmopolitan and successful family numbering about 3,000 species of trees, herbs and shrubs. The flower has the basal parts fused into a cup with petals, sepals and numerous stamens being attached to the cup's rim. The rose family includes a number of economically important fruits such as the cherries, apricots, peaches, plums, apples, pears, strawberries, blackberries, loganberries and raspberries. Other species are highly prized household and garden plants. Roses are extensively cultivated as landscaping and ornamental plantings. The Venus' flytrap, famous for capturing insects by closing its cage-like leaves, is also in this family.

Family Fabaceae—The Legumes. This is the third largest family of dicots with over 13,000 species. Legumes are a cosmopolitan family, having representatives everywhere a land plant can grow. The flowers are either radial or bilateral in symmetry. The bilateral flowers are complex with two keeled petals enclosing the pistil, two wing petals which are flanked by banner petals on the sides. Stamens are fused and form a tube around the ovary. The fruit is a legume. Many legume species are important pulse crops, including peas, beans, lentils, and peanuts. Others are important cover and pasture species such as alfalfa and sweet clover while still others provide products such as licorice, wattle, carob, indigo and logwood. Common landscape ornamentals in this

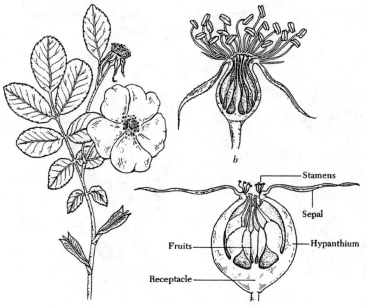

Figure 23–12 The organization of a rose (a) stem, leaves, and flower (b) sectioned flower (c) rose hip with enclosed fruits. *Source: Harold C. Bold and John W. La Claire II. The Plant Kingdom (1987), Prentice-Hall, p. 233.*

family include the lupines, locusts, *Catalpa* and sensitive plant. About 90 percent of the legume species exhibit leaf movements, of which the sensitive plant is the most outstanding example.

Family Euphorbiaceae—The Spurges. These are plants of tropical and temperate habitats. The flowers are generally small and inconspicuous. They have stamens and pistils produced as separate flowers and lack a corolla. The female flower is elevated on a stalk with the male flowers arranged around it. Examples of spurges include the *poinsettia*, *cassava* (farinha), tapioca, para rubber tree, Mexican jumping beans and the crown-of-thorns.

Family Cactaceae—The Cactuses. These succulents are indigenous only to the Americas but they have been widely introduced in other parts of the world as landscape ornamentals. The cacti number about 1500 species. The showy flowers have numerous stamens, petals and sepals. The sepals are colored like the petals and the

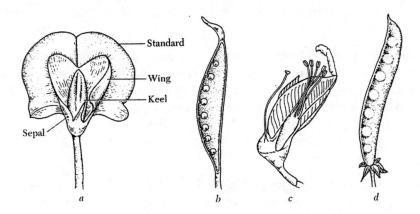

Figure 23–13 From flower to fruit in the sweet pea (Lathyrus odoratus) (a) single flower (b) fruit (c) carpel (pistil) enlarging to form fruit (d) mature fruit. *Source: Harold C. Bold and John W. La Claire II. The Plant Kingdom (1987), Prentice-Hall, p. 234.*

Figure 23–14 The castor oil plant. *Source:* Jim Harter (1988), p. 307.

Figure 23–15 A prickly pear cactus plant. *Source:* Jim Harter (1988), p. 51.

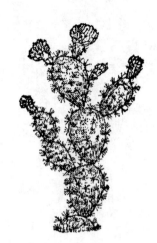

ovary develops into a berry. The leaves are reduced and the stem typically has protective thorns. The cacti are widely used as household and garden ornamentals. The succulent tissues of many cacti are a food source.

Cacti also store water which can be extracted by pulping the tissues. The Peyote are small button-like plants with a carrot-like tap root. They produce several secretions that can be made into drugs including mescaline which is a powerful hallucinogen. They have been used in religious ceremonies by several native American groups.

Ecologically, many cacti have proven to be hardy and robust species. For example, the prickly pear cactus (*Opuntia*), common and widespread in the southwest deserts of North America, was introduced as a garden ornamental in Australia during the late 1800's. It escaped and quickly became established in the wilds. Within a few decades this seemingly incongruous cactus had spread rapidly, ultimately covering enormous areas of good pasture and farmland with a thick and nearly impenetrable tangle of cactus growth. Its spread was finally halted by deliberately introducing a cactus moth, *Cactoblastis cactoium*, from North America, whose larvae tunneled through *Opuntia* feeding on its tissue. Within a short time the cacti withered and died and the cactus infestation was effectively checked and then almost eliminated. This deliberate introduction of a predator to control a pest species is an excellent example of **biological control.**

Family Lamiaceae—The Mints. The mints comprise a large family with 3,000 or more species. They are characterized by stems having a square cross section, opposite leaves and bilateral flowers. Also they smell minty, especially when the leaves and stems are crushed. Included here are many spices such as rosemary, thyme, sage, oregano, marjoram, basil, lavender, catnip, peppermint, spearmint and horehound. Other useful mints include vinegar weed, salvias, coleus and chia. Menthol, used in medications, is produced from mint oil.

Family Solanaceae—The Nightshades. Nightshades number about 3,000 species and are mostly in the tropics of South and Central America. The flowers have petals fused together at the base and filaments of stamens fused to the corolla so they appear to be arising from it. The superior ovary develops into a berry or capsule. The nightshades include many familiar plants such as the tomato, white potato, eggplant, pep-

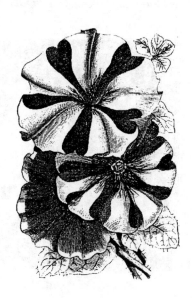

per, tobacco and petunia. The nightshades are also the source of several important drugs such as belladonna, atropine, scopolamine and hyoscyamine.

Family Apiaceae—The Carrots. The 2,000 members of the carrot family are mostly from the Northern hemisphere. They all have aromatic foliage and small numerous flowers, arranged in umbels. Plants that we use in this family include dill, celery, carrot, parsley, caraway, coriander, fennel, anise, and parsnip.

Family Cucurbitaceae—The Pumpkins. This small family of 700 species consists mostly of tropical forms. The pumpkins are prostrate or climbing herbaceous vines with tendrils. The flowers have fused petals and an inferior ovary with three carpals. The flowers are imperfect with male and female flowers on the same plant. Some are dioecious with only one sex on each vine. Included here are pumpkins, squashes, cucumbers, cantaloupes, watermelons, vegetable sponge and gourds.

Family Asteraceae—The Sunflowers. This huge and successful family has over 20,000 species. The asters and sunflowers and their relatives comprise the largest family of all of the flowering plants. The individual flowers (florets) are tiny and arranged in compact inflorescenses so they resemble a single flower. Because of the showy flowers, many garden varieties belong to this group, including sunflowers, daisy, dandelions, lettuce, endive, chicory, Jerusalem artichoke, dahlia, chrysanthemum, marigold, thistle and yarrow.

Figure 23–18 Carrots. Source: Jim Harter (1988), p. 296.

Figure 23–19 The flower structure of Helianthus, a sunflower (a) capitulum, or inflorescence (b) detail of a disc flower (c) detail of a ray flower. *Source:* Harold C. Bold and John W. La Claire II. *The Plant Kingdom* (1987), Prentice-Hall, p. 210.

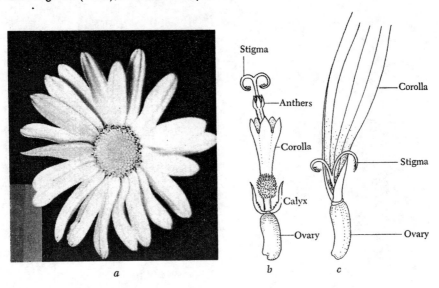

Figure 23–20 Gourds. *Source:* Jim Harter (1988).

Figure 23–21 A sunflower. *Source:* Jim Harter (1988), p. 72.

CLASS MONOCOTYLEDONAE— THE MONOCOTS

Most of the monocots have a single monocotyledon on their embryo. Monocot leaves are usually long, with parallel venation, as exemplified by leaves of grasses and lilies. Other monocot characters include the fact that their flowers are usually arranged in parts of threes, i.e., three each of stamens, sepals, petals and carpels, and the vascular bundles are scattered throughout the stem rather than being restricted to a single ring, as found in the dicots.

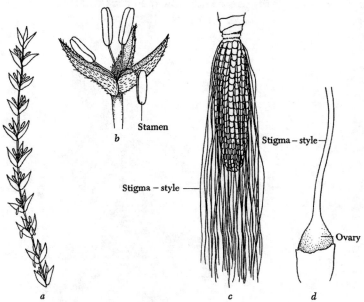

Figure 23–22 The structure of a typical corn grass, Zea mays (a) young stalk (b) single staminate flower (c) inflorescence of young ear of corn (d) single pistilate flower with stigma-style. *Source:* Harold C. Bold and John W. La Claire II. *The Plant Kingdom* (1987), Prentice-Hall, p. 209.

Figure 23–23 Grasses. *Source:* Jim Harter (1988), p. 118.

Family Poaceae—The Grasses. This family of flowering plants numbers about 8,000 species. Familiar examples of the grass family include bamboo, millet, rice, sugar cane, rye, sorghum, oats, corn and wheat. Grasses have a complex and often greatly reduced flower. The reduction of petals and sepals serves to facilitate pollination of grass flowers by the wind. The economic value of grasses rank them among the most important of all plants for humans. All the cereal grains and some other plants belong to this group, including wheat, rye, barley, oats, rice, corn, sugar cane and sorghum.

Grasses also comprise the dominant species of ecologically important grassland ecosystems of the world. Large expanses of grasslands occur on most continents. In North America grasslands are called prairie, in South America the pampas, in Africa the veld and in Eurasia the steppes.

Family Liliaceae—The Lilies. This family includes about 2,000 species, most of which are abundant in the tropics and subtropics. The flowers are usually large and all parts are in multiples of three with sepals usually colored the same as the petals. Many are ornamentals, but some economi-

Figure 23–24 A day lily. *Source:* Jim Harter (1988), p. 150.

Figure 23–25 The magnificent orchid. *Source:* Jim Harter (1988), p. 178.

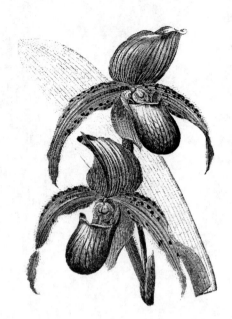

cally important vegetables, spices and fiber plants are in this family, including onion, leek, garlic, asparagus, sarsaparilla, squill, meadow saffron, bowstring hemp and aloe.

Family Orchidaceae—The Orchids. This huge family has over 35,000 species and is most abundant in the tropics. The flowers are usually exceptionally showy and specialized. Many of the orchids are epiphytes, that is, plants that live on other plants. Orchid flowers usually have three sepals and three petals with a lip petal differing from the other two. Many orchids are prized as ornamentals, but the vanilla orchid is used to produce vanilla flavoring.

Key Words and Phrases

angiosperms
monocot
pollination
megaspore
micropyle
synergids
female gametophyte
pollen sac
carpel
parthenocarpy
monecious
double fertilization
endosperm

seed ferns
heterosporous
coevolution
ovule
polar nucleus
antipodals
male gametophyte
apomixis
inferior ovary
imperfect flowers
dioecious
seed
generative nuclei

dicot
pollinators
fertilization
integument
egg
embryo sac
anther
exine
superior ovary
perfect flowers
fertilization
fruit
tube nucleus

Selected References and Resources

Cronquist, A. 1988. *The Evolution and Classification of Flowering Plants.* Wm. C. Brown, Publishers. Dubuque, Iowa.

Cullen, J. 1997. *The Identification of Flowering Plant Families.* Cambridge University Press. New York.

D'Arcy, W. G., and R. C. Keating. 1996. *The Anther.* Cambridge University Press. New York.

Faegri, K., and L. vander Pijl. 1972. *The Principles of Pollination.* 2nd. Edition. Pergamon Press. Elmsford, New York.

Friis, E. M., W. G. Chaloner, and P. R. Crane. Eds. 1987. *The Origin of Angiosperms and Their Biological Consequences.* Cambridge University Press. Cambridge.

Hickey, M., C. King, and S. M. Walters. 1997. Common Families of Flowering Plants. Cambridge University Press. New York.

Huxley, A. 1987. *Plants and Planet.* Viking Press. New York.

Johri, M. B. Ed. 1984. *Embryology of Angiosperms.* Springer-Verlag. New York.

Mabberley, D. J. 1997. *A Portable Dictionary of the Vascular Plants.* 2nd. Edition. Cambridge University Press. New York.

Mathias, M. E. Ed. 1982. *Flowering Plants in the Landscape.* University of California Press. Berkeley, California.

Proctor, M., and P. Yeo. 1972. *The Pollination of Flowers.* Taplinger Publishing Company. New York.

Rudall, P. 1992. *Anatomy of Flowering Plants.* Cambridge University Press. New York.

Sporne, K. R. 1974. *Morphology of Angiosperms.* Hutchinson University Library. London.

Tathtajan, A. L. 1969. *Origin and Dispersal of Flowering Plants.* Oliver and Boyd. Edinburgh.

Review and Discussion Questions

1. Use a flow chart to review events in the formation of the male and female gametophytes.
2. Describe how the color and shape of flowers attract specific insects as pollinators.
3. Flowers and their pollinators coevolved. Exactly what does that mean?
4. Discuss the ecological importance of legumes.
5. Discuss the ecological importance of grasslands. Why are they sometimes considered to be the most productive as well as the most human modified of all ecosystems?
6. Take a walk through the flower garden of a nearby nursery or the school greenhouse and classify each of the plants as monocots or dicots based on their flower and leaf characteristics alone.
7. How does male and female gametophyte development in angiosperms differ from that previously seen in the gymnosperms?
8. What structures and processes have contributed to angiosperms becoming the dominant plants?

9. Discuss the concept of alternation of generations and the role of mitosis and meiosis in the life cycle of angiosperms.
10. Discuss the differences in reproduction between the two seed-bearing divisions of plants, the angiosperms and the gymnosperms.

Chapter 24

Foods and Medicines from Plants

Food and Agriculture

THE FIRST FARMERS

The earliest humans were hunter-gathers that gathered edible roots, berries and other fruits, nuts, and seeds, tubers, and collected edible fungi. They hunted small animals with stones and clubs and scavenged the remains of large animals whenever possible. To them, life was a constant and not always successful search for food. If they found food they survived, if not they starved to death. When food was plentiful human numbers increased but when food was scarce their numbers diminished.

The invention or discovery of agriculture helped guarantee a more stable food supply, thereby eliminating much of the uncertainty associated with hunting and gathering. This assured food supplied by agriculture produced several interrelated events that provided enormous benefit for humans. First, agriculture stabilized the previously nomadic peoples which now had to remain in an area for most of the year to attend their agricultural fields and harvest the crops. Second, since agriculture produces large amounts of food with minimal labor, fewer people were needed to work agricultural plots. One of the main benefits is that a portion of the population is freed from the need to obtain food and can be employed in other tasks such as construction work, as priests, and as entertainers. No doubt this led directly to the development of the sciences. Third, leisure time is now available for other pursuits.

Exactly how the first farmers learned to sow and harvest wild plants is unknown, lost in the long-ago mists of antiquity. Conjectures suggest that they may have noticed the growth of certain food plants on garbage heaps or perhaps they were able to correlate food plants and their seeds with certain types of soil and then crudely duplicated conditions that resulted in a more assured, steady crop of plants. This would probably not have been difficult, since many of the first cultivated plants were weeds that could grow under relatively poor soil conditions. It is also possible that farming began only after it was noticed that plants such as tomatoes could be grown again and again if the seeds were kept over winter and subsequently planted. Of equal interest is how our distant ancestors learned to make bread and other foodstuffs from cereals as well as use the harvested products from many other plants. It is not immediately obvious, for example, that a handful of wheat seeds can be ground into flour and baked into bread.

Whenever the origin and whatever the steps involved, agriculture originated more or less simultaneously in several parts of the world between 20,000–11,000 years ago and became widespread amongst most of the peoples of the world by 5000–1000 years ago.

ORIGINS AND WORLD-WIDE INTRODUCTIONS OF FOOD PLANTS

All food crops have their origin in wild plants that were initially selected by the first farmers for cultivation. Some cultivars such as carrots, berries, and various fruits are almost exactly like their wild counterparts except that the edible part is larger as a result of centuries of selection of the best growing varieties on many local scales. Other cultivars are so different that it is difficult to recognize their wild origin.

Another interesting aspect of early agriculture was the spread of the most desirable plants from one region to another. The first sustained agriculture began in the Fertile Crescent of the Middle East, a region that extends roughly from modern Syria southward through the Tigris and Euphrates Rivers. Wheat and barley were the first crops and sometime later, lentils, peas, and vetch were added. Agriculture soon spread northward into the Black Sea region, eastward into Asia, and southward into the land of Egypt and beyond to Africa. Crops of wheat and barley were next introduced north and west into Europe.

The discovery and colonization of the New World and Australia led to many further introductions of food plants in both directions, from the old world to the new world and from the new world to the old world. The pioneers that colonized North America brought their own food crops, fruits, vegetables, and forage plants with them but also adopted and adapted many of the native cultivars, especially maize, potatoes, and tomatoes, all of which ultimately were introduced into Europe where they became important food crops, especially potatoes which was originally an important food crop cultivated in the northern Andes of South America. Additional foods cultivated by the native peoples of Latin America and adapted by the European explorers included chili peppers, tomatoes, cocao, pineapple, squashes and pumpkins, and kidney beans and lima beans. Cotton and tobacco were two New World plants also favored by the early explorers.

Similar introductions occurred with the colonization of Australia and the larger Oceanic Islands of the Pacific, mostly in the form of cereal crops; today Australia is one of the most important wheat producers in the world.

Agriculture also brought selective changes in plants used for farming as certain strains and varieties were selected for planting and other varieties that were less useful were ignored or discarded. The ears of corn and the roots of carrots, for example, are many times larger and more edible than those found in the original wild species of corn and carrots. Another of the many examples of active selective processes at work by farmers from ancient times to the present is seen in wheat. The ancestral varieties from which wide scale wheat farming eventually sprang were weak stemmed and had seed heads that fell apart at maturity. Farmers deliberately used wheat species or individuals of species that had firm stalks and seeds that stuck together for easy harvesting.

CONTRIBUTIONS OF CROPS AS FOOD FOR HUMANS

Plants provide over 80 percent of calories for an ever growing human population but only six of the 235,000 species of plants known to science contribute most of the calories. Another 3000 species are gathered or cultivated or have been historically used by native peoples and about 150 have been more widely cultivated. In terms of their caloric contribution, the six most important plants as food sources—in order of importance—-are the cereals rice, wheat, corn along with potatoes, sweet potatoes, and manioc. Of these rice is the single most consumed crop in the pantropics of the world while wheat, corn, and potatoes are staples of north temperate regions. Ten additional plants that figure heavily as food sources in certain areas of the globe include sugar cane and sugar beets, barley, sorghum, soybeans, bananas, yams, and coconuts.

Table 24–1 Examples of origin of world food plants.

Place of Origin	Example
Southeast Asia	Cotton, rice, coconut, cane sugar (New Guinea), tea, soybeans
India, Tropical Asia	Bananas, mangos, taro
Latin America	Corn, potatoes, tomatoes, pineapples, papaya, peanuts, tobacco, sweet potatoes, cocoa, squashes, kidney beans, lima beans, chili peppers, tobacco
Africa	Coffee, wheat, vanilla (Madagascar), oil palms, millet, sorghums
East Indies, IndoMalaysia	Oranges, mandarins, grapefruits, lemons

FOOD CROPS: CEREALS

All cereals are grain crops and all grain crops are grasses belonging to the grass family, the Poaceae or Gramineae. Cereals rank as the most important of all food crops, providing over half of the world's food calories and a substantial portion of the world's protein for human diets. The major foods produced from the grains of cereals include breads, pasta, and noodles. Nutrients obtained from grains include carbohydrates, of which starch comprises about 75%, protein, oils, essential minerals, vitamin B, and vitamin E, and fiber. Although grains provide about 8-15% protein, most grains lack sufficient quantities of certain essential amino acids such as lysine. Hybridization of grain varieties has produced several high-lysine cultivars that are currently grown in certain areas of the world. Other important grain products include animal feed in the form of hay, straw, silage, and forage.

The food that is harvested from cereals is **grain**, which is a kind of fruit. A grain is a one-seeded type of fruit called a **caryopsis** which develops from a fertilized ovary. Each grain is surrounded and protected by an outer coat that consists of the fused ovary wall and seed coat. Most of the interior is comprised of a starchy **endosperm** used to nourish the growing **seed embryo** which lies at one end of the endosperm. The outermost layers of the endosperm has a high protein content and is called **aleurone**.

Only the grains of cereal plants are harvested, the remainder of the plant, called straw or chaff, is either plowed under the soil as mulch or harvested for use as silage or other livestock food. Most harvested grains are processed by milling in which the grain coat and aleurone layers, collectively called bran, are mechanically removed. The remaining endosperm is further processed into flour. White bread, for example, comes from processed wheat in which the starchy endosperm has been ground into flour after the bran has been removed. In turn, the bran may be used as bran flakes in breakfast cereals and bran breads, or as livestock food.

Rice is the single most important food source, providing nutrition for more than half of the world's human population and cultivated on nearly 10 % of all arable land. It is estimated that rice is a dietary staple for 1.6–2 billion people, almost all from the pantropical areas of the world.

Rice is a grass of hot, rainy tropics and subtropics and is extensively cultivated in India, Southeast Asia, Japan, and the Phillippines where some 95 % of the rice crop is grown. Lesser centers of rice production include Africa, Latin America, and the United States. Because rice comprises 80–90 % of the human diet in these countries the growing of rice dictates much of their agricultural and social structure. A rainy climate is essential for the growing of rice which must be flooded (in rice paddies) for most of the growing season. In some areas peoples obtained dual benefits from the fact that flood rice paddies attract a variety of warm water fish that are then harvested with the rice crop, thereby simultaneously providing a meat and cereal source.

Most rice is still laboriously harvested by hand, then the husks are removed to produce brown rice or whole grain rice which is then further milled by removing the bran to produce white or polished rice. The enormous quantity of hulls generated by milling rice are used as animal feed, fertilizer, and biofuels. The bran is used as food for hogs and other livestock. The bran has also proven to be a good source of an oil extract that reduces blood cholesterol levels. Unfortunately for humans, milling of rice removes most of the vitamin thiamine, loss of which causes a deficiency disease called **beri-beri**.

Wheat is an annual grass that is widely cultivated in the temperate regions of the world. The United States, Canada, Russia, Australia, and Argentina are all centers of wheat cultivation but China, France, Turkey, and Pakistan are also important producers. Most wheats are cultivated for flour used in making breads and other bakery products. Wheat is also valued because the seeds contain gluten, a sticky protein substance that acts like an organic glue to hold bread together as it is formed into pastries and baked.

Hybridization of wheat along with the production of rice and corn varieties made possible the Green Revolution. Among the thousands of cultivars known there are two major types of cultivated wheat; bread wheat and durum wheat. About 90 % of the wheat crop is bread wheat which is also known as spring wheat although some varieties are planted in winter. Bread wheat is milled to produce hard wheat which is used for breads and soft wheat used for making pastries, cakes, cookies, and biscuits.

Wheat breads are made by baking a mix of flour, water, and salt to which is added yeast to leaven or ferment the baking bread. Yeast activity releases carbon dioxide which makes the bread rise. This, in turn, is made possible because of the extraordinarily elastic properties of gluten. Lack of yeast in the mixture results in flat, unleavened breads.

Durum wheat is also called macaroni wheat which grows well in arid and semiarid or drought-like conditions. Centers of duram wheat production include North Africa and Latin America. Duram wheat flour is much used in the preparation of noodles for spaghetti, macaroni, and lasagne.

Corn, which is also called maize or Indian corn was widely cultivated by Central and North American Indians for thousands of years before the arrival of European colonists.

Columbus brought seeds of corn back to Europe on his return voyage and today corn is cultivated on every continent under a wide variety of climate conditions. Corn is actually a large, coarse grass that bears both male and female flowers. The male flowers form the tassels and are borne at the top of the stem. The kernel represents the swollen ovary of the female flower. Corn silk is actually a very long style that extends from each kernel to the tip of the corn husk, near the tassels.

The three most common varieties of corn are field corn, sweet corn, and popcorn. Dent corn—so named for the dent in the kernel—is one of several types of field corn that is grown for livestock feed, corn meal, corn syrup, and more recently for the preparation of gasohol which is increasingly used as an automobile fuel. Sweet corn differs from field corn in having higher sugar and lower starch concentrations in the kernels, thereby making it more tasty to humans. Baby corn is another popular commercial corn grown mostly in Thailand but widely exported for use in Oriental cooking. Baby corn is harvested just before pollination and fertilization so it contains mostly water which makes it popular among perennial dieters.

Nearly 50% of the world's corn is grown in the Corn Belt of the United States which extends from Indiana and Ohio northward into Michigan, Minnesota, Wisconsin, and South Dakota, southward into Kentucky, Missouri, and Kansas, and westward across Illinois, Iowa, and Nebraska. Other important corn producing regions include parts of Brazil and Argentina in South America, the Po Valley of Italy, the Danube of central Europe, and parts of China.

Some of the many other cereal crops include oats, barley, rye, millets, sorgham, and wild rice. Rye and oats are cool-temperate plants mostly grown as crops in the northern hemisphere. Originally from Armenia, rye is now widely cultivated over much of northern Europe and across Russia principally as a food crop for animals although some is used in the production of the strongly flavored and densely textured black rye breads such as pumpernickel. Nutritionally, rye is most valued for its mineral and fiber content. Some rye is also used in the preparation of alcoholic beverages including beer in Russia, gin in the Netherlands, and rye whiskey in England and North America. During the Middle Ages of Europe there were occasional outbreaks of a disease called St. Anthony's Fire. Some of the symptoms inflicted on persons affected with this disease included gangrene, the sudden withering of limbs, abortion, hallucinations, and sometimes death. Modern medicine has traced the disease to an ergot fungus parasite of rye which is extremely poisonous to humans.

Despite being the most nutritious of all the cereals, oats, which contain up to 20% protein and 10% unsaturated oils, are mostly cultivated as pasture crops, hay, and silage for livestock feed. Oats are a common ingredient in certain cereal grain breads and pastries, in porridge, oatmeal cookies, and oatmeal. The last, oatmeal, has become increasingly popular as a breakfast cereal with the realization that it significantly lowers blood cholesterol levels.

Along with wheat, barley was one of the very first cereal crops to be domesticated in the Fertile Crescent about 6000–8000 years ago. Unlike rye and oats, barley grows under a wide variety of climate conditions and major production centers are now found in Eurasia, Africa, and North America. Although some barley production is used in whole grain breads and other baked goods most of the barley is grown for livestock feed. Barley is also important in the production of hops used to make beer.

The sorghums and millets are grain crops of semiarid and arid habitats of Africa and Asia. Sorghum is an important staple food for millions of African natives. The two most common products of sorghum include beer and bread. Millets provide a flat bread in Ethiopia and other parts of Africa and a pasture crop in the Southeastern United States.

Flax is yet another cereal that was once widely cultivated for food but is now mostly used for plant fibers for weaving of linen cloth. Some native peoples, of Ethiopia, for example, still include the edible flax seeds in their diet.

FOOD CROPS: THE LEGUMES

Legumes are pulse plants that belong to the pea family, the Leguminosae, also sometimes called the family Fabaceae. Legumes are named for their fruit, which is a pod or seed that is called a legume. As crops, legumes are second in importance only to the cereals and are cultivated throughout the world. Both legumes and grasses were among the very first plants to be cultivated.

Food obtained from cultivating legumes include the beans or pulses (beans, fava beans, peas, chick-peas, lentils), oilseeds (soya), spices, sprouts, and leaves. The seeds of legumes are typically high in starches (40–90%) and proteins (20–40%) and are especially important sources of the amino acid lysine which is often lacking in cereals. Because of their high quality protein content the legumes are sometimes called "poor man's meat." However, legumes are deficient in sulfur-containing amino acids such as cystine and methionine so a diet combining cereals and legumes is needed to fulfill our basic amino acid dietary requirements.

Legumes are excellent sources of plant oils and many minerals including calcium, magnesium, iron, phosphorous, zinc, copper, and potassium. Beans, peas, and other pulses provide B-vitamins such as thiamin, riboflavin, folic acid, pantothenic acids, and niacin. The nutrient relationships between cereals and beans reflected in long farming traditions throughout the world; farmers cultivated maize and common beans, wheat and lentils in Europe and Western Asia, millet, sorghum and cowpeas in Africa, and rice and soya bean in China and Southeast Asia.

In addition to being desirable crop plants, legumes are ecologically of great value because their root nodules contain *Rhizobium* nitrogen-fixing bacteria that incorporate atmospheric nitrogen into organic compounds used by the plants. The accumulation of nitrogen-containing organic compounds from legumes dramatically increases soil fertility and legumes are often used as green manure. Ancient farmers were aware of the contribution of legumes to soil fertility and initiated a systematic alteration of planting cereal crops one year and legume crops the next year. This practice of crop rotation has continued to the present time.

Some of the major legume crops include beans, peas, and peanuts. Economically marketable beans include kidney beans, lima beans, navy beans, wax beans, and butter beans but a wide variety of beans are grown world wide under a variety of climate and soil conditions. Beans are an important source of protein which may comprise 17–31%. The edible component of most beans is the dried fruit but bean sprouts of mung beans are used in Oriental cooking and both pods and seeds of green beans and wax beans are consumed.

The common or French bean is the most important and widely cultivated of the pulse crops. Its origin can be traced to the mountains of Central America and Peru where it still grows wild as a climbing vine. It is still cultivated in these original areas of its range as well as in tropical Africa, India, and Southeast Asia. This is the bean of baked beans, kidney beans, navy beans, pinto beans, and many other commercial names. Kidney beans are a favorite in the United States where they are mostly used in chili dishes and bean salads. Lima beans and pinto beans are New World crops, the former named after the capital of Peru. The brown and pink pinto beans are the key ingredient in refried beans and other Mexican bean dishes.

The faba bean or broad bean is still another important temperate pulse crop now cultivated in over 50 countries including China, which produces most of the world's crop of faba beans. Other names for faba beans include Windsor bean, field bean, and horse bean, the last because its pods are large.

Lima beans are also called butter beans and Madagascar beans. Like most of the other beans, lima beans are native to Latin America and were cultivated by Incas and other South American tribes at least 5000 years ago. Currently, the United States is the world's largest producer of lima beans but Africa and Asia are also cultivation centers. With their high protein and carbohydrate content, the lima bean is a favorite in succotash and other vegetable dishes. Dried beans are ground into a flour that is used for noodles and bread in the Orient.

Pea is a cool season climbing vine crop that has long been cultivated and is now the second most important legume crop. Its origin as a domesticated pulse crop date from 8000 years ago in Asia and eastern Mediterranean. Greeks, Romans, and the early Britains used it as a food crop eaten fresh or dry. China and Russia are the leading producers of dry peas, the United States and Great Britain lead in the production of green peas. Peas are a nutritious food containing 18–23% protein and about 60% carbohydrates. Most peas are consumed fresh, cooked, canned, or frozen. Pea seeds have also been ground into flour for puddings and soups. The hulls are ground for fiber additive and the residue is an animal feed.

The chick pea is the third of the three most important pulse crops. First cultivated in the Fertile Crescent of the Middle East, chick-pea continues to remain an important crop in the Middle East, Mediterranean region, and India. In addition to being eaten fresh, frozen, or canned.

Lentils are another pulse cultivated very early, about 8000 years ago in the Fertile Crescent region of the Near East. Lentils grow best in warm and dry climates. Although widely cultivated modern centers of production include India, Spain, Ethiopia, Syria, and Turkey. Lentils are an important snack food but also widely used in soups or ground into lentil flour for use in soups, breads, and pastries.

Other important legume crops include peanuts, soybeans, tamarind, and fenugreek. Peanuts are also known as ground nuts, monkey nuts, or goobers. Although native to South America they are now very widely cultivated and are an important cash crop in the southern states. Centers of cultivation include India, China, Burma, and Indonesia.

Unlike most other legume crops, after fertilization, the flowering stalk of peanuts twists downward into the soil where the peanut fruit matures as a pod containing two seeds. Although not the best food to combat obesity, peanuts are especially rich protein (25–30%) and plant oils (45–50%). Peanuts are especially rich in oleic acids and linoleic acids. The United States ranks as the most important peanut consumer with over 1 billion pounds harvested annually. About half is used to make peanut butter and the rest is used in snack foods such as candies. Peanuts are also harvested for peanut oil which is in margarine and salad dressing, the remainder being used for livestock feed.

Soybeans are a major crop source in Asia and in some ways the Old World equivalent of peanuts but their popularity in North America is increasing and soybeans are farmed in the Midwest. Today, soybean is used for soups, soymilk, tofu, cheeses, yogurt, and other dairy products as well as an important livestock feed. Tamarind and Fenugreek are spices and seasonings.

Carob flour is used in making cookies, bread, cakes, and carob chocolate. Carob is a temperate Mediterranean tree of the legume family that is grown in Greece, Italy, Spain, France, and Israel. The legume is harvested and the pulp, which is high in sugars and fats, is extracted and ground into the flour.

The term vegetable refers to a wide variety of plant products that are harvested for food other than fruits and seeds, although some vegetables, e.g., tomatoes are technically fruits. Different types of foods commonly called vegetables include plant stems (potatoes), roots (cassava), and leaves (cabbage). Generally, vegetables are neither as colorful as fruits nor as sweet but are instead eaten with meat and fish.

Some of the more important families of vegetables include the carrot family, the Apiaceae (carrots and parsnip), the tomato or Solanaceae family (tomato, potato), and the Cruciferae family (turnip, cabbage, kale). These can be divided into root vegetables and leafy vegetables, although many types of vegetables such as potatoes are "rootlike" underground stems rather than above ground plants.

Carrots are economically one of the most important of all root vegetables, being eaten raw, cooked, or processed into carrot juice. All of the hundreds of cultivars of carrot originated from the wild carrot which is still a common weed plant of Eurasia and North America. Cultivation of carrots probably began in the Near East, possibly in Afghanistan, and during the long agricultural history the slender yellowish taproot of wild carrots has gradually been transformed into the familiar red-orange carrot root of today. Carrots are especially valued for their vitamin A content and are also high in carotenes.

Although the fleshy root of **parsnip** is less desirable than that of carrots it is still a valuable root crop cultivated in the United States and Europe. Parsnips are harvested for the food value of their tap roots, for the parsnip leaves that are used to garnish foods, and for the parsnip wine which is a local favorite in some parts of Europe.

Potatoes are native to the Andes of South America and have been cultivated there for centuries. They have been widely introduced in other parts of the world and today potatoes rank as the most important of the tuber crops although it should be noted that potatoes are actually underground stems. In many temperate areas of the world the volume of potatoes grown and harvested exceeds that of cereal crops. Potatoes have proven to be a valued crop because they grow well in cool and wet locations with poor soils. Although potatoes are mostly water (78%) they are nutritionally rich in carbohydrates and low in fat and protein. Tropical varieties of tuber plants include sweet potatoes and cassava.

Originally native to Latin America and certain Pacific islands, notably Hawaii and New Zealand, sweet potatoes are now widely cultivated in Asia and Africa. Despite their name, sweet potatoes are not closely related to true potatoes. Sweet potatoes are in the Convolvulaceae family—which includes the morning glories. Furthermore sweet potatoes are a modified root while potatoes are a true tuber, or modified stem.

Cassava root (also called manioc) is a tropical tuber that which was originally from South America about 2000 years ago and is now widely cultivated in Africa, India, and Southeast Asia. In tropical regions it is a dietary staple that comprises about a forth of the caloric intake. Cassava is a tall Euphorbiaceae shrub (to 3 meters in height) harvested for its root which is ground into powder and then mixed to form a paste which can be baked into a type of bread or used as an additive or thickener in soups and sauces. Cassava is a dietary staple of tropical peoples of the Americas. In the United States a popular prepared form of cassava is called tapioca. Nutritionally, cassava is comprised of 35% starches and lesser amounts of vitamin C. Another important food crop in Asia is **taro** which is cultivated for its starchy tubers. Probably from southeast Asia, taro belongs to the Arum family and was brought into cultivation even before rice. A related species, *Xanthosoma*, of the New World tropics was brought to Hawaii and other Pacific Islands several thousand years ago and is the source of poi, a dietary staple of many of the peoples of the Pacific islands.

Two of the more important salad roots include radishes and beetroots. **Radishes** are an ancient cultivar, first known from Egypt and then somewhat later appearing in China and Japan. These members of the crucifer or mustard family are typically small leafy vegetables harvested only for their fleshy, edible bulb-like root. Some of the more important varieties of radishes include western radishes which produce the small radishes that are a favorite salad component, Oriental radishes which are flavorful additions to soups and sauces, and rat-tailed radishes of Asia which are cooked or pickled.

Beetroots are widely grown for their roundish dark green or red root that is high in sugars and pigments. Beetroots are used to make the traditional borsch soups of Russia and Poland. Although still an Asian and Mediterranean favorite, beets are now widely cultivated, especially in the United States.

FOOD CROPS: LEAFY, STEM, AND FLOWER VEGETABLES

Some of the many and most familiar examples of leafy vegetables include spinach, chard, orache, lettuce, chicory, cabbage, and endive. Familiar vegetables that are less well known as leafy vegetables include the onions and related members of the Allium Family, in which the edible leafy bases cluster around a central bulb. Vegetables such as celery, asparagus, rhubarb, bamboo shoots, fennel, and angelica are actually leaf stalks of flowering plants. Still other vegetables such as globe artichokes, okra, cauliflower, and broccoli represent clusters of flowering heads that are harvested and consumed as green vegetables.

Still other "vegetables" such as cucumbers and their relatives are actually fruits. All will be discussed in more detail in the section that follows.

The several dozen cultivars of **onions** and their relatives, the chives, leeks, and garlic, are an excellent example of leafy vegetable that resembles an underground root crop. Almost all of the onions and related plants have a long history of cultivation and use, both as food crops and as medicines. Onions were one of the most common crops of classic peoples. Egypt, the countries of the Fertile Crescent, the Greeks and Romans all valued the onion as an important agricultural crop. The characteristic odor of this group of plants comes from volatile sulfur-containing oils. Medically, they were important herbs used in the treatment of intestinal worms, high blood pressure and both fungal and bacterial infections.

Onions are used in an amazing number and variety of ways in food preparations. They can be eaten fresh, frozen, canned, roasted or pickled but mainly onions are used as a very effective and desirable flavoring agent in soups, salads, sauces, and in the preparation of meats, poultry, fishes, and prepared dishes.

The Egyptians and other ancient peoples of the Mediterranean region cultivated **lettuce** thousands of years ago as a salad vegetable. It remains today the most popular of all salad vegetables, as much for its contribution of roughage to a diet as for its taste. Because it grows well in a wide range of climates, from temperate to tropic, lettuce is available throughout the year, a factor that may well contribute to its popularity. Although nutritionally low in carbohydrate and protein content, lettuce does contain appreciable amounts of minerals, especially potassium, vitamin B-carotene, and some vitamin E and vitamin C.

If lettuce is the most popular leafy vegetable then **spinach** may well be the most "unpopular" popular leafy vegetable of all. It is thought to have originated in Persia several thousand years ago but since very widely cultivated throughout the world. Spinach is nutritionally valued for its vitamin content, mostly vitamins B, C, and E, carotenes, and minerals and is now eaten fresh or cooked or mixed in salads.

Cabbages are yet another native of southern Europe and the greater Mediterranean region and are now widely cultivated on every continent. The main cultivars include wild cabbage, head cabbage, red cabbage, and spring cabbage. In addition to being a salad ingredient for those that like cabbage salads rather than lettuce salads the leaves of head cabbage can be shredded and fermented to make sauerkraut. Flower cabbages were developed in Japan and are strictly used for landscape ornamentals.

Celery is an example of a vegetable that is actually the leaf stalk or petiole of the celery plant. Wild celery is a biennial plant native to Europe and possibly Asia. It has long been used as a medicinal plant that herbalists recommend to reduce both excess gas and arthritis and its leaves were said to sweeten the blood and cure scurvy if eaten in the spring. As a culinary, celery is used mostly for salads and soups.

Asparagus is the young shoot or spear that emerges in spring and is cut in mid-summer before maturity. It was cultivated by the Ancients of the Mediterranean region and is now grown commercially and in gardens all over the world. Connoisseurs consider asparagus cooked and served with butter or white sauce to be one of the most desirable of all stalk vegetables.

Bamboo shoots are new stems of bamboo plants that are harvested very early in their growth. They are widely cultivated in the Orient and prepared by boiling to remove the stem sheaths, after which they can be eaten raw or canned.

Rhubarb is a perennial that may have originated in Siberia and China and then introduced into Europe. Originally, rhubarb was an herbal medicine taken as a mild laxative. Cultivation of rhubarb for food probably began in Europe in the Middle Ages. Its stalks have a sweet tartness that makes them attractive for rhubarb pies, preserves, cookies, and rhubarb wine.

Artichoke, Brussels sprouts, okra, broccoli and cauliflower all represent vegetables that are actually flowering heads or buds. Brussels sprouts are dense buds that resemble miniature cabbages. Artichoke, more correctly known as **globe artichoke**, is a perennial thistle member of the compositae family which is now widely cultivated. The globular flower heads are the part of the plant that is harvested and eaten.

Cauliflower is another of the many important members of the Brassica group of plants that are consumed in enormous quantities throughout the world. The edible part of cauliflower is the swollen flower head borne on the single stem. **Broccoli** is similar to cauliflower but the edible portion is comprised of several flower heads rather than the single flower head of cauliflower.

Cucumbers and cucumber-like plants are traditionally considered vegetables although the edible portion is a fruit. A number of **cucumbers** and cucumber-like plants that belong to the Cucurbitaceae family are cultivated. These include cucumbers, gherkins, melons, summer squashes, winter squashes, and pumpkins. Technically, these plants produce fruits because the melon is a pepo. However, in parts of their range the roots and leaves may be eaten as well, so the fruit is also a vegetable.

The **cucumber** is a wild, straggler of a ground vine that originated in the Himalayas 3000 years ago but is now widely cultivated throughout the world. Cucumbers are harvested before they ripen and are eaten raw or cooked. Although water content is high, cucumbers consist of about 2% carbohydrates, some vitamin C and vitamin B complex, and carotenes.

The gherkins of Europe are actually a small cucumber but true **gherkins** originate from Africa and were introduced into the West Indies during the colonization period. Most cultivated gherkins are picked fresh and pickled.

Pumpkins and winter squashes are a South American fruit that probably originated in Peru. Pumpkins especially have become completely associated with Halloween but pumpkin pie is consumed throughout the year raw, roasted, or cooked. Like all members of the Curcubitae, pumpkins are mostly water with small amounts of starches, other sugars, vitamins, minerals, and some carotenes.

FOOD CROPS: VEGETABLE OILS

The salad oils and seed oils extracted from plant seeds are called vegetable oils. Useable amounts of oils can be extracted from about 200 species of plants but only 12 species are of any commercial importance. Depending on species, the seeds of oilseed plants can yield from 18–50% oils although some oils such as sunflower oil and olive oil are actually extracted from fruits. Plant oils are extracted from seeds and fruits in several different ways but pressing is one of the more common processes. After the oil had been drained and collected the residue material is called presscake. Presscake is rich in protein and generally used as an animal feed.

Some of the more important plant oils include coconut oil, sunflower oil, olive oil, palm oil, corn oil, soya bean oil, and cocoa oil. Plant oils are very widely used in cooking, in salad dressings, and in the manufacture of margarine. To make margarine, the vegetable oil is hardened by adding hydrogen.

Sunflowers of the genus *Helianthus* were first domesticated several thousand years ago by native peoples of central North America for their edible seeds and were cultivated at least 3000 years ago by natives. Now they are one of the more important sources of vegetable oils although their seeds continue to be eaten as a popular snack. They were introduced into Europe in the 16th century and into Russia somewhat later. The seeds yield about 40% or more polyunsaturated oil, much of which is linoleic acid, along with about 20% protein. Commercial centers of sunflower seed oil are Russia, the United States, and Argentina. Sunflower oil is used as a cooking oil and also to garnish salads. It is one of several plant oils used as an industrial lubricant and also has been tested for use as a biofuel.

Other oil producing plants include cotton and safflower. Cotton seed oil is pressed from the seed after the cotton fiber is removed. The oil is used mostly for cooking. Safflower oil is another seed oil (oil extracted from the seeds of the safflower plant) that shows promise for a variety of uses.

Along with its cultivation as a valuable food source, soya bean also is harvested for its oil content. The seeds of soya bean are best known for their protein content, about 30–50%, but they also contain 15–25% oil, much of it in the form of linoleic and oleic acids.

FOOD CROPS: FRUITS

Fruits are extremely important in human diets and are considered one of the four major food groups. Botanically, fruits are the fertilized ovary containing seeds that have matured. In a larger sense fruits are ovaries that contain or lack seeds. Harvested fruits are world-wide in distribution. Some tropical fruits include pineapples, bananas, dates, coconuts, and breadfruit. Fruits of temperate climates include cherries, plums, peaches, apples, oranges, and grapes.

Fruits are important sources of many vitamins (Vitamin C, B, and E) and vitamin precursors such as carotenes. They are the major source of Vitamin C. Other important dietary components of fruits include minerals, especially calcium, iron, and potassium, organic acids such as malic acid and citric acid, and a variety of organic volatiles such as esters and alcohols. Fruits are also desired for their high fiber content. Most fruits have a low fat content and are lacking in protein.

Although a wide range of plants including herbs, shrubs, trees produce fruits the most widely harvested and used come from shrubs or small trees of the family Rosaceae (apples, cherries, plums, pears, strawberries) and the family Rutaceae (lemons, grapefruits, oranges).

Virtually all of the world's fruits can be eaten raw or cooked or included as ingredients in pies and pastries, and as sweeteners in dairy products and beverages. Many fruits can also be added to culinary dishes because of their color and aroma.

Tomatoes are actually fruits and not vegetables. The tomato originated in South America and was extensively cultivated in Mexico. The Spanish explorers introduced the plant into Europe where it became known as the love plant or golden apple plant. Its popularity assured its continued spread and tomato is now grown everywhere in gardens and cultivated extensively around the world. Important commercial centers of tomato cultivation include the United States, Italy, Russia, China, and Egypt. The tomato fruit is a berry comprised mostly of water (to 90%) but it also contains small amounts of carbohydrates, some potassium and other minerals, carotenes, and vitamins E, C, and the B vitamin complex.

Bananas are a tree-like herbaceous plant that originated in the humid tropical lowlands of Southeast Asia, possibly India or New Guinea. They are now very widely cultivated, especially in tropical and subtropical regions of Africa and South America where they are called **plantains**. Both locally and on the world market the several hundred cultivars of bananas rank as one of the most important of all fruits. In parts of Africa and Latin America bananas are a staple food. About one half of banana production is consumed fresh or in desserts and the other half is fried, baked, or roasted. Sugars comprise about 20% of bananas which also contain relatively large amounts of vitamin C and potassium. Bananas are also sliced and dried as banana chips which are very high in starches. Although sold everywhere, the starchy fruits of bananas are a dietary staple of many pantropic peoples. Seeds must be removed from the wild varieties but almost all of the marketable cultivated bananas are seedless.

Apples have been cultivated for at least 3000 years and still remain one of the world's most popular fruits. The apple is probably the most widely distributed of all tree fruit crops, especially in temperate regions of the world. The historical traditions of apples date from Adam and Eve, which partook of the forbidden fruit (when Adam bit into the apple it stuck in his throat, giving rise to the prominent Adam's apple seen in males). Apples were also the favorite fruit of Aphrodite, the Greek goddess of fertility, and newlyweds shared an apple in hopes of a fruitful and fertile marriage. Apples remain a widely cultivated fruit today and are still the most popular fruit in North America. About 7000 varieties of apples are recognized, of which 100 kinds are grown commercially. The fruit of the apple is actually a pome. Apples provide a good source of sugars and are used mostly as snack food and as ingredients in pies but apple cider remains as popular as ever. Crab apples are used in pies, jams, and jellies.

The 20 species of **pears** are also a popular tree fruit crop of temperate regions of the world. Like apple, the fruit of pears is a pome. About 20 species are recognized. Pears have a long history of cultivation, dating from 4000 years ago in China. Pears remain a very popular tree fruit crop with about 5000 recognized cultivars.

The cultivation of **peaches** can be traced back some 4000 years ago from the mountainous areas of China and Tibet. Peaches spread from the Orient to the Middle East and eventually to Greece by 300 years BC. Its ever increasing popularity as a fruit has led to the widespread cultivation of some 2000 cultivars of peaches in Europe, the United States, Turkey, Japan, and parts of Central and South America. Peaches are also a popular and widely cultivated garden fruit. Peaches are harvested and consumed fresh, canned, or frozen. They can be made into jams and jellies, in ice cream, and in desserts. Nutritionally, peaches are high in potassium, vitamin C, malic acid and citric acid. **Nectarines** are a smooth-skinned variety of peach. In fact, some peach trees may bear a few nectarines on them. Nutritionally, nectarines are similar to peaches.

Cherries, **peaches**, and **apricots** are closely related and all are grouped in the genus *Prunus*. Their fruit is a one-seeded drupe that consists of a thin skin and a fleshy interior surrounding a single central stone that contains and protects the seed. Two species of cherries are cultivated; most cherry orchards grow the sweet cherry which is a medium-sized tree closely related to wild sweet cherry. Centers of cherry orchards are the United States, and several western European countries including Germany, Spain, France, and Russia. Cherries are eaten fresh, frozen, or canned. They are a snack food but also used in various dishes, especially desserts. The fruits of another popular cherry have a tart, almost bitter taste and are called sour cherries. Sour cherries are processed into pies, jellies, and jams. Apricots are thought to have originated in China and are now very widely cultivated. Their nutritional content is similar to that of peaches.

Citrus fruits are commercially important tropical and subtropical small and medium-sized trees that belong mostly to the family Rutaceae. The fruit is called a hesperidium and consists of an outer rind and an inner spongy-like fleshy fruit separated by thin partitions. Common citrus fruits include **oranges** and **lemons**. Although both consist mostly of water they do contain sugars, carotenes, citric acids, dietary fiber, and vitamins. A number of essential oils and fatty acids can be extracted from the rind. Citrus fruits are especially rich in vitamin C but also contain vitamin B and vitamin E. The three types of oranges that are widely cultivated are the sweet orange, blood orange (so-called because of its blood red fleshy interior), and the naval orange, which is a naval-like tip.

Oranges are probably the most popular of the citrus fruits. They originated in China and were later introduced in Europe. Oranges accompanied Columbus to the New World on his second voyage and were cultivated shortly thereafter. Today, the centers of orange cultivation are the United States, Brazil, and Spain.

Lemons also originated in Southeast Asia but are now widely cultivated in orchards and gardens. The United States, Italy, Spain, Brazil, and Argentina are centers of lemon cultivation. Because of their tartness lemons are not consumed as a fruit but they are very important cooking ingredients and are also used in the preparation of beverages such as lemonade.

Grapefruit seems to have a New World origin, possibly in the West Indies. Today, it is mainly cultivated along the southern subtropical or warm temperate parts of the United States but Cuba, Argentina, South Africa, and the West Indies also have sizable grapefruit plantations. Like almost all of the commercially important citrus fruits, grapefruit can be eaten fresh, frozen, or canned. It is probably the most popular breakfast fruit in the United States. Although somewhat tart to the taste, grapefruit contributes sugars, citric acid, and vitamin C.

Tangerines are yet another citrus fruit that seems to have originated in China. Also called mandarins, the two may represent separate species as the flesh of tangerines is red and that of mandarins is yellow in color. Centers of cultivation of tangerines include the United States, Japan, Mediterranean Europe, Brazil, and South Africa. Like oranges, tangerines are eaten fresh or the segments are canned. They are still sold locally as clementines and are a popular fruit around Christmas.

The **lime** is a small tree that may have originated in India and are mostly used for flavoring and other cooking ingredients. Centers of lime cultivation include the West Indies, Brazil, Egypt, and Mexico. Limes are known for their high concentrations of vitamin C and in the days of sailing ships limes were carried to guard against **scurvy**.

The 60 species of **grapes** are mostly temperate and north-temperate vines. Some are vigorous climbing vines extending upwards 15–22 meters or more, depending on height of the host tree. No doubt humans have harvested wild grapes for centuries as an important autumn food and drink. In fact, North America was first named Vineland by Leif Erickson and his followers that settled at L' Anse au Meadows in modern New-foundland.

The culture of grapes is called **viticulture** and dates from ancient Cyprus, Jericho, and other Middle Eastern sites—all of which have yielded examples of grape cultivation. Greeks and especially the Romans introduced the cultivation of grapes throughout the Mediterranean and later northward into Roman Britain. Spanish explorers dating from Columbus onward introduced grape culture first in South America and later into North America. Modern cultivars may number some 10,000 varieties or more. Grapes are high in sugars (about 15–25 percent). Additional nutrients include acids, mostly tartaric acid and malic acid along with smaller quantities of vitamin C. Modern cultivation of grapes yields about 70% for wine, 20% as table desserts and snacks, and 10% for rains, currants, and other dried grape products.

Some tropical fruits of importance include **pineapples** and **mangos**. **Pineapple** is originally from tropical South America but is now widely cultivated in many tropical and subtropical areas of the world including Thailand and the Phillippines, Malaysia, Ivory Coast and South Africa, the United States and Mexico. The fruit is consumed fresh or frozen, canned, or processed into pineapple juice. Fresh pineapple has a high vitamin C content. Dried pineapple has a high sugar content of 70%. Some pineapple is distilled to produce alcohol and some is fermented to produce vinegar. Wastes are used for animal feed and for fertilizer.

Mango is an important tropical fruit that has been grown for several thousand years. The mango tree grows to about 40 meters in height and bears rosettes of mangos. Each mango is actually a round drupe up to 30 cm in length. Originally from the Himalayas of India and Burma, mangos have been widely introduced in tropical countries including Malaysia and Southeast Asia, East Africa and West Africa, and Central America and Brazil. The mango fruit is eaten fresh, canned, dried, or pulped for juices, jellies, jams, and desserts. Mango is high in vitamin C, carotenes, and contains about 15% sugars.

Three of the more important tropical vegetable fruits include papaya, breadfruit, and avocado pear. **Papaya** is the fruit of a tall, tree-like herbaceous plant originally from the tropics of Central America, especially Costa Rica and southern Mexico. It is an important tropical fruit and is a good source of sugars, vitamin C, and carotenes. An enzyme called papain is extracted from young fruits and used as a meat tenderizer. A papaya drink is popular but the fruit is also used as a fresh or dried fruit, in salads, ice creams, jams, and jellies.

The **breadfruit** is a tropical tree of the Pacific that long remained a staple of Pacific islanders. Made famous by the Bounty expedition to Tahiti (Mutiny on the Bounty), breadfruit has since become an important West Indies crop.

The **avocado pear** is a tall, evergreen tree originally native to Central America but now cultivated in most of the tropical areas of the world including Brazil, South Africa,

Israel, Florida, and California. Avocado is a popular fruit that is more often eaten in salads and used as an ingredient in a variety of dessert and salad dishes. Oils extracted from avocado are used in the preparation of shampoos and other cosmetics.

Many species and varieties of berries are harvested directly from the wild or are cultivated. Strawberries, blackberries, raspberries, and blueberries rank among the more important berries consumed.

Strawberries are perennial herbaceous plants that spread by sexual reproduction but also by extending an extensive network of runners from which new plants arise. Botanically, the edible fruit of a strawberry is an achene. Although strawberries are gathered in the wild, the cultivated strawberry is a North American hybrid first introduced into Europe, later throughout much of the world. Today, strawberries are very widely cultivated but major centers include California, Spain, Italy, and France. Nutritionally, strawberries have a very high water content near 90% along with 10% sugar and some vitamin C, malic acid, and citric acid. Strawberries are a popular snack and dessert fruit and also much used as an ingredient in pastries and ice cream.

Berries of the genus *Rubus* include blackberry, boysenberry, raspberry, and wineberry along with many hybrids and cultivars. The *Rubus* fruit is a drupe or aggregation of drupelets attached to a single, conical receptacle. Fruits of red raspberry and black raspberry and their hybrids have been gathered for centuries. Commercial centers include Russia, eastern Europe, and the Pacific coast of the United States. Raspberries are a very popular dessert food and also are used in pastries, ice cream, jams, and jellies. Blackberry is a prickly stemmed and very scrubby plant that grows wild. Commercial centers include the Pacific Northwest, Arkansas, and New Zealand. Like other berries, the fruit of blackberry is consumed fresh, canned, frozen or made into jams and jellies. Blackberry wine is a popular beverage in parts of Europe and an occasional treat in parts of North America.

Olives, **figs**, **dates**, and **pomegranates** are quite possibly the oldest of all fruits to be cultivated. Early neolithic sites from the Near East have yielded both olives and figs. The olive is a small evergreen fruit tree of warm and dry Mediterranean climates. The olive was brought into cultivation as early as 10,000 years ago in the Fertile Crescent region and spread quickly to Greece, Italy, France and Spain. It is still widely cultivated in those areas but the United States and Argentina are also important olive growing areas as well.

The fruit of the olive has a thin skin, a fleshy pulp, and a stony kernel. Unripe olives are green but as the fruit matures it turns a purple-black. Olives are eaten fresh, and as salad and dessert fruits. Olives contain relatively high amounts of oil, to 40%, of which oleic acid is a major component. Extracted by presses, the oil is a favored cooking oil. The first oil extracted is called virgin olive oil. After further presses to extract olive oil, the remaining waste is used as animal feed.

Figs were an important cultivated crop in Egypt nearly 5000 years ago. The cultivated fig is a large shrub or small tree some 2–5 meters tall. The fig is considered a compound fruit comprised of numerous drupes. Commercially, some of the most popular fig fruits require pollination by a fig wasp to develop, consequently baskets containing figs are set out in orchards to attract and facilitate the life cycle of this wasp. The fig tree is adapted to warm and subtropical regions of the world. While figs are still a staple in the Middle East other centers of fig cultivation today include the southern United States, Greece, Spain, Italy, and Portugal. Nutritionally, the fig contains about 10% sugars along with high levels of potassium.

Pomegranates may have originated in Iran but have also been widely introduced and are now cultivated for export in Egypt, India, Peru, and Spain. The fruit of the pomegranate is a berry which is pulped into juice, combined with walnuts to make a sauce, syrup, or fermented into wine.

Like figs, date palms were among the first fruits to be cultivated some 5000-6000 years ago in the Middle East. Dates, figs, olives, and grapes were among the dietary staples of that time and those peoples. Date palms are subtropical trees that grow to 25 meters in height in hot and dry climates. A mature date palm can produce up to 100 kilograms of dates each year, making them an exceptionally important fruit food source. Commercial centers of fig production still include the Middle East, especially Iraq, Iran, and Egypt, North Africa, Mexico, and the United States. Dates remain a mainstay of food in the Middle East and North Africa where they are consumed in cakes and other pastries, as flavorings for beverages, and as desserts.

FOOD CROPS: NUTS AND NUT-LIKE FRUITS

The edible kernel of a fruit is called a nut. Examples of nuts include peanuts, walnuts, pecans, pistachios, almonds, Brazil nuts, and cashews. Almost all nuts are enclosed in a hard, protective, outer shell which must be opened and discarded to obtain the kernel which represents the endosperm of the seed. Cultivated nuts actually fall into three botanical categories; **true nuts** such as hickory nuts, **drupes** which include walnuts, almonds, and coconuts, and **capsules** such as the Brazil-nut.

Most nuts are cooked and then eaten but some such as walnuts and pistachios are consumed raw. Nuts are also important ingredients in prepared dishes, in ice creams, and as flavorings. Peanuts are probably the most popular nut snack food but peanuts are legumes rather than true nuts. Of the true nuts, walnuts, pecans, and almonds are mostly used in cooking.

Nuts are cultivated world wide and also collected from the wild in many areas. Examples of nuts collected rather than cultivated include hickory nuts, chestnuts, and hazelnuts. They are a major source of protein which often comprises to 30% of the kernel. About 70% of the kernel consists of plant oil although some nuts such as walnuts are unusual in containing 60% starch. In addition, most nuts are valuable sources of many minerals including calcium, iron, potassium, and sodium as well as vitamin B and vitamin E. A percentage of the peanut and almond harvest is allocated for the extraction of oils.

Some of the more important nut trees of warm and subtropical climates include Brazil nuts, cashew-nuts, and pine kernels. Brazil-nuts are seeds of a tall rain forest tree of Amazonia that may reach 50 meters in height. These are collected from the wild rather than cultivated. The nuts contain 17–20% protein, to 70% fat, much of which is oleic acid oil. Most Brazil-nuts are gathered for trade in Brazil but Peru, Columbia, Bolivia, and Venezuela are also exporters.

The **cashew** is a medium-sized tropical tree that also probably originated in Brazil but was widely introduced by the Portugese into territorial holdings and trade-centers including India, Sri Lanka, and Mozambique. In addition to its value as a snack food, cashew-nuts are also used in the preparation of juices, wine, liquor, jams, and jellies. Cashew nuts also contain a shell liquid used in the industrial production of resins.

Pine kernels are the seeds of small pines which can be extracted and used locally by native peoples for centuries. The pueblo peoples of the American Southwest gathered and stored pine nuts and the Hopi and Navajo peoples of today still gather pine nuts. The thin shell is removed and the kernel, which is high in unsaturated fat and protein, is eaten or made into puddings and soups.

Table 24–2 Major food crops of the world.

Group	Examples	Nutrients
Cereals	rice, wheat, corn, sorghums, rye, oats	carbohydrate calories and proteins
Legumes	beans, peas, peanuts, soybeans, lentils, chick-peas, lima beans, pinto beans, mung beans,	proteins, oils, iron, potassium, zinc, copper, calcium, zinc, magnesium, B-vitamin complex
"Root Crops,"	potato, sweet potato, cassava	starch, oils, fatty acids
Spices	cinnamon, nutmeg, pepper, mustard	————
Herbs	cherries, oranges, lemons, mangos	————
Fruits	citrus fruits, bananas	carbohydrates, minerals, especially iron and potassium, oils and fatty acids
Sugar Crops	sugar cane, sugar beets, sugar maple	carbohydrates, notably simple sugars and starches
Nuts and Nut-like Fruits	walnuts, cashews, pecans, Brazil nuts, pistachios, almonds	high quality protein, minerals including calcium, iron, sodium, potassium, vitamins B and E, oils,

Nut trees of temperate climates include **hickory nuts**, the **almond,** and **filbert nut**. Hickory nuts are still gathered from the wild rather than cultivated. Originally from the Mediterranean region, the almond was possibly the earliest nut tree cultivated, from 3000 years ago to the present. The kernel is very nutritious, containing 40–60% oil and about 20% protein. In addition to being a snack and dessert food, almond products include almond butter, paste, and ice-cream. Almonds are still widely cultivated in the Mediterranean region but California is now the largest producer of almonds. Filberts were originally gathered in southern Europe and the Mediterranean where they are now cultivated, especially in Turkey, Spain, and Italy. The filbert kernel contains high protein and oil content which is used as a snack food and in confectionaries.

Several important nut trees of temperate climates include **walnuts, pistachios,** and **pecans**. Nuts of all of these are classified as drupes. Seeds of about 15 species of walnuts are still collected from wild trees but the Persian walnut or common walnut is commercially cultivated in a number of countries. The common walnut is a valuable commodity because of its high protein and oil content. Walnuts are canned, eaten fresh, or used as an ingredient in pastries, confectionaries and ice cream. The kernel is also rich in vitamins B, E, and vitamin C. The shell is ground into a flour used in the plastics industry while the oil is an ingredient in the preparation of certain types of paints.

Native to North America, the pecan is a tall tree widely cultivated in the United States, Mexico, South Africa, and Australia. The kernel is especially rich in fats, to 70% of which 80% is oleic acid, along with 18–20% protein. Although pecan pie is a familiar favorite pecans are much used as snack food, desserts, and in ice cream.

Pistachio is a medium-sized tree to 10 meters tall of the Middle East and Southeast Asia. California is an important cultivation center in North America. Pistachios are highly regarded as one of the most desirable of all nuts as snack food. The nuts contain 18% protein and 56% unsaturated oil and are marketed in the shell.

Coconut from the coconut palm originated in the Pacific tropics and is now widely cultivated in the tropical and subtropical regions of the world, especially in East Africa, Panama, and Asia.

A coconut tree grows 20-30 meters in height, matures at 6-7 years, and thereafter produces 50-100 nuts per year for about 80 years. The coconut fruit consists of a fibrous hull or shell, a mesocarp more fibrous than fleshy, and a hard shell or endocarp. After harvesting, the coconut is dehusked and the interior nut is split open to get to the endosperm milk and coconut meat. Coconut meat is rich in carbohydrates, fats, and proteins. It is either eaten fresh or dried to produce copra, which can be further processed to extract coconut oil that is used in soap, margarine, cosmetics, and in the preparation of confectionaries. Coconut milk is extracted by squeezing the endosperm through a sieve. Coconut milk is not the same as the milky coconut water, which consists mostly of water, sugar, vitamins and minerals.

Almost all of the coconut tree proves useful. Leaves are woven into thatch roofs, the shells formed into handy drinking utensils and fibers tied into baskets and the trunks are carved into dugouts.

SPICES AND FLAVORINGS

Spices are defined as strongly flavored or aromatic parts of plants that are usually essential oils extracted from roots, stems, leaves, buds, fruits, or seeds. The use of spices for flavoring of cooked foods dates from ancient civilizations and probably into prehistory. Originally, most of the valued spices came from the fabled spice islands of the East Indies and the demand for spices spurred the great Age of Exploration as European explorers sought new trade routes to the East. In fact, the age of exploration which led directly to the discovery of the New World was actually part of a larger attempt to find new trade routes to the Spice Islands of the East Indies. Columbus actually set out on a journey to the Spice Islands, discovering the Americas quite by accident.

Nutmeg is a flavoring obtained from the dried outer seed coverings of a tropical evergreen tree that originally grew only in the Spice Islands. Although nutmeg was originally gathered from wild trees, commercially important nutmeg is now obtained from plantations. Major sources of nutmeg today include Granada in the West Indies and Indonesia. Nutmeg was a popular flavoring for beverages such as eggnog, coffee and as a garnish for rice puddings and many other desserts. During colonial times nutmeg was the center of a brisk trade, especially in New England and Connecticut is still known as the nutmeg state.

Another widely used flavoring is **cinnamon**, which is processed by grinding the bark of a tropical evergreen cinnamon shrub that grows in Sri Lanka, the Malagasy Republic, and the Seychelles, all in the Indian Ocean. Cinnamon is a great flavoring ingredient in apple pies, coffee, cinnamon pastries, and puddings but is also used in the preparation of sauces and confectionery. Curry powder is also a cinnamon product.

Vanilla was used as a cocoa flavoring by the Aztecs, then adopted by the Conquistadores who introduced it to Europe. Vanilla is obtained from the unripe fruits of a tropical orchid that grows throughout much of Latin America and is prepared by first drying the unripe fruits and then allowing them to ferment. Although still an important Latin American export the center of vanilla production has shifted to Madagascar, Reunion Island, and Indonesia. Vanilla is used to add flavor in vanilla pudding, in some pastries, and to flavor beverages. Much of the demand for vanilla is now satisfied by the production of a synthetic volatile ester called vanillin which is derived from processed wood pulp.

Peppers are technically fruits that have long been considered the most desirable of all spices and were some of the spices that drove the spice trade. Pepper actually describes two kinds of spices; white and black pepper are climbing vines belonging to the Piperaceae family while Chillies come from the tomato family, the Solanaceae, and are bushy plants.

Pepper is actually a berry-like fruit called a drupe produced by a tropical vine from India where it still occurs in the wild. The spice trade centered around two kinds of pepper, black pepper and white pepper. Black pepper is obtained from grinding the dried fruit while white pepper comes from grinding the stone and seed of the pepper fruit. Although now much more widely cultivated, especially in Brazil, Indonesia, and India, pepper is still one of the most important of all spices. Pepper spice comes from alkaloids and volatile oils in the fruit.

Sweet pepper, chilli, and paprika are all cultivars of *Capsicum*, a bushy tropical plant that can also be cultivated in subtropical and warm-temperate climates. Well known cultivars include bell pepper, one of the larger members, paprika, which is dried and ground into a powder that is typically a cooking ingredient added to eggs, potatoes, cheeses, and other products. Hungarian paprika is added to Hungarian goulash. Chillis are strong-tasting cultivars that are dried and ground into chilli powder or curry powder. The value of peppers is in their alkaloids which flavor food, although they do contain some amounts of sugars, fats, and proteins.

Still other spices (or flavorings) include the **mustards** which are mostly derived from the seeds of mustard plants that belong to the Cruciferae family. The three main types of mustards include black mustard, white mustard, and brown mustard. Although black mustard seeds were once ground into table mustard the Indian mustard or brown mustard is now more important and widespread. White mustard is combined with brown mustard to produce the familiar table mustard. Mustards are mostly used as an applied spice layered on hot dogs, hamburgers, ham slices and similar sandwiches.

Cloves are dried, unopened flower buds of a tall evergreen tree originally of the East Indies and Indonesia. Spice Island trade brought their introduction into China and India and later into Madagascar and Europe. Cloves are a spicy flavoring for sauces, pickles, hams, apple cider, and other highly flavored foods and beverages. An oil extracted from cloves is used as a food and beverage flavoring and also for perfumes.

Allspice is named because its flavor seems to include many different spices including cloves, cinnamon, and nutmeg. Also called pimento, allspice is obtained from unripe berries of a small tropical tree.

Capers are unopened flower buds of a spiny shrub native to North Africa and the Mediterranean region. The caper has been cultivated for thousands of years and is used in sauces and as a flavoring for meats. Capers are also used as garnishes, as condiments, and the buds can be pickled.

Saffron is the world's most expensive spice, mostly because it takes a huge amount of flowers to produce a small amount of spice. In fact, 70,000 dried saffron flowers must be harvested to produce a pound of saffron spice. Products of saffron include food coloring agents and essential oils that act as flavoring agents in sauces such as the French *bouillabaisse* and the Spanish *paella*.

Many tuberous flavoring plants such as ginger, liquorice, and horse-radish, can be identified as either spices and herbs. Of these, **horse-radish** is a perennial herb member of the mustard family, originally cultivated in western Asia but now very widely grown. The horse-radish flavoring is obtained from the ground tap-root which is ground and mixed with water to produce the familiar whitish sauce. Horse-radish is a pungent flavoring used with meat and fish dishes and sometimes as an ingredient of cooking sauces.

Ginger is a slender herbaceous plant from Asia. It has been so long cultivated that it is apparently no longer found in the wild. For centuries India and China have used ginger as both a medicine and herb. The ginger spice is actually the ground root or rhizome of the plant and is used in syrups, sauces, powders, and in the production of ginger beer.

Liquorice is a wild perennial herb of the pea family that is native to the Middle East and was well known to the ancient Greeks and Romans. Modern cultivation centers include Italy, Spain, Turkey and Russia. Unlike most spice plants, liquorice must grow for 3-5 years before the rhizomes and roots can be harvested and their flavoring extracted. Liquorice is used as an ingredient and flavoring in confectionaries, pastries, beverages and making liquorice candy sticks.

HERBS

In contrast to spices, herbs are usually leafy parts of herbaceous plants although some such as bayleaf are leaves of woody plants. Both herbs and spices have long been used in burial and related preservation practices. Like spices, the herbs are used mostly as flavorings in cooking and preparation of a variety of foods. Many, but not all, of the most widely used herbs are members of the mint family (Menthaceae) and parsley family (Apiaceae). Important mints used for herbs include **rosemary, thyme, basil, mint, lemon balm,** and **sage**. Members of the parsley family used as herbs are dill, fennel, coriander, caraway, and anise. Some herbs of local importance include the leaves of wormwood and western sage called tarragon.

Bay laurel is actually a member of the avocado or laurel family. The leaves of laurel are harvested and a volatile oil called cineole is extracted for use as a flavoring and preservative. Bay laurel is also famous because its leaves were once formed into a crown that adorned victorious athletes and award-winning scientists and authors, hence the derivation of the name poet laureate, for example.

Rosemary originates from the Mediterranean region but has been widely introduced. It is an erect bushy shrub with dark green leaves and violet flowers. Rosemary herb is used mostly as a flavoring for meats, poultry, and fish and in soups, sauces, and salads. The pungent oil of rosemary is used in the perfume industry and in cosmetic preparations.

Basil is a slender, erect annual originally from India and is now produced commercially in Italy and grown in pots in other parts of the world. Also called sweet basil, this herb is widely used as a flavoring in meat, poultry, and fish dishes and in tomato sauces such as pesto sauce.

Lemon balm is a perennial herbaceous plant of the Mediterranean region that was grown long ago by the Egyptians and later the Greeks and Romans. Its lemon scented leaves are used as herb flavoring for a variety of dishes including omelettes, liqueurs, and wines.

Both **summer savory** and **winter savory** are natives to the Mediterranean region. Summer savory is a bush, winter savory an herb plant. Like most of the other herbs discussed in this section, both of the savory herbs are used as flavorings for meats and other prepared dishes.

SUGAR CROPS

Plants grown for their sugar content are known as sugar crops. Those parts of sugar crop plants especially rich in carbohydrates are harvested and processed and the remainder of the plant is used as fertilizer. The major plant sugars obtained from sugar crops include glucose, fructose, maltose, and sucrose. Most of the sucrose is used as a sweetener in both foods (e.g., pies and cakes) and beverages (e.g., soda pop), as a preservative in fruits, and as a bulking agent for certain pastries. Some sugars are also widely used as antioxidants.

Worldwide, about 65% of harvested sugar comes from **sugar cane** and roughly 35% from **sugar beet**. In the United States sugar beets provide almost all of the refined sugar. Sugar obtained from sugar maple is a distant third sugar crop in volume harvested.

Sugar cane is a tall, coarse grass to 6 meters in height (nearly 23 feet) that grows well in tropical and subtropical environs. Both India and Brazil grow large quantities but it is also widely cultivated in Florida and a number of islands in the West Indies. The stem of sugar cane is harvested for its white refined sugar and consists of about 17–20% sucrose. Sugar cane is harvested by removing the leaves or canes, which are then crushed in a watery mixture which is purified and centrifuged to remove the sugar crystals from the molasses. The sugar crystals are 96–99% sugar which is nearly 100% sucrose. The molasses is produced as a separate product for baking use, animal feed, or for making rum. The cane residue can be used in making paper and cardboard, as animal feed, and—more recently—for manufacturing fuel.

Sugar beet is a temperate plant that may have evolved from the sea beet that grows wild along the coasts of Western Asia and southern Europe. This near relative of beets is widely cultivated in Europe and along the Gulf Coast in the United States. A member of the chenopod family, the roots of sugar beet are harvested and processed by centrifugation to separate the white sugar from molasses and residue. Molasses is used for animal feed and for industrial fuel production. The remainder is called filter cake and is used as a manure fertilizer.

Extraction of sugar from **sugar maple**—a temperate tree—is quite seasonal and of limited consumption but still is highly desirable as the prime ingredient in maple syrup manufacture which is so much in demand in North America. The tapping of sap was a tradition of certain native peoples of North America who cut channels in the bark in late winter and early summer and then collected the flowing sap which was then boiled to concentrate the syrup. A seasonal maple syrup industry continues to thrive in New England.

Increasingly, sugar substitutes obtained from corn are being used as sweeteners and other replacements for sugar. The value of this crop is increasing, especially as more and more sucrose is being fermented to produce ethyl alcohol which is being eyed as an alternative to gasoline for use in automobiles.

FOOD FROM PALMS AND CYCADS

Palms are exceptionally common plants over much of the tropics and subtropics. Sago starch is harvested from several palm species for use in breads or as a stuffing or starchy additive to soups and stews. The most important species is sago palm, a tall, to 33 feet (about 10 meters) native of New Guinea. Much of the food is harvested from wild sago palm although some is grown in plantations. This palm flowers once in its lifetime, at about 10–15 years of age. Flowering time is preceded by mobilization of starch resources. Just before flowering time the palm is felled and the wood cut away to expose the starchy pith which is then removed and pulverized to yield the useable starch which is then either boiled, dried, roasted, or fried. There is a small commercial trade in export of pearl sago made from this palm which can be used in puddings and pastries.

Other palms also provide a host of food products such as sugary sweeteners for beverages, palm wine, and palm oil, the last a kind of vegetable oil. The young terminal buds of certain warm tropical species are harvested as palm cabbages in Thailand and Latin America.

Several cycads are also harvested for their pithy starch content in Japan, Sri Lanka, and India. The starch is ground into a paste used for bread and soups.

Masticatories

Masticatories are plant foods that are chewed but not swallowed. The classic example of a common masticatory is chewing gum. The essential ingredient of chewing gum is the dried latex from the bark of the tropical sapodilla tree, found in the New World tropics of North America. The latex is extracted from trees grown in the wild by natives or from plantation trees for the commercial production of chewing gum.

Betel nuts are probably chewed by more people than even the ever-popular chewing gum. Betel nuts are derived from the betel palm tree which grows wild in the tropics of Southeast Asia, the East Indies, and Polynesia. Betel nuts may be plucked from the tree and chewed or sliced into strips that are wrapped in pepper leaves. They remain in great demand among tropical peoples as a breath sweetener and are said to aid in digestion.

Cola nuts are harvested from the cola tree which grows wild in tropical Africa. Cola nuts may be chewed like betel nuts or chewing gum or may be used as a flavoring in the preparation of beverages such as cola drinks. Cola is often used as a stimulant because it has a high caffeine content. Cola is commercially a very important ingredient in coca-cola and other beverages manufactured in the United States.

Beverages

A number of plants are produced for drinking liquids that are derived from fruits or other plant substances. Major drinks include tea, coffee, chocolate, and cocoa. Most of these contain a stimulant called caffeine. Drink flavorings derived from plants also include lemonade, lime, orange, raspberry, sarsaparilla, birch, and many others. Worldwide the two most commercially important beverages are coffee and tea. Both contain large amounts of an alkaloid stimulant called **caffeine**.

Tea is prepared from the dried leaves of a small subtropical tea plant originally native to the Irrawaddy River of Burma. Its use spread northward into Southeast Asia and China, then much later into Japan. Tea has been extensively cultivated in China for 2000-3000 years. It is now grown in some 50 subtropical and tropical countries of the world including India, East Africa, Sri Lanka, and southern Russia. Preparation of tea for markets involves cutting and fermenting the terminal bud and a few leaves just below the terminal bud. The leaves are fermented to change the phenols into tannins and volatile alcohols that give tea its distinctive flavor and aroma. The leaves of green tea, which is produced mainly in China and Japan, are not fermented.

Coffee is commercially probably the world's most important beverage. It is brewed from the beans (seeds) of the coffee tree which are harvested and ground into coffee grains. The coffee plant originated in the highlands of Ethiopia and was subsequently introduced to Middle East, then Europe, and ultimately Central and South America. Today, Brazil is the largest exporter of coffee. Coffee seeds are extracted from their shell, roasted, dried, and then mechanically ground or hulled. The granules are infused in hot water to give the characteristic coffee drink. Instant coffee is made from dried powder or water soluble granules. Coffee is also used as an ingredient in ice cream, ice coffee, and other desserts such as coffee cake. Although widely consumed coffee contains few nutrients other than, of course, water.

Chicory is a weed-like plant with beautiful sky-blue flowers. It grows wild as a weed in the more temperate regions of the Northern Hemispheres. Chicory has been used as a flavoring for coffee and other drinks for several hundred years. The root is gathered, chopped, roasted, and ground into a powder which is then added as the flavoring. Although it is often gathered from the wild, cultivation centers are mainly in France, Germany, and Holland.

The leaves of the **dandelion** weed have been gathered and used for beverages and for flavorings for hundreds of years. Dandelion wine, obtained from the flowers, is probably the best-known and most widely consumed product obtained from dandelions but the leaves are also gathered for salads.

Almost all alcoholic beverages are obtained from plants. **Wines** represent fermented grapes, beer is from barley and hops, sake is from rice, and mead is from fermented honey. In fact, the old Anglo-Saxon word "honeymoon" originally referred to the quantities of honeyed mead consumed by the newlyweds. Other plant-derived drinks include gin and whisky which is distilled from grains, vodka from potatoes, and rum from sugar cane.

Cocoa is a wild New World tropical tree originally from Amazonia. It was collected and later cultivated by Central American natives for the preparation of cocoa beverages. They introduced cocoa to Columbus who in turn introduced it to Europe where cocoa became a very popular drink. The commercial product cocoa is obtained from the dried beans which are first roasted and then the shells are removed and the embryo is extracted. The embryo is ground into a cocoa mass consisting of two important products, cocoa butter and cocoa powder. Cocoa powder is an ingredient in ice cream, cakes, and milk. Chocolate is made by combining cocoa butter, cocoa powder, sugar, and milk. The shells and other wastes are used as fertilizer and animal feed. Unlike coffee and tea, both chocolate and cocoa are nutritious and are especially rich in fatty acids, proteins, and sugars.

Narcotics

Narcotics are defined as substances that induce various mood changes when smoked or ingested. Most narcotics are derived from plant substances such as alkaloids and fall into one of three categories; stimulants, hallucinogens, or depressants. Some stimulants are like diet pills, exciting the nervous system, reducing fatigue, and increasing levels of activity. Other narcotics are hallucinogens that act as mind-altering drugs, inducing a dreamlike state of euphoria and unreal feelings of well-being. Depressants dull mental activity and slow thought processes thereby producing a general "dumbing down" in which sensory perception and mental activity is greatly slowed.

The peoples of ancient Babylonian and Egyptian civilizations valued **opium** for its mystical effects. Opium along with a number of important drugs including morphine, papaverine, noscapine, heroin, and codeine are all obtained from the milky juice found in seed capsules of the opium poppy. The seed capsule is cut open and the juice removed and dried into a latex form that yields morphine. One of the most effective pain killers known and is used extensively as an anesthetic in all surgical procedures, morphine somehow diminishes the sensation of pain in the thalamus, the pain-receptor center of the brain. Before the addictive nature of morphine was recognized it was widely used in all types of medicines from before the time of the American Civil War. So many wounded veterans became addicted to morphine that it was called the Soldier's Disease.

Morphine was named after the Greek god Morpheus, the god of dreams, revealing its true properties. Morphine depresses the brain center that controls respiration, and heavy users may die of respiratory failure. Before the advent of modern narcotics, morphine was the drug of choice of many intellectuals and poets such as Edna St Vincent Millay who succumbed to her morphine addiction. Both codeine and papaverine are nonaddictive alkaloids. Codeine is frequently an ingredient in cough syrups, hypnotics, and analgesics while papaverine is prescribed to relieve muscle spasms.

Heroin is a highly addictive alkaloid derived from processed morphine. Both heroin and morphine are mind-altering and hallucinogenic drugs that may induce feelings of euphoria, nightmares, and visions.

For thousands of years the native peoples of Latin America chewed the leaves of the cocoa plant to relieve stress and pain. Studies revealed that cocoa leaves contain a strong narcotic called **cocaine**. They are now illegally harvested in the highlands of Peru, Bolivia, and Ecuador and processed to produce a white powder called cocaine.

Unlike most drugs which are alkaloids, marijuana is an organic chemical found in the leaves and seeds of Cannabis.

Tobacco is prepared from the dried leaves of a large, coarse annual member of the grass family. Leaves of the plant contain nicotine which, when chewed, smoked, or eaten relieves tension and stress. A plant of New World origins, tobacco was introduced to European settlers by North American Indians who had long cultivated the plant for use in certain religious ceremonies. Although the use of tobacco is legal except where no smoking signs are posted, smoking and chewing tobacco has been scientifically proven to be addictive and is also dangerous to health. Smokers have been shown to have much higher risks of lung cancers. Furthermore, research has shown that even secondary smoke can cause an increase in cancer risk.

Table 24–3 Examples of narcotic plants.

Plant	Family	Parts	Psychoactive Substances
Fly Agaric	Agaricaceae	basidiocarp	muscimole
Belladonna	Solanaceae	roots and leaves	atropine
Morning Glory	Convolvulaceae	seeds	ergine, isoergine
San Pedro cactus	Cactaceae	stems	mescaline
Cocoa	Erythroxylaceae	leaves	cocaine
Marijuana	Cannabinaceae	leaves, seeds	tetrahydrocannabinol
Opium Poppy	Papaveraceae	unripe fruit	morphine, codine

That plants are possibly the single most important natural source of drugs used for medicinal purposes has long been recognized. In fact, much of the early interest in botany centered on the search for plants that contributed useful healing properties. In every corner of the world every early culture had shamans and medicine men and women that were able to identify plants from which healing brews, teas, and edible extracts could be derived. The curative properties of many of these traditional species have been incorporated in the manufacture of modern medicines from the common aspirin used to cure headaches and body aches to digitalis which has proven significant in the treatment of a variety of heart ailments. Today the search for new plant medicines continues across the tropical rain forests as ethnobotanists evaluate and document the ability of traditional and folklore medicines to cure diseases.

ACTIVE COMPONENTS OF PLANT MEDICINES

Almost all medicines derived from plants belong to a class of organic chemicals called secondary plant compounds which are metabolic products not normally used as plant structural or enzymatic components. Plant physiologists initially considered secondary plant compounds to be waste products but a thorough review of their properties has shown that almost all are actually manufactured by plants as chemical defenses to deter herbivores. The two most common categories of secondary plant compounds used for medicines include **alkaloids** and **glycosides**.

Alkaloids

The several thousand types of alkaloids are named for their alkaline or basic chemical characteristics. Chemically, most alkaloids also contain nitrogen components and have a bitter taste. Examples of alkaloids include ephedrine, morphine, caffeine, cocaine, and nicotine. Plants from which alkaloids are extracted include ephedra along with members of the coffee family (*Rubiaceae*), nightshade family (*Solanaceae*) and the legume family (*Fabaceae*). Most plant alkaloids are stimulants and alkaloids specifically used for medicines typically cause pronounced physiological changes in the nervous system.

Glycosides

Of secondary importance to alkaloids as medicinal sources, the glycosides are chemical compounds that consist of a sugar molecule bound to another molecule. The sugar molecule is usually—but not always—glucose and the bound molecule may be a fatty acid or protein. Familiar examples of glycosides include certain steroids, saponins, cyanogenic glycosydes, and cardioglycosides. Like virtually all plant-derived medicines, glycosides can be deadly in large doses; that is, the difference between a toxic drug and a medicine is often simply controlling the amount of the dose.

Cardioglycosides are derived from the milky sap of such plants as milkweed and oleander. The sap is deadly if directly consumed but correct dosages of cardioglycosides are used to treat a variety of heart ailments including heart failure. Saponins also are deadly if uncontrolled. An important saponin obtained from yams is diosgenin which is used in the manufacture of cortisone and progesterone.

SOME EXAMPLES OF PLANT MEDICINES

The innumerable examples of plant medicines include aloin, atropine, quinine, digitoxin, ephedrine, gingko, salicin, and taxol. The derivation and uses of some of these will be further described below.

Aspirin

Aspirin is best known as an **analgesic**, or pain killer. Derived from the bark of willows *(Salix)*, aspirin is the most widely used of all plant medicines. Americans consume some 80 million pills a day and the rest of the world is not far behind. The treatment of aches and pains with a tea steeped in willow bark was known to many ancient peoples including the Greeks and Romans, who treated fevers, aches and pains, and gout. Native American peoples also prepared infusions made with willow bark to soothe sore throats and aching bones. The use of willow bark was so well known throughout Europe that early chemists conducted experiments to isolate and identify the active chemical ingredient. After numerous attempts by French and German chemists a glycoside was finally identified as the working ingredient and called salicylic acid, after the genus of willows from which it was extracted. In addition to willows, other important sources of salicylic acid include the shrub meadowsweet and the herb wintergreen.

Physicians value aspirin for three medicinal properties, as an **analgesic**, or pain killer, as a **antipyretic**, or fever-reducing drug, and as an **anti-inflammatory** medicine. In recent years aspirin has also been widely heralded for its role in sharply reducing heart attacks and strokes. Use of the aspirin has also been linked with the reduction of colon cancer. Evidence strongly supports the contention that in older males an aspirin a day helps prevent heart attacks. Furthermore, a prescribed aspirin regimen following a heart attack or stroke significantly reduces the chances of a second attack.

Although widely hailed and even more widely used as a wonder drug the use of aspirin by some people can cause unwanted symptoms because aspirin can irritate the lining of the stomach, causing upset stomach, especially severe if aspirin is taken on an empty stomach. Because of the side affects, sodium bicarbonate has been added to salicylic acid to make the very popular buffered aspirin.

Quinine

Quinine is an alkaloid extract from the Fever Bark Tree that grows on the eastern slopes of the Andes Mountains of South America. Actually one of a group of about 36 alkaloids found to occur in the Fever Bark Tree, quinine is an extract from the bark and was used by the Incas to cure malaria, one of the world's deadliest and most dreaded tropical diseases. European explorers quickly adopted the use of quinine and its chemical relatives and introduced the fever bark tree in the East Indies and the Phillippines. The advent of several synthetic substitutes for quinine including primaquine and chloroquine have largely replaced quinine use, although it is still cultivated for local use. Quinine works by destroying the protozoan parasite in the blood stream. The demand for quinine resulted in vigorous collecting of wild plants which were threatened with extinction until 1820, when two French scientists were able to synthesize this plant alkaloid in the laboratory.

Reserpine

This alkaloid is an extract from the roots of a low evergreen shrub called snakeroot, which is native to the East Indies, Sri Lanka, and India. Snakeroot was named because its roots are long and coiled, thereby resembling a coiled snake. Because of this, the root was used to cure snakebite and insect stings. Later it was prescribed to cure mental illness. Because a tea brewed from its leaves had a calming affect, reserpine is thought to reduce anxiety and blood pressure. Modern medicine has revealed that reserpine is an alkaloid that acts as a sedative to calm the central nervous system, thus the long-associated traditions about snakeroot are based on fact.

Digitalis

This glycoside medicine is extracted from foxglove, a common flower with rows of attractive, bell-shaped flowers. The medicinal use of digitalis was first discovered in the mid 18th century by an English physician named Withering who prescribed it for the treatment of dropsy, a form of edema or bloating. Further analysis of foxglove yielded some 30 glycosides of which two, digitoxin and digoxin are used for treatment of heart conditions and marketed under the name of digitalis. Digitalis is used to treat congestive heart failure; correct dosages increase the strength of heart contractions and reduce or eliminate atrial arrhythmias. Unlike many other plant-derived medicines, digitalis has not been chemically synthesized and must be obtained from harvested foxglove plants.

Cortisones from Yams

Cortisones are steroid chemicals produced by the adrenal cortex in humans that play an important role in reducing inflammation. Yams have proven to be an important natural source of cortisone steroids. Yams are tropical and subtropical vines that are best known for the large, edible tubers that they produce. Chemical tests revealed that yams are excellent sources of natural cortisone steroids.

Cortisones are widely prescribed for the treatment of inflammation, Addison's Disease, bursitis, gout, bowel disease, skin diseases, and rheumatoid arthritis. Prior to the discovery that yams contain commercially useable quantities of cortisone, bovines such as oxen and cattle were the major sources. Cortisones were extracted from bile acids in these animals, processed and purified. The use of yams as cortisone sources has dramatically decreased the costs of this medicine.

Atropine

Atropine is an alkaloid derived from the roots and leaves of the belladonna plant, a poisonous member of the nightshade or tomato family. Belladonna is also the source of two other important medicinal alkaloids, hyoscyamine and scopolamine. Historically, extracts of belladonna were called the devil's herb or sorcerer's herb, and were used to dilate the eyes of ladies, giving them a wide-eyed appearance. Belladonna, in fact-means "beautiful lady."

As a medicine, atropine is used as a cardiac stimulant, a treatment for certain kinds of organic poisoning, and to dilate the pupils of the eye during opthalmic surgery. Belladonna is still cultivated in Europe for its medicinal extracts.

Ginseng Acids

Extracts from the roots of ginseng have long been known to improve mental powers and reduce fatigue. Chemical tests revealed that the key ingredients of ginseng are panax acid and panaxin. The use of ginseng may have originated in Manchuria and Korea, and still remains a common herbaceous perennial in use there. Native tribes of North America also reputedly used ginseng to reduce fatigue and stress among other purposes, notably as a contraceptive.

The use of ginseng as a natural medicine has become so popular that the plant was collected so vigorously that it is now rare and threatened with extinction over much of its range. This resulted in the commercial cultivation of ginseng in Wisconsin, Minnesota, and other central states.

Table 24–4 Examples of some plants used for medicines.

Common Name	Plant Family	Ingredient	Medicinal Use
Periwinkle	Apocynaceae	vinblastine	blood cancers; lymphoma and leukemia, Hodgkin's disease
Pacific Yew	Taxaceae	taxol	breast cancer, ovarian cancer
White willow	Salicaceae	salicin (aspirin)	pain, fever, hypertension
Snakeroot	Apocynaceae	reserpine	hypertension
Feverbark Tree	Rubiaceae	quinine	malaria
Foxglove	Scrophulariaceae	digitoxin	congestive heart failure
Ephredra	Ephedraceae	ephedrine	bronchitis
Eucalyptus	Myrtaceae	eucalyptol	cough suppressant
Ginkgo	Ginkgoaceae	ginkgolides	Alzheimer's disease
Opium poppy	Papaveraceae	morphine	pain
Chaulmoo Tree	Flacourtiaceae	ethyl oils	leprosy, skin diseases
Penicillium	Aspergillaceae	penicillin	antibiotic
Ephedra	Gnetaceae	ephedrine	low blood pressure
Coca	Erythroxylaceae	cocaine	local anesthetic
Mayapple	Berberidaceae	podophyllin	cancer, warts

EXAMPLES OF POPULAR HERBAL MEDICINES

Herbal medicines employing the medicinal benefit of a variety of herbs that have been shown through tradition to be useful treatments for certain ailments. In practice, many natural remedies rely strongly on folklore and tradition rather than medical approval and should not be taken without first consulting a physician. Furthermore, these alternative therapies should never be used as a substitute for genuine medicines. Granted all of the above, many herbal medicines are still recommended as natural therapy for a wide variety of ailments.

Garlic

This popular member of the onion family is a favorite flavoring of gourmet cooks, especially in the preparation of Italian dishes. Garlic connoisseurs claim that eating garlic lessens cholesterol levels and helps reduce heart disease and cancer. A four year study conducted in Germany lends support to these ideas, indicting that garlic opens narrowed arteries which is the first and most elemental step in reducing risk of heart attack. Another study conducted at the University of North Carolina found that garlic eaters were 47% less likely to develop stomach cancer and had 31% less incidence of colon cancer compared to non-garlic eaters. As with any treatment, too much garlic can produce unwanted affects. Because it dilates blood vessels and reduces blood clots garlic should not be eaten at least two weeks before an operation.

Ginkgo

This extract from the ginkgo tree is recommended to reduce the onset of Alzheimer's Disease in elderly folk and enhance memory in all ages. It may also eliminate the annoying problem of tinnitus, or ringing in the ears experienced by some people. Some herbalists claim that ginkgo can reduce the incidence and severity of Alzheimer's Disease but this has been disputed by some medical authorities. Like garlic, ginkgo is an anticoagulant and should not be taken at least several weeks prior to an operation.

Horse Chestnut

Horse chestnut is a large, coarse tree with five lobed leaves and large, round seed fruits. Gathered fresh from the tree or from beneath the tree is unwise because the seeds are poisonous. Commercial preparations detoxify the seeds and provide tablets containing just the right amount of dosage of the active organic substance called aescin. Horse chestnut taken correctly help reduce hemorrhoids, strengthen walls of capillary blood vessels, and noticeably reduce the intensity of varicose veins.

Saw Palmetto

This small palm is fairly common in Florida and along the Gulf Coast. The herbal extract is obtained from the date-like fruits and offered in commercial tablet form. The pills offer some relief from swollen prostate or benign prostatic hyperplasia. However, prostrate problems should always be referred to a physician for diagnosis and treatment.

Eucalyptus

This tall tree which may reach over 100 meters in height is native to Australia but has since been widely transplanted into almost every temperate region of the world including California, South Africa, and North Africa. Its herbal qualities come from a pungent, aromatic oil extracted from its leaves. The oil is an antiseptic and is also used for treatment of bronchial congestion and asthma, mostly via steam inhalations. Eucalyptus oil is also an important ingredient in cough syrup and cough drops.

Echinacea or Coneflower

The roots and rhizome of the black Sampson or purple coneflower were used by the Plains Indians of North America to treat snakebite and toothaches. Later, they were thought useful as an antibiotic, antiseptic, and a drug to restore health and happiness. Herbalists still suggest that tinctures of this very attractive flower can be used to alleviate cold and flu symptoms and, in fact, Echinacea is the most popular of all herbal medicines in terms of annual sales. The herb is considered safe when administered in prescribed dosages but people with organ transplants and autoimmune diseases such as lupus and rheumatoid arthritis should not take it.

Bloodroot

One of the earliest of our spring flowers, this member of the poppy family is named for its bright red sap which contains a number of medically important alkaloids.

Although bloodroot is very poisonous a tea brewed from its rhizome has shown multiple uses including an antiplaque mouthwash, and emetic. Bloodroot also helps relieve congestion caused by flu and colds. Some authorities suggest that bloodroot is an anticancer agent.

Black Cohosh

Also known as black snakeroot, this wildflower of the buttercup family has a long history of herbal use. Indians used a poultice of the rhizome to treat snakebite (hence its common name). Herbalists recommend black cohosh as a mild sedative and for treatments of menopause but this dates from Indian preparation of a tea taken to alleviate menstrual cramps, hence the derivation of yet another common name of squawroot for this plant.

Witch Hazel

An alcohol or water based extract from the twigs and bark of this woodland shrub is one of the most popular of all herbal skin applications when applied as a topical antiseptic and astringent.

Feverfew

Also known as Bachelor's button, feverfew is an attractive chrysanthemum thought to cure fever or at least reduce fever intensity. A tea made from its leaves is also recommended by herbalists for reducing tension, diarrhea, and as a cold treatment. Because of its strong, penetrating odor, sprays of feverfew are also sometimes used to purify the air in homes.

Culver's Root

This member of the snapdragon family was used by American Indians as a blood cleanser and body purifier. The Puritans believed that it helped cure tuberculosis and Cottan Mather used this plant for his daughter's tuberculosis.

Boneset

This tall streamside flowering plant with its leaves penetrated by the main stem enjoys a very long history of herbal use. American Indians prescribed a hot tea of boneset leaves for breakbone fever, a flu-like disease characterized by aching bones. The tea also is taken to relieve fever and as a laxative and diuretic.

Selected Key Words and Phrases

pulses	alkaloids	glycosides	oilseeds	scurvy
legumes	aleurone	heroin	tobacco	vegetable
bran	codeine	opium	fruit	masticatories
caryopsis	endosperm	cocaine	spices	herbs
grains	beri-beri	marijuana	tuber crops	root crops

Selected References and Resources

Blackwell, W. H. 1990. *Poisonous and Medicinal Plants.* Prentice-Hall. Englewood Cliffs, New Jersey.

Culpeper, N. 1995. Reprinted 1995. *Culpeper's Complete Herbal.* Wadsworth Reference Library. Hertfordshire, England.

HerbalGram, the journal of the American Botanical Council. *www.herbalgram.org.*

Kent, N. L., and A. D. Evers. 1994. *Technology of Cereals.* 4th edition. Pergamon Press. Oxford and New York.

Macaleb, R., and the Herb Research Foundation. Prima Publishing Company. New York, New York.

Macrae, R., R. K. Robinson, and M. J. Sadler. (Eds.) 1993. *Encyclopedia of Food Science, Food Technology, and Nutrition.* 8 volumes. Academic Press. New York

Reader's Digest Association. 1986. *Magic and Medicine of Plants.* Reader's Digest Corporation. Pleasantville, New York.

Vaughan, J. G., and C. A. Geissler. 1997. *The New Oxford Book of Food Plants.* Oxford University Press. Oxford and New York.

Review and Discussion Questions

1. Many vegetarians actually supplement their diet with certain animal products such as eggs and milk. Strict vegetarians, however, eat only plants. What nutrient risks do strict vegetarians face and what kinds of plants must be included in their diet to avoid nutrient deficiencies?

2. Exactly what chemical and physiological changes do highly addictive drugs such as cocaine induce in drug addicts that make them so compulsive?

3. What is the major factor involved in using secondary plant products from poisonous plants as medicinal drugs for the treatment of certain human ailments and diseases?

4. List and describe the most famous and best known examples of herbs long used as cures by native peoples that have proven to be medically effective

GLOSSARY

abscisic acid (ABA)—a plant hormone that inhibits growth. It is involved in causing dormancy, with other hormones, in plants.

abscission—the process whereby leaves, flowers, and fruits are separated from a plant after the development of an abscission zone at the base of their attachments to the main stem.

abscission zone—region at the base of a leaf of other plant organ or structure where the cells break down prior to, during, and ultimately causing the separation of the leaf or other structure.

accessory pigment—any of several pigments such as carotenoids or xanthrophyls in higher plants that captures light energy and transfers a portion of that energy to chlorophyll.

achene—a fruit with a single seed in which the seed is attached to the ovary only at the seed base.

acid—a chemical compound that contains hydrogen ions and combines with bases to form salts.

active transport—the movement of a substance across a plasma membrane and against a diffusion gradient. In the process energy is expended by the cell.

adenine—one of the four nitrogenous bases found in DNA, RNA, and other organic molecules of the plants and animals.

adhesion—attraction of separate substances caused by molecular attractive forces between them, causes clinging.

adventitious—budlike structures that develop on roots or stems, function as roots.

aeciospore—reproductive spore produced by fruiting body of rusts.

aerenchyma—parenchyma tissue with large intercellular spaces which entrap air, often found in aquatic plants.

aerial root—special kind of root produced by stem meristematic tissue of aerial plants, may penetrate soil, bark, or debris of canopy.

aerobic respiration—any living process that requires free oxygen.

agar—a gelatinous material found in some red algae that is used as a culture medium for bacteria.

agaric—a family of basidiomycete club fungi.

aggregate fruit—a kind of fruit derived from a flower with many pistils.

akinete—reproductive cells of some algae, commonly thick-walled.

albuminous cell—supportive cells of phloem usually found in certain conifers.

algin—a gelatinous material found in some brown algae. Algin is used in many food products and pharmaceutical, industrial, and household preparations.

alkaloid—nitrogen based organic chemicals produced by plants for defense against herbivores.

allele—an alternate form of a gene.

allelopathy—(also **allelopathic agent**)—chemicals secreted in soil or air to inhibit growth of other, would-be competitive plants.

allophycocyanin—blue respiratory pigment found in blue-green algae.

alternation of generations—a plant life cycle in which there is an alternation between the haploid gametophyte and diploid sporophyte stages.

amino acid—an organic compound containing nitrogen, and forming a basic building block of a protein molecule.

amyloplast—kind of leucoplast in which starch grains are formed.

anabolism—synthesis or manufacture of molecules.

anaerobic respiration—respiration in the absence of oxygen. In the process hydrogen is removed from glucose during glycolysis and is combined with an organic ion instead of oxygen.

anisogamy—also known as heterogamy, sexual fusion of two gametes in which one is larger than the other.

angiosperm—a seed plant with flowers, in which the seed is produced in an ovary that matures into a fruit.

annual—a plant with a life cycle that is completed in one growing season.

annual ring—the record in a tree trunk of a single season's production of xylem by the vascular cambium.

annulus—a layer of cells that form one margin of a fern sporangium. As the cells of this layer expand they cause the sporangium to spring open and disperse the spores. Also, annulus is a term applied to a membranous ring around the stipe of a mushroom.

anther—the male part of a flower in which pollen is produced. This is the top part of a stamen, the pollen-bearing part of a stamen.

antheridiophore—a structure that holds an antheridium.

antheridium—the male gamete producing structure of some algae, fungi, bryophytes, and lower vascular plants.

anthocyanin—a pigment found in cell sap that can alter color due to pH. In acid conditions it is red and in basic conditions it is blue.

anthophyta—another name for flowering plants.

antibiotic—a substance produced by plants, usually fungi that destroys or interferes with the life processes of other living organisms.

anticodon—set of three nitrogenous bases in transfer RNA that bonds with three complementary nitrogenous bases on the messenger RNA template.

antipodal—or antipodals, cells that are opposite the micropylar end of the embryo.

apical dominance—the hormonal suppression of growth of lateral buds on a stem allowing one apical bud to become dominant.

apical meristem—an area of mitotic division at the end of a root or stem.

apomixis—a process of reproduction whereby an organism is produced without sexual reproduction.

archegoniophore—a structure that holds an archegonium.

archegonium—a multicellular female gamete producing structure in bryophytes, lower vascular plants and gymnosperms.

areole—in cacti, a lateral that produces leaves.

ascocarp—in ascomycte fungi, a fruiting body that bears asci.

ascus—finger-like projections on sac fungi in which a row of ascospores is formed.

asexual reproduction—a form of reproduction in which gametes are not used, e.g., budding.

assimilation—the conversion of raw materials into structure by cells.

atactostele—vascular cylinder in plants comprised of scattered vascular bundles.

atom—the smallest divisible unit of an element that still exhibits the characteristics of that element.

ATP-adenosine triphosphate—an energy rich molecule containing three phosphate groups held by high energy bond. ATP is the most important chemical substance for the storage of energy by cells.

autosome—a nonsexual chromosome.

autotroph—an organism that manufactures it owns food.

auxin—a hormone that regulates growth. Auxins are produced naturally by plants and synthetically by industry.

auxospore—large cells produced in diatoms during sexual reproduction.

axil—an angle formed between a stem and a leaf petiole. This is the area in which axillary buds are produced.

axillary bud—this kind of bud occurs in a leaf axil.

B

bacillus—cylindrical or rod-shaped bacteria.

backcross—a genetic cross between an offspring and one of its parents.

bacteriophage—a form of virus which uses a bacterium as a host.

bark—outer tissues of a woody stem formed by cork cells of the cork cambium.

base—a chemical compound that dissociates in water to release hydroxyl (OH-) ions. Bases combine with acids to produce salts.

basidiospore—a vegetative reproductive body produced by club fungi.

basidium—one of many club-shaped structures in which basidiospores are produced in club fungi.

benthic—plants or animals that live attached to the bottom of aquatic habitats.

berry—a kind of thin-skinned fruit that forms from a compound ovary and normally contains more than one seed.

betacyanin—purple plant pigments that are sometimes found in flowers, leaves and other parts of flowering plants.

biennial—a plant with a two year life cycle.

binomial nomenclature—first developed by Linneaus, this is the naming of plants and animals with two names, genus and species.

biological clock—system of time keeping in plants, using environmental cues to determine events in the life history of the plant.

biological controls—a process whereby natural enemies and inhibitors are used to combat insect pests and undesirable destructive organisms.

biome—giant subcontinental ecosystems consisting of similar biotic communities.

biosphere—portion of the hydrosphere, lithosphere and atmosphere where life exists on earth.

biotechnology—the use of organisms, and or their parts for the uses and benefits of humankind.

biotic community—a group of plants, animals, that form a natural grouping or association.

blade—the flattened part of a leaf or seaweed.

bond—an electromagnetic force that holds atoms together as compounds.

botany—the science that includes the study of plants.

botulism—a poisoning by ingesting toxins produced by botulism bacteria.

bract—a leaf-like structure that is modified to carry seeds or sporangia.

bran—a kind of cereal but technically, the thin, outer layer of the seed coat typically comprised of fibers.

bryophyte—the group of primitive green land plants including mosses, liverworts and hornworts.

bud—terminal region of a shoot which gives rise to a leaf or flower, also an immature flower.

budding—a process of reproduction in which a new cell develops from the side of a mature cell in yeasts.

bud scale—bladeless leaf that forms a protective cover over a bud.

bulb—a storage organ that develops underground and consists of a modified stem with fleshy storage leaves that surround it.

bundle scar—a marking at the node of a stem. It is created by the leaf petiole and vascular bundles when the leaf drops at abscission.

bundle sheath—a ring of parenchyma and / or sclerenchyma cells that surround a vascular bundle.

C

callus—a form of undifferentiated tissue that develops over injuries on stems and roots.

Calvin cycle—see dark reactions.

calyptra—a growth of tissue from the archegonial wall of some mosses. It forms a cap over the capsule.

calyx—a collective term for that part of a flower containing the sepals.

cambium—a kind of meristem that produces secondary tissues such as xylem and phloem and cork cambium.

capillary water—that water that is held in the soil despite gravitational force against it.

capsule—a kind of dry fruit that splits variously when mature.

carbohydrate—an organic compound that contains carbon, hydrogen, and oxygen, with hydrogen being twice as common as oxygen and carbon atoms.

carpel—a flower part including the ovule-bearing part of the pistil.

caryopsis—a kind of non splitting dry fruit with the pericarp tightly fused to the seed.

Casparian strip—a band of suberin forming a series of radial coils around part of xylem cells.

cell—the basic structural and functional unit of a living organism. Cells in plants are characterized by having protoplasm surrounded by a cell wall.

cell cycle—the sequence of events involved in the cell division.

cell membrane—see plasma membrane.

cell plate—a molecular structure forming the precursor of the middle lamella in a cell wall. They form between future daughter cells during telophase.

cell sap—the liquid contents of a cell vacuole.

cell wall—the outer layer of a plant cell.

centromere—a dense constricted area on a chromosome to which a spindle fiber is attached.

chemiosmosis—a theory that energy is provided from phosphorylation by protons being "pumped" across inner mitochondrial and thylakoid membranes.

chiasma—the X-shaped configuration produced when two chromatids of homologous chromosomes become attached to each other during prophase I of meiosis.

chlorenchyma—a kind of tissue composed of parenchyma cells containing chloroplasts.

chlorophyll—kinds of green pigments containing magnesium and necessary for trapping light in photosynthesis.

chloroplast—a cell organelle containing chlorophyll, and found in cells of organisms that carry on photosynthesis.

chromatid—one of the two DNA strands of a chromosome, that are held together by a centromere.

chromatin—the mass of DNA and proteins found in chromosomes.

chromoplast—a kink of plastid that contains pigments other than chlorophyll, usually including yellow to orange.

chromosome—a cellular structure consisting of genes composed of DNA and proteins. Chromosomes occur in cell nuclei and appear during mitosis and meiosis.

cilium—a short hairlike organelle found on the cells of unicellular aquatic organisms. Normally cilia function in movement or propulsion.

circadian rhythm—a daily rhythm of activity or growth found in plants and animals.

cladophyll—a flattened stem that resembles a leaf.

class—a taxonomic category of classification occurring between a division and an order.

climax vegetation—a vegetational type that can perpetuate itself indefinitely at the end of ecological succession.

coenocytic—cells or organisms that have nuclei not separated from one another by cell walls. This condition is found in many fungi.

cohesion-tension theory—a theory that states that the rise of water in plants is due to a combination of cohesion of water molecules in capillaries and tension on the water columns brought about by transpiration.

coleoptile—a seedling structure that forms a protective sheath surrounding the emerging shoot in the grasses.

coleorhiza—a protective sheath in a seedling that surrounds the emerging radicle of grasses.

collenchyma—a kind of tissue formed from cells with unevenly thickened walls.

colloid—a substance consisting of a solution in which fine particles are permanently mixed.

community—a collective term for sum total of living organisms in a common environment and interacting with each other.

companion cell—a kind of specialized cell derived with a sieve-tube element from the same parent cell. It is found in angiosperm phloem and controls the activity of the sieve-tube element.

compound leaf—a leaf with its lamina divided into separate leaflets.

conidium—an asexually produced fungal spore formed outside of a sporangium.

conifer—a kind of gymnospermous tree that bears its seeds in cones.

conjugation—a process in green algae that allows the fusion of isogametes. Conjugation also occurs in fungi, protozoa and bacteria.

conjugation tube—a tube between two filaments of algae that permits the transfer of a gamete between adjacent cells.

cork—a kind of tissue composed of cells whose walls are impregnated with suberin. Cork forms the outer layer of tissue of an older woody stem and is produced by cork cambium.

cork cambium—a narrow cylindrical sheath of cells between the exterior of a woody root or stem and phloem. It produces cork cells exteriorly and phelloderm interiorly.

corm—a kind of thickened food-storage stem that is surrounded by papery nonfunctional leaves.

corolla—a collective term for the petals of a flower.

cortex—the tissue of a stem that is primary tissue composed mainly of parenchyma, and extends between the epidermis and vascular tissue.

cotyledon—an embryo or seed leaf that either stores or absorbs food.

covalent bond—an electromagnetic force provided by pairs of electrons that are shared by two or more atomic nuclei, thus holding the atoms together.

crossing-over—the exchange of genetic material between corresponding segments of chromatids of homologous pairs during prophase I of meiosis.

cuticle—a waxy or fatty layer in the outer walls of epidermal cells.

cutin—the waxy or fatty substance of which a cuticle is made.

cyclosis—the streaming of cytoplasm within a cell, caused by the contraction of microfilaments.

cytochrome—an iron-containing pigment found in mitochondria and involved in molecular activity in the electron transfer chain.

cytokinesis—the process of cell division.

cytokinin—a growth hormone involved in cell division and aging in plants.

cytology—the science of the study of cells.

cytoplasm-the protoplasm of a cell exclusive of the nucleus.

cytoplasmic streaming—the movement of protoplasm as in cyclosis.

D

dark reactions—a series of chemical reactions, occurring in the stroma of chloroplasts, that takes carbon dioxide and energy from the light reactions of photosynthesis, and produces sugars. Because the reactions don't need light they are referred to as the dark reaction.

day-neutral plant—a plant that does not require a specific photoperiod length for flowering.

deciduous—refers to plants that shed leaves annually.

decomposer—an organism that reprocesses organic material into substances capable of being reused by other organisms.

development—embryonic changes in plant structure creating growth and differentiation of cells to form tissues and organs.

dicotyledon—a class of angiosperms in which seedlings develop with two cotyledons.

dictyosome—another name for Golgi body.

differentially permeable membrane—a membrane through which different substances can pass at different rates.

differentiation—the development of an unspecialized cell into a cell with a more specialized function.

diffusion—the process whereby molecules or particles move from a region of high concentration to a region of low concentration.

digestion—a process whereby enzymes convert complex substances into simpler form.

dihybrid cross—a genetic cross involving two different characteristics.

dikaryotic—club fungi cells that have a pair of nuclei in each cell.

dioecious—plants with flowers or cones that are unisexual.

diploid—a condition in cells in which two sets of chromosomes are present.

diuretic—a substance that increases the flow of urine.

division—the largest undivided taxonomic category of classification of plants within a kingdom.

DNA-deoxyribonucleic acid—the chemical form of genetic information in cells and viruses.

dominant—a member of a pair of genes that expresses itself in the phenotype regardless of the other gene in the pair.

dormancy—a period of time during which seeds, buds or bulbs are inactive regardless of environmental conditions.

double fertilization—in angiosperms, the simultaneous fertilization of the sperm and egg to form a zygote and the fertilization of a second sperm and polar nuclei to form endosperm.

drupe—a kind of simple fleshy fruit in which the single seed is surrounded by a hard endocarp.

E

ecology—a biological science that studies the relationships of organisms to each other and to their environment.

ecosystem—a system of living organisms and their abiotic environment.

egg—a female gamete.

elater—a strap-like appendage on a horsetail (*Equisetum*) spore. The function of elaters is to assist spore dispersal.

electron—a negatively charged particle in an atom.

element—a molecular structure composed of one kind of atom.

embryo—the multicellular growth that results from a zygote. It is an immature sporophyte.

embryo sac—the female gametophyte of angiosperms, in which most forms have eight nuclei which will ultimately form a zygote and endosperm of the seed.

enation—a small bump on the stems of whisk ferns that represents leaf-like outgrowths.

endocarp—the innermost layer of a pericarp or fruit wall.

endodermis—in angiosperms, a single layer of cells that surrounds the vascular stele in roots and some stems.

endoplasmic reticulum—a cell organelle composed of interlined double membrane channels that are lined with ribosomes. Fats and proteins are manufactured here.

endosperm—a form of stored food tissue found in angiosperm seeds. It is formed from the fusion of a sperm and polar nuclei in the embryo sac.

energy—the capacity to do work; kinds of energy include heat, light, and kinetic.

enzyme—a protein molecule that speeds up chemical reactions and in the process is not altered.

epicotyl—that part of a seedling found above the cotyledons.

epidermis—the outer layer of cells, of leaves, stems and roots.

epiphyte—a plant that grows on another organism without parasitizing it.

ergotism—a disease that results from the ingestion of food made with flour containing ergot fungus.

essential element—one of 18 elements generally considered essential to the normal growth, development, and reproduction of most plants.

ethylene—a gas that inhibits plant growth and promotes the ripening of fruit.

eukaryotic—cells that have organelles with membranes and a nucleus with chromosomes.

eutrophication—the accumulation of nutriments in a body of water leading to an increase in algae and other organisms.

exine—the outer layer of a pollen grain.

exocarp—the outermost layer of a fruit wall or pericarp.

eyespot—the small cell organelle found in motile unicellular organisms, that is sensitive to light.

F

F₁ or first filial generation—the offspring of a cross between two parents.

F₂ second filial generation—the offspring of organisms within the F_1.

family—a taxonomic classification category between genus and order.

fat—an organic compound containing carbon, hydrogen, and oxygen but with much less oxygen than in carbohydrates.

fermentation—a anaerobic chemical process in which glucose is broken down to form ethyl alcohol or lactic acid.

fertilization—the fusion of two gametes to produce a zygote.

fiber—a dead long cell with thick-walls.

filament—thread-like colony form in algae and fungi, also the stalk of a stamen.

fission—cell division in bacteria, blue-green algae, and related organisms.

flagellum—a thread-like cell organelle extending from motile unicellular organisms. Its main function is locomotion.

floret—a flower that is a part of an inflorescence in Asteraceae and Poaceae.

florigen—a mystery substance or hormone that may cause a plant to flower.

follicle-a kind of dry fruit that splits along one side.

food chain—a sequence of organisms in a community that are dependant upon one another for food.

foot—the basal part of the bryophyte sporophyte.

fossil—the remains or impressions of any natural object that has been preserved after death.

frond—a fern leaf.

fruit—a mature ovary usually containing seed, and consisting of an endocarp, mesocarp and exocarp.

fucoxanthin—a brown pigment found in brown algae.

G

gametangium—a plant structure in which gametes are formed.

gamete—a sex cell that contains one half the chromosome number.

gametophore—a stalk holding a gametangium.

gametophyte—a plant generation which is haploid and produces gametes.

gemma—a small cup like growth on the gametophyte of bryophytes. Tissue removed from it can produce a new plant.

gene—a segment of a DNA molecule that can be inherited.

generative cell—an angiosperm cell in the male gametophyte that divides to produce two sperms. In gymnosperms it divides to produce a sterile cell and a spermatogenous cell.

genetic engineering—the artificial introduction of genes into another organism to create a life system useful to humankind.

genetics—the biological science that deals with heredity.

genotype—the genetic makeup of an organism. It may contain genes that are not physically expressed.

genus—a taxonomic category of classification between a family and a species.

gibberellin—a plant hormone that affects growth. It acts with auxins and is useful for causing elongation of stem.

gill—a flattened plate in the cap of a club fungus. The basidia form the free border of the gill.

gland—a mass of plant tissue that secretes something.

glycolysis—a chemical process in the mitochondria of cells in which glucose is converted to pyruvic acid.

golgi body—a cell organelle in which material is accumulated and packaged. Also called a dictyosome.

grain—a seed of grasses, also called a caryopsis.

granum—a cellular structure found in chloroplasts. It consists of stacks of thylakoids and contains chlorophyll.

gravitational water—the water that is affected by gravity and drains from the soil after a rain.

gravitropism—the growth response of a plant to gravity.

ground meristem—plant tissue that forms all primary tissue types except epidermis and vascular steles.

growth—the process whereby an organism increases in size.

guard cell—one of two cells that surround the stoma.

guttation—a process whereby a plant will exude liquid water from leaves as a result of root pressure.

gymnosperm—a group of plants with naked seeds.

H

haploid—a set of chromosomes in which none of the chromosomes occur in pairs.

haustoria—the protrusion of fungal hyphae from the main mass of the plant.

heartwood—dark colored wood whose cells are soaked with resins and have stopped functioning in the conduction of water.

herbaceous—plants that lack wood.

herbal—a botany book that stresses the medicinal uses of plants.

herbarium—a collection of dried plants stored and catalogued for research.

heterocyst—an enlarged thick walled cell found in filaments of some kinds of algae.

heterospory—the production of spores of two sizes by a plant.

heterotrophic—an organism that must ingest food to obtain nutrients.

heterozygous—a pair of genes of differing strengths for the same characteristic.

holdfast—a growth of tissue or a cell used by a plant to hold on to a substrate.

homologous chromosomes—chromosomes that will pair and share genes for the same characters.

homozygous—a pair of genes of the same strength for a character.

hormone—an organic chemical that is produced in one part of the organism is transported to a different area where it has an affect on something.

hybrid—the offspring of parents that differ in gene type.

hydathode—a structure at the tip of a leaf that loses water in guttation.

hydrolysis—the chemical process whereby water combines with substances and breaks them down to simpler form.

hydrosere—a succession of habitats that begins in a wet habitat.

hygroscopic water—water that is chemically bound to soil particles and thus is not available for plant use.

hypha—a single thread-like growth of a fungal mycelium.

hypocotyl—the portion of a seedling that is beneath the cotyledons and above the radicle.

hypodermis—the layer of cells beneath the epidermis in the cortex of some plants.

hypothesis—an educated guess. An explanation for an observation that must be tested experimentally.

imbibition—the swelling of something because it has absorbed water which adheres to the internal surfaces.

indusium—in ferns, a small umbrella-like covering over the sori.

inferior ovary—in a flower, an ovary which is beneath the attachment areas for the calyx, corolla and stamens.

inflorescence—a group of flowers that emerge as a cluster from one stem.

inorganic—refers to non living. In chemical sense is that group of chemical compounds that are not hydrocarbons.

integument—the outermost layer of an ovule. It normally develops into a seed coat.

intermediate-day plant—a plant that will not flower if the photoperiod is too long or too short.

internode—the region of a stem between two nodes.

ion—an atom or molecule that is electrically charged due to the gain or loss of electrons.

isogamy—the process of producing gametes of both sexes that are identical in size. The condition occurs in some algae and fungi.

isotope—one or more forms of an element that share similar chemical properties but have different neutron numbers in their nuclei.

K

kingdom—the highest taxonomic category of classification. Five kingdoms are recognized.

knot—the base of a branch that has been trapped by trunk growth.

Krebs Citric Acid Cycle—a complex series of chemical reactions occurring in mitochondria, in which pyruvic acid is degraded to form hydrogen, carbon dioxide and electrons.

L

lamina—blade of a leaf.

lateral bud—a growth of a bud from the leaf axil.

laticifer—cells and ducts that secrete latex in some plants.

leaf—flattened plant organ specialized for photosynthesis or storage and equipped with mesophyll, vascular bundles and or stomata.

leaf gap—a break in the vascular bundle above the point where the vascular tissue enters a leaf.

leaflet—a subdivision of a compound leaf.

leaf scar—the scar left on a twig when a leaf is dropped during abscission.

leaf trace—see leaf gap.

legume—a dry fruit that splits along two seams.

lenticel—a spongy group of cells occurring in periderm that allow the passage of gas in and out of the plant.

leucoplast—a kind of plastid which lacks pigment and stores starch.

light reactions—the chemical reactions that begin the process of photosynthesis. They occur in the grana of the chloroplast and are responsible for trapping light and creating energy from it.

lignin—an organic chemical that impregnates cell walls in some cells to harden them. Lignin is a major component of wood.

ligule—a tiny spike-like projection at the base of the sporangiophore in some lycophyte strobili.

linkage—two or more genes located on the same chromosome and usually inherited together.

lipid—the general term for the organic class of compounds called fats.

locule—the cavity within an ovary or sporangium.

long-day plant—a plant that does not flower unless there is an increase in the length of the photoperiod.

M

mass flow hypothesis—see pressure-flow hypothesis.

megaphyll—a leaf containing branching veins.

megaspore—a spore that is large in size for that plant and develops into a female gametophyte.

megaspore mother cell—a diploid cell that undergoes meiosis to produce megaspores.

meiocyte—see megaspore mother cell.

meiosis—a series of two nuclear divisions resulting in the change of a diploid cell into four haploid cells.

meristem—a region in a growing plant in which mitosis occurs.

mesocarp—the middle area of a fruit. Normally this is the flesh between the endocarp and the exocarp.

mesophyll—parenchyma cells between the upper and lower epidermal layers of a leaf.

metabolism—the chemical processes that occur in an organism.

microfilament—a cell organelle formed from protein and involved with holding the organelles in place in the cytoplasm. Microfilaments are also involved with cytoplasmic streaming.

microphyll—a leaf that is small in size and has a single unbranched vein lacking a leaf gap.

micropyle—an opening in the integuments of an ovule, through which the sperm and pollen tube enter the embryo sac.

microspore—a small spore that develops into a male gametophyte.

microspore mother cell—a diploid cell that undergoes meiosis to produce four microspores.

microsporophyll—a modified leaf that contains the organs that produce microspores.

microtubule—a tubular cell organelle formed from protein and functioning as conduction pathways for materials within the cell.

middle lamella—a layer of pectin that holds two adjacent cell wall layers together.

midrib—the main vein of a pinnately veined leaf.

mitochondria—cell organelles that contain enzymes that function in the Krebs cycle and the electron transport chain.

mitosis—the division of cell nuclei during cell division. Results in two identical cells being formed.

mixture—the combination of two or more ingredients that retain their separate identities within the substance.

molecule—the smallest unit of an element or compound above the atom level.

monocotyledon—one class of angiosperms characterized by seedlings with one cotyledon.

monoecious—a flower or plant with organs of both sexes in the same plant.

monohybrid cross—a genetic cross involving a single pair of genes.

monokaryotic—club fungi cells with a single nucleus in each.

motile—cells capable of independent movement.

multiple fruit—a fruit formed from the many flowers in an inflorescence.

mushroom—the sexual phase in the life cycle of a club fungus.

mutation—any change in the structure of gene or chromosome that can be inherited.

mycelium—a growth of fungal hyphae.

mycorrhizae—a mass of fungi growing around the roots of plants. The fungi have a symbiotic relationship with the plant.

N

n—haploid or having one set of chromosomes.

NAD—nicotinamide adenine dinucleotide. A molecule that temporally stores energy during respiration.

NADP—nicotinamide adenine dinucleotide phosphate. A molecule that temporally stores energy during the light reactions of photosynthesis.

nastic movement—the non-directed movement of a flat plant organ with the organ alternately bending up and down.

neutron—an uncharged particle in the nucleus of an atom.

node—an active area of growth on a stem. Leaves and buds form here.

non-meristematic tissue—tissue in which the cells have differentiated and no longer go through mitosis.

nucellus—ovule tissue in which the embryo sac forms.

nuclear envelope—the porous membrane around the nucleus.

nucleic acid—an organic compound such as DNA or RNA.

nucleolus—a round body in the nucleus of the cell. It contains RNA and protein.

nucleotide—a structural unit of DNA and RNA.

nucleus—a cell organelle containing chromosomes which functions to control the cells' functions.

nut—a one-seeded dry fruit with a hard pericarp and a cup or series of bracts at the base.

O

oil—a liquid form of fat.

oogamy—a form of sexual reproduction in algae in which the female gamete is non-motile and larger than the motile male gamete.

oogonium—a female sex organ in some algae and fungi.

operculum—the cap or lid on a moss capsule or sporangium.

orbital—the location and path of an electron around the nucleus of an atom.

order—a taxonomic category of classification between a class and family.

organelle—a membrane bound molecular structure in a cell that functions like an organ.

organic—pertaining to living things. In chemistry, molecules made mostly of carbon and hydrogen.

osmosis—the diffusion of water through a differentially permeable membrane from an area of high concentration to an area of low.

ovary—a flower part forming the enlarged base of the pistil and containing one or more ovules. When fertilized it contains seeds and forms a fruit.

ovule—a structure in the ovary of angiosperms that contains a female gametophyte and when fertilized will develop into a seed.

palisade mesophyll—the top rows of mesophyll forming distinct regular rows of cells just under the upper epidermal layer in leaves.

palmately compound, palmately veined—leaves with leaflets or veins radiating out from a common point.

parenchyma—common plant cells that are thin walled and with large vacuoles.

parthenocarpic—seedless fruits developing from unfertilized ovaries.

passage cell—a thin walled cell in the endodermis.

pectin—a form of carbohydrate that is used to make the middle lamella of cell walls.

pedicel—the stalk of a flower within an inflorescence.

peduncle—the stalk of a single flower.

peptide bond—a chemical bond found in protein. They link amino acids together.

perennial—a plant that lives for more than two years.

pericarp—the sum total of tissue layers that form a fruit.

pericycle—a layer of cells in roots, between the endodermis and the phloem. It is responsible for branching in the root.

periderm—the outer bark formed from cork.

peristome—teeth-like projections around the opening of a bryophyte sporangium.

petal—a flower part of the corolla, that is often showy and colored.

petiole—the stalk of a leaf.

pH—hydrogen ion concentration. An indication of the degree of acidity or alkalinity.

phellogen—cork cambium.

phenotype—the outward expression of a gene. What the organism looks like.

pheromone—a chemical produced by one organism and used to communicate with another organism.

phloem—vascular tissue that conducts food.

photon—a unit of light energy used in photosynthesis.

photoperiodism—the process of inducing flowering or other activities in a plant by changes in the length of daylight.

photosynthesis—the process whereby light, carbon dioxide and water, in the presence of chlorophyll, are converted to simple sugars or starch. Oxygen is released as a byproduct. Chlorophyl molecules are phytochrome-special pigments that absorb light. They are located in the cytoplasm.

pilus—a kind of conjugation tube in bacteria.

pinna—leaflets of compound leaves. Also a subdivision of a fern frond.

pinnately compound, pinnately veined—with leaflets or veins that arise from both sides of a common central rachis or vein.

pistil—the female part of a flower, an ovary, style and stigma.

pit—a hole or depression in cell wall.

pith—undifferentiated parenchyma tissue found in the center of dicot stems and the center of monocot roots. It is often used for storage.

plankton—the sum total of free floating, mostly microscopic organism in the ocean.

plant anatomy—the botanical science that deals with the structure of plants.

plant community—all the plants inhabiting a common environment and interacting with each other.

plant ecology—the botanical science that studies the activities of plant communities.

plant geography—the botanical science that studies the distribution of plants over the face of the earth.

plant morphology—the botanical science that studies the development and form of plants.

plant physiology—the botanical science that studies the metabolic activities and life processes of plants.

plant taxonomy—the botanical science that studies the classification, naming and identification of plants.

plasma membrane—the cell membrane of a cell. A double lipid layer that forms the outer boundary of a cell.

plasmid—circular rings of DNA material that are found in some bacterial cells.

plasmodesmata—strands of cytoplasm that extend through pores in the cell wall to connect adjacent cells.

plasmodium—the colonial form of a slime mold. It consists of a slimy like liquid containing many nuclei.

plasmolysis—the shrinking of the protoplast of a cell due to a loss of water.

plastid—a cell organelle that manufactures or stores. Examples include leucoplasts and chloroplasts.

plumule—the terminal end of a seedling. It contains the seedling's apical meristem.

polar nuclei—the nuclei in the embryo sac of an angiosperm that are going to fuse with a sperm to produce endosperm.

pollen grain—the structure formed from a microspore of an angiosperm or gymnosperm. It is the delivery system for sperm.

pollen tube—a growth of the pollen grain that carries the sperm to the female gametophyte in seed plants.

pollination—the process of transferring pollen from an anther to a stigma.

polymer—a large molecule composed of many similar units. Large carbohydrate and lipid structures may be polymers.

polyploidy—the condition of having two or more sets of chromosomes in a cell.

pome—a simple fleshy fruit in which the flesh of the fruit is derived mostly from the receptacle.

population—a group of organisms of the same species occupying an area at the same time.

pressure-flow hypothesis—the theory of food transport in plants. Substances in solution flow along concentration gradients between sources of food and sinks where food is utilized.

primary consumer—animals that feed directly on producers. Herbivores.

primary tissue—that tissue produced by the apical meristem in a seedling. It consists of epidermis, cortex, primary xylem and phloem and pith.

primordium—the beginning of a plant organ. A structure at its earliest developmental stage.

procambium—that primary meristem that gives rise to primary xylem and phloem.

producer—a green plant. An organism that has the ability to trap solar energy and form material that consumers can use.

prokaryotic—the condition in primitive cells of not having a well developed nucleus, or organelles encased in membranes.

protein—an organic chemical compound in which there is hydrogen, carbon, oxygen and nitrogen. Structurally proteins are formed from chains of amino acids.

prothallus—the gametophyte growth stage of ferns.

protoderm—the primary meristem that forms the epidermis.

proton—a positively charged particle in the nucleus of atoms.

protonema—a branched or thread-like growth from the spore of a bryophyte. It forms the gametophyte stage.

protoplasm—a general term for the living material that makes up a cell.

pruning—the removal of terminal parts of a plant to assist growth, transplanting or elimination of disease.

pyrenoid—a small structure in the chloroplasts of some algae. They are involved with starch accumulation.

pyruvic acid—the organic compound formed in glycolysis and degraded in the Krebs cycle.

Q

quiescence—the condition of a seed that will not germinate or grow until the environmental conditions needed for growth are met.

R

rachis—the central stalk or axis of pinnately compound leaves or fronds.

radicle—the part of a seedling that forms the root.

ray—groups of specialized parenchyma cells that extend radially outward from the vascular stele. The main function of these cells is conduction of food or water.

receptacle—the expanded portion of a peduncle or pedicel on which the part of a flower are attached.

recessive—the weak gene in a pair of alleles. Its phenotypic expression is masked when a dominant gene for that characteristic is present.

red tide—the development of large populations of dinoflagellates that tinge the ocean water red and produce toxins harmful to humans and other organisms.

reproduction—the formation of new organisms by either sexual or asexual processes.

resin canal—a tube or duct found in conifers and some angiosperms, that is filled with resin.

respiration—the process of breaking down sugar in cells to produce energy and release waste products such as carbon dioxide and water. In the process of aerobic respiration oxygen is required.

rhizoid—root-like structure of algae, fungi, bryophytes and some angiosperms that function to anchor the plant and absorb nutriments. They differ from true roots in lacking xylem and phloem.

rhizome—an underground stem, root-like in appearance, but with nodes and internodes.

ribosome—cellular organelles associated with endoplasmic reticulum and also occurring free in the cytoplasm. They are rich in RNA and are the site for protein synthesis.

RNA—ribonucleic acid. RNA is involved in cells in the synthesis of proteins.

root—specialized plant organ modified for anchoring plants to the soil and absorbing nutriments. In structure roots contain xylem and phloem and absorb through specialized cells called root hairs.

root cap—a growth of protective cells at the tip of a root.

root hair—a specialized epidermal cell that protrudes into the soil to absorb nutrients.

runner—a stolen.

S

salt—a chemical produced by the union of an acid and a base.

samara—a dry fruit in which the pericarp produces wings that allow the free fruit to twirl in the wind.

saprobe—an organism such as a fungus that obtains its food directly from non-living organic material.

sapwood—the lightly colored wood in a tree trunk, that is still functioning to carry water.

science—the search for truth by using the powers of observation, recording and classifying facts.

sclerid—a form of sclerenchyma cell that contains pits in the cell wall and is used by plants to provide strength to structure.

sclerenchyma—plant tissue formed from thick-walled cells which provide strength for regions of the plant.

secondary consumer—a carnivore, an animal that feeds on a herbivore.

secondary tissue—tissue that forms from vascular cambium or cork cambium.

secretory cell—plant cells that produce or excrete material that is used outside the cell.

seed—a plant embryo surrounded by integuments, including a seed coat.

seed coat—that layer of integument that forms the outer layer of the seed.

semipermeable membrane—same as differentially permeable membrane.

senescence—the process of breakdown in cells in plants that produces death of the cell.

sepal—a flower part that resembles a leaf and functions as a bud scale in the unopened flower. It is part of the calyx.

sessile—something that is attached directly by the base rather than a stalk.

seta—the supporting stalk of a bryophyte capsule.

sexual reproduction—the formation of a new organism by the union of sperm and egg.

short-day plant—a plant that flowers when the length of the photoperiod is shorter than the critical photoperiod.

sieve-plate—the end of a sieve-tube element of phloem, with many holes. Sieve-plates lie adjacent to each other when phloem cells are connected end to end.

sieve-tube—phloem vessel cells arranged end to end.

sieve-tube element—one cell in sieve-tube column of phloem.

silique—a dry fruit that splits along two sides and bears seeds on a central stalk within.

simple leaf—a leaf in which the blade is undivided into leaflets.

solvent—a chemical in which other substances are dissolved.

sorus—a cluster of fern sporangia.

species—the basic taxonomic unit of classification. A population of organisms that share unique characteristics and exhibit reproductive isolation from their closest relatives.

sperm—the male gamete in sexual reproduction.

spice—an organic substance derived from a plant and used to flavor or season food and drink.

spindle—a cell organelle that develops during mitosis and meiosis. Spindle fibers are microtubules that attach between centromeres and centrioles or the poles of the cell.

spine—protective pointed plant organs derived from a stem, modified leaf or leaf stipule.

spongy mesophyll—loose aggregation of cells in the main structure of a leaf. This tissue contains many air spaces.

sporangiophore—the stalk that holds a sporangium.

sporangia—reproductive bodies that produce spores.

spore—in green plants it is a reproductive body that develops into the gametophyte generation. In bacteria spores can be resistant stages that enable the bacterium to survive under difficult conditions.

spore mother cell—a cell in a sporangium that undergoes meiosis to produce spores.

sporophyll—a modified leaf that holds a sporangium.

sporophyte—that stage of the plant life cycle which is diploid and derived from a zygote.

stamen—male portion of a flower, consisting of a filament and an anther.

stele—the vascular tissue in the center of a stem. The middle of stele may also contain pith.

stem—a plant organ that has a vascular stele, nodes and internodes.

stigma—the top of the pistil in a flower that is where pollen is deposited.

stipule—appendages at the base of a leaf.

stolon—a horizontal stem that grows along the ground.

stoma—the opening of a stomata on a leaf.

strobilus—a collection of sporophylls on a common stalk. Found in lycophytes and horsetails.

stroma—the material in a chloroplast where the dark reaction takes place in photosynthesis.

style—that portion of the pistil of the flower that connects the stigma with the ovary.

suberin—a lipid produced by cells for waterproofing. Common in cork cells of the bark.

succession—the development of an ecological sequence of plant communities until a climax community is reached.

sucrose—a kind of sugar produced in photosynthesis. It is a disaccharide consisting of fructose and glucose.

superior ovary—an ovary in a flower that is above the calyx, corolla and stamens.

symbiosis—a relationship between two unrelated organisms that benefits one or both of them.

syngamy—the combining of two gametes.

T

tendril—a coiling modified leaf or stem that serves as a holdfast.

thallus—an unorganized multicellular flat plant organ that lacks roots, stems and leaves.

thylakoid—disk shaped units in the grana of chloroplasts, onto which chlorophyll molecules are attached.

tissue—a group of cells of a similar type functioning together.

tracheid—a kind of xylem in which the cells are tapered and have many pits.

transpiration—the evaporation of water from the stomata of plants.

tropism—a plant organ behavior created in response to an external stimulus.

tuber—an underground stem that is enlarged with parenchyma cells and used for storage.

turgid—the condition of a cell that has become swollen with water.

turgor movement—the changes in plant structure due to loss or gain of water, that result in movement.

turgor pressure—the pressure against a cell wall that water exerts in the cell.

U

unisexual—the type of flower that has the organs of only one sex.

V

vacuole—a space within the cytoplasm of a cell, surrounded by cell membrane and occupying up to 90% of the cell's volume. Also called a tonoplast.

vascular bundle—the conduction tissue of a plant, consisting of xylem and phloem.

vascular cambium—the narrow layer of cells that forms vascular tissue, secondary xylem to the inside and secondary phloem to the outside.

vascular plant—a plant that has xylem and phloem conducting vessels.

vein—a vascular bundle in a leaf.

venter—the enlarged area of the archegonium where the egg is located in mosses.

vessel—a tube that conducts something. In plants vessels are either xylem or phloem.

vessel element—a single cell within a xylem vessel.

virus—a tiny particle with a nucleic acid core and a protein sheath. These can only reproduce in living cells.

vitamin—a chemical substance necessary for normal growth and metabolism in living systems.

W

whorled—the condition of three or more leaves emerging from a node on a stem.

X

xerosere—the plant community succession that begins with bare rock.

xylem—a plant tissue that forms vessels and conducts water.

Z

zoospore—a mobile spore in algae and fungi.

zygote—a fertilized egg.

Index

Botany Workbook

Please Read

The function of this workbook is to provide you with an in-depth review of all major concepts covered in each of the chapters. The workbook is set up in three sections which correspond to the topics covered in each of three tests that are typically offered during the semester. The format and types of questions presented in the workbook are similar to—but of course not exactly—the same questions that will appear on the tests. They offer a good review and also a good preparation. More precisely, the self-quiz sections enable you to judge your level of preparation and how much further preparation is needed for you to satisfactorily complete the in-class tests.

Each of the workbook sections should be completed without looking up answers in the text or lecture notes. After you have answered all the questions, then check your answers by looking up the information in the appropriate chapters.

Completing the Self-quiz Sections

The workbook sections are organized so that they can be torn out and handed in to the instructor as a completed unit, if requested. The essay questions should be answered on separate pages, which should be attached to any materials to be turned in to the instructor. Do all of your work in pencil. For essay questions the instructor may ask you to include a list of the citations that you referenced.

Check with your instructor for complete instructions about workbook assignments.

TEENA